Manual of Housing Law

Andrew Arden QC founded Arden Chambers in 1993 to provide a centre for specialist practice, primarily in the area of housing law, together with local government and property. The set has been described in Chambers and Partners as 'a trailblazer ... extremely well-regarded and strong in its niche areas of local government, property and housing' and in Legal 500 as 'a pre-eminent set for housing law'.

Andrew Arden QC has appeared in many of the leading cases in housing law over the past 30 years. He is author or editor of the principal practitioner texts on housing law, including the *Encyclopaedia of Housing Law, Housing Law Reports, Journal of Housing Law, Arden & Partington's Housing Law, Local Government Constitutional and Administrative Law* (all Sweet & Maxwell), *Quiet Enjoyment* and *Homelessness and Allocations* (LAG).

Andrew Dymond is a barrister and founder member of Arden Chambers. He advises and represents both public and private sector clients, including leaseholders, tenants and the homeless, local authorities, private registered providers, registered social landlords and private landlords. Andrew is deputy general editor of the *Housing Law Reports*, an editor of *Arden & Partington's Housing Law* and a member of the editorial board of the *Journal of Housing Law*.

Available as an ebook at www.lag.org.uk/ebooks

The purpose of the Legal Action Group is to promote equal access to justice for all members of society who are socially, economically or otherwise disadvantaged. To this end, it seeks to improve law and practice, the administration of justice and legal services.

Manual of Housing Law

TENTH EDITION

Andrew Arden QC and Andrew Dymond

Legal Action Group
2017

Tenth edition published in Great Britain 2017
by LAG Education and Service Trust Limited
National Pro Bono Centre, 48 Chancery Lane, London WC2A 1JF
www.lag.org.uk

All previous editions published by Sweet & Maxwell (part of Thomson Reuters (Professional) UK Limited
First edition 1978 (Housing: security and rent control)
Second edition 1983
Third edition 1986
Fourth edition 1989
Fifth edition 1992
Sixth edition 1997
Seventh edition 2003
Eighth edition 2007
Ninth edition 2012

British Library Cataloguing in Publication Data. A CIP catalogue record for this book is available from the British Library.

This book has been produced using Forest Stewardship Council (FSC) certified paper. The wood used to produce FSC certified products with a 'Mixed Sources' label comes from FSC certified well-managed forests, controlled sources and/or recycled material.

print ISBN 978 1 908407 98 6
ebook ISBN 978 1 908407 99 3

Typeset by Regent Typesetting, London
Printed in Great Britain by Hobbs the Printers, Totton, Hampshire

Preface

Quiet Enjoyment: protection from rogue landlords, 8th edn; *Manual of Housing Law*, 10th edn and *Homelessness and Allocations*, 10th edn

Background

For the first time, these three books are being published contemporaneously and by the same publisher.

Historically, the first of these books started life as *Housing: security and rent control*, in 1978, originally paired with *Housing: repairs and improvements*, by Tom Hadden (1979). Both were published by Sweet & Maxwell, as have been all subsequent editions of the *Manual of Housing Law* (as it became from the second edition in 1983, expanded to include the material in *Repairs and Improvements*). The first edition of *Quiet Enjoyment, remedies for harassment and illegal eviction*, co-authored with Martin Partington, was published by LAG, also in 1978, a booklet rather than a full-length book. The first edition of *Homelessness and Allocations*, under the title *The Homeless Persons Act*, followed from LAG in 1982. Over the years, I have been joined by a number of co-authors; there was a small number of editions of the LAG books which I did not write. Here I find myself, still writing them just shy of 40 years after they were first published, the books still in use.

Until the mid-1970s, the term 'housing law' was in scant use: it was a term applied to a sub-division of planning law and on occasion merited a mention in landlord and tenant or local government. The subject covered the powers and duties of local authorities, mainly in relation to slum clearance (by area or individual unit), the provision of public housing and related matters such as improvement grants. Reflecting the growth of legal aid, the introduction of law centres and the underlying social demand for rights, housing law began to develop in the early 1970s – largely through the pages of the *LAG Bulletin* (as *Legal Action* was then called) – bringing together all the law as it affected the use of a property as a home, whether derived from private rights or from the public powers and duties conferred or imposed on local authorities, whether formally identified as housing or because it impacted on housing in practice.

At that time, LAG did not publish many full-length books; hence the observation that *Quiet Enjoyment* was initially no more than a booklet. This was one reason why the *Manual* was published by Sweet & Maxwell, one of the two leading legal publishers. Sweet & Maxwell had, however, given the subject a further boost when, in the same year as the first edition of what became the *Manual* was published, it decided to expand the coverage of the *Encyclopaedia of Housing Law and Practice* to reflect the new vision of housing law.

The topics taken into the subject through the efforts of these two publishers included the Rent Acts (governing private sector security and harassment/illegal eviction), leasehold enfranchisement and extension, matrimonial law so far as it affected the family home on domestic breakdown, environmental health (statutory nuisance and other provisions affecting housing), social security, mobile homes, judicial review (enjoying its own period of unprecedented growth, itself in part a reflection of the same rise in rights awareness), as well as some planning law, compulsory purchase, conveyancing, landlord and tenant, contract and tort. Subsequent significant developments include the mass of law directly or indirectly reflecting policies on anti-social behaviour, much of it focused on housing, enhanced long leaseholder rights, human rights and the divergence of housing law as between England and Wales.

Sweet & Maxwell continues to publish the *Encyclopaedia*, along with the *Housing Law Reports*, the *Journal of Housing Law* and *Arden & Partington's Housing Law*; but for a change of direction in relation to titles such as the *Manual*, it would have remained in its list – regardless of legalities, it would not have been right to seek to move it after the publisher had done so much for the subject, as it continues to do through these other titles; and, while I am delighted both to bring the *Manual* 'home' to LAG and to be able to publish it as part of a discrete set, it would be wrong not to mark the departure by expressing my own gratitude for its support for the title over so many years.

Books

The three books have had different aims. Since the 1970s, the *Manual of Housing Law* has sought to provide a guide to housing law as described above, for a fairly wide array of interested individuals: the practitioner starting out in housing law; the non-specialist practitioner who needs occasional but ready access to the subject; lay advisers; students both of housing and of law; housing officers in local authorities and other social housing providers; environmental health officers working in housing; and, local councillors with a remit or interest in the subject.

Without claiming to describe all the detail of the subject, the intention has remained the same: to enable the reader to understand housing law as a whole, to know where to find it and to know how to apply it, whether to the problems of individuals or to the policies and practices of landlords and local authorities. This has been the essential approach to housing law as a subject: it exists not for its theory but to be applied.

While the focus of *Quiet Enjoyment* and *Homelessness and Allocations* has been on particular – and particularly important – aspects of the subject, that approach is also at their core, although their target audiences have been somewhat different, aimed primarily at actual and emerging specialist practitioners, specialist lay advisers and specialist officers in local authorities rather than students and others: the emphasis has nonetheless throughout been on practical application of the law. Hence, each of them contains specimen documentation to help the adviser bring cases into court as quickly as they usually need (although this did not arrive in *Homelessness and Allocations* until the seventh edition, the second one following the introduction of the right of appeal on a point of law to the county court by Housing Act 1996, before which it was uncommon for judicial review applications to be prepared by anyone other than relatively experienced public law counsel).

Status

It is this central approach of practical application which generated the proposition that the fundamental starting-point in relation to any housing law problem or discussion requires identification of the *status* of the occupier, which is to say the class of occupational right both at common law and under statute which determines the body of rights, duties and remedies to which the occupation is subject, without which the occupier's entitlements are unknown and, of as much importance, without which the implications are uncertain as to how a problem or other matter should be addressed so as to achieve the greatest gain in living conditions for the occupier while averting the worst consequences, in particular eviction and rent increases.

The number of statuses has long been a problem. Even during the 1970s, there were Rent Act protected and statutory tenancies subject to full and partial exceptions, furnished tenants, tenants with resident landlords, restricted contracts, tenants and licensees exempt from any protection, Rent (Agriculture) Act 1976 tenancies and licences for tied workers in agriculture and forestry, as well as residual controlled tenancies dating from before repeal of the previous security and rent regime in 1957. Moreover, there were housing association tenancies within rent regulation but outside security and other lettings wholly outside both, primarily local authority tenancies but also those from other bodies, such as New Town Development Corporations and the Crown.

The Housing Act 1980 introduced the secure tenancy for most public sector tenants – and licensees – as well as for those in the remainder of the social rented sector, ie housing associations and trusts, together with its own schedule of exceptions, full and qualified; at the same time, it sought to revivify the private rented sector by means, first, of new protected shorthold tenancies and, secondly, a class of new-build letting called assured tenancy, modelled on the security available to business tenants under the Landlord and Tenant Act 1954 Part 2, the latter of which attracted negligible interest. In addition, the 1980 Act brought tenants of the Crown into Rent Act security and rent control if the property was under the management of the Crown Estate Commissioners.

In 1988, the modern assured tenancy was introduced for the fully private sector as well as for housing association and trust tenants, together with assured shorthold tenancies and assured agricultural occupancies, again subject to their own exceptions; the regime also replaced the short-lived new-build 1980 Act predecessor of the same name. In 1996, introductory tenancies were added to the secure tenancy regime. Subsequent developments include demoted tenancies (from both secure and assured status) and family intervention tenancies. In 2011, the dawn of putative localism brought with it the flexible tenancy – in effect, a shorthold secure tenancy albeit for somewhat longer periods than usual in the private sector. The year 2016 brought the distinction between old (existing) secure tenancies and new secure tenancies (which are not secure at all), which is, as it were, still waiting at the platform for the government to set in motion.

I should add that, obviously, this reflects wholesale disregard in England for the Law Commission's *Renting Homes: The Final Report* (2006), the proposals by Martin Partington and his team, *inter alia* to reduce the number of available forms of rental occupation of residential property to two (standard contract and secure contract) and for model contract terms. These were, however, taken up by the Welsh Government, which accepted the recommendations (revisited in *Renting Homes: a better way for Wales*, May 2013) and enacted them in the Renting Homes (Wales) Act 2016, also yet to be brought into force.

As I wrote in the Introduction to the ninth edition of the *Manual*:

> ... [H]ousing law is a subject in a state of constant evolution (if not revolution) and, if this history is anything to go by, is probably destined so to remain. ... That makes it difficult to keep up with. Furthermore, law is rarely retrospective. Accordingly, one set of rules does not replace another, so much as two (or ten) sets co-exist for a period. And, as this is about where people live, that can commonly mean decades rather than years.

Concept, complexity and consistency

Although housing law's approach is practical rather than theoretical, that does not mean that there is no underlying concept: its *purpose* was to seek a housing focus for housing cases, however they were categorised in law, to ensure that decisions reflect awareness that what is in issue is someone's home, not merely property, local authority discretion or an abstract interpretation of statute. This is not to say that the subject is one that 'belongs' exclusively to occupiers, although there was undoubtedly a significant element in its origins which was intended to redress an historical imbalance; the idea was to ensure that all those involved in housing share that purpose as a common, guiding principle, not only to enhance the rights of occupiers but to help all the subject's 'clients' or 'constituents' better to understand how housing cases are likely to be treated in the courts and housing law itself is likely to develop.

The exponential growth in the number of statuses, this most fundamental aspect of housing law and its key structural foundation, has, however, posed a continuing problem in terms both of this purpose and of these books; it has complicated the subject and made it more and more difficult to understand, to write about and to apply, especially as tenancies can and do last for a very long time indeed and tenants may remain in the same accommodation not merely for years but for decades, which means that even law which ceased to apply to new tenancies 20–30 years ago may still be applicable to some older tenants (or their successors) and may still need to be considered. Moreover, old laws may sometimes remain applicable to a new tenancy granted to an existing tenant, in the same or different premises, to prevent tenants being talked into exchanging one set of rights for another, less favourable set.

Status is, however, not the only source of complexity and obfuscation. Central governments of all parties have micro-managed housing law, using it both as an economic tool, which may be expected, and as a political football, responding to populist perceptions without regard to its purpose: this has been particularly acute in the areas of immigration and anti-social behaviour. Given that it is only rarely, and only more recently, that this involves the removal of existing rights, this piles more and more layers of law on top of one another, so that rights turn not merely on status, but increasingly on when something occurred, eg the array of rules governing discharge of duty to homeless applicants depending on when an application was made. There is also something of a ping-pong between criminal and civil law: at points in time, functions which may properly be thought to belong to the criminal law – again, in particular in relation to anti-social behaviour – have been passed to local authorities and other social housing providers, while measures to tackle unlawful immigration have been handed out not only to those landlords but to all; at other times, functions which have historically been issues of civil law – eg trespass and unlawful sub-letting – have been criminalised.

Nor is it only governments who have lost sight of any central concept of housing law: courts have increasingly been led by so-called 'merits', that most subjective of approaches, without regard to the need to preserve any kind of over-arching principle or consistency of approach. Sometimes, this has been motivated by the best of intentions – to jettison archaic rules which are unacceptable in a more modern, human rights-oriented climate. Sometimes, it has been solely motivated by consideration of cost to the public purse. Sometimes, it has been motivated by a largely uninformed assumption as to what will advance the interests of housing. Sometimes, a return to abstract interpretation has countered the positive gains that a housing focus has otherwise achieved – for example in relation to the powers of local authorities to enforce standards in the (ever-increasing and much troubled) private sector.

This is not the place to pursue an analysis of these developments. While it has always been true that the outcome of very few cases has ever been capable of certain prediction, it is now the position, more widely than at any time I have known in my career as legal practitioner and writer, that how an issue will be determined by the courts depends predominantly upon who determines it and how the merits are perceived. Even leaving aside the effects of constant legislative change, this undermines consistency and increases the complexity of housing law. Sad to say, housing is being reduced to a set of detailed rules, not dissimilar to the intricacies of social security legislation, a subject with which it is increasingly coming to have in common an absence of access to qualified advice.

Current editions

This, then, is the climate in which these new editions are published and in which they have had to be re-considered. In earlier editions, chapter 1 of the *Manual* tied classes of occupation to their security of tenure, which is their first and foremost concern: by the last edition, the growth of statuses meant that this approach had become too unwieldy and it had proved necessary to separate class of occupation from security and eviction, a problem that further developments would have exacerbated. Moreover, a substantial chunk of *Quiet Enjoyment* – a subject to which status is critical – would need to be given over to describing the numerous different ways in which people occupy rented accommodation, adding to its length, even though much of its readership is sufficiently familiar with most of them not to need more than occasional reference to the issue. Aspects of homelessness law itself also depend on status: in particular, whether someone is homeless (defined in terms of rights of occupation) and whether someone is intentionally homeless (often turning on whether there was a right to remain in accommodation). It is also central to the new assessment and initial help duties which will come in with the Homelessness Reduction Act 2017.

As the books are now all under one roof and published together, it has been possible to introduce an element of rationalisation: status in *Quiet Enjoyment* now relies exclusively on the *Manual*, affording more space for the considerable body of new law which has emerged over the last few years to reflect the resurgence in private renting and to control the abuses to which it has given rise: I no more foresaw that *Quiet Enjoyment*, newly suffixed *Protection from rogue landlords*, would come back into its own any the more than I ever expected to see the term 'rogue landlords' enshrined in statute. *Homelessness and Allocations* also relies on the *Manual* for status where appropriate, as well as for other questions, eg whether a valid section 21 notice has been served on an assured shorthold tenant.

The *Manual* provides an introduction to the new laws protecting tenants from abuse; *Quiet Enjoyment* considers them in close detail. Both have been restructured. The *Manual*, as mentioned, had already separated out classes of occupation from security of tenure and eviction; in addition, protection from rogue landlords has now been separated out from anti-social behaviour, which is more largely about the conduct of occupiers. The *Manual* includes a wholly new chapter on mobile homes and houseboats, a subject which had slipped out of coverage but that needs to be brought back in as more and more people resort to them as a permanent home for want of being able to afford either owner-occupation or even renting. Naturally, the book continues coverage of rents, other rights (such as leasehold enfranchisement and right to buy), domestic breakdown, regulation of social landlords and housing conditions, including contract and tort, housing standards, environmental health, overcrowding, multiple occupation and licensing.

Quiet Enjoyment for the first time separates out eviction and harassment, as the law on the latter grows to reflect increased awareness of the many different ways that some people set out to distress others and seeks to protect victims. Mobile homes and houseboats are also afforded treatment. There are wholly new chapters on tenancy deposits, licensing of landlords, banning orders and a range of additional duties in respect of rented property many of which impact on a landlord's rights to take advantage of reduced security but which, in turn, may in practice give rise to additional unacceptable and unlawful conduct towards tenants when they are enforced, eg duties in relation to gas, fire, electricity and smoke alarms. As before, there are separate chapters on bringing civil and criminal proceedings, and the traditional collection of case reports on awards of damages is retained and updated, albeit now to be found in an appendix.

The *Manual* also outlines homelessness and allocations law, which *Homelessness and Allocations* addresses fully. The structure of the latter has not changed: an introduction to policy, an outline of the law, detailed consideration of the key concepts – eligibility, homelessness, priority need, intentionality, local connection, protection of property – followed by chapters on enquiries and decisions (including review), discharge of homelessness duties, allocations, enforcement by way of appeal to the county court and judicial review, other provisions to which recourse may need to be had in order to secure housing by way of social and child care provisions, strategy, practice, aid and advice, and criminal offences.

The two key changes since the last edition are the separate development of homelessness in Wales under the Housing (Wales) Act 2014 Part 2, and the Homelessness Reduction Act 2017, through which England adopted some of the changes which Wales had already introduced. The new duties in England include the extension from 28 days to 56 of the period during which a person is threatened with homelessness (dating, where appropriate and as qualified, from service of a valid notice under Housing Act 1988 s21), the introduction of a new assessment duty and consideration of support to ensure that applicants have or retain suitable accommodation, including reasonable steps to be taken by authorities to help applicants secure that accommodation does not cease to be available for their occupation, as well as a new initial duty requiring authorities to take reasonable steps for 56 days to help applicants to secure accommodation, regardless of whether they are in priority need. These developments have added to the increasing complexity of the subject and result in significant changes to chapter 10, on discharge.

Otherwise, the book continues the approach taken in previous editions so far as concerns the development of the law: every detail of homelessness and allocations law is recorded, analysed and applied; nothing which has gone before, however revised by the courts, has been wholly abandoned even if relegated to footnote or analysis reduced to reflect current lack of importance; nothing is divorced from its history and evolution. Experience has shown that cases come back again and again – as true as it may well be of other areas of law, homelessness and allocations have a marked tendency to shift with the winds: nothing is ever finally overruled or permanently irrelevant.

In addition to the structural changes and coverage of new law, in both England and Wales, the opportunity has been taken to reconsider the text of each book. Too often, later editions take for granted what has been written previously, focusing instead on the need to bring books up to date: these books have been no less guilty of this than others. It is not merely that it can leave text feeling stale so much as it can cause a loss of focus or even coherence: the branches can so change the tree that it is not the same picture at all. I have therefore undertaken a line by line – and paragraph by paragraph – revision which I hope will recover some of the freshness which I strove to achieve 'back in the day'.

I extend my thanks to my co-authors, to LAG and, in particular, our publisher Esther Pilger, as well as to colleagues in Chambers and on other publications with which I am associated, and, as always, to my very long-standing writing partners – and friends – Professors Martin Partington CBE, QC (Hon) and Caroline Hunter. My wife and daughter have suffered the stresses and strains of my legal writing – including these books – for far too long for either thanks or apology to make up for what it has cost them. Finally, I should like to dedicate this set of books to the late Pat Reddin, since the early

1970s the go-to housing surveyor of choice in housing disrepair cases both for tenants and for social landlords, who died in April 2015: he is missed both as professional colleague and close friend over the whole of the time-span I have been discussing in this Preface; he remains uppermost in my thoughts and emotions.

The law is predominantly stated as at 30 April 2017, although it has been possible to add a small number of subsequent amendments during the publication process. Two key developments which were due prior to the General Election, which these books have therefore been unable to accommodate, are: the commencement of the Homelessness Reduction Act 2017 (for which no date had been set); and, the introduction of banning orders under the Housing and Planning Act 2016 ss14 and 15 (which had been expected to be implemented from 1 October 2017), although the provisions of each have been fully described so far as available.

Andrew Arden QC
Arden Chambers
London

21 May 2017

Contents

Table of cases

McNerny v Lambeth LBC (1989) 21 HLR 188, [1989] 19 EG 77, CA	11.131
McPhail v Persons, Names Unknown [1973] Ch 447, [1973] 3 WLR 71, CA	1.144, 2.246
Magnohard Ltd v Earl Cadogan [2012] EWCA Civ 594, [2012] HLR 31	4.17
Mainwaring v Trustees of Henry Smith's Charity [1998] QB 1, (1996) 28 HLR 583, CA	4.10
Makisi v Birmingham CC [2011] EWCA Civ 355, [2001] HLR 27	10.154
Malekshad v Howard De Walden Estates Ltd (No 1) [2002] UKHL 49, [2003] HLR 31	4.16
Malpas v St Ermin's Property Co Ltd (1992) 24 HLR 537, (1992) 64 P&CR 436, CA	4.17
Manaton v Edwards (1986) 18 HLR 116, [1985] 2 EGLR 159, CA	2.218
Manchester CC v Benjamin [2008] EWCA Civ 189, [2008] HLR 38	2.117
Manchester CC v Finn [2002] EWCA Civ 1998, [2003] HLR 41	2.126
Manchester CC v Higgins [2005] EWCA Civ 1423, [2006] HLR 14	2.105
Manchester CC v Lawler (1999) 31 HLR 119, CA	2.98
Manchester CC v Pinnock [2010] UKSC 45, [2011] HLR 7	1.319, 2.107, 2.183, 2.251, 7.46
Manel v Memon (2001) 33 HLR 24, [2000] 2 EGLR 40, CA	2.207
Mann v Cornella (1980) 255 EG 403, CA	1.277
Mansukhani v Sharkey (1992) 24 HLR 600, [1992] 33 EG 65, CA	2.218
Marath v MacGillivray (1996) 28 HLR 484, [1996] EG 22 (CS), CA	2.91, 2.170
Marchant v Charters [1977] 1 WLR 1181, [1977] 3 All ER 918, CA	1.122
Marcroft Wagons Ltd v Smith [1951] 2 KB 496, [1951] 2 All ER 271, CA	1.42, 1.43, 1.272
Martin v Smith (1873–74) LR 9 Ex 50	1.19
Mason v Skilling, *see* Skilling v Arcari's Executors—	
Matharu v Matharu [1994] 2 FLR 597, (1994) 26 HLR 648, CA	1.130
Mathew v Bobbins (1981) 41 P&CR 1, (1980) 256 EG 603, CA	1.135
Mei Ling Lin v Barnet LBC [2007] EWCA Civ 132, [2007] HLR 30	10.205
Melville v Bruton (1997) 29 HLR 319, [1996] EG 57 (CS), CA	5.54
Metropolitan Housing Trust v Hadjazi [2010] EWCA Civ 750, [2010] HLR 39	2.98
Metropolitan Properties Co Ltd v Cordery (1980) 39 P&CR 10, (1979) 251 EG 567, CA	1.71

R (Ahmad) v Newham LBC, 2009 [2009] UKHL 14, [2009] HLR 31	10.205, 10.206
R (Best) v Chief Land Registrar [2015] EWCA Civ 17, [2015] HLR 17	1.145
R (C) v Lewisham LBC [2003] EWCA Civ 927, [2004] HLR 4	10.151
R (CN) v Lewisham LBC [2014] UKSC 62, [2015] HLR 6	1.313
R (Conville) v Richmond upon Thames LBC [2006] EWCA Civ 718, [2006] HLR 45	10.100
R (Edwards) v Birmingham CC [2016] EWHC 173 (Admin), [2016] HLR 11	10.33
R (G) v Barnet LBC [2001] EWCA Civ 540, (2001) 33 HLR 59	10.175
R (Hackney LBC) v Rottenburg [2007] EWHC 166 (Admin), [2007] Env LR 24	13.13
R (Haysport Properties Ltd) v West Sussex Registration Area Rent Officer [2001] EWCA Civ 237, (2001) 33 HLR 71	3.68
R (J (Ghanian citizen)) v Enfield LBC [2002] EWHC 432 (Admin), [2002] HLR 38	10.186
R (JL) v Secretary of State for Defence [2013] EWCA Civ 449, [2013] HLR 27	1.327, 2.255
R (Jakimaviciute) v Hammersmith and Fulham LBC [2014] EWCA Civ 1438, [2015] HLR 5	10.192, 10.194
R (Keyu) v Secretary of State for Foreign and Commonwealth Affairs [2015] UKSC 69, [2016] AC 1355	8.36
R (Kilby) v Basildon DC [2007] EWCA Civ 479, [2007] HLR 39	4.120
R (Limbuela) v Secretary of State for the Home Department [2004] EWCA Civ 540, [2004] HLR 38	10.29
R (Lusamba) v Islington LBC [2008] EWHC 1149 (Admin)	10.40
R (Mahmood (Yaser)) v Secretary of State for the Home Department [2001] EWHC Admin 632	8.35
R (Mani) v Lambeth LBC [2003] EWCA Civ 836, [2004] HLR 5	10.184
R (Morris) v London Rent Assessment Committee [2002] EWCA Civ 276, [2002] HLR 48	2.80
R (Morris) v Westminster CC (No 3) [2005] EWCA Civ 1184, [2006] HLR 8	10.186
R (Moseley) v Haringey LBC [2014] UKSC 56, [2014] 1 WLR 3947	4.91
R (O) v Barking and Dagenham LBC [2010] EWCA Civ 1101, [2011] HLR 4	10.29
R (Peat) v Hyndburn BC [2011] EWHC 1739 (Admin)	14.27
R (Regas) v Enfield LBC [2014] EWHC 4173 (Admin), [2015] HLR 14	14.27, 14.67
R (Spath Holme Ltd) v Secretary of State for the Environment, Transport and the Regions [2001] 2 AC 349, (2001) 33 HLR 31, HL	3.57

Table of statutes

Table of statutory instruments

Health Protection (Part 2A Orders) Regulations 2010 SI No 658—	
reg 3	13.78
Health Protection (Part 2A Orders) (Wales) Regulations 2010 SI No 1544—	
reg 3	13.78
Homelessness (Decisions on Referrals) Order 1998 SI No 1578	10.139
Homelessness (Intentionality) (Specified Categories) (Wales) Regulations 2015 SI No1265	10.70
Homelessness (Priority Need for Accommodation) (England) Order 2002 SI No 2051	10.50
Homelessness (Review Procedure) (Wales) Regulations 2015 SI No 1266	10.153
reg 5(2)	10.157
Homelessness (Suitability of Accommodation) (England) Order 2003 SI No 3326	10.120
Homelessness (Suitability of Accommodation) (England) Order 2012 SI No 2601	10.118
Homelessness (Suitability of Accommodation) (Wales) Order 2015 SI No 1268	10.118, 10.120
Homelessness (Suitability of Accommodation) Order 1996 SI No 3204	10.62, 10.117
Housing (Empty Dwelling Management Orders) (Prescribed Exceptions and Requirements) (England) Order 2006 SI No 367—	
reg 3	14.137
Housing (Preservation of Right to Buy) Regulations 1993 SI No 2241	4.70
Housing (Replacement of Terminated Tenancies) (Successor Landlords) (England) Order 2009 SI No 1262	12.132
Housing (Replacement of Terminated Tenancies) (Successor Landlords) (Wales) Order 2009 SI No 1260	12.132
Housing (Right to Acquire) (Discount) Order 2002 SI No 1091	4.75
Housing (Right to Acquire) (Discount) (Wales) Order 1997 SI No 569	4.75
Housing (Right to Acquire) Regulations 1997 SI No 619	4.75
Housing (Right to Buy) (Information to Secure Tenants) (England) Order 2005 SI No 1735	4.113
Housing (Right to Buy) (Information to Secure Tenants) (Wales) Order 2005 SI No 2681	4.113
Housing (Right to Buy) (Limit on Discount) (England) Order 2014 SI No 1378	4.56
Housing (Right to Buy) (Limits on Discount) (Wales) Order 1999 SI No 292	4.56
Housing (Right to Buy) (Prescribed Forms) Regulations 1986 SI No 2194	4.58
Housing (Right to Buy) (Prescribed Forms) (Wales) Regulations 2015 SI No 1320	4.56

Table of European legislation and conventions

Abbreviations

ALMO	arm's length management organisation
ASBA 2003	Anti-social Behaviour Act 2003
ASBCPA 2014	Anti-social Behaviour, Crime and Policing Act 2014
ASBI	anti-social behaviour injunction
BA 1984	Building Act 1984
CA 1989	Children Act 1989
CCA 1974	Consumer Credit Act 1974
CCA 1984	County Courts Act 1984
CDA 1998	Crime and Disorder Act 1998
CJPA 2001	Criminal Justice and Police Act 2001
CLA 1977	Criminal Law Act 1977
CLRA 2002	Commonhold and Leasehold Reform Act 2002
CPA 2004	Civil Partnership Act 2004
CPR	Civil Procedure Rules 1998
CRA 2015	Consumer Rights Act 2015
CSA 1968	Caravan Sites Act 1968
CSCDA 1960	Caravan Sites and Control of Development Act 1960
DA 2015	Deregulation Act 2015
DPA 1972	Defective Premises Act 1972
EA 1989	Electricity Act 1989
ECHR	European Convention on Human Rights
ECtHR	European Court of Human Rights
EDMO	empty dwelling management orders
EPC	energy performance certificate
EqA 2010	Equality Act 2010
EPA 1990	Environmental Protection Act 1990
FLA 1996	Family Law Act 1996
GA 1986	Gas Act 1986
HA 1985, 1988, 1996, 2004	Housing Acts
HAA 1985	Housing Associations Act 1985
HCA	Homes and Communities Agency
HGCRA 1996	Housing Grants, Construction and Regeneration Act 1996
HHSRS	housing health and safety rating system
HMO	house in multiple occupation
HPA 2016	Housing and Planning Act 2016

HRA 1998	Human Rights Act 1998
H&RA 2008	Housing & Regeneration Act 2008
HSWA 1974	Health and Safety at Work, etc Act 1974
H(W)A 2014	Housing (Wales) Act 2014
IA 2014	Immigration Act 2014
IAA 1999	Immigration and Asylum Act 1999
LA 1980	Limitation Act 1980
LA 2011	Localism Act 2011
LASPO 2012	Legal Aid, Sentencing and Punishment of Offenders Act 2012
LCA 1973	Land Compensation Act 1973
LGA 1972, 2000	Local Government Acts
LGHA 1989	Local Government and Housing Act 1989
LPA 1925	Law of Property Act 1925
LP(MP)A 1989	Law of Property (Miscellaneous Provisions) Act 1989
LRA 2002	Land Registration Act 2002
LRA 1967	Leasehold Reform Act 1967
LRHUDA 1993	Leasehold Reform, Housing and Urban Development Act 1993
LSVT	large scale voluntary transfer
LTA 1927, 1954, 1985, 1987, 1988	Landlord and Tenant Acts
MCA 1973	Matrimonial Causes Act 1973
MFPA 1984	Matrimonial and Family Proceedings Act 1984
MHA 1983	Mobile Homes Act 1983
MH(W)A 2013	Mobile Homes (Wales) Act 2013
NA 1996	Noise Act 1996
NIAA 2002	Nationality, Immigration and Asylum Act 2002
NOP	notice of proceedings
NSP	notice seeking possession
PEA 1977	Protection from Eviction Act 1977
PHA 1936	Public Health Act 1936
PHA 1997	Protection from Harassment Act 1997
PRP	private registered provider of social housing
PSHFA 2013	Prevention of Social Housing Fraud Act 2013
PSO(W)A 2005	Public Services Ombudsman (Wales) Act 2005
RA 1977	Rent Act 1977
RAC	rent assessment committee
RH(W)A 2016	Renting Homes (Wales) Act 2016
RRO 2002	Regulatory Reform (Housing Assistance) (England and Wales) Order 2002
RSL	registered social landlord
SSWB(W)A 2014	Social Services and Well-being (Wales) Act 2014
ToLATA 1996	Trusts of Land and Appointment of Trustees Act 1996
TRO	tenancy relations officer
UCTA 1977	Unfair Contract Terms Act 1977
WIA 1991	Water Industry Act 1991
WRWA 2016	Welfare Reform and Work Act 2016

CHAPTER 1

Classes of occupation

continued

Introduction

1.1 The starting point of any study of housing law is the 'status' of a person in premises, that is to say the class of occupation he or she enjoys which will determine his or her rights in relation not only to the all-important question of security of tenure and eviction, but also to such matters as rent, repairs and numerous other terms governing occupation of accommodation.

1.2 In turn, determining the class of occupation involves three questions. First, there are the different rights which people enjoy in relation to the use of land (including houses, flats and other buildings), which they own or occupy, which have primarily been developed by decided case-law over many years and embodied in the common law, although because one of these (commonhold) is relatively new and has been introduced by statute, we refer to them as 'basic concepts'. This gives us the legal concepts on which statutory classes of occupation – or protection – bite. The second part of the status issue is therefore to identify within (or across) these basic concepts those to whom the benefits of each body of statutory protection apply.

1.3 Finally, regardless of pursuant to what basic concept and under what statutory class of protection someone occupies accommodation, there remains the question of whether occupation amounts to occupation as a 'home' for the purposes of Article 8 of the European Convention on Human Rights (ECHR), within the meaning given to that expression by the European Court of Human Rights.

1.4 If it does so, the Human Rights Act (HRA) 1998 may – and usually will – add a layer of protection, at least where the landlord is a public authority for the purposes of that Act (normally a local authority, private registered provider of social housing or registered social landlord). This requires a court to consider for itself whether action being taken by the landlord – or in some circumstances whether the landlord's failure to take action – is in breach of that Act, in which case, the court may refuse to allow the landlord to take that action, eg to evict, or may require the landlord to take action, eg to repair.

1.5 There is a great deal of scope for criticism of such a complex approach to something as fundamental as housing rights and the Law Commission – the body charged with proposing major reforms to the law – did devise proposals for a substantially simpler system of 'Type 1' and 'Type 2' rights of occupation, meaning those with full and those with only limited security, which was intended to do away with some, if not all, of this difficulty: see *Renting Homes: The Final Report*, Commission Consultation Paper No 297. It is, however, unlikely that these proposals will be put into effect for some time (if ever) in England but they have been adopted in Wales in the Renting Homes (Wales) Act 2016, although the provisions will still not come into force for some time.

1.6 It is only when the exercise of ascertaining what status an occupier enjoys has been carried out that it is possible to say which substantive rights and duties bind which occupiers and/or landlords. In this chapter, therefore, we propose to address this issue in isolation: it is necessary in order to address the critical questions which arise, and which are addressed in subsequent chapters, ie security of tenure; payments; other rights; disrepair; unlawful conduct; domestic breakdown; regulation of social landlords; homelessness and allocations and housing conditions. While this does mean that much of this chapter is devoid of direct reference to substantive issues – what each class of occupation *means* in practice – the alternative is to tie this issue of status to each substantive issue, which in turn makes for a much more complex study. This chapter should, therefore, be read with this in mind, that its true value is only once it comes to be applied to other issues – and its presence is essentially for reference back from those issues when they arise.

Basic concepts

Freehold

1.7 'Freehold' is, to all intents and purposes, outright ownership. In principle, a freehold lasts forever. There are numerous constraints on what a freehold owner can do, eg planning law, environmental health law, other provisions allowing public authorities to interfere or even compulsorily to purchase the property in question, as well as provisions in private law so far as what is done affects neighbouring occupiers; moreover, a freehold owner may sometimes be subject to an agreement allowing someone else to exercise rights over his or her land or constraining how he or she may use it.

1.8 Other ways in which a freehold owner-occupier might lose his or her right of ownership – and, therefore, occupation – is if he or she goes into bankruptcy and the trustee in bankruptcy forces the sale of his or her home; or, a court might transfer the property in the course of the breakdown of a relationship. Subject to these – and analogous – qualifications, however, freehold is the highest form of ownership of land and, therefore, the greatest occupational right anyone can enjoy.

1.9 Although it is possible to own a flat by way of freehold ownership, it is neither common nor effective. The reason for this is that owners of flats need to ensure that they all contribute to the upkeep of the building as a whole, eg roof repairs and cleaning of the common parts. An obligation to do this is a 'positive' obligation. While positive obligations can be embodied in covenants which neighbouring freeholders can impose on one another, they are usually only enforceable against the original parties who do so (*Rhone v Stevens*, 1994). Accordingly, such a covenant imposed on a freehold owner of a flat is not enforceable after its sale and, therefore, will quickly fail to provide a sound basis for upkeep of the building (as more and more flats are sold and the positive covenants fail). Leases (below) are far more effective for this purpose and, for this reason, it is exceptionally rare for a flat to be owned on a traditional freehold basis.

Leasehold and commonhold

1.10 If someone owns or occupies housing otherwise than as a freeholder, there is a limited number of ways in which he or she can do so. Until recently, an occupier could be a tenant – which is in practice to say that possession of the housing has been passed to him or her for a period (or periods) of time usually for a monetary payment – or he or she could merely have permission to use it, known as licence, or he or she might even be a trespasser. To that small group, there has recently been added a little used right, known as commonhold, which is addressed under this heading.

Long leasehold

1.11 Tenancy comes in many shapes and sizes. Most people are familiar with the weekly or monthly tenancy available either from a social or a private landlord, which runs on until determined, usually by notice to quit. In addition, people are familiar with the relatively short fixed-term tenancy, which could be for, eg a number of months or a small number of years. Finally, people are familiar with a different type of tenancy, which is usually referred to as leasehold and which is for a much greater number of years, indeed could be for up to hundreds of years.

1.12 Such leasehold occupation is – strictly – merely another form of tenancy and the essential elements of tenancy considered under the next heading apply to it, as do many of the observations made in relation to, eg joint tenancy, subtenancy and assignment. Nonetheless, it is viewed as a form of owner-occupation, both because the rights which are enjoyed by a long leaseholder – a term confined to leases in excess of 21 years – are much greater than those of other tenants, and because it usually only arises on payment of a sum of money, whether to the landlord for its grant or to the existing leaseholder for its assignment, ie its transfer.

1.13 On an assignment, it does not matter how much time there is to run on the lease: the incoming occupier steps into the shoes of the outgoing occupier. It is the length of the interest itself, ie the lease, not the length of occupation left under it, which determines whether or not it is a long lease. Furthermore, the problem discussed in relation to traditional freehold ownership of flats, of enforcing positive obligations or covenants against subsequent owners (see para 1.9), does not arise where flats are owned on a leasehold basis. Positive covenants are enforceable by the landlord against each assignee, at least provided that they 'touch and concern' the land (*London Diocesan Board v Phithwa*, 2005), as do covenants requiring the tenant to keep the flat in repair and to contribute to the costs of maintaining the block.

1.14 Most long leases are of flats, although they can also be of houses, eg if the landlord wants to retain it as part of an estate or else to generate a continuing income, or if the person granting the long lease him- or herself only has a long lease of the building in question.

1.15 The leaseholder will pay what is usually a small, annual ground rent to a landlord and a service charge. The leasehold interest may be lost in any of the circumstances illustrated in relation to freehold (see para 1.8), and in theory will come to an end when the period itself runs out (but, in practice, there will normally be a form of statutory protection available and there are other rights, including to buy the freehold or extend the lease of a house (see paras 4.15–4.38), or to stay on until the lease is replaced with a periodic tenancy – see paras 2.73–2.83).

Commonhold

1.16 The Commonhold and Leasehold Reform Act (CLRA) 2002 introduced a new form of ownership for flats, 'commonhold'. Commonhold is a form of collective freehold, applicable to flats. Under the commonhold system, the freehold of the common parts is owned by a 'commonhold association', which is a company whose members are the owners of the flats. The flats are then owned on a freehold basis, ie without any limitation of time (see para 1.7). The rights and obligations of the flat owners and the commonhold association are dealt with in a document called the 'commonhold community statement', overcoming the difficulties associated with the enforcement of positive traditional obligations under freehold ownership (see para 1.9).

Tenancy

1.17 Tenancy is the normal arrangement by which one person comes to occupy premises which someone else owns or controls. It is customarily granted in exchange for a monetary payment: rent. The person to whom the rent is paid is the landlord: the landlord may own the freehold (see para 1.7), or may him- or herself be a long leaseholder or only a tenant. Indeed, the landlord may have no interest at all, but simply have been in a practical position to grant a tenancy, whether or not having a right to do so: save in exceptional circumstances (see para 1.125), he or she will still be the landlord so far as concerns the tenant, provided what was granted amounts to a tenancy in law (*Bruton v London & Quadrant Housing Trust*, 1999).

1.18 While in theory there is a number of different types of tenancy, there are in practice only two with which we are concerned: the periodic tenancy (which means a tenancy from period to period, eg weekly, monthly, quarterly, even annually) and the fixed-term tenancy (which may be for as little as, say, a month but – as noted above (see para 1.11) could also be not merely for decades but for hundreds of years). While considerably different rights exist as between these two main types of tenancy – and, in particular, between long leases (those for more than 21 years – see para 2.72) and periodic or shorter fixed-term tenancies, they all qualify as tenancies in law.

1.19 Under this heading we are, however, primarily concerned with fixed-term tenancies which are not long leases, which were addressed under the last heading. Periodic tenancies do not need to be in writing; subject to exceptions (see paras 1.189 and 1.249), however, fixed-term tenancies for a term in excess of three years must be created by a deed – Law of Property Act (LPA) 1925 ss52(1), 54(2). To qualify as a deed, a document must be signed both by the parties and by witnesses to their signatures and must say that it is intended to be a deed (Law of Property (Miscellaneous Provisions) Act (LP(MP)A) 1989 s1). A written agreement for a tenancy for a term in excess of three years not created by a deed takes effect as an 'equitable tenancy' if it is signed by both parties (*Walsh v Lonsdale*, 1882; LP(MP)A 1989 s2). Between the landlord and the tenant, an equitable tenancy is, however, as effective as if it was made by deed but the tenant needs to ensure that the lease is recorded against the landlord's title at the Land Registry so that it is binding on a new landlord if the property is sold. If only created orally, however, it will take effect as a periodic tenancy provided that the tenant moves in and pays rent on a periodic basis (*Martin v Smith*, 1874), in which case (if the tenant is still in occupation) it will also bind a new landlord, even if not so registered.

1.20 Certain tenancies have to be registered with the Land Registry. Formerly, under the Land Registration Act (LRA) 1925, only long leases for a term of more than 21 years (see para 1.12) had to be registered (LRA 1925 s123(1)(b)). LRA 1925 was replaced by LRA 2002. With effect from 1 October 2003, subject to exceptions (see paras 1.189 and 1.249) it has been necesssary to register any lease granted on or after that date for a term of more than seven years (LRA 2002 s4(1)(c)). If it is not registered, the tenancy is still enforceable between the landlord and the tenant as an equitable tenancy (see para 1.19) and, if created by deed (see para 1.19), it will still be a fixed-term tenancy.

1.21 A registered tenancy is binding on any purchaser of the property. If it is not registered, the tenancy will still be binding on a purchaser if it has been recorded as a caution or a notice against the landlord's title (LRA 2002 Sch 12 paras 1 and 2). If not so recorded, the purchaser will be bound by the tenancy if the tenant is in occupation of the property at the date of sale, unless, prior to the sale, the purchaser asked the tenant about why he or she was in occupation of the property and the tenant failed to disclose the existence of the tenancy (LRA 2002 Sch 3 para 2).

Essential qualities of tenancy

1.22 For there to be a tenancy, it has to be possible to show that four essential qualities exist. If one or more of them is missing, then the agreement cannot be a tenancy, and for this reason will necessarily be the lower occupational right known as licence (*AG Securities v Vaughan*, 1988) – see paras 1.114–1.130. The four qualities are as follows.

Identifiable parties

A landlord and a tenant

1.23 There must be a landlord and a tenant. This does not mean that the tenant must know the identity of the landlord, eg where agents have granted the tenancy on behalf of the landlord. It means that a person cannot be a tenant either of him- or herself, or of premises or land which have no owner or other person in control (*Rye v Rye*, 1962).

1.24 A person can, however, be a tenant of a company of which he or she is a director, or an employee, or even of which the tenant is the major shareholder, and a person can be a tenant of a partnership of which he or she is one of the partners. In such a case, it would be wrong to refer to the tenant alone as the owner: he or she is only the owner when taken together with the other partners. The same applies to trustees or joint owners (*Rye*).

Identifiable premises

A tenancy of premises

1.25 There must be premises of which to constitute a tenancy. Those premises can be as little as a single room, or as much as hundreds of acres of land. It is not, however, possible to be a tenant of only part of some premises or land, eg a shared room not broken up into parts.

1.26 It is possible to be a joint tenant of premises with another (see paras 1.48–1.58), but if genuinely separate agreements have been independently reached with the landlord conferring separate rights to occupy, eg a room, on separate persons, this cannot be tenancy because there is no identifiable part of the premises of which to have a tenancy and – because they are separate – the occupiers are not acting or occuping jointly. Even if the two – or more – individuals occupying were to divide up the room between themselves, they would still have to have access to the door in common.

Period of tenancy

Tenancy and time

1.27 One cannot have a tenancy in respect of which there is no period of time involved. That is exactly what tenancy is: a slice of time in the exclusive use of the premises belonging to another. There must be both an ascertainable date of commencement, and an ascertainable period for which it is to run, both of which must be capable of being established before the lease takes effect (*Prudential Assurance Co Ltd v London Residuary Body*, 1992; *Mexfield Housing Co-operative Limited v Berrisford*, 2011). Thus, fixed-term tenancies state that the tenancy commences on a specified date and either give a date for the end of the tenancy or state that it is to last for a period of time, eg a year or six months, from the commencement date. Sometimes, one party is, or both parties are, given the right to determine the tenancy before the end of the term by serving notice referred to as a 'break clause', eg a tenant may be given the right to end a one-year fixed term after six months. This does not conflict with the rule that the period of the tenancy must be ascertainable.

1.28 The need to identify the period of the tenancy does not mean that a tenancy cannot in practice be granted for an indefinite time, which is normally what happens when a periodic tenancy is granted. In these cases, the period for which the tenancy has been granted is the time of the periodic tenancy, eg one week, but the tenancy is automatically renewed from week to week until determined, usually by notice to quit (see para 2.49). Accordingly, a term of the tenancy which inhibits the right of either the landlord or the tenant to serve notice to quit is invalid and ineffective in law because it prevents the tenancy from being for an identifiable term (*Prudential*, *Mexfield*). Historically, an agreement which granted a person possession of a property for an unascertainable period was treated as a form of freehold interest which lasted for the remainder of that person's life. Such a 'tenancy for life' interest can no longer exist and now takes effect as a tenancy for a 90-year fixed term, which may be determined by one month's notice after the tenant's death or in accordance with the terms of the agreement (LPA 1925 s149(6); *Mexfield*).

Exclusive possession

The tenant's use

1.29 Exclusive possession means that the arrangement conveys to the tenant the use to the exclusion of all others of the premises in question, including the landlord (or anyone else the landlord claims to try to let in). Exclusive possession is the most important, and on occasion (albeit now only rarely) can be the hardest to establish of the four essential qualities of tenancy, because even a licensee (see paras 1.114–1.130) can have exclusive occupation of premises and yet be considered no more than licensee.

Rights of entry

1.30 Exclusive use is not destroyed because the landlord retains some right to visit – for example, to inspect for disrepair, or to collect the rent – nor, for example, because under the terms of the tenancy the landlord provides cleaning of the premises, and a cleaner has occasional access to the premises to carry out his or her duties. Such functions are visits to the premises, or services performed to or in the premises, but they are not use of them as such. Indeed the express reservation of a right to enter for limited purposes tends to confirm that the occupier has exclusive possession, for otherwise it would be unnecessary to spell out the right: *Bruton v London & Quadrant Housing Trust*, above.

Unrestricted access

1.31 If, however, the extent of services is such that the access has to be unrestricted, ie not limited to particular times or occasions, the arrangement will, rather, be that of lodging, a form of licence (see para 1.35).

The control test

1.32 It may be that in the normal management of a hotel or hostel, the landlord reserves the right to shift occupiers from room to room, as occasion demands. If so, the occupier cannot be described as having exclusive possession of the premises, even though he or she may have exclusive use of whatever room he or she is occupying for the time being. This is the 'control' test: because the landlord controls even the internal use of the premises, the tenant does not have exclusive possession.

Avoidance and sham

1.33 Statutory rights – in particular, security of tenure – normally attach to tenancies rather than to lesser rights (ie licence). It is accordingly on a finding of tenancy that landlords have directed the most concerted attacks. The reservation of a right for the landlord him- or herself to use the premises, not merely to visit them, or else a right to put some other person in to use them, would, if a genuine term of the arrangement, effectively destroy the idea of exclusive possession (*Somma v Hazelhurst*, 1978). Today, however, the courts are much quicker and more astute to appreciate that such terms may not be genuine but a 'sham' (or pretence or false label) designed to avoid the protection that attaches to tenancies. If so, the courts will not uphold the term (see para 1.53). A sham arises when a document claims one thing, but the reality or actuality is, and was intended to be, something quite different, eg creating the (false) impression that a group of occupiers are not joint tenants.

1.34 This issue of avoidance came to a head in the case of *Street v Mountford*, 1985, in which, following an earlier line of Court of Appeal authority, the landlord argued that there was no tenancy because none was intended (see para 1.40); accordingly the occupier was a licensee (see paras 1.114–1.130). The House of Lords attacked the development of this 'intention' test in favour of the more traditional approach which had previously prevailed, pursuant to which the court decides for itself what the intention is, by reference to whether the rights that have granted amount to tenancy.

> In order to ascertain the nature and quality of the occupancy and to see whether the occupier has or has not a stake in the room or only permission for himself personally to occupy, the court must decide whether upon its true construction the agreement confers on the occupier exclusive possession. If exclusive possession at a rent for a term does not constitute a tenancy then the distinction between a contractual tenancy and a contractual licence of land becomes wholly unidentifiable.

1.35 It said:

> In the case of residential accommodation there is no difficulty in deciding whether the grant confers exclusive possession. An occupier of residential accommodation at a rent for a term is either a lodger or a tenant. The occupier is a lodger if the landlord provides attendance or services which require the landlord or his servants to exercise unrestricted access to and use of the premises. A lodger is entitled to live in the premises but cannot call the place his own ...
>
> If on the other hand residential accommodation is granted for a term at a rent with exclusive possession, the landlord providing neither attendance nor services, the grant is a tenancy; any express reservation to the landlord of limited rights to enter and view the state of the premises and to repair and maintain the premises only serves to emphasise the fact that the grantee is entitled to exclusive possession and is a tenant ... There can be no tenancy unless the occupier enjoys exclusive possession; but an occupier who enjoys exclusive possession is not necessarily a tenant. He may be owner in fee simple, a trespasser, a mortgagee in possession, an object of charity or a service occupier. To constitute a tenancy the occupier must be granted exclusive possession for a fixed or periodic term certain in consideration of a premium or periodical payments. The grant may be express, or may be inferred where the owner accepts weekly or other periodical payments from the occupier.

Lodger or tenant? Attendance or services

1.36 The sort of attendances or services (see also para 1.302) which would mean that the occupier is a lodger rather than a tenant might include daily room-cleaning, emptying rubbish, changing sheets periodically, the provision of meals (see also para 1.303) or other 'housekeeping-type' activities (*Huwyler v Ruddy*, 1996).

The three hallmarks of tenancy

1.37 The House of Lords identified three hallmarks of tenancy: exclusive occupation of residential accommodation, payment and term, ie periods or length of tenancy.

> Unless these three hallmarks are decisive, it really becomes impossible to distinguish a contractual tenancy from a contractual licence save by the professed intention of the parties or by the judge awarding marks for drafting ... The only intention which is relevant is the intention demonstrated by the agreement to grant exclusive possession for a term at a rent. Sometimes it may be difficult to discover whether, on the true construction of an agreement, exclusive possession is conferred. Sometimes it may appear from the surrounding circumstances that there was no intention to create legal relationships. Sometimes it may appear from the surrounding circumstances that the right to exclusive possession is referable to a legal relationship other than a tenancy. Legal relationships to which the grant of exclusive possession might be referable and which would or might negate the grant of an estate or interest in the land include occupancy under a contract for the sale of the land, occupancy pursuant to a contract of employment or occupancy referable to the holding of an office. But where as in the present case the only circumstances are that residential accommodation is offered and accepted with exclusive possession for a term at a rent, the result is a tenancy.

A fork by any other name

1.38 The question is determined not by what name the parties put on the agreement, but by to what the agreement is considered to amount in law.

> It does not necessarily follow that a document described as a licence is, merely on that account, to be regarded as amounting only to a licence in law. The whole of the document must be looked at and if, after it has been examined, the right conclusion appears to be that, whatever label has been attached to it, it in fact conferred and imposed on the grantee in substance the rights and obligation of a landlord, then it must be given the appropriate effect, that is to say, it must be treated as a tenancy agreement as distinct from a mere licence... The important statement of principle is that the relationship is determined by the

> law, and not by the label the parties choose to put on it ... It is simply a matter of ascertaining the true relationship of the parties. (Jenkins LJ in *Addiscombe Garden Estates v Crabbe*, 1958.)

1.39 Or, as it was put graphically in *Street*:

> ... [t]he manufacture of a five-pronged implement for manual digging results in a fork even if the manufacturer, unfamiliar with the English language, insists that he intended to make and has made a spade.

Paying arrangement

1.40 In every case, one should ask whether the arrangement is the normal arrangement by which one person comes to occupy someone else's premises for use as a home, customarily paying rent in money for the right. If it is, then this is likely to be a tenancy however the parties have described it, and whatever they may have said that their intentions were:

> ... the courts must pay attention to the facts and surrounding circumstances and to what people do as well as to what people say. (*AG Securities v Vaughan*, 1988).

1.41 Once the occupier is paying for the accommodation, then there must be some overriding reason which prevents the occupation being that of tenancy. Strictly, it is not even necessary to pay rent in order to establish that there is a tenancy (*Ashburn Anstalt v Arnold*, 1989), but the courts do tend to look sceptically in this day and age at any arrangement purporting to be tenancy under which no rent is paid (*Heslop v Burns*, 1974) and will only be prepared to treat it as a tenancy if they can find some other consideration by way of discernible benefit to the landlord in exchange for the tenancy.

Holding over

1.42 The analysis thus far addresses what might be called 'new' or 'original' arrangements. The position may be somewhat different when a tenancy is brought to an end but the tenant stays on, perhaps paying for use and occupation, even though he or she has no right to do so under any contract or statutory protection. Thus, in *Marcroft Wagons v Smith*, 1951, a woman had lived with her parents in a cottage for 50 years. Her father was the original tenant and, on his death, his wife was entitled, by the law then in force, to 'succeed' to the tenancy (see para 1.279). Only one such succession was, however, permitted and, on the death of her mother, the daughter faced eviction. She asked for the tenancy to be granted to her but the landlords refused, although they permitted her to remain in occupation while she found somewhere else to live, during which period they continued to charge her the same weekly rent as her mother had been paying. It was – albeit with some hesitation – held, in substance, that there had been no intention to create a new contract. The court emphasised that this could only be the result where the would-be tenant was already in occupation of the premises at the time at which the arrangement was made; if an arrangement on those lines was offered to someone not living in the premises, it would still constitute tenancy (*Street v Mountford*, 1985).

New tenancy v statutory protection

1.43 The result of *Marcroft*, and a number of cases which followed it, has been that when a tenancy comes to an end, but the occupier stays on for a period of time paying a weekly sum of money, the courts have not necessarily assumed a new tenancy agreement. If the reason why the occupier has gone on paying, and the landlord accepting, rent is because there is a statutory right to remain in occupation, ie statutory protection, the courts will assume that what is intended by the payment and acceptance of rent is the exercise of the statutory right to remain, rather than a new tenancy (*Clarke v Grant*, 1950), with whatever statutory consequences the particular legislation has in mind (see chapter 2).

Disputed right to remain

1.44 If there is a dispute between the parties as to whether or not the occupier is entitled to remain in occupation, then – even if the occupier continues to pay the rent and the landlord to accept it pending resolution of the dispute – the courts might not assume a new tenancy (*Longrigg, Burrough and Trounson v Smith*, 1979).

1.45 While, therefore, it is true that the normal inference to be drawn from payment and acceptance of rent is that there is a tenancy (*Lewis v MTC (Cars)*, 1975; see also *Street v Mountford*, 1985), some particular or peculiar explanation or 'special circumstance' why the landlord is leaving an occupier in his or her premises, and on that account accepting money, may well lead the the courts to find that there is no tenancy, and consequently that there is only a licence.

1.46 When a person stays on after the termination of a tenancy without a new tenancy, 'rent' is properly called 'mesne profits', and landlords frequently declare that money will only be accepted as such, although such a declaration is not decisive as to whether or not a new tenancy has been created. On the other hand, the fact that the payment is called 'rent' will also not be decisive (*Westminster City Council v Basson*, 1990).

Charity

1.47 An occupier who is 'an object of charity' is not a tenant even if he or she has exclusive possession (*Street v Mountford*, 1985 (see para 1.34)), reflecting the need quickly to move occupiers who no longer qualify for assistance from the charity's property. Accordingly, occupiers of almshouses are licensees rather than tenants (*Gray and others v Taylor*, 1998). This lack of security has been held held not to breach Articles 8 (right to respect for family life and home) or 14 (non-discrimination) ECHR (*Watts v Stewart*, 2016).

Joint tenancy

1.48 A joint tenancy occurs wherever more than one person shares the tenancy. Joint tenants do not each have a different part of, for example, a flat or a house: they are all equally entitled to share possession of the whole of it. Between them, they must establish the four essential qualities of tenancy (*AG Securities v Vaughan*, 1988); but they need not establish them (and, in particular, exclusive possession) as against each other. Joint tenants are, unless the agreement states to the contrary (*AG Securities v Vaughan*, 1988; *Demuren v Seal Estates*, 1978), each liable for the whole rent of the premises, so that if a landlord can only trace one of them, that one will be obliged to pay any and all rent outstanding (though he or she may subsequently be able to recover shares from any of the missing joint tenants). Where there is no joint liability for the rent this may prevent a joint tenancy arising, and the occupiers may only be licensees (*Mikeover Ltd v Brady*, 1989). When one joint tenant dies, the other or others become the tenant or remaining joint tenants by a 'right of survivorship' (*Birmingham City Council v Walker*, 2007).

Joint tenancy v sole tenancy

1.49 It is possible, however, that people who assume that they are joint tenants are not so in law. For example, a group of friends take a flat together but only one of them is named in, or signs, the agreement, if any, or only one of them is named on the rent book. At first sight, the law would assume that the named occupier was the sole tenant, and that his or her sharers were either his or her subtenants (see para 1.59) or licensees (see paras 1.114–1.130), most likely the latter

(*Monmouth BC v Marlog*, 1994). There is some merit to this approach, for as between the members of the group, it is unlikely that they will have wanted the formality of landlord and subtenant. Most likely, they are sharing the outgoings, perhaps even buying food together, and living as one household. This would suggest licence rather than subtenancy. Subtenancy may be established, however, if there is clear evidence of separate living).

1.50 It is possible to upset this first impression with evidence that the entry of one name only was either an oversight or intentionally inaccurate, by showing that the landlord was contracting with the whole group, and that it was clearly intended, as between themselves and as between them and the landlord, that they should all have equal rights in the premises. This might be evidence by the fact that they each pay the rent for the whole of the premises to the landlord in turn and/or that references were sought from each of them individually. Although not impossible, it is nonetheless difficult to upset the first impression created by a written indication that the tenancy belongs to only one of the sharers (*Hanstown Properties Ltd v Green*, 1978).

Non-exclusive occupation

1.51 One problem that has arisen in the context has been caused by the use of the evasive device of 'non-exclusive occupation agreements,' pursuant to which the landlord insists on entering into a series of separate contracts with each occupier, granting to each the right to use the premises in question in common with others, but not to use a particular part of the premises. In this way, the landlord seeks to avoid a finding of tenancy of some part of the premises as against him or her, and – because the agreements are all separate – seeks also to avoid a finding of joint tenancy of the whole of the premises between him- or herself and the group. With the availability of new forms of tenancy which do not carry long-term security of tenure (particularly the assured shorthold tenancy – see para 1.246), landlords are less inclined to use such devices. Nonetheless, they are still in some use.

1.52 Such evasive devices often purport to retain for the landlord a right to come and live in the premises him- or herself, or else to select new occupiers as and when one or other of the original group departs, hence destroying the quality of exclusive possession (see para 1.27). Such arrangements could be genuine, eg if the landlord effectively runs a small-scale 'hostel', and chooses the occupiers him- or herself. Such an arrangement, if genuine, will create a series of individual licences, or, if specific rooms are allocated to individual occupiers, may create separate tenancies of the individual, specific rooms (*AG Securities v Vaughan*, 1988).

Genuine or sham

1.53 Sometimes, however, these arrangements are not genuine. In *Street v Mountford*, three cases in which the lower courts had upheld non-exclusive occupation agreements as genuine were said to have been wrongly decided, and to be obvious sham arrangements which the courts should have treated as tenancies. The matter was considered again by the House of Lords in *Antoniades v Villiers; AG Securities v Vaughan*, 1988. Save where the agreement was, unusually, a genuine arrangement between the landlord on one hand, and separate individuals on the other, as in *Vaughan* itself, the House of Lords reiterated that pretences devised to get around statutory protection would not be upheld. The courts should look at all the circumstances, including the relationship between the occupiers before they approached the landlord, the negotiations and, so far as the written agreement is alleged to be a pretence or sham, even after they have taken up occupation. If the reality is that the occupiers are to use the premises as a home together, paying a rent for it, then the arrangement must be construed as a (joint) tenancy, no matter what documents have been drawn up.

Earlier cases

1.54 This accorded with earlier case-law on residential protection.

> It has been said before, and it must be said again, that in the consideration of questions arising under the Rent Acts, the court must look at the substance and reality of a transaction, not its form. (*Viscount Simonds, Elmdene Estates v White*, 1960).

1.55 In one case, *Samrose Properties v Gibbard*, 1957, Lord Evershed MR said that a court must always ask itself:

> Whether the transaction, viewed as a whole and according to the substance of it, is in truth one which ... is on that side of the line which frees the premises from the impact of the Acts, or whether, so regarded, the transaction is one which is of the mischief which the Acts were designed to avoid.

Subsequent cases

1.56 There has been a number of subsequent Court of Appeal decisions which have sought to apply the principles laid down by the House of Lords in *Antoniades* and *AG Securities*. In two of them (*Stribling v Wickham*, 1989, and *Mikeover Ltd v Brady*, 1989), the court found that the arrangements were genuine licences, while in three others (*Nicolaou v Pitt*, 1989; *Aslan v Murphy*, 1989 and *Duke v Wynne*, 1989), the agreements were all found to be pretences and the occupiers held to be tenants. (The rise of the assured shorthold tenancy (see para 1.246) probably explains why there have been few such cases since.)

Replacement occupiers

1.57 Once joint tenancy is established, there can still be problems. Commonly, in the course of time, one or more of the original occupiers will move on to alternative accommodation. What, then, is the position of new occupiers, assuming that they are selected by the occupiers themselves and not by the landlord? If a new occupier is selected by the landlord, this will afford the landlord evidence that he or she is in overall possession of the premises and that there is no tenancy at all.

1.58 If the landlord consents, a new occupier may become a joint tenant with the others. If he or she does not, then the existing occupiers cannot impose a new party to the tenancy on the landlord against his or her will. The new occupier must therefore be either the subtenant (see para 1.57) or licensee (see paras 1.114–1.130) of the existing and remaining joint tenants. Unless the new occupier enjoys the four essential qualities of tenancy (see paras 1.22–1.29), as against the existing joint tenants – which will be unusual – it is likely that he or she will be no more than their licensee. The court will look closely at the arrangement and, unless there is clear evidence of separate living, it is likely to be inclined to view another occupier as a sharer, or as a lodger, and in either event therefore a licensee, even though rent is paid, rather than as a subtenant (*Monmouth BC v Marlog*, 1994).

Subtenancy

1.59 It is entirely possible that a person's landlord is him- or herself no more than a tenant of another. In such a case, the 'middle' tenant is known as a 'mesne' (pronounced 'mean') tenant, and the 'lower' tenant as the subtenant. Many more people are subtenants than realise it. As noted above (see para 1.12), someone who owns on a long lease is a tenant, so that the tenant of an owner who holds only on a long lease is a subtenant. There are major property holdings still in existence in which a series of interests and sub-interests are held on leasehold. It is not only possible but common for there to be many 'intervening' interests by way of superior leasehold between an actual occupier and the ultimate freeholder.

Continuation of mesne tenancy

1.60 So long as the mesne tenancy continues to exist, the subtenant is in no different a position than any other tenant. His or her landlord (the mesne tenant) must serve notice to quit to terminate the subtenancy in the normal way, and the subtenancy may fall into any of the classes of protection discussed below. This is so even in the case of a Rent Act (RA) 1977 protected tenant whose contractual tenancy comes to an end so that he or she becomes what is known as a statutory tenant which is not in law a true tenancy at all (see para 1.269).

Termination of mesne tenancy

1.61 Difficulties arise once the mesne tenant's interest comes to an end. In such a case, the question to be decided is whether the subtenant has any right to remain in occupation as against the superior landlord. This will depend on three factors:

1) whether there is any statutory protection afforded to the subtenant;
2) whether or not the subtenancy is a legal or illegal subtenancy; and,
3) how the mesne tenancy comes to an end.

Statutory protection

1.62 As we shall see, there is a number of different types of statutory protection. Each of them has to be considered separately.

Housing Act (HA) 1985 and Housing Act 1996 Part 5

Tenants within this class of protection are secure (see para 1.160), introductory (see para 1.210) or demoted (see para 1.252) tenants; they are the tenants of local authorities and other public bodies (see paras 1.164–1.165). Even if the landlord is only a tenant – including leaseholder – of someone else, it is only in the most rare case that it will enjoy any statutory protection against its landlord, so rare that it may for this purpose be disregarded. Nor is any statutory provision made to protect its tenants. Nor is any statutory provision made to protect the subtenants of its tenants. Accordingly, when the mesne tenancy is determined, the issue depends on whether or not the subtenancy is legal or illegal and on how the tenancy comes to an end.

Housing Act 1988

Tenants within the protection of HA 1988 are tenants either of a private landlord or of a private registered provider (PRP) or registered social landlord (RSL) (see paras 1.162–1.163), and are known as assured tenants (see para 1.220), whether fully assured or assured shorthold (see para 1.246). The landlord him- or herself or itself will not normally be assured, because the tenant under an assured tenancy must be an individual, and in occupation as an only or principal home. If the landlord is a tenant – including leaseholder – of another, and his or her or its tenancy is determined, then his or her or its legal subtenants will become the tenant of that other and will become his or her or its assured tenants depending on the application of the usual tests for determining that question (see paras 1.62–1.73). This applies 'down the line.' Accordingly, while an occupying, assured tenant's own subtenant will not normally be assured (because there is an exemption for those living in the same building as his or her resident landlord (see para 1.235(10)), if the resident landlord's assured tenancy ends, the legal subtenant may become an assured tenant.

Rent Act 1977

Rent Act tenants are those whose tenancies date from before the introduction of assured tenancy by HA 1988, on 15 January 1989 (see para 1.220). Unlike HA 1988 (see above), there is no requirement that the tenant is an individual and there is initially no occupation requirement, so that it is entirely possible that both landlord and tenant have tenancies within RA 1977. If the landlord's interest determines, his or her or its legal subtenants then become the tenant of the landlord directly (RA 1977 s137). As regards the subtenant of an occupying protected tenant, it is also possible that he or she will be excluded because his or her landlord (the occupying mesne tenant) lives in the same building (see para 1.277(1)), but this may not apply in the case of some, older subtenancies (see para 1.277(1)). The principle that subtenancies come to bind the superior landlord when the mesne tenancy ends also (see above, HA 1988) applies 'down the line,' but it only applies to legal subtenants who are within RA 1977, so that the line stops at a tenant who is not (*Stanley v Compton*, 1951).

Note. As foreshadowed (see para 1.60), RA 1977 protected tenancies may be contractual or what is called statutory (see para 1.269): if the subtenancy was statutory rather than contractual, so it will remain as against the superior landlord (*Keepers & Governors of the*

Free Grammar School of John Lyon v Jordan, 1995). Where a subtenant of furnished accommodation becomes the tenant directly of a superior landlord by operation of s137, then the landlord is entitled to disclaim responsibility for the provision of furniture, if he or she does so in writing within six weeks of the subtenant becoming his or her tenant (s138).

Notification

1.63 A Rent Act protected tenant who creates a lawful Rent Act protected subtenancy is obliged to notify the landlord of this in writing, within 14 days of doing so, stating details of the subtenancy, including the name of the subtenant and the rent he or she is paying under the subtenancy (RA 1977 s139). There is no analogous obligation under HA 1985 or HA 1988.

Legal or illegal subtenancy

Illegal subtenancy

1.64 In determining whether or not, on the termination of an intervening, mesne tenancy, the subtenant becomes the superior landlord's tenant directly much turns on whether the subtenancy is 'legal' or 'illegal'.

1.65 There is only an illegal subtenancy if the terms of the mesne tenancy include a prohibition on sub-letting (see chapter 4). Most written tenancies include such a term, and many weekly or monthly tenancies granted in the last few years, and for which the terms are to be found in printed rent books provided by the landlord, will also be subject to such a prohibition. Even a rent book issued for a period subsequent to the grant may be used as evidence of a prohibition (*RC Glaze v Alabdinboni*, 1992). The particular, statutory rights of HA 1985 secure tenants and HA 1988 assured tenants to sub-let – at all and/or with consent – are considered in chapter 4 (see paras 4.127 and 4.144–4.146).

1.66 Some prohibitions on sub-letting are absolute, ie they simply state that it is not permitted. Some are qualified, ie they state that it is not permitted without the consent of the landlord. The law implies into a qualified prohibition a condition that such consent will not unreasonably be withheld and, if unreasonably withheld, that the consent will be treated as given (Landlord and Tenant Act (LTA) 1927 s19; *Balls Brothers Ltd v Sinclair*, 1931. *Note*: this is not so where the power to sub-let is implied by HA 1988 s15, into a HA assured tenancy – see para 4.144).

Withholding of consent

1.67 There can only be an unreasonable withholding if there has been a request, and a refusal before the sub-letting is granted (*Barrow v Isaacs*, 1891; *Eastern Telegraph Co v Dent*, 1899). It is withholding which is prohibited, however, so that if the tenant seeks consent but the landlord fails to reply after a reasonable time, consent has been withheld (*Wilson v Fynn*, 1948). Nonetheless, it can be risky to rely on a court finding that a withholding has been unreasonable, so that someone seeking to use a right to sublet is well advised to seek consent and, when it is withheld, to seek a declaration from the court that the withholding is unreasonable, before granting the subtenancy (*Mills v Cannon Brewery Co*, 1920).

Landlord and Tenant Act 1988

1.68 If the tenant seeks consent in writing, then the position is additionally affected by the Landlord and Tenant Act (LTA) 1988. This Act applies only where the covenant is a qualified covenant (see para 1.66). Where a written application is made, the landlord owes the tenant a duty to reply within a reasonable time, either consenting, or else giving written notice either of a refusal, in which case the reasons must be stated, or of a 'conditional consent', in which case the conditions must be stated. An unreasonable condition is not permitted. Under the Act, the burden is on the landlord to show: that he or she replied within a reasonable time; that any condition attached is reasonable; and, that a refusal is reasonable.

1.69 Whether or not a withholding is reasonable will turn on the facts of each case (*Lee v Carter*, 1948) including the impact of statutory protection (*West Layton Ltd v Ford*, 1979). The reasonableness of withholding consent is not confined to questions about the proposed subtenant but can include consideration of the landlord's own interests, provided they are interests to which a reasonable landlord would have regard (*Leeward Securities Ltd v Lilyheath Properties Ltd*, 1983), eg questions of good estate management, rather than an attempt to extract some benefit outside of the tenancy, such as an unanticipated surrender (*Rayburn v Wolf*, 1985). The burden is on the tenant to show unreasonable withholding of consent (*Rayburn*).

Waiver of illegality

1.70 Even if an illegal subtenancy is created, however, it is possible that it will subsequently be 'legalised'. This can happen because the landlord learns of the illegal sub-letting and yet 'waives' the breach of the term of the tenancy by continuing to accept rent from the mesne tenant as if nothing had happened. Waiver requires that the landlord knew that there had been an actual sub-letting, not merely, eg that a friend had come to live with the mesne tenant, but once the landlord is aware of the basic facts which show that subletting has occurred, the acceptance of one payment of rent may be sufficient to waive the breach.

1.71 The knowledge of the landlord's employees, agents or officers is imputed to the landlord, so that if one such person knows of the illegal sub-letting and the landlord continues to accept rent, there will have been waiver (*Metropolitan Properties Co v Cordery*, 1979). In one case, the issue of proceedings to gain access to the flat to inspect it, pursuant to the terms of the lease, was held to have waived an existing breach of the covenant not to sublet, of which the landlord was already aware (*Cornillie v Saha*, 1996).

1.72 Once waiver has occurred, the subtenant becomes a legal subtenant as if in the first place he or she had been allowed in lawfully.

No advantage of own wrong

1.73 A tenant who lets illegally cannot him- or herself subsequently take advantage of it (*Critchley v Clifford*, 1962) by claiming not to be bound by it. It is, after all, his or her wrong, or breach, not that of the subtenant. It is no ground for the eviction of a subtenant by the mesne tenant that the letting was illegal.

Termination of mesne tenancy

1.74 There is one exception to the limits described above as to when a subtenancy can survive the mesne tenancy, which is if the mesne tenant surrenders (see paras 2.24–2.28) to the landlord, and the landlord accepts the surrender (*Parker v Jones*, 1910). In this case, the subtenant becomes the landlord's direct tenant regardless of whether or not the subtenancy is illegal, and regardless of statutory protection.

1.75 This arises by operation of common law and may also be said to operate by way of waiver, ie of the illegality (see paras 1.70–1.72), although – exceptionally – it is a waiver that takes place even though the landlord does not know of the existence of the subtenant. By accepting the surrender, the landlord is deemed to have waived any breaches by the tenant and to have taken over the tenant's liabilities, which include the subtenancy. By this means, a subtenant may acquire statutory security in appropriate circumstances, eg where a local authority had let premises as a business, part of which had been sublet residentially, and the mesne business tenant surrendered (*Basingstoke & Deane BC v Paice*, 1995). *Note*. As foreshadowed in para 1.60, there is a distinction under RA 1977 between a tenancy which is still contractual and one that has become what is called statutory (see para 1.269). There can be no surrender of a mesne tenancy within RA 1977 which is a statutory tenancy, because a statutory tenancy is not a true tenancy at common law (*Solomon v Orwell*, 1954).

Termination of subtenancy

1.76 If the subtenancy is not to become a tenancy directly held from the superior landlord, whether by statute or surrender, the subtenancy automatically determines, without any need for notice or other steps, on the determination of the mesne tenancy (*Moore Properties (Ilford) v McKeon*, 1976). *Note*. A subtenant, even one who is an illegal subtenant, can, however, apply for relief from forfeiture: LPA 1925 s146(4), and see paras 2.37–2.46.

Subtenancy and licence

1.77 The foregoing discussion applies to subtenants. Not everyone living with a tenant will be a subtenant; he or she may be a lodger or sharer, ie a licensee (see paras 1.114–1.130). Whether or not a person is the licensee or subtenant of another will be a question of fact based on the normal considerations, but it is true to say that where the parties are living in the same premises, the court will look closely at the arrangement and, unless there is clear evidence of separate living, is unlikely to find subtenancy (see paras 1.49 and 1.58).

Assignment

1.78 The term 'assignment' has been used before, to describe the purchase of a long lease from the existing leaseholder (see paras 1.12–1.13). The same may in theory occur in connection with the shorter forms of tenancy with which this heading is concerned; that is to say that one tenant may assign the tenancy to another. An assignee steps into the shoes of the outgoing tenant and occupies on exactly the same terms.

1.79 The rights of HA 1985 secure, introductory and demoted and HA 1988 assured (including assured shorthold) tenants to assign are described in chapter 4. As foreshadowed in para 1.60, there is a distinction under RA 1977 between a tenancy which is still contractual and one that has become what is called statutory (see para 1.269):

only a contractual tenancy can be assigned, ie not a RA statutory tenancy (chapter 4; *Jessamine Investment Co v Schwartz*, 1976).

1.80 If there is nothing in the terms of the tenancy or of a statute prohibiting assignment, then it is permissible. Most tenancy agreements and rent books do, however, include such prohibitions which, like subtenancies (see para 1.66), may be absolute or qualified. As with qualified covenants prohibiting subtenancies (see para 1.66), the law implies a condition that the landlord will not unreasonably withhold consent to an assignment (LTA 1927 s19(1)). The issues concerning withholding of consent discussed in relation to subtenancies (see para 1.67), including the effect of LTA 1988 (see paras 1.68–1.69), likewise apply to requests for consent to an assignment (*Straudley Investments Ltd v Mount Eden Land Ltd (No 1)*, 1996).

1.81 Strictly, assignment should be by formal deed, but there can be an assignment if the transaction is in writing, in a document that sets out all the express terms, and which is signed (LP(MP)A 1989 s2).

1.82 An assignment not by deed, though binding as between the two tenants who are party to it, will not bind the landlord unless he or she accepts the assignment, eg by payment and acceptance of rent, in much the same way and to the same extent as if he or she were deemed to have waived a breach of a covenant (see paras 1.70–1.72) or at least to the extent that the law considers that it would be inequitable to allow the landlord to deny the assignment (*Rodenhurst Estates v Barnes*, 1936), ie that the landlord is 'estopped' from doing so (see paras 1.129–1.130).

1.83 A purported assignment that is neither by deed, nor in writing, signed and setting out the express terms, cannot be effective against the landlord. To sustain a tenancy against the landlord, the assignee has to show that by his or her actions the landlord has accepted him or her as a new tenant in place of the old; in effect, that the old tenancy has been surrendered (see paras 2.24–2.28) and a new tenancy has been accepted in its place in a similar way to which a tenancy may be granted by a landlord as a result of his or her conduct (see paras 1.40–1.41).

Landlords

1.84 **Identity.** It has already been noted that someone may be another person's landlord even though he or she is the tenant of another (see para 1.59). That is not an identity issue, although it gives rise to status issues. The identity of a landlord may, however, not be known if the letting is through an agent, or if there is a transfer of the landlord's interest.

1.85 **Weekly tenancy**. A landlord under a weekly tenancy (but no other) is obliged to provide a rent book or similar document, and commits a criminal offence if he or she does not do so (LTA 1985 ss4, 7). Under this Act, any tenant can, in writing, ask the person who last received rent under the tenancy for the full name and address of the landlord. If the person to whom the demand is made fails to reply, also in writing, within 21 days, he or she commits an offence. This may be important information if, for example, the tenant wants to commence proceedings against an absentee landlord and cannot do so without first establishing his or her identity. Both of these offences should be reported to the council's tenancy relations officer (TRO): see chapter 5.

1.86 **All tenancies**. Under LTA 1987 s48, all landlords of premises which are, or include, dwellings must provide the tenant by notice with an address in England or Wales at which tenants' notices may be served on him or her, until compliance with which duty rent is not due: the notice must be in writing, but may be by means of inclusion in a tenancy agreement, or in a rent book (*Rogan v Woodfield Building Services Ltd*, 1994).

1.87 **Purchase subject to existing interests**. When a person purchases property, he or she generally does so subject to existing interests in it. A tenancy is an interest in property as, indeed, is a subtenancy, and even an illegal subtenancy. Whether the purchaser is bound by an existing tenancy depends on the nature of the tenancy. As already noted (see para 1.20), certain tenancies have to be registered with the Land Registry: any tenancy granted on or after 1 October 2003 for a term of more than seven years and any tenancy granted before that date for a term of more than 21 years. If such a tenancy is not registered, it is only binding on purchaser in two circumstances. First, the purchaser will be bound by the tenancy if it has been recorded at the Land Registry as a caution or notice against the landlord's title (LRA 2002 Sch 12 paras 1 and 2). Secondly, it will be binding if the tenant is in occupation of the property at the date of the sale, unless, prior to the sale, the purchaser asked the tenant about why he or she was in occupation of the property and the tenant failed to disclose the existence of the tenancy (LRA 2002 Sch 3 para 2). A tenancy which does not have to be registered is binding on purchaser (LRA 2002 Sch 3 para 1). *Note*. A contractual licence (see para 1.127) is not an interest in property; it is a personal right, and it does not bind a purchaser (*Ashburn Anstalt v Arnold*, 1989). In some circumstances, however, where the licence creates an estoppel (see paras 1.129–1.130), a purchaser may be bound by it (*Inwards v Baker*, 1965).

1.88 **Notification.** Before a tenant starts to pay rent to the new landlord, the old landlord should write to him or her, authorising the changeover, and will remain liable as landlord until either he or she or the new landlord does so (LTA 1985 s3).

1.89 **Change of ownership: other issues.** The new landlord takes subject to all the old landlord's rights, liabilities and duties. He or she also takes liable to any knowledge the old landlord had, eg such knowledge as would found a claim for waiver of an illegal subtenancy (see paras 1.64–1.66). A tenancy dates from its original grant, and there is no new tenancy on change of ownership. There are special statutory provisions relating to change of ownership which determine whether or not a tenant still has a resident landlord for the purposes of either HA 1988 (see para 1.233(10)) or RA 1977 (see para 1.277(1)). In addition, there are special provisions governing the transfer of ownership from local authorities (see para 1.205) which may affect the occupier's statutory protection.

Mortgages

1.90 **Freeholders**, long leaseholders and commonholders may have had sufficient money to buy their properties outright but most people acquire property in which they propose to live with a mortgage.

1.91 **Charges.** A mortgage is a form of 'charge', which, in general terms, is a right over someone else's property which provides security for money owed to the person with the benefit of the charge. Charges arise in a number of circumstances. If someone obtains judgment for a debt against a home owner who continues to refuse to pay, he or she can apply to the court for a 'charging order' over the house and, ultimately, use that order to force the sale of the house to meet the debt out of the proceeds. Often, statutes provide that, where a local authority is entitled to require a landlord to carry out works but he or she fails to do so, the authority can do the works in default and recover them from the landlord; the costs of the works become a charge on the landlord's property (see para 11.28).

1.92 **Priority.** There may be a number of charges over one property in favour of different people. The charges are ranked in order of priority, usually governed by the date of the charge, the earliest ranking highest. On sale of the property, the proceeds are used to meet each charge in order of priority.

1.93 A mortgage is a loan against the security of an interest in the house or a flat. The money is usually borrowed in order to buy the property, although sometimes it may be for carrying out repairs or improvements. Sometimes people raise money by way of mortgage because they are in other financial difficulties or want money for their businesses. If a person falls into arrears with his or her mortgage repayments, eviction may follow (see paras 2.14–2.18).

1.94 Strictly, the borrower is known as the mortgagor, and the lender as the mortgagee. As these terms can lead to confusion, however, the former are referred to as the owner-occupier or borrower and the latter as the mortgage company or lender. (It need not be a company as a matter of law but it almost invariably will be in practice).

1.95 It will not in practice be possible to obtain a mortgage on a leasehold property unless there is at least a 30-year period to run on the lease. This is because mortgage companies need security for their loans and must calculate what they can recover by resale of the property, should the occupier fall into arrears on the mortgage at any given point in time. (This is one of the advantages of – and reasons for – commonhold: see para 1.16).

Types of mortgage

1.96 There are two principal sorts of mortgage: capital repayment and endowment.

Capital repayment

1.97 A capital repayment mortgage is a loan which requires repayment in periodic amounts. Although it is not an essential part of a capital repayment mortgage, most mortgage companies insist that there is included in the package an element of insurance, called the mortgage protection policy. This provides insurance against the death of the owner-occupier, in which case the insurance will pay off any outstanding mortgage and so leave the property unencumbered for the next of kin.

1.98 The two essential parts of the repayments are capital repayment and interest (commonly at a variable rate, though it can be fixed or, eg fixed for a period of time). Monthly payments are assessed at an amount slightly larger than the interest due on the original capital loan. This means that at the beginning of a mortgage repayment period, most of the payment is interest, and only a small amount of it is capital repayment. As the capital decreases, however, a decreasing proportion of the repayments goes to interest (still based on the original loan) and an increasing amount to capital.

Endowment

1.99 The monthly payment under an endowment mortgage is a sum assessed in two parts only: interest and life assurance premium. Subject to fluctuations in the mortgage interest rate, both these amounts remain the same. There is no capital repayment. Instead, the life assurance premium is calculated to produce a sum that, either at the end of the period for which the mortgage has been taken out, or on the death of the owner-occupier, will be sufficient to pay off the whole of the capital outstanding. There are other benefits which may be included in an endowment mortgage arrangement, but they are decreasingly popular because the sums produced by the premium have in recent years proved insufficient to pay off the capital, leaving the owner-occupier to make up the balance.

Tenants of landlords with a mortgage

1.100 Because a landlord (whether or not freeholder or leaseholder, and whether or not in residential occupation) may have a mortgage, it is necessary to consider the position of that landlord's tenant or tenants. If the landlord falls into arrears with mortgage repayments, the mortgage company may 'foreclose' and, in effect, take the property over. It is in this situation that problems will arise for the tenant.

1.101 As long as the borrower remains in possession, the tenant's position is wholly unaffected by the existence of a mortgage on the property, even if the tenancy is granted in contravention of its terms (*Church of England Building Society v Piskor*, 1954). There are commonly such terms in a mortgage.

Prior tenancy

1.102 If a person owns property before taking a mortgage on it, then whether a tenancy existing at the date of the mortgage is binding on the mortgage company depends on the nature of the tenancy. As already noted (see para 1.20), certain tenancies have to be registered with the Land Registy: any lease granted on or after 1 October 2003 for a term of more than seven years and any lease granted before that date for a term of more than 21 years. If such a tenancy is not registered, it will only be binding on the mortgage company in two circumstances. First, it will be binding on the mortage company if it has been recorded at the Land Registry as a caution or notice against the landlord's title (LRA 2002 Sch 12 paras 1 and 2). Secondly, it will be binding if the tenant is in occupation of the property at the date of the mortgage, unless, prior to execution of the mortgage, the mortgage company asked the tenant about why he or she was in occupation of the property and the tenant failed to disclose the existence of the tenancy (LRA 2002 Sch 3 para 2). If the tenancy does not have to be registered, it is binding on the mortgage company (LRA 2002 Sch 3 para 1). Where the tenancy is binding on the mortgage company, once the company takes possession, the tenant becomes its tenant, just as if it had bought or otherwise acquired the landlord's interest (see para 1.87).

Illegal tenants

1.103 Almost all mortgage deeds (except those specifically for 'buy to let') prohibit the creation of tenancies, and as the majority of tenancies from people who have a mortgage are in fact created after the mortgage, there are many tenants who are – in this sense – 'illegal' tenants. This does not avail the landlord, or afford him or her any additional right to evict the tenant: as with illegal sub-letting, it is his or her wrong, not that of the tenant (see para 1.73). If the mortgage company obtains possession against the borrower (see paras 2.4–2.18), however, then no matter whether the tenant is statutorily protected or not, he or she has no right of occupation as against the mortgage company, even though the mortgage company knew of the illegal tenancy but continued to accept repayments (*Dudley and District Benefit Building Society v Emerson*, 1949; *Britannia Building Society v Earl*, 1989). There is no analogy with waiver of illegal sub-letting (see paras 1.70–1.72).

1.104 Assured tenants under HA 1988 (see para 1.220) and protected or statutory tenants under RA 1977 (see para 1.258) are, however, given some rights by the Mortgage Repossessions (Protection of Tenants etc) Act 2010 (see para 2.17).

New tenancy?

1.105 It is theoretically possible – although in practice now rare – that, after getting possession, the mortgage company either actively agrees to accept the continued presence of the tenant and takes on the tenancy, or does so by implication by taking rent from the tenant over such a long period that the only inference that can properly be drawn is that it is treating the tenancy as binding upon itself (*Taylor v Ellis*, 1960; *Stroud Building Society v Delamont*, 1960).

Trust

1.106 A trust is what arises when property is held in the name of one person for the benefit of another. This could be freehold, leasehold, commonhold or even a tenancy. When property is held on trust, the ownership is subject to the trust, meaning the purposes of the trust and the interests of the beneficiaries. Property can be held on trust for the benefit of a number of individuals including one of the trustees him- or herself. A person, for example, could buy a house and put it on trust for the use of him- or herself and his or her spouse and/or children. The person could not subsequently dispose of the property, unless all the beneficiaries consented.

1.107 **Trusts of land.** Property is automatically considered to be held on trust whenever two or more people own land or premises jointly. Such a trust is now governed by the Trusts of Land and Appointment of Trustees Act (ToLATA) 1996, which regulates all trusts of land.

1.108 The effect of a trust of land is that any of the joint owners (trustees) can apply to force the property to be sold, even against the wishes of the other party. This is a necessary provision for the value of a half-share in a house will be non-existent if it is not possible to force a sale at will, nor as a matter of land policy would it be desirable to allow any kind of land – including housing – to be indefinitely 'locked' between parties in dispute. These rights are additional to the special provisions available to married partners, and are of most relevance where people have been cohabiting without being married, or where non-cohabitants (eg a small group of friends) purchase property together.

1.109 **Powers of the courts.** Whenever property is held on trust, or is alleged to be held on trust, the court has power to declare whether or not it is held on trust, and in what proportions or for whose benefit, and can also make orders which affect what should happen to the property in question.

1.110 It is not only the parties who can apply to the court, but also someone else with an interest, eg a mortgagee (ToLATA 1996 s14). In deciding what order to make (including whether the property should be sold), the court must take into account the following (ToLATA 1996 s15): the intention of the person or persons who created the trust; the purposes for which the property is held, eg whether the property is a family home; the welfare of any children living in the property; and, the interests of any mortgagee of the property.

1.111 **How trusts arise.** A trust sometimes arises under a formal deed. It may also arise if one person buys property, but factually for the benefit of another. It also arises if one person comes to own property either wholly or in part with someone else's money. In the case of a house or flat, this might arise because, for example, one person has – without becoming a joint owner – made direct contributions to the purchase such as putting up all or part of the purchase price of the property, or all or part of the deposit on a property purchased under mortgage, or has simply contributed to the mortgage repayments, or if he or she has contributed to maintenance or improvement of the property in such a way as to increase its value.

1.112 Where there is such a direct contribution, but it was made without any common intention – on the part both of owner and contributor – to share an interest in the property, the trust is known as a resulting trust (*Lloyds Bank Plc v Rosset*, 1990). Where the common intention was that the contribution would result in a share of the property, the trust is known as a constructive trust, even if there was no common intention as to the extent of the shares (*Drake v Whipp*, 1995). A common intention is one that is shared and expressed between the parties, as distinct from an intention which one or other party had in his or her or her own mind but that was never communicated to the other (*Springette v Defoe*, 1992).

1.113 **Declaration of trust.** It follows that if two people are living together, whether or not married or in a civil partnership, one of whom has made such a direct contribution, the law has power to intervene at a time of break-up and make an appropriate declaration: for example, that the house is held for the benefit of the other person, or that he or she or she has an interest in it. In the case of a resulting trust, that the beneficial interest is proportionate to the direct contributions (*Pettitt v Pettitt*, 1969). In the case of a constructive trust, however, quantification of the beneficial interest is not confined to consideration of direct contributions; the court looks at the conduct of the parties as a whole to determine what they intended (*Jones v Kernott*, 2011; *Stack v Dowden*, 2007; *Gissing v Gissing*, 1971; *Capehorn v Harris*, 2015; *Barnes v Phillips* 2015).

Licence

1.114 **Permission.** While the normal arrangement whereby one person rents, as a home, property belonging to or under the control of another is that of tenancy (see paras 1.17–1.58), there is a number of arrangements of less formality, which are known as licences. The term 'licence' means 'permission', whether used in connection with housing, driving a car, or selling alcohol (*Thomas v Sorrell*, 1673). A licence is a personal right, rather than an interest in land, and therefore cannot be transferred to someone else. (The inclusion in an agreement of a prohibition on assignment may be taken as an indication that the agreement was intended to create a tenancy, as there would be no other reason for including the term in a licence). In the housing context, it is used to describe one who is not a trespasser (because he or she has permission to occupy) but who is neither a freeholder, leaseholder or commonholder, nor a tenant. Were it not for 'licences', there would be no term appropriate for people such as family, friends or casual guests.

1.115 **Family**. The most common example of licence is a person living in property which is either owned or rented by a member of the family, eg a parent. The non-owner, or non-tenant, is in this circumstance in law a licensee. Similarly, a cohabitant is a licensee of his or her partner, if it is the partner who owns or who is the tenant of the accommodation in which they live. Technically, if one spouse or civil partner is the owner or tenant of the home in which they live, the other spouse or partner is only his or her licensee, although it has been said that, both as a matter of practice (because of the extent of rights as between spouses) and as a matter of good taste, it is inappropriate to consider one spouse as the licensee of another (*National Provincial Bank v Ainsworth*, 1965). The special position of spouses, civil partners and cohabitants will be considered in the context of relationship break-up in chapter 7.

1.116 **Sharing.** Some people are quite obviously no more than licensees of another. Common sense dictates that a friend who comes to stay for a while is not to be considered a tenant, while at the same time he or she cannot be a trespasser because he or she is there at the host's invitation. This does not change simply because, for example, the guest is invited to stay for several weeks and even agrees to pay some sort of contribution towards the housekeeping expenses, or indeed, an amount of rent, although at this last stage the agreement is beginning to border on some sort of formal arrangement. Where two people move into accommodation, one named as tenant and the other not, it is likely that the latter will be viewed as no more than a sharer, and therefore licensee, of the other (*Monmouth BC v Marlog*, 1994 – see paras 1.49, 1.58 and 1.77).

1.117 **Long-stay hotel occupation**. There are other arrangements, however, where it is less immediately obvious whether a person is to be considered a licensee or a tenant. If someone goes to stay in a hotel for a few days, for example, it would not be considered that he or she had become a tenant of the hotel. But what if he or she had made his or her home over a number of years in the hotel? There are many who live for considerable periods of time in hotels, who have nowhere else to live and who regard the hotel as a home. In *Luganda v Service Hotels*, 1969 the Court of Appeal considered that, nonetheless, such an occupier was only a licensee and did not become a tenant. A similar view was reached in *Brillouet v Landless*, 1996.

1.118 **Hostels.** In the same way, the occupier of a hostel is usually considered a mere licensee, eg a YWCA hostel, as in *R v South Middlesex Rent Tribunal ex p Beswick*, 1976, or one of the many hostels which exist not primarily to provide housing for people, but to help those who have had some sort of difficulty, such as drug addicts, mental patients, ex-prisoners, to reach the point at which they can manage on their own: *Trustees of the Alcoholic Recovery Project v Farrell*, 1977.

1.119 The distinction which may be drawn between hostels and houses of bedsitting-rooms is that in a hostel there is normally a resident housekeeper or manager, and the occupier is bound to obey rules and regulations which interfere, far more than normal housing management rules, with the occupier's way of life. See, for example, *Westminster City Council v Clarke*, 1992, where a hostel provided accommodation for vulnerable single homeless men.

1.120 **Old people's home.** *Abbeyfield (Harpenden) Society v Woods*, 1968 affords another example. The society ran an old people's home, consisting of single rooms for which the old people paid a weekly rent. The project could only exist satisfactorily so long as each of the occupiers was self-sufficient. Once an elderly person required constant care and attention, it was no longer possible for him or her to go on living there. There were no facilities for the provision of such assistance and, clearly, in a house containing nothing but the elderly, the consequences could be serious. It was held that the occupier was a lodger, ie a licensee, not a tenant.

1.121 **Acts of kindness.** Acts of kindness or generosity are not acts from which tenancies spring. In *Booker v Palmer*, 1942, a city family was provided with accommodation in the country during the war. They later suggested that they had become tenants of the property, but the Court of Appeal applied what it termed a 'golden rule' of interpretation of such matters: that the courts will not impute intention to enter into legal relations (including tenancy), where the spirit of the arrangement is family or friendly.

1.122 'Intention' is, however, a difficult test to apply: see the discussion of the reasoning of the House of Lords in *Street v Mountford*, 1985 (see para 1.37). Thus, in *Marchant v Charters*, 1976, there was a house of bedsitting-rooms: each of the occupiers had cooking facilities and equipment in his or her own room, the rooms were furnished, and the occupiers lived wholly separate lives; that is to say there were no communal facilities. The house was expressed to be let and was actually let 'to single men only', and there was a resident housekeeper with whom an arrangement could be made for the provision of evening meals, although this was not an obligatory part of the arrangement and was not a facility of which the occupier in question had availed him- or herself. None of these circumstances would individually have caused the arrangement to be considered only a licence. Indeed, many thought at the time that, even taken together, there was nothing to distinguish the arrangement from a conventional bedsitting-room letting, which lettings had always been considered to constitute tenancies, rather than licences, and there was (and is) nothing exceptionable in the idea of a tenancy of a single room (*AG Securities v Vaughan*, 1988). Nonetheless, it was held that, in the individual circumstances of the case, the occupier was no more than a licensee.

1.123 At the time, it was said that this was because the parties to the agreement would not have intended a tenancy, with all the formal consequences as to grant of separate possession (ie the statutory protection given to certain tenants, see para 1.62) that this implies. This 'intention' test is what was subsequently rejected by the House of Lords in *Street v Mountford*, 1985, which returned to a much more traditional approach to the distinction between tenancy and licence, described as lying 'in the grant of land', including housing, 'for a term at a rent with exclusive possession'. In substance, the House of Lords was reiterating the proposition that 'intention' did not mean the wishes or intentions of one or other, or even both, of the parties but the intention that the law would impute to the parties on the basis of the nature of the arrangement they had actually made.

1.124 **Evasion of protection**. In addition, however, a person will be only a licensee if the rights which he or she has been given are simply not enough to amount in law to tenancy, for want of the four essential qualities (see para 1.52 – *AG Securities v Vaughan*, 1988), including the grant to the occupier of 'exclusive possession' of the premises (see para 1.29). One device by which landlords have sought to avoid the impact of statutory protection by arguing that a letting comprised a licence rather than a tenancy was the agreement which came to be known as the 'non-exclusive occupation agreement' (see paras 1.51–1.52). Another device was 'rental purchase', whereby a person was allowed into occupation as a licensee, paying money towards purchase but not enjoying the status of owner until the whole of the purchase price has been paid. Such schemes are extremely rare – if still in use – and are therefore not considered. Whatever the scheme, there is now high authority (*AG Securities v Vaughan*, 1988, HL) for the proposition that the courts should lean against shams or pretences designed to defeat statutory protection (see paras 1.53–1.56).

1.125 **Lack of capacity**. As noted, the fact that a person has no interest in the land does not prevent him or her granting a tenancy of it (see para 1.17). That said, where the grantor is acting under statutory powers, eg emergency powers in wartime (*Minister of Agriculture and Fisheries v Matthews* (1949), the purported grant of a tenancy may only take effect as a licence because the terms of the statute limit the grantor's powers (*Redbank Schools v Adullahzadeh*, 1995).

1.126 **Trespass and licence**. A person who is a trespasser but who is subsequently given permission to remain on the premises may well be considered a licensee. A person whose licence is brought to an end becomes, technically, a trespasser. However, most of the recent laws relating to trespass (see para 1.145) do not affect those who entered as licensees but subsequently became trespassers.

1.127 **Bare and contractual licence**. Licensees may be termed 'bare licensees', or may be termed 'contractual licensees'. One who is, by arrangement, paying a fixed sum of money for the right of occupation will be a contractual licensee. A friend, member of the family or cohabitant, even although he or she may be paying some amount by way of contribution to household expenses, will normally be considered a bare licensee.

1.128 **Fixed-term licences**. There are a few arrangements which may be described as 'fixed-term' licences, which is to say that the period for which the right of occupation has been granted is fixed in advance.

1.129 **Licences and estoppel**. In some cases, a rather different form of licence may be created which continues for the life of the occupier. This may occur where the occupier has incurred expenditure or otherwise acted to his or her detriment, in the belief that he or she had a right or interest in the property, and the owner of the land has encouraged that belief, so creating what is known as an 'estoppel'. Thus, for example, an owner of a house may let a child into occupation, lead him or her to believe that the property will one day be transferred to him or her, and – in reliance on that belief – the child may expend money improving the property and/or may forego an alternative opportunity to acquire housing. In such circumstances, a trust will not arise because there is no intention to create an interest, nor a contribution to the purchase price (see para 1.111). Instead, it is said that the parent is 'estopped' from denying the child's right to occupy.

1.130 Once the estoppel is established, it may be enforced by recognition of an irrevocable licence to occupy (*Inwards v Baker*, 1965; *Matharu v Matharu*, 1994). Where it becomes impossible for the licence for life to continue, eg because of an irretrievable breakdown in relations between the licensee and an owner with whom he or she is sharing the house, the courts adopt a flexible approach and make the minimum order necessary to do justice (*Baker v Baker*, 1993).

Tied accommodation

1.131 **Job-related accommodation.** Many people who live in premises they do not own are occupying accommodation which 'goes with the job'. Such people are not merely the obvious classes of service occupier or tenant, such as resident housekeepers, porters, au pairs, live-in help, caretakers, etc but also people such as the managers of pubs and many who work in off-licences, and employees of some industries and of local authorities, who may, eg offer accommodation to key workers, such as teachers and social workers, as an inducement to work in a particular area. The accommodation is often job-related and the right to it customarily ends when the job itself is brought to an end.

1.132 This section is concerned only with accommodation which is job-related, not with accommodation offered as an inducement but which is not otherwise tied contractually to the employment, to which normal principles will apply.

1.133 **An additional test.** Job-related accommodation occupies its own place in housing law. Clearly, occupiers are not trespassers, nor of course are they freeholders, leaseholders or commonholders, and so they must, of definition, be either tenants or licensees. There are, however, particular tests which apply to this distinction when job-related accommodation is in question, which are additional to those already discussed (see paras 1.22–1.58). A job-related occupier who is a licensee is called a 'service occupier', while one who is a tenant is called a 'service tenant'.

1.134 It is important to stress this: a person might appear to qualify as a service tenant by application of one of the particular, job-related tests, and yet lack one of the four essential qualities of tenancy (see paras 1.22–1.32), or else be a licensee for some other reason (see paras 1.114–1.130), eg because on taking up new employment in a strange area, the employer offered to provide temporary accommodation as a favour; unless, however, one of the tests already considered applies, the test which follows will determine whether occupation is by way of tenancy or licence.

1.135 **A single arrangement**. For this purpose, it is assumed that the employment and the housing arrangements were reached as part of an overall package and are connected. It is entirely possible that a tenant subsequently becomes his or her landlord's employee. The tenancy would not normally become a service tenancy, any more than it would if someone subsequently rented accommodation from his or her employer. It is possible, however, that a landlord who has become someone's employer will offer a new arrangement which, if accepted, could become one of a licence (*Scrimgeour v Waller*, 1980). In deciding whether the new arrangement is valid, the courts will not take into account the inequality of bargaining power between the parties (*Mathew v Bobbins*, 1980), although they will recognise that a mere statement of intention is not binding, and may have been signed by the occupier because he or she had little choice (*AG Securities v Vaughan*, 1988).

1.136 **The test of necessity**. A person living in job-related accommodation will be a service occupier if it is necessary for him or her to live in the premises in question in order to carry out his or her employment duties (*Smith v Seghill Overseers*, 1875; *Street v Mountford*, 1985), or – at least – if it is a requirement of the contract of employment that he or she do so, which requirement is imposed at the least for the better performance of employment duties (*Fox v Dalby*, 1874; *Glasgow Corp v Johnstone*, 1965; *Wragg v Surrey CC*, 2008), not merely as an arbitrary regulation, or whim, on the part of the employer (*Gray v Holmes*, 1949).

1.137 The fact that it is merely convenient for the employee to reside in the premises in question is not sufficient for it to be for the better performance of his or her duties (*Ford v Langford*, 1949; *Chapman v Freeman*, 1978).

1.138 If neither of the factors above applies, then the occupier will normally be a service tenant.

1.139 **Tied accommodation and rent**. One common problem which occurs in connection with occupiers of tied accommodation is in establishing whether or not they are paying rent for their accommodation, which may in turn come to be relevant to whether or not they qualify for statutory protection. Some will actually be doing so, ie they will be handing over a sum of money which will normally be entered as received in a rent book. Others may have an agreement as to how much rent they are paying for their accommodation, but this may be deducted from their wages at source. So long as the amount is quantified, they will still be treated as paying rent (*Montagu v Browning*, 1954).

1.140 Others may not have any agreed quantification of rent but receive lower wages than they would normally get for the job in question on account of the provision of accommodation. Whether rent is actually being paid or not should not affect whether they are considered tenants or licensees, contrary to the normal presumption that one who pays no rent is not a tenant (*Heslop v Burns*, 1974), but it may affect whether or not they can enjoy statutory protection (see paras 1.233(3) and 1.277(6)).

Trespass

1.141 **Absolute trespass.** A trespasser is one who occupies premises without any permission at all to do so. Permission given by anyone in a position to grant it will prevent someone being a trespasser.

1.142 **Permission.** For example, a freeholder or leaseholder may give permission to occupy property, but so also may his or her agent, or a director of a company which owns property, or even someone who is him- or herself no more than a tenant. A tenant is in a position to give permission because – so long as his or her tenancy lasts – he or she, rather than the landlord or the owner, has possession of the premises (see para 1.29). It follows, therefore, that a landlord cannot give someone else permission to occupy premises if he or she has already let them to a tenant.

1.143 **Squatting.** Squatting is a common term for occupying property as a trespasser. Sometimes people who enter as squatters are then given permission to remain. There is little popular distinction between those who squat without permission, and those who use short-life property with permission, but there is considerable difference in law: those without permission are trespassers; those who have permission are 'licensees' (*GLC v Jenkins*, 1975; see also *Camden LBC v Shortlife Community Housing*, 1992).

1.144 The term 'squatter' is therefore not one which it is appropriate to use in discussion of housing *law*, although in one case in which it was used (*McPhail v Persons Unknown*, 1973) the description given was consistent with trespass, rather than licence. This does not mean that all squatters are trespassers, simply that if the term is to be used in law it must be confined to those who squat without permission.

1.145 **Criminal trespass.** The Legal Aid, Sentencing and Punishment of Offenders Act (LASPO) 2012 s144, introduced a new offence of trespass in residential premises. The offence is committed where: a person is in a residential building as a trespasser, having entered it as a trespasser; the person knows, or ought to know, that he or she is a trespasser; and, the person is living in the building or intends to live there for any period. A residential building is any structure or part of a structure (including a temporary or moveable structure which, before the time of entry, was designed or adapted for use as a place to live in). The offence is not committed by a person holding over after the end of a lease or licence (even if he or she leaves and re-enters the building). The offence is punishable in the magistrates' court by a maximum of 51 weeks' imprisonment and an unlimited fine. The fact that residential trespass is a criminal offence does not prevent a trespasser from obtaining title to land through adverse possession (see para 1.146; *R (Best) v Chief Land Registrar*, 2015).

1.146 **Adverse possession.** A trespasser can acquire the interest in land of the person entitled to possession of it – usually the freeholder or a long leaseholder – if he or she has been in 'adverse possession' of the land for a certain period of time. To be in adverse possession, a trespasser must have both factual possession of the land and an intention to possess it to the exclusion of the whole world, including the person legally entitled to possess it (*JA Pye v Graham (Oxford) Ltd*, 2002). In a residential context, if a trespasser replaces the existing locks to the front door so the person entitled to possession cannot get in, he or she takes factual possession and demonstrates the necessary intention (*Lambeth LBC v Blackburn*, 2001). The fact that, if asked to do so, the trespasser would have been willing to pay for his or her occupation of the land does not show an absence of the requisite intention (*Pye, Blackburn*).

1.147 It is not necessary for the same person or group of persons to be in adverse possession for the whole period. As long as the period of adverse possession is continuous, the adverse possession of successive trespassers may be added together (*Asher v Whitlock*, 1865).

1.148 **Tenants.** If a tenant, however, takes possession of neighbouring land belonging to his or her landlord, he or she is not in adverse possession. Rather, the tenant is said to be 'encroaching' on the landlord's land and cannot acquire the landlord's interest (*Smirk v Lyndale Developments Ltd*, 1974).

1.149 **Time required.** The length of adverse possession required depends in part on whether land is 'registered' or 'unregistered' land (LRA 2002), a topic that is in itself outside the scope of this book, although it may be said that most land is by now registered. Registration of interests in land was phased in across regions of England and Wales under LRA 1925, which was replaced by LRA 2002. The scheme for registered land has applied to the whole of England and Wales since 1 December 1990. The requirement to register interests in land is only triggered by transfers of the land or granting certain interests in it, eg some tenancies (see para 1.20). Consequently, some land which has not changed hands for many years remains unregistered.

1.150 **Unregistered land.** If the land is unregistered land, the trespasser – either by his or her own or by successive occupation – must establish 12 years adverse possession of the land. If he or she does so, the person entitled to possession cannot evict him or her and the trespasser takes his or her interest in of the land: Limitation Act (LA) 1980 ss15 and 17. (The European Court of Human Rights has held that the right to acquire someone else's interest through adverse possession is not a violation of that person's right to enjoyment of his or her possessions under Article 1 of the First Protocol ECHR – *Pye v UK*, 2007).

1.151 **Registered land.** LRA 2002 changed the law in relation to registered land. The provisions of LRA 2002 are not retrospective, so it is necessary to consider the position both before and after the date on which the Act came into force (13 October 2003).

1.152 **Pre-13 October 2003 entitlement.** If the trespasser was in adverse possession for 12 years before 13 October 2003, the person otherwise entitled to possession is, as a matter of law, treated as having held the land on trust for him or her at that date. On that date, that trust was replaced by both a statutory right to be registered as the owner and a defence to any claim for possession (LRA 2002 Sch 12 para 18). The 'issue' on any such claim to registration or possession will be the same as in relation to unregistered land – had the trespasser accumulated 12 years of what is properly called adverse possession?

1.153 **Post-13 October 2003 entitlement.** If the trespasser cannot establish 12 years' adverse possession before 13 October 2003, then (whenever the adverse possession started) he or she must apply to be registered as entitled to the interest of the person who otherwise held it, which he or she may do after as little as 10 years' adverse possession (LRA 2002 Sch 6 para 1). The person otherwise entitled then has the option (Sch 6 para 3) – which he or she will normally take – of asking for the application to be dealt with by a special procedure (Sch 6 para 5), under which the trespasser will have to show not only adverse possession but one of a limited number of circumstances (to be found in Sch 6 para 4) amounting to additional reasons as to why he or she should acquire the title. One such arises from a boundary dispute, ie where a person seeks to acquire title to a strip of land of which he or she has taken possession by moving his or her boundary fence onto a neighbour's land. In general terms, the other special reasons relate to cases where the trespasser claims to have acquired an interest in the property through estoppel (see paras 1.129–1.130).

1.154 If successful in doing so, the trespasser will be entitled to registration. If unsuccessful, he or she cannot make another application for another two years. On such a second application, the trespasser only has to establish that he or she has been in adverse possession for 12 years. In practice, however, the trespasser's first application will prompt the person otherwise entitled to take possession proceedings against the trespasser before expiry of the additional two-year period.

1.155 **Tolerated trespassers.** In *Burrows v Brent LBC*, 1996, the House of Lords coined a new – and contradictory – form of status: the 'tolerated trespasser'. At that time, where a possession order was made against a secure tenant under HA 1985 (see para 1.160), the tenancy came to an end on the date for possession specified in the order. Thus, if the order was an outright order (see para 2.120), the tenancy ended on the date specified in the order; if the order was postponed on terms (see para 2.121), the tenancy ended on breach of the terms. In such circumstances, landlords were nonetheless often prepared to give the tenant another chance by way of a new agreement to clear the arrears.

1.156 At common law, such a person could not be described as a trespasser: so long as he or she complied with the agreement, he or she had the landlord's express permission to be there. He or she would therefore on the face of it be a licensee (see para 1.114). The 'policy' difficulty for the courts was that – as will emerge (see para 1.168) – local authority security of tenure under HA 1985 applies as much to most licensees as to tenants. Accordingly, the House of Lords came up with the new term to prevent the occupier from automatically regaining security. After the possession order became effective, the former tenancy was said to be 'in limbo'. The tenant could apply to the court to revive the tenancy, eg on payment of the arrears, but until he or she did so the tenancy did not exist and neither the landlord or the tenant was able to rely on its terms, eg the occupier could not sue for breach of repairing covenant (chapter 11).

1.157 This new status proved to be highly problematic (see *Knowsley Housing Trust v White*, 2008). Accordingly, the Housing and Regeneration Act (H&RA) 2008 Sch 11 amended HA 1985 so that a secure tenancy only comes to an end once the possession order is executed (see para 2.126). Existing occupiers – provided certain conditions were fulfilled – were deemed to occupy under new tenancies from the date on which the amendments came into force: 6 April 2009 (see paras 2.128–2.132). This effectively abolished the status of tolerated trespasser. *Note.* H&RA 2008 also amended HA 1988 expressly to provide that assured tenancies (see para 1.220), including assured shorthold tenancies (see para 1.246), come to end on execution of the order. That amendment proved to be unnecessary as the House of Lords came to hold that this was how HA 1988 worked in any event, contrary to previous decisions of the Court of Appeal, which had wrongly held that they ended in the same way as under HA 1985: *Knowsley*).

1.158 Although the tolerated trespasser as envisaged in *Burrows* accordingly no longer exists, it is thought that a similar status may apply in those cases where the courts refuse to allow a landlord to execute a possession order under HRA 1998, even though the tenancy itself has come to an end (*Hounslow LBC v Powell*, 2011): this could arise, for example, where a non-secure tenancy has been held from a local authority (see para 1.180), but the court decides that it would be disproportionate to allow them to evict the occupier. To avoid this result, the Supreme Court has suggested that the court can also set aside the notice to quit so that the tenancy is reinstated (*Powell*).

Statutory classes of protection

1.159 Against this background, we turn now to consider the statutory classes of protection which apply primarily to tenants but in some cases also to licences, and which comprises the second main stage in identifying the status of an occupier, as an essential element in identifying what his or her rights are, considered in the following chapters.

Secure tenants and licensees

1.160 The expression 'secure' is confined to tenants and licensees enjoying statutory protection under HA 1985, consolidating the introduction of security of tenure for local authority and housing association tenants for the first time since the Second World War by HA 1980, when the right to buy was also introduced. In some ways, the former was a concomitant of the latter, for the degree of hostility towards right to buy by some authorities meant that, without security of tenure, some of those who sought to exercise it might well have been met with notice to quit and eviction.

Landlords

1.161 The issue of who is within HA 1985 is complicated by the way in which treatment of social housing tenants has changed. Originally, tenants and licensees of registered housing associations and trusts (as the non-local authority providers of social housing were then called) were within the same regime as local authority tenants and licensees (and those of a small number of other public bodies such as New Town Corporations): all were secure. Tenants of charitable housing trusts (see para 8.5) were secure whether or not the trust was registered. HA 1988, however, 'moved' registered housing association and charitable housing trust tenants (*note: not* licensees) into the same (new) regime – 'assured tenancy' – as was introduced by that Act (with effect from 15 January 1989) for the private sector. Accordingly, there is a big difference for the tenants and licensees of such bodies depending on when their rights of occupation began.

Registered providers of social housing

1.162 By 'registered' in the last paragraph, is meant then registered with the Housing Corporation: the advantage of registration was that it qualified the association or trust for grant aid, although it also subjected the body to a regulatory scheme. Following changes made by HA 1996, such landlords became known as 'registered social landlords' (RSLs). Following changes made by H&RA 2008 in England, such landlords became known as 'private registered providers of social housing,' or 'PRPs'. H&RA 2008 then abolished the Housing Corporation in England and replaced it with the Tenant Services Authority (TSA). On 1 April 2012, the Localism Act (LA) 2011 abolished the TSA and transferred its functions to the Homes and Communities Agency (HCA), operating by a special committee. *Note.* In a White Paper, *Fixing our broken housing market*, February 2017, the government announced its intention to relaunch the HCA as Homes England in the summer of 2017).

Wales

1.163 From devolution in Wales in 1989, Welsh RSLs ceased to be regulated by the Housing Corporation but have instead been regulated by the National Assembly for Wales; with effect from 1 April 2010, the National Assembly's responsibilities for RSLs passed to the Welsh Ministers. They remain RSLs rather than PRPs.

Local authorities

1.164 Local authorities for housing purposes are: district councils; county and county borough councils (in Wales); London borough councils and the Common Council of the City of London; although county councils may, with the consent of the secretary of state, also exercise housing powers. Unitary authorities are likewise housing authorities. Initially, local authorities were not regulated by the TSA. With effect from 1 April 2010, however, English local housing authorities were automatically registered with it and became registered providers of social housing but, of course, not 'private'. Following the abolition of the TSA on 1 April 2012, they are now registered with the HCA.

Other public bodies

1.165 Urban development corporations fulfil functions similar to those of local authorities, and their tenants are likewise normally secure. Tenancies of certain other public bodies, such as the police and fire services are also secure (HA 1985 ss4(1), 79). In some circumstances, tenants of the HCA may be secure, eg where they become the landlord under an existing secure tenancy (HA 1985 s80(2A)–(2E)).

Pre- and post-15 January 1989 private registered provider and registered social landlord tenants

1.166 As noted, tenants and licensees of registered housing associations and charitable housing trusts were initially within the secure regime of HA 1980 (see para 1.161), but were then moved to the assured regime of HA 1988. Accordingly, we are in principle only concerned under this heading with the tenants of PRPs or RSLs if the tenancy from such a landlord began before the commencement (15 January 1989) of HA 1988 Part 1. (A tenancy may have been granted before that date by a local authority, which then transfers its housing to a PRP; such a tenancy will not remain secure – see para 1.205).

Exceptions

1.167 A tenancy granted by a PRP or an RSL or a charitable housing trust on or after that date can, however, still be secure if one of the following circumstances applies.

1) **Pre-Act contract.** It was entered into pursuant to a contract for its grant which preceded that date.
2) **New tenancy to former tenant.** It is the grant of a new tenancy (not necessarily of the same premises) to a person who was a former

tenant of the same landlord, or one of a number of joint (see para 1.48) such tenants.

3) **Suitable alternative accommodation.** It is the grant of a tenancy resulting from an order for possession against a secure tenant, on the ground of suitable alternative accommodation (see para 2.114); and
   a) the premises in question are those which the court has found to be suitable; and
   b) the court directs that the new tenancy should be a secure tenancy on the basis that an assured tenancy will not provide sufficient security.
4) **New town corporation to housing association.** It falls within a small class of tenancy formerly held by a new town development corporation, and passed into housing association ownership before 31 March 1996. *Note.* All new town corporations have now been wound up.
5) **Defective premises.** The tenancy is one granted under special provisions (HA 1985 Part 16) dealing with buying back premises that have been designated as defective in their design (not covered in this book): HA 1988 s34.

Secure licensees

1.168 As noted (see para 1.160), secure protection applies not only to tenants but also to licensees, whether or not granted for a monetary payment (HA 1985 s79(3)), ie whether or not bare or contractual (see para 1.127). Licences within HA 1985 are, however, only those which effectively grant the occupier the equivalent of exclusive possession (*cf* para 1.29). Where the landlord retains the right to move tenants to other rooms, as is commonly the case in agreements for a letting of a room in a hostel, the licence will not be within the Act (*Westminster City Council v Clarke*, 1992).

Temporary licenses

1.169 Nor does the inclusion of licences extend to a licence granted as a temporary expedient to a person who entered the premises the subject of the licence, or other premises, as a trespasser (HA 1985 s79(4)), eg those who illegally entered unused public sector property awaiting demolition but – to avoid unnecessarily leaving property empty – who were then allowed to remain or else who were offered somewhere else temporarily.

1.170 Under this heading, save where a distinction is drawn, references to secure tenancy include licences brought into security by section 79.

Preconditions

Let as a separate dwelling

1.171 A secure tenant is one to whom residential accommodation is let as a separate dwelling (HA 1985 s79), under which both the landlord conditions and the tenant conditions are fulfilled, and which is not excluded from security under the schedule of exceptions (HA 1985 Sch 1). Premises which are let with no element of shared living accommodation (see para 1.172) will be a 'dwelling' for these purposes, provided that the tenant occupies them as his or her home. It does not matter if they do not include any kitchen facilities, although the premises probably have to be big enough to sleep in, ie for a bed (*Uratemp Ventures Ltd v Collins*, 2001).

Shared living accommodation

1.172 Thus, there cannot be a secure tenancy where living accommodation is shared because there is no letting 'as a separate dwelling': *Central YMCA HA Ltd v Saunders*, 1990; *Curl v Angelo*, 1948). Living accommodation for these purposes means a living-room, rather than a bathroom or lavatory (*Cole v Harris*, 1945) or, probably, a kitchen, unless it is big enough to eat in (*Neale v Del Soto*, 1945; *Central YMCA*; *Uratemp v Collins*, 2001). (There remains some doubt about whether a kitchen that is not big enough to sit and eat in comprises living accommodation). For this purpose, it does not matter whether or not anyone else is actually sharing living accommodation at any particular time; it is sufficient if the terms of the letting are such that it is genuinely within contemplation – or there is a real prospect – that the occupier will have to share living accommodation with another at some future date (*Gray v Brown*, 1992).

Land

1.173 If the property is let together with land, it will be treated as part of the letting unless it is agricultural land exceeding two acres (HA 1985 s112). An agricultural holding itself is specifically excluded (see para 1.180(12)).

Landlord condition

1.174 The landlord condition now is that the landlord under the tenancy is: a local authority; an urban development corporation or a housing co-operative as defined (HA 1985 s80(1)). The section only applies to housing co-operatives set up under a housing management agreement (as defined in HA 1985 s27B) (HA 1985 s80(4)).

Former secure landlords

1.175 As noted above (see para 1.161), a number of other landlords were formerly listed in HA 1985 s80(1) until removed by HA 1988. They were: the Housing Corporation itself (now replaced by the HCA); a housing trust which is a charity; registered housing associations (other than co-operative housing associations, ie fully mutual housing associations – see para 8.8), which are now PRPs or (in Wales) RSLs; and unregistered housing associations which are co-operative associations (HA 1985 s80(1), (2), prior to amendment). Tenants of such landlords whose tenancies were granted prior to commencement of HA 1988 Part 1 (15 January 1989) remain secure.

Tenant condition

1.176 The tenant condition is that the tenant is an individual, as opposed to a corporate body, eg a company, and that the tenant occupies the dwelling-house as his or her only or principal home (HA 1985 s81). If the tenancy is a joint tenancy, then at least one of the joint tenants must be an individual as opposed to a corporate body, and at least one of the joint tenants must be in occupation as an only or principal home (HA 1985 s81).

1.177 To establish occupation as an only or principal home may not require actual physical occupation (*Crawley BC v Sawyer*, 1987). Where the tenant is no longer in occupation, however, he or she is under the burden of showing that he or she intends to return to the property, and must substantiate this through visible signs of that intention (*Ujima HA v Ansah*, 1997; *Amoah v Baking and Dagenham LBC*, 2001; *Hammersmith and Fulham LBC v Clarke*, 2001; *Islington LBC v Boyle*, 2011). If the tenant sub-lets the whole of the property, however, he or she loses security and does not regain it even if he or she moves back into the property after the subtenancy has ended (HA 1985 s93); cf. the position for assured tenants (see para 1.230) and statutory tenants (see para 1.292).

1.178 A tenant does not necessarily lose security if he or she ceases to occupy as an only or principal home temporarily, so long as he or she is so occupying when the tenancy purports to end (*Hussey v Camden LBC*, 1994), ie he or she may be able to resume sufficient occupation between service and expiry of notice to quit. As a notice to quit needs time to take effect (see para 2.49), if the tenant does return in time, he or she can become secure again.

1.179 On the breakdown of a relationship, the tenancy may be in the sole name of the departing partner. If the couple are married or in a civil partnership, the occupation of the remaining partner is deemed to be that of the one that left so that the tenant condition is satisfied despite the tenant's departure (Family Law Act 1996 s34; see para 7.11). This does not apply if the partners were merely cohabiting but it is possible for the remaining cohabitee to obtain an occupation order which has the same effect (see para 7.24), albeit only on a temporary basis (see para 7.26).

Exceptions

1.180 There are, however, numerous exceptions from security in HA 1985 Sch 1.

1) **Long leases**. Long leases, ie leases for a period in excess of 21 years (para 1).
2) **Introductory tenancies**. Tenancies which are granted under an introductory tenancy regime, and which have not moved into security pursuant to those provisions (para 1A; see paras 1.210–1.219).
3) **Demoted tenancies**. A demoted tenancy which arises following a demotion order made by the court (para 1B; see paras 1.252–1.260).
4) **Employee accommodation**. Premises occupied under a contract of employment which requires the tenant to occupy the dwelling-house for the better performance of his or her duties (see para 1.136), where the tenant is an employee of the landlord, or of a local authority, or an urban development corporation (para 2). This is not necessarily the same as a service occupancy (see para 1.133) because it allows one public sector landlord to house the employee of another.

   Also within this exception are premises provided to policemen and women free of rent and rates under the Police Act 1996, and premises rented to firemen and women in consequence of employment, where the contract of employment requires him or her to live close to a particular station (para 2).

A requirement to occupy will not be implied, unless the occupation is in fact necessary for the tenant's employment duties to be carried out (*Hughes v Greenwich LBC*, 1993; *Surrey CC v Lamond*, 1998).

If occupation continues after employment ceases, it will be a question of fact whether the tenancy is still referable to the employment in question, or whether there has been an agreed or intended change in the nature or purpose of the occupation (*South Glamorgan CC v Griffiths*, 1992; *Elvidge v Coventry City Council*, 1993; *Greenfield v Berkshire CC*, 1994).

4) **Temporary use of employee accommodation**. Where premises have been occupied under the last exception at any time in the previous three years, the landlord can let them out in other circumstances, without the occupier becoming secure, provided:
   (a) the landlord gives the occupier notice that this exception will apply; and
   (b) (i) in the case of a local authority landlord, the landlord has not notified the tenant that he or she is to become secure, and
   (ii) in the case of any other landlord, the tenancy, or tenancies, do not themselves extend more than three years beyond the last time when the premises were occupied under a para 2 exception.
5) **Development land**. Premises on land acquired for development, being used pending development for temporary housing accommodation, ie short-life user (para 3).
6) **Homeless persons accommodation**. A tenancy granted to a person under HA 1996 Part 7 or Housing (Wales) Act (H(W)A) 2014 Part 2 (see para 10.86) is not secure until the landlord notifies the tenant that he or she is to be a secure tenant (para 4).
7) **Asylum-seeker accommodation**. A tenancy granted to an asylum-seeker under the Immigration and Asylum Act (IAA) 1999 Part 6 is not secure until the landlord notifies the tenant that it is to be (para 4A).
8) **Family intervention tenancy**. (para 4ZA; see paras 1.262–1.266).
9) **Job-mobility accommodation**. Temporary accommodation granted to a person not resident in the same district or London borough as the premises, granted for the purposes of enabling that tenant to take up employment or an offer of employment within that district or London borough, or within an adjoining district or London borough, while looking for permanent accommodation.

Before the grant of the tenancy, the landlord must notify the tenant that this exception applies. In the case of a local authority landlord, the exception lasts until the landlord notifies the tenant that he or she is to become secure. In the case of any other landlord whose tenants are secure, the exception only applies for one year, or less if – during that year – the landlord notifies the tenant that he or she is to be a secure tenant (para 5).

10) **Sub-leasing schemes**. Sub-lettings under leasing schemes are not secure. These are schemes under which the landlord takes a lease from a private sector landlord, ie one whose tenants would not be secure if granted a direct tenancy (see paras 1.161–1.165), which is either for a fixed term or else is granted on terms that the lease will come to an end when required by the landlord (*Haringey LBC v Hickey*, 2006).

    This scheme enables public landlords to take lettings of residential accommodation which would otherwise be left vacant by the private sector landlord, in order to lease it on to others, typically to the homeless pending their allocation of a permanent home (para 6).

11) **Accommodation pending works for non-secure tenant**. Temporary accommodation provided to a tenant who is not a secure tenant, while works are executed to his or her usual home, is not secure (para 7).

12) **Agricultural holdings**. Agricultural holdings within the Agricultural Holdings Act 1986 or farm business tenancies within the Agricultural Tenancies Act 1995 are not secure, if occupied by the person in control of the holding or business (para 8).

13) **Licensed premises**. Tenancies are not secure if of premises which consist of or include premises licensed for the sale of intoxicating liquor for consumption on the premises (para 9).

14) **Student lettings**. Student lettings are not secure if granted to enable the tenant to attend a designated course at an educational establishment and the landlord has, before the grant of the tenancy, notified the student that the exception applies.

    A designated course is one designated by the secretary of state for this purpose. This exception ceases at any time:

    (a) in the case of a local authority landlord, if the landlord has notified the tenant that he or she is to become secure; and
    (b) in the case of any other landlord, until six months after he or she ceases to attend the educational establishment, or – if the tenant fails to take up his or her place on the course – six

months after the grant of the tenancy (para 10), or if the landlord notifies the tenant that he or she is to be a secure tenant.

15) **Business lettings**. Business tenancies within LTA 1954 Part 2, the main legislation concerned with business lettings, are not secure (see para 11). Such tenancies can include residential accommodation, eg a shop with accommodation above; even a house may be let for a business and so come within LTA 1954 rather than residential security. The following points may be noted.
    (a) It is not possible for a tenancy which was originally let for a business purpose to become a letting within HA 1985, for it will not have been let 'as a dwelling' (*Webb v Barnet LBC*, 1988) unless there is an agreed change to residential use (*Russell v Booker*, 1982), but it is possible for a tenancy which was originally let as a dwelling under a secure tenancy to become a business letting and so move from HA 1985 protection into that of LTA 1954 Part 2 (HA 1985 Sch 1 para 11).
    (b) Such a move will happen if the predominant use of the premises is, or becomes, business use (*Cheryl Investments Ltd v Saldanha*, 1978), or if the business purpose can be said to be more than incidental to the residential occupation (*Wright v Mortimer*, 1996).
    (c) Such a move will not necessarily happen merely because there has been some amount of business use, perhaps ancillary to offices elsewhere (*Royal Life Saving Society v Page*, 1978), although it is not decisive (in favour of business use in the premises in question) that no business is carried out from elsewhere (*Wright*).
    (d) Merely taking in lodgers will not convert the tenancy into a business letting (*Lewis v Weldcrest*, 1978).
    (e) The business activity must be part of the reason for, and the aim and object in, occupying the house, not merely an incidental hobby which made some money (*Gurton v Parrot*, 1990). It is always a question of fact and degree.
    (f) Where the main purpose of the tenancy is to provide a place from which the tenant can trade, however, the fact that it also provides him or her with a home does not prevent the tenancy from being a business tenancy (*Broadway Investments Ltd v Grant*, 2006).

16) **Almshouses.** Almshouses occupied under a licence from a charity are not secure (para 12).

Flexible tenancies

1.181 A secure tenant has security of tenure, described in chapter 2, which in substance means that, to recover possession, a landlord has both to prove a ground for possession and, often, that it is reasonable to make the order sought (see paras 2.84–2.107). Thus, a secure tenancy may last for many years, during which a tenant's needs may change, eg a family house may become under-occupied once the tenant's children have grown up and left. At a time of acute shortage of social housing, the government considered that local authorities and PRPs should be able to grant tenancies which can be ended more easily so that they can maximise use of their housing accommodation for those most in need of it.

1.182 In England, with effect from 1 April 2012, the Localism Act (LA) 2011 introduced the flexible tenancy, which is a secure tenancy for a fixed term of at least two years. As a flexible tenancy is a form of secure tenancy, the tenant enjoys same the rights as any other secure tenant, discussed in chapter 4 (with the exception of rights relating to improvements: see paras 4.152–4.154). During the fixed term, he or she has the same protection as any other secure tenant (see paras 2.84–2.86). At the end of the fixed term, however, if the landlord decides not to grant a new tenancy, possession can be obtained without the need to establish a ground for possession (see paras 2.96–2.117).

PRPs

1.183 As noted (see paras 1.161–1.162), PRPs can no longer grant secure tenancies so they are also unable to grant flexible tenancies. PRPs now grant assured tenancies under HA 1988 (see para 1.220). Such tenancies are usually fully assured, in which case the tenant has security of tenure similar to that of a secure tenant. Assured tenancies can also be shorthold, in which case the landlord can obtain possession without the need to establish a ground for doing so (see paras 2.195–2.208). The intention of LA 2011 is that, if PRPs do not wish to grant fully assured tenancies but do want to grant tenancies which are equivalent to flexible tenancies, they will grant assured shorthold tenancies for a term of at least two years.

Tenancy strategy

1.184 As authorities and PRPs will be able to grant a wider range of tenancies, LA 2011 introduced a new requirement for English local housing authorities to maintain a tenancy strategy (LA 2011 s150). This must summarise the matters that both the authority and PRPs in its area must take into account when formulating policies on the kinds of tenancies they grant, when they grant a tenancy of a particular kind, the length of their fixed-term tenancies and the circumstances in which they will grant a new tenancy after an existing one has come to an end (s150(1)).

1.185 The strategy had to be published by 12 January 2013 (LA 2011 s150(4)). It must be kept under review and may be modified (s150(5)). Any modification must be published (s150(6)). Before adopting or modifying a strategy, the authority must consult every PRP providing social housing in its district (s151(1)). In preparing or modifying a strategy, the authority must have regard to its allocation scheme (see para 10.200) and its homelessness strategy (see para 10.10); London borough councils must also have regard to the London housing strategy published by the Greater London Authority (s151(3)). A copy of the strategy must be available at the authority's principal office for inspection at all reasonable hours, free of charge, and provided to members of the public on request, on payment (if required) of a reasonable charge (s151(7)).

Creating flexible tenancies

1.186 A secure tenancy is a flexible tenancy if it is granted for a fixed term of not less than two years and, before it was granted, the landlord served notice on the tenant stating that it would be a flexible tenancy (HA 1985 s107A(2)).

1.187 A flexible tenancy may also arise following an introductory tenancy (see para 1.210), provided that, before granting the introductory tenancy, the tenant was notified that, at the end of his or her trial period, the tenancy would become flexible (see para 1.214; HA 1996 s137A). The notice must specify the length of the term of the flexible tenancy and the other terms of that tenancy (s137A(2)). A flexible tenancy can also arise following a demoted tenancy (see para 1.260) or a family intervention tenancy (see para 1.265).

Review

1.188 A prospective tenant under flexible tenancy has the right to request a review of the length of the term being offered (HA 1985 s107B(1), (2)). The only ground for review is that the proposed term does not accord with the landlord's policy, which is formulated in accordance with the tenancy strategy (s107B(3); see para 1.184). The request for a review must be made within 21 days of the offer of the tenancy or, if the flexible tenancy is to follow an introductory tenancy (see para

1.187), of the notice served on the tenant, although this time limit may be extended by agreement (s107B(4)). The landlord is obliged to carry out a review if one is requested (s107B(5)). Procedure on review is governed by regulations to be made by the secretary of state (s107B(6)); Flexible Tenancies (Review Procedures) Regulations 2012 SI No 695. A request for a review must give grounds for the review and specify whether an oral hearing is requested. If so, the landlord must give at least five days' notice of the date and time of the hearing. The tenant has the right to be represented at the hearing and may give evidence and cross-examine any witnesses. If a hearing is not requested, the landlord must notify the tenant that he or she can make written representations. In either case, if the decision is to be made by an officer, he or she must be someone senior to the original decision-maker. A challenge to a review decision can only be made on the limited grounds available on judicial review (see paras 8.23–8.28).

Formalities

1.189 Although tenancies for a fixed term of more than three years usually have to be created by deed (see para 1.19), this rule does not apply to flexible tenancies (LPA 1925 s52, as amended by LA 2011). Tenancies for a fixed term of more than seven years usually have to be registered with the Land Registry (see para 1.20) but this rule does not apply to flexible tenancies (LRA 2002 ss4(5A) and 132).

Housing and Planning Act 2016

1.190 In England, the Housing and Planning Act (HPA) 2016 will amend HA 1985 so that, once the provisions are in force, almost all new secure tenancies will be for a fixed term. Existing periodic tenancies will become known as 'old-style' secure tenancies. If a landlord moves an old-style secure tenant to a new property, it will have to grant him or her an old-style secure tenancy of that property. Otherwise, a landlord will only be able to grant an old-style secure tenancy where the new tenant is exercising the right to a mutual exchange (see para 4.135) and in circumstances to be set by the secretary of state in regulations (new HA 1985 s81B).

1.191 The new secure tenancies will be similar to flexible tenancies. The minimum term is two years. The maximum is ten, unless the proposed tenant's household includes a child under nine, in which case the landlord can grant a tenancy which will expire on the date of the child's nineteenth birthday. A prospective tenant will have a right to a review of the length of the term being offered (new HA 1985 s81D; see para 1.188) and, where the term is more than three years it will not be necessary for it to be created by deed (see para 1.189).

Succession

1.192 When a tenant dies, there may be succession to the secure tenancy (HA 1985 s89). In England, LA 2011 amended the rules governing succession; the law in Wales is slightly different. Currently, the amendments do not apply if the tenancy was granted before 1 April 2012, but, once provisions in HPA 2016 Sch 8 are brought into force, the amendments will also apply to tenancies in England granted before that date.

One succession

1.193 There can only be one succession to a tenancy in Wales or to a pre-1 April 2012 tenancy in England (HA 1985 s87). Where a tenancy in England was granted after that date, the number of permissible successions is determined by the terms of the tenancy agreement (HA 1985 s86A(4)), but there is no requirement for there to be more than one.

Joint tenancy

1.194 If the tenancy is a joint secure tenancy, however, there is no such succession. Rather, on the death of one tenant, the tenancy devolves on the remaining tenant(s) under the right of survivorship (*Solihull MBC v Hickin*, 2010) (see para 1.48). There can be no statutory succession after a secure tenancy has devolved in this way (HA 1985 s88). Prior to 3 October 1980, however, when HA 1980 introduced secure tenants (see para 1.160), local authority tenants were not secure and there was no statutory succession so that if the first death occurred before that date, it did not qualify as a statutory succession and succession under the statute (now HA 1985) is therefore permissible (*Birmingham City Council v Walker*, 2007).

Qualifying successor

1.195 Only a qualifying person can succeed. In relation to pre-1 April 2012, tenancies in England and tenancies in Wales, person qualifies if, at the time of the death of the secure tenant, the would-be successor was occupying the dwelling-house as his or her only or principal home (see para 1.176) and he or she was either the deceased tenant's spouse or civil partner; or another member of the deceased tenant's family (HA 1985 s87). In England, if the tenancy was granted on or after 1 April 2012, only spouses, civil partners and those in an equivalent relationship have the right to succeed (HA 1985 s86A(1)), ie other family members do not do so. Landlords may, however, grant wider succession rights in their tenancy agreements (s86A(2); see para 1.193) not only to family members but also to other categories of person, eg carers.

Residing with

1.196 For pre-1 April 2012 tenancies in England, and tenancies in Wales, in the case of anyone other than a spouse or civil partner, it is also necessary to show that the would-be successor had been residing with the deceased tenant for at least 12 months before his or her death. 'Residing with' means more than 'living or staying at' the premises, although does not necessarily require so much as permanent or indefinite residence (*Swanbrae v Elliott*, 1987; *Hildebrand v Moon*, 1989). Mere physical presence in the tenant's premises, however, is not sufficient; there must be a settled intention to make a home with the tenant (*Freeman v Islington LBC*, 2009). A period of absence does not necessarily break the continuity of residence. It depends on the nature and extent of the continuing connection with the premises throughout the period of absence and the quality of the intention to return, ie how firm and whether it is to return to reside as a home (*Camden LBC v Goldenburg*, 1996).

1.197 A cohabitee only qualifies to succeed to a pre-1 April 2012 tenancy in England or a tenancy in Wales as a family member (see para 1.200) and must therefore satisfy the 12-month residence test. This difference in treatment between spouses/civil partners and cohabitees has been held not to breach Articles 8 (right to respect for family life and home) or 14 (non-discrimination) ECHR (*R (Turley) v Wandsworth LBC*, 2017). In relation to tenancies granted in England on or after 1 April 2012, however, cohabitees and spouses/civil partners can succeed without showing the 12-month residence requirement.

1.198 The qualification of 12 months' residence with the deceased tenant does not have to have been at the property to which succession is being sought (*Waltham Forest LBC v Thomas*, 1992). Thus, if the tenant came to stay with, say, a child in that child's home, but – less than 12 months before the end of the tenant's life – parent and child moved back into the parent's home – the child will still be able to succeed.

Choice of successor

1.199 There can be no joint succession: *Newham LBC v Phillips*, 1997. Where there is a number of potential qualifying successors, the deceased tenant's spouse or civil partner takes precedence, but otherwise the qualifying persons may agree amongst themselves who is to take over the tenancy. If they cannot do so, the landlord is entitled to choose. There is, however, no obligation to notify the landlord who is the agreed successor (*General Management v Locke*, 1980).

Member of family

1.200 Members of the family are defined (HA 1985 s113) as: spouses, parents, grandparents, children, grandchildren, siblings, uncles, aunts, nephews and nieces; including step-relations, half-relations and illegitimate children and persons living together as husband and wife.

1.201 '[L]iving together as husband and wife' means more than merely living together in the same household (*City of Westminster v Peart*, 1991). A homosexual couple can be considered to be living together as husband and wife, even if not civil partners. A minor can succeed to a secure tenancy: *Kingston upon Thames RLBC v Prince*, 1998. As a minor cannot hold a legal interest in land, however, the tenancy must be held on trust for him or her.

1.202 The list of family members is exhaustive. Accordingly, a more distant relative (*Wandsworth LBC v Michalak*, 2002) or a foster child who was not adopted by the tenant (*Sheffield City Council v Wall*, 2010) cannot succeed to a secure tenancy. The limit on the list of family members who may succeed does not breach Articles 8 (right to respect for family life and home) or 14 (non-discrimination) ECHR (*Michalak* and *Wall*).

No qualifying successor

1.203 If there is no one qualified to succeed on the death of the tenant under the statutory rules, the tenancy may yet remain secure if a court orders its transfer under one of a number of family statutes governing both partners and children, eg where a court makes such an order in favour of a person who did not fulfil the residential requirements, or in favour of a former spouse (likewise not residing with the deceased tenant) (see paras 7.3–7.38). Otherwise, the tenancy will cease to be secure once it has vested – pursuant to the rules applicable to the ordinary devolution of property (including tenancies) on death – and it is known that the vesting is not pursuant to one of those statutes (HA 1985 ss89, 90). In the interregnum, it therefore remains secure.

Loss of security

1.204 Leaving aside an order for possession made by a court (see para 2.84), the tenant giving notice to quit or surrendering, or the tenant dying without anyone qualifying to succeed him or her (see para 1.198), there is a number of circumstances in which security can be lost.

1.205 First of all, security will be lost if there is a change of landlord, and the new landlord does not fulfil the landlord condition (see paras 1.164–1.165). This is now common when local authorities dispose of their stock to a PRP, under the scheme known as Large Scale Voluntary Transfer (LSVT).

1.206 Secondly, security will be lost if the tenant ceases to occupy the premises as his or her only or principal home (see para 1.176).

1.207 In addition, a secure tenancy is incapable of assignment (see para 1.78) unless: the assignment is pursuant to an order of the court under one of a number of family provisions (see paras 7.3–7.38), governing both partners and children; the assignment is to someone who qualifies to take over the tenancy on the tenant's death as a successor (see para 1.198); or the assignment is pursuant to the 'right to exchange' (HA 1985 s91 – see paras 4.135–4.143). Any other assignment will therefore cause security to be lost.

1.208 If the secure tenant sublets the whole of the premises, either at one go or piecemeal, security is also lost, even if the sub-letting is to a person who qualifies as a successor (HA 1985 s93). An arrangement which amounts to no more than a licence (see paras 1.114–1.130) will, however, not cause the loss of security (*Hussey v Camden LBC*, 1994).

1.209 In any of these cases, once security is lost it cannot be regained (HA 1985 ss91, 93), eg by evicting a subtenant or by reassignment. Security will not, however, normally be lost by bankruptcy (Insolvency Act 1986 s283(3A)).

Introductory tenants

1.210 Introductory tenants are tenants (or licensees) who would otherwise be secure, but for the adoption by the landlord of an introductory tenancy scheme (HA 1996 s124(1)): the only landlords able to adopt such a scheme are local authorities. Because it was not introduced until 1996, it does not concern lettings by PRPs or RSLs (see para

1.162) not even in those few circumstances when they may – *post*-14 January 1989 – yet grant a secure tenancy (see para 1.167). (Such landlords may grant assured shorthold tenancies instead, even if to be followed by a fully assured tenancy – see paras 1.248, 1.250(1). These are commonly referred to as 'starter tenancies'). The purpose of an introductory tenancy scheme is to allow the landlord to offer a trial or probationary period of tenancy without the tenant becoming secure, essentially to see how the tenant behaves: accordingly, the first phase of the tenancy is excluded from secure protection (see para 1.180). If at any time the landlord decides to cease operating the scheme (without prejudice to its reintroduction: HA 1996 s124(5)), an introductory tenancy automatically becomes secure (HA 1996 s125(5)(c)). If a scheme is in place, all the authority's new tenants (subject to a small number of exceptions – see para 1.213), will initially be introductory tenants.

1.211 **Who may be an introductory tenant**? Currently, only a periodic tenant (or licensee) can be introductory but in England, once amendments made by HPA 2016 are in force (see para 1.190), new introductory tenancies will be for a fixed term. Only someone who would otherwise be a secure tenant can be introductory, so that someone who would be excluded from full security (see para 1.180) will also be excluded from being an introductory tenant (HA 1996 s124(2)); indeed, if during the life of the tenancy, the tenant (or, if joint tenants, all of them) cease to occupy the property as an only or principal home – which will cause the loss of security (see para 1.206) – so also will it cause the loss of status as an introductory tenant. The regime does not apply to those whose tenancies are granted pursuant to a contract entered into before the decision was made to adopt the regime (HA 1996 s124(3)).

1.212 **Licensees**. As with secure tenancy (see para 1.168), the introductory tenancy regime is applicable to licences, other than those granted as a temporary expedient to people who entered the property, or other land, as a trespasser (HA 1996 s126). References below to secure or introductory tenant therefore include secure or introductory licensee.

1.213 **Exclusions**. If, immediately before the tenancy is granted, the tenant (or, if joint tenants, one or more of them) was a secure tenant of any premises (of any landlord, whether or not the same) (HA 1996 s124(2)(a)), or a fully assured tenant (see para 1.220) of a PRP or RSL (but not a mere assured shorthold tenant – see para 1.246), again of any premises (HA 1996 s124(2)(b)), the tenancy cannot be introductory.

1.214 **Period of introductory tenancy.** The intention is that introductory tenants will become secure tenants unless the tenancy (or licence) is determined while the regime still applies to the tenant – 'the trial period' (HA 1996 s125(1)). In England, a landlord can notify the tenant before he or she is granted an introductory tenancy that – on completion of the trial period – he or she will have a flexible tenancy, the length of which must be specified in the notice (see para 1.187; HA 1996 s137A). The trial period initially lasts for one year starting with the date when the tenancy was entered into or, if later, the date on which the tenant was first entitled to take possession under it (HA 1996 s125(2)). Where there are two (or more) introductory tenancies in immediate succession, or where the tenant formerly held an assured shorthold tenancy (see para 1.246) from a PRP or RSL – in neither case necessarily of the same premises – the earlier period (or periods) counts (or count) towards the trial period (HA 1996 s125(3)). Where there are joint tenants, one or more of whom has an earlier period to be taken into account than the other or others, it is the earliest starting date which is to be applied: HA 1996 s125(4).

1.215 **Extension.** The landlord can, however, extend the trial period for a further six months (HA 1996 s125A, added by HA 2004). Before doing so, the landlord must – at least eight weeks before the original expiry date – serve a notice of extension on the tenant. That notice must give reasons for the landlord's decision to extend, and notify the tenant of his or her right to a review, which must be requested within 14 days. The extension becomes effective if the tenant fails to request a review or if the decision is confirmed on review. A challenge to a review decision can only be made on the limited grounds available on judicial review (see paras 8.23–8.28).

1.216 **Succession.** The succession provisions are similar to those applicable to secure tenancies (see paras 1.192–1.203), and the succession will be to an introductory tenancy (HA 1996 ss131–133). If there is no one entitled to succeed under the statutory provisions (HA 1996 s133(3)), then once the tenancy has vested pursuant to the normal provisions applicable to the devolution of property on death, it will cease to be introductory but will not become secure. This is not so, however, if it is vested by an order of a court using powers under one of a number of family statutes, governing both partners and children, in which case the tenancy may remain introductory, notwithstanding the absence of a qualifying successor, eg if it is vested by the court in a child who had not been residing with the tenant, or a former spouse (likewise not residing with the deceased tenant) (see paras 7.3–7.48). In the interregnum, it will therefore remain introductory.

1.217 **Cessation of introductory tenancy.** Unless the tenancy has terminated, or the introductory tenancy scheme is abandoned, the tenancy becomes secure at the end of the trial period unless before that time something has happened that means that the tenancy would not otherwise be secure, eg cessation of occupation as an only or principal home, or someone other than a local authority becomes the landlord (HA 1996 s125(5)). As with secure tenancies, on relationship breakdown, the occupation of the remaining partner is deemed to be that of a departing sole tenant, so that security of tenure is not lost (see para 1.179). Security will not be acquired if the tenant dies and if there is no one entitled to take over as a secure tenant (see para 1.216). Like secure tenancies (see para 1.207), introductory tenancies are incapable of assignment (HA 1996 s134(1)), unless the assignment is in pursuance of a court order made under one of a number of family statutes, governing both partners and children (see paras 7.3–7.48), or else it is to a person who would be qualified to succeed to the introductory tenancy (see para 1.116) (HA 1996 s134(2)). Any other assignment will therefore cause security to be lost.

1.218 Critically, however, a tenancy will not become secure if proceedings for possession have been commenced and are not finally resolved (HA 1996 s125(7)).

1.219 Once a tenancy ceases to be introductory, it cannot become introductory again (HA 1996 s125(6)).

Assured tenants

1.220 The Housing Act 1988 introduced a new regime of security of tenure and (limited) rent control for private sector tenants, defined to include the tenants of what were then housing associations but are now PRPs (England) and RSLs (Wales) and charitable housing trusts (see para 8.5), in place of the Rent Acts, which had been the source of security of tenure and rent control in the rented sector since 1915, albeit much changed over the years. HA 1988 assumes that all tenants to whom property is let as a separate dwelling (on or after the commencement of HA 1988 Part 1: 15 January 1989) are assured tenants if they fulfil the qualifying conditions, unless there is some factor which takes them out of HA assured protection (HA 1988 s1).

Landlords

Exempt landlords

1.221 Those landlords whose tenants are not assured are (HA 1988 Sch 1 para 12): local authorities, including district and county councils, county borough councils (in Wales), unitary authorities, London Borough Councils, the Common Council of the City of London and the Council of the Isles of Scilly; a police authority or fire service; an urban development corporation; a waste disposal authority; and, in England, a fully mutual association housing association, ie where the rules restrict membership to people who are tenants or prospective tenants of the association, and preclude the grant or assignment of tenancies to persons other than members. In Wales, a fully mutual housing association can grant an assured tenancy but, before the tenancy is granted, the association must give the tenant written notice that the tenancy will be assured. Tenants of fully mutual housing associations can also neither be secure tenants under HA 1985 (see para 1.270), nor protected tenants under RA 1977 (see para 1.175) and so, save for tenants in Wales who have been given the appropriate notice, have no security of tenure (*Nettleton Road Housing Co-operative Ltd v Joseph*, 2010).

1.222 Tenants of the Crown or a government department are not assured unless the tenancy is under the management of the Crown Estate Commissioners (HA 1988 Sch 1 para 11). Tenants of the Welsh Ministers are likewise excluded as are some tenants of the HCA (see para 1.165) (HA 1988 Sch 1 para 12).

Pre- and post-15 January 1989 PRP and RSL and charitable housing trust tenants

Assured or secure?

1.223 A tenancy which is a secure tenancy cannot be an assured tenancy (HA 1988 Sch 1 para 13). Accordingly, those described above as falling within HA 1985, even though granted on or after 15 January 1989, will be secure rather than assured (see para 1.160).

Licensees

Tenancy

1.224 For there to be an assured tenancy, there must be a tenancy (see paras 1.22–1.32), ie unlike secure status (see para 1.168), the Act does not apply to licences (see paras 1.114–1.130).

Preconditions

Let as a separate dwelling

1.225 The tenancy must be of a dwelling-house let as a separate dwelling, as with secure tenancy (see para 1.171).

Sharing living accommodation

1.226 While in principle this would exclude a tenancy where there is sharing of living accommodation (see para 1.172), if the living accommodation in question is shared with someone other than the tenant's own landlord, it will not prevent the tenancy qualifying as assured (HA 1988 s3).

1.227 If the tenant shares, or may have to share, living accommodation with his or her landlord, however, there is no letting as a separate dwelling and no saving statutory provision. This arrangement should not be confused with the position of a resident landlord, with his or her own separate home elsewhere in the same building, which is subject to its own express exclusion (see para 1.233). The proposition applies, rather, where the landlord and the tenant share living accommodation, ie neither of them has his or her own separate dwelling. In that case, there is no letting as a separate dwelling, no *prima facie* assured tenancy, and the resident landlord exclusion never comes into play.

1.228 There may be no letting as a separate dwelling, even if the landlord does not actually live in the premises, but – whether or not he or she has actually ever exercised the right or whether or not he or she has a current intention to do so – sharing with his or her tenant was in contemplation at the time of the letting, the right to do so was reserved, and there is, at the lowest, a real prospect of the landlord doing so at some future date (*Gray v Brown*, 1992).

Land

1.229 If the property is let together with other land, then provided that the main purpose of the letting is the provision of a home for the tenant or, where there are joint tenants, at least one of them, the other land is treated as part of the tenancy but, if it is not, the tenancy is treated as if it was not let as a separate dwelling (HA 1988 s2). Specific provision is made, however, for the exclusion of agricultural land and holdings (see para 1.233).

Tenant condition

1.230 The tenant must be an individual rather than a company or other corporation, or if a joint tenancy, all the joint tenants must be individuals; and, the tenant, or if a joint tenancy at least one of them, must occupy the dwelling as an 'only or principal home,' as with secure tenancy (see para 1.176) (s1(1)). As with secure tenancies, on relationship breakdown, the occupation of the remaining partner is deemed to be that of a departing sole tenant, so that security of tenure is not lost (see para 1.179). If the landlord is a PRP or RSL, as under a secure tenancy, security is lost if the tenant sub-lets the property and cannot be regained (HA 1988 s15A; see para 1.177). In any other case, however, security is not necessarily lost if the tenant sub-lets the property, if he or she can establish that an intention to return to the premises once the subtenancy has ended (*Ujima Housing Association v Ansah*, 1998). If the subtenancy is a breach of a term of the tenancy agreement, the landlord may nonetheless be able to seek possession (see para 2.169(3)).

Avoidance of assured tenancy

1.231 Because of the availability of the assured shorthold tenancy (see paras 1.246–1.250), devices designed to defeat assured tenancy based on this requirement are rare, although they could still be considered desirable by a landlord seeking to avoid the limited rent jurisdiction of the Rent Assessment Committee (see paras 3.30–3.38), eg by letting to a company, as whose licensee the tenant occupies (*Firstcross Ltd v East West Ltd*, 1980; *Tetragon Ltd v Shidash Construction Co Ltd*, 1981; *Hilton v Plustitle Ltd*, 1988). It is likely that the court will treat the arrangement as valid unless it believes that the company – to the landlord's knowledge – took the tenancy as agent or nominee for the tenant. The question to be asked in such a case is whether the company letting is genuine (*Kaye v Massbetter*, 1990). The principles governing sham, false label and pretence (see paras 1.33–1.41) will apply. Likewise, the courts are unlikely to permit avoidance of the requirement of residence by the tenant by permitting the landlord to put the tenancy in one person's name for the real use of another (*Cove v Flick*, 1954; *Dando v Hitchcock*, 1954), if satisfied that the arrangement was a device (*Feather Supplies v Ingham*, 1971).

1.232 Otherwise, one person cannot suddenly step forward and say that he or she is the true tenant, and the named tenant no more than his or her agent, without this having been known to the landlord (*Hanstown Properties Ltd v Green*, 1977).

Exceptions

1.233 There is a number of exceptions from security.

1) **Prior tenancy**. A tenancy entered into before, or under a contract which pre-dates, the commencement of HA 1988 will be either HA 1985 secure or RA 1977 protected (see paras 1.160, 1.269) (HA 1988 Sch 1 para 1).
2) **High-rateable value or rent**. Some premises have such a high-rateable value or rent that they are considered to be beyond the need for protection (HA 1988 Sch 1 para 2). It is the part of the premises which the tenant occupies which must be valued, not the whole house in which the tenancy is situated. A block of flats will often, as a whole, have too high a rateable value for HA 1988 purposes, but each individual flat will not.

   A tenancy granted before 1 April 1990, will not be an assured tenancy if the premises had a rateable value in excess of £1,500 (Greater London) or £750 (elsewhere) (HA 1988 Sch 1 para 2A). A tenancy granted after 1 April 1990, will be excluded at any time when the rent is greater than £100,000 a year (HA 1988 Sch 1 para 2, as amended by Assured Tenancies (Amendment) (England) Order 2010 SI No 908 and Assured Tenancies (Amendment of Rental Threshold) (Wales) Order 2011 SI No 1409).
3) **No or low rent**. HA 1988 is not designed to apply to those who purchase long leases (see para 2.72) and pay only a small, annual ground rent (HA 1988 Sch 1 para 3). This exclusion applies where the annual ground rent is less than two-thirds of the rateable value of the premises (HA 1988 Sch 1 para 3B) or, in the case of a tenancy which has been granted after 1 April 1990 and is for a property which had no rateable value on 31 March 1990, where the rent is £1,000 or less a year in Greater London or £250 or less elsewhere (HA 1988 Sch 1 para 3A).

   Specifically disregarded in ascertaining the rent is any part of the rent which is expressed to be payable in respect of rates, services, management, repairs, maintenance or insurance, unless, even although so expressed, the rent could not have been regarded as so payable (HA 1988 Sch 1 para 2(2)).

   Tenancies at no rent are also excluded (HA 1988 Sch 1 para 3). It has been held that rent must mean payment of rent in money if the tenancy is to be brought within protection, ie not payment in goods or services (*Hornsby v Maynard*, 1924). There is, however, some authority for the proposition that if goods or services represent a quantified, or agreed amount which would otherwise be payable by way of rent, the Act may apply (*Barnes v Barratt*, 1970). Where there is a true service tenancy (see para 1.131) and an amount of rent between a landlord/employer and his or her tenant/employee has been agreed but is merely deducted at source, this will be sufficient payment of rent for the purposes of protection (*Montagu v Browning*, 1954).

4) **Business lettings**. Tenancies subject to the business protection of LTA 1954, are outside of residential protection (see para 1.180) (HA 1988 Sch 1 para 4).
5) **Licensed premises**. Tenancies are not assured if of premises which consist of or include premises licensed for the sale of intoxicating liquor for consumption on the premises (HA 1988 Sch 1 para 5).
6) **Agricultural land**. A tenancy which includes agricultural land of more than two acres let together with the dwelling-house is not assured (HA 1988 Sch 1 para 6).
7) **Agricultural holdings**. Agricultural holdings within the Agricultural Holdings Act 1986 or farm business tenancies within the Agricultural Tenancies Act 1995 are not assured, if occupied by the person in control of the holding or business (HA 1988 Sch 1 para 8).
8) **Student lettings**. A tenancy will not be an assured tenancy if the landlord under the tenancy is a specified educational institution and the tenant is following or intends to follow a course of study at that or another specified educational institution (HA 1988 Sch 1 para 8).
9) **Holiday lettings**. If the purpose of the tenancy is use as a holiday home, then the tenancy will not be assured (HA 1988 Sch 1 para 9).

   This is a class of exception which had been widely used as a device to defeat the Rent Acts (see para 1.277) and is sometimes still used to seek to avoid statutory protection. The mere fact that someone has been compelled to sign an agreement alleging falsely that the tenancy is for a holiday purpose does not make it so as a matter of law. The principles relating to sham or 'false label' (see paras 1.33–1.41) will apply to determine whether the agreement was a mere device to exclude protection, although occupiers should be aware that once they have signed such an agreement, the burden of proof is on them to displace the inference that the tenancy is not protected: *Buchmann v May*, 1976. In *R v Rent Officer for Camden LBC ex p Plant*, 1980, the landlord was found to have known, either before the first or the second of two consecutive 'holiday' lettings, that the occupiers were students so that the letting was not a holiday letting. What is a holiday is a question of fact and common sense.

10) **Resident landlord**. This is in practice in some ways the most important exception, allowing people to grant a tenancy in their own homes, without finding that the tenant has acquired the full security of tenure (see para 2.158) that accompanies assured status. This exception was originally developed under the Rent Acts (see para 1.277) and operates in a similar fashion under HA 1988 (HA 1988 Sch 1 para 10).

The exclusion applies to premises let which are part of a building and, unless the landlord's dwelling itself forms part only of a flat, which building is not a purpose-built block of flats. At the time of the grant of the tenancy, the landlord must have occupied, as his or her only or principal home (see para 1.176), another dwelling forming part of the same building (or, where the dwelling forms part only of a flat, another part of the same flat).

Same building does not cover, eg a terrace of houses, but will include one house within that terrace and may include a house which has had an extension added, even if there is no internal connection between the house and extension (*Griffiths v English*, 1981; *Lewis-Graham v Conacher*, 1991).

The term 'purpose-built block of flats' means exactly what it says. A house converted into flats, no matter how long ago, or however separately the living units are now constructed (*Barnes v Gorsuch*, 1982), will not be a purpose-built block (*Bardrick v Haycock*, 1976; *Griffiths*), even if there are separate entrances. If the building is a purpose-built block, then it avails the landlord not at all that he or she lives in one and the tenant lives in another flat – the tenant will be assured (all other considerations being equal).

A corporate landlord, eg a landlord which is a company, a trust or a partnership, cannot qualify as a resident landlord for these purposes because it cannot occupy as a home. It is, however, expressly provided that occupation by one of two or more joint landlords is enough to keep the tenant from being an assured tenant. There are additional provisions to prevent the tenant being assured when the landlord is a trustee, and it is the beneficiary who is resident.

For the landlord to take advantage of this exclusion, he or she must establish that, since the commencement of the tenancy, he or she has at all times used the other part of the building or flat which he or she occupies as an only or principal home. There are two circumstances, however, when residence is deemed to continue without such occupation.

(a) If the landlord sells the house, residence will be treated as continuing for a further 28 days. If, during that time, the new owner serves notice that he or she intends to move into the premises for use as a home, then he or she has a total of six months in which to do so, during which period residence by the landlord will likewise be treated as continuing. If, by the end of the six months, the new owner has not taken up residence, the tenant will become an assured tenant and will so remain even when the owner moves in, for there will not have been continual residence (or deemed residence) since the start of the tenancy. During the deemed period, the landlord cannot evict otherwise than as if the tenant was assured, ie if there are grounds.

(b) On the death of a resident landlord, the executors effectively have two years during which the fact that there is no resident landlord will be disregarded. During this period, however, the landlord's executors may freely evict as if there was still a resident landlord.

Note. The two periods – six months to move in and two years on death – may be added together: *Williams v Mate*, 1982.

11) **Exempt landlords**. This has been addressed above (see para 1.221).

12) **Asylum-seeker accommodation**. A tenancy granted to an asylum-seeker under the IAA 1999 Part 6 is not assured (HA 1988 Sch 1 para 12A).

13) **A family intervention tenancy**. A family intervention tenancy granted by a PRP is not assured (see para 1.262). (HA 1988 Sch 1 para 12ZA).

14) **Other classes of protection**. A tenancy which remains Rent Act protected (see para 1.269) or Housing Act secure tenancy is not assured (see para 1.160) (HA 1988 Sch 1 para 13).

15) **Homeless persons accommodation**. When seeking to house homeless families under the interim housing duties imposed on them by HA 1996 Part 7 and H(W)A 2014 (chapter 10), local authorities will commonly seek to use accommodation provided by other landlords, whether social landlords or wholly private.

In order to ensure that the homeless do not obtain security when being housed under these duties, HA 1996 s209 and H(WA) 2014 s92 provide that a tenancy granted in pursuance of arrangements with authorities in the discharge of one of the interim duties: accommodation pending enquiries (HA 1996 s188; H(W)A 2014 s68 – see para 10.83; accommodation for the intentionally homeless (HA 1996 s190) – see para 10.99; accommodation pending or following a local connection referral (HA 1996 s200; H(W)A 2014 s82) – see para 10.103; accommodation pending appeal to county court (HA 1996 s204; H(W)A 2014 s88 – see para 10.164) is not assured at all for a period of 12 months (from notification of decision, or decision on review or appeal), unless the tenant is notified by the landlord that the tenancy is to be either an assured tenancy or an assured shorthold tenancy (see para 1.246).

Succession and assignment

Periodic tenancies

1.234 There is a limited right of statutory succession to a periodic assured tenancy, similar to that available to secure tenants under HA 1985 (see para 1.181). On the death of a periodic assured tenant, his or her spouse, a civil partner or a person who has been living with the tenant as husband or wife or as a civil partner, can succeed, provided that immediately before the tenant's death the would-be successor was occupying the dwelling-house as his or her only or principal home (see para 1.176) (HA 1988 s17(1)).

1.235 In addition, as a result of amendments made by LA 2011, PRPs in England can include wider succession rights in their periodic tenancies (HA 1988 s17(1A)). Thus, for example, a tenancy agreement could give succession rights to other members of the tenant's family or carers or permit more than one succession (s17(1E)).

Fixed-term tenancies

1.236 There is no statutory right of succession to any fixed-term, assured tenancy in Wales, or to a fixed-term assured tenancy in England unless the tenancy was granted by a PRP on or after 1 April 2012, for a term of at least two years. Where there is no statutory right of succession, the position is governed by the terms of the will or the law on intestacy (see para 1.240).

1.237 In England, as a result of amendments made by LA 2011, if the tenancy was granted by a PRP on or after 1 April 2012, spouses, civil partners, and those in an equivalent relationship have a right to succeed to a fixed term assured tenancy, provided that it was granted for a term of at least two years and immediately before the tenant's death the would-be successor was occupying the dwelling-house as his or her only or principal home (HA 1988 s17(1A)). In addition, PRPs can include wider succession rights in fixed-term tenancies granted for a term of more than two years (s17(1C)), eg giving succession rights to other members of the tenant's family or carers. Such agreements can can also permit more than one succession (s17(1E)).

Limits on succession

1.238 The general rule is that here can be no statutory succession if the deceased was him- or herself already a successor, whether by reason of this statutory succession provision, or by reason of a succession under RA 1977 to an assured tenancy (see para 1.279), or because of inheritance (HA 1988 s17(2)). The only exception is where the terms of a tenancy granted by a PRP allow more than one succession (see paras 1.235, 1.237).

Joint tenants

1.239 Statutory succession only applies to a sole tenancy (HA 1988 s17(1), (1A), (1B)); on the death of one joint tenant, the other or others becomes or become the sole tenant or remaining joint tenants, by the right of survivorship (see para 1.48) – accordingly the statutory provision does not apply (HA 1988 s17(2)(b)).

Devolution by will or on intestacy

1.240 Where there is no statutory succession, a tenancy can pass under a will or according to the normal rules which govern intestacy, and if the inheritor occupies as an only or principal home, the tenancy will still be assured, but as there is to be a mandatory ground for possession available against the successor (provided the proceedings are brought within time limits: see para 2.170) it may be of little value.

Assignment and subletting

1.241 The rights of an assured tenant to assign the tenancy or sublet are primarily governed by the terms of the tenancy agreement but specific rules apply to assured periodic tenancies (see para 4.144).

Loss of security

1.242 Leaving aside an order for possession made by a court (see para 2.158), or the tenant giving notice to quit or surrendering, or the death of the tenant with no qualifying successor, there is a number of circumstances in which the tenancy may cease to be assured. Protection under HA 1988 may also be lost if the premises are made the subject of a prohibition or demolition order under HA 2004, because of their condition (see paras 12.33 and 12.46).

1.243 First of all, the tenancy will cease to be assured if the premises are bought by one of the public landlords described above whose tenants are not assured (see para 1.221). The tenancy will usually then become a secure tenancy.

1.244 Secondly, the tenancy will cease to be assured if the tenant ceases to occupy the premises as his or her only or principal home (see para 1.176).

1.245 Thirdly, the exclusions from assured status (see para 1.233) do not necessarily apply once and for all, eg resident landlord, low rent. A tenancy may therefore move in to, or out of, being assured.

Assured shorthold tenants

1.246 A fully assured tenancy will confer security of tenure, described in chapter 2, which in substance means that, in order to recover possession a landlord will have both to prove a ground for possession and, often, that it is reasonable to make the order sought (see paras 2.168–2.170); an assured shorthold tenancy is an assured tenancy (so that those grounds for possession are also available in respect of it) in respect of which all that the landlord needs to show is that an appropriate notice has been served (see para 2.187) and, where applicable, that the landlord has complied with certain regulatory requirements (see paras 2.203), ie in substance, there is no security of tenure and the landlord will, subject to compliance with this minimal procedural requirement, be able to obtain a court order for possession.

1.247 In the private sector, the assured shorthold has largely replaced the sort of evasive devices considered earlier (company lets – see para 1.231; holiday lettings – see para 1.233). In the social housing sector, where the landlord is a PRP or an RSL, it is commonly used in the same way as introductory tenancies (see paras 1.210–1.219) are used by local authorities, ie for the purpose of a trial or period, or as a probationary tenancy.

1.248 **Tenancies created on or since 28 February 1997**. All assured tenancies – fixed-term or periodic – granted on or after 28 February 1997 are automatically assured shortholds, unless (HA 1988 s19A and Sch 2A) certain conditions are fulfilled.

1) **Prior notice**. The tenancy will be fully assured if the prospective landlord serves notice on the prospective tenant before the

tenancy is entered into stating that it is not to be an assured shorthold (see *Andrews v Cunningham*, 2007).

2) **Subsequent notice**. The tenancy will become fully assured if the landlord serves notice on the shorthold tenant after the tenancy has been entered into that it is no longer to be shorthold. (See *Saxon Weald Homes Ltd v Chadwick*, 2011, in which a notice sent by mistake nevertheless converted an assured shorthold into a fully assured tenancy.)
3) **Term of agreement**. The tenancy will be fully assured if the tenancy agreement itself contains a provision that it is not to be shorthold.
4) **New tenancy for existing tenant**. The tenancy will be fully assured if granted to a person who (or, if joint tenants, one of whom) immediately beforehand was an existing (fully) assured tenant (or one of a number of assured joint tenants) by someone who (or, if joint landlords, one of whom) is the existing landlord (or one of a number of joint landlords), even if in different premises. The purpose is to protect tenants against being deprived of rights they already enjoy in respect of their landlords. A tenant may, however, not wish to have a fully assured tenancy (eg because he or she does not wish to remain long term and/or the landlord makes it worth his or while to give up existing security – perhaps in order to move into better premises). Accordingly, in order to allow tenants to agree to enter into an assured shorthold, the tenancy will be shorthold if the tenant serves notice before the (new) tenancy begins stating that he or she agrees that it will be assured shorthold. To ensure that the tenant is aware of the rights he or she is giving up, the notice must be in a prescribed form which warns him or her of the effect of giving the notice; see Assured Tenancies and Agricultural Occupancies (Forms) (England) Regulations 2015 SI No 620, form 3, Assured Tenancies and Agricultural Occupancies (Forms) Regulations 1997 SI No 194, form 8 and *Kahlon v Isherwood*, 2011.
5) **Transfer of secure tenancy**. Where a secure tenancy is transferred to a PRP or RSL – whether by way of Large Scale Voluntary Transfer or otherwise, see para 1.205) – and becomes assured (see para 1.222), it will become fully assured, not an assured shorthold.
6) **Termination of long lease**. Provided qualifying conditions are fulfilled, on the expiry of a long lease, the tenant will be entitled to become an assured tenant (see para 2.78). That tenancy will be fully assured, not shorthold.

7) **Termination of non-shorthold fixed term**. Where a periodic assured tenancy comes into being following a fixed-term fully assured tenancy (see para 2.158) it will remain fully assured.
8) **Assured agricultural occupancy**. The position of workers in agriculture and forestry is considered under its own heading (see para 1.304). Where this means that a worker has what is called an assured agricultural occupancy, it is fully assured rather than assured shorthold.

1.249 **PRPs and LA 2011**. Following changes in the law by LA 2011, PRPs commonly grant assured shorthold tenancies for two years or more (see para 1.183). Although tenancies for a fixed term of more than three years usually have to be created by deed (see para 1.19), this rule does not apply to assured shorthold tenancies granted by PRPs (LPA 1925 s52, as amended by LA 2011). In addition, although tenancies for a fixed term of more than seven years usually have to be registered with the Land Registry (see para 1.20), this rule does not apply to assured tenancies granted by PRPs (LRA 2002 ss4(5A) and 132). Special rules apply for regaining possession against such fixed-term assured shorthold tenants (see para 2.187).

1.250 **Tenancies created prior to 28 February 1997**. While all assured tenancies granted on or after 28 February 1997, are shorthold unless one of the foregoing conditions applies, the opposite was true beforehand, when all assured tenancies were fully assured unless certain conditions had been fulfilled.

1) **Notice**. The landlord (or, if joint landlords, one of them) had to serve a notice stating that the assured tenancy was to be shorthold. The notice had to be served in the form prescribed by Assured Tenancies and Agricultural Occupancies (Forms) (Regulations 1988 SI No 2203 or in a form susbstantially to the same effect – (HA 1988 s20(2)). Landlords commonly made mistakes in completing this form but not all mistakes invalidated the notice (*Ravenseft Properties Ltd v Hall*, 2001).
2) **Fixed term**. In addition to service of notice, the tenancy had to be for a fixed term of not less than six months (containing no power for the landlord to determine the tenancy within that period, otherwise than by way of forfeiture, ie for breach – see para 2.29): HA 1988 s20(1).
3) **Subsequent periodic tenancy**. When the initial shorthold tenancy came to an end, a periodic tenancy came into being, of the same or substantially the same premises, which was also an assured shorthold tenancy unless the landlord (or, if joint landlords, one

of them) served (or serves) notice stating that it is no longer to be considered a shorthold tenancy (HA 1988 s20(4)).

4) **New tenancy for existing tenant**. To prevent a landlord persuading a fully assured tenant to enter into a new arrangement which is shorthold, a tenancy was not shorthold if, immediately beforehand, the person to whom it is granted (or if joint tenants, one of them) was a fully assured tenant of the same landlord (even if in different premises) (HA 1988 s20(3)).

1.251 **Succession, assignment and sub-letting**. An assured shorthold tenancy is merely a form of assured tenancy and the usual rules relating to succession (see para 1.234), assignment and sub-letting (see para 1.241) apply equally to shortholds.

Demoted tenants

1.252 An introductory tenancy is a trial period at the start of a tenancy which must be completed before security of tenure is obtained (see para 1.210); an assured shorthold tenancy is likewise usually something with which the tenant begins his or her occupation, which may be replaced by a fully assured tenancy (see para 1.248(2)). A demoted tenant is a secure tenant (or licensee) or an assured tenant from whom protection under either scheme has been taken away for a period, pursuant to a demotion order, before allowing him or her to regain protection.

1.253 **Anti-social Behaviour Act 2003**. Demotion orders were introduced by the Anti-social Behaviour Act (ASBA) 2003. Unless the court considers it just and equitable to dispense with the requirement to do so, the landlord must serve the tenant with a preliminary notice in a form prescribed by the secretary of state or Welsh Ministers (contained in Secure Tenancies (Notices) Regulations 1987 SI No 755, as amended), or substantially to the same effect (HA 1985 s83(1); HA 1988 s6A(5)), which warns the tenant that demotion proceedings are to be brought. The notice must specify the date after which the proceedings may be begun. The specified date must not be earlier than the date when the tenancy could have been brought to an end by notice to quit (see para 2.49). The notice ceases to be in force 12 months after that date, ie if the proceedings have not been brought within that time, it lapses and if the landlord still wishes to seek a demotion order, it will have to serve a new notice (HA 1985 s83(4A)).

1.254 A demotion order can only be made if the court is satisfied that the tenant, or a person residing or visiting the dwelling has either engaged in, or threatened to engage in, conduct capable of causing a nuisance or annoyance to any person which directly or indirectly relates to or affects the housing management functions of the authority or has engaged in conduct which involves using or threatening to use for an unlawful purpose housing accommodation owned or managed by the authority or by the PRP or RSL (HA 1985 s82A(4); HA 1988 s6A(4)).

1.255 The court can only make an order if it considers it reasonable to do so: HA 1985 s82A(4)(b); HA 1988 s6A(4). Various factors are relevant to this question, many of which are also relevant to the making of a possession order, eg effect on neighbours, severity of the conduct and degree of fault on the tenant's part (see paras 2.104–2.105). The effect on the tenant will be relevant, ie the fact that after the order is made, the landlord can obtain possession not only for further antisocial behaviour but for any reason, including rent arrears.

1.256 **Replacement of tenancy.** A demotion order does not convert an existing secure tenancy into another tenancy. Instead it terminates the existing secure tenancy and replaces it with a new, demoted tenancy (HA 1985 s82A(8)(a)). By contrast, a demotion order against a tenant of a PRP or RSL (whether secure or assured) causes the tenant to become a demoted assured shorthold tenant (HA 1985 s82A(8)(b); HA 1988 s6A(11)). Demoted tenancies and demoted assured shorthold tenancies are periodic. If the original tenancy was periodic, the period of the demoted tenancy is the same; if the original tenancy was fixed-term, the demoted tenancy is weekly periodic (HA 1985 s82A(5), (6); HA 1988 s6A(8), (9)). The parties to the tenancy and the rent are the same as under the prior tenancy (HA 1985 s82A(5); HA 1988 s6A(8)). Rent arrears (or credit) outstanding under the prior tenancy transfer to the new tenancy (HA 1985 s82A(3); HA 1988 s6A(3)). The landlord may serve a statement of any other terms which are to govern the demoted tenancy or demoted assured shorthold tenancy (HA 1985 s82A(7); HA 1988 s6A(10)).

1.257 **Demotion period.** The intention is that the tenant will regain security of tenure unless the tenancy is determined during the demotion period. That period lasts one year starting with the date on which the demotion order takes effect (HA 1996 s143B(1); HA 1988 s20B(2)). In contrast to the trial period for introductory tenants (see para 1.215), the period cannot be extended.

1.258 **Succession.** The succession provisions for demoted tenants are similar to those applicable to secure tenancies (see paras 1.192–1.203); the succession will be to a demoted tenancy (HA 1996 s143H). If there is no one entitled to succeed under the statutory provisions, then once the tenancy has vested pursuant to the normal provisions applicable to the devolution of property on death, it will cease to be demoted (HA 1996 s143B(2)(c)). This is not so, however, if it is vested by an order of a court using powers under one of a number of family statutes, governing both partners and children (see paras 7.7–7.48), in which case the tenancy may remain demoted, notwithstanding the absence of a qualifying successor, eg if it is vested by the court in a child who had not been residing with the tenant, or a former spouse (likewise not residing with the deceased tenant) (HA 1985 ss89, 90). In the interregnum, it will therefore remain demoted (HA 1996 s143J). The rules relating to succession to a demoted assured shorthold tenancy are those which apply to assured shorthold tenancies generally (see para 1.251).

1.259 **Cessation of demoted tenancy.** Unless terminated, a demoted tenancy becomes secure or assured at the end of the demotion period, unless before that time something has happened which means that the tenancy would not otherwise be secure or assured, eg cessation of occupation as an only or principal home, or – in the case of a local authority tenancy – if someone other than a local authority becomes the landlord (HA 1996 s143B; HA 1988 s20B(2)). (Security may also not be re-acquired if the tenant dies and if there is no one entitled to take over as a secure tenant or an assured tenant – see para 1.258). The tenancy will not become secure or assured, however, if proceedings for possession have been commenced and are not finally resolved (HA 1996 s143B(3); HA 1988 s20B(3)).

1.260 In England, where a demotion order is obtained against a flexible tenant (see paras 1.181–1.189), or an assured shorthold tenant who had a fixed term of at least two years (see para 1.183), at the end of the demotion period, the tenant will once again become a flexible tenant, or fixed-term assured shorthold tenant, provided the landlord serves notice to that effect before the end of the demotion period (HA 1996 s143MA; HA 1988 s20C). The notice must state that the tenancy will be for a specified term of at least two years and set out the other terms of the tenancy (HA 1996 s143MA(3); HA 1988 s20C(3)).

1.261 **Assignment and sub-letting.** The rights of a demoted tenant to assign or sub-let are governed by the terms of the tenancy agreement, which will usually prevent both. Demoted assured shorthold tenant's rights to assign or sub-let are the same as for other assured shorthold tenants (see para 1.251).

Family intervention tenants

1.262 **Anti-social behaviour.** Family intervention tenancies were introduced by H&RA 2008 as another means to address anti-social behaviour. The intention of the scheme is to provide a home for a tenant where his or her household receives 'behaviour support services' with the aim of ensuring that his or her behaviour, or that of his or her children, improves. Sometimes the landlord may offer the tenant a family intervention tenancy of his or her existing home. Often, however, the tenancy is of premises in a 'core unit' where a group of families work with support services.

1.263 Who may grant family intervention tenancies? The scheme only applies in England and family intervention tenancies can only be granted by local authorities or PRPs (see para 1.162).

1.264 **Conditions.** A family intervention tenancy cannot be secure or assured (HA 1985 Sch 1 para 4ZA; HA 1988 Sch 1 para 12ZA). For a tenancy to be a family intervention tenancy it must satisfy the following conditions.

1) **Anti-social behaviour.** The tenant must be a person against whom a possession order has either been made, or against whom – in the landlord's opinion – an order could have been made, on any of the anti-social behaviour grounds (see paras 2.98(2), (3) and 2.169(5)) or domestic violence (see paras 2.98(3) and 2.157(6)).
2) **Prior notice.** Before granting the tenancy the landlord must give the tenant a notice stating: the reasons for offering the tenancy; the dwelling to be let; the main terms of the tenancy (including any requirements for the tenant to engage in behaviour support services); the security of tenure available under the tenancy and any loss of security of tenure which will result from the tenant entering into the agreement; that the new tenant is not obliged to enter into the tenancy and that, if the tenant has an existing tenancy, there is no obligation on him or her to surrender it; any likely action by the landlord if the new tenant does not enter into the tenancy or surrender any existing tenancy.

1.265 **Changing status.** A family intervention tenancy becomes secure or assured if the landlord serves notice to this effect on the tenant (HA 1985 Sch 1 para 4ZA(2); HA 1988 Sch 1 para 12ZA(2)). In England, a notice may instead provide that, if the tenant was originally a flexible tenant (see paras 1.181–1.189) or an assured shorthold tenant (see para 1.246), the tenant will again become a flexible tenant or an assured shorthold tenant (HA 1985 s107A(3); HA 1988 s20D). In the case of a former flexible tenant, the notice must state that the tenancy will be for a specified term of at least two years and set out the other terms of the tenancy (HA 1985 s107A(3)(d)).

1.266 Such security of tenure as a family intervention tenant enjoys is considered below (see paras 2.188–2.194). The status is one without security, so – in the absence of notice that the tenancy is to become secure or assured – no particular provisions need to be considered governing its loss otherwise than by possession proceedings.

Housing Act 1980 assured tenancies

1.267 The term 'assured tenancy' was first used in HA 1980 and reflected a policy of encouraging the private sector to build housing for rent, with a system of protection modelled on the mechanism applicable to business lettings under LTA 1954 Part 2. The policy was not successful and, subject only to minor qualification and to those lettings at the time being kept alive under the adapted LTA 1954, all HA 1980 assured tenancies were converted into HA 1988 assured tenancies from the commencement of HA 1988 Part 1 (15 January 1989) (HA 1988 ss1, 37). These HA 1980 tenancies will not be considered further.

Rent Act protected tenants

1.268 Rent Act protection was first introduced in 1915, and in one form or another, much changed, was the principal form of statutory protection in the private rented sector until 1988. In chapter 2, it will be seen that secure (see para 2.87), assured (see para 2.158), introductory (see para 2.148) and demoted (see para 2.177) tenancies cannot be brought to an end except by execution of an order of the court, in the first two cases only on specified grounds for possession. This model of how to confer protection was based on the approach adopted in relation to business lettings under LTA 1954, rather than the means used under the Rent Acts, in which the tenancy can come to an end in any of the normal ways in which it can end at common law, eg notice to quit (see para 2.49), forfeiture (see para 2.23), expiry of fixed term (see para 2.26) – but is followed by a personal 'right of irremovability' (subject to the grounds for possession considered in chapter 2 (paras 2.218–2.229) and to the other ways in which that right may cease – see paras 1.287–1.289).

1.269 **Protected and statutory tenancy**. Strictly, the term Rent Act protected tenant refers to a tenant within Rent Act protection who is still a contractual tenant (RA 1977 s1), ie one whose contract of tenancy has not come to an end in one of the ways described. A person continuing in occupation thereafter, pursuant to the right of irremovability, has what is known as a 'statutory tenancy' (RA 1977 s2), which the tenant can enjoy so long as he or she continues to occupy the property as 'a' residence (not necessarily 'only or principal'): see further below (see paras 1.280–1.293). Provided this residence test is satisfied, a statutory tenancy arises, even if it was the tenant who determined the tenancy by notice to quit, although in this circumstances, the landlord may be able to recover possession (case 5; see para 2.218(4)).

Landlords

1.270 The tenants of the following landlords will not be Rent Act protected: local authorities; PRPs and RSLs; charitable housing trusts (RA 1977 ss14–15). Most of these tenants will, however, if *pre*-Housing Act 1988 (see para 1.162), be secure tenants; otherwise they will usually qualify as assured (see para 1.220). Tenants of the Crown and a government department will not be protected unless the property is under the management of the Crown Estate Commissioners (RA 1977 s13). Tenants of a housing management co-operative (a body formed to manage or lease land belonging to, eg a local authority or housing association) will also not be protected (RA 1977 s16). Other kinds of housing co-operative are usually PRPs or RSLs or are fully mutual housing associations (see para 8.6) and are therefore exempt (RA 1977 s15).

Pre- and post-15 January 1989 tenants

1.271 The general rule is (see para 1.220) that there can be no new protected tenancies after commencement of HA 1988 Part 1, but this does not apply in the following cases (HA 1988 s34).

1) **Pre-Act contract.** The tenancy was entered into pursuant to a contract for its grant which preceded that date.
2) **New tenancy to former tenancy**. The tenancy has been granted to a person who was a former protected or statutory tenant of the same landlord, or one of a number of joint protected or statutory tenants (not including a shorthold tenant – see para 1.294), not necessarily of the same premises. This was intended to prevent

tenants with existing Rent Act protection being deprived of by it by their landlords. Unlike the case of an assured tenant granted a new assured shorthold, there is no provision for the tenant to serve notice waiving this protection (see para 1.248(4)).

3) **Suitable alternative accommodation.** The tenancy will be protected if it has been granted as a result of an order for possession made by a court on the ground of suitable alternative accommodation (see para 2.218(10)), of the premises which the court has found suitable, and the court directs that the new tenancy should be a protected tenancy because it considers that an assured tenancy would not afford sufficient security of tenure.
4) **New town corporation to private ownership**. The tenancy falls within a small class of tenancy formerly held by a new-town development corporation, which passed into the private sector prior to 31 March 1996. *Note.* All new town corporations have now been wound up.

Licensees

Tenants only

1.272 Only tenants can enjoy full Rent Act protection, not trespassers or licensees (see, eg *Marcroft Wagons v Smith*, 1951), nor, except as described in chapter 2 on owner-occupiers. Landlords commonly sought to avoid the effects of Rent Act protection by granting licences (see paras 1.33–1.41). A licensee whose contract began before commencement of HA 1988 (15 January 1989) may, however, be a restricted contract, within the jurisdiction of the Rent Tribunal (see paras 1.298–1.307).

Preconditions

Let as a separate dwelling

1.273 The Rent Act only applies to tenancies under which a dwelling was let as a separate dwelling (see para 1.171).

Sharing living accommodation

1.274 Accordingly, if the tenant shares living accommodation (see para 1.172) with his or her landlord, it cannot be a protected tenancy. This issue is extremely unlikely to arise in connection with a tenancy commencing after 14 August 1974, because it could only apply to a situation in which, on the one hand, the landlord used the premises, but, on the other, he or she did not establish sufficient residence to qualify as a resident landlord (see para 1.277(1)). It may, however, be relevant to an argument over whether or not the tenant was Rent Act protected at the beginning of the tenancy if the landlord took up residence shortly before 14 August 1974, and is trying to establish that the tenancy was not Rent Act protected at that date.

1.275 A tenant sharing living accommodation with his or her landlord, whose tenancy began before commencement of HA 1988 (15 January 1989), will have a restricted contract and be subject to the jurisdiction of the Rent Tribunal (see paras 1.298–1.305).

1.276 As with assured tenancy (see para 1.226), the fact that a tenant is sharing living accommodation with other tenants only, does not affect protection at all (RA 1977 s22).

Exceptions

1.277 There is a number of exceptions from Rent Act protection.

1) **Resident landlord**. The principal exception applies to resident landlords (see para 1.233(10) for the same exception in relation to assured tenancies). Although long ago, it remains necessary to consider this in relation to a tenancy which commenced before 14 August 1974, when the resident landlord exception was introduced, and those which have commenced since. Before that date, the fact that there was a resident landlord did not keep a tenant out of protection, unless he or she was sharing living accommodation with the tenant (see para 1.274), although many tenants with landlords living in the same house or flat would not have been protected for a different reason, the former exception, the furnished tenancy (see further below).

   On or after 14 August 1974

   We start with those tenancies which commenced on or after 14 August 1974. For a landlord to take advantage of this exception, he or she must establish that (subject to the provisions governing change of landlord described below), he or she has at all times since the commencement of the tenancy used the other part of the building which he or she occupies as a residence (RA 1977 s12). The definition applies where the landlord and the tenant occupy different parts of the same building (not being a purpose-built block of flats), or else (even if a purpose-built block of flats) that they occupy different parts of the same flat. These conditions are defined in the same way as under HA 1988 (see para 1.233(10)).

The degree of residence is the same as that which a statutory tenant must establish in order to sustain a statutory tenancy (see paras 1.290–1.295) (RA 1977 Sch 2). Briefly, it requires that premises are being used as a home, even if not the only home. A person may for short periods cease to use premises as a residence and still be treated as sustaining legal residence, provided both that he or she fully intends to return to live in the premises, and that he or she has left some physical sign of occupation in the premises, eg furniture, belongings, family. The law accepts that a person may have more than one residence at a time, but purely token residence will not suffice: a landlord cannot simply keep one room in a house, or in several houses, in order to keep his or her tenants out of protection. It is likely that residence by one of two or more joint owners/landlords would, however, be considered enough to keep the tenant out of protection.

Because of this requirement for residence, a corporate landlord, ie a landlord which is, eg a company, trust or partnership, cannot 'reside' at all because such a landlord has no natural life (*Hiller v United Dairies (London)*, 1934).

If the landlord sells the house, residence will nonetheless be treated as continuing for a further 28 days. If, during that time, the new owner serves notice that he or she intends to move into the premises for use as a home, he or she has a total of six months in which to do so, during which period residence by the landlord will likewise be treated as continuing (RA 1977 Sch 2). If, by the end of the six months, the new owner has not taken up residence, the tenant will become a Rent Act protected tenant and will so remain, even when the owner moves in, for there will not have been continual residence since the start of the tenancy.

If the contractual tenancy comes to an end within this period, on the one hand no statutory tenancy will arise, but on the other, the landlord cannot during this period evict other than as if the tenant was a statutory tenant (RA 1977 Sch 2). At the end of the period, the new landlord can simply evict (*Landau v Sloane*, 1981).

The position is somewhat different on the death of a resident landlord. In such circumstances, the executors effectively have two years in which the fact that there is no resident landlord will be disregarded (RA 1977 Sch 2). The two periods (two years and six months) may be added together (*Williams v Mate*, 1982). During this period, the landlord's executors may freely evict.

In certain circumstances, a tenant who would appear to have been excluded from protection because of a resident landlord may in fact be protected. In order to prevent a landlord tricking a tenant out of protection, RA 1977 s12 provides that a tenant who was formerly a Rent Act protected tenant under a previous tenancy of the same or another part of the building remains a Rent Act protected tenant. This, however, is only so where the presence of the resident landlord is the only reason for exclusion from protection, not where he or she is excluded for other reasons. Likewise, it will not apply if the tenant was not a protected tenancy under a previous tenancy, ie if he or she was excluded for some other reason.

Pre-14 August 1974

The resident landlord exception replaced an exception for furnished tenants. The general policy of Parliament is to allow people with protection to keep it. Accordingly, where there was a furnished tenancy in a house or flat with a resident landlord as at the commencement of RA 1974, the tenant moved from being excluded from protection for one reason (furniture) to exclusion for another (resident landlord). This still left to be addressed the tenant who was protected (because his or her tenancy was not furnished, nor was he or she sharing living accommodation with his or her landlord) before commencement, who was not to be deprived of his or her rights once the new test came into force.

As the question can still arise as to whether or not a tenant was protected before RA 1974 came into force (*Mann v Cornella*, 1980), it remains necessary briefly to consider what comprised a furnished tenancy. The law did not treat any amount of furniture, however small, as taking a tenant out of protection. The landlord had to provide enough furniture that the value to the tenant of the furniture formed a substantial proportion of the whole rent paid under the tenancy. *Note.* It is the value to the tenant which has to be calculated, in calculating which regard may be had to the social conditions prevailing at the time, ie the fact that the tenant lost the valuable asset of a protected tenancy, while the landlord gained the ability to evict his or her tenant with little or no difficulty, so that even a lot of furniture could have little actual value to the tenant: *Woodward v Docherty*, 1974.

Valuation involves a valuation of the furniture, with a proportion (usually 20 per cent) representing a fair return to the landlord. This sum must then be compared to the rent, ascertained as at the commencement of the tenancy. Courts will normally view anything over 20 per cent as substantial, anything between 15 per cent and 20 per cent as probably substantial, anything between 15 per cent and 10 per cent as possibly substantial, and anything below 10 per cent as insubstantial (see *Nelson Developments Ltd v Taboada*, 1992).

If the tenancy – thus approached – was furnished, then it was not protected and, as noted above, the test is whether the resident landlord test has been fulfilled since 14 August 1974. If not furnished, then it became protected and the tenant remains protected, even though there has been a resident landlord in the building since 14 August 1974.

2) **Attendances**. A tenancy under which the tenant is provided with attendances (RA 1977 s7) is not protected, provided that the value to the tenant of the attendance forms a substantial proportion of the whole rent (RA 1977 s7). The substantiality test is the same as that applicable to that for furniture.

   Attendance means personal service performed in the premises in question for the tenant, eg room cleaning, changing the sheets, doing the tenant's laundry, etc (*Palser v Grinling*, 1947; *Nelson Developments Ltd v Taboada*, 1992). The term does not include the provision of gas or electricity, or hot water, nor does it include cleaning of the common parts of a house in multiple occupation, eg hallways, stairs, bathroom, lavatory, etc (*King v Millen*, 1922). The provision of a resident housekeeper does not mean that the tenant is necessarily provided with attendances, although it is likely. If it does so, then the full amount of the wages of the resident housekeeper should not be attributed to the tenants, as a whole, even apportioned between them, for the presence of a resident housekeeper is considered to be of value also to the landlord. Window-cleaning is another service which is considered to be partly of value to the landlord and partly an attendance upon the tenant (*Engvall v Ideal Flats*, 1945).

   Note. Tenants whose tenancies precede the commencement of HA 1988 Part 1 (15 January 1989), and who are excluded from protection for either of the above reasons, will have a restricted contract, subject to the jurisdiction of the Rent Tribunal (see para 1.298).

3) **Board**. A tenant who, under the terms of his or her tenancy, is provided with any amount of board cannot be a Rent Act protected tenant (RA 1977 s7). Board means more than a mere morning cup of tea (*Wilkes v Goodwin*, 1923), but as little as a continental

breakfast has been upheld as the provision of board for this purpose, provided that at least some services are involved in preparing it and it includes the provision of crockery and cutlery with which to eat it (*Otter v Norman*, 1988). *Note*. Tenants whose tenancies precede the commencement of HA 1988 Part 1 (15 January 1989), and who are excluded from protection for the above reason, will have a restricted contract, subject to the jurisdiction of the Rent Tribunal (see para 1.298), unless the value of the board to the tenant forms a substantial part of the whole rent.

4) **Low rent**. As under the HA 1988 (see para 1.233(3)), RA 1977 is not designed to protect those who purchase long leases and pay only a small, annual ground rent (RA 1977 s5). A low rent is defined in the same way as under HA 1988 (see para 1.233(3)).
5) **Student lettings**. A tenancy will not be protected if the landlord under the tenancy is a specified educational institution, and the tenant is following or intends to follow a course of study at that or another specified educational institution (RA 1977 s8).
6) **No rent**. If no rent is paid under the terms of the tenancy, the tenancy cannot be protected (RA 1977 s5). The same issues as to the meaning of rent apply here, as under HA 1988 (see para 1.233(3)).
7) **Holiday letting**. If the purpose of the tenancy was used as a holiday home, then the tenancy will not be protected (RA 1977 s9). This is an exemption which was widely used as a device to defeat the Rent Acts. It is considered in relation to the same exemption as it arises under HA 1988 (see para 1.233(9)).
8) **High-rateable value**. This exemption operates in the same way as under HA 1988 (see para 1.233(2)), save that for tenancies granted after 1 April 1990, the threshold is £25,000 in both England and Wales (RA 1977 s4). Under RA 1977, this exception is presumed to be so unlikely to apply that it does not do so unless the landlord shows the contrary (RA 1977 s4(6)).
9) **Agricultural and other land**. A tenancy which qualifies as an agricultural holding will not be protected (RA 1977 s10); nor will a tenancy where the dwelling is let together with other land exceeding two acres (RA 1977 ss6, 26).
10) **Shared-ownership leases**. A shared-ownership lease (ie one where the tenant owns a share in the freehold or superior lease, and pays a rent proportionate to the share he or she has not acquired), as defined, is not protected (RA 1977 s5A).

11) **Licensed premises.** If the tenancy is of the premises which qualify as licensed premises, it will not be protected (RA 1977 s11).
12) **Business lettings.** As with secure (see para 1.180(15)), and assured (see para 1.233(4)) tenancies, business tenancies are excluded from protection (RA 1977 s24).

Succession

Statutory tenancy by succession

1.278 Normally, a tenant will be first a contractual tenant (and, as such, a protected tenant) and subsequently become a statutory tenant (see para 1.269). This may not be the case, however, when a protected tenant dies and his or her spouse, civil partner, or someone who was living with the tenant as husband or wife or as a civil partner, succeeds to the tenancy (RA 1977 s2). In such circumstances, the successor becomes a statutory tenant at once, even if the deceased still had a contractual tenancy.

Rent Act succession to Housing Act assured tenancy

1.279 Succession to a tenancy where the tenant died on or after the commencement of HA 1988 Part 1 (15 January 1989), is subject to the following rules.

1) **Priority to spouse/civil partner.** If the tenant who died was married or in a civil partnership, his or her spouse or civil partner will have priority in the succession, provided he or she was living in the dwelling-house at the time of death; for these purposes, persons who have been living together as husband and wife or as if they were civil partners are included (RA 1977 Sch 1 para 2, as amended).
2) **Member of family.** If there is no spouse or civil partner to succeed, any member of the family who was residing in the dwelling-house at the time of the tenant's death and for two years beforehand is entitled to succeed to the tenancy, but the tenancy will become an assured tenancy (see paras 1.220–1.246), not a Rent Act protected or statutory tenancy (RA 1977 Sch 1 para 3, as amended). 'Residing with' has the same meaning as in relation to a secure tenancy (see para 1.196).

   Unlike for a secure tenancy (see para 1.200), 'member of the family' is not statutorily defined and may be given a wide meaning. It is not used in any technical sense but in a popular sense (*Langdon v Horton*, 1950; *Brock v Wollams*, 1949). The hallmarks of family membership are essentially that there should be a degree of mutual interdependence, of the sharing of lives, of caring and love, of commitment and support. In respect of legal relationships these are presumed; in other relationships, these are capable, if proved, of creating membership of the tenant's family (*Fitzpatrick v Sterling HA*, 1999).

3) **Death of spouse or civil partner successor.** On the death of a spouse or civil partner who was a successor, someone who was a member of the family (of both the original tenant and the successor) residing in the dwelling-house at the time of the successor's death and for two years beforehand is entitled to a 'second succession', but likewise only to an assured tenancy (RA 1977 Sch 1 para 6, as amended).

   Note. There were transitional provisions governing deaths within the first 18 months following the commencement (15 January 1989) of HA 1988 Part 1 under which a member of the family residing with the deceased for six months before the commencement date was treated as having resided for two years.

Loss of security

Expiry of contractual tenancy

1.280 The distinction between a contractual tenancy and a statutory tenancy has already been described (see para 1.269). There is no requirement for occupation during the contractual tenancy: that only arises once the tenancy becomes statutory. Hence, even a corporation can be a protected tenant; but it cannot be a statutory tenant: this was the genesis of the use of corporate tenancies designed to defeat protection, or the grant of a tenancy to one person for the use of another, considered in relation to assured tenancy (see paras 1.231–1.232).

1.281 How tenancies come to an end is considered in chapter 2, as it is commonly the first stage in the process of eviction, even though many tenancies today (secure, assured, introductory, demoted and assured shorthold) cannot be brought to an end otherwise by court order, not least because even those provisions involve the preliminary service of a notice which, in the case of a periodic tenancy (see para 1.18) cannot be earlier than the tenancy could otherwise be brought to an end (see para 2.49), nor can possession be sought against a fixed term such tenancy (see para 1.18) unless either it has expired (see para 2.23) or else in the same circumstances as those in which it could be brought to an early end (see paras 2.24–2.59).

1.282 In the case of a protected (ie contractual – see para 1.269) tenancy, however, there is no requirement for a court order to bring it to an end and convert it into a statutory tenancy: that is achieved by using the normal means of terminating tenancies (see paras 2.23–2.59). In addition, however, a periodic protected tenancy may be brought to an end by a notice of increase of rent in the proper form (*Aristocrat Property Investments v Harounoff*, 1982), specifying a date for the increase to take effect no earlier than a notice to quit could have taken effect (see para 2.51). If it complies with these requirements, it will have the effect of converting the protected tenancy into a statutory tenancy (RA 1977 s49).

Former tenant

1.283 It is the person who immediately before termination was the protected, contractual tenant who becomes the statutory tenant (RA 1977 s2). Accordingly, if the tenant goes bankrupt while the tenancy is still contractual, the contract of tenancy may vest in his or her trustee in bankruptcy. When then determined, the bankrupt cannot become the statutory tenant because immediately before determination he or she was not the tenant, ie the trustee was (*Smalley v Quarrier*, 1975). If, however, the contractual tenancy was determined before bankruptcy, the statutory tenancy does not vest in the trustee because it is not a true tenancy, only a 'status of irremovability' (*Jessamine Investments Co v Schwartz*, 1976). Accordingly, the bankrupt can remain in possession as a statutory tenant (*Sutton v Dorf*, 1932).

1.284 At one time, contractual tenancies invariably vested in the trustee. The position today is that Rent Act protected tenancies will not do so unless the trustee elects to adopt the tenancy (HA 1988 s117), and the bankrupt tenant will otherwise be permitted to retain the tenancy in his or her own name. This averts the worst effects of this rule while retaining the trustee's right to vest the contractual tenancy in him- or herself, eg if the rent is too high. Nor does this provision apply where the tenancy is one in respect of which a premium may lawfully be charged (see para 3.124) because it has a value which the trustee can realise: in such a case, the contractual tenancy still vests in the trustee.

Joint tenants

1.285 If there were joint contractual tenants (see para 1.48), each will acquire the personal right of statutory tenancy (*Daejan Properties Ltd v Mahoney*, 1995), and, if only one remains, he or she will be able to sustain it alone (*Lloyd v Sadler*, 1977).

Termination of statutory tenancy

1.286 Once the protected, ie contractual, tenancy (see para 1.269) has been brought to an end, however this is done, there is no need for any further notice to be served to bring the subsequent statutory tenancy to an end, no matter how long it has subsisted since termination. No new contractual tenancy comes into being unless there is evidence that it was intended, eg because the landlord and the tenant agreed to vary some term of the tenancy other than rent, and it is sufficiently substantial to warrant description as a new tenancy. The tenant simply occupies as a statutory tenant until such time either as a court orders possession to be given up to the landlord or the statutory tenancy itself comes to an end.

1.287 Leaving aside an order for possession made against the statutory tenancy by a court (see para 2.217), the tenant leaving or the death of the tenant with no qualifying successor, there is a number of circumstances in which the statutory tenancy may end. Protection under RA 1977 may also be lost if the premises are made the subject of a prohibition or demolition order under HA 2004, because of their condition (HA 2004 s33) (see paras 10.33 and 10.46), or become illegally overcrowded under HA 1985 (RA 1977 s101) (see para 14.7).

1.288 First of all, the tenancy will cease to be statutory if the premises are bought by one of the public landlords described above whose tenants are not within Rent Act protection (see para 1.270). The tenancy will usually then become a secure or an assured tenancy.

1.289 Secondly, if the tenant ceases to occupy the premises as a residence, the statutory tenancy will come to an end. A statutory tenancy only comes into and remains in being, so long as the tenant is in residence.

Regular and personal use

1.290 Residence for the purpose of the Rent Acts is not the residence as an only or principal home required for a secure tenancy (see para 1.176) or an assured tenancy (see para 1.230) but use as 'a' home. Use as a home means 'a substantial degree of regular personal occupation by the tenant of an essentially personal nature' (*Herbert v Byrne*, 1964). The tenant may be using the premises as a home, even if he or she is also using somewhere else in the same way, ie a statutory tenant may have two homes. The question is whether the tenant is keeping on the premises in question 'as a mere convenience' (*Beck v Scholz*, 1953) or whether in fact he or she is using both places as homes, even if he or she only visits one or other of them infrequently (*Langford Property Co v Tureman*, 1948).

Continuous residence

1.291 The residence must be continuous although, as with resident landlords (see para 1.277(1)), this does not mean that the tenant must constantly be living in the premises; rather, it means that he or she must still be able to claim that the premises are in his or her use as a home, even if not as an only home. If a tenant is absent from premises for a longish period of time, eg a few months, there may, on the face of it, be a claim that he or she has abandoned use of the premises as a home (*Brown v Brash*, 1948), and if sufficiently prolonged it may be said to put the tenant to having to prove continued residence (*Roland House Gardens v Cravitz*, 1974).

Intention to return

1.292 Regardless of whether a person is laying claim to two homes or not, a person who absents him- or herself from premises for a longish period of time can still claim to be a statutory tenant of them so long as he or she intends to return at some time in the future to use the premises as a home, and leaves in the premises some visible signs of that intention (*Brown v Brash*, 1948). There must be both intention to return and some indication of it. A tenant who claims that he or she intends to return subject to a condition, eg works by the landlord, will not be considered a statutory tenant unless he or she can be said to have a reasonable expectation that it will be fulfilled (*Robert Thackray's Estates Ltd v Kaye*, 1988). Indication of intention could be belongings or furniture, or even leaving a friend in occupation to 'keep the place warm'. But simply leaving a friend in occupation without any intention to return to live there him- or herself will not be sufficient to maintain the claim to be a statutory tenant of the premises. In contrast with the position under a secure tenancy (see para 1.177), however, security can be maintained even if the premises have been sub-let (*Leslie & Co Ltd v Cumming*, 1926) but if the sub-letting is a breach of a term of the tenancy agreement, the landlord may seek possession under case 6 (see para 2.218).

Residence – spouses and civil partners

1.293 As with secure tenancies and assured tenancies, on relationship breakdown, if the departing partner is the statutory tenant, security is nevertheless maintained by the occupation of the partner who remains until the marriage or civil partnership is actually ended (see paras 1.179 and 1.230; Family Law Act 1996 s30(4) – see para 7.11). *Note.* Even before statutory provisions were introduced to protect remaining partners, case law established that an abandoned wife's occupation was sufficient to maintain protection under the Rent Acts (*Wabe v Taylor*, 1952) for as long as the marriage lasted (*Metropolitan Properties Co v Cronan*, 1982; *Lewis v Lewis*, 1985).

Protected shorthold tenancies

1.294 The protected shorthold tenancy was introduced by HA 1980, and abolished by HA 1988 (when it was replaced in practice by the assured shorthold tenancy – see paras 1.246–1.250). It is possible for protected shorthold tenancies still to remain in existence. The essence of the protected shorthold is that it adds a ground for possession (see para 2.223) – that the tenancy was shorthold and that the appropriate notice has been served – to those otherwise available in respect of Rent Act protected or statutory tenants, which is a mandatory ground, which is to say that it does not also require the landlord to prove to the court that it is reasonable to make the order sought. (The shorthold tenant is also subject to those other grounds for possession – see paras 2.217–2.219).

1.295 **Conditions**. The protected shorthold tenancy (HA 1980 s51), is a tenancy which is in all other respects a fully Rent Act protected tenancy (see paras 1.268–1.293), granted after 28 November 1980 (when these shorthold provisions were brought into force), which fulfilled the following conditions.

1) **Fixed term**. The tenancy had initially to be fixed-term tenancy (see para 1.18), not one that was periodic (see para 1.18), granted for a minimum of one-year and a maximum of five (HA 1980 s52(1)). A tenancy granted on one date, but expressed to have commenced on an earlier date, would only be considered to fulfil the minimum/maximum time limits if they were fulfilled from the date when the tenancy was actually granted, rather than from any such earlier date (*Roberts v Church Commissioners for England*, 1971; *Brikom Investments Ltd v Seaford*, 1981).
2) **No break clause**. There can have been no provision in the agreement for bringing the tenancy to an end by the landlord, other than by way of forfeiture (see paras 2.29–2.44) for non-payment of rent or breach of some other term of the tenancy (HA 1980 s52(1)(a)). Thus, a 'break clause' (see para 1.27) allowing the landlord to give notice in the middle of, or any other time during, the term would defeat the shorthold.

A clause which allowed a landlord to forfeit if the tenant went bankrupt was construed as creating an obligation on the part of the tenant not to go bankrupt, with the effect that the tenancy was still shorthold (*Paterson v Aggio*, 1987).

3) **Prior notice**. Before the tenancy was granted, the landlord must have given the tenant a valid shorthold notice (HA 1980 s52(1)(b)). The notice must have been in the prescribed form. A notice given after the tenancy began will not suffice.

   On proceedings for possession under the shorthold ground, a court can, however, waive the requirement for notice if it considers that it is just and equitable to do so (HA 1980 s55(2)) (see para 2.223). This would in effect retrospectively deem the tenancy to have been a shorthold. The court should only use this power when the omission to serve notice was known to the tenant, perhaps known to be an oversight or accident of which the tenant now seeks to take advantage in a way that the court considers unmeritorious, or if the notice was in only slightly the wrong form.

   In *RJ Dunnell Property Investments Ltd v Thorpe*, 1989, where the tenancy agreement had stated that the letting was a protected shorthold but no notice had in fact been served, a decision to dispense with notice was upheld by the Court of Appeal. It should not be used, however, to take away from a tenant full security where the tenant had reason to believe that was what he or she enjoyed.

4) **Registered rent**. In some cases, either there must have been a registered rent (see para 3.59) at the commencement of the tenancy, or the landlord must have secured a certificate of fair rent (now no longer available) by the time the tenancy was granted (HA 1980 s52(1)(c)).

5) **Previous Rent Act protected or statutory tenant**. The tenancy was not granted to a person who, immediately before the grant, was a Rent Act protected or statutory tenant (see para 1.269) of the same premises (HA 1980 s52(2)). This is designed to prevent landlords persuading existing tenants to sign shorthold agreements. It only protects the tenant if the new tenancy was of exactly the same premises as the pre-existing tenancy. Thus, another flat in the same building would not prevent the tenancy being shorthold, nor even would a new agreement in respect of, for example, the same premises less or plus one room (*Gluchowska v Tottenham BC*, 1954).

1.296 **Notice by tenant.** Although the landlord could not give notice during the fixed-term period of the shorthold (see para 1.295(2)), the shorthold tenant is entitled to do so, even if the written agreement purports to prohibit him or her from doing so (HA 1980 s53(1)). Any clause purporting to penalise the tenant for giving notice, eg imposing an additional payment, is wholly void and of no effect (HA 1980 s53(2)). The notice may be given at any time during the fixed term: if the fixed term was for more than two years, the notice must be of three months; if for two years or less, it need only be of one month; in either event, it must be in writing (HA 1980 s53(1)).

1.297 **Continuation of protected shortholds.** A protected shorthold tenancy is technically only a shorthold during the initial fixed-term tenancy (HA 1980 s52(5)). This is technical, because the landlord retains the right to recover possession under the additional shorthold ground (see para 2.223) indefinitely (*Gent v De La Mare*, 1987).

Restricted contracts

1.298 Restricted contracts were a form of subordinate security, under (in its last form) RA 1977. The largest class of occupiers with restricted contracts were tenants who would have been Rent Act protected but for the presence of a resident landlord (see para 1.277(1)). In addition, those provided with sufficient attendances to take them out of full Rent Act protection (see para 1.277(2)) or board, provided it is not substantial (see para 1.277(3)), had restricted contracts. Hostel-dwellers also frequently had restricted contracts, as indeed did some of those in long-stay hotels. The class did not normally cover lettings from public landlords, nor family and friendly arrangements.

1.299 **Licensees.** Both tenants and licensees could have restricted contracts: *Luganda v Service Hotels Ltd*, 1969. The arrangement must, however, be contractual, ie it has to be intended to be binding on the parties. There must, however, be exclusive occupation. Any tenant will of definition have exclusive occupation (see para 1.29). A hostel-dweller with his or her own room will usually have exclusive occupation sufficient to amount to a restricted contract (*R v South Middlesex Rent Tribunal ex p Beswick*, 1976). A hostel-dweller who is given a room to share with another will not have exclusive occupation, unless the occupiers approached the hostel together and took the room jointly. In every case, it will be a question of fact whether or not an occupier has exclusive occupation. It will not be missing just because, for example, a landlord retains a key to the room, or because one of the landlord's employees comes in to clean. There will still be enough exclusive occupation for these purposes if, in addition to the exclusive use of at least one room, there is shared use of other rooms (RA 1977 s19), even if those shared rooms constitute 'living accommodation' (see para 1.172).

1.300 **Post-14 January 1989.** No new restricted contracts could be created on or after the commencement of HA 1988 (15 January 1989), subject to the following exceptions (HA 1988 s36).

1) **Pre-Act contract.** The tenancy or licence was entered into in pursuance of a contract made before the commencement of the Act.
2) **Variation.** If the terms of a restricted contract have been varied after the Act came into force then, unless it was a variation of rent, the question of whether or not it was a new contract has to be addressed in the same way as for, eg a new tenancy. If the variation was of the amount of rent payable, then the contract is treated as a new contract (and, therefore, not restricted) unless it either was a variation (increase or reduction) ordered by the Rent Tribunal (see para 3.82–3.83) or a variation agreed by the parties in order to conform to a rent already registered by the Rent Tribunal, in which case the contract is treated as the same, continuing restricted contract (HA 1988 s36).

1.301 **Landlords.** There is no restricted contract if the landlord under the letting (tenancy or licence) is a government department, a local authority or the Crown, unless the property is under the management of the Crown Estate Commissioners (RA 1977 s19(5)(d)). Likewise, if the landlord under a tenancy was an RSL, housing trust, the Housing Corporation, or a housing co-operative (RA 1977 s19(5)(e)). Note that this only excludes *tenants*, and does not prevent *licensees* of such landlords from using the powers of the Rent Tribunal, if they otherwise qualify (see para 1.299).

1.302 **Preconditions.** There are two ways in which restricted contracts were defined: by general definition and by specific definition.

1) **General definition.** Restricted contracts are those 'contracts ... whereby one person grants to another person, in consideration of a rent which includes payment for the use of furniture or for services, the right to occupy a dwelling as a residence' (RA 1977 s19). 'Services' includes attendances (see para 1.277(2)) and board (see para 1.277(3)) as well as the provision of heating or lighting, the supply of hot water and any other privilege or facility connected with the occupancy of a dwelling, other than a privilege or facility necessary for the purposes of access to the premises let, the

supply of cold water or sanitary accommodation (RA 1977 s85). Furniture means any amount of furniture.

2) **Specific definition.** Even if a tenant does not qualify under the foregoing definition, the tenants of resident landlords who are excluded from full Rent Act protection for that reason (see para 1.277(1)) have restricted contracts, even if no furniture or services are provided (RA 1977 s20).

   Those who are excluded from full protection because they share living accommodation with their landlords (see para 1.172) are also included regardless of the provision of furniture or services (RA 1977 s21).

1.303 **Exclusions.** There are certain conditions which exclude an occupier from the definition of restricted contract (RA 1977 s19):

1) **Rateable values.** There is no restricted contract if the rateable value of the (occupier's part of the) premises exceeds £1,500 (Greater London) or £750 (elsewhere). This is highly unlikely to be the case.
2) **Regulated tenancy.** There is no restricted contract if the letting created a protected tenancy (see para 1.268). This ensured that there was no overlap between full Rent Act protection and Rent Tribunal restriction (*Baldock v Murray*, 1980).
3) **Board.** There is no restricted contract if, under the terms of the letting, the occupier is provided with board and its value to the occupier forms a substantial proportion (see para 1.277(1)) of the whole rent paid. What constitutes board has already been considered (see para 1.277(3)). If any board is provided, a tenancy cannot be Rent Act protected, but if the value of the board forms an insubstantial proportion of the rent then it can be restricted. Board may be hard to value and is almost certainly worth more than the mere cost of the food.
4) **Holiday lettings.** There is no restricted contract if the letting is for the purposes of a holiday (see para 1.277(7)).

Agricultural and forestry workers

1.304 Under HA 1988 Part 1 chapter 3, agricultural and forestry tied workers, ie those living in accommodation belonging to their employers (see paras 1.131–1.140), whose occupation commenced on or after 15 January 1989, enjoy a measure of protection, notwithstanding that they may well have licences rather than tenancies. Under the Rent (Agriculture) Act 1976, protection largely similar to that under

RA 1977 is available to agricultural and forestry tied workers whose rights of occupation precede the commencement of HA 1988 Part 1.

1.305 It is not possible in this book to consider these provisions in any detail, but the following points may be noted.

1) **Tenants and licencees.** The provisions of both 1988 and 1976 Acts apply not only to service tenants but also to service occupiers.
2) **No rent.** The fact that such occupiers will not usually be paying rent does not take them out of protection.
3) **Period of employment.** It is usually necessary to show that the employee has been an agricultural worker (though not necessarily with the same employer) for 91 out of the 104 weeks preceding the date when it is claimed that either Act applies.

1.306 The structure of each Act allows a landlord to make application to the local authority to provide re-housing 'in the interests of efficient agriculture'.

1.307 Agricultural workers not within these provisions may get some temporary security for up to a year, under the Protection from Eviction Act (PEA) 1977 s4, by way of time granted by the court before a possession order takes effect (see para 2.209).

Excluded tenants

1.308 If a tenant is not within any of the categories discussed above (see paras 1.160–1.307), his or her rights to remain in occupation are limited. In most cases it remains necessary for the landlord to obtain a court order before evicting a tenant (PEA 1977 s3 – see para 2.237). In the case of 'excluded tenants', however, once the tenancy has been terminated in one of the permissible ways (see paras 2.20–2.58) it is not even necessary for the landlord to obtain a court order.

1.309 **Excluded tenancies and licences.** The following are excluded tenancies (PEA 1977 s3A).

1) The tenant shares any accommodation (other than storage space, passages, corridors or other means of access, ie a bathroom or lavatory is accommodation for this purpose, *cf* para 1.172) with the landlord, who was him- or herself in occupation of another part of the premises as an only or principal home (see paras 1.176–1.178) both before the tenancy was granted and at the time it comes to an end.
2) The tenant shares any accommodation (other than storage space, passages, corridors or other means of access, so that again a

bathroom or lavatory is included) with a member of the family of the landlord, who was in occupation of another part of the premises as an only or principal home (see paras 1.176–1.178) both before the tenancy was granted and at the time it comes to an end, and immediately before the tenancy was granted and at the time it comes to an end, the landlord occupies, as his or her only or principal home, premises in the same building (not being a purpose-built block of flats: see para 1.233(10).

3) The tenancy was granted as a temporary expedient to someone who originally entered premises as a trespasser, ie a former squatter who is granted a tenancy for a period of time.
4) The tenancy was a holiday letting (see para 1.233(9)) or was granted other than for money or money's worth, ie was not a commercial arrangement.
5) The tenancy was granted in order to provide accommodation under IAA 1999 Part 6.

Excluded licencees

1.310 **Former licensees.** Once a licence (see paras 1.114–1.130) is terminated, PEA 1977 s3 (see para 2.212) also protects former licensees who have occupied under restricted contracts (see para 1.298) commencing on or after 28 November 1980, former service occupiers (see para 1.131) who were granted some exclusive occupation of their accommodation under the employment arrangement (PEA 1977 s8), and all other former licensees other than those with 'excluded licences'.

1.311 **Excluded licensees.** This has the same meaning as 'excluded tenancy' (see para 1.309), in each case including anyone lawfully living with such a licensee at the end of the occupancy.

1.312 **Hostels.** In addition, a licence of part of a hostel is also excluded if it is provided by one of a specified number of public bodies, including local authorities, PRPs, RSLs, development corporations and charitable housing trusts (see para 8.5) (PEA 1977 s3A(8)).

1.313 **Homeless persons.** In a judicial extension to these provisions, it has been held that accommodation provided by way of licence (see para 1.114) as a temporary measure to a homeless person, eg pending inquiries into his or her application for assistance (see para 10.83) or following a decision that he or she is intentionally homeless (see para 10.99), is not, normally, 'occupied as a dwelling under a licence' because of the transience of the occupation (*R (CN) v Lewisham LBC*, 2014). Such licence arrangements do not, therefore, have the protection of PEA 1977. It has, however, been suggested (although not yet decided) that if the letting is by way of tenancy, the accommodation will be protected (*Desnousse v Newham LBC*, 2006).

Renting Homes (Wales) Act 2016

1.314 As noted earlier (see para 1.5), in Wales, the Law Commission's proposals for the simplification of the number of classes of occupation have been adopted in the Renting Homes (Wales) Act (RH(W)A) 2016, although the Act is unlikely to come into force for some time because much preparatory work needs to be done in anticipation of the transition to the new regime.

1.315 In essence, there will be two forms of 'occupation contract' (RH(W)A 2016 s7). No distinction is drawn between a tenancy or a licence (RH(W)A 2016 s1). 'Secure contracts' will be periodic and will be granted by 'community landlords', ie local authorities, RSLs, PRPs and certain other public bodies (RH(W)A 2016 s9), and provide similar security of tenure to that enjoyed by secure tenants (see para 2).

1.316 The other form of contract is the 'standard contract', which can be fixed-term or periodic (RH(W)A 2016 s1), and which have similar security of tenure to assured shorthold tenancies (see para 2.195–2.208). All other landlords are referred to as 'private landlords' (RH(W)A 2016 s9) who will grant standard contracts (RH(W)A 2016 s1). Community landlords will be able to grant standard contracts in limited circumstances (RH(W)A 2016 Sch 3), which are similar to the exceptions to full security of tenure under HA 1985 Sch 1 (see para 1.180).

1.317 Of the classes of occupier considered (see paras 1.158–1.309), only tenants with full protection under RA 1977 will retain their existing status the Act comes into force. All other existing tenants will become occupiers under either secure or standard contracts. In broad terms, existing secure tenants and fully assured tenants of RSLS or PRPs will become occupiers under secure contracts; all other tenants and licences will become occupiers under standard contracts (RH(W)A 2016, Sch 12).

1.318 One of the core objectives of the Law Commission's report was to promote a 'consumer-protection' approach to housing law. The Welsh Ministers will provide model contracts setting out the parties' statutory rights and responsibilities (RH(W)A 2016 s29) so that both landlords and tenatns have a clearer understanding of their position.

Human Rights Act 1998 and judicial review

1.319 Article 8 ECHR – imported into domestic law by the Human Rights Act (HRA) 1998 – confers a right of respect for the home which is, in principle, offended by an eviction, even if otherwise in accordance with the terms of a tenancy or licence, or of a trespasser (*Harrow LBC v Qazi*, 2003; *Kay v Lambeth LBC*, 2006). In turn, respect requires – in principle – that a body independent of the landlord reaches its own decision, on the facts as it finds them, of whether or not the eviction is 'proportionate,' meaning that it is reasonable remedy having regard to its purpose, eg to recover arrears, because of nuisance or to let the property to someone else (*Manchester City Council v Pinnock*, 2010; *Hounslow LBC v Powell*, 2011).

1.320 **Home**. It does not require much to establish that occupation is as a home for the purposes of the Convention, such as to attract the right to respect afforded by Article 8. It does not require that the occupation is lawful in domestic law (*Buckley v UK*, 1996; *Hounslow v Powell*, 2011). Indeed, it is not even necessary for the property to be currently occupied. A property is a person's home if he or she can show 'sufficient and continuous links' with it (*Gillow v UK*, 1986; *Kay v Lambeth LBC*, 2006). Thus, a house in which a couple had lived for five years, and to which they intended to return at some point, remained their home notwithstanding that they had a house elsewhere (*Gillow*). A house remained a husband's home notwithstanding that he or she had moved out of it following separation from his or her wife (*Wiggins v UK*, 1976). Land on which a person intends to build a house to live in is not, however, a home (*Loizidu v Turkey*, 1996). Nor, where a family of travellers unlawfully camped on land for two days, could the site possibly be their home (*Kay*).

1.321 **Public authorities**. It is, however, only a public authority which is required to act compatibly with a Convention right: HRA 1998 s6(1). 'Public authority' includes a court and any person whose functions are functions of a public nature: HRA 1998 s6(2).

1.322 Local housing authorities are public authorities. Other 'social landlords', such as housing associations, are assumed to be public authorities when managing (including allocating and evicting from) social housing, provided that they have had at least some public funding, whether or not for the property in question (*R (Weaver) v London & Quadrant Housing Trust*, 2009).

1.323 Outside of HRA 1998, public authorities or bodies are susceptible to the principles of domestic judicial review (see paras 8.23–8.28), which have been evolved by the common law over the years, sometimes referred to as domestic public or administrative law. There is no definition of public authority or body for this purpose: any authority or body which is set up by statute or derives its authority from statute will qualify – the essence of domestic judicial review is that when Parliament confers a power, it assumes it will be exercised 'properly', not abused, and the principles of domestic judicial review define what is proper for this purpose.

1.324 Merely because a body is one defined by Parliament, eg a PRP or RSL, does not, however, mean that it derives its authority from statute (although if a PRP or RSL is within HRA 1998, it will be susceptible to principles of domestic judicial review in relation to those functions as well – see para 1.322). The authority or body does not have to be established by Parliament: even a self-regulator created by an industry (to reflect public interest in its proper conduct, without – and often in order to pre-empt – legislation) may be considered to serve a sufficient public purpose to merit application of these principles.

1.325 The right to rely on these principles are therefore available to all those affected by the decisions or action of a local authority, the Crown, a government department, or other bodies such as an urban development corporation, the HCA – if a matter in respect of which susceptible to a Convention challenge – a PRP or RSL, whether a freeholder (see para 1.7) seeking to resist, eg planning or compulsory purchase, a long leaseholder (see para 1.18) whose landlord may be a public authority, tenant, licensee or even a trespasser.

1.326 Because these principles are applicable across the range of decisions that a public authority may make in housing, they are considered in relation to social landlords, in chapter 8. It may be noted, however, that an unlawful decision by a public authority or body may be challenged by seeking permission in the High Court to bring a judicial review, which is a particular kind of procedure which cannot be commenced without permission and which must be commenced without delay and in any event (unless there are reasons to extend time) within three months of the decision in question.

1.327 Further, an individual affected by the decision can usually raise its unlawfulness as of right, by way of defence to any action being taken by the authority or body against him or her, eg by defending possession proceedings on the basis that the decision to issue them was unlawful (*Bristol DC v Clark*, 1975; *Cannock Chase DC v Kelly*, 1978; *Barber v Croydon LBC*, 2010; *R (JL) v Secretary of State for Defence*, 2013; *Leicester City Council v Shearer*, 2013): not only is there no requirement for permission, but this right is available without limit of time.

1.328 **Private landlords**. The Supreme Court has held that a tenant of a private landlord cannot avail him- or herself of Convention rights, at least once a court is involved *(McDonald v McDonald,* 2014). Although there are some cases in which the European Court of Human Rights assumed that a private tenants could avail themselves of the Convention rights (see, in particular *Zehentner v Austria,* 2009), the Supreme Court took the view that these cases did not directly address the issue. A subsequent case in the European Court of Human Rights involving repossession by a mortgage lender supports the Supreme Court's approach (*Vrzić v Croatia,* 2016).

CHAPTER 2

Security of tenure and eviction

continued

Introduction

2.1 The expression 'security of tenure' is generally taken to refer to the rights given to occupiers to remain which have been conferred by the law – enacted by Parliament – and which are additional to those which the parties have agreed between themselves by contract, whether long leasehold, fixed-term or periodic tenancy, or licence. The starting-point, however, is always the contract: even where Parliament appears to have substituted statutory means of determining a tenancy for those which would have applied under the contract, it will invariably mean that no *fewer* rights than would have been available under the contract will still be available.

2.2 In this chapter, therefore, we consider how the basic rights of occupation considered in chapter 1 (see paras 1.7–1.154) may be brought to an end, followed by how occupation pursuant to the statutory classes of protection may be ended; finally, we consider the constraints on eviction which, in practice, may serve to extend occupation by requiring a landlord or other person entitled to possession to take court proceedings before evicting. Unlawful eviction itself is, however, dealt with in chapter 5.

Freeholders

2.3 Because of their position, freeholders are, however, considered in a class of their own, for in principle no one else has a right – in private law – to determine the right of occupation. A freeholder (see para 1.7) without a mortgage can only be permanently displaced by, eg 'state' action such as compulsory purchase by central or local government, because the condition of the property or the way it is used entitles a local authority to an order prohibiting its occupation (see para 12.33), because the property is transferred on domestic breakdown (see para 7.3), because of bankruptcy or in similar circumstances, many of which are outside the ambit of this book.

2.4 **Repossession.** Many freeholders will, however, have a mortgage and this can lead to eviction. Although all mortgage deeds contain a variety of terms, eg not to create tenancies – or tenancies other than of a particular type, eg only those without security – in the property without permission, it is usually only when an occupier falls into arrears with the repayments that the company has the right to take action to evict the borrower, and to dispose of the property.

2.5 **Sale.** If such an order is made, then absent agreement to the contrary, either the mortgage company or the owner-occupier may apply for an order for the property to be sold (under the Law of Property Act (LPA) 1925 s91). Thus, if a mortgage company wishes instead to rent the property out until the market picks up, the owner-occupier can apply to the court to force the mortgage company to sell in order to prevent interest continuing to accrue (*Palk v Mortgage Services Funding Plc*, 1992). Usually, however, an order for sale at the request of the owner-occupier will be refused if the mortgage company can demonstrate a tangible benefit of which it will be deprived, although this will not include either its own policy considerations or the power to conduct the sale through its own agents and solicitors (*Barrett v Halifax BS*, 1995).

2.6 **Whether bound by mortgage.** The mortgage company will, however, have to be able to show that the mortgage is binding on those against whom it seeks possession. It will not be binding on someone with a prior interest, eg a prior tenant (see para 1.102), or a spouse or civil partner with a prior right of occupation under the Family Law Act 1996 (see paras 7.9–7.27), unless there has been an effective agreement to subordinate that right to the subsequent mortgage company (*Woolwich BS v Dickman*, 1996). Likewise, if there are joint owners on the face of the deeds, or as a result of a trust (see paras 1.106–1.113), all those who have an existing right must be shown to be bound by the mortgage before the company will be able to exercise its rights.

2.7 **Securing someone else's loan.** These issues commonly arise when a home is put up as security for a loan, which may not itself be for housing purposes but, eg for a business purpose. Where one person puts up his or her own home as security, then the position is no different than in any other case where one individual borrows against the security of his or her house or flat. Problems arise where one person – who wants to borrow the money – needs the agreement of a joint owner or someone else with a prior right to use the property as security.

2.8 **Undue influence.** Where agreement to the security has been procured by a third party (such as a spouse, civil partner, cohabitee or employer) using undue influence, misrepresentation or another legal wrong, it may not be binding if the lender had actual notice of the wrong or the surrounding circumstances were such that the lender should have made inquiries to satisfy itself that the agreement was not procured by a legal wrong. In some relationships, eg parent/child, solicitor/client, undue influence will automatically be presumed (and therefore the lender should make inquiries of the person providing the security) in any transaction which is to the disadvantage to the third party, unless it can be shown that he or she entered into it with 'full, free and informed thought'.

2.9 This presumption does not, however, automatically apply to husbands and wives or to civil partners. To show undue influence in such cases, it is necessary to have evidence that the transaction was wrongful 'in that it constituted an advantage taken of the person subjected to the influence which, failing proof to the contrary, was explicable only on the basis that undue influence had been exercised to procure it' (*National Westminster Bank Plc v Morgan*, 1985; *Royal Bank of Scotland v Etridge (No 2)*, 2001).

2.10 **Effect on lender.** Where the lender is under the duty to make inquiries (see para 2.8), then it will, in order to avoid being affected by the wrong and unable to enforce its security, have to show that it had taken reasonable steps to satisfy itself that the third party has entered into the arrangement freely and in knowledge of the true facts, which will normally mean warning him or her – at a meeting not attended by the borrower – of the amount of the potential liability, and of the risks involved, and advising him or her to take independent legal advice (*Barclays Bank Plc v O'Brien*, 1993). Even if the lender does not meet with the third party, the lender will also be protected against the wrongdoing if it has confirmed with the third party that he or she has a solicitor acting for him or her, and has confirmation from the solicitor that the third party has been appropriately advised (*Royal Bank of Scotland*).

2.11 **Pre-action Protocol.** The Civil Procedure Rules (CPR) 1998, which govern the conduct of court proceedings, include a number of 'pre-action protocols' which are intended to ensure that parties settle their disputes without resorting to the courts. Under the protocol for mortgage possession claims, as soon as the borrower falls into arrears, the mortgage company must write to him or her informing him or her of the amount of the arrears and of the total outstanding under the mortgage (including any interest). Both parties are expected to take all reasonable steps to try to agree a timetable for paying off the arrears.

2.12 If no agreement can be reached, or if any agreement is made but the borrower breaches it, the mortgage company may issue possession proceedings, although the protocol advises that this should only be done as 'a last resort'. Where the borrower is proposing to sell his or her home, the company should consider postponing the issue of proceedings. It should also discuss the possibility of extending the term of the mortgage or changing the type of mortgage, ie in a way that reduces the burden and/or the arrears.

2.13 **Possession proceedings.** If all negotiations fail, the next step is for the mortgage company to issue possession proceedings in the county court. In theory, a mortgage company can obtain possession without a court order (*Ropaigealach v Barclays Bank plc*, 1998, in which the house was empty when the bank took possession because it was being refurbished). In practice, however, lenders almost invariably take court proceedings. The court is not obliged to grant the possession order immediately. It has power to grant an order suspended on condition that the occupier continues to pay current instalments under the mortgage, and a fixed amount off the arrears, or it may stay execution or postpone the date for giving up possession. Once an order has been executed, however, there are no further powers of stay, suspension or postponement, unless there are grounds on which to set aside the warrant for possession, or it is considered to be an abuse of the process of the court, or oppressive to execute it (*Cheltenham & Gloucester BS v Obi*, 1994).

2.14 **Suspended orders.** The court will only exercise the discretion to suspend if it is of the view that the arrears can be cleared in a reasonable time (Administration of Justice Act 1970 s36; *Town & Country Building Society v Julien*, 1991). If it does not think so, then the order will be final, but will usually be suspended for at least 28 days to give the occupier time to start making alternative arrangements. While it has been said that an order may be deferred for a short period, eg three months, in order to enhance the prospects of sale by the occupier (*Target Home Loans Ltd v Clothier*, 1992), this is not a rule of law, and if there is evidence that a sale could take place in a longer period, there is no reason why a court should not allow it (*National & Provincial BS v Lloyd*, 1995).

2.15 **Reasonable time to clear arrears.** There is no formal definition of reasonable time. The courts used normally to consider one year a reasonable time in which to clear the arrears (*Cheltenham & Gloucester BS v Grant*, 1994). The court should now take as its starting point the full period of the mortgage, and determine whether or not it would be possible for the owner-occupier to maintain payment of the arrears by instalments over that period. This approach requires the court to consider: how much the borrower can reasonably afford to pay (currently and in the future); whether a difficulty is temporary and for how long it is likely to last; what the reason is for the arrears; the remaining term; any relevant contractual terms; the type of mortgage; over what period it is reasonable to expect the lender to recoup arrears of interest; and, any other reasons affecting the security which should influence the length of the period (*Cheltenham & Gloucester BS v Norgan*, 1995). A borrower who asks the court for time to pay must provide the court with full and up-to-date information about his or her expenditure and income (*Jameer v Paratus AMC*, 2012).

2.16 **Consumer Credit Act 1974.** Loans of less than £15,000, unless made by local authorities or building societies (and certain other exempt organisations), are regulated by the Consumer Credit Act (CCA) 1974. Where the creditor is seeking repayment or possession, the court may make a 'time order' to reschedule payment of the debt (CCA 1974 s129). The court must consider whether it is just to make the order, and where possession proceedings are involved this relates to the whole outstanding balance under the mortgage (*Southern & District Finance v Barnes*, 1995). The court also has power to alter the rate of interest (CCA 1974 s136).

2.17 **Tenants.** Assured tenants (see paras 1.220–1.251), and protected or statutory tenants (see paras 1.269–1.293) are given additional rights by the Mortgage Repossessions (Protection of Tenants) Act 2010. Where the mortgage company claims possession against the borrower, the tenant may apply to the court for the possession order, or execution of the order, to be postponed for up to two months (in total: there can be more than one application, but no more than two month in all). In deciding whether to exercise this power, the court must have regard to the circumstances of the tenant, including any breaches by him or her of the tenancy agreement. The court may require the tenant to make payments to the mortgage company.

2.18 **Public authorities.** If the mortgage 'company' is a public authority, as is not uncommon if the freehold has been bought as a result of the right to buy (see para 4.46), the freeholder may be able to invoke either the Human Rights Act (HRA) 1998 or the principles of domestic public law to resist an eviction (see paras 2.250–2.257), although it must be said that it is highly unlikely that either will avail the occupier save where the conduct of the authority is particularly outrageous.

Commonhold

2.19 Commonholders own the freeholds of their flats (see para 1.16) and if they own their flats without a mortgage can only lose their homes in limited circumstances (see para 2.3). A commonholder is therefore in a much stronger position than a leasehold owner of a flat. If a leaseholder fails to pay his or her service charges, the landlord may ultimately forfeit (see paras 2.29–2.44) the lease and obtain possession. A commonhold association has no such right. If a commonholder does not pay charges, its only remedy is to sue for the debt in the usual way. The commonholder can only lose his or her home if he or she continues to refuse to pay the debt and the association obtains and enforces a charging order on the flat (see para 1.91).

Termination of common law rights of occupation

2.20 The common law classes of occupation are tenancy and licence: trespass is not a right – to the contrary, it is occupation without right although there are circumstances in which trespassers can remain in occupation either in the short term or for much longer or even, ultimately, by acquiring the property through the law of adverse possession (see paras 1.146–1.154); the eviction of trespassers is accordingly dealt with in its own section of this chapter (see paras 2.243–2.249). The rights of long leaseholders and of fixed-term tenants are different from those of periodic tenants, and those of licensees from tenants.

Leaseholders

2.21 A leasehold interest may be long (more than 21 years – see para 2.72) or not; in principle, the position so far as concerns termination is the same. Save in the case of an excluded tenancy (see paras 1.308–1.309), a landlord must seek a court order before evicting a leaseholder or tenant (or anyone lawfully living with him or her at the end of the tenancy) (see para 2.240); the landlord commits an offence if he or she evicts without an order (see para 5.5).

2.22 **Mortgages.** A long lease (see para 2.72) will commonly have been bought with a mortgage: the position stated in relation to mortgages of freeholds is also applicable to such leases (see paras 2.4–2.18).

2.23 **Expiry of time.** The normal way a lease comes to an end is because the time runs out. There is, at common law, nothing more to be said about it: at the end of the term, the leaseholder ceases to be a tenant, although in practice, statutory protection of one kind or another will almost invariably allow the leaseholder to remain.

2.24 **Surrender.** As well as expiry, another common way of bringing a lease to an end is for the leaseholder or tenant to 'surrender' it. It occurs, commonly, when the landlord agrees to the tenant's wish to leave accommodation before the end of a fixed term and in such circumstances will usually conform to the legal requirement that a formal declaration of surrender be drawn up.

2.25 **Operation of law.** Surrender can also, however, occur by operation of law if the tenant performs some unequivocal act of surrender, such as returning the keys to the landlord, or removing from the premises all signs of occupation, including furniture, belongings and any family or friends – or animals – who were living with him or her (*Chamberlain v Scalley*, 1992).

2.26 In deciding whether there has been such an unequivocal act of surrender, the subjective intentions of the tenant, eg as to whether the tenant intends to give up his or her rights to the tenancy are irrelevant; it is the conduct objectively assessed which is crucial (*Zionmor v Islington LBC*, 1997).

2.27 **Acceptance of act.** It is an essential feature of surrender by operation of law that the landlord accepts the acts as a surrender. The landlord is not obliged to do so and can continue to consider the tenant liable for rent and other responsibilities in the premises. Abandonment of occupation might be considered a surrender (*R v Croydon LBC ex p Toth*, 1987), but only where the landlord unequivocally accepts it as such (*Preston BC v Fairclough*, 1982). The landlord's conduct as a whole must be taken into account (*Brent LBC v Sharma*, 1992). The grant of a new tenancy to someone else will evidence acceptance of a surrender of the previous tenancy (*Tower Hamlets LBC v Ayinde*, 1994). There can even be surrender, by clear agreement, without quitting occupation (*Dibbs v Campbell*, 1988).

2.28 **Joint tenants.** One joint tenant cannot surrender without the consent of the other(s) (*Leek and Moorlands Building Society v Clark*, 1952).

2.29 **Forfeiture.** The other common way of bringing a leasehold or fixed-term tenancy to an end is 'forfeiture'.

2.30 There can be no forfeiture unless it is provided for in the lease or tenancy agreement. Commonly, the lease will allow the landlord to claim that a lease or tenancy has automatically been forfeit when rent has been in arrears for a stated period of time, eg 14 days. It is usually also part of an agreement that forfeiture will occur if some other breach of the tenancy takes place.

2.31 **Re-entry.** When there is a forfeiture, the landlord claims to 're-enter' the premises (although he or she cannot in practice do so because of the rules governing the eviction of residential tenants (see para 2.240) so that forfeiture therefore has to be effected by proceedings for possession). A court has power to order 'relief' from forfeiture, if the breach of the tenancy has been remedied, eg arrears of rent have been paid off.

2.32 **Demands for payment.** Any demand for payment of rent, service charges or administration charges must contain the name and address of the landlord and, if that address is not in England or Wales, an address in England or Wales at which notices can be served; if the demand does not include this information, the payments demanded are not due (Landlord and Tenant Act (LTA) 1987 s47) and the landlord will not be able to forfeit the lease if the tenant does not pay.

2.33 **Ground rent.** Long-leaseholders (see para 2.72), usually have to pay a small rent, commonly referred to as 'ground rent', in addition to the service charges payable under their leases. The tenant does not become liable to pay ground rent unless the landlord has served a notice on him or her containing prescribed information (Landlord and Tenant (Notice of Rent) (England) Regulations 2004 SI No 3096 or Landlord and Tenant (Notice of Rent) (Wales) Regulations 2005 SI No 1355), specifying the amount owed, and stating a date by which it must be paid, which date must be not less than 30 days nor more than 60 days after notice is given and not before the date on which the rent became due under the lease (Commonhold and Leasehold Reform Act (CLRA) 2002 s166).

2.34 **Service and administration charges.** Long leases also sometimes provide that service charges are recoverable as if they were rent; whether or not they do so, they also usually provide that the lease may be forfeit for non-payment of service or administration charges. Forfeiture in such cases is now prohibited unless the amount of the charge has been agreed or admitted by the tenant or has been determined by a court, by the First-tier Tribunal (in England) or by the leasehold valuation tribunal (in Wales) or by arbitration (Housing Act (HA) 1996 s81).

2.35 **Long leaseholders and arrears.** In addition, CLRA 2002 s167 limits forfeiture of long leases for arrears of rent, service or administration charges: if the amount of arrears is less than £350 or has been owed for less than three years, the landlord will not be permitted to exercise the right of re-entry or forfeiture.

2.36 **Breach of other term.** Likewise, landlords of long leaseholders cannot seek forfeiture unless the fact that there has been a breach of the lease has been admitted by the tenant or has been determined by a court, by the First-tier Tribunal or leasehold valuation tribunal or by arbitration (CLRA 2002 s168).

2.37 **Relief from forfeiture.** Any forfeiture of residential premises in which anyone is living must be by way of court proceedings

(Protection from Eviction Act (PEA) 1977 s2). This includes forfeiture of tenancies of premises which are partly commercial and partly residential (*Patel v Pirabakaran*, 2006). It is normally in the course of these proceedings that relief is sought. Relief may be sought by the tenant (LPA 1925 s146(2)), or a subtenant or a mortgage company (LPA 1925 s146(4)).

2.38 Where the forfeiture is for a reason other than arrears of rent, a preliminary notice must be served, identifying the breach, calling for remedy (if the breach is remediable) and demanding compensation (where applicable) (LPA 1925 s146(1)). A breach of a positive covenant, ie a term requiring the tenant to do something, is usually remediable and the notice should set out what action the tenant has to take. A breach of a negative covenant, ie a covenant prohibiting the tenant from doing something, may be remediable even though the tenant cannot undo what he or she has done in the past (*Savva v Houssein*, 1996). For example, a breach of a covenant prohibiting anti-social behaviour may be remedied by the tenant committing no further anti-social acts, although if the behaviour is very serious the landlord may take the view that the breach is incapable of remedy (*Telchadder v Wickland (Holdings) Ltd*, 2014).

2.39 It has been held that arrears of service charges are not rent arrrears even if the lease reserves the service charges as rent: accordingly, the requirement to serve a preliminary notice under LPA 1925 s146 (see para 2.38) applies (*Freeholders of 69 Marina, St Leonards on Sea v Oram*, 2011). This decision conflicts with an earlier decision (*Escalus Properties Ltd v Robinson*, 1996), and it has been doubted whether *69 Marina* correctly states the law).

2.40 The courts are chary of laying down general principles governing relief (*Hyman v Rose*, 1912), although remedying the breach will usually be necessary, and will always be needed if the breach is non-payment of rent (*Barton, Thompson & Co v Stapling Machines Co*, 1966), though time will usually be allowed in which to do so. There will usually be no relief from forfeiture for breach of a covenant not to use premises for an immoral purpose (*British Petroleum Pension Trust Ltd v Behrendt*, 1986). Relief from forfeiture is not available to an assured tenant (*Artesian Residential Developments Ltd v Beck*, 1999; see para 2.159).

2.41 **Waiver.** There will be no right to forfeit if the breach has been waived, eg waiver of illegal sub-letting (*Cornillie v Saha*, 1996; see paras 1.70–1.72). Waiver occurs where the landlord has the right to forfeit but then does something which recognises the continued existence of the tenancy (*Kammins Ballrooms Co v Zenith Investments*

(Torquay) Ltd, 1970). A landlord can expressly agree to waive a breach but it is more usually implied from his or her conduct. The most common act of waiver is a demand for, or acceptance of, rent in knowledge of the breach. *Note.* It is only a demand for, or acceptance of, rent falling due *after* the right to forfeit has arisen which waives the breach; moreover, acceptance of a payment of arrears which fell due *before* the right to forfeit arose does not amount to waiver, even if the payment is accepted after the right to forfeit has arisen (*Re Debtors Nos 13A10 and 14A10 of 1995*, 1995). The point in each case is that the act has to affirm continuation of the tenancy *after* the landlord had the right to to forfeit it.

2.42 **Effect of relief.** Relief may be granted in the High Court, if that is where the forfeiture proceedings are brought, but may also be granted in the county court. The effect of relief is to reinstate the lease as if there had been no forfeiture (*Hynes v Twinsectra Ltd*, 1995; *Rexhaven Ltd v Nurse*, 1995). Relief may be granted in relation to only part of the premises that are subject of the lease (*GMS Syndicate v Elliott (Gary) Ltd*, 1982).

2.43 **Rent arrears and relief.** Where proceedings are brought in the county court, and the breach in question is non-payment of rent (but not service charges even if reserved as rent in the lease – see para 2.39), there is automatic relief if all the arrears and the costs of the action are paid into court at least five days before the hearing; otherwise, the order for possession must provide at least four weeks before it takes effect, and there will again be automatic relief if all the rent and costs are paid into court. These provisions do not apply if the forfeiture is for, or also for, any other breach (County Courts Act (CCA) 1984 ss138–140).

2.44 If not obtained automatically, relief for arrears may still be available from the county court, as a matter of discretion, on an application made within six months of execution, ie even if afterwards (CCA 1984 s138).

2.45 While relief – including for non-payment of rent – may also be sought in the High Court (Senior Courts Act 1981 s38), that procedure cannot be used to secure relief after execution of the possession order, in order to circumvent the six-month limitation in the county court (*Di Palma v Victoria Square Property Co Ltd*, 1985). A subtenant seeking relief likewise cannot circumvent the requirements of section 38 by seeking relief (outside the six-month period) by application to the High Court (*United Dominions Trust v Shellpoint Trustees*, 1993).

2.46 **Relief and disrepair.** There is additional power to apply for relief from a section 146 notice which is concerned with an alleged failure to comply with a covenant requiring internal decorative repairs (LPA 1925 s147). In the case of a lease of at least seven years, with at least three years left to run, the Leasehold Property (Repairs) Act 1938 prevents forfeiture for such a breach without the prior leave of the court (see para 11.103).

Periodic tenancies

2.47 **Eviction.** Save in the case of an excluded tenancy (see paras 1.308–1.309), a landlord must seek a court order before evicting a tenant (or anyone lawfully living with him or her at the end of the tenancy) (see para 2.240); an offence is committed if the landlord evicts without an order (see para 5.5). Moreover, most tenants have some form of statutory protection, which is considered below (see paras 2.72–2.233).

2.48 **Surrender.** Surrender (see paras 2.24–2.28) may also occur in the case of a periodic tenancy, when a periodic tenant wishes to quit without going through the formality of serving notice to quit. The principles considered above (several of which derive from surrender of a period tenancy) apply.

2.49 **Notice to quit.** Notice to quit is the normal means by which a periodic tenancy is brought to an end by a tenant; it is also the normal means for a landlord to bring it to an end, save so far as a landlord is prevented from using it by statute (see paras 2.84, 2.149 and 2.158). Notice to quit is a formal and technical document, to which old common law rules apply, as well as modern regulations introduced by legislation.

2.50 **Invalid notice.** It is not uncommon for, in particular, tenants to give an invalid notice to quit. An invalid notice to quit may nonetheless be treated as valid by the party who receives it, at least in so far as the technicalities of the common law are concerned; alternatively, a landlord who receives an invalid notice from the tenant may treat it as a surrender. If the tenant subsequently changes his or her mind about departing, whether after notice to quit or surrender, the landlord will still have to take court proceedings to evict the tenant and in some cases might not be able to do so (see para 2.218(4)). An invalid notice to quit served by one of a number of joint tenants (see paras 1.48–1.58) cannot be treated as valid by the landlord (*Hounslow LBC v Pilling*, 1993).

2.51 **Requirements of notice to quit.** All notices to quit residential tenancies, other than 'excluded tenancies' which began on or after the commencement of HA 1988 Part 1 (15 January 1989) (see paras 1.308–1.309), must be in writing, must be of a minimum length of four weeks (PEA 1977 s5; *Hounslow LBC v Pilling*, 1993), and the notice must expire on either the last day or the first day of a period of the tenancy. The four weeks include day of service or day of expiry (*Schnabel v Allard*, 1966). The rent day is normally the first day of the tenancy, in the absence of evidence that it is some other day. The notice must also be at least as long as a full period of the tenancy (so that a monthly tenancy requires a full calendar month's notice. Exceptionally, a periodic annual tenancy only requires six months' notice).

2.52 **Saving clauses.** A notice to quit which is of insufficient length will not become valid at a later, correct time, but will be wholly invalid. Because of this need for accuracy, many notices to quit, especially those from landlords to tenants, add a saving clause, which will read something like this: '. . . on the 9th day of December 2016 or at the end of the period of your tenancy expiring next four weeks after service of this notice upon you'.

2.53 Such a saving clause is valid and if 9 December 2016 was neither the first nor the last day of a period of the tenancy, the notice to quit would take effect on the next of those two possible days, four weeks after service: see, eg *Bradford Community Housing Ltd v Hussain*, 2009.

2.54 **Service of notice to quit.** Service of a notice to quit has to be personal. Most service is effected by post, although some service is carried out by leaving it at the premises. It is not validly served until the tenant him- or herself receives it, or it is left with a tenant's spouse or some other person who may be treated as the tenant's agent for this purpose, eg someone left by the tenant in possession or control of the premises (*Harrowby v Snelson*, 1951).

2.55 If the tenancy itself expressly requires service of a notice to quit in order to determine it, however, it will be sufficient if the notice is left at the last known place of abode of the tenant (LPA 1925 s196; *Wandsworth LBC v Atwell*, 1995; *Enfield LBC v Devonish*, 1996). The Local Government Act (LGA) 1972 s233, which permits postal service of notices required or authorised to be given 'by or under any enactment', does not, however, apply to common law notices to quit (*Enfield*).

2.56 **Contents of notice to quit.** A notice to quit must identify the premises which are the subject of the tenancy, so that a notice given for the wrong address will be invalid. Minor defects in description, such as specifying a back garden that does not exist, are unlikely to invalidate the notice; and if a notice to quit identifies the wrong address, it may be validated by a covering letter sent to the right one. On the other hand, a notice to quit two rooms was held invalid where the tenant was tenant of only one (*Jankovitch v Petrovitch*, 1977).

2.57 The notice must be addressed to the tenant, although if only the first name is wrong this will not be enough to invalidate it. It may be enough to specify only one of two or more joint tenants (see para 1.45) and it is certainly enough to serve one only of the joint tenants. The notice must state that it is given by or on behalf of the landlord, unless it is given by an agent acting in the normal course of his or her business on the landlord's behalf when serving the notice.

2.58 **Prescribed information.** In addition, a notice to quit from a landlord to a tenant must contain specified information, also in writing. Without this information the notice is invalid. The information is as follows (Notices to Quit, etc. (Prescribed Information) Regulations 1988 SI No 2201) although it does not have to be in the same form of words (*Beckerman v Durling*, 1981; *Swansea CC v Hearn*, 1990).

a) If the tenant or licensee does not leave the dwelling, the landlord or licensor must get an order for possession from the court before the tenant or licensee can lawfully be evicted. The landlord or licensor cannot apply for such an order before the notice to quit or notice to determine has run out.
b) A tenant or licensee who does not know if he or she has any right to remain in possession after a notice to quit or a notice to determine runs out can obtain advice from a solicitor. Help with all or part of the cost of legal advice and assistance may be available under the Legal Aid Scheme. He or she should also be able to obtain information from a Citizens' Advice Bureau, a Housing Aid Centre or a rent officer.

2.59 **Subtenants.** If the mesne and subtenancies (see para 1.59) are not both Rent Act protected (see paras 1.268–1.293), or if the subtenancy is not Housing Act assured (see paras 1.220–1.251), or if the subtenancy is illegal (see paras 1.64–1.73), so that neither Rent Act (RA) 1977 s137 nor HA 1988 s18 applies (see para 1.62), and if there is no surrender by the tenant (see paras 2.24–2.28), the subtenancy automatically determines, without notice or forfeiture, on the determination of the mesne tenancy (*Moore Properties (Ilford) v McKeon*, 1976). A subtenant, even one who is an illegal subtenant, can, however, apply for relief from forfeiture (see para 2.37).

2.60 **Joint tenants.** If a joint tenancy is periodic, one joint tenant can serve notice to quit and bring the contractual tenancy to an end

(*Greenwich LBC v McGrady*, 1983; *Hammersmith & Fulham LBC v Monk*, 1991). Service of the notice by one joint tenant does not infringe the other tenant's right to quiet enjoyment of possessions (Article 1 of the First Protocol to the European Convention on Human Rights (ECHR)) or his or her right to respect for his or her home (Article 8 ECHR) (*Sims v Dacorum BC*, 2014). The notice to quit must, however, be valid if it is to have this effect, and cannot simply be 'treated as valid' by the landlord (see para 2.50). Nor can a joint leaseholder or fixed-term tenant surrender without the consent of the other or all the others (see para 2.28).

2.61 This technique is commonly used where a local authority wants to re-house one of the joint tenants, together with the children, without leaving the other – usually the man – in accommodation now much larger than he or she needs (*Crawley BC v Ure*, 1995). The right to serve a notice to quit is not affected by matrimonial homes and occupation rights under the Family Law Act 1996 (*Harrow LBC v Johnstone*, 1997 – see para 7.12). See also para 7.6 on preventing service of a notice to quit in matrimonial cases.

Licensees

2.62 **Eviction.** Licensees may be termed 'bare licensees', or may be termed 'contractual licensees' (see para 1.127). One who is, by arrangement, paying a fixed sum of money for the right of occupation will be a contractual licensee. A friend, member of the family or cohabitant, even although he or she may be paying some amount by way of contribution to household expenses, will normally be considered a bare licensee. Save in the case of an 'excluded licensee' (see paras 1.310–1.313), which will include most family or friendly arrangements, and those whose licences were granted as a temporary measure to a homeless person (see para 1.313), it is necessary to obtain a court order before evicting the former licensee (see para 2.241) and a person who fails to do so will commit an offence: see chapter 5. Some licensees whose licences began before the commencement of HA 1988 Part 1 (15 January 1989) are entitled to refer their contracts to the Rent Tribunal, and in the case of some now long-standing licences the tribunal has power to allow more time to leave premises occupied under licence (see para 2.230).

2.63 So long as the licence remains in existence, the licensee cannot be turned off the premises. Once the licence comes to an end the person who is immediately entitled to possession of the premises in question, who may be the owner of the premises, a landlord or may only be a tenant of the premises, can reclaim possession from the former licensee, save in the case of a licence which attracts security of tenure under HA 1985 (see para 1.168), but unless the licence has been duly brought to an end, the person who seeks possession is not entitled to reclaim it the property.

2.64 **Fixed-term licences.** No notice be given to bring a fixed-term licence to an end because, in effect, the notice has been given at the outset of the arrangement: it expires according to its terms.

2.65 **Non-fixed term licences.** Many licences are not for a fixed period but exist from week to week, even from day to day, but possibly as much as from month to month. In such cases, it is necessary to give notice in order to bring the arrangement to an end. It may be that some agreement about the length or form of notice has been reached while arranging the licence in the first place, eg one month's notice in writing. This is not a necessary element of a licence. If there is such an agreement, it would indicate that the licence was a contractual, not a bare licence. Where there is such an agreement in force, then the licence cannot be determined except in accordance with it: the law will not support a breach of contract (*Winter Garden Theatre (London) v Millennium Productions*, 1947).

2.66 **Reasonable notice.** Whether or not there is such agreement, however, the law additionally implies into every licence, whether bare or contractual, a term that it will not be brought to an end without 'reasonable notice' being given. This means that a licence agreement which contractually provided for, eg one day's notice, would not be brought to an end in one day, unless the law considered one day a reasonable time (*Minister of Health v Bellotti*, 1944).

2.67 **Written notice.** In the case of a periodic licence of a dwelling, other than an 'excluded licence' (see paras 1.310–1.313) or the homelessness exception (see para 1.313), the law now requires written notice of a minimum period of four weeks, which contains specified information. The information is the same as for a notice to quit a tenancy (see para 2.58).

2.68 **Reasonable time.** What is a reasonable time is a question of fact. It will depend on the circumstances, eg how long the licensee has been in occupation, how much furniture or property he or she has in the premises, size of family, what alternative arrangements have been or could be made, even the time of day or night could affect it. In one case, where a man had been living as the owner-occupier's lodger for about five years, the Court of Appeal suggested that a reasonable notice period was a number of weeks (*Gibson v Douglas*, 2016). In addition, behaviour may affect what the law views as a reasonable time for determination of a licence. A violent licensee will not be given much time at all, eg a violent man who is cohabiting with the woman who is the tenant or owner-occupier cannot expect a matter of weeks in which to leave, even if he or she has lived in the property for years.

2.69 **Alternative requirements.** The rule may be shortly stated in this way: a licensee is entitled to a reasonable period of notice or a contractually agreed period of notice, or in the case of a periodic licence which is not an 'excluded licence' (see paras 1.310–1.313) four weeks' notice, whichever is the longest. In most cases (other than excluded licences), court proceedings for eviction are required (see para 1.241).

2.70 **Tied accommodation and termination.** A service licence which is expressly terminable on the cessation of employment comes to an end without any requirement of notice (*Ivory v Palmer*, 1975). Notice in accordance with PEA 1977 (see para 2.67) is not, therefore, required (*Norris v Checksfield*, 1991).

2.71 **Alternative procedures.** Proceedings in the civil courts are governed by the Civil Procedure Rules. CPR 55 sets out the procedure for possession proceedings. A claim against a former licensee may be brought by ordinary possession action, or by a special, speedy form of procedure originally intended for trespassers, but also applicable to former licensees: CPR r55.1(a). If these speedy proceedings are used, then the person seeking to evict the former licensee must establish that the licence had come to an end before the application was issued at the court (*GLC v Jenkins*, 1975). The inference of the argument in that case is that where normal possession proceedings are used, the landlord need only show determination of the licence by the date of the hearing, but this would not seem to be correct as *Minister of Health v Bellotti* (see para 2.66) refers to the need for sufficient time for the licensees to remove themselves and their possessions and find alternative accommodation before proceedings were instituted, so that there is no difference. The proceedings can be used against an illegal subtenants (*Moore Properties (Ilford) Ltd v McKeon*, 1976; paras 1.64–1.72), although not against an illegal tenant of a borrower (*London Goldhawk Building Society v Eminer*, 1977; para 1.103). Nor should these proceedings be used where there is a triable issue (*Cooper v Varzdari*, 1986), eg that the licence is a sham arrangement concealing a tenancy (*Crancour Ltd v Da Silvaesa*, 1986 – see paras 1.33–1.41) or that the occupier is a tenant holding over (*Henderson v Law*, 1984 – para 1.40).

Statutory security

Long leaseholder security

2.72 'Long leases' are those for more than 21 years: LTA 1954 s2(4); Leasehold Reform Act (LRA) 1967 s3(1); LTA 1987 s59(3); Local Government and Housing Act (LGHA) 1989 Sch 10 para 2(3); CLRA 2002 s76(2) (although – except under LTA 1954 or LGHA 1989 – the expression can include a lease under the 'right to buy' provisions of HA 1985, even if it is for less than 21 years. This can only arise in extremely rare circumstances, eg where the authority is itself a lessee and there is less than 21 years to run on its own lease). Although the lease must (normally) be for more than 21 years, the leaseholder need not have been in occupation for that period; it means that the right *under which he or she occupies* is or was for that period, ie someone who take an assignment of a long lease is still a long leaseholder even if there remain less than 21 years of the lease to run (see para 1.78). Time runs from when the lease was originally granted (*Roberts v Church Commissioners for England*, 1971), and not from any earlier date to which it may have been backdated.

2.73 **LTA 1954; LGHA 1989 Sch 10.** So long as the occupier is using the premises, or part of them, as his or her home at the end of the lease, the lease will not come to an end, and the occupier can remain in occupation indefinitely because it is automatically continued by statute (either under LTA 1954 or LGHA 1989). This is not so, however, if the landlord under the lease is one of the public landlords whose tenants cannot be Housing Act assured (see paras 1.221–1.222) or Rent Act protected (see para 1.270). At the end of a long lease from a local authority, therefore, eg under the right to buy (see paras 4.46–4.73), the occupier will only have rights in relation to eviction, including such rights (if any) as can be procured under HRA 1998 (see paras 2.250–2.255).

2.74 **Pre-1 April 1990 leases.** If the lease began before 1 April 1990, but terminated before 15 January 1999, the protection available will be that of a statutory tenant (see paras 1.269–1.293; paras 2.216–2.222) under RA 1977, provided that all other qualifying conditions for a statutory tenancy (see paras 1.277–1.282) are fulfilled with the exception of the fact that the tenancy is at a low rent, which is to be disregarded (LTA 1954 s2(1), (5)). There is, however, an additional ground for possession, if the landlord can prove that he or she proposes to demolish or reconstruct the whole or a substantial part of the premises in question (LTA 1954 s12).

2.75 **Use as a home.** The most essential element of protection under LTA 1954 is that at the end of the lease, the premises are being used by the tenant as his or her home, to the same extent as is necessary to sustain a Rent Act statutory tenancy (see paras 1.290–1.293). Protection may, however, extend to only part of the premises (LTA 1954 s3(2)), eg if the tenant occupies only one part, and does not intend to resume possession of the remainder, perhaps a part which he or she has sublet (*Regalian Securities v Ramsden*, 1981).

2.76 **Procedure.** During the last year of a long lease, the landlord can take action in the county court to try to secure a pre-determination of whether or not the tenant is going to enjoy protection (LTA 1954 s2(2)). If he or she does not follow this procedure, then the tenancy automatically continues, at the old – and usually low – rent, until brought to end by notice from the landlord (LTA 1954 s3), indicating either that he or she intends to seek possession on one of the available grounds (see para 2.74; paras 2.218–2.219), or proposing a statutory tenancy to commence at a specified date (LTA 1954 s4), identifying the proposed terms of the statutory tenancy, which will include the proposed rent, and dealing with the question of 'initial repairs' (LTA 1954 s7; see paras 11.66–11.69).

2.77 Once the statutory tenancy has come into existence, it may later end in exactly the same way as one which arises under RA 1977 (see paras 1.260–1.284; 2.191–2.199).

2.78 **Termination post-15 January 1999.** For tenancies which were not brought to an end by the landlord under the LTA 1954 before 15 January 1999, ie which are not terminated until after 15 January 1999, the tenancy will not become statutory, but will fall to be dealt with in the same way as those leases which commenced on or after 1 April 1990 (LGHA 1989 Sch 10 para 3(2)).

2.79 **Post-1 April 1990 leases.** The protection available to these leaseholders (as well as to those which commenced earlier but terminated on or after 15 January 1999) is (by LGHA 1989) that of an assured tenancy under HA 1988.

2.80 **Procedure.** LGHA 1989 continues the existing tenancy until the landlord serves a notice either proposing an assured monthly periodic tenancy or giving notice of seeking possession (LGHA 1989 Sch 10 para 4(5)). A notice proposing a new tenancy must propose a new rent which must be sufficient to ensure that it is no longer at a 'low rent', and must either state that it is to be on the same terms as the long tenancy or propose new terms (LGHA 1989 Sch 10 para 4(5), (6)). The new rent may be above the maximum level for an assured tenancy (£100,000 per annum – para 1.233(2)), which – if upheld by the First-tier Tribunal (in England) or the rent assessment committee (in Wales) (see para 2.79) – will accordingly take the tenant outside protection (*R (Morris) v London RAC*, 2002).

2.81 **Terms.** If the tenant wishes to dispute the proposed rent and terms of the new tenancy he or she must serve a notice on the landlord within two months, making his or her own proposals. If no agreement can be reached, the matter may be referred by either party to the First-tier Tribunal (in England) or the rent assessment committee (in Wales), which have similar powers as under HA 1988 (see para 3.33; LGHA 1989 Sch 10 paras 11, 12). In setting the rent, the tribunal or committee must disregard any improvements carried out by the tenant during the long lease but such improvements *will* be taken into account in any *subsequent* rent increase during the assured tenancy (see para 3.35; *Hughes v Borodex Ltd*, 2010). An interim monthly rent may be proposed by the landlord, which the tenant may also appeal to the tribunal or committee (LGHA 1989 Sch 10 para 6).

2.82 **Possession.** Where a notice of seeking possession is served, it must state the ground or grounds. The landlord may rely on some of the HA 1988 grounds, ie Ground 6 (see para 2.158(6)) and the discretionary Grounds 9 to 15 (see para 2.157) – LGHA 1989 Sch 10 para 5(1). In addition, provided his or her interest was not purchased after 18 February 1966, the landlord may also be able to obtain possession if he or she can prove that the premises are needed for occupation by the landlord, any child over 18 or his or her parents or parents-in-law and that it is reasonable to make the order – LGHA 1989 Sch 10 para 5. In such a case, the landlord must also satisfy a 'greater hardship' test, ie that – having regard to all the circumstances of the case, including the availability of other accommodation to either landlord or tenant – greater hardship would be caused by granting than by refusing the order (LGHA 1989 Sch 10 para 5).

2.83 **Option to stay or go.** The notice proposing a new tenancy or seeking possession must give the tenant the option either to elect to remain or to indicate willingness to give up possession. Any application for possession must be made within two months of the tenant's election, or, if there is no reply, within four months of the landlord's notice (LGHA 1989 Sch 10 para 13). The tenant may, at any time and regardless of whether he or she has elected to remain, give one month's notice to terminate the tenancy (LGHA 1989 Sch 10 para 13(4)).

Secure tenants

Contractual security

Contractual security – periodic tenancy

2.84 If a secure tenancy is a periodic tenancy (see para 1.18), the landlord cannot bring it to an end at all: only the court can do so (HA 1985 s82(1)), only on specified grounds and only after the landlord has followed the appropriate preliminary procedure, which commences with a notice of seeking possession (NSP). If a tenant has ceased to sustain sufficient occupation to be secure (see paras 1.172–1.175), it will have ceased to be a secure tenancy and the NSP procedure will be inapplicable, so that notice to quit in the ordinary way has to be served (see paras 2.49–2.58).

Contractual security – fixed-term tenancy

2.85 If the tenancy is a fixed-term tenancy (see para 1.18), it can only be forfeited by court order and, even if it expires by effluxion of time, there will come into its place an automatic periodic tenancy, on the same terms as the preceding fixed-term tenancy; the periods are the same as those for which rent was paid under the preceding fixed-term tenancy (HA 1985 s86).

2.86 The only exceptions to this latter proposition are if the landlord and the tenant agree a new fixed-term tenancy to follow the first fixed-term tenancy, or if the court orders possession to be given up at the end of the fixed term in forfeiture proceedings (see paras 1.29–1.44), or if the court makes a demotion order, in which case a periodic demoted tenancy or demoted assured shorthold tenancy (depending on the identity of the landlord) replaces the fixed-term tenancy (see para 1.252). On proceedings to forfeit a fixed-term secure tenancy, the court has a choice of orders: it may determine the fixed term, but not order the tenant out, in which case the periodic, secure tenancy will follow (HA 1985 s86(1)); or, it may grant a possession order, in which case it will not.

Continuation until possession

2.87 In the case of a periodic tenancy, whether originally periodic or following a fixed term, the tenancy itself continues until the possession order is executed (HA 1985 s82(2)) or a court makes a demotion order (see para 1.256). An NSP must also be served before possession can be sought of a fixed-term tenancy. The NSP has effect with respect to any periodic tenancy arising on the termination of the fixed term by virtue of HA 1985 s86 (see para 2.85) (HA 1985 s83(6)).

Notice of seeking possession

Notice of seeking possession (NSP)

2.88 The court can only make an order for possession on specified grounds, and only if either the landlord has followed the proper procedure, or the court considers it just and equitable to dispense with the requirement for a notice (HA 1985 s83). The only exception to this is the absolute ground for possession based on anti-social behaviour, for which there is a different procedure (see paras 2.110).

Just and equitable

2.89 Whether or not it is just and equitable to dispense with the NSP depends on all of the facts and circumstances both those in which there was an omission to serve the notice and otherwise affecting both landlord and tenant (*Bradshaw v Balwin-Wiseman*, 1985; *Kelsey Housing Association v King*, 1995).

Effectiveness of NSP

2.90 The NSP must normally specify a date after which legal proceedings may be issued (HA 1985 s83(4)(a)). The NSP then remains in force for one year following that date (HA 1985 s83(4)(b)). The specified date must not be earlier than the date when the tenancy could have been brought to an end by notice to quit (see para 2.49) (HA 1985 s83(5)).

Contents of notice

2.91 The NSP must be in the form prescribed by the secretary of state, or substantially to the same effect (Secure Tenancies (Notices) Regulations 1987 SI No 755), and it must specify the grounds on which the court will be asked to terminate the tenancy and make a possession order (HA 1985 s83(2) – paras 2.96–2.117). The particulars must be sufficient to enable the tenant to know what he or she has to do in order to put matters right, eg they must specify an amount of arrears (*Torridge DC v Jones*, 1985; *Mountain v Hastings*, 1993, *cf Marath v MacGillivray*, 1996). In cases where Ground 2A (domestic violence: para 2.98(4)) is being relied on, the incidents of violence should be particularised: *Camden LBC v Mallett*, 2001. An error in the particulars does not, however, invalidate the notice, provided it sets out what the landlord intends in good faith to prove (*Dudley MBC v Bailey*, 1990).

The court has power (HA 1985 s84(3)) to allow additional grounds to be specified, or for the grounds to be altered, which includes power to alter or add to the particulars (*Camden LBC v Oppong*, 1996).

Nuisance and annoyance

2.92 When reliance is placed – in whole or part – on Ground 2, Nuisance and Annoyance (see para 2.98(2)), the notice must state that proceedings for possession may be commenced immediately, and must specify a date by which the landlord wants the tenant to give up possession (HA 1985 s83(3)). Again, however, that date must not be earlier than when the tenancy could have been brought to an end by notice to quit (HA 1985 s83(5)). The difference allows the landlord to start proceedings under Ground 2 earlier than in other cases. These specific provisions in relation to Ground 2 do not apply to notices served on fixed-term tenants (HA 1985 s83(6)).

2.93 The court cannot entertain proceedings for possession in a case to which Ground 2 is relevant unless the NSP is still in force at the time the proceedings are begun (HA 1985 s83A(1)), which means one year after the date specified (see para 2.90) as that by which the landlord wants the tenant to give up possession (HA 1985 s83(3)).

Other cases

2.94 In any other case, the court cannot entertain proceedings for possession unless the proceedings are commenced after the specified date (HA 1985 s83A(2)), and the NSP is still in force at the time the proceedings are begun, which is for one year from that date (HA 1985 s83(4)).

Domestic violence

2.95 Ground 2A allows recovery of property where there has been domestic violence leading to the departure of one of a couple (married, civil partners, or who have been living together as husband and wife or civil partners), one of whom is, or both of whom are, a tenant of it (see para 2.98(4)). If this ground is to be used, the court is not to entertain proceedings for possession unless satisfied that the landlord has served – or has taken all reasonable steps to serve – a copy of the NSP on the partner who has left (HA 1985 s83A(3), (4)). If the case is one in which Ground 2 (above) is also specified, however, the court may dispense with this additional service requirement, if just and equitable (see para 2.89) to do so (HA 1985 s83A(5)).

Grounds for possession

2.96 The most significant element in security law is the grounds for possession. These fall into four classes (HA 1985 ss84(2) and 84A): where the landlord must prove both a specified ground for possession and that it is reasonable to make the order; where only the ground has to be proved; where not only must the ground be proved by the landlord, but the landlord must also prove that suitable alternative accommodation will be available for the tenant; and, where not only must the ground by proved by the landlord, but the landlord must also prove both that it is reasonable to make the order and that suitable alternative accommodation will be available for the tenant. Where reasonableness is required, the ground is known as a 'discretionary' ground; where it is not, it is 'mandatory'.

2.97 The grounds for possession are set out in HA 1985 Sch 2 and HA 1985 s84A. These provide an exhaustive code of the grounds on which a landlord may bring a secure tenancy to an end (*Islington LBC v Uckac*, 2006).

Ground plus reasonableness

2.98 When reasonableness has to be shown, the court has a wide discretion what sort of order to make, as between outright and postponed (see paras 2.120–2.127). The grounds are as follows.

1) **Rent unpaid or breach of term of tenancy**. Ground 1 is available where rent due from the tenant has not been paid, or an obligation of the tenancy has been broken or not performed. There will be no arrears if the tenant has exercised the right to set-off an amount against the landlord's breach of his or her repairing obligations (see paras 11.84–11.86), although if the tenant does so wrongly there will be a ground for possession (whether or not it is then likely that it will be reasonable to make the order tending to depend on whether or not the tenant has the money to pay the arrears: para 2.101).

   It will usually be unreasonable to make the order if the tenant has paid off the arrears by the date of hearing (*Hayman v Rowlands*, 1957), although in some circumstances, eg a long history of non-payment, it may still be possible (*Bird v Hildage*, 1948).

   The second part of the ground is available where there has been a breach of any other term of the tenancy. Only breach of a term of the tenancy gives rise to the claim, not breach of some additional, ancillary agreement, eg a personal undertaking (*RMR Housing Society v Combs*, 1950). Failure to pay charges due under the tenancy which are not rent falls with this part of the ground (eg water charges, *Rochdale BC v Dixon*, 2011; *Lambeth LBC v Thomas*, 1997). In *Heglibiston Establishments v Heyman*, 1977, it was held that cohabitation did not amount to a breach of a covenant prohibiting immoral user. In *Sheffield City Council v Jepson*, 1993, and *Green v Sheffield City Council*, 1993, orders were made or upheld for breaches of terms prohibiting the keeping of pets in blocks of flats. There will be no breach of a term of the tenancy if there has been a waiver of the breach (see paras 1.70–1.72).

2) **Nuisance and annoyance**. Ground 2 is available where the tenant or any person residing in or visiting the dwelling-house has been guilty of conduct causing or likely to cause a nuisance or annoyance to others residing, visiting or otherwise engaging in a lawful activity in the locality. Nuisance here does not necessarily mean nuisance in a technical legal sense (see paras 11.134; 5.50(3)), but in a natural sense; in any event, annoyance is a term with a wider meaning, although it must be conduct that would annoy an ordinary occupier (rather than one who is especially sensitive) (*Tod-Heatly v Benham*, 1888; *Harlow DC v Sewell*, 2000).

   Where the allegation is one of nuisance by members of the family or visitors, there does not need to be any personal fault on the part of the tenant (*West Kent HA v Davies*, 1998; *Bryant v Portsmouth CC*, 2000), although the extent of personal fault will be relevant to the question of 'reasonableness' (see para 2.105).

   What is meant by 'locality' is a question of fact in every case. It may be part of, or the whole of an estate (*Manchester City Council v Lawler*, 1998), or a wider area.

   The Anti-social Behaviour, Crime and Policing Act (ABCPA) 2014 extended Ground 2 so that it is now also available where the tenant or any person residing in or visiting the dwelling-house has been guilty of conduct causing or likely to cause a nuisance or annoyance to the landlord or a person employed in connection with the landlord's housing management functions and the conduct is directly or indirectly related to or affects those functions. It is not necessary for the conduct to take place in the locality of the tenant's home so the ground would apply where, eg a tenant was abusive to staff at a housing office.

   Ground 2 also applies where the tenant or any person residing in or visiting the dwelling-house has been convicted either of using the dwelling-house or allowing it to be used for immoral or illegal purposes, or of an indictable offence in, or in the locality (see penultimate para) of the dwelling.

Immoral use will normally lead to an order for possession, though not invariably (*Yates v Morris*, 1950). 'Allowing' includes both positively giving permission and failing to take preventative steps (*Kensington and Chelsea RLBC v Simmonds*, 1996). 'Indictable offence' means an offence which, if committed by an adult, is triable in the Crown Court on indictment, even if it may also be prosecuted in the magistrates' court (Interpretation Act 1978 Sch 1). The landlord may even rely on an offence committed before the tenancy was granted: *Raglan Housing Association Ltd v Fairclough*, 2007.

Illegal use only applies when the use of the premises has something to do with the conviction, even if the offence was not one which as a matter of law necessarily involved the use of the premises. Nonetheless, the use of the premises must have been part of the facts leading to the conviction, rather than only incidentally the site of the commission of the offence (*S Schneiders & Sons Ltd v Abrahams*, 1924). A conviction for possession of cannabis at the premises will be unlikely to lead to an order, especially as it would mean the imposition of a double penalty (*Abrahams v Wilson*, 1971).

Landlords of secure tenants have other powers to combat anti-social behaviour which may be used as an alternative – or in addition – to possession proceedings, eg demotion order (see paras 1.252–1.261), family intervention tenancy (see paras 1.262–1.266), or anti-social behaviour injunctions (ASBIs) (see paras 6.3–6.27). Landlords often use their powers to apply for ASBIs as an alternative to seeking possession immediately, to see if the order results in an improvement in behaviour so that eviction becomes unnecessary. Failure to use one of these alternative remedies before seeking possession does not, however, mean that it is not reasonable to make a possession order (see para 2.105).

Such orders can also be used in conjunction with eviction proceedings. Thus, when the NSP is served or proceedings are issued, an ASBI can be used to protect witnesses who will be giving evidence against the tenant pending trial of the possession claim. If the tenant is evicted, an ASBI can be used to ensure that the tenant does not return to the area to harass the neighbours who gave evidence against him or her (*Swindon BC v Redpath*, 2009).

Under the Equality Act (EqA) 2010, when evicting a tenant a landlord must not discriminate on the ground of disability (EqA 2010 s35), which can include mental illness: where the tenant's behaviour is attributable to a mental illness, it may not be reasonable to make an order (see paras 2.99–2.105), depending on the severity of the behaviour and the prospects of the tenant responding to treatment (*Croydon LBC v Moody*, 1999).

If the landlord knows of the tenant's disability, evicting him or her because of anti-social behaviour which is a consequence of his or her mental illness is potentially discriminatory, although the landlord will usually be able to justify bringing possession proceedings on the ground that they were necessary to protect the tenant's neighbours (EqA 2010 s15). The court should consider what other steps could have been taken by the landlord to address the tenant's behaviour, such as obtaining support from social services (*Stephenson v Birmingham City Council*, 2016).

3) **Anti-social behaviour.** Ground 2ZA was added by the ABCPA 2014 in response to the riots which took place in the Summer of 2011. It applies where the tenant or an adult residing in the tenant's home has been convicted of an indictable offence (see Ground 2) committed at the scene of a riot (as defined in Public Order Act 1986 s1(1)) which took place anywhere in the UK. The ground only applies in England.
4) **Domestic violence.** Ground 2A applies where a property was occupied – whether on their own, or together with others – by a married couple, civil partners, or a couple living together as husband and wife or as civil partners, one of whom is a tenant, or both of whom are tenants, of it, one of whom has left because of violence or threats of violence towards (usually) her or a member of her family who was residing with her immediately before she left the other, and the court is satisfied that the partner who has left, ie the victim of the violence, is unlikely to return. (See also the added requirements for notice: above, para 2.95). Note, however, that the violence which causes the partner to leave does not have to take place while the couple were living together (*Metropolitan Housing Trust v Hadjazi*, 2010).
5) **Deterioration of premises or furniture.** There are grounds for possession where the premises or common parts, or any furniture provided by the landlord in the premises or common parts, have deteriorated owing to the acts, neglect or default of the tenant, or of someone living with him or her (Grounds 3 and 4). No order will be made on either of these grounds if the default was that of a subtenant or lodger and before the hearing the tenant has taken such steps as are available in order to evict him or her.

6) **Deception**. There is a ground for possession where the tenant is the person, or one of the persons, to whom the tenancy was granted, and the landlord was induced to grant the tenancy by a false statement knowingly or recklessly made by the tenant or by a person acting at the tenant's instigation, ie obtaining a tenancy by deception (Ground 5).

   Although the false statement must induce the grant of the tenancy, this will be assumed where the statement was 'material', ie where it was likely to affect the landlord's decision to grant a tenancy (*Windsor & District Housing Association v Hewitt*, 2011). As such an allegation is of a quasi-criminal nature (and if the tenancy was granted under Part 6, an actually criminal nature, *cf* para 10.219), it will accordingly require a high standard of proof. Once proved, the judge may, in deciding whether it is reasonable to grant possession (see paras 2.99–2.105), take into account the need to discourage dishonest applications generally (*Rushcliffe BC v Watson*, 1991 and see also *Shrewsbury & Atcham BC v Evans*, 1997; *Lewisham LBC v Akinsola*, 1999).

   If the tenancy was granted to two persons, eg cohabitants, spouses, one of whom has departed, the ground is only available against the remaining tenant if he or she was guilty of the false statement or had instigated the deception by the departed tenant. Once the tenancy has been assigned (see paras 1.78–1.83), this ground is no longer available (*Islington LBC v Uckac*, 2006).

7) **Premium on exchange**. Ground 6 relates to the 'right to exchange' (see paras 4.135–4.143). It arises if the tenancy arose by exchange, to which either the tenant, or a member of his or her family (see paras 1.200–1.202) from whom he or she has taken over the tenancy, was a party and a 'premium' was paid in connection with the exchange (whether to, or by the tenant or member of his or her family). In the case of a member of the family, he or she must still be living in the property with the tenant. Premium means money or other pecuniary consideration, eg goods.

8) **Conflict with other purposes**. Ground 7 governs employment-related accommodation (not excluded from security, *cf* para 1.180(4)), and is available where the premises are part of, or in the grounds of, a building held by the landlord for non-housing purposes, the letting was in consequence of employment, and the tenant or someone residing in the property has been guilty of conduct, such that, having regard to the purposes for which the main building is held, it would not be right for the tenant to remain in occupation.

9) **Accommodation pending works**. Ground 8 arises where the secure tenant of one set of premises is asked to move to another while works are carried out. It is only available if the terms of the move included an undertaking that the tenant would move back once works were completed, and the works are now completed and the original property ready for reoccupation. The requirement of reasonableness (see paras 2.99–2.105) allows the tenant to argue, eg that the works have not been done as agreed, or that they have taken so long that he or she has now set down new roots in the alternative property and ought not to have to move back again.

Reasonableness

2.99 Where the ground is discretion so that it must also be reasonable to make the order sought, it is an additional requirement which the court must consider in every case (*Peachey Property Corp v Robinson*, 1966). Whether or not it is reasonable to make an order has to be determined having regard both to the interests of the parties and to the interests of the public (*Cresswell v Hodgson*, 1951; *Battlespring v Gates*, 1983). There is no general restriction, save relevance, as to what the court can take into account under this heading (*Cresswell*), which is to be considered as at the date of the hearing (*Rhodes v Cornford*, 1947).

Arrears

2.100 Even where arrears are of charges owed to a third party, such as water charges being collected by the landlord which the tenancy requires the tenant to pay, it may nonetheless be reasonable to make an order for possession, and a judge should not limit him- or herself to doing so only in 'exceptional circumstances' (*Lambeth LBC v Thomas*, 1997; *Rochdale BC v Dixon*, 2011).

Arrears and disrepair

2.101 In *Lal v Nakum*, 1981, a tenant withheld rent on account of an alleged breach of repairing obligation by the landlord (chapter 11), which allegation he did not sustain in court. He had, however, saved the withheld rent and could have paid it all at once: nonetheless, the court made an outright order for possession. The Court of Appeal set this aside. On the other hand, where a tenant lost a counterclaim for disrepair and was unable to make any provision to pay off the arrears in *Haringey LBC v Stewart*, 1991, the Court of Appeal upheld the outright order for possession.

Long-term tenants

2.102 In *Woodspring DC v Taylor*, 1982, a couple had lived in their house for 24 years. The man lost his or her employment and suffered a heavy tax demand; the woman had diabetes and was attending a blood specialist. The Department of Health and Social Security took over their rent payments, and were paying £1 per week off the arrears. Until their recent difficulties, the Taylors had always been good tenants. The county court judge made an order for possession, but the Court of Appeal had 'difficulty in understanding how anyone could have made an order turning them out of their home'.

Rent arrears pre-action protocol

2.103 Before commencing possession proceedings, a social landlord (including a local authority, PRP or RSL) should comply with the pre-action protocol for rent arrears claims under the CPR. In general terms, this requires the parties to make efforts to reach agreements for the payment of the arrears without having to go to the court. The court may take into account any unreasonable failure by the tenant to comply with the protocol, when considering whether it is reasonable to make an order. Failure to comply by the landlord may result in his or her claim being dismissed.

Reasonableness – anti-social behaviour

2.104 In cases under Ground 2 (nuisance and criminal behaviour: para 2.98(2)), the court must always take into account the effect that the tenant's behaviour has had on neighbours, the continuing effect of that behaviour, and the effect that it would be likely to have if it is repeated: HA 1985 s85A; *Woking BC v Bistram*, 1993; *Kensington and Chelsea RLBC v Simmonds*, 1996; *Darlington BC v Sterling*, 1996; *Newcastle City Council v Morrison*, 2000; and *West Kent HA v Davies*, 1998. In severe cases, such as drug dealing from the premises or racial harassment, it will only be in exceptional circumstances that it is not reasonable to make an order (*Bristol City Council v Mousah*, 1997; *Davies*; *Sandwell MBC v Hensley*, 2007).

2.105 The fact that the nuisance was committed by someone other than the tenant does not mean it is not reasonable to grant possession (*Simmonds*; *Sterling*; *Camden LBC v Gilsenan*, 1998; *Portsmouth City Council v Bryant*, 2000). This is so even where alternative remedies, such as an ASBI (see paras 6.3–6.27), are available against the perpetrator (*Morrison*; *Manchester City Council v Higgins*, 2005).

Reasonableness – impact of homelessness

2.106 While it is right for a judge to consider the effect of a possession order in rendering a tenant homeless, it is wrong for the judge to consider the possible outcome of any application made by the tenant as a homeless person, eg that the tenant may be intentionally homeless (see para 10.52), as that is a matter for the local authority with responsibility for the homeless (*Mousah*; *Sterling*; *Shrewsbury & Atcham BC v Evans*, 1997; *Lewisham LBC v Akinsola*, 1999; *Watford BC v Simpson*, 2000; *cf Croydon LBC v Moody*, 1999).

Reasonableness – impact of Article 8 ECHR

2.107 The test of proportionality in relation to the ECHR (see paras 1.319 and 2.250–2.255) is in practice identical to reasonableness (*Pinnock v Manchester City Council*, 2010): accordingly, Article 8 ECHR adds nothing to it.

Absolute ground for anti-social behaviour

2.108 ABCPA 2014 introduced a new ground for possession based on anti-social behaviour (HA 1985 s84A). In contrast with Grounds 2 (see para 2.98(2)) and 2ZA (see para 2.98(3)), the landlord does not have to show that it is reasonable to make an order.

2.109 The landlord must prove that one or more of five conditions is made out. In each case, a court will already have made certain findings against the tenant.

1) Condition 1 is that the tenant, or a person residing in or visiting the dwelling-house, has been convicted of a 'serious offence' committed in or in the locality (see para 2.98(2)) of the dwelling-house, or committed elsewhere either (a) against a person with a right to reside in, or occupy housing accommodation in the locality of, the dwelling-house or (b) against the landlord or a person employed in connection with the exercise of the landlord's housing management functions, where the offence directly or indirectly related to or affected those functions. The serious offences are specified in HA 1985 Sch 2A and include a range of crimes involving violence, sexual abuse, possession of weapons, damage to property and drugs.
2) The tenant, or a person residing in or visiting the dwelling-house, has been committed for breaching an anti-social behaviour injunction made under ABPCA 2014 s1 (condition 2) or has been convicted of breaching a criminal procedure order under ABCPA 2014 s30, ie an injunction made against him or her following a

conviction for an offence (condition 3). Under each conditions, the breach must either have occurred in, or in the locality of, the dwelling-house, or if the breach occurred elsewhere, the term of the order which was breached must have been intended to prevent conduct capable of causing a nuisance or annoyance to a person with a right to reside in, or occupy housing accommodation in the locality of, the dwelling-house or must have been intended to prevent conduct capable of causing nuisance or annoyance to the landlord, or a person employed in connection with the exercise of the landlord's housing management functions, and directly or indirectly related to or affected those functions.

3) The dwelling-house has been the subject of a closure order (see para 6.28) and access to the dwelling-house has been prohibited by the closure order or under a closure notice (see para 6.30) for a continuous period of more than 48 hours (condition 4).
4) Condition 5 is that the tenant, or a person residing in or visiting the dwelling-house has been convicted for breaching the terms of an abatement notice (see para 13.15) or breaching an order to abate a statutory nuisance (see para 13.18) and the nuisance concerned was noise emitted from the dwelling-house.

Notice

2.110 The landlord must serve a notice on the tenant before bringing the claim (HA 1985 s83ZA); the court has no power to dispense with this requirement – cf para 2.89. If the landlord also wishes to rely on any of the grounds for possession in Schedule 2 (see para 2.98), it may do so in the same notice, in which case it must specify the ground(s) and give particulars. There is no prescribed form (see para 2.91) but the notice must state that the court will be asked to make an order for possession under section 84A, give reasons for the landlord's decision to apply for the order, inform the tenant of any right he or she may have to request a review of the landlord's decision and the time within which the request must be made (see para 2.112), specify the date after which possession proceedings may be commenced, and inform the tenant that, if he or she needs help or advice about the notice, he or she should take it immediately to a Citizens Advice Bureau, a housing aid centre, a law centre or a solicitor. If the tenancy is periodic, the specified date must be not earlier than the date when the tenancy could have been brought to an end by notice to quit (see para 2.51). In the case of a fixed-term tenancy, the specified date must be at least one month after the date of the notice.

2.111 The notice must include details of the conviction, court decision or closure order relied on. In the case of conditions 1, 2, 3 or 5, the notice must be served within 12 months of the date of the decision relied on. If condition 4 is relied on, the notice must be served with three months of the date of the closure order. The claim for possession must be commenced within 12 months of the date specified in the notice.

Review

2.112 If the landlord is a local authority, the tenant has a right to request a review of the decision to seek possession against him or her (HA 1985 s85ZA). A request for a review must be made within seven days of service of the notice. Detailed provision is made for the review procedure in the Absolute Ground for Possession for Anti-social Behaviour (Review Procedure) (England) Regulations 2014 SI No 2554 and the Secure Tenancies (Absolute Ground for Possession for Anti-social Behaviour) (Review Procedure) (Wales) Regulations 2014 SI No 3278. On completion of the review, the landlord must notify the tenant in writing of its decision, giving reasons for it. The review must be completed, and the tenant notified of the outcome, before the date when proceedings for possession may be begun (see para 2.110).

Ground plus suitable alternative accommodation

2.113 In relation to this category of ground for possession, it is not necessary also to show reasonableness but instead it must be shown that suitable alternative accommodation is available. Once satisfied on both points – ground and suitable alternative accommodation – the court has no discretion whether or not to make the order or to suspend or postpone it (see paras 2.123–2.126). The grounds are as follows.

1) **Overcrowded accommodation**. The first ground under this class is Ground 9, and arises when the dwelling currently occupied is overcrowded within the meaning of HA 1985 Part 10, in such circumstances as to render the occupier guilty of an offence (see para 14.5). In relation to this ground only, it should be noted that alternative accommodation is not to be deemed unsuitable solely because it offends the space standard described in chapter 14 (see para 14.3(2); HA 1985 Sch 2 Pt 4 para 3).
2) **Redevelopment**. Ground 10 is available when the landlord intends, within a reasonable time of seeking possession, either to demolish or reconstruct the building, or part of the building, which

includes the dwelling in question, or to carry out work on the building, or on land let together with the building, and (in either case) cannot reasonably do so without obtaining possession. The landlord has to be able to show an established, settled and clearly defined intention to do the works and that possession is needed in order to execute them (*Wansbeck DC v Marley*, 1987).

3) **Approved development area**. Ground 10A applies when the landlord, within a reasonable period of obtaining possession, intends to sell with vacant possession, but it is available if, and only if, the property is in an 'approved development area'. In England, if the landlord is a local authority, approval to a development area for this purpose must be obtained from the secretary of state; if a PRP, it must be obtained from the HCA. In Wales, local authorities and RSLs must obtain approval from the Welsh Ministers. There is provision for a dwelling which falls partly within, and partly outside of, such an area.
4) **Conflict with charitable purposes**. Ground 11 is available only to a landlord which is a charity within the meaning of the Charities Act 2011, and the tenant's continued occupation of the dwelling would conflict with the objects of the charity, ie where the charity has a specific purpose, such as the assistance of the elderly or the disabled, and neither the tenant nor anyone living with him or her any longer qualifies for such a description.

Suitable alternative accommodation

2.114 Unless the landlord is the local authority seeking possession, a certificate of the local housing authority for the area that suitable accommodation will be provided by that authority will be conclusive evidence that the accommodation so provided is suitable (HA 1985 Sch 2 Pt 4 para 4). Otherwise, alternative accommodation will only be suitable if it is of premises to be let as a separate dwelling (see para 1.171) under a secure tenancy (see para 1.160–1.209), or under an assured tenancy (see para 1.220–1.245), other than an assured shorthold (see paras 1.246–1.251) or one subject to any of the mandatory grounds for possession (see para 2.170) or a protected tenancy (see para 1.268–1.293), other than one subject to any of the mandatory grounds for possession (see para 2.219), including shorthold (see para 2.223) – HA 1985 Sch 2 Pt 4 para 1.

2.115 The requirement is that suitable alternative accommodation *will* be available when the possession order takes effect so the landlord does not have to make an offer of suitable accommodation before the possession hearing nor does the accommodation have to be available at the date of the hearing (*Reading BC v Holt*, 2013). The court can therefore make a possession order on condition that a property of a particular type will become available before the tenant is evicted. The court should take great care when considering whether a conditional order is appropriate, particularly where the tenant is vulnerable, and the order should include a time limit within which the accommodation must be provided (*Holt*).

2.116 The accommodation must, in the opinion of the court, be reasonably suitable to the needs of the tenant and his or her family. The court must, on this, have regard to: the nature of the accommodation usually provided by the landlord to persons with similar needs; distance from the place of work or education of the tenant or members of his or her family; distance from the home of the family or any member of the tenant's own family, eg relatives who require or provide support, if proximity is necessary to the well-being of either relative or tenant; the needs (as regards extent of accommodation, which in an appropriate case can include a garden: *Enfield LBC v French*, 1984) and means of tenant and his or her family; the terms of the accommodation; and, if furniture has hitherto been provided, whether furniture is to be provided in the alternative accommodation, and its nature (HA 1985 Sch 2 Pt 4 paras 1 and 2). This schedule of matters to which regard is to be paid is not exhaustive; the weight to be given to each is a matter of degree in each case (*Enfield LBC*).

Ground plus suitable alternative accommodation plus reasonableness

2.117 In this class, the landlord must prove that the ground is available and applicable, *and* that suitable alternative accommodation (see para 2.114–2.116) will be available, *and* that it is reasonable to make the order sought (see paras 2.99–2.107). When reasonableness has to be shown, the court has a wide discretion what sort of order to make, as between outright and postponed (see paras 2.120–2.127), although it would be highly unusual to find that it was reasonable, and that suitable alternative accommodation is available, and yet postpone an order otherwise than for a fixed period of time. The grounds are as follows.

1) **Non-housing property required for employee**. Ground 12 applies where the property forms part of, or is in the grounds of, a non-housing building, or in the grounds of a cemetery, was let in consequence of employment, and the property is now reasonably required for a new employee.

2) **Adapted housing.** Ground 13 applies to dwellings which have features which are substantially different from ordinary houses, designed to make the house suitable for the occupation of a physically disabled person. The ground is only available if there is no longer a physically disabled person of the class for whom it was provided in occupation (who need not be the tenant, but could be a member of his or her family), and the landlord requires it for occupation of one such disabled person.
3) **Required for persons with special needs.** Ground 14 is available only to housing associations (see para 8.4) or housing trusts (see para 8.5) engaged in letting property to specific categories of persons who, for reasons other than poverty, have particular difficulty satisfying their housing needs, eg ethnic groups, battered women, young people, the mentally handicapped. This ground is only available when either there is no longer such a person in occupation (whether as tenant or not), or the local authority is offering the tenant a secure tenancy elsewhere, and in either case the landlord requires the dwelling for occupation by a person of the class it is engaged in assisting.
4) **Sheltered accommodation.** Ground 15 applies to 'sheltered accommodation', ie houses or flats in a group which are in practice let to people with special needs, and in close proximity to which a social service or other special facility is provided, eg for elderly people or the disabled. As under the last two grounds, the ground is only available when there is no longer a person of the designated class in occupation, and the premises are required for occupation by such a person.
5) **Under-occupation.** Grounds 15A (England) and 16 (Wales) are available when the tenant has succeeded to the secure tenancy on the death of a previous tenant (see paras 1.192–1.203). They are not available when the successor tenant is the spouse or civil partner of the deceased secure tenant. They are only available when the accommodation afforded by the dwelling is more extensive than is reasonably required by the successor, which is to be judged at the date of the hearing rather than the date of succession (*Wandsworth LBC v Randall*, 2007): accordingly, if additional people have moved in during the interval, they have to be considered.

Although the notice of seeking possession (see para 2.88) should be served *no earlier* than six months after the death of the previous tenant and *no later* than 12 months after his or her death, the court has power to direct that these time limits run from the date on which the landlord first became aware of the tenant's death. This power was added by Localism Act (LA) 2011 as a result of *Newport CC v Charles,* 2008, in which the landlord did not give notice within 12 months of the tenant's death because the successor had managed deliberately to conceal the death from the landlord which, before the amendment, was effective to prevent the authority using the Ground.

In deciding whether it is reasonable to make an order for possession, the court must take into account the age of the tenant, his or her length of residence in the dwelling-house, and any financial support he or she gave to the previous tenant: see *Bracknell Forest BC v Green,* 2009. Where the tenant has applied to exercise his or her right to buy (see paras 4.46–4.73), it may nevertheless be reasonable to make an order, given the demands on local authority housing stock and the fact that the tenant will be able to buy the alternative accommodation which will made be available to him or her (and which will, of definition, be suitable) (*Manchester City Council v Benjamin,* 2008).

Orders for possession

2.118 Once the court is satisfied that a ground for possession has been proved and, if necessary, that it is reasonable to make an order for possession and/or that suitable alternative accommodation is available, it must make an order for possession. There are three types of order: outright, postponed and suspended. An order may only be postponed or suspended where possession is sought on any of the discretionary grounds, in relation to which the court must also be satisfied that it is reasonable to make an order (Grounds 1–8: para 2.98; and Grounds 12–16; para 2.117) (HA 1985 s85(1)).

2.119 In some circumstances, the landlord is obliged to accept payments from a spouse or ex-spouse, civil partner or former civil partner and some cohabitants and former cohabitants: see paras 7.13 and 7.27. If so, that person may also apply for the order to be postponed or suspended: *Penn v Dunn,* 1970.

Outright orders

2.120 An outright order grants possession to the landlord after some finite period of delay, eg two or four weeks. Once the period of delay granted by the court has run out, the landlord can issue a bailiff's warrant (see para 2.133) and there may be a further period of delay before any actual eviction. If the basis of the order is one where the landlord did not need to prove reasonableness – ie where only the ground and that suitable alternative accommodation is available need be proved (see para 2.113) – the order must be made to take effect in two weeks time unless exceptional hardship would be caused, in which case time may be extended to a maximum of six weeks (HA 1980 s89), a time limit considered compatible with the right to respect for the home under Article 8 ECHR (*Hounslow LBC v Powell*, 2011).

Postponed and suspended orders

2.121 The court may decide that a possession order should be made but that the tenant should have the opportunity to remain in occupation provided that he or she complies with certain terms, eg to pay the current rent and pay something off the arrears or not to commit acts of nuisance and annoyance to neighbours. In such cases, the court may make a 'postponed' or 'suspended' possession order.

Rent arrears – period of postponement or suspension

2.122 A court should not make an order producing an indefinite postponement or suspension, disappearing into the 'mists of time' (*Vandermolen v Toma*, 1981; *Taj v Ali*, 2000), although in *Lambeth LBC v Henry*, 1999, a period of 23 years was upheld by the Court of Appeal. Indeed, the desirability of allowing tenants to remain in occupation paying off arrears over lengthy periods of time was part of the rationale behind the abolition of the status of the tolerated trespasser (see paras 1.155–1.158 – *Austin v Southwark LBC*, 2010).

Bankruptcy

2.123 If the tenant is bankrupt or subject to a debt relief order – an order providing a period during which creditors cannot enforce debts – the court may still make a suspended possession order but the terms must be limited to payment of the landlord's costs and payment of future rent instalments: the tenant cannot be required to pay sums off the arrears which are subject to the bankruptcy or debt relief order (*Sharples v Places for People Homes Ltd*, 2011).

Postponed or suspended orders – anti-social behaviour

2.124 In cases under Ground 2 (see para 2.98(2)), it may be appropriate to postpone or suspend the order (*Kensington and Chelsea RLBC v Simmonds*, 1996; *Greenwich LBC v Grogan*, 2001; *Portsmouth City Council v Bryant*, 2000; *Castlevale Housing Action Trust v Gallagher*, 2001; *Sheffield City Council v Shaw*, 2007). In considering whether postponement or suspension is appropriate, the judge must consider future conduct. Before suspending an order, the judge must be satisfied that there is a sound basis for believing that the anti-social behaviour will cease (*Birmingham City Council v Ashton*, 2012; *City West Housing Trust v Massey*, 2016). There is no point suspending an order if the inevitable outcome will be future breaches (*Canterbury CC v Lowe*, 2001; *Sandwell MBC v Hensley*, 2007; *Leeds and Yorkshire Housing Association v Vertigan*, 2010). Even if the tenant's conduct has improved significantly by the time of the hearing, it may still be appropriate to make an outright possession order where the past conduct was sufficiently serious (*Lambeth LBC v Howard*, 2001).

Conditions

2.125 Conditions may be imposed on any adjournment, stay, suspension or postponement. In all cases, the court will order payments of rent and of any arrears that there may be unless it will cause exceptional hardship to the tenant or would otherwise be unreasonable, (HA 1985 s85(3)). In *City West Housing Trust v Massey*, 2016, the tenant allowed her partner to grow cannabis in her home. The judge suspended the order on condition that the tenant had to allow her landlord to inspect her home on not less than two hours' notice. Although the Court of Appeal approved the condition, it held that conditions in a suspended order should not require social landlords to do more than is reasonable, particularly having regard to their limited resources.

Variation of conditions

2.126 Where a postponed or suspended order is made under one ground for possession, eg rent arrears, and another ground for possession, eg anti-social behaviour, subsequently becomes available, it is not necessary for the landlord to commence new proceedings. The court has the power to add conditions to the existing order in respect of the new ground (*Manchester City Council v Finn*, 2002).

Discharge

2.127 If conditions are complied with, eg to clear arrears, it is worth the tenant's while to apply for discharge, rather than leaving on the court file an order which might later be activated erroneously and with inadequate warning to the tenant, or which the landlord might seek to use in respect of a new ground without needing to issue new proceedings (see para 2.126).

Tolerated trespass

2.128 As already noted (see paras 1.155–1.158), until amendments made by the Housing & Regeneration Act (H&RA) 2008, if the tenant breached the terms of an order, the tenancy came to an end and the tenant became a 'tolerated trespasser'. This meant that the tenant could lose his or her tenancy even if he or she was late with only one rent payment. Accordingly, in *Bristol City Council v Hassan*, 2006, the Court of Appeal provided for a new form of order, referred to as a 'deferred date' postponed order, under which the court did not fix a date for possession but instead postponed the date of possession to a subsequent date to be fixed by the court; thus, the tenancy continued even if the terms of the order were breached. If the tenant failed to keep to the terms of the order, the landlord could apply for a date for possession to be fixed. The procedure for the application is set out in CPR PD 55A(10).

2.129 As the H&RA 2008 has now amended HA 1985 so that the tenancy does not come to an end until a warrant is executed (see para 2.87), the form of order used is now of much less significance and courts rarely make deferred date orders.

2.130 On 6 April 2009, under the provisions of the H&RA 2008 Sch 11 someone who was then a tolerated trespasser would have become a tenant under a new, replacement tenancy, provided that he or she was occupying the premises as his or her only or principal home (see paras 1.172–1.175) throughout the period between the date on which he or she became a tolerated trespasser and 6 April 2009. The terms and conditions of the replacement tenancy are those of the original tenancy, modified to reflect any changes in the level of payments while the tenant was a tolerated trespasser.

2.131 Although the occupier got a new tenancy, however, that tenancy is subject to the terms of any order which applied to his or her former tenancy. For example, if the original possession order was suspended on terms that the tenant paid current rent plus £10 per week off the arrears, the replacement tenancy is also subject to those terms. If the tenant breaches those terms, the landlord can rely on the existing possession order and need not issue fresh proceedings. For certain purposes, the replacement tenancy is treated as a continuation of the original tenancy, eg if the tenant was a successor (see para 1.192) under the original tenancy, he or she remains a successor under the replacement tenancy. In addition, the court has power to treat in the tenancy as if it were a continuation in claims brought by either party for a breach of the terms of the original tenancy: this is primarily intended to allow the tenant to be able to claim for damages for disrepair during the period when he or she was a tolerated trespasser, which he or she would otherwise not have been able to do (*Lambeth LBC v Rogers*, 1999).

2.132 If the property was transferred to a landlord who was not capable of granting secure tenancies, eg a PRP, the replacement tenancy is an assured tenancy (see paras 1.220–1.245) – Housing (Replacement of Terminated Tenancies) (Successor Landlords) (England) Order 2009 SI No 1262 or Housing (Replacement of Terminated Tenancies) (Successor Landlords) (Wales) Order 2009 SI No 1260.

Warrant for possession

2.133 Orders for possession are executed by means of a warrant for possession (CPR 83.26; *Haniff v Robinson*, 1992), which entitles the court bailiff to take possession of the property. The position used to be that, once the landlord became entitled to enforce the possession order, eg because the tenant had breached the terms of a suspended order, the landlord could simply request the court to issue a warrant. A change in the rules in April 2014 means that where the landlord considers that the tenant has breached the terms of a postponed or suspended possession order, the court's permission for a warrant to be issued needs to be obtained, giving the tenant the opportunity to argue that the order has not been breached or to ask for further postponement or suspension (CPR 83.2(3); *Cardiff Council v Lee*, 2016).

2.134 The powers to suspend or postpone (see paras 2.121–2.127) can be exercised at any time before execution of the warrant for possession. Even if a warrant for possession has been issued, the court can still suspend execution of the warrant. After the warrant has been executed, however, the court can no longer do so. The tenant can only get back into the property if he or she can show that there are grounds to set aside the original order, eg he or she had no notice of the proceedings, or if the warrant can be set aside because it was an abuse of the process or oppressive to proceed with it (*Governors of Peabody Donation Fund v Hay*, 1986; *Leicester City Council v Aldwinckle*, 1991; *Hammersmith and Fulham LBC v Hill*, 1994; *Barking and Dagenham LBC v Saint*, 1999; *Southwark LBC v Sarfo*, 1999; *Hammersmith and Fulham LBC v Lemeh*, 2001; *Lambeth LBC v Hughes*, 2000). Oppression in the execution of a warrant requires unfair use of the court's procedures, or action by a person which is open to criticism as unfair use (*Jephson Homes HA v Moisejevs*, 2000).

Application to suspend warrant

2.135 Where a tenant applies to suspend a warrant for possession, it is open to the landlord to adduce evidence of a ground – or grounds – of possession different to those relied upon at the original hearing, even if those grounds had existed when the original order was made: *Sheffield City Council v Hopkins*, 2001. In that case, the original order had been made on the grounds of rent arrears. When the tenant failed to pay the arrears in accordance with the order, a warrant was issued and the tenant applied to suspend it. It was held that the landlord could adduce evidence of nuisance to resist the tenant's application to suspend the warrant. Where the new ground was already available at the time of the original possession action, however, the landlord will usually only be allowed to raise the matter if the tenant was warned at the time that the landlord had decided only to bother proceeding on the one ground, so that he or she will have been aware that the other could still subsequently be used to give rise to eviction (*Hopkins*).

Flexible tenants

2.136 **Termination by tenant.** During the fixed term of a flexible tenancy, the tenant has the right to terminate the tenancy (see paras 1.181–1.189) by serving notice on the landlord (HA 1985 s107C(2)). The notice must specify a date on which the tenancy will come to an end which must be at least four weeks after the date of the notice (s107C(3)). The landlord may agree a shorter notice period or to dispense with notice altogether (s107C(4)). The tenancy comes to an end on the date specified in the notice (or the date agreed between the parties) unless the tenant is in rent arrears as of that date or is otherwise in breach of a condition of the tenancy (s107C(5)).

2.137 **Termination by landlord – during fixed term.** A flexible tenancy is a form of secure tenancy: during the term it may be determined in the same way as any other fixed-term secure tenancy (see paras 2.85–2.86): HA 1985 s107D(10).

2.138 **Termination by landlord – death of tenant.** If a secure tenancy passes under the tenant's will or intestacy to a person who qualifies to succeed to the tenancy (see paras 1.192–1.202), then that person becomes the secure tenant. If, however, it passes to a person who is not qualified to succeed, or it is known that when the tenancy passes to succeed it will be to such a person, the fixed-term tenancy ceases to be secure and the new tenant has only contractual security. In the case of a lengthy fixed term, which might be granted to a flexible tenant, this could mean that the landlord would be prevented from obtaining possession for some time.

2.139 Amendments introduced by LA 2011 accordingly allow a landlord to obtain possession before expiry of the fixed term. The landlord has to establish that the tenancy has been disposed of in the course of the administration of the tenant's estate and that the tenancy has ceased to be secure (HA 1985 s90(5), (9)). The landlord must give the tenant four weeks notice: (s90(7)(a), (8)). The tenancy ends when the order is executed by warrant for possession: (s90(10)).

2.140 **Termination by landlord – expiry of fixed term.** After the fixed term of a flexible tenancy has expired, the landlord has a right to possession provided that three conditions are met (HA 1985 s107D(1)). First, the landlord must have given the tenant not less than six months' notice that it does not propose to grant another tenancy on expiry of the fixed term, giving reasons for that decision and informing the tenant of his or her right to request a review (s107D(3)). Secondly, on or before the last day of the fixed term, the landlord must have given the tenant not less than two months' notice that possession is required (s107D(4), (5)). Thirdly, no new tenancy must have been granted to the tenant after the expiry of the fixed term (s107D(2)).

2.141 **Review.** A request for a review of a landlord's decision not to grant a new tenancy must be made within 21 days of notification that no new tenancy is to be granted (HA 1985 s107E(1)). The landlord must conduct a review if one is requested (s107E(2)). The review must, in particular, consider whether the landlord's decision accords with its policy on the circumstances in which it will grant a further tenancy on expiry of a flexible tenancy (s107E(3), para 1.188). Procedure on review is governed by regulations (s107E(4); Flexible Tenancies (Review Procedures) Regulations 2012 SI No 695) (see para 1.184). On completion of the review, the landlord must notify the tenant in writing of its decision and, where the original decision is confirmed, reasons must be given (s107E(6), (7)).

2.142 **Court's powers.** A court can only refuse to grant possession if a review has been requested and the court is satisfied that it was not carried out or that the review decision is 'otherwise wrong in law': HA 1985 s107D(6). Accordingly, the tenant can challenge the review decision on conventional grounds of public law (see paras 8.23–8.28). A tenant may also defend the claim on the basis that eviction would not be proportionate and therefore would be in breach of his or her right to respect for the home under Article 8 ECHR (*Hounslow LBC v Powell*, 2011), or would amount to unlawful discrimination against him or her under EqA 2010 (see paras 2.250–2.259). For the general principles applying to a proportionality defence, see paras 2.250–2.255. If possession is refused, the court may give directions regarding the holding of a review (or a further review) (HA 1985 s107D(7)).

2.143 **Orders and warrants.** When an order is made, there is no power to postpone or suspend it nor any power to suspend execution of the warrant: it must be made to take effect in the same way as an order against a secure tenant on the mandatory grounds (see para 2.120), ie within two weeks or six in cases of exceptional hardship (HA 1980 s89).

Housing and Planning Act 2016

2.144 As noted (see paras 1.190–1.191), once HPA 2016 is brought into force, all new secure tenancies in England will be for a fixed term. The rules governing termination of such tenancies will be similar to those which currently apply to flexible tenancies (see paras 2.136–2.143).

2.145 **Termination by tenant.** The tenant's right to terminate a new style fixed-term tenancy will be the same as that currently enjoyed by flexible tenants (see para 2.136; new HA 1985 s86F).

2.146 **Termination by landlord – during fixed term.** During the fixed term, the landlord will be able to end the tenancy by obtaining a possession order on any of the grounds available against secure tenants (see paras 2.98–2.117). In contrast to the current position for fixed-term secure tenants (see para 2.86), including flexible tenants (see para 2.137), it will not be necessary for the landlord also to obtain an order forfeiting the fixed term (new HA 1985 s82(A1), (A2)).

2.147 **Termination by landlord – expiry of fixed term.** The procedure governing possession against new style fixed-term tenants after the end of the fixed term are the same as those for flexible tenants (see paras 2.140–2.142) (new HA 1985 ss86A–86E).

Introductory tenants

2.148 **Terminating the tenancy.** Like the secure tenancy (see para 2.85), an introductory tenancy (see paras 1.210–1.219) can only be brought to an end by obtaining an order of the court, in which case the tenancy comes to an end on the date when the possession order is executed (HA 1996 s127, as amended by H&RA 2008). The provisions also apply to a licensee who qualifies as introductory (see para 1.212) although as this is rare, reference is only made to tenants.

2.149 **Notice of proceedings.** The court cannot make an order for possession unless there has first been served a notice of proceedings ('NOP'), which states that the court is to be asked to make an order, sets out the reasons for the decision to apply for it, and specifies a date after which the proceedings may be begun, being a date no earlier than when the tenancy or licence could be brought to an end by a notice to quit (see para 2.51) given on the same date as the NOP (HA 1996 s128(1)–(4)).

2.150 The proceedings cannot be begun before that date (HA 1996 s128(5)). The notice must inform the tenant: of the right to seek an internal review of the decision, and the time within which the review may be sought (HA 1996 s128(6)); and, that if the tenant needs help or advice about the notice, and what to do about it, that he or she should take it immediately to a Citizens Advice Bureau, housing aid centre, law centre or solicitor (HA 1996 s128(7)). The information does not have to be contained in a single document, so that notice was validly given where the advice to the tenant about to seek assistance was included in a leaflet enclosed with another document which included all the other information (*Islington LBC v Dyer*, 2017).

2.151 **Reasons.** While there are no 'grounds for possession' (see paras 2.96–2.97), the landlord has to give its reasons for the decision to seek an order (HA 1996 s128(3)). This means that the reasons must be good reasons, in the sense that all public authorities (see paras 1.321–1.327) must reach decisions which accord with the principles of public law (see paras 8.23–8.28), eg they cannot be absurd, irrational or whimsical, or reached in bad faith, nor can they disregard relevant considerations or take into account irrelevant matters.

2.152 **Review.** The tenant is entitled to apply for an internal review of the decision to seek an order; the application must be made within 14 days of the date on which the NOP is served (HA 1996 s129(1)). The landlord is bound to carry out a review which has been properly asked for (HA 1996 s129(2)). The secretary of state has power to decide the procedure to be followed on a review (s129(3), (4)). The current regulations (Introductory Tenants (Review) Regulations 1997 SI No 72) require that a review is carried out by a person who was not involved in the decision to apply for possession and, if made by an officer, that the officer is senior to the officer who made the original decision. There are also detailed provisions about the right to make representations, depending on whether or not a hearing is held. If there is a hearing, the tenant has a right to attend with the assistance of representation. The tenant has the right to call witnesses, and may put questions to any person who gives evidence.

2.153 **Notification.** The landlord has to notify the tenant of the outcome of the review and, if it is to uphold the decision to evict, of the reasons (HA 1996 s129(5)). The review must be completed, and the tenant notified of the outcome, before the date when proceedings for possession may be begun (see para 2.149) (HA 1996 s129(6)).

2.154 **Challenge.** If the review upholds the decision to evict, the tenant may challenge that decision by judicial review in the High Court. He or she can also challenge the decision in the county court as a defence to the claim for possession and/or seek to argue that eviction would not be proportionate and therefore would be in breach of his or her right to respect for the home under Article 8 ECHR (*Hounslow LBC v Powell*, 2011 – see paras 2.250–2.255). In claims against introductory tenants, it is only in highly exceptional cases that a proportionality defence will be available, given that the authority will have had to provide a fully reasoned decision for deciding to end the tenancy and the tenant will have had the opportunity to challenge that decision on review (*Powell*). In an appropriate case, the tenant may also be able to argue that eviction would amount to unlawful discrimination against him or her under EqA 2010 (see paras 2.258–2.259).

2.155 **Proceedings and status as introductory tenant.** Proceedings may not be completed before either an introductory tenancy would otherwise become secure because of the expiry of the trial period (see paras 1.217–1.218) or circumstances arise such that the tenancy ceases to be secure, so that the tenancy would also cease to be an introductory tenant (see para 1.217) (HA 1996 s130(1)). In either case, the tenancy remains an introductory tenancy until the proceedings are finally determined by a court, withdrawn or abandoned (including on appeal), and the date arrives when the tenant has to give up possession pursuant to the court order (HA 1996 s130(2), (5)).

2.156 If no order is made, the normal rules will apply to determine whether the tenancy is still introductory. If the tenancy would have ceased to be introductory because of a change of landlord, or the introductory tenancy regime is abandoned (see para 1.217), then the tenancy will cease to be introductory notwithstanding the proceedings, but the landlord may continue with the proceedings as if the tenancy was still introductory (HA 1996 s130(3)). If no order is then made, the tenant may become secure (or assured if a change of landord).

2.157 **Orders and warrants.** The position is the same as for flexible tenants (see para 2.143).

Assured tenants

Contractual security

Continuation by contract – periodic tenancy

2.158 Security of tenure under HA 1988 operates closer to HA 1985 than RA 1977, in so far as a periodic contractual tenancy cannot be brought to an end by the landlord other than by executing a possession order or by obtaining a demotion order (see para 1.252) (HA 1988 s5), so that there is no division between a contractual and a 'statutory' tenancy as in the case of a Rent Act protected tenancy (see para 1.269). The periodic tenancy can, however, still be brought to an end by the tenant in the normal way, ie by notice to quit (see paras 2.47–2.56) or surrender (see paras 2.24–2.28). An assured tenancy can also be ended by a demotion order, which replaces the fully assured tenancy with an assured shorthold (see para 1.256).

Continuation by contract – fixed-term tenancy

2.159 In the case of a fixed-term assured tenancy which contains a forfeiture clause (see para 2.30), the tenancy cannot be brought to an end by the landlord by the exercise of that power (HA 1988 ss5(1) and 45(4)). Instead of forfeiture, the landlord may obtain an order of the court to determine the tenancy as if it was a periodic tenancy (HA 1988 ss7, 8).

2.160 A fixed-term tenancy may contain a break clause, allowing the tenant to leave early (see para 1.27). If the tenant exercises this, the fixed term will end (HA 1988 s5(1)). A tenant may also surrender a fixed-term tenancy (HA 1988 s5(2)), which will also terminate the fixed-term tenancy. A deed of surrender, notice or any other document which would bring the fixed-term tenancy to an end, or an undertaking an obligation to do an act which would cause it to cease to be assured (eg requiring the tenant to cease to occupy as an only or principal home during a last period, so that it is not assured when it expires), entered into or given before the grant of that tenancy will be invalid and ineffective (HA 1988 s5(5)).

2.161 If the fixed term ends because its time expires, then – unless the tenant voluntarily leaves or the landlord and the tenant agree a new tenancy to start on the determination of the old, whether that is a new fixed term or a new period tenancy (HA 1988 s5(4)) – there will automatically come into being a 'statutory periodic tenancy', which will continue until determined by a court, on specified grounds, in the same way as a tenancy that had been periodic all along. Again, a deed of surrender, notice or any other document which would bring the statutory period tenancy to an end, or an undertaking an obligation to do an act which would cause it to cease to be assured (eg ceasing to occupy as an only or principal home once it arises), entered into or given before it comes into being will be invalid and ineffective (HA 1988 s5(5)).

Notice of seeking possession

Notice of seeking possession

2.162 As under HA 1985 (see para 2.88), in place of notice to quit, the landlord has to serve a notice of seeking possession, specifying the ground he or she intends to rely on, before he or she can seek an order for possession (HA 1988 s8). A notice of seeking possession can be served during a fixed-term tenancy, to take effect in relation to the following statutory periodic tenancy (HA 1988 s8(5)).

Contents of notice

2.163 The notice must be in the form prescribed, must inform the tenant that the landlord intends to bring proceedings on the grounds specified, and must inform the tenant that the proceedings will begin no earlier than a date specified in the notice, but no later than 12 months from service of the notice. The prescribed form is, in England, Assured Tenancies and Agricultural Occupancies (Forms) (England) 2015 SI No 620, form 3; in Wales, it is Assured Tenancies and Agricultural Occupancies (Forms) Regulations 1997 SI No 194, form 3. The discussion of contents of notices, relative to secure tenants, is equally applicable to assured tenants, including the need to specify the ground relied on and particulars of it (see para 2.91).

Domestic violence and service

2.164 There are added requirements where the domestic violence ground (Ground 14A) is relied on (HA 1988 s8A), analogous to those applicable to secure tenants (see para 2.95).

Just and equitable

2.165 The court can, however, dispense with a notice of seeking possession if it considers it just and equitable (see para 2.89) to do so (other than when possession is sought on the mandatory Ground 8, governing arrears above a specific level – see para 2.170(10)).

Grounds

2.166 Unless the court dispenses with the notice, or the court gives permission to alter or add to the grounds, possession can only be ordered on a ground specified in the notice (HA 1988 s8(2)).

Commencement of proceedings

2.167 Proceedings cannot commence before the later of the following: two weeks; or, if possession is sought on Grounds 1, 2, 5–7, 9 or 16, two months; or, if a periodic tenancy, the earliest date when a notice to quit could have expired; or, if reliance is placed on Ground 14, the date of service of the notice (HA 1988 s8(4)). If a notice is served relying on Ground 7A (absolute ground for anti-social behaviour), the notice must be served within 12 months of the day of the court decision or closure order relied on (s8(4D). Where the landlord is relying on conditions 1, 2, 3 or 5 (see para 2.109), the notice must be served within 12 months of the date of the court decision. If condition 4 is relied on, the notice must be served with three months of the date of the closure order.

Grounds for possession

Discretionary and mandatory grounds

2.168 As under HA 1985 (see paras 2.96–2.97) and indeed under RA 1977 (see paras 2.218–2.219), grounds for possession against an assured tenant (HA 1988 s7 and Sch 2) are either discretionary or mandatory. The mandatory grounds are set out in Sch 2 Pt 1; the discretionary grounds are set out in Sch 2 Pt 2.

Ground plus reasonableness

2.169 The discretionary grounds for possession are those where the landlord has to prove that it is reasonable to make the order: the law on reasonableness is the same as under HA 1985 (see paras 2.99–2.107), save that where reasonableness has to be proved and the landlord is private rather than a PRP or RSL, it is likely that issues of public interest (see para 2.99) will play less of a part, if any. The grounds are as follows.

1) **Suitable alternative accommodation**. Ground 9 applies when suitable alternative accommodation is available or will be available for the tenant when the order takes effect.

   Suitable alternative accommodation is defined in HA 1988 Sch 2 Pt 3. A certificate from the local authority that the tenant will be re-housed by it is conclusive that suitable alternative accommodation will be available (although not necessarily that it is reasonable to make the order).

   In the alternative, a landlord can him- or herself provide another private tenancy, or obtain one for the tenant from another landlord. The Schedule regulates such details as suitability for the needs and means of the tenant and his or her family as regards extent and character, or its similarity to the existing accommodation, or its proximity to work (*Yewbright Properties v Stone*, 1980).

The character of the new premises can be a determining factor. In *Redspring v Francis*, 1972, it was held that premises on a busy road, next door to a fish and chip shop, were not suitable for a tenant who had hitherto been living in a quiet residential street. The extent of the facilities and amenities in an area, including shops, open space, transport, etc will also influence a decision. Alternative accommodation will never be suitable if it will result in overcrowding, even if the tenant's present premises are overcrowded.

Suitable alternative accommodation may consist of part only of a tenant's present premises, eg if one room is sublet or disused (*Mykolyshyn v Noah*, 1970). If the part of the premises which the landlord is seeking to recover is used at all, eg as a study or workroom or a spare room for visiting family, it is extremely unlikely that the court would allow this ground for possession to be used, in effect to reduce the size of the premises subject to the tenancy (*MacDonnell v Daly*, 1969).

The landlord must still establish that it is reasonable to make the order. A court will frequently refuse, even where the alternative premises are apparently suitable, because of, eg the age of the tenant. An order may well be made subject to undertakings from the landlord to do specific works to the new premises, or else to pay for various removal or other expenses. If such undertakings are given but are not fulfilled, the tenant can apply to the court to set aside or discharge the order, or else make a claim for any amount owing.

The new tenancy must either be assured (see paras 1.220–1.245), excluding tenancies in respect of which notices under Grounds 1–5 have been given (see para 2.170(1)–(5)), and excluding an assured shorthold tenancy (see paras 1.246–1.251), or else must afford security equivalent to that enjoyed by an assured tenant.

2) **Arrears of rent**. Grounds 10 and 11 are the discretionary grounds (but see para 2.170(10) for the mandatory ground) dealing with rent arrears. Ground 10 applies when rent is in arrears both at the date when the proceedings for possession are commenced, and at the date of service of the notice of seeking possession (see para 2.162), unless such notice is waived by the court (see para 2.165). It will not be available if there are no arrears at the date of hearing.

Ground 11 is available where, regardless of whether there are current rent arrears, and regardless of whether there were arrears at date of service of notice of seeking possession (or of issue of proceedings or date of hearing), the tenant has persistently delayed paying rent.

Whether or not there are arrears may be affected by the question of set-off for disrepair or a counter-claim (see paras 11.84–11.88)).

3) **Breach of term of tenancy**. Ground 12 applies when the tenant has broken an obligation of the tenancy (see para 2.98(1)).
4) **Deterioration of premises or furniture**. Grounds 13 and 15 are available when the dwelling-house or common parts, or furniture provided in the premises or the common parts, has deterioration as a result of the neglect or default of the tenant or someone else residing in the property (whom no steps have been taken to try to remove) (see para 2.98(4)).
5) **Nuisance and annoyance**. Ground 14 applies to nuisance, annoyance and convictions (see para 2.98(2)). Ground 14ZA, which is only available in England, applies where there has been a conviction at the scene of a riot (see para 2.98(3)).
6) **Domestic violence**. Ground 14A is the domestic violence ground (see para 2.98(4)).
7) **Service tenancies**. Ground 16 is available when the property was let to the tenant in consequence of his or her employment (see paras 1.131–1.140) and the tenant has ceased to be in that employment.
8) **Deception**. Ground 17 applies to tenancies induced by a false statement (see para 2.98(6)).

Mandatory Grounds

2.170 In relation to this category of ground for possession, it is not necessary also to show reasonableness. Once satisfied of the ground, the court has, accordingly, no discretion whether or not to make the order or to suspend or postpone it (see paras 2.121–2.127). The grounds are as follows.

1) **Absentee owner-occupiers**. Ground 1 concerns absentee owner-occupiers. The ground is, however, available in relation to a subtenant, even though the landlord is him- or herself the tenant of another.

   The ground is available to a landlord who has (or, if joint landlords, one of whom has) formerly occupied the property as his or her only or principal home (see paras 1.172–1.175). It is also available to a landlord who requires (or, in the case of joint landlords, one of whom requires) occupation of the property as his or her or his or her spouse's or civil partner's only or principal home, although not if the would-be occupier bought the premises (for money or money's worth) with the tenant already in occupation.

This ground is only available to a landlord who has served notice no later than the beginning of the tenancy, warning the tenant that the ground might be used against him or her. If the landlord fails to do so, however, the court may waive this requirement if it thinks it just and equitable to do so, eg if the tenant had oral notice, although such other factors as mutual hardship and time in occupation are also relevant (*White v Jones*, 1993). Persistent late payment of rent may also be relevant (*Boyle v Verrall*, 1996).

2) **Mortgaged property**. Ground 2 is available when the property is subject to a mortgage granted before the beginning of the tenancy, and the mortgage company has become entitled to exercise the power of sale under the mortgage (see para 2.5) and requires possession in order to sell with vacant possession. Again, there must have been notice to the tenant no later than the beginning of the tenancy that this ground might apply but the the court also has power to waive notice on the basis that it is just and equitable to do so.
3) **Out-of-season holiday letting**. An out-of-season fixed-term letting for not more than eight months, of premises occupied within the previous 12 months for a holiday (see para 1.233(9)), is subject to a mandatory ground for possession, providing notice was given to the tenant no later than the beginning of the tenancy that the ground would apply (Ground 3). There is no power for the court to waive the notice requirement.
4) **Off-season student letting**. An off-season fixed-term letting for not more than one year, of premises occupied within the previous 12 months as a student letting (see para 1.233(8)), is likewise subject to a mandatory ground for possession, provided notice was given no later than the beginning of the tenancy that the ground would apply (Ground 4). There is no power for the court to waive the notice requirement.
5) **Ministers of religion**. Ground 5 is a special ground, applicable to property occupied or formerly occupied by ministers of religion.
6) **Demolition**. Possession can be obtained under Ground 6 by a landlord who intends to demolish or reconstruct the whole or a

substantial part of the premises, or carry out substantial works on them. The following conditions must be fulfilled.

(i) The work cannot reasonably be carried out with the tenant in occupation either because the tenant will not agree to a variation in terms, such as would allow sufficient access and facilities to permit the work to be carried out, or no such variation is practicable in the light of the intended works; or

(ii) The tenant will not agree to accept an assured tenancy of part only of the property, such as would permit the landlord to carry out the works, or no such 'part-property' arrangement would be practicable.

The ground is similar to that available under HA 1985; in particular, a landlord's plans have to be clear and certain before the ground is available (see para 2.113(2)). This ground is also available in the case of a PRP, RSL or charitable housing trust (see para 8.5) where the person intending to do the works is not the landlord under the tenancy but a superior landlord. This ground is not available, however, to a landlord who has bought the property for money or money's worth with the tenant in occupation, or when the assured tenant has become an assured tenant by succession under RA 1977 (see para 1.279).

7) **Inherited tenancy**. Ground 7 is available in the case of a periodic tenancy (including a statutory periodic tenancy: para 2.161), and, in England only, a fixed-term tenancy. It applies when the tenancy has devolved not on statutory succession (see para 1.234) but under the will of the tenant, or on the tenant's intestacy, and proceedings for possession are commenced no later than one year after the death of the former tenant (or, if the court so permits, one year after the court considers that the landlord – or in the case of joint landlords, one of them – became aware of the death of the former tenant).

It is expressly provided that if the landlord continues to accept rent from the successor, it will not amount to the creation of a new tenancy (see paras 1.40–1.41), unless there is a variation in the amount of rent, the terms of the tenancy, its periods or the property itself.

The availability of Ground 7 against fixed-term tenants in England reflects the fact that PRPs may decide to grant fixed-term assured tenants contractual rights of succession (see para 1.237).

8) **Anti-social behaviour**. Ground 7A is the absolute ground for anti-social behaviour and is the same as against secure tenants (see para 2.98(3)).

9) **Illegal immigrants**. Ground 7B was added by the Immigration Act 2016 and is available where the secretary of state has notified the landlord that the tenant, or one more joint tenants, or any other adult occupying the dwelling-house, is disqualified from doing so because of his or her immigration status. (See below paras 2.233–2.236).

10) **Two months' or 8 weeks' rent arrears**. Ground 8 concerns rent arrears (and is to be compared with the discretionary grounds – para 2.169(2)). This ground is available if both at the date of service of the notice of seeking possession (see para 2.162) and at the date of hearing of the action, there are at least eight weeks' rent arrears (if the tenancy is weekly or fortnightly), or two months' rent arrears (if the tenancy is monthly).

    At the hearing, unless the tenant can raise a defence to the arrears, the court must order possession. In exceptional circumstances, it can, however, adjourn the proceedings. The fact that the arrears may be attributable to a local authority failing to process a housing benefit claim is not considered such an exceptional circumstance (*North British Housing Association v Matthews*, 2004). If no notice has been served pursuant to LTA 1987 s48 (see para 1.86), rent will not yet be due and, therefore, cannot be in arrears (*Marath v MacGillivray*, 1996). Nor will there be arrears if there is a valid set-off for disrepair (or other breach) (see paras 11.84–11.88), but there will be arrears at the date of NSP even if there is a counter-claim (see para 11.84) which is not a set-off, eg a debt owed by the landlord to the tenant which does not relate to the tenancy, although (arguably) there may not be by the time the hearing ends, ie if a (sufficient) award is made on the counter-claim.

Rent arrears

2.171 It will therefore be appreciated that there are three grounds governing rent arrears, one mandatory (Ground 8; para 2.170(10)), while the other two are discretionary (Grounds 10 and 11; para 2.169(2)). Possession may be sought on both the mandatory and discretionary grounds in the same proceedings. Unless, on the face of the order, it has been made on the mandatory Ground 8, the court will retain its added powers (see paras 2.174–2.176) to suspend the order or a warrant for possession: *Capital Prime Plus Plc v Wills*, 1998. When making an order under Ground 8, the court therefore needs to ensure that it is made clear on its face: *Diab v Countryside Rentals 1 Plc*, 2001.

Forfeiture

2.172 In the case of a fixed-term tenancy which contains a forfeiture clause (see para 2.30), the court can only make an order for possession on the discretionary grounds in Sch 2 Pt 2, other than Grounds 9 or 16 (see para 2.169), or on Grounds 2 or 8 of the mandatory grounds in Sch 2 Pt 1 (see para 2.170) (HA 1988 s7), and then only if the forfeiture clause itself permits the lease to be ended on that ground. The landlord does not, and cannot (see paras 2.159), bring the claim as a claim for forfeiture, nor do the provisions for relief from forfeiture (see paras 2.37–2.46) apply (*Artesian Residential Developments Ltd v Beck*, 1999).

Misrepresentation

2.173 Where possession is ordered on any ground, and it can later be shown that the order was obtained by misrepresentation or concealment of a material fact, the landlord can be ordered to compensate the tenant (HA 1988 s12).

Orders for possession

2.174 The position governing orders for possession when made on a discretionary ground is the same as for secure tenants (see paras 2.118–2.127), save that under HA 1988, assured tenancies end when the order for possession is executed, so that amendments by the H&RA 2008 to achieve the same effect were unnecessary (see para 1.57), with the result that tolerated trespass did not arise in the same way as for secure tenants (see paras 2.128).

2.175 In the case of discretionary grounds, the court's powers to postpone, suspend or vary an order are the same as under HA 1985 (see paras 2.121–2.127 – HA 1988 s9). Otherwise, ie where the order is made on mandatory grounds – the court must make an outright order, subject to the same limit (two weeks save in a case of exceptional hardship, when it may be extended to six) as under that Act (HA 1980 s89; para 2.120).

Warrant for possession

2.176 The position governing warrants is the same as for secure tenants (see paras 2.133–2.135).

Demoted tenants

2.177 **Terminating the tenancy.** Like the secure tenancy (see para 2.85), a demoted tenancy (see paras 1.252–1.261) can only be brought to an end by obtaining an order of the court, in which case the tenancy comes to an end on the date when the possession order is executed (HA 1996 s127, as amended by H&RA 2008). As some licensees are treated as secure tenants (see para 1.168), they may also be demoted but as this is rare, reference is only made here to tenants.

2.178 **Notice of proceedings.** The scheme for possession proceedings against a demoted tenant is similar to that for introductory tenants. The court cannot make an order for possession unless there has first been served a notice of proceedings ('NOP'), which states that the court is to be asked to make an order, sets out the reasons for the decision to apply for it and specifies a date after which the proceedings may be begun, being a date no earlier than when the tenancy could be brought to an end by notice to quit (see para 2.51) given on the same date as the NOP (HA 1996 s143E).

2.179 The proceedings cannot be begun before that date (HA 1996 s143E(4)). The notice must inform the tenant: of the right to seek an internal review of the decision and the time within which the review may be sought (HA 1996 s143E(2)(e)); and, that if the tenant needs help or advice about the notice, and what to do about it, that he or she should take it immediately to a Citizens Advice Bureau, housing aid centre, law centre or solicitor (HA 1996 s143E(5)).

2.180 **Reasons.** Similar considerations arise in relation to the reasons given for eviction as arise in relation to the decision to evict an introductory tenant (see para 2.139).

2.181 **Review.** The tenant is entitled to apply for an internal review of the decision to seek an order but the application must be made within 14 days of the date on which the NOP is served (HA 1996 s143F(1)). The landlord is bound to carry out a review which has been properly asked for (HA 1996 s143F(2)). The procedure to be followed on a review is governed by either the Demoted Tenancies (Review of Decisions) (England) Regulations 2004 SI No 1679 or the Demoted Tenancies (Review of Decisions) (Wales) Regulations 2005 SI No 1228. The requirements mirror those for introductory tenancies (see para 2.152).

2.182 **Notification.** The landlord has to notify the tenant of the outcome of the review and, if it is to uphold the decision to evict, of its reasons (HA 1996 s143F(5)). The review must be completed, and the tenant notified of the outcome, before the date when proceedings for possession may be begun (para 2.178) (HA 1996 s143F(6)).

2.183 **Challenge.** As with introductory tenancies (see para 2.154), if the review upholds the decision to evict, the tenant may challenge the decision by way of judicial review in the High Court; he or she can also challenge the decision in the county court as a defence to the claim for possession; he or she can also ask the county court to reach its own decision that eviction would not be proportionate and would therefore be in breach of his or her right to respect for the home under Article 8 ECHR, so that the tenancy should not be determined (*Pinnock v Manchester City Council*, 2010; see paras 2.250–2.255). It is only in highly exceptional cases that a proportionality defence will be available to a demoted tenant, given that there will already have been a hearing at which the court will have decided that it was reasonable (and therefore proportionate) to make a demotion order and that the tenant will have been given the authority's reasons for deciding to evict him or her and the opportunity to challenge the decision by a review (*Pinnock*). In an appropriate case, the tenant may also be able to argue that eviction would amount to unlawful discrimination against him or her under EqA 2010 (see paras 2.258–2.259).

2.184 **Proceedings and status as demoted tenant.** Proceedings may not be completed before either a demoted tenancy would otherwise become secure because of the expiry of the demotion period (see para 1.257) or circumstances arise such that the tenancy ceases to be secure, so that the tenancy would also cease to be a demoted tenant (see paras 1.259–1.260) (HA 1996 s143G(2)). In either case, the tenancy remains a demoted tenancy until the proceedings are finally determined by a court, withdrawn or abandoned (including on appeal), and the date arrives when the tenant has to give up possession pursuant to the court order (HA 1996 s143G(1), (2)).

2.185 If no order is made, the normal rules will apply to determine whether the tenancy is still demoted. If the tenancy would have ceased to be demoted because of a change of landlord (see para 1.259), then the tenancy will cease to be demoted notwithstanding the proceedings, but the landlord may continue with the proceedings as if it was still demoted (HA 1996 s143G). If no order is then made, the tenant may become secure (or assured if a change of landlord).

2.186 **Orders and warrants.** The position is the same as for flexible tenants (see para 2.143).

2.187 **Demoted assured shorthold tenants.** A demoted assured shorthold tenancy (see para 1.256) is merely a type of periodic assured shorthold tenancy and the usual rules for determining such a tenancy on the shorthold ground (see paras 2.195–2.208) – as well as the rules in relation to the court's powers (see para 2.208) – apply. In contrast to demoted tenants (see paras 2.180–2.181), there is no requirement for the landlord to give reasons for eviction or to conduct a review. That said, such tenancies are granted by PRPs or RSLs, who in evicting tenants are acting as public authorities (see para 1.322), so that a tenant may be able challenge a decision to evict by way of judicial review or defend it in the county court either on traditional public law grounds or on the basis that eviction would be in breach of his or her right to respect for the home under Article 8 ECHR. In an appropriate case, the tenant may also be able to argue that eviction would amount to unlawful discrimination against him or her under EqA 2010 (see paras 2.258–2.259). PRPs and RSLs are therefore well-advised to ensure that they have proper procedures in place for making and recording eviction decisions to be able to meet any challenge which may arise.

Family intervention tenants

2.188 **Terminating the tenancy.** Family intervention tenancies (see paras 1.262–1.265) are never fixed-term and may be terminated by notice to quit (see paras 2.49–2.58). Where the landlord is a local authority (rather than a PRP or an RSL), however, there are additional procedural requirements.

2.189 **Local authority notice to quit.** Before serving notice to quit, the authority must serve a notice on the tenant which must state that the authority has decided to serve notice to quit, explain the effect of a notice to quit, give reasons for the authority's decision to serve notice, say when the authority is intending to serve notice to quit, inform the tenant of his or her right to request a review of the authority's decision, within the period of 14 days beginning with the service of the notice, and tell him or her how he or she may obtain advice in relation to the notice (H&RA 2008 s298(1), (2)).

2.190 **Review.** The tenant is entitled to apply for a review of the authority's decision similar to that available to an introductory (see para 2.152) or demoted (see para 2.181) tenant (H&RA 2008 s298(3)). Procedure on review is governed by Family Intervention Tenancies (Review of Local Authority Decisions) (England) Regulations 2008 SI No 3111, which are in similar form to the provisions governing a review requested by an introductory tenant (see para 2.152).

2.191 **Notice to quit.** If on review the authority decides to uphold its decision to evict the tenant, it may terminate the tenancy by notice to quit. The notice to quit must, however, include advice to the tenant on how he or she may obtain assistance in relation to it (H&RA 2008 s298(7)).

2.192 **Challenge.** As with introductory tenancies (see para 2.154) or demoted tenancies (see para 2.171), if the review upholds the decision to evict, the tenant may challenge the decision by way of judicial review or in the county court as a defence to the possession claim. Likewise, he or she may also argue that eviction would be disproportionate and in breach of his or her right to respect for the home under Article 8 ECHR (see paras 2.250–2.295). By analogy with introductory and demoted tenants, it is likely that such a challenge will only be available in highly exceptional circumstances, given that a family intervention tenant is a former secure or assured tenant who either has had a possession order for anti-social behaviour made against him or her or who voluntarily accepted the tenancy in the realisation that such a possession order would be made (see para 1.254).

2.193 **Registered providers and registered social landlords.** There is no express requirement for a PRP or RSL to conduct a review of a decision to evict a family intervention tenant or to give reasons for the decision to evict. As in the case of decision to evict demoted assured shorthold tenants, however, such landlords are well advised to have proper procedures in place to meet any challenge to their decision that may arise, not least because they will usually be susceptible to the provisions of HRA 1998 (see paras 1.321–1.322).

2.194 **Orders and warrants.** The position is the same as for flexible tenants (see para 2.135).

Assured shorthold tenants

2.195 **Mandatory ground.** The assured shorthold tenancy works by the addition of a mandatory (see para 2.96) ground for possession, so that the landlord still enjoys all the other grounds (see paras 2.169–2.170). As will be seen, the ground is that the landlord has served the tenant with the appropriate notice requiring possession under HA 1988 s21 (see para 2.203).

2.196 **Deregulation Act 2015.** HA 1988 was extensively amended by the Deregulation Act (DA) 2015. These amendments do not apply in Wales, nor do they currently apply to a tenancy granted before 1 October 2015. From 1 October 2018, however, the amendments will apply to all assured shorthold tenancies in England whenever they were granted.

2.197 **Restrictions on mandatory ground.** In a number of circumstances, the landlord cannot use the mandatory ground.

1) Where the tenancy is of an HMO or other dwelling which has not been licensed in accordance with HA 2004 (see para 14.103).
2) In Wales, where the landlord is a private landlord and is not registered with Rent Smart Wales (see paras 14.74–14.80) or, if registered, does not have a licence (14.81–14.85), unless the dwelling is being managed for the landlord by a licenced managing agent (see paras 14.86–14.87).
3) Where the tenant has paid the landlord a deposit and he or she has failed to deal with in accordance with a tenancy deposit scheme (see para 3.150).
4) In England, where the landlord is in breach of a 'prescribed requirement' (HA 1988 s21A). The prescribed requirements currently only apply to tenancies granted on or after 1 October 2015, and are that the landlord must provide the tenant free of charge with an energy performance certificate for the dwelling (under Energy Performance of Buildings (England and Wales) Regulations 2012 SI No 3118 (see para 13.56) and a gas safety certificate (see paras 11.106–11.108) (Assured Shorthold Tenancy Notices and Prescribed Requirements (England) Regulations 2015 SI No 1646). From 1 October 2018, however, the prescribed requirements will apply to all assured shorthold tenancies in England whenever they were granted.
5) In England, where the landlord has failed to give the tenant prescribed information about the rights and responsibilities of a landlord and a tenant under an assured shorthold tenancy, contained in *How to rent; the checklist for renting in England*, published by the DCLG (HA 1988 s21B; Assured Shorthold Tenancy Notices and Prescribed Requirements (England) Regulations 2015 SI No 1646). This booklet may be given to the tenant in hard copy or an electronic version may be sent to his or her email address if the tenant has notified the landlord (or a managing agent) that he or she will accept notices and other tenancy documentation by email. The obligation to provide this information currently only relates to tenancies granted on or after 1 October 2015, but from 1 October 2018, it will apply to all assured shorthold tenancies in England whenever they were granted.
6) Where the provisions in the Deregulation Act 2015 relating to 'retaliatory eviction' apply (see paras 2.198–2.202).

2.198 **Retaliatory eviction.** DA 2015, ss33 and 34, contain provisions intended to ensure that landlords cannot avoid carrying out repairs to their properties by evicting their assured shorthold tenants. These provisions only apply in England and do not currently apply to tenancies granted before 1 October 2015, but will apply to all tenancies in England from 1 October 2018, whenever they were granted.

2.199 A notice requiring possession given within six months of the landlord being served by a local authority with an improvement notice (see paras 12.18–12.26) or a notice of emergency remedial action (see paras 12.30–12.32) under HA 2004 (DA 2015 s33(1)) is invalid. The authority's notice must either relate to the tenant's dwelling or to common parts of the building in which it is situated, provided that the landlord has a controlling interest in those common parts and their condition is affecting the tenant's enjoyment of the dwelling or of any common parts which he or she is entitled to use (s33(10), (11)). In the case of a suspended improvement notice (see para 12.22), the six months runs from the date on which the suspension ends.

2.200 A notice requiring possession is also invalid in the following circumstances (DA 2015 s33(2)).

1) The tenant complained in writing to the landlord, or his or her managing agent, about the condition of the dwelling and either the tenant received no response within 14 days, or if there was a response, it did not tell the tenant what the landlord proposed to do and give a reasonable timescale for taking action.
2) The tenant then complained to the local authority about the same defect in the condition of the dwelling.
3) The authority served an improvement notice (see paras 12.18–12.26) or a notice of emergency remedial action (see paras 12.30–12.32) under HA 2004.
4) If the notice requiring possession was not given before the tenant's complaint to the local authority, it was given before the authority served the improvement notice or notice of emergency remedial action.

2.201 Where the notice is invalid under these provisions, the court must strike out possession proceedings based on it (DA 2015 s33(6)) but if a possession order is made before the local authority notice is served, this does not provide a ground setting it aside (s33(7)).

2.202 **Exceptions.** The retaliatory eviction provisions do not apply if any of the following applies (DA 2015 s34).

1) The defective condition of the dwelling giving rise to the authority's notice is caused by the tenant's failure to use the dwelling in a tenant-like manner (see para 4.111(3)).
2) When the notice requiring possession is given, the dwelling is genuinely on the market for sale.
3) The landlord is a PRP.
4) The landlord has a mortgage and the lender requires possession to sell the dwelling.

2.203 **Notice requiring possession – fixed term tenancies.** There are two forms of notice, both of which must give the tenant at least two months' notice in writing that the landlord requires possession of the dwelling (HA 1988 s21(1), (4)). A notice under section 21(1) may only be used if the tenancy was a fixed-term tenancy but can be given during the term or after it has expired and may therefore be used to end a statutory periodic tenancy (see para 2.161) (*Spencer v Taylor*, 2013). The alternative form of notice under section 21(4) can be used to end a periodic tenancy (whether contractual or statutory). The notice must state that possession is required under section 21(4). In Wales, and in England, if the tenancy was granted before 1 October 2015, this form of notice must also end on the last day of a period of the tenancy (*McDonald v Fernandez*, 2003; *Notting Hill Housing Trust v Roomus*, 2006). A particular date need not be specified – it is sufficient to state that possession is required after the end of the period of the tenancy which ends more than two months after service of the notice (*Lower Street Properties v Jones*, 1996; *Spencer v Taylor*, 2013). If a date is specified, it must be no earlier than the tenancy could otherwise have been brought to an end by notice to quit (see para 2.51). In England, if the tenancy was granted on or after 1 October 2015, it is sufficicent to give two months' notice (HA 1988 s21(4ZA)). This will apply to all tenancies in England from 1 October 2018.

2.204 In England, for both forms of notice, there are additional requirements if the tenancy was granted on or after 1 October 2015, which will also apply to all assured shorthold tenancies in England from 1 October 2018. First, a prescribed form must be used (HA 1988 s21(8); Assured Shorthold Tenancy Notices and Prescribed Requirements (England) Regulations 2015 SI No 1646, form 6A). Secondly, the notice must not be given within four months of the commencement of the tenancy (or, if one shorthold of the same or substantially the same premises with the same landlord and tenant has followed another, within four months of the date when the original shorthold was granted) (HA 1988 s21(4B)).

2.205 **PRPs – fixed term.** A PRP bringing a claim for possession against an assured shorthold tenant whose tenancy is for a fixed-term tenancy for two years or more (see para 1.183) has to serve an additional notice. The PRP must give the tenant at least six months' notice that it does not propose to grant another tenancy at the end of the fixed term (HA 1988 s20D). The notice must tell the tenant of how to obtain help or advice.

2.206 **Public law defences.** Although PRPs and RSLs normally grant full assured tenancies, they now often grant assured shorthold tenancies, the most common of which are 'starter tenancies,' in the same way that local authorities grant introductory tenancies (see paras 1.210–1.219). The landlord grants an assured shorthold for a 'trial period', usually one year. If this trial period is successful, the landlord then notifies the tenant that his or her tenancy has become assured (see para 1.248(2)). If the tenant breaches the terms of his or her tenancy agreement during the trial period, the landlord is able to use the mandatory procedure. Furthermore, PRPs will make greater use of longer-term assured shorthold tenancies now that the provisions of LA 2011 are in force (see para 1.183) As PRPs and RSLs can be public authorities (see paras 1.321–1.322), it may be possible for the tenant to defend the possession claim on the basis that the decision to evict him or her was irrational or not proportionate (see paras 2.250–2.257).

2.207 **Accelerated procedure.** CPR 55 provides an accelerated possession procedure enabling landlords to recover premises let under an assured shorthold tenancy without a hearing. The procedure cannot be used if the landlord is making any other claim in the proceedings, eg for arrears of rent. If the tenant wishes to dispute the claim for possession, he or she must complete the form of reply within 14 days of service of the application. On consideration of the application and the reply (if any), the judge may order possession without a hearing. If the judge is not satisfied that the claim was served, or that the claimant landlord is entitled to possession, he or she may fix a day for a hearing and give case management directions. A hearing day must be fixed if the documents filed by the claimant might arguably disclose a defect in his or her claim, or where, on its face, the defendant's reply raises an issue which, if true, would constitute an arguable defence to the claim for possession (*Manel v Memon*, 2000).

2.208 **Orders and warrants.** No order on the shorthold ground may be made so as to take effect any earlier than six months after the shorthold was granted (or, if one shorthold of the same or substantially the same premises with the same landlord and tenant has followed another, after the original shorthold was granted) (HA 1988 s21(5)). Otherwise, the position is the same as for flexible tenants (see para 2.143) ie the order must be made to take effect within two weeks (or six in cases of exceptional hardship) and there is no power to suspend execution of the warrant (HA 1980 s89).

2.209 **Abandonment.** In England, once HPA 2016 Part 3 is in force, if a dwelling let under an assured shorthold tenancy has been abandoned, the landlord will be able to end the tenancy without a court order. The landlord can only do so if the 'unpaid rent condition' is satisfied and the landlord has given three warning notices and a final notice (HPA 2016 s57).

2.210 The unpaid rent condition is that there are at least eight weeks' rent arrears (if the tenancy is weekly or fortnightly), or two months' rent arrears (if the tenancy is monthly) (HPA 2016 s58(1); *cf* the mandatory rent arrears ground against assured tenants (see para 2.170(10)).

2.211 The landlord has to give three warning notices (HPA 2016 s59). Each warning notice must be given to the tenant, any person named in the tenancy agreement as someone who is entitled to live in the dwelling, and anyone who the landlord knows paid a tenancy deposit (see paras 3.135–3.150) on the tenant's behalf (s59(2)). All three warning notices must explain that the landlord believes that the dwelling has been abandoned and warn that the landlord intends to bring the tenancy to an end if he or she does not receive a written response before a specified date (s59(4)). The specified date must not be before the end of a number of weeks after each notice is given: eight weeks (first notice); four weeks (second notice); and, five days (third notice). The first notice can be given before the unpaid rent condition (see para 2.210) is met but the unpaid rent condition has to be met for a second notice to be given. If the tenant pays *any* rent at all before the final notice is given, the landlord is unable to serve a final notice (ss57(b), 58(2)). If, however, no rent is paid and the third warning notice expires, the landlord can serve a final notice bringing the tenancy to an end (s57).

2.212 A first or second warning notice, or a final notice, may be given by: delivery to the person concerned; leaving it at the dwelling; leaving it, posting it or emailing it to a contact address which that person has provided; or, in the case of the tenant only, leaving it or sending it to postal addresses provided by anyone who has agreed to guarantee the tenant's obligations under the tenancy (HPA 2016 s61). The third warning notice must be fixed to a conspicuous part of the dwelling (s59(3)).

2.213 After the tenancy has been brought to end, the county court may nonetheless, on application by the tenant, reinstate the tenancy if it considers the tenant had a good reason for failing to respond to the warning notices (HPA 2016 s60). The court may make such order as it thinks fit for reinstating the tenancy. Any such application must be made within six months of the day on which the final notice was given.

Rent Act protected and statutory tenants

Contractual security

2.214 No tenant can be evicted, whether lawfully in fact or by court proceedings, so long as the tenancy has not been brought to an end. In the case of a tenant within the protection of the Rent Act, this means the contractual tenancy (see para 1.261) rather than the statutory tenancy (see para 1.261) which will continue so long as the tenant is in residence. The contractual tenancy may have come to an end by expiry of a fixed term (see para 2.23), by notice to quit (see paras 2.47–2.56) or by forfeiture (see paras 2.29–2.44). It is unlikely to have come to an end by surrender (see paras 2.24–2.28) if the tenant is still living in the premises, although not impossible, eg where the tenant changed his or her mind at the last moment, perhaps because an alternative arrangement fell through.

Notice of increase of rent

2.215 A tenant's rent may have been increased by notice under the provisions of RA 1977 (see para 3.75). A notice of increase of rent can double as a notice to quit so as to bring the tenancy to an end and replace it with a statutory tenancy (RA 1977 s49). To operate dually in this way, a notice of increase must be in the proper form (*Aristocrat Property Investments v Harounoff*, 1982) and specify a date for the increase to take effect no earlier than a notice to quit could have taken effect (see para 2.51). It will then convert the contractual tenancy into a statutory tenancy.

Statutory tenancy

2.216 Once the tenancy is statutory, no notice need be given by the landlord in order to terminate it before seeking possession: to the contrary, so long as the tenant is in residence (see paras 1.290–1.293), the statutory tenancy subsists and will continue until the tenant is evicted by the court (*Haniff v Robinson*, 1992). If the tenant abandons possession, the statutory tenancy will end and the landlord will be able to recover possession without a court order, but the landlord will need to be absolutely certain that the tenant has quit altogether, for there is otherwise a real risk of committing an offence (see para 5.5). As the tenant can sustain a statutory tenancy by means of intention to return, coupled to visible signs of it (see para 1.292), it follows that if there is *anything* in the property that suggests that the tenant *might* return, or *anyone* (eg subtenant, licensee), the landlord should only evict by way of seeking an order.

Grounds for possession

Discretionary and mandatory grounds for possession

2.217 As under HA 1985 (see paras 2.96–2.117) and HA 1988 (see paras 2.168–2.169), the court may order possession only where the landlord makes out either a discretionary ground for possession (RA 1977 s98 and Sch 15 Pt 1), ie one where in addition to the provisions of the ground, the landlord must also provide that it is reasonable to make the order sought, or a mandatory ground for possession (RA 1977 s98 and Sch 15 Pt 2).

Discretionary grounds

2.218 The discretionary grounds for possession are those in relation to which the landlord must prove that it is reasonable to make the order, as well as proving that the details of each case are applicable. Reasonableness has been considered (see paras 2.99–2.103); under RA 1977, it is analogous to the position under HA 1988 when the landlord is not a PRP or RSL (see para 2.169), ie public interest forms a smaller part of the equation than when the landlord is one of those bodies (or a local authority under HA 1985). The discretionary grounds are as follows.

1) **Rent arrears and breach of term of tenancy**. Case 1 is available where either the tenant is in arrears with his or her rent, or the tenant has broken a term of the tenancy (see para 2.98(1)).

   Breach of a condition attached to a grant of consent to improve (see para 4.155) can constitute a breach of a term of the tenancy for these purposes (HA 1980 s83).

2) **Nuisance, annoyance, illegal or immoral user**. Conviction for immoral, or illegal, user is also a ground for possession, as is nuisance and annoyance to adjoining occupiers (Case 2).

   This ground is narrower than the extended corresponding grounds in HA 1985 and HA 1988 (see paras 2.98(2), 2.169(5)).

The nuisance or annoyance must be to an adjoining occupier but this does not mean that the occupier's property is necessarily physically contiguous: it means the same as 'neighbour' (*Cobstone Investments Ltd v Maxim*, 1985).

3) **Deterioration of premises or furniture**. Cases 3 and 4 concern deterioration of the premises, or of any furniture provided by the landlord, attributable to the acts, neglect or default of the tenant, or someone living with him or her (see para 2.98(4)). (Unlike HA 1985 and HA 1988 grounds, these cases do not cover deterioration of common parts or furniture situated in common parts.)
4) **Tenant's notice to quit**. Case 5 is peculiar to RA 1977 and is available when the tenant has given notice to quit the premises, in consequence of which the landlord has contracted to sell or let the property, or has taken any other steps as a result of which he or she would be seriously prejudiced if the tenant were to remain. It reflects the proposition (see para 1.269) that even if the tenant has given notice to quit, a statutory tenancy will arise if he or she is still in residence (see paras 1.290–1.293).

   For this to to apply, the notice to quit must be valid (see para 2.49–2.58) (*De Vries v Smallridge*, 1927).
5) **Assignment or sub-letting**. Case 6 is available when the tenant, without the consent of the landlord, has assigned (see paras 1.78–1.83) or sublet (see paras 1.59–1.77) the whole of the premises, whether the sub-letting is in one go, or bit by bit.

   Commonly, the tenant will in any event lose his or her statutory tenancy if he or she does this, for want of residence, although this is not inevitable, as the tenant may be intending to return (see para 1.292).

   The case is available even if there was no prohibition in the tenancy agreement on sub-letting (*Regional Properties Co v Frankenschwerth*, 1950). Consent may, however, be express or implied, and may be before or even after the assignment or sub-letting, at any time before hearing (*Hyde v Pimley*, 1952), so that cases on waiver of illegal sub-letting here (see paras 1.70–1.72) may be relied on by way of analogy.
6) **Overcharging subtenant**. If the rent for the subtenancy has been registered (see paras 3.63–3.64), or if the First-tier Tribunal (in England) or a rent assessment committee (in Wales) has fixed a rent for the subtenancy (see para 3.72–3.73), it is a ground for possession against the tenant that he or she has overcharged the subtenant (Case 10).

7) **Required for employee.** Case 8 is available in relation to a service tenant (see paras 1.131–1.140). The letting must have been in consequence of the employment, the tenant must have been in the landlord's employment, and the property must now be reasonably required by the landlord for the occupation of someone else in his or her full-time employment, or for someone with whom a contract of employment has been agreed, conditional upon the provision of accommodation.

   In one case, the landlord was one person, but the employer was a partnership, of which the landlord was but one member: Case 8 did not apply (*Grimond v Duncan*, 1949).

8) **Required by landlord.** Case 9 is applicable where the property is reasonably required by the landlord for occupation as a residence by him- or herself, any of his or her children over the age of 18, his or her parents or the parents of his or her spouse or civil partner.

   This case is not available if the landlord became the landlord by purchasing the property with the tenant already in occupation (*Newton v Biggs*, 1953). Purchase does not carry any technical meaning but covers what a reasonable person would consider a purchase (*Ammadio v Dalton*, 1991). It does not include a transfer 'in consideration of mutual love and affection' (*Mansukhani v Sharkey*, 1992).

   A landlord cannot use this case if his or her true intention is to gain vacant possession in order to sell, no matter how reasonably he or she wishes to do so. The landlofd must want the property for living in it (him- or herself or for one of the other permitted occupiers) for some reasonable period, definite or indefinite (*Rowe v Truelove*, 1976).

   Under this case, if the landlord is comprised of two or more joint owners, they must all wish to live there before it can apply (*McIntyre v Hardcastle*, 1948). It is not necessary, however, for any son or daughter for whom the property is required to be the child of both joint owners; it is sufficient if he or she is the child of any one of them (*Potsos v Theodotou*, 1991).

   This case is often referred to as 'greater hardship' because RA 1977 provides a particular defence to a claim under it, that – having regard to all the circumstances of the case, including the availability of other accommodation to either landlord or tenant – greater hardship would be caused by granting than by refusing the order (RA 1977 Sch 15 Pt 3). The burden of proving the defence lies on the tenant (*Sims v Wilson*, 1946), and he or she must, at the lowest, produce evidence of attempts to find other accommodation in order to discharge it (*Alexander v Mohamadzadeh*, 1985).

Where there are joint tenants, hardship to all of them must be taken into account. The court must consider hardship long term, so that if a tenant who is to be re-housed by a local authority (chapter 10) will suffer some short-term inconvenience, it is unlikely to amount to 'greater hardship' (*Manaton v Edwards*, 1985). The extent to which either landlord or tenant will be eligible for re-housing under HA 1996 Part 7 or H(W)A 2014 Part 2 (see chapter 10) may accordingly be decisive under this case.

9) **Illegal immigrants**. Case 10A is equivalent to Ground 7B in HA 1988 (see para 2.170(9)), but in contrast with Ground 7B, it is a discretionary rather than mandatory ground for possession. Given the limited circumstances in which new RA tenancies can be created (see para 1.271), it is unlikely to arise in practice.

10) **Suitable alternative accommodation**. The final 'ground for possession', in relation to which reasonableness must still, and additionally, be shown, does not appear in the schedule of discretionary grounds (RA 1977 Sch 15) but functions in the same way. It is available when the landlord can provide or obtain suitable alternative accommodation for the tenant (RA 1977 s98).

    This definition of this phrase (RA 1977 Sch 15 Pt 4) is in similar terms to HA 1988 (see para 2.157(1)). Accordingly, a certificate from the local authority that the tenant will be re-housed by it is conclusive that suitable alternative accommodation will be available (RA 1977 Sch 15 Pt 4 para 3). If the court seems likely to make an order on this ground, it will be in the tenant's interests to seek a ruling that the tenancy of the new premises should be Rent Act protected, rather than Housing Act assured tenancy (see para 1.271(3)).

Mandatory grounds

2.219 There are 10 mandatory grounds for possession, those which, if proved, leave the court no alternative but to make an order for possession. The grounds are as follows.

1) **Owner-occupiers**. Case 11 is available to absentee owner-occupiers, ie someone who before the letting had occupied the premises as a residence, although it may be noted that the case is available against a subtenant, ie the landlord may him- or herself be a tenant of another. The requirement of former residence can be fulfilled by previous intermittent residence, or something less

than permanent residence (*Naish v Curzon*, 1984). Such residence does not have to be as a home (see para 2.170(1); *Mistry v Isidore*, 1990).

This case is only available to a landlord who has served notice at the commencement of the tenancy, warning the tenant that the case might be used against him or her, although the court has power, if it thinks it just and equitable to do so, to waive this requirement.

The case is only available if the landlord has not let the property out since he or she last occupied the premises as a residence, otherwise than on terms that include service of one such notice at commencement, although again this requirement may be waived by the court. There are additional criteria which must also be fulfilled (below).

2) **Retirement homes**. Case 12 is available to a landlord who has bought property and intends to retire to it once he or she ceases regular employment.

Again, notice must have been served at the commencement of the tenancy, warning the tenant that the case might be used, and again the property must not have been let out to another since the landlord bought it without the service of such a warning notice, although, again, the court has power to waive the requirements, if just and equitable to do so.

The court should not exercise this power unless the tenant knew at the outset that he or she had only limited security, ie it should only be used where the failure was largely technical (*Bradshaw v Baldwin-Wiseman*, 1985; see also *White v Jones*, 1993). The fact that the occupiers signed licence agreements, which the landlord later conceded amounted to the grant of a tenancy, is not sufficient on its own to make it just and equitable to dispense with notice (*Ibie v Trubshaw*, 1990). There are additional criteria which must also be fulfilled (below).

3) **Member of armed forces**. Case 20 is available to a landlord who, both at date of purchase and of letting, is a member of the armed forces: the same requirements of notice, both to tenant and to anyone else to whom the property has been let other than the present tenant, are imposed, though may be waived by the court, again in limited circumstances. There are additional criteria which must also be fulfilled (below).

Applicability of additional criteria. Assuming that a landlord falls within one of the three cases set out above, he or she must go on to prove certain additional matters. There are seven, but they are not all equally available or applicable. Under Case 11, the landlord must be able to show the second, fourth, fifth, sixth or seventh; under Case 12, the landlord must be able to show the third, fourth, fifth, sixth or seventh; under Case 20, the landlord must be able to show the first, fourth, fifth, sixth or seventh. The additional matters are as follows:

(i) The property is required as a residence for the owner.
(ii) The property is required as a residence for either the owner or for any member of his or her family who lived with the owner when last he or she occupied the property as a residence.
(iii) The owner has retired from regular employment and requires the property as a residence.
(iv) The owner has died, and the dwelling is required as a residence for a member of his or her family who was living with him or her at the time of death.
(v) The owner has died, and the dwelling is required by his or her successor in title, either to live in, or to sell with vacant possession.
(vi) The property is subject to a mortgage granted before the tenancy was granted, and the lender requires vacant possession in order to sell the property under the power of sale, ie for default (by the landlord).
(vii) The dwelling is not reasonably suitable to the needs of the owner, having regard to his or her place of work, and he or she wants to sell it with vacant possession, and use the proceeds of sale to buy somewhere more suitable (RA 1977 Sch 15 Pt 5).

Requirement for residence. Where the landlord is in fact two people, ie joint owners, the necessary qualifications can be fulfilled by just one of them (*Tilling v Whiteman*, 1979), so that, eg both do not need to show they want to come and live in the house.

In each case, the landlord need only show that he or she requires the property, rather than 'reasonably requires' the property. 'Requires' means no more than *bona fide* wants, and genuinely intends, to occupy as a residence either at once or at any rate within a reasonable time (*Kennealy v Dunne*, 1976).

Once the wish to return to the property has been established, it does not matter if the landlord can be shown to want to sell it as and when he or she can (*Lipton v Whitworth*, 1993).

4) **Out of season holiday lettings.** Case 13 applied where the letting was for a fixed term of not more than eight months; the tenant must have been given notice at the commencement of the letting that the case could be used against him or her; and, within the 12 months preceding the commencement of the letting, the property was occupied under a holiday letting (see para 1.233(9)). This case dealt, in effect, with 'out-of-season' holiday lettings. In view of the time requirement, although in theory someone could have remained in occupation as a statutory tenant ever since, it is extremely unlikely that it will be applicable to any current tenants, and it has in practice expired.
5) **Off-season student lettings.** Case 14 concerned property normally used for student lettings (see para 1.277(5)). The letting in question had to be for a fixed term of not more than 12 months; the tenant had to have been given notice at the commencement of the letting that the case may be used against him or her; and, within the 12 months preceding the commencement of the letting, the property was occupied under a student letting. Again, for time reasons this case has for all practical purposes expired.
6) **Ministers of religion.** Case 15 is applicable to property occupied or formerly occupied by ministers of religion.
7) **Agricultural land.** Cases 16–18 are applicable to agricultural land.

Misrepresentation

2.220 If an order for possession is made under either Case 8 (see para 2.218(7) or Case 9 (see para 2.218(8)), and it is later made to appear to the court that the landlord obtained the order by misrepresenting circumstances to the court or by concealing some material fact, the court has power to order the landlord to pay damages to the tenant (RA 1977 s102). A mere change of mind is not the same as a misrepresentation, however, and will not be enough.

Orders for possession

2.221 In the case of discretionary grounds, the court's powers to postpone, suspend or vary an order are the same as under HA 1985 and HA 1988 (see paras 2.121–2.127; RA 1977 s100); likewise, the court's powers are as limited as under those two Acts where no security attaches or a mandatory ground is available (see para 2.120; HA 1980 s89).

Warrant for possession

2.222 The position governing warrants is the same as for secure tenants (see paras 2.133–2.135).

Protected shorthold tenants

2.223 **Mandatory ground for possession.** Case 19 is a mandatory ground for possession available against a protected shorthold tenant (see para 1.286) or former protected shorthold tenant (see para 1.296) so long as the original shorthold tenant remains the tenant of the premises (HA 1980 s54(3)). The landlord must show not only that the preliminary conditions were fulfilled (see para 1.295), save in so far as he or she hopes to rely on the court's discretion (see para 1.295(3)), but also that since the end of the original shorthold tenancy, ie the termination of the original fixed period (see para 1.295(1)), there has been no further grant of a tenancy of the premises to anyone other than the original shorthold tenancy.

2.224 **Warning notices.** In addition, the landlord must comply with the 'warning' notice provisions (*Ridehalgh v Horsefield*, 1992). The purpose of the warning notice provisions is to ensure that the tenant is not constantly subject to the likelihood of proceedings. Accordingly, before applying for possession under Case 19, the landlord must serve the appropriate notice. These notice provisions do not, however, need to be fulfilled once the tenancy has become statutory (see para 1.269) if grounds for possession (see paras 2.218–2.219) other than case 19 (see para 2.223) are used instead. The landlord can only commence proceedings within three months after the expiry of the notice (RA 1977 Sch 15 Case 19(b)). The notice must be in writing and must state that proceedings may be brought under Case 19 after it expires. The notice must give a minimum of three months but can be for longer. It may be served during the last three months of the fixed term, or else during the same three months of any succeeding year, and no earlier than three months after the expiry of the last notice.

2.225 **Warning provisions exemplified.** These provisions are difficult to untangle. They are best approached by way of illustration. A fixed term was granted on 1 April 1988 to expire on 31 March 1990. A warning notice may be served at any time between the beginning of January and the end of March during 1990 or any subsequent year in which the ground remains available to the landlord. It must give the tenant at least three months: if served on January 1, therefore, proceedings could commence on 1 April; if not served until 1 March, however, they could not commence before 1 June. If the landlord gave longer than three months, the proceedings could not be commenced before the time allowed expires.

2.226 **Commencement of proceedings.** Once the notice expires, the landlord must bring proceedings within three months, or else the notice lapses. The landlord cannot serve a further notice during these three months. Thus, if the notice was for three months, and was served on 1 January, proceedings must be commenced between 1 April and 30 June, and during that time no further notice can be served. Accordingly, 1 July would be the earliest date when a new notice could be served, but as the notice can only be served during the January–March 'season', the landlord cannot serve a further notice until 1 January next. If, however, the landlord gives nine months, from 1 January, he or she can commence proceedings at any time between 1 October and 30 December. If the landlord fails to do so, he or she can serve a new notice immediately after 30 December, as: (a) he or she will be back in the notice season and (b) three months will have passed since the notice lapsed.

2.227 **Eviction season.** It follows that while it is true that a tenant cannot be subject at any given moment to proceedings for possession under Case 19, the landlord has a generous discretion to select his or her eviction (as opposed to notice) season, and may in practice, by careful choice of the length of notice, keep the tenant in the position where proceedings are always looming, or to be anticipated.

Restricted contracts

2.228 **Lettings pre- and post-28 November 1980.** The security provisions governing restricted contracts are completely different in relation to contracts starting before 28 November 1980 (the date when the relevant parts of HA 1980 came into force), and in relation to contracts starting on or after that date.

2.229 **Pre-1980 Act security.** Even if rent is not the real issue, security of tenure is obtained by application to the First-tier Tribunal (in England) or a rent assessment committee (in Wales) for consideration of the rent, plus security. The tribunal's jurisdiction is initiated by application for a rent registration. An occupier can only apply for security of tenure (together with the rent to be considered) if a notice bringing the right of occupation to an end has been given and has not yet expired. This means that a fixed-term agreement cannot be referred to the tribunal or committee for security of tenure.

2.230 **Suspension and deferral of notice to quit.** The existence of a pre-1980 restricted contract is now so unlikely that the provisions are set out here only in outline. Where the landlord has served a valid notice to quit, and the rent has been referred to the tribunal, the notice is automatically suspended (RA 1977 s104). If a notice has been served before application, then the tribunal or committee will not only decide what rent is payable under the letting, but also when the notice should take effect (RA 1977 s104). The tribunal or committee can defer the notice for up to six months at a time. Before the six months run out, there is nothing to stop an occupier applying for more time. The tribunal or committee may order no security at all, or a period shorter than six months. Deferral is automatic once the rent has been registered (RA 1977 s103). The landlord is entitled to apply during the period of deferral for a reduction in security, which will be granted if there has been misconduct, eg non-compliance with the contract, by the tenant (RA 1977 s106).

2.231 **Post-1980 Act security.** The position relating to these contracts is very different. The jurisdiction of what was then the Rent Tribunal over security was entirely abolished (RA 1977 s102A). In its place, the county court has a more limited power; to allow suspension of an order for possession to a maximum of three months from the date of its order (RA 1977 s106A). If the court grants less than three months initially, it can on a later application grant further suspension, to a maximum of three months from the date of the original order. These powers may be exercised not only for the benefit of the tenant or licensee, but also for the benefit of his or her spouse or ex-spouse (RA 1977 s106A(5), (6)). The court's power may be exercised on terms or conditions, which must include terms as to payment of rent and of any arrears, unless the court considers that to do this would cause exceptional hardship or would otherwise be unreasonable. The power is not confined to a former periodic restricted contract, but extends to one that was fixed-term.

Agricultural and forestry workers

2.232 As noted in chapter 1 (see paras 1.304–1.307), agricultural and forestry workers will, subject to appropriate conditions, enjoy either assured protection under HA 1988 or RA security, under Rent (Agriculture) Act 1976; for reasons of space, it is not possible to describe these provisions here. Where an agricultural tenant (or licensee other than under an excluded licence) has occupied premises not within either of these provisions has occupied accommodation under the terms of his or her employment, he or she will enjoy a measure of protection against eviction (PEA 1977 s4(1), (2A)). The provisions apply to the tenant or, if he or she has died, his or her surviving spouse or civil partner (or, if none, a member of his or her family living with him or her at the time of his or her death) (PEA 1977 s4(2)). The provisions allow a court to suspend execution of a possession order on such terms and conditions, including conditions as to the payment by the occupier of arrears of rent, mesne profits and otherwise as the court thinks reasonable (PEA 1977 s4(3)), and in some circumstances require the court to do so (PEA 1977 s4(4)).

Illegal immigrants

2.233 The Immigration Act (IA) 2016 amended IA 2014 to include provisions designed to prevent landlords from letting property to illegal immigrants. A person who does not have leave to enter or remain in the United Kingdom is disqualified from having the 'right to rent' residential premises (IA 2014 s21). Leave to enter or remain in the country may also be made conditional on the person not having the right to rent. An exception is made for nationals of the EEA and Switzerland so that, eg a national of an EEA state does not lose the right to rent on losing his or her job. The provisions apply to 'residential tenancy agreements', defined to include licences (IA 2014 s20), but do not apply to a tenancy or licence granted before 1 December 2016 (IA 2014 s35).

2.234 A landlord under a residential tenancy agreement commits a criminal offence if *any* adult in the dwelling (not just the person named in the agreement) who is disqualified from the right to rent residential premises occupies the property, if the landlord knows, or has reasonable cause to believe, that the occupier does not have the right to rent (IA 2014 s33A(1)–(3)). It is a defence for the landlord to show that he or she has taken reasonable steps to terminate the agreement within a reasonable time of first discovering that the occupier was, or might be, disqualified from renting accommodation (IA 2014 s33A(6)). The offence is punishable in the Crown Court by a maximum of five years' imprisonment and an unlimited fine, or in the magistrates' court by a maximum of one year's imprisonment and an unlimited fine (IA 2014 s33C).

2.235 To enable the landlord to obtain possession quickly, if the secretary of state notifies the landlord that *all* the occupiers are disqualified from the right to rent, any provision giving the tenant or licensee security of tenure is disapplied. The landlord can simply serve a notice in the prescribed form (Immigration (Residential Accommodation) (Termination of Residential Tenancy Agreements) (Guidance etc) Regulations 2016 SI No 1060, giving the 28 days' notice (IA 2014 s33D). Once the notice has expired, it can be enforced as if it was a High Court order, ie there is no need for the landlord to take possession proceedings.

2.236 If any of the occupiers are *not* disqualified from the right to rent, a ground for possession will be available against an assured tenant under HA 1988 (see para 2.170(9)) or a protected tenant under RA 1977 (see para 2.218(9)).

Eviction

2.237 Those who are not within any of the classes of security considered above occupy without any statutory security, although – if they have any right of occupation – be it tenancy (including long leases) or licence – it will always be necessary to determine that right before the occupier can be evicted. The rules relating to determination or expiry of a tenancy or licence have been described above (see paras 2.20–2.71). Notices to quit or to terminate a licence must normally be in writing, contain prescribed information and be of a minimum period of four weeks, and are also subject to the other common law rules described: if the tenancy commenced on or after 15 January 1989, when HA 1988 Part 1, came into force, however, the requirement for a minimum period and for writing, and for prescribed information, has been waived for 'excluded tenants' and 'excluded licencees' (see paras 1.308–1.313), so that only compliance with common law is required.

2.238 Further, there are statutory provisions which mean that the landlord – or person seeking possession – may have to take proceedings for an order for possession before the occupier can be evicted (absent which, the person carrying out the eviction will commit the offence of unlawful eviction: paras 5.5–5.12).

2.239 In addition, as foreshadowed in chapter 1 (see paras 1.319–1.328), either the ECHR and/or the principles of domestic public law and/or EqA 2010 may be prayed in aid, either to vitiate a decision to evict or perhaps even to procure a ruling that no eviction is possible, at any rate in current circumstances or for a period of time. As these provisions are additional to the statutory constraints on eviction, they will be considered at the end of this section.

Tenants

2.240 All former tenants are entitled to remain in occupation until such time as a court order is obtained against them (PEA 1977 s3), save for those who qualify as 'excluded tenants' (see paras 1.308–1.309). Tenants of local and other public authorities, and of PRPs and RSLs, may, however, be assisted by HRA 1998 and/or domestic public law (see paras 2.50–2.259). The limited powers of the court in relation to the order for possession and warrant are as described in relation to flexible tenants (see para 2.143), ie two weeks or a maximum of six in cases of exceptional hardship (HA 1980 s89).

Licensees

2.241 All former licensees whose licences began after the commencement of HA 1980 s69 (28 November 1980) other than those with 'excluded licences' (see paras 1.310–1.313) are also protected by PEA 1977 s3. This includes former service occupiers (see paras 1.131–1.140) provided that they were granted at least some exclusive occupation of their accommodation under the employment arrangement (PEA 1977 s8).

2.242 **Use of speedy procedures.** Proceedings may be brought against any former licensee under the speedy procedures provided by CPR 55 (see para 2.71).

Trespassers

2.243 Unless they have been in occupation for long enough to claim a right by adverse possession (see paras 1.146–1.154), trespassers have no rights of occupation. Court proceedings can be taken against them at any time, without any warning, and special, speedy procedures can, and usually will, be used: CPR 55. They do, however, enjoy some protection against violent eviction, which is considered (along with other forms of unlawful eviction) in chapter 5.

2.244 **Proceedings for possession.** These procedures do not even require the landlord to identify the occupiers. A landlord can issue proceedings against a named person on his or her own, or against persons unknown, or against both a named person and persons unknown. A claim is issued, stating the landlord's interest in the property, that the property in question has been occupied without his or her consent and, if the claim is also against persons unknown, that the landlord does not know the names of some or all of the people on the property.

2.245 **Orders for possession.** The claim is served by personal service, save in the case of persons unknown, where it can be served by fixing the summons to the door of the premises. Once it has been served, there need only be a delay of five days, in the case of residential premises (otherwise two), before a court hearing.

2.246 If the court finds that the occupiers are, indeed, trespassers, then it is obliged to make an immediate order for possession (*McPhail v Persons Unknown*, 1973; *Boyland & Son Limited v Rand*, 2006) not even subject to the normal 14-day delay to which, for example, a final order against a secure, or indeed any other tenant, will normally be subject (see para 2.120). Although it has been suggested (*Kay v Lambeth LBC*, 2006) that this rule may have to be relaxed in light of a trespasser's rights under Article 8 (see para 2.250), the Supreme Court has yet to decide the issue.

2.247 **Eviction.** Landlords will still normally need to effect eviction by using court bailiffs, which may provide some slight delay of, perhaps, a week or 10 days. When bailiffs attend on an eviction, they must turn out of the premises all those people found there, whether or not they were parties to the proceedings, or even if they moved into the premises between the date of the court order and the actual eviction, unless an occupier can claim to have some separate right of occupation, eg a tenant who is on the premises (*R v Wandsworth County Court ex p Wandsworth LBC*, 1975).

2.248 **Interim possession.** The interim possession order provides an even quicker remedy, allowing for a hearing only three days from the application to court. An application for an interim possession order may only be made against persons who have entered the premises without the applicant's consent (CPR 55.21). An application for such an order must be made on the prescribed form, and the applicant must give specific undertakings, in particular as to damages and putting the defendant back into possession if it turns out the interim possession order was wrongly granted. The court hearing date may be set at any time after three days from the making of the application. For the hearing to go ahead, there must be evidence that the order has been served on the defendant.

2.249 **Order and breach.** An interim possession order requires the defendant to vacate the premises within 24 hours. The order must also fix a return date (for a full hearing) not less than seven days after the date on which the interim order was made, and the order expires on this return date. Eviction takes place through the police, rather than the court bailiffs. Failure to leave is a criminal offence, as is returning to the premises to which the order applies within 12 months, or knowingly or recklessly giving false information in order to obtain or resist such an order: Criminal Justice and Public Order Act 1994 ss76, 75.

Human Rights Act 1998

2.250 Even after a notice to quit has expired, a property can remain a 'home' for the purposes of Article 8 ECHR (see paras 1.319–1.320); the same is true of any other occupation – whether a former licensee or a trespasser, if there is sufficient occupation as a home, he or she may be able to argue that his or her eviction would be disproportionate under Article 8 (see para 1.319). Only public landlords – whether public (including local) authorities or PRPs and RSLs – and not private landlords are within it (*McDonald v McDonald*, 2014; paras 1.321–1.322).

2.251 In *Manchester City Council v Pinnock*, 2010, and *Hounslow LBC v Powell*, 2011, the Supreme Court made a number of points about defences to claims for possession based on proportionality.

1) **The occupier must raise the issue.** The court need only consider whether a possession order is proportionate if the question is raised by the occupier. If so, the court should initially consider it summarily and, if satisfied that the point would not succeed, should dismiss the defence. The issue should only be further entertained only if the court is satisfied that it is seriously arguable that consideration of Article 8 could affect the order that it might make.
2) **High threshold**. The threshold for raising an arguable case on proportionality is a high one which will succeed in only a small proportion of cases. Public landlords hold their housing stock for the benefit of the whole community and are best placed to decide how it should be used. In the great majority of cases, the court should proceed on the basis that the authority has sound reasons for seeking possession
3) **Justification**. Eviction can be justified on the basis that it both vindicates landlords' rights of ownership and enables them to comply with their duties in relation to allocation and management of their housing stock, eg fair allocation of housing, refurbishment of sub-standard accommodation, moving people who are in accommodation that exceeds their needs and moving vulnerable people into sheltered or warden-assisted housing;.
4) **Evidence**. In the overwhelming majority of cases, there is no need for an authority to explain and justify its reasons for seeking

possession. It is entitled to possession under the relevant domestic legal framework and is to be assumed to be acting in accordance with its housing management duties. If they choose to do so, landlords can inform the court of any particularly strong or unusual reasons that they may have for claiming possession. Such reasons must be pleaded and may require evidence.

2.252 In *Corby BC v Scott; West Kent Housing Association v Haycraft*, 2012, two defences based on proportionality failed to reach the requisite, high threshold. In *Corby*, the tenant relied on the fact that she had cleared her arrears before the hearing and had suffered a serious assault in the previous year. The court held that the assault was irrelevant because she had not suffered any injury which made it particularly harmful for her to be evicted. Paying off the arrears before the hearing could only assist a tenant in an extraordinary case. In *Haycraft*, the tenant's medical condition was irrelevant because there was nothing to suggest that it would worsen if he were homeless. The fact that he had recently married and had a child so that he would probably be re-housed by the local authority if evicted (see chapter 10) did not mean that an order should not be made.

2.253 Where the occupier lived with the tenant before the tenant died but is not entitled to succeed to the tenancy (see paras 1.203 and 1.240), it will usually be proportionate to make a possession order (*Birmingham City Council v Lloyd*, 2012), even if the defendant lived with the tenant for many years (*Holley v Hillingdon LBC*, 2016).

2.254 Where anti-social behaviour is committed at the defendant's home, it will usually be proportionate to make an order even if the defendant is not directly involved (*Fareham BC v Miller*, 2013), athough if the anti-social behaviour ceased a long time before the possession hearing it may not be proportionate to evict the defendant (*Southend on Sea BC v Armour*, 2014).

2.255 If proportionality was considered by the court when it made the possession order, or if the occupier failed to raise the issue at the hearing, it will usually be an abuse of process for the occupier to challenge the subsequent decision to enforce the possession order on the basis that eviction would be disproportionate, unless there has been a fundamental change in the occupier's circumstances (*R (JL) v Secretary of State for Defence*, 2013; *Lawal v Circle 33 Housing Trust*, 2014).

Domestic public law

2.256 There is also the possibility of impeaching a decision of a public authority (including a PRP or RSL if in relation to a function within the HRA 1998 – para 1.307) to commence or to pursue possession proceedings – even against a trespasser – under the principles of domestic public law (see paras 8.23–8.28), whether by seeking judicial review in the High Court in order to seek an order quashing the decision and/or preventing the authority acting on it and/or ordering it to take a new decision, or by defending the proceedings for possession on the basis that they are unlawful.

2.257 If the occupier raises the defence in the county court, it is for him or her to show that the authority has not complied with the requirements of domestic public law and details of the allegations must be given; a bald statement by the occupier that he or she 'has done nothing wrong' is not sufficient to raise a defence (*Cannock Chase DC v Kelly*, 1978). Where a real issue is raised about the decision to evict, the authority needs to provide a clear explanation about how it reached its decision (*McGlynn v Welwyn Hatfield DC*, 2009). Where the initial decision to evict was flawed, however, then provided that mistake is corrected by the time of the possession hearing, the occupier will have no public law defence (*Central Bedfordshire Council v Taylor*, 2009). Such defences have succeeded where authorities have failed to follow their own policies, as in *Croydon LBC v Barber*, 2010, where the authority failed to follow its procedure for dealing with a tenant with mental health problems and in *Leicester City Council v Shearer*, 2013, where the authority did not consider its policy on granting a tenancy to the wife of a deceased tenant who was not entitled to succeed to the tenancy (see para 1.203).

Equality Act 2010

2.258 As already noted (see para 2.98(2)), under EqA 2010, in evicting a tenant a landlord must not discriminate on the ground of disability (EqA 2010 s35), which can include mental illness. If the landlord knows of the tenant's disability, evicting him or her because of behaviour which is a consequence of his or her mental illness is potentially discriminatory, although the landlord may be able to justify bringing possession proceedings (EqA 2010 s15).

2.259 If the defendant raises a defence based on disability discrimination, it will rarely be appropriate to order possession summarily and the court can only do so if the landlord can establish that: the defendant has no real prospect of establishing that he or she has a disability; or, it is clear that possession is not being sought because of something arising in consequence of a disability; or, ordering possession plainly represents a proportionate means of achieving a legitimate aim, eg protecting the defendant's neighbours (*Akerman-Livingstone v Aster Communities Ltd*, 2015). In deciding whether an order is justified, the court should consider what other steps could have been taken by the landlord to address the tenant's behaviour, such as obtaining support from social services (*Stephenson v Birmingham City Council*, 2016).

CHAPTER 3

Rent and other charges

continued

Introduction

3.1 Rents and other charges are, in the first instance, governed by the letting arrangement, be it long leasehold, tenancy (fixed-term or periodic) or licence: one of the principal benefits of a fixed-term tenancy is the limit on rent during its term, or pending exercise of a rent review clause. (Such a rent review is outside the scope of this book, as it is uncommon in housing). It has also been noted (see para 1.85) that weekly tenants are entitled to a rent book or similar document, the non-provision of which is a criminal offence: this will identify the initial rent. In most housing cases, the provisions of the tenancy or other arrangement are relatively straightforward, and do not call for additional comment. This chapter is, rather, concerned with the statutory provisions which limit rents and other charges, without which security of tenure would of course be valueless. The provisions governing rents are primarily to be found in the Housing Act (HA) 1985, HA 1988, the Rent Act (RA) 1977 and the Welfare Reform and Work Act (WRWA) 2016. The Landlord and Tenant Act (LTA) 1985 contains the main provisions governing service charges. The chapter also deals with payment for utilities, charges made by lettings agents, premiums and deposits.

Rents

Local authority rents

3.2 Local authority tenants (and licensees) may be secure, or not (see paras 1.160–1.180). Although the mechanism for increasing rent is different depending on whether or not the tenant is secure, the underlying principles are the same, and the effect is the same.

3.3 **Reasonable rents.** Local authorities are bound to charge reasonable rents and to review their rent levels from time to time; in setting their rent levels, they must have regard to the principle that rents of property of one class or description should bear broadly the same proportion to private sector rents as the rents of houses of any other class or description (HA 1985 s24), eg houses with more rooms or those with gardens generate higher private sector rents than those with fewer rooms or no gardens, so that local authority rents should – broadly – likewise charge more.

3.4 **Ring-fencing.** Local authorities have a long history of discretion in relation to their decisions as to what comprises a 'reasonable' rent.

The provisions of the Local Government and Housing Act (LGHA) 1989, however, severely limited the theoretical freedom which local authorities enjoyed over rent levels, by requiring that an authority's Housing Revenue Account be balanced (s76), and limiting what can be credited and debited to it so as, above all, to exclude any contribution from an authority's general fund, ie by the body of local taxpayers generally, but also to prevent rents subsidising local taxes, each of which was believed to have been used politically: this is the policy known as 'ring-fencing of the account' (see s75 and Sch 4).

3.5 **Social and affordable rents**. Nonetheless, rents of most local authority housing, called 'social rents,' are significantly below market rent because they are set in accordance with guidance from the secretary of state or the Welsh Ministers: *Guidance on Rents for Social Housing*, DCLG (May 2014) and *Policy for social housing rents*, Welsh Government (December 2013). In England, authorities are permitted to charge higher than social rents, called 'affordable rents', which are up to 80 per cent of market rent, but only for new properties delivered as a result of an agreement with the Homes and Communities Agency (HCA).

3.6 **Welfare Reform and Work Act 2016**. In England, the WRWA 2016 ss23–27 require local authorities to decrease rents year-on-year for certain tenants. Detailed provision is made in the Social Housing Rents (Exceptions and Miscellaneous Provisions) Regulations 2016 SI No 390. The requirement is that during the financial years beginning April 2016, 2017, 2018 and 2019, the amount of rent payable must be at least one per cent less than the rent payable in the preceding 12 months. In the case of tenancies let under affordable rents (see para 3.5), it is the whole of the rent, including any service charges, which must be reduced; for a tenancy let on a social rent (see para 3.5), any service charge is disregarded and can even be increased, and only the remaining 'net rent' is to be decreased. A number of types of tenancy are excluded from these provisions, including certain types of supported housing and low cost home ownership accommodation (see para 8.11).

3.7 **Secure tenants**. The rent under a fixed-term secure tenancy, including a flexible tenancy (see paras 1.181–1.189) and a fixed-term licence, and, once the relevant part of the Housing and Planning Act (HPA) 2016 is in force, under a new-style secure tenancy (see paras 1.190–1.191), can only be increased (if at all) in accordance with its own terms, eg pursuant to a rent review clause in the tenancy agreement. Unless there is provision in the agreement allowing the rent to be increased (HA 1985 s102(1)(b)), the rent can only be increased once a periodic tenancy following the fixed term has arisen (see para 2.85), at which point it may be increased in the same way as the rent for any other periodic secure tenancy. Rent cannot be increased on account of tenants' (lawful) improvements (see paras 4.152–4.154) (HA 1985 s101).

3.8 The authority may increase the rent of a secure tenant by notice of increase, served at least four weeks or one period of the tenancy (whichever is the longer, eg a monthly tenancy requires a full month) – or licence – before it is due to take effect (HA 1985 s103); if the tenant gives a valid notice to quit before the date on which it is to take effect, it does not do so unless the tenant or licensee, with the written agreement of the landlord, withdraws his or her notice to quit before that date (HA 1985 s103(6)). It may not be open to an occupier to do so, as – on re-application for housing – he or she may be susceptible to a finding that he or she has become homeless intentionally, subject to consideration of the affordability of the new rent (see para 10.52). For the purpose of these increase provisions, rent includes rent itself, and payments in respect of the rent, or of payments in respect of services or facilities provided by the landlord or of payments in respect of rates (HA 1985 s103(3)).

3.9 **Non-secure occupiers.** Where a periodic tenancy (nb *not* a licence) is non-secure, notice may be given at least four weeks beforehand, advising the tenant of his or her right to terminate the tenancy and of the steps to be taken to do so (HA 1985 s25), a similar (but in the detail not quite identical) provision to section 103 (see para 3.8). Again, a tenant needs to consider the risk of a finding of intentional homelessness before doing so. Introductory tenants (see paras 1.210–1.219) are expressly brought within HA 1985 ss102 and 103 (HA 1985 s111A), which therefore includes licensees qualifying as such (see para 1.212), although demoted (see paras 1.252–1.261) and family intervention (see paras 1.261–1.266) tenants are not, so that the authority needs to rely on section 25. It would seem that to effect an increase for a non-secure licensee, the authority would have to determine the licence and offer a new one but in practice this can occur by individual agreement, given the lack of security available to the licensee.

3.10 **Challenging local authority rents.** There has been a number of attempts to challenge the amount of local authority rent levels in the courts (both by those who think they are too high, and by those who think they are too low), most of which have failed, although in theory the principles of public law (see paras 8.23–8.28) are applicable. It could also in theory be argued that a rent increase which would in practice force someone to leave would be challengeable under Article 8 of the European Convention on Human Rights (ECHR), but this is a remote prospect and would be likely to require such a gross increase that it would be challengeable in domestic public law in any event.

Housing association rents

3.11 **Pre-15 January 1989 tenancies.** Tenancies which began before the commencement (15 January 1989) of HA 1988 Part 1 (see para 1.161), granted by housing associations (see para 8.4), housing trusts (see para 8.5) and the Housing Corporation (in the terminology of the time – now PRPs, RSLs and the HCA – para 1.162), although excluded from Rent Act protection by sections 15 and 16 of RA 1977 (see para 1.270), were and are subject to the same 'fair rent' system as those private sector tenants (RA 1977 Pt 6). The same is true of those tenancies from such landlords which, although granted after that date will, for one of the reasons set out in para 1.167, not become Housing Act assured tenancies but remain within all or part of an earlier regime of protection.

3.12 **Secure or non-secure.** The fair rent system is applicable whether the tenant in question is secure or not (see paras 1.160–1.180).

3.13 **Increase of rents.** Where the fair rent system is applicable, a rent registered under the fair rent system will form the rent limit for such a tenancy (see para 3.53; RA 1977 s88). Where the tenancy is secure, HA 1985 s103 will be available with which to effect an increase (see para 3.8); where it is not, there is a similar power in RA 1977 s93.

3.14 **Register.** Although there is a separate part of the register for housing associations and other such bodies (RA 1977 s87), the same general principles will apply (*Palmer v Peabody Trust*, 1974) on the determination of their fair rents as other Rent Act protected and statutory tenants (see paras 3.53–3.61). It is not necessary to consider the operation of the fair rent system in relation to these tenancies discretely as the system is largely the same as that to be considered in relation to the Rent Act (see paras 3.53–3.76), and variations in detail are relatively minor.

3.15 **Pre-15 January 1989, non-secure licensees.** There is no rent control applicable.

3.16 **Post-14 January 1989 tenancies.** Tenancies granted by PRPs (England – para 1.162) and RSLs (Wales – para 1.163) after commencement of HA 1988 will normally be assured tenancies (see paras

1.220–1.245) or assured shorthold tenancies (see paras 1.246–1.251). They are in principle subject to the same statutory rent provisions as are applicable to other, private sector assured tenants (see paras 3.20–3.41) and assured shorthold tenants (see paras 3.42–3.48). As a matter of government policy, however, they will charge below market rents: in England, these are in accordance with guidance from the HCA (*Rent Standard Guidance,* April 2015) and – as with local authorities in England (see para 3.5) – are usually either social or affordable rents. The guidance that applies to local authorities in Wales (see para 3.5) also applies to RSLs.

3.17 In England, the WRWA 2016 (see para 3.6) applies, requiring PRP rents to decrease year-on-year for certain tenants in the same way as for local authorities. The HCA (with the consent of the secretary of state) may, however, direct that it should not apply, or only apply for a period or subject to a lesser amount, if it considers that compliance would jeopardise the financial viability of the PRP: WRWA 2016 s25).

3.18 **Non-assured tenants and licensees**. There is no statutory rent control over the rents of those tenants who are not assured (see para 1.233) or licensees (see para 1.224), nor are there any statutory provisions governing how their rents may be increased.

3.19 **Challenging PRP/RSL rents**. PRPs and RSLs may be public authorities whose decisions in the course of managing their social housing are subject both to the ECHR (see paras 1.321–1.322) and, in the same circumstances, to the principles of domestic public law (see paras 1.323–1.327) (*R (Weaver) v London & Quadrant Housing Trust,* 2009). In theory, this could affect their rent increases but it is highly unlikely when there are statutory provisions governing most of them, they are normally designedly low rents (see para 3.15), and in any event the courts would intervene only in an extreme case.

Assured tenancies

3.20 **Starting-point**. The starting-point of such rent control as is applicable to assured tenancies (see paras 1.220–1.245) is that what has been agreed is payable; there is no concept analogous to 'registered rents' under RA 1977 (see para 3.53), by which an existing registration might override the rent agreed at the commencement of the tenancy. Thereinafter, the position must be considered discretely in relation to fixed-term (see para 1.18) and periodic (see para 1.18) tenancies.

Fixed-term tenancy

3.21 In the case of a fixed-term assured tenancy, there is no means for varying the rent, save so far as the agreement itself provides, until such time as the agreement becomes a statutory periodic tenancy (see para 2.161).

Statutory periodic tenancy

3.22 Under a statutory periodic tenancy, the terms are *prima facie* the same as under the fixed term, and its periods the same as those for which rent was paid under the fixed term (HA 1988 s5; *Church Commissioners v Meya*, 2006). Within one year of the termination of the fixed term, however, either landlord or tenant may serve notice on the other, in prescribed form, proposing different terms and, if considered appropriate, a variation of rent to reflect the variation of terms (HA 1988 s6). The prescribed form is either, in England, Assured Tenancies and Agricultural Occupancies (Forms) (England) Regulations 2015 SI No 620, form 1, or, in Wales, Assured Tenancies and Agricultural Occupancies (Forms) Regulations 1997 SI No 194, form 1.

Tribunal/committee

3.23 Once such a notice has been served, the landlord or the tenant on whom it has been served has three months within which to refer it to the First-tier Tribunal (in England) or the rent assessment committee (in Wales) (HA 1988 s6). If the notice is not referred, then the proposed terms, and rent, become the terms (and rent) of the statutory periodic tenancy (HA 1988 s6(3)).

3.24 If there is a reference, the Tribunal or committee has to consider the proposed terms, and determine whether they, or some other terms (dealing with the same subject-matter as the terms proposed), might reasonably be expected to be found in an assured periodic tenancy of such a property, on the basis of the following two assumptions: that the tenancy began on the coming to the end of the former fixed term; and, that the tenancy was granted by a willing landlord on the terms (other than those now under review) that apply to that tenancy (HA 1988 s6(4)). The committee must also disregard the fact that there is a sitting tenant (HA 1988 s6(6)).

3.25 Even if the notice proposing the new terms did not include a proposal for the variation of rent to reflect them, the Tribunal or committee is entitled to adjust the rent to take account of adjustment of the terms (HA 1988 s6(5)). Unless the landlord and tenant agree otherwise, the Tribunal or committee decides from when the new terms and rent apply, save that in the case of the rent, it cannot specify a date which is earlier than any date proposed in the original notice (HA 1988 s6(7)).

3.26 The tribunal or committee is not bound to continue with the process if the landlord and the tenant give notice in writing that they do not wish it to do so; nor need it continue if the tenancy ends before it reaches its determination (HA 1988 s6(8)).

No notice

3.27 If no variation of terms (and rent) is proposed within the one-year time limit (see para 3.22), then rents are dealt with in the same way as other periodic tenancies.

Periodic tenancy

3.28 In the case of a periodic assured tenancy, and in the case of a statutory periodic tenancy to which the foregoing provisions (see paras 3.22–3.27) do not apply, either because no variation of terms is proposed or because the one-year time limit from the previous fixed term has expired, a variation of rent procedure applies, albeit that it can only be initiated by a landlord seeking an increase (HA 1988 s13), ie if the tenant considers the existing rent too high, there is nothing he or she can do (reflecting the 'agreement' basis that is the starting-point of assured tenancy rents – para 3.20).

3.29 This procedure is not available, however, if the periodic tenancy (not being a statutory periodic tenancy following a fixed term) contains its own provisions for determining increases (HA 1988 s13(1)). Such terms sometimes fix the increase by reference to an index-linked formula but this is not necessary and the provision can merely require that the rent be determined by the landlord with reference to, eg a market rent for the property (*Contour Homes Ltd v Rowen*, 2007). In such a case, the Tribunal or Committee will not be able to intervene. Statutory periodic tenancies following a fixed term are within the statutory procedure even if they did have their own provision for determining increases (*London District Properties Management Ltd v Goolamy*, 2009).

Statutory process for increase of rent

3.30 To obtain an increase by the statutory process, the landlord must serve notice on the tenant, in the prescribed form, proposing a new rent to take effect at the beginning of a period of the tenancy. The period must itself commence no earlier than: a minimum period (see para 3.31) after service of the notice; and – other than in the case of a statutory period tenancy – the date that falls 52 weeks after the date on which the tenancy began; and if there has been a previous increase under the statutory process, the appropriate date (see para 3.32) (HA 1988 s13(2)). The prescribed form is either, in England, Assured Tenancies and Agricultural Occupancies (Forms) (England) Regulations 2015 SI No 620, form 4, or, in Wales, Assured Tenancies and Agricultural Occupancies (Forms) Regulations 1997 SI No 194, form 4D.

3.31 The 'minimum period' is six months in the case of a yearly tenancy; one month in the case of a tenancy the periods of which are less than a month, eg weekly or four-weekly; or in any other case, eg quarterly tenancy or six monthly tenancy, one period of the tenancy (HA 1988 s13(3)).

Appropriate date

3.32 The appropriate date is either: 52 weeks after the date on which the last increase took effect; or 53 weeks after that date if the 53rd week after the date of the last increase began more than six days before the first increase after February 1993. The point of this cumbersome and complicated rule is to allow landlords to increase rents on the same day in each year, eg the first Monday in April, rectifying a problem (but without retrospective effect) which had been identified in HA 1988 as enacted, which provided that a full year had to pass between increases. This produced difficulties for landlords with weekly periodic tenants who increase rents on the first rent day at the beginning of a particular month each year – usually, April, or or immediately after the beginning of a new financial year.

Effect of notice

3.33 The new rent will take effect unless before the beginning of the (minimum) period specified, the tenant refers the notice to the First-tier Tribunal (England) or the rent assessment committee (Wales), by application in the prescribed form, or else the landlord and the tenant agree a different rent (HA 1988 s13(4)). The prescribed form is, in England, Assured Tenancies and Agricultural Occupancies (Forms) (England) Regulations 2015 SI No 620, form 6, or, in Wales, Assured Tenancies and Agricultural Occupancies (Forms) Regulations 1997 SI No 194, form 5.

Decision

3.34 If the rent is referred to the tribunal or committee, it has to decide: what rent the property concerned might reasonably be expected to obtain on the open market, by a willing landlord letting an assured tenancy of the same periods, beginning at the period specified in the notice, the terms (other than rent) of which are the same and in respect of which the same notices (if any) under Sch 2 Grounds 1–5 (mandatory grounds for possession; para 2.170) have been served (HA 1988 s14(1)). The fact that there is a sitting tenant must be disregarded (HA 1988 s14(2)(a)).

Improvements

3.35 The tribunal or committee must also disregard: any increase attributable to a 'relevant improvement' by a person who – at the time it was carried out – was the tenant (not necessarily the current tenant); and, any reduction in value attributable to the tenant's failure to comply with the terms of his or her tenancy (the tenant's failure only applies to the current tenant and not any predecessor: *N & D (London) Ltd v Gadson*, 1991): HA 1988 s14(2).

3.36 An improvement is not to be disregarded, ie is not a 'relevant improvement', if it was an improvement which the tenant was required to carry out under a term of the tenancy or any other 'obligation' to the landlord (unless the obligation arose as a condition of consent given by the landlord on a request by the tenant to execute works) (HA 1988 s14(2)). A relevant improvement is otherwise one carried out either during the current tenancy, or else carried out no more than 21 years before the date of service of the notice proposing the rent increase, during which 21 years the property has always been subject to an assured tenancy, on the termination of which the tenant (or if joint tenants, one of them) did not quit (HA 1988 s14(3)).

3.37 These are the only improvements to be disregarded: the tenant will have to pay for others, by way of increased rent. The definition of relevant improvements can operate harshly for a former leaseholder who became an assured tenant following the expiry of his or her long lease (see paras 2.77–2.81). In setting the initial rent for the tenancy under the provisions which apply to former leaseholders, improvements carried out during the long lease are to be disregarded (see para 2.81) but they are then taken into account in the first statutory increase during the statutory periodic tenancy, thereby potentially leading to a significant rent increase which may even cause the tenancy to cease to be assured because it is at too high a rent (see para 1.233(2) – *Hughes v Borodex Ltd*, 2010).

Powers of tribunal/committee

3.38 In addition to paying the rent, the tenant may be required to pay service charges, eg for communal heating or hot water. In this context, there are two types of service charge: 'fixed' and 'variable'. A variable service charge is where the tenant agrees to pay a proportion of the landlord's actual costs of providing the service, albeit that the tenancy agreement may require the tenant to pay a specified sum on account pending the landlord's calculation of the actual costs during a particular period. The tribunal or committee does not have power under HA 1988 to determine the amount of any variable service charge (HA 1988 s14(4)) but the tenant will have the right to challenge its reasonableness on application under LTA 1985 to either the tribunal (England) or leasehold valuation tribunal (Wales) (see para 3.89). A fixed service is not necessarily a charge which is fixed 'for all time'. Rather, it means that a specific charge is provided for in the tenancy agreement and there is no reference to the tenant paying a proportion of the landlord's actual costs. When determining the rent, the the tribunal or committee is concerned with both the rent and any fixed service charges and must also take into account council tax if the landlord is paying it on the tenant's behalf (HA 1988 s14(4)).

3.39 If there are both a notice seeking an increase in rent and a notice proposing a variation of terms (see paras 3.23–3.27) before the tribunal or committee at the same time, which can only be in the case of a former fixed-term tenancy, and the notice proposing a variation of terms specifies a date no later than the proposed rent increase, the applications can be heard together. When doing so, the tribunal or committee is bound to decide the variation of terms before it decides the new rent as this may affect what rent should be paid (HA 1988 s14(6)).

3.40 Unless the landlord and the tenant otherwise agree, the new rent takes effect from the date specified in the notice of increase unless it appears to the tribunal or committee that it would cause undue hardship, in which case it may determine a later date (but no later than its decision): HA 1988 s14(7).

3.41 The tribunal or committee is not bound to continue with the process if the landlord and the tenant give notice in writing that they do not wish it to do so; nor need it continue if the tenancy ends before it reaches its determination (HA 1988 s14(8)).

Assured shorthold tenancies

3.42 Assured shorthold tenants are subject to the normal provisions governing rents applicable to Housing Act assured tenants generally (see paras 3.20–3.41), with the qualification that the tenant is able (to a limited extent) to refer the rent to the First-tier Tribunal (in England) or the rent assessment committee (in Wales (HA 1988 s22) even though the landlord is not seeking an increase (see para 3.28).

3.43 In the case of a pre-1996 Act assured shorthold (see para 1.248), this power is only available once, and it is not available if the initial fixed-term tenancy has already expired so that the tenancy has become periodic. After that, only a request for an increase can trigger the reference. In the case of a post-1996 Act assured shorthold, the power is only available during the first six months from the commencement of the original tenancy, and is otherwise likewise reliant on a request for an increase from the landlord.

3.44 **Comparison with other rents.** Moreover, a decision by the tribunal or committee to fix a rent under this additional power arises only if satisfied (a) that the rent under the assured shorthold tenancy is significantly higher than rents under other assured tenancies (whether or not shorthold), and (b) that there are sufficient other assured tenancies with which to make a comparison (HA 1988 s22). If it refuses to make a determination, however, the tenant may still re-apply in the future, if it seems that other rents are now available with which to make a comparison, or much lower, because the power will not have been exercised even the once.

3.45 **Procedure.** Rent for this purpose excludes any variable service charges (see para 3.38) but includes any fixed service charges and any amount payable for council tax (HA 1988 s22(5)). A reference may be withdrawn by written agreement between the landlord and the tenant.

3.46 If the tribunal or committee does proceed to a determination, it will decide from when it is to take effect, which cannot be earlier than the date of the application (HA 1988 s22(4)(a)). Any excess rent over the determination is irrecoverable from the tenant (HA 1988 s22(4)(b)).

3.47 Once the rent has been determined, the landlord cannot serve a notice seeking an increase (see para 3.30) for a year after the determination takes effect (HA 1988 s22(4)(c)).

3.48 Note that the secretary of state has power to disapply this additional means of referring a rent to the tribunal or committee (HA 1988 s23).

Rent Act protected and statutory tenants

3.49 **Contractual tenancy**. So long as the contractual tenancy subsists, whether fixed-term or periodic (see para 1.18), the rent payable by a protected tenant will be limited by its terms. The provisions to be considered below are additional.

3.50 **Rent in advance**. Whether protected (contractual) or statutory, and whether or not a rent is registered in respect of the premises (see para 3.59), it is illegal for a landlord to demand rent further in advance than the beginning of the period for which it is payable, ie the first day of a week for which a weekly rent is paid, or the first day of a month for which a monthly rent is paid (RA 1977 s126). If the tenancy is yearly, then the landlord cannot charge the year's rent earlier than halfway through the year for which it is due.

3.51 A tenant can recover any money improperly demanded too far in advance, for up to two years after it was paid. This probably does not mean that the landlord is not entitled to receive the rent at the time when it would be lawful to ask for it, although the point has never been tested in law. If so, then this provision would probably only be of use to a protected or statutory tenant who has been charged a considerable amount in advance, or by way of defence to an action for arrears, or part of them, based on rent improperly charged in advance, ie because it is, in law, not yet due and therefore not in arrears.

3.52 **Rent protection**. All tenants within Rent Act protection (see paras 1.268–1.293), whether contractual or statutory, are entitled to protection of their rents according to a system known as the 'fair rent system'. It is necessary to consider: what the fair rent is; how it applies to a tenancy; and, the rent limit.

Fair rent

Rent officers

3.53 A fair rent is one that a rent officer – employed by the Valuation Office Agency (in England) or Rent Officers Wales – considers fair for the premises and tenancy in question and registers as such. An appeal from the rent officer lies to the First-tier Tribunal (England) or the rent assessment committee (Wales) – the same bodies which govern assured tenancy rents (see para 3.23); they will themselves apply the same principles (see para 3.54) as the rent officer. The rent includes any fixed payments for furniture or services (RA 1977 s71(1)) and any payment for council tax (RA 1977 s70(3A). Variable service charges (see para 3.38) are treated differently (RA 1977 s74): if the rent officer is satisfied that the clause which allows the landlord to vary the amount of the charge in accordance with his or her actual costs of providing the services is reasonable, he or she must enter the amount of the charge separately in the rent register (see para 3.59) as a variable amount (s74(4)).

Statutory considerations

3.54 The Rent Act contains guidelines as to what should be considered a fair rent (RA 1977 s70). The rent officer is obliged to take into account all the circumstances (other than personal circumstances) and in particular the age, character, and locality of the residential accommodation, its state of repair, if any furniture is provided for use under the tenancy, the quantity, quality and condition of the furniture, and any premium, or sum in the nature of a premium, which has been or may be lawfully required or received on the grant, renewal, continuance or assignment of the tenancy (RA 1977 s70(1)). Critically and centrally to the concept of fair rent, he or she must also assume that there is no scarcity of dwellings in the locality (RA 1977 s70(2)). It is this which means that fair rents are below – sometimes well below – the market rent (or what, when the Rent Acts were the principal form of rent control, would have been the market rent but for their intervention).

1) **Disregard of personal circumstances.** The most common example of a personal circumstance is the tenant who is in straitened circumstances, or the landlord who claims that he or she cannot afford to keep the property in repair. Another example might be that of an elderly person who finds it more inconvenient to live at the top of a flight of stairs than would a hypothetical, average tenant; or a tenant with children who feels the lack of a garden.

   The presence or otherwise of a garden, or the fact that a flat is at the top of, perhaps, a long flight of stairs, will, however, affect the value of the premises themselves in any event, just not more so because of the particular characteristics or circumstances of the present tenant.

   The extent of a tenant's security of tenure, (eg notice under mandatory ground – para 2.219) or the fact that the landlord is a PRP or RSL – to whose tenants these provisions in some circumstances also apply (see paras 3.11–3.12), is a personal circumstance if the approach being taken to assessment is by means of valuing the property (*Palmer v Peabody Trust*, 1974; *Spath Holme v*

Greater Manchester & Lancashire RAC, 1995 – para 3.55), but not if a comparables approach to determination of a fair rent (see para 3.60) is adopted (*Spath Home*).

2) **General conditions in locality**. Although it is not permissible to take into account the tenant's financial circumstances, it is possible for a rent officer to consider the general level of wages throughout a particular locality (*Guppy's (Bridport) Ltd v Carpenter*, 1983).

   It is up to the rent officer to determine just what he or she will consider the locality for the purposes of the determination (*Palmer v Peabody Trust*, 1974). This could benefit a tenant of whatever income, living in a working class district, but, equally, could act to the detriment of a poor tenant living in an area that is, or that has become, predominantly middle class.

3) **Age, character and locality**. Whether or not premises are on a noisy street is obviously relevant. Consideration of locality means more than just what part of town premises are in, but also whether they are near other amenities, such as parks and recreational facilities, public transport and good shopping centres. In other words, all the factors that would normally be considered as affecting the value of living in particular premises or that would tend to push rents up or down (*Metropolitan Property Holdings v Finegold*, 1974).

   State of repair is very important; if premises are in such a bad condition that they are not even habitable, or perhaps only in part habitable, then there is nothing to stop a rent officer determining a purely nominal rent for the premises as a whole, or attributing a purely nominal amount to the uninhabitable part (*McGee v London RAPC*, 1969) although he or she is not obliged to do so (*Williams v Khan*, 1981).

4) **Disrepair; furniture**. The rent officer must disregard disrepair or defects attributable to a failure by the tenant or his or her predecessor in title to comply with any terms of the tenancy; the rent officer must also disregard any improvements carried out, otherwise than under the terms of the tenancy, by the tenant or his or her predecessor in title, and – if furniture is provided – either any improvement to it or deterioration in its condition due to ill-treatment, attributable to the tenant or his or her predecessor in title (or, in the case of deterioration, attributable to ill-treatment by anyone living with the tenant) (RA 1977 s70(3)).

5) **Scarcity value.** The major element which the rent officer must disregard, that forms the cornerstone of the fair rent system, is 'scarcity value'.

It is scarcity, more than anything else, which pushes up the price of property and rents. In order to avoid scarcity value, the rent officer is obliged to adopt the assumption that there are not substantially more people seeking any particular sort of accommodation in the locality than there is such accommodation available (RA 1977 s70(2)). Locality for these purposes is very much larger than that relevant for ascertaining locality under section 70(1) (see para 3.54(3)): *Queensway Housing Association Ltd v Chiltern Thames and Eastern RAC*, 1998.

Adjusted market rent

3.55 Following HA 1988, there was, for the first time since the introduction of fair rents in 1965, the growth of a body of market rents (see para 3.34). This impacted on Rent Act fair rents, which had hitherto functioned by comparison with other fair rents registered by rent officers (rather than with a market demand which had itself been distorted by the fair rent system itself). Indeed, 'comparables' (as they were known) had hitherto been held to be the best evidence of a fair rent (*Mason v Skilling*, 1973). Building on this new market, a number of judicial decisions in the following decade required more emphasis to be placed on the market, albeit adjusted to accommodate the statutory criteria, in place of the earlier focus on the existing body of comparable fair rents.

3.56 Following these decisions, it may be said that a fair rent had become the market rent for a property adjusted for scarcity (see para 3.54(5)) and having regard to (or disregarding) the matters specified in the statute: *Curtis v London RAC*, 1999; *Spath Holme v Greater Manchester and Lancashire RAC (No 1)*, 1995. The expression is 'fair' rent, which is not (necessarily) the same as a 'reasonable' rent (*BTE Ltd v Merseyside and Cheshire RAC*, 1991; *Spath Holme*). Comparables remain an alternative approach only where there continues to be no, or an inadequate, market on the basis of which to proceed.

Maximum increases

3.57 The new approach led to substantial increases in rent and, in turn, to the Rent Acts (Maximum Fair Rent) Order 1999 SI No 6, made under LTA 1985 s31. This set a maximum increase on all fair rents registered since 1 February 1999, fixing them by reference to a formula using the RPI (see *Compatriot Holdings Ltd v London Rent Assessment*

Committee, 2009, for how the RPI is to be used). A challenge to the legality of this Order was rejected by the House of Lords in *R v Secretary of State for the Environment ex p Spath Holme Ltd*, 2000, in which it was held that the Act did not violate the freeholder's right to quiet enjoyment of its possessions under Article 1 of the First Protocol ECHR (*James v UK*, 1986).

Current position

3.58 Accordingly, the current position is that the determination of the fair rent involves consideration of the market rent, followed by adjustment for the statutory considerations, followed by limitation (if needed) by the RPI-based formula. If there is no market on the basis of which to determine the rent, then comparison with other registered rents would remain a correct approach, but the RPI-based formula would still be applicable.

Rent register

3.59 Both the Valuation Office Agency (England) and Rent Officers Wales are obliged to maintain a rent register, which is open for public inspection. This contains details of all rent registrations in force. Normally these are rents which will have been registered by a rent officer since 1965, when the fair rent system was introduced (Rent Act 1965). There is one exception to this. Prior to 14 August 1974, furnished tenancies were subject to the Rent Tribunal (see para 1.277) and rents may have been registered in respect of them by that body (see paras 3.80–3.83). When RA 1974 came into force, such rent registrations were deemed to be fair rents and were included in the fair rent register (RA 1977 Sch 24).

Comparables

3.60 The rent register contains the documentary part of the experience which the rent officer will apply to any particular application. In the past, the practice of rent officers was to look at the register to see if there were any previous registrations for properties of similar size, in similar areas, and with any other similarities. These were what has been referred to above (see para 3.56) as 'comparables', formerly considered the best evidence of a fair rent (*Mason v Skilling*, 1973).

Market-rent comparables

3.61 As already stated, the starting point for setting a fair rent today is the market rent: *Curtis v London RAC*, 1998. Accordingly, where there are good market rent comparisons available (from assured and assured shorthold tenancies – paras 3.20; 3.32), these should be used in preference to relying on the register: *Curtis*; *Spath Holme Ltd v Greater Manchester and Lancashire RAC*, 1995; *Northumberland & Durham Property Trust v London RAC*, 1998. Comparables from the register remain an appropriate approach, however, when there is no such market.

Application of fair rents

3.62 A fair rent comes to apply to a tenancy in one of two ways. Either a rent was already registered for the premises, or an application for a registration is made after the tenancy starts. Given that new protected tenancies can only be created by a court (see para 1.271(3)), in which case all parties are likely to be professionally advised, the first limb now has little application. Nonetheless, housing arrangements can and do last for a very long time, and a lengthy tenancy may only recently have expired, in relation to which there was a registered rent at the beginning, unknown to the tenant who has been paying more ever since. For that reason, the law remains fully stated for the time being.

Existing registered rent

3.63 If there was a registration before the tenancy started, then the amount registered will have been the maximum rent under the protected tenancy, even if the tenancy agreement was for a higher figure (RA 1977 s44), until such time as there was a new registration (see para 3.67). (If, however, the tenancy agreement was for a lower sum, that would – contractually – have prevailed).

3.64 This is so even if the nature of the letting had changed, eg from unfurnished to furnished or vice versa, unless the change is to the structure of the premises such that it can no longer be called the same dwelling-house (*Rakhit v Carty*, 1990). The rent only applies, however, to exactly the same premises, ie not premises which have been enlarged by the addition of a room, nor even premises reduced in size by letting them less one room (*Gluchowska v Tottenham BC*, 1954).

Cancellation of registration

3.65 In order to end the registration, application may have been made to cancel it:

i) at least two years after the last registration, at a time when the premises are unlet, by the person who would be the landlord if it were let; or

ii) pursuant to a rent agreement taking effect at least two years after the last registration, by the landlord and tenant jointly under a fixed-term tenancy on which there was at least one year to run, who agreed on a higher rent which was approved by the rent officer (RA 1977 s73).

Recovery of excess

3.66 Assuming no such (proper) cancellation, the registered rent remained the maximum payable and any excess recoverable for up to two years after it was paid, either by deducting it from future rent owing, or by a normal civil action (RA 1977 s57). *Note*. This provision was first introduced into the Rent Acts to overcome *Sharp Bros & Knight v Chant*, 1917, in which it was held that the tenant could not recover the excess because it was paid under a mistake of law rather than fact and, as the law then stood, only payments made under a mistake of fact could be recovered at common law: the law has now changed so that payments made under a mistake of law are recoverable (*Kleinwort Benson Ltd v Birmingham City Council*, 1996). Seeking recovery in this way rather than under the statute may therefore be more advantageous to the tenant as he or she could go back six years rather than two.

New registration

3.67 Either landlord or tenant, or both jointly (RA 1977 s68), can apply for registration of a rent. There cannot normally be an application for a new registration until a period of two years has elapsed since the last, even if there is a new tenancy or, indeed, even if there is a new landlord (RA 1977 s67). Thus, two parties can find themselves bound by a registration secured by two completely different parties.

Early application

3.68 There are three exceptions to the two-year bar.

1) **Joint application**. Where a landlord and a tenant apply jointly for a new rent to be registered, this may be in less than two years.
2) **Landlord's application**. A landlord may apply on his or her own, one year and nine months after the last registration, but the new rent cannot come into force until two years have elapsed.
3) **Change of circumstances**. There can also be an application before the expiry of two years, by either party, if there have been such substantial changes in the terms of the tenancy of the condition of the premises or furniture, that, in all the circumstances, the rent last registered is no longer fair.

A change in the condition of the premises can be as a result of repairs carried out by the landlord, even where the landlord was obliged to carry them out under the terms of the tenancy agreement or because he or she was required to do them by a local authority (see para 10.18): *R v West Sussex Registration Area ex p Haysport Properties Ltd*, 2001.

On an application based on change of circumstances, the rent officer does not, however, merely consider the changed circumstances and reduce or increase accordingly, but considers the whole rent anew (*London Housing and Commercial Properties v Cowan*, 1976).

This provision is therefore only likely to be of use to a landlord who has, for example, installed some facility, such as a hot water system, since the last registration. A tenant who applies because of deterioration may well find that the amount by which the rent ought to be decreased on its account is not as great as the amount by which the rent has increased, in respect of the rent of the tenancy, because of inflation and the passage of time. On the other hand, on a landlord's application for a higher rent because of an improvement, a tenant should not hesitate to point out any deterioration or other new circumstances, eg reduced local amenities, which might prevent too great an increase.

Procedure

3.69 The party making the application completes the appropriate forms, which are available from the Valuation Office Agency (England) or Rent Officers Wales and from most aid or advice agencies. The applicant is obliged to state what is the fair rent that he or she wishes to have registered. The forms will be sent to the other side, eg the landlord on a tenant's application, who will have an opportunity to comment and to put his or her own point of view.

3.70 If there are joint tenants or, indeed, joint landlords, then either they must all sign the application form or one must sign as agent for the others (*Turley v Panton*, 1975; *R v Rent Officer for Camden LBC ex p Felix*, 1988).

Inspection and consultation

3.71 Although the rent officer is not obliged to do so, he or she will normally visit the premises. The rent officer will hold a consultation which may be during a visit (if any) or at a different time at his or her office. The rent officer would not normally volunteer to hold a consultation if the rent has previously been registered, and there is no change other than the passage of time, but he or she must do so if either party asks for one. The consultation is informal and it is not usual for parties to be represented. The decision will be in writing.

First-tier Tribunal and rent assessment committee

3.72 If either party is dissatisfied with the rent registration, he or she may appeal to the First-tier Tribunal (England) or a rent assessment committee (Wales) (RA 1977 Sch 11). When the tribunal or committee hears an appeal, it does not start with the decision of the rent officer and decide whether he or she is right or wrong; rather, it starts all over again for itself. It, too, will normally inspect the premises in question and will usually hold a consultation which will be slightly more formal than that before the rent officer, and will always be at its office, not at the premises.

Appeal from tribunal or committee

3.73 There is no appeal from the decision of the tribunal or the committee, unless it can be shown to have acted wrongly in law, whether by the wrongful inclusion or exclusion of some consideration or otherwise, in which case the decision could be appealed (on that basis only) to the High Court. If asked to do so, the RAC is bound to give its decision, and the reasons for it, in writing (Tribunals and Inquiries Act 1992 s10).

Relevant date

3.74 The date when the registration is finally made, whether by rent officer or tribunal or committee, is known as the relevant date (RA 1977 s67(5)), and it affects the date when a new application can be made (see para 3.67). The rent applies to the tenancy from the relevant date (RA 1977 s72).

Effecting an increase

3.75 The landlord cannot claim an increase unless the amount is within the contractual rent (RA 1977 s44) or else he or she has brought the contractual tenancy to an end, either by notice to quit (see paras 2.49–2.58) or, in the case of a fixed-term tenancy, by forfeiture (see paras 2.29–2.46), or if the fixed-term has expired (see para 2.23). The landlord can use a notice of increase in the proper form (*Aristocrat Property Investments v Harounoff*, 1982), to claim the new rent, specifying a date no earlier than the date when the contractual tenancy could have been brought to an end; this has the effect of terminating a periodic tenancy (RA 1977 ss45, 49).

Rent limit

Maximum rent

3.76 The rent limit is the term used to describe the maximum amount which a landlord can claim from the tenant.

1) **Contractual period.** During the contractual period of the tenancy, the rent limit is either the registered rent or the contractual rent, whichever is the lower (RA 1977 s44).

   If there is no registered rent, then the limit is the contractual rent. Any increases up to the amount of the contractual limit can be imposed without notice of increase, but in order to exceed the contractual limit, the tenancy must be determined (as and when it can be).

   Where there is no registered rent, the parties may agree to an increase by means of a rent agreement (RA 1977 s51). Such an agreement will, however, only be valid if it is in writing, and if at the head of the document there appears a statement in writing or print, no less conspicuous than that used elsewhere in the agreement, that the tenant is not obliged to enter into the agreement and that his or her security of tenure will not be affected if he or she refuses (RA 1977 s51(4)). The statement must also advise the tenant of his or her right to apply to the rent officer at any time, then or even immediately after it has been signed, for registration of a fair rent.

   An agreement which does not comply with these terms is invalid (RA 1977 s54) and the excess paid can be reclaimed by the tenant for up to one year after it was paid, as an ordinary civil debt or by deduction from the rent (RA 1977 s57). It may be possible to reclaim it for up to six years, not under the statute but as a claim for mistake (see para 3.66).
2) **Statutory period: pre-registration.** By the time the contractual tenancy comes to an end, there may still be no registered rent. In this case, the landlord is confined by the former contractual rent limit until such time as he or she applies for registration of a fair rent (RA 1977 s45). If the result of an application is an increase, then the landlord must first serve a notice of increase (RA 1977 ss45, 49).

   The landlord can, however, increase the rent without applying for registration on account of the costs of providing services or furniture (RA 1977 s47). The tenant may be able to challenge the amount claimed in the county court (RA 1977 s47(2)).

3) **Statutory period: post-registration.** Once a rent has been registered for the premises, then this becomes the rent limit and cannot be increased except by a new application and, where applicable, notice of increase (RA 1977 s45). It is, however, possible to pass on increases in the cost of providing services without a new application, provided that the rent officer has agreed that the service element should be entered on the register as variable and has endorsed the landlord's proposed terms for calculating any future variations (see para 3.53).

Protected shorthold tenancies

3.77 **Need for registered rent.** Under RA 1977, there had, at the time the tenancy was granted, either already to have been a registered rent (see para 3.59), or a certificate of fair rent, in relation to the premises (HA 1980 s52(2)(c); para 1.295(4)). Registration of fair rents has already been considered (see paras 3.53–3.75). The certificate of fair rent was repealed with the introduction of HA 1988: it was usually used by a landlord intending to let out premises on a fully Rent Act protected tenancy after the execution of works, who wanted to know what was likely to be his or her return on the property – the same procedure used to be available to a landlord intending to let out on a protected shorthold tenancy, even though no works were to be carried out by him or her beforehand.

3.78 If the landlord let out the premises on a protected shorthold tenancy when there was only a certificate of fair rent then, prior to full registration, no more rent should have been charged than stated in the certificate; and, the landlord had to apply for full registration within 28 days of the beginning of the tenancy (HA 1980 s52(1)(c)).

3.79 **Waiver of need for registered rent.** The secretary of state reserved powers under the Act to waive the requirement for a registered rent or a certificate of fair rent (HA 1980 s52(4)). This power was used this power in 1981 to waive the requirement outside London (SI 1981/1578) and from 1987, throughout the whole of the country (SI 1987/265).

3.80 Even if there was a failure to comply with the registered rent requirement so that the letting was not strictly a protected shorthold tenancy (see para 1.295), the court may still order possession on the shorthold ground (see para 2.200), provided that it is just and equitable to do so (HA 1980 s55(2)). This power is only likely to be used when there has been a technical defect, or an application pursued a matter of days late. It is highly unlikely to be used if a very high rent has been charged but may be where the failure was an honest mistake, and the rent set was fully acceptable to both parties (*RJ Dunnell Property Investments Ltd v Thorpe*, 1989).

3.81 Where a rent was already the subject of a certificate or registered, the tenant could still apply for registration him- or herself (see paras 3.67–3.69) and if the rent officer registered a rent lower than that stated in a certificate, it is the lower rent that would be payable from registration (see para 3.76).

Restricted contracts

3.82 **Reasonable rents.** In respect of all restricted contracts, the Rent Tribunal (or, now the First-tier Tribunal (England) and the rent assessment committee (Wales) (HA 1980 s72(2)) could – and where they still exist, can – fix a reasonable rent (RA 1977 s78), which is to say, a rent which it considers reasonable in all the circumstances. There are no guidelines analogous to those to which the rent officer must pay heed, but, under different legislation, it was once said that it would not be reasonable to make a tenant pay for general shortages in the availability of accommodation, ie scarcity value (*John Kay Ltd v Kay*, 1952) although that point of view is unlikely to prevail today were the question to arise. An application may be made in respect of any letting within the jurisdiction of the tribunal or committee, so long as the letting lasts, and it can reduce, confirm or increase the existing rent. It can do this in respect of a periodic letting, or a fixed-term letting, and irrespective of any contractually agreed rent. The likelihood of such an application now being made is so rare that we do not consider the procedure any further.

3.83 The rent fixed by the tribunal or committee is entered into a register and, if such a registered rent one exists in respect of the letting, forms the only rent limit which binds the landlord (RA 1977 s81), other, of course, than the actual terms of the agreement, eg for a fixed term at a specified rent.

Agricultural and forestry workers

3.84 Rents for agricultural and forestry workers within the Rent Act scheme (see para 1.304) are governed by a fair rent scheme similar to that which applies to protected tenants under RA 1977 (see paras 3.57–3.76; Rent (Agriculture) Act 1976 ss11–14). The provisions for determining rents for an assured tenancy (see paras 3.20–3.42) apply to assured agricultural occupancies under HA 1988 (see para 1.304), save that where a tribunal or committee is setting a rent for a property, it determines the market rent for an assured agricultural occupancy (HA 1988 s24(3), (4)).

Other tenants and licensees

3.85 There is no rent control for other tenants and licensees: they are confined by their contracts, whether fixed-term or periodic. In the former case, unless the agreement itself contains a review provision, the landlord will not be able to increase the rent, even with the occupier's agreement (for it is central to the agreement not only that the occupier can *stay* for the fixed-term, but at what rent he or she is entitled to do so), and if there is such an increase, the occupier may be able to recover it on the basis that there was no consideration, ie because he or she already had a continuing right to occupy (at the former rent). In the latter case, if the landlord seeks an increase without wishing to evict the occupier and the occupier wishes to remain, then while in theory the landlord has to serve notice to quit or terminate, in practice the parties will agree the new rent, which will be enforceable on the basis that the landlord has foregone the opportunity to evict (which the landlord under the fixed-term arrangement did not enjoy). If the landlord is a local authority, however, a notice of increase procedure is available (HA 1985 s25 – para 3.9).

Trespassers

3.86 **Damages.** Leaving the peculiar position of the former tolerated trespasser aside (see paras 1.155–1.158), trespassers pay no rent. On an eviction, the court can order damages for use and occupation, but only if normal proceedings are used, not the special, speedy provision available (see para 2.71).

Service charges

3.87 **Landlord and Tenant Act 1985.** Most long leases and many shorter tenancies allow the landlord to levy service charges independently of the rent. Disputes about their amount and the quality of the work carried out or of services provided are extremely common. LTA 1985 ss18–30A, govern their levy and recovery.

3.88 **Service charge.** The Act applies to all charges payable for services, repairs, improvements, maintenance or insurance or the landlord's costs of management, which vary or may vary in accordance with their cost (LTA 1985 s18). It does not apply to tenancies from local authorities, unless they are long leases (see para 2.72) (LTA 1985 s26) but do apply to variable service charges in assured tenancies (see para 3.38). When a rent officer is registering a fair rent for a protected or statutory tenant (see paras 1.259–1.284) whose tenancy provides for a variable service charge, he or she may note that it is to be variable, and these provisions will apply (see para 3.53) (LTA 1985 s27).

3.89 **Tribunal**. The First-tier Tribunal (England) or the leasehold valuation tribunal (Wales) has jurisdiction to determine whether charges are payable, which includes whether charges are recoverable under the terms of the tenancy agreement (see paras 3.91–3.92), whether they are reasonable (see paras 3.94–3.96) and whether the landlord has complied with other statutory requirements (see paras 3.97–3.102, 3.105) (LTA 1985 s27A). Although – if the issue is raised during court proceedings – the court also has jurisdiction to determine whether service charges are payable, it will usually be referred to the tribunal for determination (Commonhold and Leasehold Reform Act (CLRA) 2002 Sch 12 para 3). Accordingly, in what follows we only refer to proceedings before the tribunal.

3.90 The tribunal has no jurisdiction if the amount of the charge has been agreed or admitted by the tenant or has been determined in tribunal proceedings or at arbitration (LTA 1985 s27A(4)). Payment of the service charge by the tenant, however, does not of itself constitute an admission for these purposes (LTA 1985 s27A(5)).

3.91 **Tenancy agreement**. The starting-point is always whether the tenancy agreement allows the landlord to recover the costs. The agreement will usually list the works or services for which the landlord may seek reimbursement from the tenants and if the item concerned is not included, the landlord will not be able to recover those costs. For example, although most agreements will allow the landlord to recover the costs of maintaining the structure and common parts of a block of flats, older leases often do not allow recovery of the costs of improvements to a block, eg introducing new security measures such as CCTV. Some agreements, however, include 'sweeping-up' clauses allowing the landlord to recover the costs of eg 'all expenses incurred by the landlord in the interests of the good management of the block'. Such a clause may allow the landlord to recover a wide range of charges (*Sutton (Hastoe) Housing Association v Williams*, 1988 – cost of replacing wooden windows with uPVC windows allowed as part of works the landlord 'considered necessary'; *Reston Ltd v Hudson*, 1990 – legal costs allowed as part of any expenses which the landlord might 'reasonably incur'; *cf Holding & Management Ltd v Property Holding & Investment Trust Ltd plc*, 1989 – costs of improvements not works 'necessary to maintain the building as a block of first class residential flats').

3.92 The tenancy agreement will usually also include a procedure which the landlord must follow before demanding payment. Commonly, the lease will include provision for an accounting year, allow the landlord to charge in advance for the estimated service charge for a year, and provision for payment of any outstanding balance after the actual costs for that year have been calculated. Depending on its wording, such a clause may prevent the landlord from demanding charges at any other time (*Southwark LBC v Woelke*, 2013).

3.93 **Proportion**. The proportion of the total costs which each tenant has to pay may be specified in the tenancy agreement as a percentage or by reference to a formula, eg the floor space of each flat, in which case the tenant is bound by the proportion stated in the agreement. Some tenancy agreements, however, allow the landlord to decide the tenant's proportion of the total costs, usually by reference to what the landlord considers to be a 'fair' proportion. In such cases, the tenant can challenge the proportion determined by the landlord in the tribunal (*Sheffield City Council v Oliver*, 2017).

3.94 **Reasonableness**. Service charges can only be recovered so far as they are reasonably incurred and the works or services are to a reasonable standard (LTA 1985 s19).

3.95 The fact that works could have been done, or services provided, more cheaply does not of itself mean that costs are unreasonable. The tribunal should not simply impose its own decision as to what is reasonable: if a landlord chooses a course of action which leads to a reasonable outcome, the costs of pursuing that course will have been reasonably incurred even if there was a cheaper way of achieving a similar result (*Waaler v Hounslow LBC*, 2017).

3.96 Where the lease permits recovery of the costs of improvements, the tribunal must consider three factors: the extent of the interests of the leaseholders, measured by the length of the unexpired terms of their leases; the views about the improvements expressed by leaseholders during any consultation with them (see paras 3.98–3.101); and, the financial impact of the works of the works on the tenants (*Waaler*). This last factor does not require a landlord to investigate the financial means of particular tenants but calls for consideration of the general means of leaseholders in a particular block or estate.

3.97 **Grant aid**. There are provisions excluding from the amount of a service charge costs that have been met with specified types of grant-aid (LTA 1985 s20A). In addition, the secretary of state and the Welsh Ministers can issue directions to local authorities, PRPs and RSLs requiring or permitting them to waive or reduce service charges generally (HA 1996 ss219–220). Directions may require waiver or reduction where the landlord is receiving financial assistance from the secretary of state or the Welsh Ministers. Directions may differentiate between landlords or descriptions of landlords and by area. They may provide for a specific amount or proportion of reduction, or for other means of determination, and for the criteria which landlords are to take into account in determining whether to reduce and to what extent. The directions of current relevance are: Social Landlords Discretionary Reduction of Service Charges (England) Directions 2014, which impose caps on the amounts that can be recovered where works were funded by Decent Homes Backlog Funding in the 2013 Spending Round; and, Social Landlords Mandatory Reduction of Service Charges (England) Directions 2014, which gives landlords a broad discretion to reduce charges for works.

3.98 **Consultation.** Before carrying out larger scale building works or entering into long-term contracts, the landlord must consult the tenants and any recognised tenants' association (LTA 1985 s20, and Service Charges (Consultation Requirements) (England) Regulations 2003 SI No 1987 or Service Charges (Consultation Requirements) (Wales) Regulations 2004 SI No 684. In the case of building works, consultation is required where any tenant would have to pay more than £250 towards the works in question. In the case of long-term contracts, consultation is necessary before entering into a contract if it is to last for more than 12 months, and any tenant's contribution to the costs in a year would be more than £100. (Such long-term contracts could include contracts for cleaning services or managing agents).

3.99 The consultation requirements in the regulations are detailed and vary depending on a number of circumstances, eg whether the landlord is a public authority. In general terms, the process allows the tenants to comment on the proposed works or services, to have input into the choice of contractor by nominating contractors from whom the landlord must obtain estimates, to be provided with a number of estimates for the relevant costs, and to be given reasons for the landlord's choice of contractor. Where the landlord is a public authority, the value of the contract is likely to be such that it will have to be put out to tender under public procurement rules. In such cases, the tenants do not have the right to nominate contractors but may still raise concerns about the successful tenderer.

3.100 If the landlord fails to comply with the regulations, the service charge which he or she may recover from each tenant is in principle limited to either £250 (for building works) or £100 (for long-term contracts).

3.101 At any time, whether before commencement of the works or even after their completion, however, any or all of the consultation requirements may be waived by the tribunal where it is reasonable to do so (LTA 1985 s20ZA). In exercising this discretion, the tribunal is not concerned with the extent to which the landlord has failed to comply the regulations but must focus on the prejudice suffered by the tenants as a result of the landlord's failure to comply with the consultation requirements (*Daejan Properties Ltd v Benson*, 2013). Where the extent, quality and cost of the works or services are in no way affected by the landlord's failure, there is no reason not to grant dispensation. In considering whether the tenants have suffered prejudice, however, the tribunal should adopt a sympathetic approach. The tribunal can grant dispensation subject to conditions, eg requiring the landlord to reduce the amount claimed to compensate the tenants for the prejudice suffered. In particular, the tribunal can, and usually should, require the landlord to pay the tenants' reasonable costs of investigating whether they have suffered any prejudice. The financial consequence to the landlord of refusing dispensation is not, however, a relevant factor when considering whether or not to grant to dispensation.

3.102 **Stale service charges.** A landlord cannot recover service charges relating to costs which he or she incurred more than 18 months before payment is demanded from the tenant, unless, within that 18-month period, the tenant was notified in writing that those costs had been incurred and that the tenant would subsequently be required to contribute to them by payment of a service charge (LTA 1985 s20B; *Brent LBC v Shulem B Association*, 2011). Costs are incurred by the landlord not when works are done or services are provided but when the landlord is liable to pay for them, eg when the contractor has invoiced the landlord for the cost (*Burr v OM Property Management Ltd*, 2013). Where, however, as is usually the case in more modern leases, the landlord is allowed to levy on-account payments (see para 3.92) section 20B only has any effect if the on-account payments for previous years are insufficient and a balancing payment is required which relates to costs incurred more than 18 months before that balancing payment is demanded (*Charlegrove v Gilje*, 2003).

3.103 **Statements of costs.** Under LTA 1985 s21, landlords must also provide a statement of relevant costs incurred during an accounting period when requested to do so and provide documentation, eg invoices from contactors, supporting those costs. If, without reasonable excuse, the landlord fails to comply with a duty imposed by sections 21 or 22, he or she commits an offence and is liable on conviction to a fine not exceeding level 4 on the standard scale (£2,500) (LTA 1985 s25; *Taber v MacDonald*, 1998; *R v Marylebone Magistrates' Court ex p Westminster City Council*, 1999). The requirement to provide a statement of costs and supporting documents only applies to a tenant of a local authority if he or she has a long lease (see para 2.7) but an authority does not commit an offence if it fails to comply with these requirements (s26(1),(2)). Currently, failure to comply with these duties does not allow the tenant to withhold payment of service charges but amendments contained in H&RA 2008 allow regulations to be made to create a new scheme for the provision of information about service charges. If that scheme is introduced, failure to supply information in accordance with sections 21 and 22 will entitle the tenant to withhold payment of service charges until the landlord complies with its obligations under the regulations.

3.104 **Separate accounts**. At present, where landlords hold receive service charges, they are deemed to be held on trust (LTA 1987 s42). This does not apply where the landlord is a local authority (ss42(1) and 58(1)). H&RA 2008 allows regulations to be made governing how trust accounts are to be held. The regulations, which have yet to be made, may prescribe circumstances in which a tenant may withhold payment of his or her service charges where he or she has reasonable grounds to believe that the landlord has failed in his or her obligations as trustee.

3.105 **Service charge demands**. If a landlord demands payment of a service charge, that demand must be accompanied by a summary of the rights and obligations of both the landlord and the tenant in relation to service charges (LTA 1985 s21B, inserted by CLRA 2002). The wording of the summary is prescribed by the Service Charges (Summary of Rights and Obligations, and Transitional Provisions) (England) Regulations 2007 SI No 1257 or Service Charges (Summary of Rights and Obligations, and Transitional Provision) (Wales) Regulations 2007 SI No 3160. If the summary is not included, the tenant is entitled to withhold payment until the landlord provides the summary (s21B(4)).

3.106 Save in exceptional circumstances, eg where a party has behaved unreasonably, the tribunal cannot order one party to service charge proceedings to pay the other's legal costs. Leases, however, sometimes allow landlords to recover their legal costs through the service charge. If so, the tribunal has power to prohibit the landlord from seeking to recover some or all of his or her costs in this way (LTA 1985 s20C).

Administration charges

3.107 **Commonhold and Leasehold Reform Act 2002.** Many long leases require the tenant to pay the landlord's costs of granting approvals, eg to an assignment, or of providing information to third parties (prospective assignees) or to pay charges in the event of a breach of the lease, eg interest on late payment of rent or services or the landlord's costs of preparing a notice under LPA 1925 s146 (see para 2.38). Recovery of such administration charges is governed by CLRA 2002.

3.108 **Reasonableness.** Administration charges can only be recovered so far as they are reasonable (CLRA 2002 Sch 11 para 2). The First-tier Tribunal (England) or the leasehold valuation tribunal (Wales) has jurisdiction to determine whether charges are reasonable. If the amount of the administration charge is fixed under the lease – whether in a specific amount or by reference to a formula – the tribunal has power to vary the amount or formula as it sees fit (CLRA 2002 Sch 11 para 2).

3.109 **Administration charge demands.** If a landlord demands payment of an administration charge, that demand must be accompanied by a summary of the rights and obligations of both the landlord and the tenant in relation to administration charges (CLRA 2002 Sch 11 para 4). The wording of the summary is prescribed by the Administration Charges (Summary of Rights and Obligations) (England) Regulations 2007 SI No 1258 or Administration Charges (Summary of Rights and Obligations) (Wales) Regulations 2007 SI No 3162.

Estate charges

3.110 **Estate management schemes.** Some properties enfranchised under either the Leasehold Reform Act (LRA) 1967 (see paras 4.15–4.25) or the Leasehold Reform, Housing and Urban Development Act (LRHUDA) 1993 (see paras 4.27–4.34) are situated on estates, in particular the estates of some of the very large landlords in central London. Under both Acts, landlords are allowed to establish estate management schemes in order to maintain the estate's character.

Most such schemes impose estate charges on freeholders; these are similar to service charges (see paras 3.87–3.106) and administration charges (see paras 3.107–3.109).

3.111 **Reasonableness.** Estate charges can only be recovered so far as they are reasonable (CLRA 2002 s159). The First-tier Tribunal (England) or the leasehold valuation tribunal (Wales) has jurisdiction to determine whether charges are reasonable. If the amount of an estate charge is fixed under the scheme – whether in a specific amount or by reference to a formula – the tribunal has power to vary the amount or formula as it sees fit.

Heating charges

3.112 **Right to information.** There is power for the government to introduce provisions which would entitle secure tenants (only) to find out how their landlords have calculated heating charges included in the rent (HA 1985 s108). This power has not yet been brought into use.

Utility charges

3.113 Although it is increasingly common for tenants to have their own utility meters, landlords sometimes remain liable to pay for utility charges and reserve power to recover the costs from tenants (or licensees) as discrete charges under their agreements. The bodies which regulate supplies of gas, electricity and water (the Gas and Electricity Markets Authority and the Water Services Regulation Authority) must set maximum prices at which utilities can be re-sold (Gas Act (GA) 1986 s37(1); Electricity Act (EA) 1989 s44(2); Water Industry Act (WIA) 1991 s150(1)). In each case, the regulator has currently set the maximum re-sale price so that a 'consumer', which includes a landlord or licensor, cannot profit from re-selling one of these utilities. Where a tenant or licensee has been overcharged for a utility, the excess is recoverable from the landlord or licensor (GA 1986 s37(3); EA 1989 s44(4); WIA 1991 s150(5)).

3.114 Thus, a tenant who had been overcharged by her local authority landlord for water supplied to her home was able to recover the excess from the authority (*Jones v Southwark LBC*, 2016). It may, however, be noted that in *Jones*, the authority was held to have been re-selling water but local authorities have power to enter into agreements with water companies to act as their agents in collecting water charges, in which case the authority is not a consumer and the water company remains the supplier. Commonly, the payment arrangements under such agreements involve the authority paying the water company a discounted sum for the water supplied to their properties to reflect the work it has done in collecting charges from the tenants. Where this is the case, the authority is not re-selling at a profit (*Lambeth LBC v Thomas*, 1997; *Rochdale BC v Dixon*, 2011).

Accommodation agency charges

Publication of fees

3.115 The Consumer Rights Act (CRA) 2015 ss83–87, impose a duty on letting agents to publish details of their fees, including a description of the work covered by those fees and, if they are to be charged to tenants, whether it is one fee for the property or one fee per tenant, ie where a group of people take a property as joint tenants. Agents must also publish details of any redress scheme for dealing with complaints (s83(7); para 3.116). Enforcement is by local authorities (s87), subject to a right of appeal to the First-tier Tribunal (England) or the residential property tribunal (Wales) (Sch 9). An authority may impose a maximum penalty of £5,000 for breach of the duty.

Redress schemes

3.116 In England, lettings agents must be members of a 'redress scheme', which provides for complaints against members of the scheme, eg for excessive or hidden fees, to be investigated and determined by an independent person approved by the secretary of state (Enterprise and Regulatory Reform Act 2013 ss83–88). Enforcement of this duty is by local authorities who, subject to an appeal to the First-tier Tribunal, may impose a maximum penalty of £5,000 for failure to belong to a scheme (Redress Schemes for Lettings Agency Work and Property Management Work (Requirement to Belong to a Scheme etc) (England) Order 2014 SI No 2359).

3.117 In Wales, it is necessary to have a licence to carry out lettings work (see para 14.88); failure clearly to advertise fees or charging excessive fees could lead to a lettings agent losing its licence.

Unlawful charges

3.118 Under the Accommodation Agencies Act 1953 s1, it is a criminal offence either to demand or to accept any payment for registering or undertaking to register the name and requirements of a person seeking a tenancy of premises.

3.119 It is also an offence under the same section to demand or accept a payment simply for supplying or undertaking to supply to any person, addresses or other particulars of premises to let. In *Saunders v Soper*, 1974, the purpose of this provision was said to be simply to prohibit payments made for *supplying* addresses and particulars of property to let, and it was accordingly held that it did not prohibit payment for actually *finding* somewhere for the prospective tenant to live.

3.120 Both offences are punishable by a fine on standard scale 3, currently a maximum of £1,000. As well as constituting offences, such payments can be recovered as civil debts.

Premiums

3.121 A premium is a single payment usually demanded in return for the grant of a tenancy or on an assignment. Premiums are not unlawful, save where statute prohibits or limits them. Strictly speaking, when a long leaseholder sells his or her home to another, the purchase price is a premium but it is, of course, lawful. There are no restrictions on charging premiums in relation to assured tenancies, or assured shorthold tenancies.

Secure tenants

3.122 It is not unlawful for a landlord to charge a premium on the grant of a secure tenancy but in practice local authorities (and other social landlords) never do so and would be likely to be subject to challenge if they did so or to regulatory action. Where a tenancy has been assigned under the right to exchange (see paras 4.135–4.143), there is a ground for possession against a secure tenant if he or she paid a premium for his or her current premises or received one for his or her former premises (see para 2.98(9)). The premium is not, however, illegal so it is not recoverable by the person who paid it.

Protected tenants

3.123 A premium is a lump sum, or any other money payable in addition to rent, or any payment by way of a deposit, other than a deposit which is reasonable in relation to the potential liability for which it is paid and which does not exceed one-sixth of the annual rent (RA 1977 s128). It is illegal to charge a tenant a premium on the grant, continuance or renewal of a Rent Act protected tenancy (see paras 1.268–1.293) (RA 1977 s119). A tenant who has paid such a premium can sue for its return (RA 1977 s125). Such a claim must be made within six years of the payment, in the same way as for the recovery of a normal civil debt (LA 1980). Given that new protected tenancies can only be granted in limited circumstances (see para 1.271(3)), this is now only like to arise in relation to continuation or renewal.

3.124 It is also a criminal offence to require or to receive a premium. There are two main exceptions where premiums may lawfully be charged (see also RA 1977 Sch 18 for other limited exceptions). The first applied to tenancies where the landlord has no power to determine the tenancy at any time within 20 years, beginning on the date when it was granted, and the terms of the tenancy did not inhibit both the assignment and the underletting of the whole of the premises comprised in the tenancy (RA 1977 s127(2)). Such tenancies were wholly exempt from the illegal premium rules. The second exception applies where a tenancy has ceased to fall outside the low rent exception (see para 1.277(4)) because of increases. Where the tenancy was granted before 16 July 1980, a premium was lawfully required and paid on the grant of the tenancy, the tenancy was when granted a tenancy at a low rent and the terms of the tenancy do not inhibit both the assignment and the underletting of the whole of the premises comprising the tenancy, the rules relating to premiums do not apply, and are deemed never to have applied (RA 1977 s127(3A), (3B)).

3.125 **Premiums on change of tenant.** A premium might be charged by a landlord, or by his or her agent, or by an outgoing tenant. An outgoing tenant might charge for an assignment, or else for arranging to surrender his or her own tenancy to the landlord, who contemporaneously consents to grant a new tenancy to the incoming tenant. In such a case, it may well be that there is no profit to the landlord. In all of these cases, however, the premium is an illegal payment (RA 1977 s120; *Farrell v Alexander*, 1976).

3.126 **Premiums paid to or by another.** It is a premium whether a person demands that the money is paid to him- or herself, or to someone else, perhaps, for example, in discharge of a debt that the person demanding the premium owes (*Elmdene Estates Ltd v White*, 1960). Another example would be that of the outgoing tenant who agrees to assign the tenancy or arrange for a new tenancy to be granted to the incoming tenant, if the incoming tenant will pay arrears of rent that he or she owes.

3.127 **Premiums in cash or kind.** The most obvious form that a premium will take is cash. But an illegal premium might also be demanded or paid other than in cash, eg by demanding payments in kind, such as goods, or else by demanding excessive prices for fixtures, fittings or furniture.

3.128 **Premiums for fittings and furniture.** It is, however, lawful to make it a condition of the grant of a tenancy, whether by assignment or from the landlord, that an incoming tenant purchase fittings, or even furniture (RA 1977 s123). Items such as fitted carpets may well be valueless to an outgoing tenant in his or her new home, and it is considered fair that he or she should be able to insist, before the assignment or an arrangement for surrender and new grant, that the incoming tenant, as it were, takes them off his or her hands.

3.129 Only a fair price for fittings and furniture can be demanded, and the excess constitutes an illegal premium (RA 1977 s123). Anyone seeking to make an incoming tenant pay for furniture is obliged to provide an inventory of it and of the price sought for each item; failure to do so is a criminal offence (RA 1977 s124). The position is slightly different where 'fixtures' are concerned. These are items such as fitted cupboards or double glazing which effectively become a part of the premises and are valueless when removed. No tenant is allowed to remove fixtures in any event; as they attach to the premises, they become, eventually, the property of the landlord. An outgoing tenant is permitted to charge an incoming tenant the amount it cost him or her to install fixtures (RA 1977 s120).

3.130 **Other items.** An outgoing tenant is also permitted to charge what it cost him or her to do any structural alterations to the premises, any amounts paid by way of outgoings on the premises, eg advance utility charges, which are attributable to a period after he or she leaves, and any amount paid by the outgoing tenant to a former tenant which was payment for fixtures or alterations (RA 1977 s120).

Protected shorthold tenants

3.131 The premium provisions applicable to Rent Act protected tenants are also applicable to protected shorthold tenancies in the same way.

Restricted contracts

3.132 The prohibitions against premiums described above (see paras 3.123–3.129) applied to restricted contracts if there was an effective rent registration with the Rent Tribunal, ie one which applied to the letting in question (RA 1977 s122). If there was not, then there were no prohibitions on premiums.

Deposits

3.133 Landlords frequently require an incoming occupier to pay a deposit, either for furniture, for rent arrears or, for example, damage. Deposits are not illegal save where statute has intervened.

Rent Act protected tenants

3.134 Deposits were not unlawful if reasonable in relation to the purpose for which claimed *and* they did not exceed one-sixth of the annual rent (RA 1977 s128).

Assured shorthold tenants

3.135 Most private landlords require assured shorthold tenants (see paras 1.246–1.251) to pay a deposit at the commencement of the tenancy as security for the tenant complying with the terms of his or her tenancy. Commonly, the deposit is retained to cover any damage which may occur to the premises, but it may also be held to cover the last period's rent. Many tenants have had difficulty recovering deposits at the end of their tenancies.

3.136 Deposits paid in respect of assured shortholds must be dealt with under a tenancy deposit scheme (HA 2004 ss212–215C; Housing (Tenancy Deposit Schemes) Order 2007 SI No 796). The provisions apply both to landlords and to managing agents (HA 2004 s212(8)). Furthermore, as the provisions apply to any deposit paid 'in connection' with an assured shorthold tenancy (HA 2004 s213(1)), a deposit paid by someone other than the tenant him- or herself, eg the tenant's parents, must be dealt with under a tenancy deposit scheme.

3.137 The provisions of HA 2004 have been amended by both LA 2011 and DA 2015 to address problems caused by their original drafting and in response to a number of decisions, in particular *Charalambous v Ng*, 2014, which decided that the obligation to deal with a deposit under a tenancy deposit scheme even applied to deposits paid *before* the provisions of HA 2004 came into force on 6 April 2007.

3.138 There are two types of scheme: 'custodial scheme' and 'insurance scheme'.

3.139 **Custodial scheme.** Under a custodial scheme, the landlord pays the deposit to a 'scheme administrator', who holds it until the end of the tenancy. At the end of the tenancy, unless the parties reach an agreement, either may apply to the administrator for an issue between them as to how much the landlord is entitled to retain to be determined by alternative dispute resolution.

3.140 **Insurance scheme.** Under an insurance scheme, the landlord or managing agent retains the deposit during the tenancy. At the end of the tenancy, if the tenant disputes the amount that the landlord intends to keep, that amount must be paid over to the administrator pending alternative dispute resolution. Under an insurance scheme, it is the administrator who is obliged to pay the tenant the amount that he or she is entitled to recover (after dispute resolution) whether or not that amount has been paid into the scheme. Hence, it is the administrator who requires the insurance, which has to be paid by the landlord.

3.141 **Dealing with the deposit.** Subject to certain exceptions (see paras 3.144–3.145), within 30 days of receiving the deposit, the landlord or managing agent must give the tenant information about the scheme which is applicable to it (HA 2004 s213(6)) and must comply with certain terms of the scheme, referred to as the 'initial requirements' (HA 2004 s213(3)). (Originally, the time limit was 14 days but this was extended to 30 days with effect from 6 April 2012, under amendments made by LA 2011).

3.142 **Prescribed information.** The information which must be given (see para 3.141) is contained in Housing (Tenancy Deposits) (Prescribed Information) Order 2007 SI No 797 art 2, and includes: contact details for the scheme administrator; any leaflet supplied by the administrator explaining how tenancy deposits work; the procedure for repaying (or not repaying) the deposit at the end of the tenancy; what happens where either the landlord or the tenant is uncontactable at the end of the tenancy; the procedure for dispute resolution; certain details about the tenancy itself and the parties; confirmation (in the form of a certificate signed by the landlord or managing agent) that the information provided about the tenancy and the parties is true and that the tenant has been given the opportunity to confirm the truth of that information.

3.143 **Initial requirements.** The initial requirements (see para 3.141) are determined by the terms of each scheme (HA 2004 s213(4)) and accordingly vary depending on which scheme is used.

3.144 **Exceptions.** If the deposit was received *before* 6 April 2012, the prescribed information (see para 3.142) must have been given and the initial requirements (see para 3.143) of the scheme must have been complied with by 5 May 2012 (Localism Act 2011 (Commencement No 4 and Transitional, Transitory and Saving Provisions) Order 2012 SI No 628 art 16).

3.145 Specific provision is also made for what happens where the deposit was received in connection with a fixed-term assured shorthold before 6 April 2007, when the tenancy deposit schemes first came into force, and a statutory periodic tenancy (see para 2.161) which arose after that date following expiry of the fixed term and which was not replaced by a new fixed-term tenancy (HA 2004 s215A). In these circumstances, the deposit had to be protected, the prescribed information given (see para 3.142) and the initial requirements (see para 3.143) complied with by 23 June 2015. If such a periodic tenancy no longer existed on 26 March 2015, or the deposit had been returned before that date, the landlord is deemed to have complied with any requirements.

3.146 **Expiry of fixed term.** Where a deposit is paid in relation to a fixed-term assured shorthold, the tenant is treated on expiry of the term as having paid the same amount by way of a deposit in relation to either any new fixed-term tenancy replacing it or the statutory periodic tenancy that arises (HA 1988 s5; para 2.161), unless the landlord returns the deposit at the end of the previous tenancy (*Superstrike Ltd v Rodrigues*, 2013). In these circumstances, it is not necessary to serve the prescribed information or to comply with the initial requirements again provided that this was properly done in relation to the original tenancy (HA 2004 s215B).

3.147 **Non-compliance.** There are significant sanctions for failure to pay a deposit into a scheme, or deal with it in accordance with an insurance scheme, failure to provide information, or breach of the initial requirements.

3.148 **Financial penalty.** If a deposit was paid in connection with an assured shorthold tenancy on or after 6 April 2007, the tenant or the person who paid the deposit can apply to the court. If the deposit is not being held in accordance with an authorised scheme, or the prescribed information (see para 3.142) was not given or the initial requirements (see para 3.143) not complied with within 30 days (or the exceptional time limit in para 3.144), the court must order the landlord, and/or any managing agent, to pay the applicant a sum of money which is not less than the amount of the deposit together with a sum which is not more than three times the amount of the deposit and/or order the deposit to be repaid to the applicant or paid into the designated account of a scheme administrator (HA 2004 s214).

3.149 The application can be made during the tenancy or after it has ended (HA 2004 s214(2A)), reversing the effect of *Gladehurst Properties Ltd v Hashemi*, 2011). If the tenancy has ended, however, the court cannot order the deposit to be paid into the designated account of a scheme administrator (HA 2004 s214(2A), (3A)).

3.150 **Prohibition on section 21 notice.** In addition, a landlord cannot give notice requiring possession under HA 1988 s21 (see paras 2.195–2.204) if the deposit is not being held in accordance with an authorised scheme, or the prescribed information (see para 3.142) was not given or the initial requirements (see para 3.143) were not complied with within 30 days, *unless* the deposit has been returned to the tenant in full or with deductions that are agreed by the tenant, or the tenant has applied to the court under HA 2004 s214 (see paras 3.148–3.149) for return of the deposit and a penalty payment, which application has either been determined by the court, been withdrawn or settled: HA 2004 s215(1), (2), (2A).

Protected shorthold tenants

3.151 The deposit provisions applicable to Rent Act protected tenants (see para 3.134) are also applicable to protected shorthold tenancies in the same way.

Restricted contracts

3.152 The prohibitions against excessive deposits described above in relation to Rent Act protected tenants (see para 3.134) applied to restricted contracts if there was an effective rent registration with the Rent Tribunal, ie one which applied to the letting in question (RA 1977 s122). If there was not, then there were no prohibitions on deposits.

Housing benefit

3.153 Under the Social Security Contributions and Benefits Act 1992, rent rebates and allowances, together with council tax rebates, are available to assist those on income support and others with low incomes with their housing costs. This scheme for housing benefit is being gradually replaced throughout the country by universal credit under the Welfare Reform Act 2012.

3.154 The details of these support schemes are so commonly varied that it is impossible to consider them here and no purpose is served by describing either scheme in outline. There is a number of annual publications which contain current provisions.

CHAPTER 4

Other terms and rights

continued

Introduction

4.1 This chapter addresses a number of rights conferred on occupiers, depending on their status, which are additional to the rights of occupation considered in relation to security of tenure and eviction in chapter 2, and to the protection afforded in relation to rents and other charges considered in chapter 3. By and large, we are concerned here with long leaseholders (see para 2.72) and tenants, whether periodic (see para 1.18) or fixed-term (see para 1.18). The only licensees with whom we are concerned are those who are secure, and who therefore enjoy the rights of secure tenants (see para 1.168).

4.2 There is a range of rights considered in this chapter – from rights of enfranchisement, meaning the rights of long leaseholders, and of secure tenants and assured tenants of private registered providers of social housing (PRPs) and registered social landlords (RSLs), to acquire the freehold (or a long lease) of their own homes, through rights to take over management, to rights to improve, with or without grant assistance. Of particular importance are the rights given to disabled persons – and others – under (now) the Equality Act (EqA) 2010, and the rights given to all occupiers under the Unfair Contract Terms Act (UCTA) 1977 and the Consumer Rights Act (CRA) 2015. Other rights include assignment and subletting.

4.3 This chapter does not, however, consider a number of rights which are addressed under their own headings, in later chapters: disrepair in chapter 11; protection against harassment, and unlawful eviction in chapter 5; rights on breakdown of relationship in chapter 7; rights that derive from the identity of the landlord as a social landlord in chapter 8, eg to complain to the independent housing ombudsman; rights to housing assistance and in relation to the allocation of housing in chapter 10; and, the rights that derive from the possibility of action taken by local authorities in relation to housing conditions, in chapters 5 and 12–14.

Enlarging rights of occupation

4.4 A number of leaseholders and tenants enjoy the right to buy out their landlords, potentially all the way up the line to the freeholder.

Tenants

4.5 **Landlord and Tenant Act (LTA) 1987.** LTA 1987 Part 1 gives tenants of blocks of flats a 'right of first refusal' should the freeholder or a superior landlord wish to sell his or her interest in circumstances amounting to a 'relevant disposal'. The provisions apply only to flats, and there must be at least two flats in the building for them to operate. The block need not be purpose-built.

4.6 **Qualifying tenants.** Tenants, including Rent Act protected and statutory tenants (see paras 1.268–1.293), qualify to exercise the right *unless* they are: protected shorthold tenants (see paras 1.294–1.297); assured tenants, whether shorthold or not (see paras 1.220–1.251; those to whom the business security of LTA 1954 Part 2 (see para 1.180(15)) applies; or, service tenants (see paras 1.131–1.140) – LTA 1987 s3. This number of exceptions combined with the exclusion of properties owned by certain landlords (see para 4.7) in effect means that the right is confined to Rent Act tenants and private sector long leaseholders. A person who has a lease of three or more flats in the building, eg someone who has acquired for sub-letting, or who is a subtenant whose landlord is him- or herself a qualifying tenant, cannot be a qualifying tenant (LTA 1987 s3).

4.7 **Exclusions.** The provisions do not apply if the landlord is a resident landlord or an exempt landlord, or if less than 50 per cent of the flats are occupied by qualifying tenants, or if less than 50 per cent of the floor area of the building (excluding common parts) is not in (or intended for) residential use (LTA 1987 s1). 'Exempt landlords' include local authorities, urban development corporations, the Homes and Communities Agency (HCA), charitable housing trusts (see para 8.5), PRPs and RSLs (LTA 1987 s58). 'Resident landlord' is defined (LTA 1987 s58) in terms very similar to the definition in HA 1988 (see para 1.233(10)). Accordingly, the mere fact that the landlord lives in a purpose-built block of flats elsewhere in the building will not exclude the right of first refusal. Where the resident landlord exemption does apply, however, eg in a converted house, the landlord need not have been in residence since the commencement of the tenancy, but only for a period of at least one year before the prospective disposal. The residence test is as an 'only or principal residence' (see para 1.176–1.179).

4.8 **Relevant disposal.** The right of first refusal arises only in relation to a 'relevant disposal'. This means the disposal of any interest in the whole or part of the building other than one of a schedule of classes of disposal:

1) the grant of a tenancy of a single flat;
2) a disposal of an interest by way of mortgage;
3) disposal under the Matrimonial Causes Act (MCA) 1973 ss23A, 24, or 24A (see para 7.7) or the Children Act (CA) 1989 (see para 7.49), or the Civil Partnership Act 2004 Sch 5 (see paras 7.7–7.8);
4) a disposal related to a compulsory purchase;
5) a disposal under the collective enfranchisement provisions of the Leasehold Reform, Housing and Urban Development Act (LRHUDA) 1993 (see para 4.27);
6) a disposal by way of gift to a member of the landlord's family or to a charity;
7) a disposal by will;
8) a disposal to the Crown; and
9) a disposal to a company which has been 'associated' (as defined) with the landlord company for at least two years (LTA 1987 s4).

4.9 A contract to dispose is a relevant disposal (LTA 1987 s4A). A disposal by a mortgage company falls within the provisions, even if it has taken the property back from the landlord under the mortgage (s4(1A)).

4.10 **Requisite majority.** Where a relevant disposal is proposed, the landlord has to offer the tenants the right of first refusal, identifying what is on offer and its terms, including price. 'Propose' here means a state of mind somewhere between mere consideration of a course of action, and a fixed or irrevocable determination to pursue it (*Mainwaring v Trustees of Henry Smith's Charity*, 1996). The offer can only be accepted by a 'requisite majority' of the qualifying tenants, within a period of not less than two months (LTA 1987 s5). 'Requisite majority' is defined as for LTA 1987 Part 3 (see para 4.44). If the requisite majority accepts the offer, they have a further two months in which to identify a person to act on their behalf in the further transactions, and the landlord cannot sell to anyone else until the end of the 'relevant period', defined to cover the designated procedure (LTA 1987 s6).

4.11 **One year restriction on disposal.** If no one is nominated or the offer is not accepted, the landlord cannot dispose elsewhere for 12 months save on the same terms and at the same price (LTA 1987 s7): this is to prevent offers at an unnaturally high figure or on unduly onerous terms designed to put off the tenants buying.

4.12 **Nominated person.** Once a person has been nominated, the landlord may not dispose of the property except to that person, and must send out a contract within one month (LTA 1987 ss8 and 8A).

The nominated person then has two months in which to offer an exchange of contract (LTA 1987 s8A).

4.13 **Other provisions.** Other provisions deal with withdrawals and deemed withdrawals (in cases where time limits are not complied with) by both landlord and nominated purchaser and where the original proposed sale is by auction. There are also provisions to deal with a disposal which has not complied with the right of first refusal, including the possibility of forcing the purchaser to resell to the tenants (LTA 1987 ss11, 12A-12D; *Belvedere Court Management Ltd v Frogmore Development Ltd*, 1995).

4.14 **Criminal offences.** It is a criminal offence for a landlord, without reasonable excuse, to make a relevant disposal (see para 4.8) of property to which LTA 1987 Part 1 applies with liability to a fine of up to an unlimited amount (LTA 1987 s10A; LASPO 2012 s85(1)). Landlords under a duty to inform tenants of an assignment of the property (see para 1.78) must also inform qualifying tenants of their rights under LTA 1987 (LTA 1985 s3A). Failure to do so is a criminal offence, punishable by a fine of up to level 4 of the standard scale (currently £2,500).

Long leaseholders

LRA 1967

Enfranchisement and extension of long leases

4.15 Under the Leasehold Reform Act (LRA) 1967, a person who is a long leaseholder (see para 2.72) of a house, but not of a flat, can compel the landlord to extend the lease for a further 50 years beyond the date of its original termination, or may require the landlord to sell him or her the freehold (known as 'enfranchisement'). Those whose landlord is a local authority are not automatically excluded from these rights (unlike the position where statutory continuation is concerned (see para 2.73), although authorities do have additional grounds on which to oppose their exercise (see para 4.23).

4.16 These rights only apply to those houses which are not horizontally divided from any other premises, ie they do not, to any material extent, overlap, nor are they overlapped by, another property (LRA 1967 s2). Whether a part of a house above or below another property is material depends on the relationship between that part and the house, rather than with the whole of the other property; it is a question of fact and degree in each case (*Malekshad v Howard De Walden Estates Ltd*, 2002).

4.17 The house need not, however, be free-standing: it may be in a row of terraced houses. The house can be sub-divided, and even sub-let. The building must have been 'designed or adapted for living in' (LRA 1967 s2(1)); if so, the fact that it is not currently occupied for residential purposes, eg because it is in a state of dilapidation, does not prevent it from being a house (*Boss Holdings Ltd v Grosvenor West End Properties Ltd,* 2008). The building must, however, be a property which can reasonably be called a house. This ties the definition to the primary meaning of house, namely a single residence rather than a hostel or a purpose-built block of flats (*Day v Hosebay* Ltd, 2012; *Magnohard Ltd v Earl Cadogan,* 2012). A house which includes commercial premises can be a house (*Lake v Bennett,* 1969; *Tandon v Trustees of Spurgeon's Houses,* 1982) where the commercial and residential parts comprise one unit but not where the residential and commercial parts are wholly unconnected (*Henley v Cohen,* 2013). A property divided into two maisonettes with separate entrances, but which is otherwise apparently a single residence, has been held to be a house for this purpose (*Malpas v St Ermin's Property Co Ltd,* 1992).

4.18 The Act formerly only applied to tenancies at a low rent, ie a rent not more than two-thirds of the rateable value or, if there is no rateable value, a rent less than £1,000 per annum in Greater London or £250 elsewhere (LRA 1967 s4). This requirement was abolished by the Commonhold and Leasehold Reform Act (CLRA) 2002, although whether the tenancy is at a low rent affects the purchase price for the freehold (but not an extended lease) (see paras 4.22–4.25). The Act still applies only to long leases (see para 2.72).

Qualifying periods

4.19 A leaseholder must exercise these rights before the lease expires (see para 2.23) or while his or her tenancy is continued under statute (see para 2.73–2.83), up until a period of two months from when the landlord has served notice proposing a statutory or assured tenancy (LRA 1967 s3(2) and Sch 3 para 2(1)). The right may be exercised after an extension to the lease has been granted.

Occupation as residence

4.20 The former requirement that the leaseholder occupy the premises as his or her residence was abolished by CLRA 2002. There remain two exceptions: (a) where a house includes a flat let to a qualifying tenant for the purposes of LRHUDA 1993 (see para 4.29); and, (b) where the tenant occupies under a business tenancy (see para 1.180(15)). In both cases the tenant does not have the right to enfranchise unless he or she has been occupying the house or part of it as his or her only or main residence for the last two years or for periods amounting to two years in the last ten years.

4.21 It is enough to occupy only part of the premises, eg it will suffice if the occupier has the lease on a whole house, lives in part and lets out part (*Harris v Swick Securities*, 1969), provided, where necessary, that he or she occupies at least part as his or her only or main, not just 'a', residence (LRA 1967 s1; *Poland v Earl Cadogan*, 1980).

Purchase price

4.22 Failing agreement between the parties, the purchase price can be fixed by the First-tier Tribunal (in England) or the leasehold valuation tribunal (in Wales), and on appeal by the Upper Tribunal, but the procedure is complicated, and anyone intending to use it should consult a lawyer or surveyor.

4.23 Extension does not cost anything, although a new ground rent, ie low rent, which is appropriate to the value of the house as at the date when the new lease is to start, will take effect from that date (LRA 1967 s15). There are special grounds of opposition to enfranchisement or extension available to specified public landlords, including local authorities, the police and fire services and universities (LRA 1967 s28). In essence, enfranchisement can be resisted where the secretary of state or the Welsh Ministers certify that a property will be required by one of these landlords for redevelopment within 10 years.

Sooner is cheaper

4.24 Enfranchisement can be extremely cheap. If the tenancy is at a low rent, all that is being bought back is the benefit of that rent and the fairly remote possibility that the landlord will ever get the property back. If the tenancy is not at a low rent, the purchase price also includes an allowance for 'marriage value', ie the increase in the value of property which is produced by the two separate interests (the freehold and the leasehold) coming to be owned by the same person. The longer there is to run on the lease at the time notice indicating an intention to purchase is served, the cheaper the price will be, because the landlord's expectations are the more remote. It follows that in those remaining cases in which an occupier has to satisfy the residential qualification (see paras 4.20–4.21), he or she should exercise the power to enfranchise as soon as he or she has done so.

4.25 The price of enfranchisement bears no practical relation to current property values or even to the customarily (lower than vacant possession) value at which many sitting tenants are usually able to buy from their landlords.

LRHUDA 1993

Rights for leaseholders of flats

4.26 The rights of leaseholders of flats were further extended by LRHUDA 1993, to compensate for their inability to enfranchise under LRA 1967 (above), because their homes are flats, not houses. Two rights were created by LRHUDA 1993: a right to collective enfranchisement of the freehold interest in a block of flats by qualifying tenants; and an individual right to a new lease of a flat.

a) Collective enfranchisement

4.27 The right of collective enfranchisement is the right to have the freehold of the premises in which the flat is situated acquired on their behalf by persons appointed by the leaseholders for the purpose (LRHUDA 1993 s1).

4.28 **Qualifying premises**. The building to be acquired must contain two or more flats owned by qualifying tenants (see para 4.29), who must between them own at least two-thirds of the total number of flats in the building (LRHUDA 1993 s3). Where the building is not primarily in residential use or where there is a resident landlord in a building containing not more than four units, the right to collective enfranchisement is excluded (LRHUDA 1993 s4). 'Resident landlord' is defined (s4) in terms similar to the definition in HA 1988 (see para 1.233(10)). Accordingly, the mere fact that the landlord lives in a purpose-built block of flats will not exclude the right to collective enfranchisement.

4.29 **Qualifying tenants**. Qualifying tenants have to have a long lease, broadly meaning one for more than 21 years (LRHUDA 1993 s7). Certain tenants are excluded: business tenants (see para 1.180(15)), tenants of charitable housing trusts (see para 8.5); and, those whose tenancies are illegal because they have been granted by a mesne landlord in breach of a superior lease (see paras 1.64–1.69) unless that breach has been waived (see para 1.70–1.72, LRHUDA 1993 s5). Tenants of local authorities are accordingly not excluded.

4.30 **Procedure**. To make a purchase, qualifying tenants are entitled to information from their immediate landlord about those with superior interests (LRHUDA 1993 s11). Once the tenants decide to proceed they must serve an initial notice on the freeholder; this initial notice must be on behalf of tenants of not less than half of the total number of flats in the building (LRHUDA 1993 s13). Qualifying tenants who are parties to the initial notice become participating tenants.

4.31 The initial notice must state the name and address of a nominee purchaser and a proposed price, which must include not only the freehold price but also a price for any intermediate interests. The freeholder must serve a counter-notice either admitting or denying the right. The right may be denied on the basis that the freeholder intends to redevelop the premises (LRHUDA 1993 s21). If the freeholder admits the right, he or she may dispute the purchase price in a counter-notice. If the freeholder fails to serve a counter-notice, the nominee purchaser is entitled to acquire the freehold on the terms set out in the initial notice (*Willingale v Global Grange Ltd*, 2000).

4.32 **Nominee purchaser.** At the moment, there is no requirement for a specific person or type of body to fulfil the role of nominee purchaser, although in practice a company is often set up for the purpose. Amendments under CLRA 2002 provided that a specially constituted 'RTE' (right to enfranchise) company had to be used, but it is now highly unlikely that these amendments will be brought into force.

4.33 **Price.** If the price is not agreed, it is to be determined under statutory rules into which defined assumptions are built. The price has to comprise a number of elements: the freehold price, the price of any intermediate leasehold interest, and the price of other interests to be acquired. The freeholder is entitled to compensation for any loss in value to any other property he or she owns, including loss of development value (LRHUDA 1993 Sch 6). Disputes regarding price are referable to the First-tier Tribunal (England) or the leasehold valuation tribunal (Wales) (LRHUDA 1993 s24).

4.34 **Enforcement.** The right may be enforced through application to the county court. Disputes about the terms of the purchase, however, are referred to the First-tier Tribunal (England) or the leasehold valuation tribunal (Wales).

b) New lease

4.35 **Ninety-year lease.** In addition, LRHUDA 1993 gives individual tenants the right to acquire a new 90-year lease. To exercise the right, the tenant must have a long lease (see para 2.72) of premises which include a flat. A long leaseholder of more than one flat may apply to extend the lease of each of them (*Howard de Walden Estates Ltd v Aggio*, 2008).

4.36 **Procedure.** The tenant proceeds by means of an initial notice, to which the landlord must respond with a counter-notice admitting or denying the right. The right can be denied on the basis that the landlord intends to redevelop (LRHUDA 1993 s45). Disputes regarding the terms and price or the terms of the new lease may be referred to the First-tier Tribunal (England) or the leasehold valuation tribunal (Wales). Other disputes regarding progress may be referred to the county court. The tenant may withdraw (LRHUDA 1993 s52); in some circumstances of inaction by the tenant, there may be a deemed withdrawal (LRHUDA 1993 s53).

4.37 **Price and grant.** If the price or the terms of the new lease are not agreed, the dispute may be referred to the tribunal. The price is determined according to statutory assumptions, and includes compensation for the landlord (LRHUDA 1993 Sch 13). Once all the terms are agreed or determined, and the price paid, the tenant must accept – in substitution for his or her present lease – a lease for a term which will amount to 90 years from what would have been the end of the current lease, at a 'peppercorn' rent (LRHUDA 1993 s56(1)). In addition, the tenant must clear any arrears of rent or service charges which have accrued (LRHUDA 1993 s56(3)). The new lease is, in general, to be on the same terms as the original (LRHUDA 1993 s57).

c) Future rights

4.38 Once a lease has been granted, there is nothing to prevent another new lease being granted or the right to collective enfranchisement being exercised. However, all rights to statutory security of tenure (see paras 2.73–2.83) are lost (LRHUDA 1993 s59).

LTA 1987 Part 3

4.39 LTA 1987 Part 3 permits a form of 'compulsory purchase' by qualifying tenants. For this purpose a qualifying tenant must have a long lease (see para 2.72). A business tenant (see para 1.180(15)) cannot be a qualifying tenant, nor can a tenant whose lease comprises more than two flats or whose own landlord is a qualifying tenant (LTA 1987 s26).

4.40 For the provisions to operate, a specified number of flats in a building must be occupied by qualifying tenants: if less than four flats, all of them; if four to ten, no less than all but one; if ten or more, at least 90 per cent (LTA 1987 s25).

Exclusions

4.41 The provisions do not apply if more than 50 per cent of the building (excluding the common parts) is non-residential, or if there is an exempt or resident landlord. Resident landlords and exempt landlords are defined as for the purposes of Part 1 (see para 4.7).

Acquisition order

4.42 An 'acquisition order' can only be made by a court, which must be satisfied that the preconditions (above) apply and (a) that one of two sets of further conditions applies, and (b) that it considers that it is appropriate to make an order in the circumstances (LTA 1987 s29).

Alternative conditions

4.43 It is the conditions which define the purpose. The conditions are (a) where the freeholder is (and is likely to remain) in breach of his or her obligations (in respect of repair, insurance, maintenance or management) – or would be in breach if notice could be served on him or her – to such an extent that the appointment of a manager under Part 2 (see para 4.78–4.80) would not be a sufficient remedy, or (b) that there has been a Part 2 manager for at least two years (LTA 1987 s29).

Procedure

4.44 Before an application can be made to the court, a 'requisite majority' of tenants must serve notice on the landlord of the intention to apply, identifying the grounds on which the application will be made, specifying what remedial steps might be taken to avert the application within a specified reasonable period, and containing such other information as may be prescribed by the secretary of state or the Welsh Ministers (LTA 1987 s27). The court can, however, waive the requirement of preliminary notice if it considers that it is not reasonably practicable to serve one. Unless the prior notice is waived by the court, no application can be made until the period specified for remedial action has expired (s28). 'Requisite majority' means more than 50 per cent of the 'available votes'; 'available votes' means one vote for each flat involved (LTA 1987 s27(4)).

Order

4.45 If an order is made by the court, it must provide for a nominated person to acquire the landlord's interests on such terms as may be determined either by agreement between the parties or by the First-tier Tribunal (England) or the leasehold valuation tribunal (Wales) (s30). A landlord can apply for discharge of the order if the tenants do not proceed within a reasonable time, or if the number of tenants wishing to proceed falls below the requisite majority (s34). There is also provision for the procedure to be used where a landlord cannot be found (s33).

Secure tenants

4.46 Most secure tenants (including flexible tenants, see paras 1.181–1.189) have the right to buy under HA 1985. The right is available to a secure licensee (see para 1.168), although this is such an uncommon circumstance that it is not referred to further in this section.

4.47 **Qualifying period.** The right to buy arises only after a tenant has spent a specified amount of time as a secure tenant or as another public sector tenant (as defined), eg a tenant of a PRP or RSL (HA 1985 Sch 4); the time does not need to be with the same landlord, in the same premises or continuous (HA 1985 s119). In England, the qualifying period is three years (s119(A1)); in Wales, it is five years (s119(1)).

4.48 **Secure tenants.** The tenant has to be secure both when applying to buy and throughout the process (*Sutton LBC v Swann*, 1985; *Jennings v Epping Forest DC*, 1992; *Muir Group HA v Thornley*, 1992; *Bradford City MBC v McMahon*, 1993). If the an authority denies that a tenant is entitled to exercise the right to buy, he or she may apply to the county court for a declaration (HA 1985 s181). Where an authority incorrectly denies the tenant's right, there is no right to damages for breach of statutory duty (*Francis v Southwark LBC*, 2011).

4.49 **Injunction.** Once matters in relation to the purchase have been agreed or determined, the tenant may obtain an order to require the landlord to sell the property to him or her (HA 1985 s138). Although the county court has jurisdiction to determine most issues arising under the right to buy (s181), eg whether the tenant is entitled to exercise the right, disputes as to the valuation of a property are decided by the district valuer (s128).

4.50 **Purchase or eviction.** In *Bristol City Council v Lovell*, 1998, at the same time as the tenant was applying to exercise the right to buy, the authority was seeking to evict the tenant because of anti-social behaviour. It was held that it is for the court to decide in what order it hears the two conflicting applications. Following that case, specific provision has been made for suspension of the duty to proceed with the sale in anti-social behaviour cases (see para 4.66). Where possession is sought under other grounds, the court should consider the length of the tenant's residence in the property, the disruption that moving would cause, whether the tenant is in breach of the terms of his or her tenancy and whether a possession order would allow the landlord better to deploy its housing stock, eg where the property is under-occupied (*Basildon DC v Wahlen*, 2006).

4.51 **Family members**. The right may be exercised jointly with other members of the family (see paras 1.200–1.202) whom the tenant specifically identifies for this purpose (HA 1985 s123). If the tenant dies after establishing the section 123 right, such other members of the family are entitled to pursue the purchase, even if not otherwise entitled to succeed to the tenancy (see paras 1.192–1.203; *Harrow LBC v Tonge*, 1992).

4.52 **Freehold or leasehold**. If the dwelling is a house, and the landlord owns the freehold (see para 1.7), the right to buy is a right to the freehold. Otherwise, ie if the property is a flat, or if the landlord only has a lease, the right is to a lease for the appropriate term which is, normally, 125 years, although it will be less if the landlord's own remaining interest is itself not that long, in which case it will be for the remainder of the landlord's leasehold interest less five days (HA 1985 Sch 6 para 12(1), (2)). It may also be less if (since 8 August 1980) the landlord has granted any previous leases in a block of flats for the appropriate term, whether or not under the right to buy, so as to bring the new lease to an end at the same time as a previous lease (HA 1985 Sch 6 para 12(3)).

4.53 **Other matters**. There are detailed provisions governing the definition of 'house' and 'flat' (HA 1985 s183) and the exercise of these rights by joint tenants (HA 1985 s118). The definition of house is similar to that used in LRA 1967 (see paras 4.16–4.17). A dwelling which is not a house is a flat.

4.54 **Exemptions**. Some property is exempt from the right to buy (HA 1985 Sch 5), including property belonging to a charitable housing trust (see para 8.5), sheltered accommodation (*cf* para 2.117(4)) and accommodation adapted for the physically disabled (*cf* para 2.117(3)), properties of which the landlord is itself a tenant if its landlord is the Crown or the lease has less than 21 years to run (houses) or 50 years (flats), and certain properties usually let to employees.

4.55 **Discount**. The purchase price is the value of the property (HA 1985 s127) less the discount to which the tenant is entitled (s126). The amount of the discount (s129) varies depending on how long the tenant has been a public sector tenant (see para 4.47).

1) If the property is a house, the initial discount is 35 per cent (or 32 per cent if the tenancy was granted before 18 January 2005). An additional one per cent is then added for each year in excess of five years for which that the tenant has been a public sector tenant, subject to a maximum discount of 70 per cent in England or 60 per cent in Wales.
2) If the property is a flat, the initial discount, is 50 per cent (or 44 per cent if the tenancy was granted before 18 January 2005). An additional two per cent is then added for each year as a public sector tenant in excess of five years, subject to a maximum discount of 70 per cent in both England and Wales.

4.56 In addition, however, there is a maximum discount set by the secretary of state or the Welsh Ministers as an amount of money (HA 1985 s131). As at 5 April 2015, the maximum discount was set at £102,700 in London and £77,000 elsewhere in England, increasing annually in line with the consumer prices index (Housing (Right to Buy) (Limit on Discount) (England) Order 2014 SI No 1378. In Wales, the maximum discount is £8,000 (Housing (Right to Buy) (Limits on Discount) (Wales) Order 1999 SI No 292, as amended).

4.57 A discount will normally have to be repaid if the house or flat is subsequently sold within five years (HA 1985 s155). Where a sale is proposed within ten years of the purchase, however, a notice must be served on the landlord which allows it the opportunity to buy the property back (HA 1985 s156A).

4.58 **Procedure.** An application to exercise the right to buy commences when the tenant serves a notice in the prescribed form, claiming the right (HA 1985 s122). The prescribed form is RTB1 in Housing (Right to Buy) (Prescribed Forms) Regulations 1986 SI No 2194 or WRTB1 in Housing (Right to Buy) (Prescribed Forms) (Wales) Regulations 2015 SI No 1320.

4.59 On receipt of the tenant's notice, the landlord must – within a specified time – serve notice on the tenant either admitting or denying the right (HA 1985 s124(1)).

4.60 Once the tenant's right to buy has been admitted by the landlord (or if necessary determined by the county court – para 4.48), the landlord must serve a further notice on the tenant which must include the price at which it considers the tenant may acquire the freehold or a lease of the property (HA 1985 s125). The notice must be served within eight weeks of the tenant's right being admitted (see para 4.59) or determined by the county court (see para 4.48) if the freehold is to be acquired; if the tenant is only entitled to a lease, the period is twelve weeks.

4.61 The notice must also contain the terms of the proposed conveyance or lease, which must include the terms set out in HA 1985 Sch 6. The tenant may challenge any of the proposed terms in the county court but must do so before the sale is completed (*Sheffield City Council v Jackson*, 1998). Specific information must be set out in the notice, including estimates of future service charges and improvement contributions which the tenant may have to pay during a specified period which, in general terms, is the first five years after the sale is completed (HA 1985 ss125A–125C). These figures impose a cap on the amount of service charges and improvement contributions that the landlord will be able to recover during this period (HA 1985 Sch 6 paras 16A–16D).

4.62 The notice must also include a description of any structural defect known to the landlord affecting the dwelling-house (HA 1985 s125(4A)). After the right to buy has been exercised, the former tenant cannot bring a claim in negligence or misrepresentation against the former landlord for failure to include a structural defect (*Payne v Barnet LBC*, 1997) but he or she can claim for breach of statutory duty (*Rushton v Worcester CC*, 2001).

4.63 The landlord may serve a fresh notice to correct any mistake in the original notice (*Nessa v Tower Hamlets LBC*, 2010).

4.64 Within 12 weeks of the service of the landlord's notice, the tenant must serve a notice stating whether he or she intends to proceed or withdraw from the purchase (HA 1985 s125D). If the tenant fails to do so, the landlord can serve a further notice requiring him or her to do so within 28 days, although this period can be extended (s125E). If the tenant fails to comply with that notice, the application is deemed to be withdrawn.

4.65 **Non-compliance with time limits**. If the landlord fails to comply with the statutory time provision for handling the right to buy, a would-be purchaser can serve notices, the effect of which is to penalise the landlord by treating rent payments during the periods of delay as attributable to – ie as deductions from – the purchase price (HA 1985 ss153A, 153B). This includes payments by way of housing benefit (*Hanoman v Southwark LBC*, 2009).

4.66 **Anti-social behaviour**. A court can suspend a tenant's right to buy where the tenant is guilty of anti-social behaviour and the court considers that it is reasonable to make a suspension order (HA 1985 s121A). The standard of behaviour is the same as that which justifies a demotion order (see para 1.254). The period of the suspension must be specified in the order but can be extended on application to the court by the landlord if it is proved that further anti-social behaviour has taken place since the original order (s121A(2), (6), (7)). If the landlord has applied for a demotion order (see paras 1.253–1.261), or a possession order based on Grounds 2 or 2ZA (see para 2.98(2), (3)) or s84A (see paras 2.108–2.112), or a suspension order, it does not have to sell the property to the tenant pending determination of the application. If a demotion order is granted, then the tenant will lose the right to buy so long as it lasts (see para 1.259).

4.67 **Arrears.** A tenant is not able to force the landlord to complete the sale if he or she has failed to pay the rent or any other payment due from him or her as a tenant, eg service charges, provided that it has been properly demanded from him or her at least four weeks beforehand (HA 1985 s138(2)). This does not apply to arrears of council tax.

4.68 **Demolition.** Where the landlord intends to demolish the premises, it may serve a demolition notice (HA 1985 ss138A–138C). There are two types of demolition notice: initial and final. A final notice must state that the property will be demolished by a specified date, which must be no later than two years after the date of the notice. An initial notice does not have to specify a date but must say that the landlord intends to demolish the property within a period not exceeding five years. While a final notice is in force, a tenant cannot apply to exercise the right to buy. If the tenant has already made an application, the landlord is not obliged to sell the property. While an initial notice is in force, a new application to exercise the right to buy can be made but any such application, and any existing application, is suspended.

4.69 The Act does not provide any means of appealing a decision to serve a demolition notice so it can only be challenged under the limited grounds available under judicial review (see paras 8.23–8.28). If a tenant has applied to exercise the right to buy and his or her right to do so has been admitted by the landlord (or if necessary determined by the county court – para 4.48), but completion of the sale is prevented by service of a demolition notice (initial or final), the tenant is entitled to compensation from the landlord for reasonable legal and other professional costs incurred prior to the notice (HA 1985 s138C).

4.70 **Preserved right to buy.** On a transfer of land to the private sector, eg on a large scale voluntary transfer (LSVT) (see para 8.13), a secure tenant's right to buy is 'preserved' (HA 1985 ss171A–171H). Where transfer is, as is most common, to a PRP or RSL, it is the right to buy which is preserved, rather than its substitution with the right to acquire which some assured tenants enjoy (see paras 4.74–4.75). The preserved right to buy will be inapplicable if the right to buy as against the former landlord was unavailable because of HA 1985 Sch 5 paras 1–3 (charities and certain housing associations – para 4.54), or in such other cases as may be excepted by order of the secretary of state or the Welsh Ministers: HA 1985 s171A(3). The secretary of state or Welsh Ministers may by regulations modify the right to buy for these purposes, (HA 1985 s171C and Housing (Preservation of Right to Buy) Regulations 1993 SI No 2241.

4.71 The right to buy is only preserved so long as the tenant occupies the premises as his or her only or principal home (see paras 1.172–1.175). The right may be exercised by the tenant, or a qualifying successor, as defined, and may extend from the original premises to other premises to which the tenant has moved and which are rented from the same landlord (or if a company, a connected company) (HA 1985 s171B). By section 171F, a court is not to make an order for possession against a tenant or qualifying successor on the ground of suitable alternative accommodation without ensuring that any right to buy will be preserved (or that the tenant will be Housing Act secure as against the new landlord).

4.72 A subsequent disposal by the (new) landlord does not terminate the preserved right to buy, unless either the new landlord is a landlord whose tenants are Housing Act secure (so that there will be a new right to buy), or the original landlord failed to register the right as a notice on the register of land in accordance with HA 1985 Sch 9A. If the tenant loses the right due to a failure to register, he or she may recover compensation for breach of the statutory duty under HA 1985 Sch 9A. The preserved right to buy may, however, be determined on termination of the landlord's interest by a superior landlord but where this occurs because of the intermediate landlord's act or omission, there is a right to compensation (s171E). The right is not lost if the termination arises by reason of a merger, which means where someone who owns a superior or inferior interest buys the other, eg a freeholder acquires a long lease, or a leaseholder buys the freehold, including by exercise of a statutory right such as those considered in this chapter, or someone else buys both interests; it reflects the proposition that a person cannot be his or her own tenant.

4.73 **Wales.** In Wales, a local authority may apply to the Welsh Ministers for an order suspending the right to buy in the whole or part of its area initially for up to five years; the order may be extended for a maximum of another five years (Housing (Wales) Measure 2011 and HA 1985 ss122A–122B).

Assured tenants

4.74 **Right to acquire.** Although some assured tenants have the preserved right to buy where they were secure tenants of a dwelling transferred to a PRP or RSL (see paras 4.70–4.72), other assured tenants of PRPs and RSLs have a right to acquire their dwelling if it was provided with 'public money', ie it was funded in whole or in part by a grant assistance (paid by the Housing Corporation, the TSA, the HCA, the National Assembly for Wales or the Welsh Ministers) (see paras 1.162–1.163) (Housing and Regeneration Act (H&RA) 2008 ss180–181; HA 1996 s16). In addition, where a dwelling was transferred to the PRP or RSL from a landlord whose tenants are secure, someone granted an assured tenancy of it after the transfer also has the right to acquire. Assured shorthold tenants can only exercise the right if they have fixed-term tenancies of at least two years (see para 1.183) and even then cannot do so if they pay an affordable rent (see para 3.5): Transfer of Tenancies and Rights to Acquire (Exclusion) Regulations 2012 SI No 696.

4.75 **Operation.** The right to acquire essentially mirrors the right to buy (see paras 4.46–4.69), save that the secretary of state or the Welsh Ministers may adapt or modify the provisions (see HA 1996 s17 and Housing (Right to Acquire) Regulations 1997 SI No 619), which remain in force in Wales and which continue to apply in England under H&RA 2008 s184). In England, however, the maximum discount available is much lower than under the right to buy (see para 4.56) and varies depending on the area in which the dwelling is situated (Housing (Right to Acquire) (Discount) Order 2002 SI No 1091). In Wales, the maximum discount is £8,000 as under the right to buy (Housing (Right to Acquire) (Discount) (Wales) Order 1997 SI No 569). As with the right to buy (see para 4.72), a local authority in Wales can apply for the right to acquire to be suspended in their area (or part of it) for an initial period of five years, which can be extended for a maximum further five years (Housing (Wales) Measure 2011 Part 1).

Management rights

Tenants

4.76 If a landlord fails to carry out his or her obligations, the High Court has power (Senior Courts Act 1981 s37) – where it considers it just and convenient to do so – to appoint a receiver to take over the whole or part of the management of a property, including the receipt of rents and/or the execution of works.

4.77 A court will not, however, appoint a receiver under this power where the landlord is a local authority carrying out its statutory housing duties to provide and manage housing, because to do so would usurp Parliament's express decision to confer those powers on the authority (*Parker v Camden LBC*, 1985).

4.78 **LTA 1987 Part 2.** The power to appoint a receiver has been codified into LTA 1987 Part 2. Part 2 applies only to a building where there are two or more flats, where at least 50 per cent of the floor area of the building (excluding its common parts) is occupied for residential purposes, and – as under LTA 1987 Parts 1 (see para 4.7) and 3 (see para 4.41) – where the landlord is neither a resident landlord, nor an 'exempt landlord' (LTA 1987 s21).

4.79 An application for a receiver to be appointed must be made to the First-tier Tribunal (England) or the leasehold valuation tribunal (Wales). The tribunal can only make an order if it is satisfied of one of the following (LTA 1987 s24).

1) The landlord is in breach of any obligation relating to management of the property owed to the tenant under the tenancy agreement (or or would be in breach but for the fact that it has not been reasonably practicable to give the landlord notice).
2) Unreasonable service charges have been made, or are proposed or likely to be made (see paras 3.94–3.96).
3) Unreasonable administration charges have been made, or are proposed or likely to be made (see para 3.108).
4) The landlord has failed to comply with the provisions of a code of practice approved by the secretary of state or the Welsh Ministers under LRHUDA 1993 s87. In England, see *Service charge and residential management code*, RICS (2016) and *Private retirement housing code of practice*, ARHM (2016). In Wales, see *Rent only management code*, RICS (2005) and *Code of Practice for Private Retirement Housing (Wales)*, ARHM (2006).

Note. Under these first four grounds, the tribunal also has to be satisfied that it is just and convenient to make the order in all the circumstances of the case.

5) Other circumstances exist which make it just and convenient for the order to be made.

4.80 Before making an application, the tenant or tenants must serve a preliminary notice (LTA 1987 s22) informing the landlord of the intention to do so and specifying the grounds which will be relied on. Where the complaints are capable of remedy, the notice must specify a reasonable period within which steps should be taken to do so. The tribunal has power to dispense with the requirement for preliminary notice where it is not practicable to serve the landlord.

4.81 **HA 1985**. Under HA 1985, the secretary of state or the Welsh Ministers can, by regulations impose requirements on local authorities on which a tenant management organisation (TMO) serves written notice proposing that the authority makes a 'management agreement' with it (HA 1985 s27AB), for it to take over management of some of the authority's stock. The regulations may require the authority to provide or finance the provision of office accommodation and facilities, and such training, as the TMO reasonably requires in order to pursue the proposal, to arrange for feasibility studies with respect to the proposal, to provide information to the organisation, to take such other steps by way of co-operation as the regulations may provide, to arrange for ballots or polls in relation to the proposals, and define when the authority must enter into a management agreement with the TMO. The regulations also cover to what houses and land the agreement should relate, and the amounts of money that should be paid to the TMO under the agreement. The regulations may prescribe time-limits for the authority to comply with their duties.

4.82 In England, the regulations (the Housing (Right to Manage) (England) Regulations 2012 SI No 1821 define a TMO as an organisation which satisfies the following conditions: it must have written constitution which specifies the area in relation to which it seeks to enter into a management agreement with the authority; its constitution must provide that any tenant of a house in that area may become a member of the TMO and that the TMO must avoid any unlawful discrimination; it must provide that the affairs of the TMO must be conducted either by the members of the TMO at a general meeting or by a committee or board of directors elected by members of the TMO. It may contain other provisions. The regulations also govern a number of other matters, eg time, ballot, resolution of disputes by arbitration, initiation of the process stage, feasibility and development and implementation. In Wales, similar provision is made under the Housing (Right to Manage) Regulations 1994 SI No 627.

Long leaseholders

4.83 **CLRA 2002.** CLRA 2002 provides qualifying tenants of qualifying premises with a right to manage, regardless of any fault on the freeholder's part (see paras 4.76–4.80).

4.84 **Qualifying requirements.** The same qualifying requirements as under LRHUDA 1993 must be met as to premises and tenants (see paras 4.28–4.29) (CLRA 2002 ss72, 75).

4.85 **RTM company.** In order to exercise the right, the tenants must first establish a right to manage company – 'RTM company' – which accords with the requirements of CLRA 2002 ss73 and 74. The RTM company then serves notice inviting participation by tenants in the company (CLRA 2002 s78). Provided membership of the RTM company includes qualifying tenants of at least half the number of flats in the building, notice claiming the right can be served on the landlord (CLRA 2002 s79). Where the tenants' block is on an estate, they cannot form an RTM company with tenants of other blocks on the estate to obtain management of the estate as a whole: an RTM company can only acquire the right to manage one block (*Triplerose Ltd v Ninety Broomfield Road Co* Ltd, 2015).

4.86 **Procedure.** The landlord must respond with a counter-notice admitting or denying the right (CLRA 2002 s84). If there is no dispute, the right to manage arises on the date set out in the initial notice, which must be at least four months after the date of the notice. If it is denied, the matter may be determined by the First-tier Tribunal (England) or the leasehold valuation tribunal (Wales). If the tribunal determines that there is an entitlement to the right, it will arise three months from the determination (CLRA 2002 s90).

4.87 **Rights.** Once it has acquired the right to manage, the RTM company becomes responsible for management functions, ie those concerning services, repairs, maintenance, improvements, insurance and management (CLRA 2002 s96).

Secure tenants and licensees

4.88 Specific consultation with tenants (whether or not secure) may be required in a number of circumstances, eg when there are alterations to common parts for the benefit of a disabled person (see para 4.162). A more general obligation to consult secure tenants (see paras 1.166–1.180) – including secure licensees (see para 1.168), flexible tenants (see paras 1.181–1.189) and the new-style fixed term secure tenants to be introduced by the Housing and Planning Act (HPA) 2016 (see paras 1.190–1.191) – is imposed on their landlords (who may be local authorities, other public bodies, or PRPs and RSLs – paras 1.161–1.165) by HA 1985, whenever there is a new programme of maintenance, improvement or demolition, or any change in practice or policy, which is likely to affect the secure tenants of the landlord as a whole or a group of them, but excluding questions of rent, payments for services or facilities provided by the landlord (HA 1985 s105). Nor is consultation required when the authority is to enter into a management agreement with a TMO (see paras 4.81–4.82) (HA 1985 s27AB(7)).

4.89 All landlords bound by these consultation provisions (HA 1985 s114) must make and maintain consultation arrangements for notifying their tenants of proposed changes in matters of housing management, and ascertaining their views. They must publish details of these arrangements (HA 1985 s105(5)). There are similar provisions governing introductory tenancies (see paras 1.210–1.219) (HA 1996 ss136, 137) and, therefore, licensees who qualify as introductory (see para 1.212).

4.90 When the landlord seeks approval of an area for the purposes of a 'redevelopment scheme' in connection with Ground 10A (see para 2.113(3)), different consultation provisions apply (HA 1985 Sch 2 Part 5).

4.91 Where an authority is under an obligation to consult, the consultation process should be undertaken at a time when proposals are still at a formative stage, provide sufficient reasons for the proposals to allow those consulted to consider them and to make an intelligent response, provide adequate time for responding, and conscientiously take the results into account (*R (Moseley) v Haringey LBC*, 2014).

Terms

4.92 As with security and rent control, the starting-point in establishing what the terms of a tenancy or licence are is what the parties have agreed. While there is a number of common terms that have given rise over the centuries to a considerable body of law as to their interpretation, the terms are essentially idiosyncratic in the sense that the parties may prima facie seek to allocate responsibilities between themselves and/or may expressly specific items in any way they see fit. Also as with security and rent control, however, that is only a starting-point and there is a number of provisions which determine whether those terms are effective in law, or whether other terms are implied; it is also necessary to consider how terms may be varied, both at common law and otherwise. Consideration of these issues excludes those provisions which are considered in the next section (governing assignment and sub-letting – paras 4.122–4.150) and in following chapters, governing eviction or harassment (chapter 5) and disrepair (chapter 11), although some of the more general considerations may apply to those provisions, eg UCTA 1977, CRA 2015 and EqA 2010.

Unfair terms

4.93 **Application**. Although UCTA 1977 does not apply to the creation or termination of an interest in land (s1 and Sch 1), it may apply to other terms in a tenancy, and applies generally to licences. The Act only applies to a person dealing with another on his or her written standard terms of business (s3), and so is unlikely to apply, eg in the case of a resident landlord (see para 1.233(10)). With effect from 1 October 2015, section 3 no longer applies to a 'consumer contract' (s3(3)), which is now governed by CRA 2015 unless the contract was entered into before that date (see paras 4.96–4.100).

4.94 **Requirements**. Under the provisions of the UCTA 1977, a landlord may neither limit his or her own liability for breach of contract, nor claim to be entitled to offer either no service at all or a service substantially different from that which might reasonably be expected of him or her, save to the extent that is reasonable (s3). Accordingly, disclaiming liability for breach, or imposing an onerous obligation on the occupier, may be invalidated.

4.95 **Reasonableness**. For these purposes, reasonableness means that the term in question is or is not one that is fair and reasonable to include in the contract: having regard to the circumstances actually known to the parties when the contract was made, or which ought to have been so known; and having particular regard to: the relative bargaining positions of the parties, alternative possibilities, eg alternative accommodation, open to the customer, and trade or custom (UCTA 1977 s11).

4.96 **Consumer rights**. In addition to UCTA 1977, contracts are also governed by CRA 2015 Part 2, which replaced the Unfair Terms in Consumer Contracts Regulations 1999 SI No 2083. They are in similar form. CRA 2015 Part 2 applies to contracts entered into 1 October 2015, but the regulations continue to apply to contracts entered into before that date. Both implement European Council Directive 93/13; neither excludes the creation or termination of interests in land.

4.97 CRA 2015 and the regulations import a requirement of good faith into contracts between a 'seller or supplier' and a 'consumer'. A landlord may be a supplier and a tenant a consumer. The regulations apply to tenancies granted by local authorities as well as to those granted by private landlords (*Khatun v Newham LBC*, 2004).

4.98 A term is unfair if it has not been individually negotiated and if, contrary to the 'requirement of good faith', it causes a significant imbalance in the parties' rights and obligations under the contract: CRA 2015 s62; reg 5(1). There is a significant imbalance if a term is so weighted in the landlord's favour as to tilt the parties' rights and obligations significantly in his or her favour (*Director of Fair Trading v First National Bank plc*, 2001). The requirement of good faith comprises fair and open dealing (*Director of Fair Trading*). Openness means that the term must be expressed clearly and must not contain concealed pitfalls or traps. Fairness requires that the landlord should not take advantage of the tenant's weak bargaining position.

4.99 A term which required a secure tenant to pay water charges to his or her landlord, which was collecting them for the water company, has been held not to be an unfair term (*Rochdale BC v Dixon*, 2011). CRA 2015 and the regulations offer a number of illustrations of unfair terms, eg any term 'excluding or hindering the consumer's right to take legal action or exercise any other legal remedy' (CRA 2015 Sch 2 para 20; UTCC Regs Sch 2 para 1(q)).

4.100 In 2005, the Office of Fair Trading published detailed guidance on unfair terms in relation to assured and assured shorthold tenancies. That guidance has been adopted by the Competition and Markets Authority (which replaced the Office of Fair Trading). It offers a number of further examples of possible exclusions and limitations of liability which would be unfair. The Guidance also advises against terms which contain absolute prohibitions rather than those which, while requiring the tenant to seek consent from the landlord, mean that consent is not to be unreasonably withheld, although the guidance does suggest that absolute prohibitions against assignment or sub-letting are not objectionable if the tenancy agreement allows the tenant to end the tenancy early. Illustrations include prohibition on the keeping of pets or having children to visit. Many of the examples illustrate the need to ensure that the wording of a clause does not, perhaps unwittingly, restrict normal activities. Thus, a clause against the keeping of 'any inflammable materials' in the dwelling is too broad because technically it would even prevent the tenant from having s box of matches in his or her home.

Equality Act 2010

4.101 **Protected characteristics.** EqA 2010 prevents discrimination in relation to a number of 'protected characteristics': age, race, religion or belief, sex, sexual orientation, gender reassignment, marriage and civil partnership, pregnancy and maternity, and disability (EqA 2010 s4). A person is disabled if he or she has a physical or mental impairment which has a substantial and long-term adverse effect on his or her ability to carry out normal day-to-day activities (EqA 2010 s6). More detailed provision as to the meaning of disability is contained in EqA 2010 Sch 1.

4.102 **Discrimination as to terms.** Subject to an exception for 'small premises', a landlord or managing agent must not discriminate against anyone on the basis of one of these characteristics in relation to the terms on which he or she offers to let the premises (EqA 2010 s33(1)(a)) under either a tenancy or a licence (s38).

4.103 **Small premises.** In the case of small premises, it is only unlawful for a landlord or managing agent to discriminate on the ground of race, eg it is not unlawful to discriminate on the ground of sex or disability (EqA 2010 Sch 5 para 2). This exception only applies if the landlord, or one of the landlord's relatives, resides and intends to continue to reside in another part of the premises, and the premises includes parts which are shared with residents who are not members of the same household, other than storage areas and means of access (Sch 5 para 3). Relatives are defined in the same way as family members under HA 1985 (see paras 1.200–1.202 – EqA 2010 Sch 5 para 3(5)). Premises are small premises if they satisfy one of the two following tests.

> **Test 1.**The only other persons occupying the part occupied by the landlord or his or her relative are his or her household; the premises include accommodation for at least one other household; the accommodation for each of those other households is let, or available for letting, on a separate tenancy agreement; and, the premises are not normally sufficient to accommodate more than two other households.

Test 2. The premises are not normally sufficient to accommodate more than six people in addition to the household of the landlord or his relative.

4.104 **Direct discrimination.** This occurs where a person treats someone with a protected characteristic less favourably than he or she would treat a person without that characteristic (EqA 2010 s13). A requirement for a female tenant to have a guarantor for the rent, where the landlord would not require that of a male tenant, is an example of direct discrimination. Direct discrimination is only permissible if the landlord is involved in 'positive action' (EqA 2010 s158). Accordingly, housing associations which require its tenants of be of one sex only because they are providing accommodation for male ex-prisoners or mental patients is not involved in unlawful discrimination.

4.105 **Indirect discrimination.** This occurs where a person has a 'criterion or practice' which puts a person with a protected characteristic at a disadvantage compared with persons without that characteristic (EqA 2010 s19). Indirect discrimination can be justified if it is a proportionate means of achieving a legitimate aim (s19(2)(d)). A prohibition on keeping pets in the premises might discriminate against a blind tenant who has a guide dog. Such discrimination would be difficult to justify, unless the premises were wholly unsuitable for dogs. A term which required a tenant not to make noise audible outside the premises during night hours could discriminate against a person with mental health difficulties who had difficulty in controlling his behaviour when ill. In that case, however, the term is justified given that it is preventing nuisance being caused to neighbours.

4.106 As already noted (see paras 2.258–2.259), indirect discrimination may occur where a landlord decides to evict a tenant because of his anti-social behaviour if that behaviour is caused by the tenant's mental health problems.

4.107 **Enforcement.** A tenant can seek a declaration from the county court that a term is unlawful or, if the landlord seeks to enforce the term, can seek such a declaration by way of defence (EqA 2010 ss114, 119). In addition, he or she can claim damages (s119).

4.108 **Public sector equality duty.** In exercising their functions, public authorities must have due regard to the need to eliminate discrimination, harassment and victimisation based on any of the protected characteristics (see para 4.101; EqA 2010 s149(1)(a)). They must also advance equality of opportunity for those with protected characteristics (s149(1)(b)) and foster good relations with other members of society by tackling prejudice and promoting understanding (s149(1)(c),

(5)). 'Public authorities' include local authorities and also PRPs and RSLs when they are exercising functions to which HRA 1998 applies (EqA 2010 s150, Sch 19; para 1.322).

4.109 The duty to advance equality of opportunity (see para 4.108) includes having due regard to take steps to meet the needs of a persons with protected characteristics (EqA 2010 s149(3)). The duty applies not only to the formulation of policy but also to individual cases, eg an application by a homeless, disabled person for assistance (*Hotak v Southwark* LBC, 2015 and *Hackney LBC v Haque*, 2017; paras 10.22, 10.116) or a decision to evict a disabled person (*Barnsley MBC v Norton*, 2011).

Terms implied by law

4.110 There is a number of terms implied by the common law into tenancies (whether long leasehold – para 2.70; fixed-term – para 1.18; or periodic – para 1.18), regardless of their class of protection, although not licences.

4.111 Leaving aside those which are considered in subsequent chapters, governing eviction or harassment (see para 5.49) and disrepair (see para 11.52), the following may usefully be mentioned.

1) **Non-derogation from grant**. Where a tenant occupies property which adjoins that occupied by the landlord (whether actually so occupied or as a matter of law, eg common parts), it is implied that the landlord will not use his or her retained property so as to 'derogate from the grant' of the tenancy, ie in such a way as to interfere with the tenant's use of the property for the purpose for which it was let.
2) **Quiet enjoyment**. A covenant by the landlord that the tenant will be able quietly to enjoy the premises which are the subject of the tenancy is implied into every letting. The covenant can only be used, however, in relation to a complaint about conditions arising after the grant of the tenancy. The tenant takes the premises in the condition in which he or she finds them and subject to the uses contemplated for those premises. Thus, everyday noise from neighbouring flats arising because of a lack of soundproofing does not amount to a breach of the covenant (*Southwark LBC v Mills*, 1999).
3) **Use in a tenant-like manner.** The tenant is under an obligation to use premises in a 'tenant-like manner' That is to say, he or she:

> … must take proper care of the place. He must, if he is going away for the winter, turn off the water and empty the boiler. He must clean the chimneys, when necessary, and also the windows. He must mend the electric light when it fuses. He must unstop the sink when it is blocked by his waste. In short, he must do the little jobs about the place which a reasonable tenant would do. In addition, he must, of course, not damage the house, wilfully or negligently; and he must see that his family and guests do not damage it; if they do, he must repair it. But apart from such things, if the house falls into disrepair through fair wear and tear or lapse of time, or for any reason not caused by him, then the tenant is not liable to repair it. (*Warren v Keen*, 1953, *per* Denning L.J.).

Identifying terms

4.112 As noted (see para 1.19), while periodic tenancies do not need to be in writing; fixed-term tenancies in excess of three years have to be created by deed (LPA 1925 ss52(1), 54(2)). The written agreement will therefore contain the agreed terms which have been identified (see para 4.92) as the starting-point. Likewise, a landlord under a weekly tenancy must provide a rent book or similar document, which is likely to contain printed terms (see para 1.85).

4.113 **Secure tenants.** In addition, landlords under secure tenancies (see paras 1.156–1.202) must publish information which explains the effect of the express terms of their secure tenancies, the security provisions of HA 1985 and other provisions considered in this chapter (see paras 4.116–4.124), and the provisions of LTA 1985 s11 (see paras 11.52–11.63) (HA 1985 s104). Copies of this publication must be provided to secure tenants. Where the landlord is a local authority, the information regarding the security provisions of HA 1985 and repairing obligations must be provided annually. It is unclear whether this applies to secure licensees (see para 1.168) for, although prima facie included in HA 1985 Part 4, in which these provisions are to be found, they are not within the provisions of LTA 1985 s11, which only applies to tenancies (see para 11.52). Landlords are also under a duty to publish information to help tenants decide whether to exercise the right to buy (see paras 4.46–4.63) (HA 1985 ss121AA, 121; Housing (Right to Buy) (Information to Secure Tenants) (England) Order 2005 SI No 1735; Housing (Right to Buy) (Information to Secure Tenants) (Wales) Order 2005 SI No 2681). Following publication, the landlord must supply a copy of the document to its existing tenants as soon as is reasonably practicable and to all new secure tenants as soon as they take up their tenancy and thereafter provide them with a copy once every five years.

4.114 **Introductory and demoted tenants**. There are similar provisions governing introductory tenancies (HA 1996 s136) and demoted tenancies (HA 1996 s143M).

4.115 **Assured shortholds tenants.** If a *post*-1996 Act assured shorthold tenant (ie one granted on or after 28 February 1997) asks his or her landlord to do so, the landlord must provide the tenant with a written statement of any term of the tenancy which is not (already) evidenced in writing and which governs: the date on which the tenancy began or if a statutory periodic tenancy (see para 2.161), or an assured shorthold by succession (see para 1.251), the date on which it came into being; the rent and dates for payment; any rent review clause; and the length of a fixed-term shorthold (HA 1988 s20A(1), (2)).

4.116 **Rent Act statutory tenants.** A Rent Act statutory tenancy (see para 1.269) continues on exactly the same terms as the prior contractual, protected tenancy save where such terms would be inconsistent with the idea of statutory tenancy (RA 1977 s3), eg a requirement to give up possession on termination of the contractual tenancy or a right to assign or sublet the whole of the premises (*Keeves v Dean*, 1923; *Atyeo v Fardoe*, 1978), and save as regards rent (see paras 3.50–3.72).

Variation of terms

4.117 **Common law**. The general rule is that a contract may only be varied in the same way as it may be created in law (*McCausland v Duncan Lawrie Ltd*, 1997). Accordingly, a periodic tenancy which does not have to be in writing can be varied orally. As fixed-term tenancies in excess of three years have to be by deed (see para 1.19), variation therefore has to be by deed. Where the parties to such a fixed-term tenancy have purported to vary the terms by oral agreement, however, they may be able to prevent each other from resiling from it under the doctrine of estoppel (see paras 1.129–1.130).

4.118 **Variation or surrender**. In two circumstances, even though the landlord and the tenant may think that they are only varying an existing lease, the effect of the variation in law is to surrender (see paras 1.24–1.28) the existing lease and replace it with a new one. The first is an agreement to extend the length of a fixed term (*Savile Settled Estate, Re*, 1931), the second is variation of the extent of the premises is varied, eg where one set of rooms is substituted for another (*Giles v Spencer*, 1857) or where the tenant gives up one of a number of rooms comprised in the tenancy.

4.119 **Long leaseholders.** The provisions of LTA 1987 Part 4 are confined to long leaseholders (see para 2.72). These provisions permit individual leaseholders to apply to the First-tier Tribunal (England) or a leasehold valuation tribunal for a variation of the terms of a lease which fail to make satisfactory provisions governing repairs or maintenance of a flat or building or of facilities necessary to ensure that occupiers enjoy a reasonable standard of accommodation, insurance, repairs, the provision or maintenance or services, or the way service charges are computed (LTA 1987 s35). There is provision for the variation of other leases within a building to ensure consistency (LTA 1987 s36) and for 'block applications' by a specified number of leaseholders in a building: two to eight flats, no less than all but one; nine or more flats, 75 per cent in support of the application, and the application is not opposed by more than ten per cent.

4.120 **Secure tenants and licensees.** A landlord may vary the terms of a secure tenancy by notice to take effect no sooner than it could have served notice to quit (see para 2.50). Before that date, the tenant may respond with notice to quit, in which case the variation will not take effect before the tenant's departure (HA 1985 ss102, 103). A term in the tenancy agreement which purports to prevent the landlord from exercising this right of variation is of no effect if the landlord is a local authority, as it would mean that the local authority would have 'fettered its discretion' in relation to its power to change the terms, which public authorities are not allowed to do in relation to any of their powers (*R (Kilby) v Basildon DC*, 2007; para 8.28(7)).

4.121 Before any such notice is served, the landlord must serve a preliminary notice, outlining the intended variation, explaining its effect and inviting the occupier's comments (see para 4.91). The 'effect' of a variation is a matter for evaluation by the landlord, which is entitled to have regard to what is reasonably to be understood by its tenants (*Rochdale BC v Dixon*, 2011). This consultation is not necessary, however, if the variation relates to the rent payable, or any amount in respect of rates, services or facilities provided by the landlord. A notice of variation cannot vary the extent of the premises let under the secure tenancy or license.

Assignment, sub-letting and lodgers

4.122 As always, the starting-point is the tenancy or other agreement: it has already been noted that if there is nothing in the terms of the tenancy or of a statute prohibiting sub-letting or assignment (see paras 1.65,

1.80), then it is permissible, but that most tenancy agreements and rent books include prohibitions, which may be absolute or qualified. As a licence is a personal right (see para 1.114), it is not assignable; a clause in an agreement purporting to be a licence but which prohibits sub-letting might well indicate that it is really a tenancy (see para 1.114).

4.123 The requirements for a valid assignment have been considered (see paras 1.81–1.83). The requirements for a valid subtenancy are exactly the same as those of any tenancy (see para 1.17).

4.124 **Discrimination.** EqA 2010 prohibits discrimination in connection with the disposal of premises on certain protected characteristics (see para 4.91). Subject to one exception (see para 4.101), refusal by a tenant to assign his tenancy (EqA 2010 s33(1)) or refusal by a landlord to consent to an assignment, where such consent is required (see para 1.77), cannot be withheld on the basis of one of these characteristics (EqA 2010 s34). Where a tenant refuses to assign on discriminatory grounds, the prospective assignee may seek an injunction requiring an assignment and/or damages (EqA 2010 s119). If a landlord refuses consent, and the tenant wishes to assign, or indeed has already assigned, the appropriate remedy is to seek a declaration from the court that the assignment is lawful (EqA 2010 s119(2)(b)).

4.125 **Small premises.** As in the case of the terms of a tenancy, however, if the 'small premises' exception applies (see para 4.103), it is only unlawful for a tenant to refuse to assign his tenancy, or a landlord to refuse consent, on the ground of race (EqA 2010 Sch 5 para 3(2)), so that assignment may lawfully be refused on the ground of the sex, age or disability of the proposed assignee.

4.126 **Domestic breakdown.** The rights considered here are additional to those which may arise on domestic breakdown, considered in chapter 7.

4.127 **Secure tenants and licensees.** Under HA 1985, secure tenants (see paras 1.160–1.191) and licensees who qualify as secure (see para 1.168) have an absolute right to take in lodgers, and a qualified right to sublet part of their premises (HA 1985 s93). As the right is absolute, nothing more need be said about the right to take in a lodger – ie a licensee (see para 1.35) – as the tenant may simply do it, without any formality or other requirements: there is no requirement to notify the landlord. A tenant on housing benefit or universal credit – a subject not covered in this book – para 3.153 – will, however, have to notify the authority administering the scheme, as it will affect his or her entitlement.

4.128 Although the right to sublet is expressed as a negative obligation (the secure tenant shall not sublet part without the written consent of the landlord – HA 1985 s93(1)(a)), the consent is not unreasonably to be withheld, and if unreasonably withheld, is to be treated as given; accordingly, the right is in substance a positive entitlement to sublet with consent (HA 1985 s94).

4.129 The exercise of a qualified right to sublet has been considered above (see paras 1.66–1.73) but it is worth restating that, no matter how well-founded may be the anticipation of refusal, a tenant will not be able to claim unreasonable withholding without first making the request (*Barrow v Isaacs*, 1891). If the landlord fails to reply within a reasonable time, consent is deemed to have been withheld (HA 1985 s94(6)); if the landlord does refuse, a written statement of reasons for refusal must be provided (HA 1985 s94(6)). Consent may, however, still be sought after the sub-letting, and if given will then validate it (HA 1985 s94(4)). No conditions may be attached to a consent (HA 1985 s94(5)).

4.130 When considering the reasonableness of a refusal, overcrowding will be relevant (see paras 14.2–14.6), as will any proposals for works which the landlord may have and which would affect the accommodation likely to be used by the subtenant (HA 1985 s94(3)). The burden of proof always lies on the landlord to show that the withholding is reasonable (HA 1985 s94(2)), and the tenant may apply to the county court for a declaration that a withholding is unreasonable (HA 1985 s110).

4.131 **Subletting of whole.** It must be emphasised that it is only subletting of *part* of the dwelling that is permissible. If the tenant sublets the whole, he or she will cease to occupy the dwelling as his or her only or principal home and even if the tenant subsequently moves back in security of tenure will not be regained (HA 1985 s93) (see para 1.209).

4.132 In addition, where the tenant knows that it is contrary to a term of the tenancy to do so, a secure tenant commits a criminal offence if he or she sublets in such a way that the dwelling is no longer his or her only or principal home (Prevention of Social Housing Fraud Act (PSHFA) 2013 s1(1)). It is likewise an offence for a tenant dishonestly and in breach of a term of the tenancy to sublet or part with possession of the whole or part of it and to cease to occupy it as his only or principal home (s1(2)). In the case of the offence under section 1(1), it is a defence for the tenant to show that he or she did so because of violence, or threats of violence, from a person residing in, or in the locality of, the property, to the tenant or to a family member residing with the tenant immediately before he or she ceased to occupy the dwelling (s1(3)). It is also a defence to show that the person in occupation is someone who is entitled to apply to court for an order giving him or her a right to occupy the dwelling (eg an occupation order under the Family Law Act (FLA) 1996 – paras 7.15–7.27), or to have the tenancy transferred to him or her (eg under FLA 1996 s53 and Sch 7 – paras 7.32–7.34) (s1(4)).

4.133 An offence under section 1(1) is punishable in the magistrates' court by a fine up to an unlimited amount (PSHFA 2013 s1(5); LASPO 2012 s85(1)). An offence under section 1(2) is punishable in the magistrates' court by a fine up to an unlimited amount and/or up to six months' imprisonment; in the Crown Court, it is punishable by a fine up to an unlimited amount and/or imprisonment for up to two years (s1(6)).

4.134 A person convicted of either offence may be ordered by the magistrates' court to repay any unlawful profits to the landlord (PSHFA 2013 s4). The county court has power to make the same form of order on an application by the tenant's landlord (s5). The amount to be repaid is what the court considers appropriate, save that the maximum payable must not exceed the difference between the money received by the tenant from the subtenant and the money paid as rent to the landlord, ie the unlawful profit. In criminal proceedings, the amount of the fine must be deducted from the amount of the unlawful profit order (ss4(8)).

4.135 **Assignment – the right to exchange.** As an exception to the normal rule that a secure tenancy cannot be assigned (see para 1.200), all secure tenants have the right to exchange their properties with another secure tenant, whether of the same landlord or not (HA 1985 s92(1)). Although a license is – as a personal right – not assignable (see paras 1.114, 4.122), because the provisions of HA 1985 Part 4, apply to those who qualify as secure (see para 1.168), this could apply to a secure licensee in the same way as to a secure tenant as either party to the exchange, although there is a counter-argument that if a licence cannot be assigned, the provisions cannot apply: a licensee wishing to exchange in this way should take advice.

4.136 The right extends to allow an exchange with Housing Act assured tenants of a PRP or RSL, or a charitable housing trust (see para 8.5), ie those landlords whose tenants were, at one time, within HA 1985 prima facie as secure tenants (see para 1.175; HA 1985 s92(2A)). There can even be three-way exchanges, provided all are Housing Act secure tenants or have an assured tenancy from one of these landlords, and the landlord of each has consented in writing (HA 1985 s92(2)).

4.137 **Consent.** A landlord has 42 days in which to consent, and can only refuse on one of a specified schedule of grounds (HA 1985 s92(4), (5)). The landlord loses the right to reply on any of the grounds unless it replies within 42 days.

4.138 If the landlord refuses consent on some other, non-specified ground, consent is to be treated as given. This does not, however, mean that the exchange can necessarily take place. The landlord is entitled to attach one condition to any consent, including where it is being treated as having given consent: if there are rent arrears, or there is another breach of a term of the tenancy, the landlord can still require the arrears to be cleared, or the breach to be remedied (HA 1985 s92(5)). The landlord may not, however, attach any other conditions to the consent; any others that are attached may be disregarded (HA 1985 s92(6)).

4.139 There are nine grounds for refusing consent (HA 1985 Sch 3).

1) **Possession order.** Consent may be refused where either the tenant or the proposed assignee is already under a court order to give up possession.
2) **Proceedings for possession.** Consent may be refused where proceedings for possession have commenced, or NSP or a notice under section 83ZA has been served (see paras 2.88, 2.110), in relation to either tenant or proposed assignee on any of the grounds for possession which require that it is reasonable to make the order (see para 2.98).
3) **Anti-social behaviour.** Consent may be refused where a court order is in force against the tenant or proposed assignee which is based on anti-social behaviour, eg a suspended possession order, or an anti-social behaviour injunction (see paras 6.3–6.27).
4) **Large or unsuitable accommodation.** Consent may be refused where the accommodation would be too large for the prospective assignee, or otherwise not reasonably suitable to his needs.
5) **Employment related accommodation.** Consent may be refused where the premises were let in consequence of employment, and form part of, or are in the grounds of, a non-housing building or a cemetery (see para 2.117(1)).
6) **Charity.** Consent may be refused where the landlord is a charity and the proposed assignee's occupation would conflict with its objects (see para 2.98(8)).

7) **Adapted accommodation.** Consent may be refused where the property is designed for a physically disabled person, and if the proposed assignee moved in, there would be no such person in occupation (see para 2.117(2)).
8) **Special needs.** Consent may be refused where the landlord is a special needs housing association or trust, and if the proposed assignee moved in there would be no one with the relevant need in occupation (see para 2.117(3)).
9) **Sheltered accommodation.** Consent may be refused where the accommodation is sheltered and if the proposed assignee moved in, there would be no one with the relevant need in occupation (see para 2.117(4)).

4.140 **Right to exchange – new tenancy.** As a flexible tenancy is a form of secure tenancy (see para 1.182), there is nothing to prevent a flexible tenant from exchanging his or her tenancy with another secure tenant (flexible or not) by assignment. A periodic secure tenant would, however, be most unlikely to wish to exchange with a flexible tenant if he or she would lose the right to full security of tenure under HA 1985. Tenants who wish to exchange can accordingly require their landlords to grant them new tenancies of the properties so that, in effect, the status follows the tenant meaning that fully secure and flexible tenants remains so in the new home (Localism Act (LA) 2011 s158). As in the case of the right to exchange by assignment (see paras 4.135–4.136), the right to a new tenancy by exchange extends to exchanges with assured tenants (including some assured shorthold tenants) of a PRPs, or a charitable housing trust (see paras 8.5). Assured shorthold tenants can only take part if they have fixed-term tenancies for at least two years and do not pay an affordable rent (see para 3.5): Transfer of Tenancies and Right to Acquire (Exclusion) Regulations 2012 SI No 696.

4.141 **Consent.** The procedure is similar to that for exchanges by assignment. A landlord has 42 days in which to consent and can only refuse consent on one of a specified number of grounds (LA 2011 s159(1)). The landlord loses the right to reply on any of the grounds unless it replies within 42 days (LA 2011 s159(1), (3)). If it refuses consent on some other, non-specified ground, consent is to be treated as given (s159(2)). The right to be granted a new tenancy is enforceable in the county court by injunction (s159(4), (5)).

4.142 The grounds for refusing consent are the same as those for refusal to an assignment (see para 4.139) save that the landlord may also refuse consent where any rent lawfully due from one of the tenants has not been paid or another obligation under one of the tenancies has been broken or not performed (LA 2011 Sch 14).

4.143 Once the provisions of HPA 2016 introducing new-style fixed-term tenancies (see paras 1.190–1.191) are in force, a similar problem will arise in that a periodic secure tenant would be unlikely to wish to exchange with a new-style fixed-term tenant as he or she would lose his or her right to full security of tenure under HA 1985. In such a case, on a mutual exchange, the periodic tenant will be entitled to a new tenancy of the dwelling but that tenancy will not be periodic (new LA 2011 s158(8)). The landlord will be able to decide what the terms of the new tenancy will be and must inform the tenant of those terms on request (new LA 2011 s158(8), (9)).

4.144 **Assured tenants.** With two exceptions, all assured periodic tenancies (see paras 1.220–1.245), including periodic assured shorthold tenancies (see paras 1.246–1.251), are subject to a prohibition on assignment of the tenancy, in whole or part, and on sub-letting under the tenancy in whole or part, without the consent of the landlord (HA 1988 s15(1)). The prohibition is absolute, not qualified (HA 1988 s15(2); para 1.66). The first exception is if the tenancy agreement itself contains a prohibition, whether absolute or qualified, in which case it is the agreement which determines what rights there are in respect of assignment and sub-letting, not the Act. The second is if a premium is paid on the grant or renewal of the tenancy (HA 1988 s15(3)). 'Premium' has the same meaning as under RA 1977 (HA 1988 s15(4); para 3.123). The rights of an assured fixed-term tenant to assign or sub-let are governed by the terms of the tenancy agreement and the usual rules relating to assignment apply (see paras 1.78–1.83).

4.145 If an assured tenant sublets the whole of his or her dwelling, he or she will cease to occupy it as his or her only or principal home and lose security of tenure under HA 1988. As already noted (see para 1.230), if the landlord is a private landlord, the tenant may regain security if he or she moves back in but if the landlord is a PRP or RSL, security is lost if the tenant sub-lets the property and cannot be regained (HA 1988 s15A).

4.146 In addition if the landlord is a PRP or an RSL, the tenant commits an offence under PSHFA 2013, in the circumstances discussed in relation to secure tenants (see paras 4.131–4.132) (PSHFA 2013 s2) and may be liable to repay unlawful profits to the landlord (see para 4.133).

4.147 **Introductory tenants.** An introductory tenancy (see paras 1.210–1.219) – or licence (see para 1.212) – is incapable of assignment

(HA 1996 s134(1)), unless it is to a person who would be qualified to succeed (see para 1.216) to the introductory tenancy (HA 1996 s134(2)). Specific provision is also made to prevent assignment of a tenancy which was introductory but ceased to be so because the tenant no longer occupies it as his or her only principal home (HA 1996 s134(3)). Whether an introductory tenant can sublet is governed by the terms of the agreement (see paras 1.64–1.73), which will usually prohibit sub-letting.

4.148 **Demoted tenants.** A demoted tenancy (see paras 1.252–1.261) is incapable of assignment (HA 1996 s143K(1)) unless it is to a person who would be qualified to succeed (see para 1.258) to the tenancy (HA 1996 s143K(2)). As with introductory tenants, whether a demoted tenant can sub-let is governed by the terms of the agreement, under which sub-letting is usually prohibited. The rights of a demoted assured shorthold tenant (see para 2.256) to assign or sub-let are the same as for any other assured shorthold tenant (see para 4.144).

4.149 **Rent Act protected and statutory tenants.** There is no statutory prohibition on sub-letting or assignment in a contractual, protected (see para 1.269) tenancy; the position is therefore governed by its terms. Once the tenancy has become statutory, however, it ceases to be assignable, as it is not a true tenancy but only a personal right (see para 1.269). There may nonetheless be a subtenancy, if the terms of the former contractual tenancy do not prohibit it.

4.150 **Protected shorthold tenants.** A protected shorthold tenancy (see para 1.294) cannot be assigned at any time during the shorthold (see para 1.295(1)), or afterwards, ie so long as the tenant remains susceptible to use of the shorthold ground (see para 1.223) (HA 1980 s54(2)). While there is no statutory restriction on sub-letting, so that the position will depend on the terms of the tenancy, a subtenant to whom some part, or even the whole, of the premises has been let at any time while the tenant is still susceptible to use of the shorthold ground cannot avail him- or herself of RA 1977 s137 (see para 1.62(3)); HA 1980 s54(1), and so will only become the landlord's tenant directly if the circumstances would put him or her in that position at common law, ie if the subtenancy is lawful and the tenant surrenders (see paras 1.24–1.28).

Improvements

4.151 There is nothing to prevent a tenant improving the premises in which he or she lives, save the terms of the tenancy (whether long leasehold or otherwise); there will, however, commonly be either an absolute or qualified (see para 1.65) prohibition on alterations. If the covenant is expressed not to be exercisable without the landlord's consent, it is implied that such consent will not be unreasonably withheld (LTA 1927 s19(1)). Nor is the landlord allowed to charge for granting consent, unless the alterations are structural and result in a reduction in the value of the property, or legal expenses have been incurred (LTA 1927 s19(3)). The landlord may make consent conditional on the premises being reinstated to their unimproved state before the property is handed back, unless the improvement adds to the value of the property (LTA 1927 s19(2)).

Right to improve

Secure tenants and licensees

4.152 Under HA 1985, secure tenants (see paras 1.160–1.180), other than flexible tenants (see paras 1.181–1.189) and new-style fixed-term secure tenants (see paras 1.190–1.191), also enjoy a 'right to improve'. It is a term of secure tenancies – other than these excluded tenancies – that the tenant will not make any improvement without the written consent of the landlord, which consent is not unreasonably to be withheld (HA 1985 ss97–99). While cast in this negative form, the term has the effect of conferring a positive entitlement to improve where consent is available. A refusal of consent can be challenged in the county court (HA 1985 s110). The right would seem to apply to those licensees who are secure (see para 1.168) although, as this is rare, reference will only be made to tenants.

4.153 For these purposes, improvement includes addition or alteration to a dwelling, and external decorations (HA 1985 s97). If the landlord refuses consent, it is obliged to provide a written statement of reasons; in the course of any subsequent challenge by the tenant, the burden lies on the landlord to show that the refusal was reasonable, which it may do, amongst other ways, by showing that the improvement would make the dwelling, or neighbouring premises, less safe, or that it would cause him or her to incur additional expenditure, or that it would reduce the value of the house (HA 1985 s98).

4.154 Secure tenants, other than flexible tenants (see paras 1.181–1.189) and new-style fixed-term secure tenants (see paras 1.190–1.191), may be entitled to compensation for certain improvements (HA 1985 s99A). Their rent is not to be increased on account of improvements they execute (HA 1985 s101), and, on the tenant's departure, the landlord has power to reimburse the tenant for the cost of any improvements carried out (HA 1985 s100), a power it must *consider* exercising even if it has a policy of usually refusing.

Rent Act protected and statutory tenants

4.155 A Rent Act tenant has the right to carry out improvements to his home under HA 1980 s81, unless he or she has been given notice either that his tenancy is a shorthold or of a notice under Cases 11–18 and 20 of Sch 15 (see para 2.219). The right may be exercised in the same circumstances as the right to improve given to secure tenants (see paras 4.52–4.53).

Disabled persons

4.156 EqA 2010 contains rights for disabled (see para 4.101) tenants, or tenants who live with disabled persons, to carry out improvements themselves (see paras 4.156–4.159) and to require their landlords to carry out improvements to their homes to take account of the disabled person's needs (see paras 4.160–4.166).

Improvements by tenant

4.157 Improvement means addition or alteration to a dwelling, an addition or alteration to services to the dwelling, the erection of a wireless or television aerial and external decorations (EqA 2010 s190(9)). The improvement must be one which is likely to facilitate the disabled person's 'enjoyment' of his home (EqA 2010 s190(7)). Enjoyment does not mean deriving pleasure; the issue is whether the improvement would enable the disabled person to live in the premises in an ordinary lawful way as any other typical tenant would live in them (*Beedles v Guinness Northern Counties Ltd*, 2011, decided under equivalent provisions in the Disability Discrimination Act (DDA) 1995).

Right to do improvements

4.158 The right to carry out improvements under these provisions does not apply to secure tenants (see paras 1.160–1.180) or Rent Act protected or statutory tenants (see paras 1.269–1.293), who have their own rights to make improvements (see paras 4.152–4.155).

Consent

4.159 An application for consent must be made in writing; the landlord must respond within a reasonable time (EqA 2010 s190(2)). In granting consent, the landlord may impose reasonable conditions (EqA 2010 s190(2)) and any breach of such a condition is treated as a breach of the term of the tenancy (EqA 2010 s190(6)). If the landlord imposes an unreasonable condition, consent is deemed to have been unreasonably refused (EqA 2010 s190(3)). If consent is refused, the landlord must provide a written statement of reasons (EqA 2010 s190(2)); in the course of any subsequent challenge by the tenant, the burden lies on the landlord to show that the refusal or condition was reasonable (EqA 2010 s190(2)). Consent is deemed to have been given if the landlord fails to respond to the tenant's request within a reasonable time, or unreasonably withholds consent, or imposes an unreasonable condition (EqA 2010 s190(4)).

Landlords' duties

4.160 EqA 2010 imposes duties on landlords and managing agents requiring them to make 'reasonable adjustments' to premises for the benefit of disabled tenants or tenants who live with disabled persons. The duties concern the provision of 'auxiliary aids' for the disabled person or the removal or alteration of 'physical features' in the common parts. Neither of these terms is defined but the following have been specified as auxiliary aids (Equality Act 2010 (Disability) Regulations 2010 SI No 2128 reg 8): replacement or provision of a sign or notice, replacement of a tap or door handle, replacement, provision or adaptation of a door bell or door entry system, and changes to the colour of a wall, door or any other surface.

Request

4.161 A duty only arises if the tenant, or someone who lives with him or her, requests the provision of the auxiliary aid or removal or alteration of the physical feature (EqA 2010 Sch 4 paras 2(6) and 5(6)).

Auxiliary aids

4.162 The duty to provide auxiliary aids is imposed on the 'controller' of the premises, ie the landlord or his managing agent (EqA 2010 s36(3)). Where a disabled person would, but for the provision of an auxiliary aid, be put at a substantial disadvantage in comparison with persons who are not disabled, the controller must take reasonable steps to provide the auxiliary aid (EqA 2010 s20(5)). The disadvantage must relate either to the disabled person's enjoyment of the premises or to his use of facilities or entitlements provided under the tenancy (EqA 2010 Sch 4 para 2(5)). Accordingly the auxiliary aid may be required either in the tenant's dwelling or in the common parts of the building in which the tenant's dwelling is situated. The duty does not require the controller to remove or alter a physical feature (see para 4.160). The landlord or managing agent is not entitled to charge the disabled person for complying with this duty (EqA 2010 s20(4)).

Physical features in common parts

4.163 The common parts comprise the structure and exterior of the premises and any common facilities used in connection with them (EqA 2010 s36(6)). Where a physical feature (see para 4.160) in the common parts puts a disabled person at a substantial disadvantage in comparison with persons who are not disabled, there is a duty on the landlord, as the person responsible for the common parts (EqA 2010 s36(5)), to take reasonable steps to remove or alter it (EqA 2010 s20(4), (9)).

4.164 Within a reasonable period of being requested to do the work, the landlord must consult all those who would be affected by it (EqA 2010 Sch 4 para 6). If he or she decides to carry out the adaptation, he or she is entitled to require that the disabled person pays for the adaptation and any subsequent restoration (EqA 2010 Sch 4 para 7(3)) and must enter into a written agreement with the disabled person as to how it will be paid for and if (and how) the common parts will be restored to their former condition if the disabled person ceases to live at the property (EqA 2010 Sch 4 para 7).

Subtenancies

4.165 Where a tenant is a subtenant, his landlord's (the mesne landlord – para 1.59) own tenancy may prevent alterations to the premises without the superior landlord's consent. The mesne landlord is not obliged to take action until the head landlord's consent is obtained but is obliged to request it (EqA 2010 Sch 21 para 2(2)). Notwithstanding any terms in the head lease, it is implied that the mesne landlord may carry out alterations with the written consent of the head landlord, which consent is not unreasonably to be withheld (EqA 2010 Sch 21 para 3). Applications for consent are governed by the Equality Act 2010 (Disability) Regulations 2010 SI No 2128 regs 10–14. Where consent is refused, the county court has power to determine whether it has been unreasonably withheld (EqA 2010 Sch 21 para 4).

Enforcement

4.166 Failure to comply with the duty to make reasonable adjustments constitutes unlawful discrimination (EqA 2010 s21(2)). The county court has power to hear a claim that a disabled person has been discriminated against (EqA 2010 s114). The court may grant an injunction requiring the landlord to carry out the reasonable adjustments and may award damages, including damages for the disabled person's injured feelings (EqA 2010 s119).

Grants

4.167 There have long been provisions for grant-aid to be made available to people carrying out improvements, whether landlords or tenants, and the detailed provisions are often changed, to reflect new policies and the availability of public monies. Two kinds of grant are considered here: grants under the Regulatory Reform (Housing Assistance) (England and Wales) Order 2002 SI No 1860, 'the Regulatory Reform Order' or 'RRO 2002'; and, disabled facilities grants under the Housing Grants, Construction and Regeneration Act (HGCRA)1996.

Regulatory Reform Order

Types of assistance

4.168 The purposes for which assistance may be provided are to be found in article 3 of the Regulatory Reform Order 2002. For the purpose of improving living conditions in its area, a local authority may provide direct or indirect assistance to a person for the purposes of enabling him or her (RRO 2002 art 3(1)) to do any of the following:

1) to acquire living accommodation (whether within or outside the area);
2) to adapt or improve living accommodation (whether by alteration, conversion or enlargement);
3) to repair living accommodation;
4) to demolish building comprising of including living accommodation; or
5) where buildings comprising or including living accommodation have been demolished, to construct buildings that comprise or include replacement living accommodation.

Living accommodation

4.169 For these purposes, 'living accommodation' means a building or part of a building, or a caravan, boat or similar structure, occupied or available for occupation for residential purposes (RRO 2002 art 2).

Adoption of policy

4.170 Before providing assistance under the Regulatory Reform Order, an authority must have adopted a policy for the provision of assistance, of which it must have given public notice (RRO 2002 art 4). The authority must ensure that a full copy of the policy is available for inspection free of charge at its principal office at all reasonable times, and that a summary document is available by post on payment of a reasonable charge. Any assistance must be provided in accordance with the policy.

Types of assistance

4.171 Assistance may be provided in any form and may be subject to conditions, including as to repayment or making a contribution towards the assisted work (RRO 2002 art 3(3), (4)). Before imposing a condition as to repayment or contribution, the authority must have regard to the ability of the person to make the repayment or contribution.

4.172 The primary means of assistance will be a grant or a loan, although other forms of assistance, eg discounted materials or access to tool hire schemes, may also be provided. Where a loan is given, the authority may take any form of security in respect of it (RRO 2002 art 3(6)). Where the security is a charge on a property (see para 1.91), the authority may at any time reduce the priority of the charge (see para 1.92) or secure its removal (RRO 2002 art 3(7)).

Statements, advice and assistance

4.173 Before providing any assistance, the authority must provide the person with a statement in writing of any conditions attaching to the assistance, and satisfy itself that the person has received appropriate advice or information about the extent and nature of any obligation (whether financial or otherwise) to which he or she will become subject as a consequence of the assistance (RRO 2002 art 3(5)).

Consent of owner

4.174 By RRO 2002 art 5, assistance to adapt, improve, repair or demolish living accommodation may not be given unless the authority is satisfied that the owner of the living accommodation has consented to the works. The owner is the person entitled to receive a rent at an annual rate of not less than two-thirds of the net annual value (or who would be so entitled if the accommodation was let), who is not him- or herself liable as tenant of the accommodation to pay such a rent to a superior landlord. Where the accommodation is a caravan, boat or similar structure, the owner is the person currently entitled to dispose of it.

Provision of information and evidence

4.175 The authority may require a person to whom assistance has been provided or who has applied for assistance to provide it, within a reasonable period, with such information as it may reasonably require (RRO 2002 art 6). This may include information as to the person's financial circumstances. The Regulatory Reform Order does not lay down any procedures which authorities have to adopt.

Central government contributions

4.176 Contributions towards expenditure incurred in providing housing assistance may be made by the secretary of state in England, or the National Assembly in Wales (RRO 2002 art 7).

Disabled facilities grant

Nature of grant

4.177 A 'disabled facilities grant' is available for the provision of facilities for a disabled person in a dwelling, a qualifying houseboat or caravan, or in common parts of a building (HGCRA 1996 s1).

Qualifying houseboat

4.178 A qualifying houseboat is a boat or similar structure designed or adapted for use as a place of permanent habitation which has its only or main mooring within the area of a single local authority, which is moored in pursuance of a right to that mooring and which is a dwelling for council tax purposes (HGCRA 1996 s58).

Caravan

4.179 A caravan is a structure or motor vehicle designed or adapted for human habitation which is capable of being moved from one place to another (not including tents or railway stock), together with any yard, garden or additional area usually enjoyed with it (HGCRA 1996 s58, adopting the definition in Caravan Sites and Control of Development Act 1960 Part 1 – see para 9.2).

Purposes of grant

4.180 A disabled facilities grant may not be approved unless the authority is satisfied that the works are necessary and appropriate to meet the needs of the disabled occupant and that it is reasonable and practicable to carry out the works having regard to the age or the condition of the building (HGCRA 1996 s24(3)). Applications should be assessed in conjunction with the social services authority.

4.181 The grant is available if it is for one or more of the following purposes:

1) facilitating access by the disabled occupant to and egress from the premises;
2) making the dwelling, qualifying houseboat, caravan (see paras 4.178, 4.179) or building safe for the disabled occupant or other persons residing with him or her;
3) facilitating access by the disabled occupant to a room used or usable as the principal family room;
4) facilitating access to, or providing, a room used or usable for sleeping;
5) facilitating access to, or providing, a room in which there is a lavatory, bath, shower or wash-hand basin, or facilitating the use of such a facility;
6) facilitating the preparation and cooking of food;
7) improving any heating system in the dwelling to meet the needs of the disabled occupant, or, if there is no existing heating system or it is unsuitable, providing a suitable system;
8) facilitating the use by the disabled occupant of a source of power, light or heat, by altering the position of access and control or providing additional means of control;
9) facilitating access and movement by the disabled occupant around the dwelling in order to enable him or her to care for a person who is normally resident in the dwelling and who is in need of such care; and
10) other purposes specified by the secretary of state or the Welsh Ministers (HA 1996 s23(1)). In both England and Wales, these are facilitating access to a garden for a disabled occupant and making that access safe (Disabled Facilities Grants (Maximum Amounts and Additional Purposes) (England) Order 2008 SI No 1189; Disabled Facilities Grants (Maximum Amounts and Additional Purposes) (Wales) Order 2008 SI No 2370).

Constraints on commencement of works

4.182 Works for which it is intended to apply for a disabled facilities grant should generally not have been started before approval of application, unless there is good reason and must not have been completed (HGCRA 1996 s29).

Pre-conditions

4.183 An application for a disabled facilities grant must be in writing and include details of the works and at least two estimates for the costs of carrying out the works (HGCRA 1996 s2). The applicant must be at least 18 years old (HGCRA 1996 s3).

Required interest

4.184 The applicant must have the requisite interest in the property. He or she must either be an owner, defined to mean a freeholder or someone with a leasehold interest of at least five years, or be a tenant (HGCRA 1996 s19). In the case of a qualifying houseboat or park home, it is enough if he or she is an occupier of the houseboat or caravan.

Future use

4.185 An application for a disabled facilities grant must be accompanied either by an owner's certificate stating that the applicant has or proposes to acquire an owner's interest (see para 4.184) and intends that the disabled occupant will live in the property as his only or main residence for five years, or by a tenant's certificate stating that the applicant is a tenant and has the same intention (HGCRA 1996 ss21, 22).

4.186 In the case of a qualifying houseboat or caravan (see paras 4.178–4.179), an occupier's certificate is required stating that the disabled occupier intends to live in the houseboat or park home as his only or main residence for five years (HGCRA 1996 s22A).

4.187 The authority may – in the case of any of these certificates – set a shorter period of intended residence, as the health of the disabled person or other relevant circumstance permit (HGCRA 1996 s22A(2)(b)).

Approval

4.188 Authorities must, by notice in writing, approve or refuse a grant application as soon as reasonably practicable and in any event no later than six months after it has been made (HGCRA 1996 s34).

4.189 An approval must include a statement of the works eligible for grant, the amount of expenses which in the authority's opinion are properly to be incurred on the eligible works, together with any preliminary or ancillary services or charges, eg the cost of having plans drawn up, and the amount of grant which will be paid (HGCRA 1996 s34(2)).

Grant maxima

4.190 The amount of grant is means-tested (see para 4.191). Maximum amounts (HGCRA 1996 s33) have been set of £30,000 in England, and £36,000 in Wales (Disabled Facilities Grants (Maximum Amounts and Additional Purposes) (England) Order 2008 SI No 1189; Disabled Facilities Grants (Maximum Amounts and Additional Purposes) (Wales) Order 2008 SI No 2370).

Means-testing

4.191 Where the application is by an owner-occupier or a tenant, the amount of grant is reduced in accordance with regulations which are similar to those applied to housing benefit calculations, and which ascertain an amount which the applicant is treated him- or herself as being able to finance, by which the grant is accordingly to be reduced (HGCRA 1996 s30).

Landlords' means test

4.192 The means-testing provisions applicable where the application is by a landlord letting or intending to let to a disabled occupier are less prescribed. In deciding the amount of grant, the authority should have regard to the extent to which the landlord is able to charge a higher rent for the premises because of the works and such other matters as may be directed (HGCRA 1996 s31). Authorities may seek the advice of rent officers (see para 3.53) (HGCRA 1996 s31(4)).

Payment of grant

4.193 Once approved, an authority may only refuse to pay the grant in one or more of seven circumstances:

1) where the applicant ceases to be a person entitled to the grant;
2) where the authority ascertains that the amount to be paid was determined on the basis of inaccurate or incomplete information and exceeds that to which the applicant was entitled;
3) where the applicant fails to complete the works satisfactorily within the time allowed (see para 4.196);

4) where the cost of the eligible works and costs incurred on preliminary or ancillary service is less than the estimated expense;
5) where the authority ascertains that without its knowledge the works were not carried out by one of the contractors who submitted an estimate (HGCRA 1996 ss42, 43);
6) where the works are not carried out to the satisfaction of the authority; and,
7) where the applicant fails to provide an acceptable invoice, demand or receipt for payment for the works or for the preliminary or ancillary services and charges (HGCRA 1996 s37).

4.194 In such circumstances there are provisions for the recovery of grant already paid, where appropriate (HGCRA 1996 ss42, 43).

Stage payments

4.195 The authority may make the whole payment after completion of the works. Alternatively, it may make stage payments, as the work progresses, provided that no more than nine-tenths of the grant is paid before completion (HGCRA 1996 s35). The authority may specify a delayed date for payment, up to 12 months after the date of application (HGCRA 1996 s36). This is to enable authorities to stagger payments of the grant to fit their budgets. Grants may be paid directly to the contractor provided that the applicant was informed of this prior to approval of the grant (HGCRA 1996 s39).

Conditions as to completion of works

4.196 The authority may make it a condition of the grant that the works are carried out in accordance with their specifications, eg as to materials to be used. It is a mandatory condition of all grants that the works are finished within 12 months of approval, although the authority may extend this time at its discretion (HGCRA 1996 s37). It is also a mandatory condition that the works are carried out by one of the two contractors from whom estimates were submitted with the application (see para 4.183), unless the authority directs otherwise (HGCRA 1996 s38).

Compensation conditions

4.197 With the consent of the secretary of state or the Welsh Ministers, an authority may attach a condition that the applicant takes reasonable steps to pursue any relevant insurance or legal claim which relates to the premises, eg where a grant is being sought following fire damage and an insurance claim can be made (HGCRA 1996 s51).

Other conditions

4.198 Other conditions may be applied with the consent of the secretary of state or the Welsh Ministers, eg as to nomination rights, insurance or maintenance (HGCRA 1996 s52).

Voluntary repayment

4.199 An owner or mortgagee entitled to exercise the power of sale can repay the grant voluntarily. On such a repayment, all grant conditions cease to have effect (HGCRA 1996 s55).

Human Rights Act 1998

4.200 A term in a tenancy or licence agreement could be so restrictive as to interfere with a tenant's right to respect or the home and family life under Article 8 of the European Convention on Human Rights (ECHR). Likewise, a term could contravene the prohibition on discrimination in Article 8. However, given that such a term would undoubtedly be either unfair (see paras 4.93–4.100) or a breach of EqA 2010 (see paras 4.101–4.109) it is unlikely that the ECHR adds anything to a tenant's rights under domestic law.

4.201 The right of long leaseholders to acquire the freehold or an extended lease of their houses under LRA 1967 or their flats (LRHUDA 1993) interferes with a landlord's right to peaceful enjoyment of his possessions under Article 1 of the First Protocol ECHR. The policy of LRA 1967 has been held to be justified, as it was calculated to 'enhance social justice' (*James v UK*, 1986). It is probable that other enfranchisement rights would likewise be considered proportionate.

CHAPTER 5

Protection against rogue landlords

Introduction

5.1 The chapter considers a number of classes of conduct which are prohibited either by criminal or civil law or both. The classes concerned are unlawful eviction and harassment, specific to housing, a more general prohibition on harassment, and offences which may be committed by trespassers. The chapter also deals with the new provisions in the Housing and Planning Act (HPA) 2016 designed to combat 'rogue landlords', under which local authorities will be able to ban persons convicted of certain offences from being residential landlords, lettings agents or property managers. Under that Act, such persons will be recorded in a database of rogue landlords. There is a number of other provisions which are considered elsewhere which also address the conduct of rogue landlords against which occupiers have some degree of protection, including the provisions considered in chapter 2 preventing the service of, or invalidating, a section 21 notice requiring possession from an assured shorthold tenant (see para 2.197), those concerning tenancy deposits in chapter 3 (see paras 3.135–3.150), and those under the heading 'Other controls' in chapter 13, none of which are repeated in this chapter.

Unlawful eviction and harassment

5.2 The Protection from Eviction Act (PEA) 1977 s3 requires a landlord to use court proceedings to evict most tenants and licensees (see paras 1.17–1.58; 1.114–1.130). Some landlords nonetheless resort to force or other crude tactics in order to get rid of their occupiers when they want to do so, without taking proceedings in court. To counter this, there are criminal offences of harassment and illegal eviction, now to be found in PEA 1977.

5.3 In practice, however, individual occupiers may be able to get more help from the civil courts than the criminal law. Thus, there are only limited circumstances in which the magistrates' courts can make an order for compensation, and they will rarely order damages for suffering or inconvenience. Similarly, the magistrates' court has no power to make an order compelling a landlord to re-admit an evicted occupier, either immediately – which is when it will be most needed – or at all (although at the conclusion of criminal proceedings, a magistrates' court can make an order restraining further harassment or eviction – para 5.66).

5.4 The position is different in the civil courts (primarily the county courts). These courts have power to order a landlord to re-admit an evicted occupier, and they can exercise this power so quickly that an occupier may be able to get back in the same day as the eviction or as help is sought. They can also make orders restraining further harassment or eviction. At the end of a case, civil courts can make orders which remain in force indefinitely, breach of which would be contempt of court. They can also order the landlord to pay the occupier damages for actual loss suffered, for distress, shock, suffering, and for the wrong that has been done to him or her.

Criminal proceedings

5.5 The criminal offences of illegal eviction and harassment are defined in PEA 1977 s1.

> (1) In this section 'residential occupier', in relation to any premises, means a person occupying the premises as a residence, whether under a contract or by virtue of any enactment or rule of law giving him the right to remain in occupation or restricting the right of any other person to recover possession of the premises.
>
> (2) If any person unlawfully deprives the residential occupier of any premises of his occupation of the premises or any part thereof, or attempts to do so, he shall be guilty of an offence unless he proves that he believed, and had reasonable cause to believe, that the residential occupier had ceased to reside in the premises.
>
> (3) If any person with intent to cause the residential occupier of any premises–
>
> (a) to give up the occupation of the premises or any part thereof; or
>
> (b) to refrain from exercising any right or pursuing any remedy in respect of the premises or part thereof;
>
> does acts likely to interfere with the peace or comfort of the residential occupier or members of his household, or persistently withdraws or withholds services reasonably required for the occupation of the premises as a residence, he shall be guilty of an offence.
>
> (3A) Subject to subsection (3B), below, the landlord of a residential occupier or an agent of the landlord shall be guilty of an offence if–
>
> (a) he does acts likely to interfere with the peace or comfort of the residential occupier or members of his household, or
>
> (b) he persistently withdraws or withholds services reasonably required for the occupation of the premises in question as a residence,

and (in either case) he knows, or has reasonable cause to believe, that that conduct is likely to cause the residential occupier to give up the occupation of the whole or part of the premises or to refrain from exercising any right or pursuing any remedy in respect of the whole or part of the premises.

(3B) A person shall not be guilty of an offence under subsection (3A) if he proves that he had reasonable grounds for doing the acts or withdrawing or withholding the services in question.

Residential occupier

Occupation as a residence

5.6 Occupation as a residence (PEA 1977 s1(1)) is a question of fact and common sense, not law. It is not necessary to show, for example, that the occupier had sufficient residence to sustain a claim to statutory tenancy (see paras 1.290–1.293) or is occupying as an only or principal home (see paras 1.176–1.179). Someone who merely visits a friend is not residing in premises, not even if he or she stays overnight or, perhaps for a few nights. The same is no doubt true of a short-term hotel guest. Once a person begins to use premises to live in, in any normal sense of the expression, then the premises are being occupied as a residence, although not so if the accommodation is being occupied under the temporary provisions of the homelessness legislation (see para 1.313). The offence may be committed in relation to any 'premises'. This has been given a broad meaning and can be as little as a single room (*Thurrock UDC v Shina*, 1972). It has also been held to include a caravan, which had remained static for some years (*Norton v Knowles*, 1967) and premises comprising a flat with a shop below (*Patel v Pirabakaran*, 2006). There is a separate but similar scheme for protection from eviction for occupiers of mobile homes (see paras 9.15–9.22).

5.7 A person can also have two residences, eg a student who lives away from home during the term-time will normally be considered resident both at home and at college. A person does not stop residing in premises just because, for example, he or she goes away for a holiday, or for some other reason is temporarily absent. The residence will continue during such breaks as if the occupier was actually present.

5.8 All tenants (including long leaseholders – para 2.72) and licensees (see paras 1.114–1.130) including service tenants and occupiers (see paras 1.131–1.140) whose tenancies and licences have not been brought to an end are residential occupiers because they are occupying under contract (PEA 1977 s1(1)). It does not matter if the person harassing or evicting is not a party to the contract; what is in question is whether or not the occupier is a residential occupier. Secure, assured, introductory, demoted and family intervention tenants occupy both under contract and by virtue of statute (see paras 1.160–1.209, 1.220–1.251, 1.210–1.219, 1.252–1.261, 1.262–1.266) as do secure (see para 1.168) and introductory (see para 1.212) licensees. Rent Act protected tenants whose contractual tenancies have been brought to an end and who occupy as statutory tenants (see paras 1.269) do so 'by virtue of an enactment' (Rent Act (RA) 1977), and remain so protected until evicted by the bailiff (*Haniff v Robinson*, 1992).

5.9 Unless the tenancy was entered into on or after the commencement date of Housing Act (HA) 1988 Part 1 (15 January 1989) and qualifies as an 'excluded tenancy', all other former tenants (together with those lawfully living with them, even if the former tenant has him- or herself departed) are residential occupiers because there is an enactment (PEA 1977 s3) 'restricting the right of any other person to recover possession of the premises'. Section 3 also protects former licensees who have occupied under restricted contracts commencing on or after 28 November 1980 (see para 1.310), former service occupiers who were granted some exclusive occupation of their accommodation under the employment arrangement (PEA 1977 s8(2) – para 1.310), and all other former licensees other than those with 'excluded licences'. Excluded tenancies and licences are considered in chapter 1 (see paras 1.308–1.313). If an excluded tenancy or licence was entered into on or after 15 January 1989, however section 3 is disapplied and the occupier will not be within section 3 so that, the tenancy or licence having ended, there will be no restriction on the right of the landlord to recover possession nor even prohibition against harassment under PEA 1977.

Domestic arrangements

5.10 In addition, there are enactments restricting the right of another person to recover possession of premises which serve to protect deserted spouses or civil partners and, in some cases, even trespassers. The Family Law Act (FLA) 1996 (chapter 7) prohibits an owner or tenant spouse, civil partner or cohabitee from evicting the non-owning member of the couple from the matrimonial home without an order of a court. Such an order will normally be made during the course of domestic proceedings, and this subject is therefore considered in that chapter. Because, however, there is an enactment which restricts the right of some other person (the owner or the tenant) to recover possession, the remaining partner qualifies as a residential occupier for the purposes of PEA 1977, even if it is not the other partner who is attempting to recover possession from him or her.

Trespassers

5.11 The offence of violent entry under the Criminal Law Act (CLA) 1977, for the purposes of the eviction of a trespasser, is described below. In so far as a trespasser is protected from eviction by that provision, so also does it seem that he or she will be protected from eviction under PEA 1977.

Advisability of proceedings

5.12 The definition of residential occupier is, therefore, very wide indeed. It is only possible to evict certain occupiers, eg trespassers, and some former licensees and tenants, without taking court proceedings, so long as CLA 1977 is not broken, so long as no other criminal offence is committed, so long as the licence or tenancy is already at an end (*R v Blankley*, 1979), and so on. This list of reservations should deter any landlord from seeking to recover possession without taking court proceedings, for the risk of committing an offence when doing so will otherwise be very high. It is for this reason that landlords are almost invariably advised by lawyers to take court proceedings before evicting any occupier.

Acts of harassment

Intention and knowledge

5.13 The difference between PEA 1977 s1(3) and s1(3A) (see para 5.5) is that the former creates an offence when the landlord does the specified acts with the intention of causing the occupier to quit or to refrain from exercising a right, while the latter creates an offence when the landlord does those acts knowing or having reasonable cause to believe that the consequence is likely to be that the occupier quits or refrains from exercising a right.

5.14 The most common intention is that of wanting the occupier to give up possession of the premises or part of them, eg one room, and that is also the most common consequence. Harassment also commonly occurs with the other objective in mind, eg to try and deter an occupier from applying to a rent officer or to a tribunal to challenge a proposed rent increase, or to deter the occupier from complaining to an environmental health officer (see chapters 12 and 13) about the condition of the property.

Services, peace and comfort

5.15 The criminal act can also be committed in different ways: by persistently withholding or withdrawing services, such as gas and electricity, reasonably required for occupation of the premises as a residence; or by doing an act (*R v Polycarpou*, 1978) or acts, likely to interfere with the peace or comfort of the residential occupier or members of his or her household. 'Persistently' means more than just once or twice. Withholding or withdrawal of services can be justified under section 1(3B) if the landlord proves that there were reasonable grounds for it, eg that services were dangerous to use. Mere non-payment of rent or other charges by the occupier is not sufficient justification: the landlord has other remedies for this, ie to seek an order for possession.

5.16 The breadth of the definition allows the law to catch odd actions which may not be obvious acts of harassment, such as hanging around a sensitive and perhaps elderly occupier, or coming into the premises so frequently that the occupier ceases to feel secure in his or her home. The act in question does not need also to be a civil wrong (see paras 5.48–5.53), so that a criminal offence may be committed by an act with the appropriate intention, even if it does not conflict with an occupier's other rights, eg refusing to supply a replacement key when the occupier has lost his or hers (*R v Yuthiwattana*, 1984), or deliberately disconnecting the door bell or preventing use of a particular bathroom and lavatory (*R v Burke*, 1990).

Acts of eviction

Definition

5.17 Eviction can be from the whole or part of the premises in question. An offence is committed by both a successful eviction and by an attempted eviction. The defence which is available to an accused (PEA 1977 s1(2) – para 5.5) requires him or her to show that he or she both believed and had reasonable cause to believe that the residential occupier had ceased to reside in the premises: the requirement of reasonable cause means that a subjective but unreasonable belief will not be a defence. The fact that the burden of proof is on the defendant does not infringe the defendant's right to a fair trial under Article 6 of the European Convention on Human Rights (ECHR) (*Attorney-General's Ref (No 1 of 2004)*, 2004). Eviction does, however, means more than intending to lock the occupier out for only a short time, eg overnight; such an action is more likely to be one of harassment (*R v Yuthiwattana*, 1984).

Homelessness

5.18 An occupier who is illegally evicted will be homeless, and will qualify for assistance under HA 1996 Part 7 (in England) or Housing (Wales) Act (H(W)A) 2014 Part 2 (in Wales) (see chapter 10), although how much will depend on priority need (see para 10.39).

The accused

5.19 Under PEA 1977 s1(2) and (3) (see para 5.5), anyone can be charged with illegal eviction or harassment, not only a landlord or the landlord's friends or agents. It may, however, be difficult to establish the necessary intention for harassment unless the act is done by someone with connections to the landlord. On the face of it, no one else is likely to have the incentive to try to get the occupier out, still less to prevent him or her pursuing remedies.

5.20 Where section 1(3A) (see para 5.5) is alleged, the perpetrator must be, or be acting on behalf of, the landlord. Where the acts are committed by an agent, the landlord is only guilty of the offence if the agent acted at the landlord's instigation or with his or her agreement (*R v Quereshi (Mohammed)*, 2011). The acts must have been committed with the knowledge – actual or deemed – that they will cause the occupier to quit or to refrain from exercising a right or remedy. For this purpose, the definition of 'landlord' is extended (PEA 1977 s1(3C)) to include anyone who would have a right to occupation of the premises but for the occupier's protection, or a superior landlord from whom the immediate landlord derives his or her right. A prospective future occupier could qualify in this way (*Jones v Miah*, 1992).

5.21 If the harassment or eviction is performed on behalf of a limited company, a director or any officer of the company will also be guilty of an offence if he or she consented to or connived at the harassment, or it happened because of his or her negligence (PEA 1977 s1(6)).

Prosecution

5.22 Criminal proceedings are initiated in the magistrates' court although the accused may elect trial in the Crown Court.

5.23 Local authorities have power to prosecute offences under the Act (PEA 1977 s6); almost all prosecutions are brought by them, usually through a tenancy relations officer employed to deal with private sector disputes.

5.24 The police are not liable for a failure to prevent an offence being committed under PEA 1977, even where the tenant has requested them to attend (and prevent) an unlawful eviction. It has been held that they cannot be expected to inform themselves about landlord and tenant law before attending such a call: *Cowan v Chief Constable of Avon & Somerset Constabulary*, 2001.

Role of tenancy relations officer

5.25 In the event of any act of harassment or eviction, the local authority's tenancy relations officer ('TRO') – or equivalent officer – should be contacted without delay. If it is urgent, he or she may call straight round to the premises and try to sort the problem out face to face with the landlord and the occupier. Some TROs have radio-linked cars. If the matter is not urgent, the TRO may write to the landlord, warning him or her of the possible offences and penalties and inviting comment. TROs do not usually make prosecution their goal: they tend to work by way of conciliation, reinforced by the possibility of prosecution, although the degree of emphasis will vary between officers and/or authorities. A TRO cannot normally decide on his or her own initiative to prosecute: the prosecution will be handled by the local authority's legal service (internal or external).

Private prosecution

5.26 If the TRO will not prosecute, then it is still open to the individual occupier who has been harassed or illegally evicted to do so. Legal aid will not be available for a prosecution. Unsurprisingly, not many occupiers are prepared to shoulder the responsibility of a private prosecution unassisted, and run the risk of having to pay the landlord's costs if he or she is acquitted.

Penalties

5.27 The magistrates' court can impose an unlimited fine or up to six months' imprisonment, or both (PEA 1997 s1(4); Magistrates' Courts Act 1980 s32; Legal Aid, Sentencing and Punishment of Offenders Act (LASPO) 2012 s85(2)). If the accused elects trial in the Crown Court, then he or she could be fined an unlimited amount, or sent to prison for up to two years, or both (PEA 1997 s1(4)). The court may also make a restraining order (see para 5.66).

Compensation

5.28 Either court has power to award compensation for 'personal injury, loss or damage resulting from [an] offence' (Powers of Criminal

Courts (Sentencing) Act 2000 s130). The power can be used in relation to ascertainable loss, such as damaged property, time off work through injury, cost of overnight accommodation or eating out, etc and can also be used for shock, distress, inconvenience or discomfort. In the case of illegal eviction, the power will not be used for loss of the home itself, as this does not have an easily identified value. There is no limit on the amount of an award against an adult but awards against those who are under 18 are limited to £5,000 (s131). Any documentary evidence of loss sustained by the occupier, such as bills, should be brought to court.

Rent repayment orders

5.29 In England, HPA 2016 introduced a power for the First-tier Tribunal to make a 'rent repayment order' against a landlord who, on or after 6 April 2017, committed an offence of unlawful eviction under PEA 1977 s1(2) (see paras 5.5 and 5.17), or of harassment under either PEA 1977 s1(3) or s1(3A) (see paras 5.5, 5.11–5.16). An order can be made on the application either of the local authority for the area in which the offence took place or of the occupier.

Application by local authority

5.30 An authority is under a positive duty to consider making an application once it becomes aware that an offence of unlawful eviction or harassment has taken place on or after 6 April 2017 (HPA 2016 s48). If the authority decides to proceed, a notice of intended proceedings must be served, warning the landlord of the authority's intention to make the application and inviting representations within 28 days (HPA 2016 s42). The notice must give reasons for making the application and provide a calculation for the money sought.

Making an order

5.31 Whether the application is by an authority or the occupier, the tribunal must, before making an order, be satisfied that at some time within the period of 12 months ending with the date of the notice of intended proceedings, the landlord committed the offence of unlawful eviction or harassment (HPA 2016 s43). It is not, however, necessary that there has been a prosecution or conviction.

Amount of order

5.32 Where the application is by an authority, the starting-point is that the tribunal may order the landlord to repay to the authority any amount of housing benefit or universal credit received by the landlord (directly or through an agent) in respect of the rent during the period of up to 12 months before the date of the offence (HPA 2016 ss45, 51).

5.33 Where the application is by an occupier, the starting-point is that the tribunal may order the landlord to repay to the tenant the rent paid during the period of up to 12 months before the date of the offence, less any amount which was paid by housing benefit or universal credit (HPA 2016 ss44, 51).

5.34 On an authority's application, if the unlawful eviction or harassment has already resulted in a conviction, the tribunal must award the full amount of the housing benefit or universal credit (see para 5.32), and on a tenant's application, it must award the full amount of the rent less the housing benefit or universal credit (see para 5.33) (HPA 2016 s46). The only exception is where the tribunal considers that it would be unreasonable to require the landlord to pay the full amount because of exceptional circumstances (s46(5)).

5.35 If there had been no conviction, the tribunal must, in deciding the amount, have regard to the landlord's conduct, his or her financial circumstances and whether the landlord has, at any time, been convicted of any of the following offences (HPA 2016 ss44, 45): unlawful eviction under PEA 1977 s1(2) (see paras 5.5, 5.17); harassment under PEA 177 s1(3) or (3A) (see paras 5.5, 5.11–5.16); violent entry into premises (CLA 1977 s6(1)) (see para 5.72); failure to comply with an improvement notice under HA 2004 s30(1) (see para 12.25); failure to comply with a prohibition order under HA 2004 s32(1) (see para 12.40); being in control of or managing an unlicensed HMO under HA 2004 s72(1) (see para 14.97); being in control of or managing a unlicensed house to which HA 2014 Part 3, applies under HA 2004 s95(1) (see para 14.97); and, once in force, breach of a banning order under HPA 2016 s21 (see para 5.99).

Civil proceedings

5.36 Civil proceedings are brought in either the county court, usually for the area in which the incident happens, or in the High Court. Most cases of harassment and illegal eviction will be brought in the county courts, as a case which includes a claim for damages may not be started in the High Court unless the value of the claim is more than £100,000 (Civil Procedure Rules (CPR) Pt 7; CPR PD 7A para 2.1). The county court has jurisdiction to hear claims for damages under HA 1988 ss27 and 28 (see paras 5.51–5.54) even though they may exceed£100,000. If the claim includes a claim for damages for personal injury, the claim may not be started in the High Court unless the value of the claim is more than £50,000 (CPR Pt 7; CPR PD 7A para.2.2).

5.37 The county court does, however, have the jurisdiction to make any order which the High Court can, eg an injunction (County Courts Act 1984 s38). The civil remedies which may be awarded by either sort of court are injunctions; and/or damages.

Injunctions

5.38 An injunction is an order of the court, which requires a person to do, or restrain from doing, something. It will always identify the person, or persons, who is or are to be bound by it. The order must include a 'penal notice', ie a warning to the person who is subject to the injunction that he or she may be sent to prison for contempt of court if he or she does not comply with the terms of the order. If the breach is proved, the court may impose a period of imprisonment up to two years and/or an unlimited fine and may also sequester a person's assets: Contempt of Court Act 1981 s14. Given the serious consequences of a finding of contempt, the burden of proof in committal proceedings is to the criminal standard of 'beyond reasonable doubt'.

Final and interim injunctions

5.39 Injunctions are either final or interim. A final injunction is awarded at the end of a trial when the factual disputes between the parties have been resolved. The trial may not, however, take place for some months after the commencement of proceedings, and the prospect of a final injunction is of little assistance to the victim of an ongoing campaign of harassment, or someone locked out of his or her home who is sleeping rough or staying with friends. In such circumstances, the victim may apply for an interim injunction, which may be granted at any time after the commencement of proceedings in order to maintain the status quo pending the trial. In extremely urgent cases, an injunction may even be awarded on an undertaking to go through the formal process of issuing proceedings within a specified time afterwards.

Notice

5.40 The landlord will be on notice of a claim for a final injunction, because he or she will be on notice of the proceedings themselves. Normally, notice is required of an application for an interim injunction, but if a matter is so urgent that it cannot even be left for the few days necessary to give the landlord an opportunity to attend court, the court can grant a 'without-notice' interim order, ie one that is based upon the unchallenged evidence of the occupier only. This will only happen when the matter is serious, eg an actual eviction or disconnection of utilities. The courts will also only use their powers to make a without-notice order if there has been little or no delay before they are asked to do so. A without-notice order should therefore always be sought immediately. If an order is granted without notice, it will usually be for only a few days or a week, until a further hearing – on notice – at which the court can hear the other side of the case and decide whether or not the order should be continued until a full trial of the matter.

Balance of convenience

5.41 When a court is deciding whether or not to grant an interim injunction, it does not decide the full merits of the case. It only decides what order should be made, pending the full trial, on what is normally called the 'balance of convenience' (*American Cyanamid Co Ltd v Ethicon*, 1975) but which is sometimes referred to as the 'balance of justice' between the parties (*Francome v Mirror Group Newspapers*, 1984). Unless the premises have already been re-occupied by someone else, or by the landlord him- or herself, the balance in a case of illegal eviction will normally be in the occupier's favour, although it may be subject to an undertaking by the occupier to pay rent pending the trial. The balance will also almost invariably be with the occupier where harassment is in issue.

5.42 If the premises have been re-let, however, the court will not usually grant an interim injunction. In *Love v Herrity*, 1990, it was suggested that the correct approach where an evicted tenant wishes to be re-admitted to the property is for the evicted tenant to ask the court to join the new tenant as a party to the proceedings and claim possession against him or her. It was assumed that, if the eviction was unlawful, the evicted tenant has the right to possession against the new tenant because his or her existing tenancy pre-dated the new tenancy granted to the new tenancy by the landlord. The assumption is probably correct. The evicted tenant has the right to exclusive possession of the premises including as against the new tenant. This is because, if a property is let under a tenancy and the landlord grants a second tenancy of the property to a different tenant, the second tenancy is what is known as a 'concurrent' tenancy (*Sheffield City Council v Wall*, 2010). The grant of a concurrent tenancy operates as an assignment (see paras 1.78–1.83) by the landlord of his or her interest in the property to the concurrent tenant for as long as the two tenancies co-exist. It follows that the new tenant has no more right of possession against the evicted tenant than the landlord had.

5.43 Although the issue is one of a balance, the strength of a case may still affect the decision of the court. If the occupier's case is a strong one, on the face of it, then even if – for example – the landlord is in occupation, the court will be reluctant to allow him or her to benefit from what appears to be both the commission of a criminal offence and a very serious breach of the civil law, by allowing him or her to remain in occupation until trial.

Damages

5.44 Damages are not awarded until the end of the case. There are several different sorts of damages. A person can claim 'special damages' for specific sums of money, eg damage to furniture, cost of eating out or overnight accommodation, lost property, etc. These are the same sorts of damages which may be awarded in the magistrates' courts as compensation (see para 5.28). In addition, there will usually be a claim for general damages, which are for unquantified sums claimed in respect of, for example, suffering, shock, distress, physical injury, inconvenience, the lost right of occupation itself or any other harm to which a specific value cannot be attached, eg additional electricity costs because gas is cut off. After calculating an award for general damages, courts must now increase the award by 10 per cent. This principle reflects the fact that claimants can no longer have a conditional fee agreement with their lawyers (often called 'no win no fee'), ie the lawyer receives nothing if the claim fails but the lawyer receives a 'success fee' above his or her normal fee if it succeeds. The principle applies, however, even where there is no conditional fee agreement (*Simmons v Castle*, 2012). In addition, aggravated damages will be awarded to compensate for injury to proper feelings of dignity and pride, and for aggravation generally (*Ramdath v Daley*, 1993), where the manner of that which is being sued for was especially mean, unpleasant or brutal.

5.45 Finally, exemplary damages are awarded where it would appear that the landlord has evicted a tenant, calculating to him- or herself that any profit made, eg from sale of the property with vacant possession, will be more than any damages awarded. In *Cassell & Co Ltd v Broome*, 1972, Lord Hailsham LC said:

> How, it may be asked, about the late Mr Rachman who is alleged to have used hired bullies to intimidate statutory tenants by violence

> or threats of violence into giving up vacant possession of their residences and so placing a valuable asset in the hands of the landlord? My answer must be that if this is not a cynical calculation of profit and cold-blooded disregard of a plaintiff's rights, I do not know what is.

5.46 In *Drane v Evangelou*, 1977, Lawton LJ said that to deprive a tenant of a roof over his or her head was one of the worst torts (wrongs) that could be committed. It brought the law into disrespect. He also expressed his surprise that the landlord had not been prosecuted under what is now PEA 1977 s1. Lord Denning MR applied the words of an earlier case:

> Exemplary damages can properly be awarded whenever it is necessary to teach a wrongdoer that tort does not pay.

5.47 Exemplary damages cannot, however, be claimed where the claim is only based on breach of contract (see para 5.49); accordingly, if it is considered that they may be available, a claim should additionally be made in tort (see paras 5.50–5.54) if possible.

Cause of action

5.48 Neither the county court nor the High Court can make any order at all, however, until an action has been commenced (or an undertaking to commence it has been accepted – para 5.39). Public funding will generally be available to bring a civil action based on harassment or illegal eviction. In order to commence the action, however, it is necessary to show that the claimant has a 'cause of action', which may be for either breach of contract or for a tort (see para 5.4).

Breach of contract

5.49 Both tenancies (see paras 1.17–1.58) and most licences (see paras 1.114–1.130) are contracts. A licensee may sue for breach of contract or breach of a term of the contract (*Smith v Nottinghamshire CC*, 1981). A term of a contract may actually be stated, or it may be implied, although only where it is a term which is necessary for the contract to be effective. In the case of a residential licence, this will usually mean such terms as are necessary for the property to be capable of use as a residence, although standards may vary depending on the type of licence, eg a hostel licence normally implies a 'full' or 'high' standard of occupancy, but a licence to share property scheduled for demolition or refurbishment (commonly called short-life use) would probably be at the opposite end of the spectrum. The following are the contractual causes of action most relevant to eviction and harassment of a tenant.

1) **Quiet enjoyment**. Into every tenancy, there is implied, unless it is actually spelled out in the agreement, a promise by the landlord that the tenant will have 'quiet enjoyment' of the premises so long as the tenancy lasts.

   In *Kenny v Preen*, 1962, it was said that the promise was broken by an act which was an invasion of the right of the tenant to remain in possession undisturbed. This includes an actual or threatened eviction and most acts of harassment. In *McCall v Abelesz*, 1975, disconnection of utilities was described as both a breach of an implied term, and as an interference with quiet enjoyment. Any conduct by a landlord which interferes with the tenant's freedom of action in exercising rights as a tenant will be an interference with the covenant for quiet enjoyment.

   Although 'quiet' enjoyment does not necessarily signify quiet in the noise sense, excessive noise made by the landlord is capable of amounting to breach of the covenant: *Southwark LBC v Tanner*, 1999. In *Tanner*, however, the disturbance arose from tenants being able to hear their neighbours due to poor sound insulation; accordingly, there was no breach of the covenant for quiet enjoyment because the landlord had not caused the noise (other than by letting the flats, as it was obvious and intended that it would).
2) **Derogation from grant**. In addition, some actions by a landlord in common parts, or in neighbouring property under the landlord's control, could amount to derogation from grant of the tenancy to the tenant (see para 4.111(1)). This is also an action in contract.

Tort

5.50 There is a number of torts which may be available in a case of unlawful eviction or harassment.

1) **Trespass**. If there is a tenancy, the tenant has possession of the premises to the exclusion of all others including the landlord. A landlord can, therefore, trespass on the premises of his or her own tenant. There is also some legal authority for the proposition that the sort of exclusive occupation which most licensees have is enough possession for the purposes of trespass. This is because it is possession in fact, rather than legally defined possession, which matters.

   A person is a trespasser whenever he or she enters the land or premises of another without permission. It is also a trespass to place anything on someone else's property without permission. In one case, it was held to be a trespass to drive a nail into someone else's wall, which, by analogy, would apply to a landlord who nails up a door or blocks up a lock. A person is also a trespasser if he or she has permission to be on someone's premises for one purpose but uses it for another. For example, a landlord calling around to collect the rent or inspect for repairs will become a trespasser if he or she uses the occasion to abuse, threaten or harass the occupier.

A person given permission to enter must leave once he or she is asked to do so and, once a reasonable time has been given to go, becomes a trespasser (see para 1.126). Reasonable time here, as with residential licence (see para 2.68), means what is reasonable in all the circumstances and, where a person is just visiting, will normally be a matter of however long it should take to get to the door.

Anyone who trespasses can be sued for it. A landlord is liable for the torts of his or her agents, if they were committed with his or her approval or on his or her behalf. An evicted or harassed occupier can sue the landlord and, if the landlord got someone else to do the job for him or her, that person as well.

2) **Assault**. Harassment and eviction will often be accompanied by assaults. An assault is not necessarily a directly physical act. It may be no more than some gesture which suggests that the person to whom it is made is about to be attacked physically. Threatening words on their own are not an assault, and it is difficult to prove unless there has been some sort of physical attack, although this might be with a weapon, piece of furniture, or merely by shoving an occupier around. As an assault is a tort, the remarks in relation to trespass as to who may be sued apply in the same way.
3) **Nuisance**. Like trespass, this is a cause of action which can be used by someone in possession of land, which certainly includes a tenant and may include a licensee. It is, however, only the person with the interest in the land who can sue, not other family members (*Hunter v Canary Wharf*, 1997).

   A nuisance is anything which interferes with the reasonable use and enjoyment of property, eg noise, smells, even hanging about outside someone's home. Whether conduct amounts to a nuisance is to be judged in context. Loud music may not amount to a nuisance if played for a short time but it may be a nuisance if it is played persistently, or frequently or during the night (See paras 6.89–6.90 for other remedies for noise nuisance). Most acts of harassment will constitute a nuisance, although this may not be so if the act is negative, eg a withdrawal of services.

4) **Trespass to goods and conversion**. Any direct interference with another person's belongings is a trespass to goods. If belongings are actually removed, this may also be conversion. Conversion is the act of dealing with someone else's property in any manner that is inconsistent with the right of the other person to possession of it.

HA 1988 ss 27 and 28

5.51 In *McCall v Abelesz*, 1975, it was held that, even though a landlord had committed an act or offence of illegal eviction or harassment, the occupier did not necessarily have any civil remedy. Accordingly, HA 1988 s27 affords an express right to sue where either illegal eviction within the PEA 1977 s1(2) has taken place, or such harassment within section 1(3), (3A) (see paras 5.13–5.16) has been committed (after 9 June 1988), that it leads to the occupier's departure. This right is conferred on all residential occupiers, as defined (see paras 5.6–5.11), and carries an express right to damages. The action is an action in tort and is additional to any other rights, save that damages for loss of occupation are not to be awarded twice over.

5.52 The action can be brought against the landlord (but not someone acting as his or her agent – *Sampson v Wilson*, 1995), or anyone else who, but for the occupier's right to occupy, would be entitled to occupy, or any superior landlord from whom that person derives his or her right. A landlord can defend the action by showing that he or she believed, and had reasonable cause to believe, that the residential occupier had already quit, or – in the case of a departure based on withholding services – that there were reasonable grounds for the withholding (*Wandsworth LBC v Osei Bonsu*, 1998).

5.53 Damages may be reduced if the court considers that the occupier's conduct provoked the eviction or harassment, or (where eviction is concerned) if the landlord has offered to reinstate the occupier, before the proceedings under HA 1988 were begun, and the offer was unreasonably refused. (There may be unreasonable refusal even if the occupier had found somewhere else before the offer.) The offer of reinstatement must be genuine, and merely handing the tenant a key to a lock which does not work, and inviting her to resume occupation of a room which has been totally wrecked, will not suffice (*Tagro v Cafane*, 1991).

5.54 There are detailed provisions (HA 1988 s28) governing the amount of damages under the Act, designed to deprive the landlord of the financial benefit of vacant possession. No damages at all are payable, however, if, before the action is commenced, or at any time before it is finally over, the occupier is actually reinstated. Where the evicting landlord holds only an intermediate interest, that is the interest which must be valued for the purpose of preventing him or her from securing a profit (*Jones & Lee v Miah*, 1992). The nature of the interest of the tenant (*Lambeth LBC v Loveridge*, 2014), and the fact of other occupiers, should be taken into account, so that where the tenancy which has been lost is an assured shorthold in a house still occupied by other tenants, the award is likely to be quite low (*Melville v Bruton*, 1996).

Protection from Harassment Act 1997

5.55 Harassment is by no means limited to tenants suffering at the hands of their landlords. The Protection from Harassment Act (PHA) 1997 created criminal offences of harassment and the right to seek an injunction to prevent it, which rights, while available more widely, are nonetheless also available to tenants and other occupiers.

5.56 **Harassment.** PHA 1997 prohibits harassment, breach of which is actionable in both the civil and criminal courts. It creates six criminal offences: harassment; putting another person in fear of violence; stalking; stalking with fear of violence; breach of a restraining order; and breach of an injunction. The Act gives a criminal court the power to make a restraining order, which has similar effect to an injunction.

5.57 PHA 1997 s1(1) prohibits a person from:

> ... pursuing a course of conduct–
> (a) which amounts to harassment of another; and
> (b) which he or she knows or ought to know amounts to harassment of the other.

5.58 It is an offence to pursue a course of conduct in breach of this prohibition against harassment (PHA 1997 s2).

5.59 There is no exhaustive definition of harassment for this purpose. It includes, but is not limited to, alarming or causing distress to a person (PHA 1997 s7(2)). It is a matter for the court to determine on the facts of the particular case whether conduct complained about 'amounts to harassment' in the everyday sense of the word but it must be 'grave' (*Ferguson v British Gas Trading*, 2009). The prosecution must also prove that the defendant was aware that the conduct amounted to harassment or, if not, that he or she 'ought to have known'. While conduct is not defined, it includes speech. To amount to a 'course of conduct' there must be conduct on more than one occasion (PHA 1997 s7(4)).

5.60 Fear of violence. Section 4(1) makes it an offence to pursue a course of conduct which:

> causes another to fear, on at least two occasions, that violence will be used against him ... if he knows or ought to know that his course of conduct will cause the other so to fear on each occasion.

5.61 The maximum penalty in a magistrates' court is six months' imprisonment and/or an unlimited fine; in the Crown Court, the offence is punishable by a maximum of ten years' imprisonment and/or an unlimited fine (PHA 1997 s4(4)). The court may make a restraining order (see para 5.66).

5.62 **Stalking**. It is an offence for a person to pursue a course of conduct in breach of PHA 1997 s1(1), (see paras 5.57–5.59) which amounts to stalking (PHA 1997 s2A). Stalking is not exhaustively defined but examples are listed in the Act: following a person; contacting, or attempting to contact, a person by any means; publishing any material which relates or purports to relate to a person, or purports to originate from a person; monitoring the use by a person of any form of electronic communication; loitering in any place; interfering with property in the possession of a person; and, watching or spying on a person.

5.63 The offence is punishable in the magistrates' court by a maximum penalty of six months' imprisonment and/or an unlimited fine (PHA 1997 s2A(4), (5); LASPO 2012 s85(1)). The court may make a restraining order (see para 5.66).

5.64 **Stalking with fear of violence**. If the stalking causes the victim to fear, on at least two occasions, that violence will be used against him or her, or causes the victim serious alarm or distress which has a substantial adverse effect on the victim's usual day-to-day activities, the stalker commits an offence under PHA 1997 s4A, if the stalker knows or ought to know that this would be the effect of his or her actions.

5.65 The maximum penalty in a magistrates' court is six months' imprisonment and/or an unlimited fine; in the Crown Court, the offence is punishable by a maximum of five years' imprisonment and/or an unlimited fine (PHA 1997 s4A; LASPO 2012 s85(1)). The court may make a restraining order (see para 5.66).

5.66 **Restraining order.** A criminal court may impose a 'restraining order' on a defendant to protect the victim (or any other specified person) from further conduct which may amount to harassment or which may cause a fear of violence (PHA 1997 s5). The power is available where a court is sentencing or otherwise dealing with a defendant convicted of *any* offence, not just those under the PHA 1977, and is also available where the defendant has been acquitted but the court considers an order to be necessary to protect someone from being harassed by the defendant (PHA 1997 s5A). The order must describe the prohibited conduct; it may be for a specified period or until a further order is made. It is an offence for a person to do anything prohibited under a restraining order, without reasonable excuse (PHA 1997 ss5(7), 5A(2)).

5.67 **Injunction.** PHA 1997 s3 provides a civil claim for actual or apprehended harassment, as defined in section 1 (see para 5.57), allowing the victim to seek an injunction and damages. It is expressly provided that damages may be awarded for any anxiety caused by the harassment, as well as any financial loss (PHA 1997 s3(1)). Where such proceedings are taken and the civil court grants an injunction to prevent further harassment, it is a criminal offence for the defendant, without reasonable excuse, to do anything which he or she is prohibited from doing by the injunction (PHA 1997 s5(6)). This offence cannot be pursued, however, if the defendant has already been punished by the civil court for contempt of court for breach of the injunction (see para 5.38), ie the sanctions – contempt of court in the civil court and conviction in the magistrates' court – are alternatives (s3(6)).

Criminal Justice and Police Act 2001

5.68 **Harassment in the home.** The Criminal Justice and Police Act (CJPA) 2001 s42A, creates the offence of harassment in the home. The offence is committed if a person is outside, or in the vicinity of, someone's dwelling, for the purpose of representing to the resident or someone else, or of persuading the resident or that other person, that he or she should not do something he or she is entitled or required to do or that he or she should do something that he or she is not under any obligation to do (CJPA 2001 s42A). The perpetrator must either intend his or her presence to amount to the harassment of, or to cause alarm or distress to, the resident, or know or ought to know, that his or her presence is likely to result in the harassment of, or to cause alarm or distress to, the resident.

5.69 The offence is only triable in the magistrates' court. The maximum penalty is six months' imprisonment and/or a fine not exceeding level 4 on the standard scale (currently £2,500).

Trespass

5.70 Save where a trespasser may have a defence based on public law (see paras 2.256–2.257) or his or her right to respect for the home under Article 8 of the European Convention on Human Rights (see paras 2.250–2.255), the only protection that a trespasser has against eviction is that which is provided by CLA 1977, which replaced the historic law on forcible entry. The Act also, however, created offences which a trespasser may commit in connection with squatting. These offences are in addition to that already considered in relation to adverse possession (see para 1.145), of entering and remaining in residential premises as a trespasser (LASPO 2012 s144).

5.71 Anyone who commits a criminal offence under CLA 1977 in the course of evicting a trespasser who is using premises as a residence is likely also to commit an offence under PEA 1977 (see para 5.5).

Violent eviction

5.72 **Violent entry**. Any person, whether or not the landlord, who uses or threatens violence either against people or against property in order to gain entry into premises, commits an offence if, but only if, the person seeking entry knows that there is someone – whom he or she knows is opposed to the entry – who is present on the premises at the time of the attempted entry (CLA 1977 s6). The offence is not committed if the person seeking entry has lawful authority to do so, ie a court bailiff. It does not, however, constitute lawful authority that the person trying to get in has some greater interest, eg licence, tenancy or ownership of the property. The offence is punishable in the magistrates' court by a maximum of six months' imprisonment and/or an unlimited fine (CLA 1977 s6(5); LASPO 2012 s85(1)).

5.73 **Displaced residential occupier**. There is a critical exception to this offence. The offence is not committed by a person otherwise offending against its provisions if he or she is, or someone on whose behalf he or she is acting, is a 'displaced residential occupier' of the premises. A displaced residential occupier is any person, other than another trespasser, who was using the premises or part of them as a residence immediately before the trespasser entered (CLA 1977 s12).

The exception is designed to permit the owner-occupier, or tenant, who goes away on holiday and finds on his or her return that the premises have been squatted, to evict the trespassers without any need to take court proceedings and without fear of committing an offence. A displaced residential occupier – or someone acting on his or her behalf – must take care when taking advantage of this exemption not to commit any of the ordinary, criminal offences such as assault or bodily harm.

5.74 **Protected intending occupier.** A second exception is made for 'protected intending occupiers'. There are three categories of protected intending occupier (CLA 1977 s12A).

1) **Freeholder or leaseholder.** A person is a protected intending occupier if he or she has either a freehold or a leasehold interest in the property, and requires the premises for his or her own occupation. The leasehold interest must have not less than two years to run at the relevant time.
2) **Private tenant or licensee.** A private tenant (whose tenancy may be less than two years) or a licensee with a licence granted by a freeholder or leaseholder (whose lease has more than two years to run) may be a protected intending occupier if he or she requires the accommodation for his or her own occupation.
3) **Social tenant or licensee.** A person is also a protected intending occupier if he or she has been given permission to occupy the premises as a residence by a local authority, a PRP or RSL.

5.75 In each case, the protected intended occupier must produce a statement which proves his or her status as a protected intending occupier. In the first and second cases, the statement has to specify the interest which he or she has, must state the requirement for use of the premises as a residence for him- or herself, and must have been signed either in the presence of a justice of the peace or of a commissioner of oaths who has also signed the statement as a witness. In the third case, the statement must specify that the would-be occupier has been authorised to occupy the premises and that the landlord is one of the bodies referred to.

Trespass with an offensive weapon

5.76 Offensive weapon. It is a criminal offence for a person who is on premises as a trespasser, having entered as such, to have with him or her any weapon of offence, ie anything which has been made or adapted for causing injury to another (CLA 1977 s8). The offence is punishable in the magistrates' court by a maximum of three months' imprisonment and/or an unlimited fine (CLA 1977 s8(2); LASPO 2012 s85(1)).

Trespass on diplomatic or consular premises

5.77 **Diplomatic premises.** This provision was designed to deal with 'political squatting' (*Kamara v DPP*, 1973) and makes it an offence for a trespasser to enter diplomatic or consular buildings, unless the trespasser can show that he or she does not believe them to be diplomatic or consular premises (CLA 1977 s9). The offence is punishable in the magistrates' court by a maximum of six months' imprisonment and/or an unlimited fine (CLA 1977 s9(6); LASPO 2012 s85(1)).

Resisting or obstructing an officer of the court in the course of an eviction

5.78 **Resisting official eviction.** It is an offence to resist or intentionally obstruct any person who is an officer of a court executing a possession order issued by a county court or the High Court (CLA 1977 s10). This offence is only committed where the officer is executing a possession order which either was made or which could have been under one of the speedy procedures contained in CPR 55 (see paras 2.243–2.249). Accordingly, it could be committed by a former licensee. The offence is punishable in the magistrates' court by a maximum of six months' imprisonment and/or an unlimited fine (CLA 1977 s10(4); LASPO 2012 s85(1)).

Refusing to leave premises when requested

5.79 The major new offence introduced by the Act (CLA 1977 s7) made it an offence for any trespasser, who enters as such, to fail to leave premises if asked to do so by a displaced residential occupier (see para 5.73) or by a person who is a protected intending occupier (see para 5.74), who produces the required statement (see para 5.75). There can accordingly be no offence until a request has been made, although it need not be a request in writing. In either case, the displaced residential occupier or the protected intending occupier must have been kept out of occupation by reason of the trespass.

5.80 It is a defence for the trespasser to prove that he or she did not believe that the person asking him or her to leave was either a displaced residential occupier or a protected intending occupier, or that the premises in question are or form part of premises used mainly for a non-residential purpose and that he was only on that part. It is also a defence to prove that a protected intending occupier did not produce the required statement (see para 5.75).

5.81 The offence is punishable in the magistrates' court by a maximum of six months' imprisonment and/or an unlimited fine (CLA 1977 s7(5); LASPO 2012 s85(1)).

Banning orders

5.82 In England, once HPA 2016 Part 2 is in force, local housing authorities will be able to apply to the First-tier Tribunal for an order banning a landlord, lettings agent, or a managing agent, who has been convicted of a 'banning order offence', from 'letting housing', engaging in 'letting agency work' or engaging in 'property management work' (HPA 2016 ss14–16).

5.83 **Banning order offences.** The offences will be specified in regulations by the secretary of state HPA 2016 s14(3). It is likely, however, that they will include certain housing offences, such as: unlawful eviction under PEA 1977 s1(2) (see paras 5.5, 5.17); harassment under PEA 177 s1(3) or (3A) (see paras 5.5 and 5.11–5.16); failure to comply with an improvement notice under HA 2004 s30(1) (see para 12.25); failure to comply with a prohibition order under HA 2004 s32(1) (see para 12.40); being in control of or managing an unlicensed HMO under HA 2004 s72(1) (see para 14.97); being in control of or managing a unlicensed house to which HA 2004 Part 3, applies under HA 2004 s95(1) (see para 14.97); and, failure to comply with the Gas Safety (Installation and Use) Regulations 1998 SI No 2451 (see para 11.107). It is also anticipated that serious criminal offences, eg fraud, drugs, serious violence or sexual assault, will be included, where the crime is relevant to letting of residential premises.

5.84 **Letting housing.** This is defined as letting a building, or part of a building, intended to be occupied as a dwelling, under a tenancy or licence for a term of less than 21 years (HPA 2016 s56).

5.85 **Letting agency work.** This is broadly defined, to include things done by a person, in the course of a business, in response to instructions received from a prospective landlord or tenant, which relates to housing (HPA 2016 s54(3),(5)). Accordingly, a banning order does not prevent someone from being involved in letting commercial premises. A prospective landlord is a person who is seeking to find someone to whom to let housing; a prospective tenant is a person seeking to find housing to rent (HPA 2016 s54(3)). Only work done in the 'course of business' is included so that introducing a prospective tenant to a friend would not be within the definition.

5.86 **Property management work**. This is defined as things done by a person, in the course of a business, in response to instructions received from a client to arrange services, repairs, maintenance, improvements, insurance or to deal with any other aspect of management of housing let under a tenancy or licence for a term of less than 21 years (HPA 2016 s55(3)).

5.87 **Provision of information**. An authority may require any person to provide specified information for the purpose of enabling it to decide whether to apply for a banning order against him or her (HPA 2016 s19). Failure, without reasonable excuse, to comply with the request, is an offence. It is also an offence to provide false or misleading information if the person either knows that it is false or misleading or is reckless as to whether it is so. Both offences are punishable in the magistrates' court by an unlimited fine.

5.88 **Application**. Before applying for a banning order against a person, the authority must give notice of intended proceedings, informing the person of its intention to apply for a banning order against him or her and explaining why, stating the length of the proposed ban and inviting representations within a period of not less than 28 days specified in the notice (HPA 2016 s15(3)). The notice must be given within six months of the conviction for the banning order offence (s15(6)).

5.89 An application can be made against any person, individual or corporate, convicted of a banning order offence (HPA 2016 s15). Where an authority make an application against a corporation, it must also make an application against any director, or other similar officer, who was convicted of the same offence (s15(2)).

5.90 **Making an order**. Before making an order, the tribunal must consider: the seriousness of the banning order offence; any previous convictions that the person has for a banning order offence; whether the person is or has at any time been included in the database of rogue landlords (see para 5.103–5.110); and, the likely effect of the banning order on the person and anyone else who may be affected by it (HPA 2016 s16(4)).

5.91 A banning order may also ban an individual from involvement in a company or other body which carries out an activity that the person is banned from carrying out (HPA 2016 s18).

5.92 A banning order may be made subject to exceptions for some or all the period to which it relates (see para 5.93), which exceptions may be made subject to conditions (HPA 2016 s17(3)). Examples given in the Act are allowing a landlord to deal with existing tenancies and allowing letting agents to wind down their business.

5.93 **Duration.** The order must specify its duration which must be at least 12 months (HPA 2016 s17(1), (2)). An order may be varied or revoked on application to the tribunal (s20). The order must be revoked if all of the convictions giving rise to it have been overturned on appeal. Otherwise, it can be varied or revoked if some of the convictions have either been overturned on appeal or become spent under the Rehabilitation of Offenders Act 1974. The power to vary the order includes power to vary the banned activities, the length of the ban and any existing exceptions to the ban. The tribunal may also add new exceptions to the ban.

5.94 **Prohibition on transfer.** To prevent a person who is subject to a banning order from avoiding its effect, detailed provision is made prohibiting him or her from transferring his or her interest in premises to defined, associated persons, such as family members and business partners, without first obtaining the tribunal's consent (HPA 2016 s27). Any such transfer made without the tribunal's consent is void.

5.95 **Database of rogue landlords.** Any person made subject to a banning order must be entered onto the database of rogue landlords (see paras 5.103–5.110) (HPA 2016 s29(1)).

5.96 **Effect on existing and new tenancies.** A banning order does not bring an existing tenancy or licence to an end nor does it affect the validity or enforceability of any tenancy or licence subsequently entered into by the landlord (HPA 2016 s24).

5.97 **Breach – civil penalty.** As an alternative to criminal prosecution (see para 5.99), an authority may, if satisfied beyond reasonable doubt that a person has breached a banning order, impose a financial penalty on that person (HPA 2016 s23(1), (6)). If the person subject to the banning order continues not to comply with the terms of the banning order, then a further financial penalty may be imposed after six months and for each six-month period thereafter for so long as the breach continues (s23(4)). There is a maximum of £30,000 for each penalty (s23(5)).

5.98 Before imposing the penalty, the authority must give notice of its proposal to do so within six months of becoming aware that the offence has been committed (HPA 2016 Sch 1). The notice must set out the amount of the proposed penalty, and the reasons for it, and inform the person of the right to make representations, which must be made within 28 days. Once that period has expired, the authority must decide whether or not to impose the penalty by serving a final notice. Once the final notice is served, the penalty must be paid within 28 days. It is enforceable as if it were a county court judgment. There is a right of appeal to the First-tier Tribunal both against the decision to impose the penalty and as to its amount.

5.99 **Criminal offence**. It is a criminal offence to breach a banning order (HPA 2016 s21(1)). A person cannot be convicted of a breach for which he or she has been subject to a financial penalty (see paras 5.97–5.98) (s21(3)). It is a defence for a person to show that he or she had a reasonable excuse for breaching the order (s21(5)). The offence is punishable in the magistrates' court by a maximum of 51 weeks' imprisonment months and/or an unlimited fine (s21(2)). The person commits a further offence if the breach continues after the first conviction, punishable by a fine not exceeding one-tenth of level 2 on the standard scale (ie £50) for each day on which the breach continues (s21(4)).

5.100 Where the offence is committed by a corporation, then a director or officer of the corporation will also be guilty of an offence if he or she consented to or connived at the commission of the breach, or it happened because of his or her negligence (HPA 2016 s22(1)).

5.101 **Rent repayment order**. The First-tier Tribunal will be able to make a rent repayment order against a landlord (but not a lettings agent or a property manager) who is in breach of a banning order (HPA 2016 ss40–52). The procedure governing a rent repayment order for breach of a banning order is the same at that which applies to rent repayment orders made in unlawful eviction and harassment cases (see paras 5.29–5.35).

5.102 **Licensing**. A person who is made subject to a banning order may not be granted a licence under HA 2004 Part 2 (HMOs – paras 14.19–14.46) or Part 3 (selective licensing – paras 14.61–14.73) (new HA 2004 ss64(3)(aa) and s88(3)(aa)). A local housing authority must revoke a licence that is held by a person subject to a banning order (new HA 2004 ss70A and 93A).

Database of rogue landlords

5.103 In England, once the provisions of HPA 2016 ss28–39, are in force, the secretary of state must establish a database of rogue landlords, lettings agents and property managers (HPA 2016 s28). The database will be maintained and updated by local housing authorities. Each authority will have access to all of the information contained within the database, not just its own entries (s38), so that authorities can find out about rogue landlords, agents and managers who have moved into their areas from other parts of the country. Authorities may use the database for the following purposes: functions under HA 2004 (chapters 12 and 14); criminal proceedings; promoting compliance with housing or landlord and tenant law; investigating or bringing proceedings in relation to any breach of housing or landlord and tenant law; and, statistics or research (s39).

5.104 Information on the database cannot, however, be disclosed by the secretary of state to a person other than a local authority save in an anonymised form (HPA 2016 s39(2)), so that a prospective tenant or letting agent would have to ask the local authority whether a landlord is on the database.

5.105 **Persons on the database – banning orders.** An authority must make an entry onto the database if a banning order (see paras 5.82–5.102) has been made against a person (HPA 2016 s29). The entry must be removed once the banning order has expired or is revoked.

5.106 **Other persons on the database.** Authorities may also make an entry for any person convicted of a banning order offence (see para 5.83) at a time when he or she was a residential landlord, letting agent or property manager (HPA 2016 s30(1)). An entry may also be made for any person who has at least twice within a period of 12 months received a financial penalty for breaching a banning order offence but who has not been made subject to a banning order (s30(2)).

5.107 Before making an entry in the database for person, the authority must give him or her a 'decision notice' explaining that the authority has decided that it will make the entry after the end of the period of 21 days beginning with the notice (HPA 2016 s31). The notice must be given within six months of the date on which the person was either convicted of the banning order offence or received the second of the financial penalties to which it relates (s31(5)). The notice must specify the period for which the entry will be on the database, which must be at least two years, and summarise the right of appeal (see para 5.108) to the tribunal (see para 5.108) against the decision. Once the time for appealing has expired, or any appeal has failed, the entry can be made.

5.108 The authority's decision to make an entry for a person in the database, including its decision as to how long the entry will remain on the database (see para 5.107), may be appealed to the First-tier Tribunal (HPA 2016 s32). The appeal must be made before the end of the period specified in the authority's decision notice (see para 5.107), although the tribunal can extend this time limit where it is satisfied that there is 'good reason'.

5.109 **Removal and variation.** A person who is not subject to a banning order may apply to the authority in writing for the entry to be removed and/or for the period in which it is to remain on the database to be reduced (HPA 2016 s37(1)). An entry must be removed only if all of the convictions on which the entry is based are overturned on appeal. Where some, but not all, of the convictions have been overturned on appeal, or some or all of them have become spent under the Rehabilitation of Offenders Act 1974, the authority may remove the entry, or reduce the period for which it is to remain on the database, even if this results in the entry being on the database for less than two years (s36). An authority may also remove an entry, or reduce the time for which it remains on the database, in respect of a person who received two or more financial penalties (see para 5.106) if at least one year has passed since the entry was made.

5.110 Where an authority refuses to remove an entry and/or to agree to a reduction in the time that it will remain on the database, the applicant has a right of appeal to the First-tier Tribunal (HPA 2016 s37). The appeal must be brought within 21 days of the authority's notice of its decision, which must give reasons for that decision and summarise the applicant's right of appeal (s36). The tribunal can extend the 21-day time limit where it is satisfied that there is 'good reason'. On appeal, the tribunal may order the authority to remove the entry or reduce the period for which it will remain on the database.

5.111 **Power to require information.** An authority may require any person to provide information to enable it to decide whether to make an entry in respect of him or her (HPA 2016 s35). The authority may also require the information in order to complete an entry or keep it up-to-date. Failure, without reasonable excuse, to provide the information is an offence. It is also an offence to provide false or misleading information if the person either knows that it is false or misleading or is reckless as to whether it is so. Both offences are punishable in the magistrates' court by an unlimited fine.

Human rights

5.112 Although an unlawful eviction may plainly breach a person's right to respect for the home (see paras 1.319–1.320) under Article 8 of the European Convention on Human Rights (ECHR), by which public authorities (see paras 1.321–1.322) are bound, in practice, given the remedies available to a victim of unlawful eviction (see paras 5.36–5.54), it is unlikely that Article 8 ECHR adds anything to his or her rights under domestic law.

5.113 The exercise of a local authority's powers to make banning orders (see paras 5.82–5.102) and to enter a landlord, lettings agent or property manager on the database of rogue landlords (see paras 5.103–5.110), can have a significant impact on businesses and the way in which properties are used by their owners, which may be considered to breach the right to peaceful enjoyment of possessions under Article 1 of the First Protocol ECHR. That right does not, however, prevent the state from enforcing such laws as it deems necessary to control the use of property and Member States have a wide margin of discretion in relation to housing matters. Given that those affected will have been found guilty of criminal offences relating to housing management, an authority's use of these powers is likely to be compatible with Article 1.

CHAPTER 6

Anti-social behaviour

Introduction

6.1 This chapter considers a range of powers available to local authorities and other social landlords to deal with anti-social behaviour. The Housing Act (HA) 1996 gave social landlords the power to apply for anti-social behaviour injunctions (ASBIs) to protect their tenants and staff. The Crime and Disorder Act (CDA) 1998 introduced anti-social behaviour orders (ASBOs) allowing not only the police and local authorities but also, following amendments, social landlords to apply for orders preventing the commission of anti-social acts. These provisions have now been brought together into one form of injunction available under Part 1 of the Anti-social Behaviour, Crime and Policing (ABCPA) Act 2014. The chapter also considers powers of the police and local authorities to obtain closure orders in cases of serious anti-social behaviour and disorder and local authority powers dealing with noise nuisance.

6.2 Where a tenant is guilty of anti-social behaviour, a number of grounds for possession are available: nuisance and annoyance (see para 2.98(2) – secure tenants; para 2.169(5) – assured tenants; see para 2.213 – Rent Act tenants); conviction at the scene of a riot (see para 2.98(3) – secure tenants; see para 2.169(5) – assured tenants); absolute ground for anti-social behaviour (see paras 2.108–2.212 – secure tenants; para 2.170(8) – assured tenants). The injunctions described below may be used as an alternative to seeking possession to see if the behaviour improves so that eviction becomes unnecessary. They may also be used in conjunction with possession proceedings, to protect neighbours while the possession action proceeds to trial or to ensure that the evicted tenant does not return to the area after possession has been obtained, by the use of an exclusion zone (see para 6.8; *Swindon BC v Redpath*, 2009).

Anti-social behaviour injunctions

6.3 **Who can apply**. An application for an injunction can be made by a number of public authorities, including: local authorities; the police; the transport police; Transport for London; and, 'housing providers', ie PRPs, RSLs and charitable housing trusts (see para 8.5) (ABCPA 2014 ss5, 20).

6.4 **Anti-social behaviour**. There are three categories of anti-social behaviour. In two cases, only specified bodies can apply to restrain the behaviour concerned.

6.5 Any of the authorities in para 6.3 can apply for an injunction where the behaviour 'has caused, or is likely to cause, harassment, alarm or distress to any person' (ABCPA 2014 s2(1)(a)). Use of the phrase 'likely to cause' enables someone other than the victim of the behaviour to give evidence, particularly professional witnesses who can provide evidence to a court where victims feel unable to come forward for fear of reprisals or intimidation.

6.6 A local authority, a housing provider (see para 6.3) or the police can apply for an injunction where the behaviour is 'capable of causing a nuisance or annoyance to a person in relation to that person's occupation of residential premises' (ABCPA 2014 s2(1)(b), (2)).

6.7 A local authority or a housing provider (see para 6.3) can apply where the behaviour is 'capable of causing housing-related nuisance or annoyance to any person' (ABCPA 2014 s2(1)(c)). 'Housing-related' means directly or indirectly relating to the housing management functions of the authority or the housing provider (s2(3)). 'Housing management functions' are broadly defined to include any functions conferred on the authority or housing provider by legislation and its powers and duties as an owner of housing (s5(3)).

6.8 In most cases, it will be obvious that the conduct affects a landlord's housing management functions because either the perpetrator or the victim of the anti-social behaviour will be - or be living with - a tenant of the landlord. In less obvious cases, the behaviour has to be seen in context. In a case decided under HA 1996, it was held that a social landlord's housing management functions included a sense of responsibility to both their tenants and also to owner-occupiers in an area for the conduct of their tenants and others; thus, an injunction could be granted against a former tenant who was evicted for anti-social behaviour to prevent him or her from returning to continue a vendetta against a former neighbour, even though the former neighbour was an owner-occupier (having exercised the right to buy) (*Swindon BC v Redpath*, 2009).

6.9 **Defendant.** An injunction may be sought against any person aged 10 or over who has acted in an anti-social manner (see paras 6.4–6.8). The fact that an injunction can be made against someone under 18 is an exception to the general rule that injunctions cannot usually be granted against a minor unless he or she is in work (*Wookey v Wookey*, 1991; *G v Harrow LBC*, 2004).

6.10 If the defendant is under 18, the application must be made to the youth court (ABCPA 2014 s1(8)(a)). Applications against adults may be made in the High Court or the county court (s1(8)(b)).

6.11 **Consultation.** Unless made without notice to the applicant (see para 6.21), the applicant must, before making the application, inform any other body or individual whom the applicant thinks appropriate about the application (ABCPA 2014 s14), eg a PRP or RSL or charitable housing trust may wish to inform the police and/or the local authority). If the defendant is under 18, the police must consult the local youth offending team.

6.12 **Conditions for order.** Before making an injunction, the court must be satisfied that the defendant has engaged, or threatens to engage in, anti-social behaviour (see paras 6.4–6.8) and that it is just and convenient to grant the injunction to prevent the defendant from engaging in it (ABCPA 2014 s1(2), (3)).

6.13 **Terms of an order.** An order may include both prohibitions, restraining the defendant from doing something, and positive requirements to do something (ABCPA 2014 s1(4)). The court's power is extremely broad. Prohibitions commonly include restraining the defendant from specified conduct but can also prevent a person from entering a defined area, eg an estate or housing management office, or even the defendant's own home (see para 6.20).

6.14 Requirements are often included to ensure that the defendant engages with support services to reduce the likelihood of future anti-social behaviour, eg where the defendant has alcohol- or drug-related problems or suffers from mental health difficulties. Before imposing a requirement, the court must hear evidence from the body which will be responsible for supervising compliance with it, to satisfy itself that the requirement is both suitable and enforceable (ABCPA 2014 s3).

6.15 **Duration.** An injunction may be made for a specified period or else be expressed to last until it is varied or discharged, unless the defendant is under 18, in which a period of not more than 12 months must be specified (ABCPA 2014 s1(5)). Different periods may be specified for any of the terms in the injunction (s1(6)).

6.16 **Power of arrest.** A power of arrest may be attached to any term of an injunction if the court thinks that the anti-social behaviour in which the defendant has engaged, or threatened to engage, consists of or includes the use, or threatened use, of violence against other persons, or there is a significant risk of harm to other persons from the defendant (ABCPA 2014 s4). Harm includes serious ill-treatment or abuse, whether physical or not (s20).

6.17 A power of arrest allows a police officer to arrest, without warrant, any person whom the officer has reasonable cause to suspect is in breach of the order (ABCPA 2014 s9). A person arrested must be produced to the court within 24 hours.

6.18 If the authority which obtained the injunction thinks that the defendant has breached any term of the order (even if no power of arrest was attached), it may apply to the court for a warrant of arrest (ABCPA 2014 s10). The police must inform the authority once the arrest has been made and produce the defendant to court (although there is no time limit specified for doing so).

6.19 When the defendant is brought to court, if the matter is not dealt with by imposing a sentence for contempt of court (see paras 6.24–6.27), eg imprisonment or a fine, the court can remand the defendant in custody or on bail (ABCPA 2014 Sch 1). Remand in custody cannot be for more than eight days, unless the court adjourns the case for a medical report on the defendant, in which case it can remand for up to three weeks at a time if the defendant is in custody, or four weeks at a time if he or she is on bail (Sch 1 paras 5–6).

6.20 **Exclusion from home.** If the defendant is an adult, the effect of the injunction can be to exclude him or her from his own home (ABCPA 2014 s13). Such a term can only be included if the applicant is the police or a local authority, or a housing provider. If the application is by a housing provider (see para 6.3), the property in question must be owned by that provider, either as freeholder or under a lease granted for a term of not less than three years (s13(2)). An exclusion order can only be made if the anti-social behaviour in which the defendant has engaged, or threatened to engage, consists of or includes the use, or threatened use, of violence against other persons, or there is a significant risk of harm (see para 6.15) to other persons from the defendant.

6.21 **Without notice applications.** Though normally the person must be given notice of the application for an injunction, an application can be made without notice (ABCPA 2014 s6), eg where there is concern for the safety of victims or a fear that residents of estates will not co-operate and give evidence until an injunction is in place. To make a without-notice order, the court must consider that it is just to do so (s7). A without-notice order can only contain prohibitions, ie it cannot require the defendant to do something.

6.22 If the court refuses to grant a without-notice order and adjourns the application for notice to be given to the defendant, the applicant must comply with its duties to inform others (and consult the local youth offending) before the next hearing (see para 6.11).

6.23 **Variation or discharge.** The applicant authority or the defendant can apply for an order to be varied or discharged (ABCPA 2014 s8).

The court's power to vary an order includes power to add new terms, attach a power of arrest to a term, or to extend the period during which the order or power of arrest has effect. If the application is made by the body which applied for the injunction itself, it is under the same obligations to inform others (and consult the local youth offending) that apply before making an application (see para 6.11). If an application to vary or discharge an order is dismissed, no further such application can be made without the court's permission or the agreement of both parties.

6.24 **Contempt of court**. Breach of the terms of an injunction is a contempt of court, enforceable by committal proceedings in the county court or High Court under Civil Procedure Rules (CPR) 81. If the breach is proved, the court may impose a period of imprisonment of up to two years and/or an unlimited fine: Contempt of Court Act 1981 s14. (Examples of the range of sentences in anti-social behaviour cases are to be found in *Accent Foundation Ltd v Lee*, 2007; *Kirklees Council v Davis*, 2008; *Birmingham City Council v Flatt*, 2008; *Amicus Horizon Ltd v Thorley*, 2012; *Solihull MBC v Willoughby*, 2013; and, *Birmingham City Council v Gill*, 2016, but it must be borne in mind that they always turn on their own facts).

6.25 **Under 18s**. If the person in breach of the order is under 18, the youth court has a wide range of powers under which it can impose a curfew, require the defendant to wear an electronic tag, or require him or her to engage with the youth offending team (ABCPA 2014 Sch 2).

6.26 Although the proceedings for contempt of court are technically civil, the burden of proof in committal proceedings is – given the serious consequences of a finding of contempt – to the criminal standard of 'beyond reasonable doubt'. Furthermore, although civil legal aid is available to defend an application for an injunction, defending committal proceedings is governed by criminal legal aid (*Brown v Haringey LBC*, 2015).

6.27 Where incidents give rise both to criminal proceedings and to proceedings for contempt of court, the first court to impose a sentence may not allow for any sentence which may be made in the other proceedings but the second court must take into account the sentence in the first, so as to ensure that the defendant is not punished twice for the same act (*Lomas v Parle*, 2003).

Closure orders

6.28 ABCPA 2014 Part 2 Chapter 3 provides for closure orders which allow premises to be closed down where their use has resulted, or is likely to result, in nuisance to members of the public, or the premises are associated with disorder. Such orders are usually only used in very serious cases, eg where premises are being used to sell class A drugs.

6.29 **Applications.** Only a magistrates' court can make a closure order (ABCPA 2014 s80). The application can be made by either the police or a local authority.

6.30 **Closure notice.** Before applying for a closure order, the police or the local authority must consult any body or individual whom it considers appropriate (ABCPA 2014 s76(7)). Having done so, a closure notice must be served on the premises warning of the intention to make an application, which must contain specified information, including the effect of the notice (see para 6.31) (s76(5)). The notice must be fixed to the premises and must also be given to at least one person who appears to have responsibility for them (s79). Where the police are making the application, the closure notice must be authorised by an officer not below the rank of inspector (s76(1)).

6.31 A closure notice prohibits anyone from entering the premises either at all, or only at specified times or in specified circumstances, unless expressly given permission to do so in the notice (ABCPA 2014 s76(1)). A closure order cannot prohibit people who habitually live on the premises or the owner of the premises from gaining access, so the notice must permit them to do so (s76(3)). An owner is a freeholder or any person granted a lease for a term of not less than three years (s92). Before issuing a closure notice, the police or local authority must make reasonable efforts to inform people who live in the premises (habitually or not), and any person who either has control or responsibility for them or an interest in them, that a closure notice is to be served. Save in certain specified circumstances, a closure notice remains in force for 24 hours (s77). At the same time that the notice is issued, an application must be made to the magistrates' court which must hear the application within 48 hours (s80).

6.32 **Closure order.** The magistrates may make an order if satisfied that: a person has engaged, or (if the order is not made) is likely to engage, in disorderly, offensive or criminal behaviour on the premises; or the use of the premises has resulted, or (if the order is not made) is likely to result, in serious nuisance to members of the public; or that there has been, or (if the order is not made) is likely to be, disorder near those premises associated with the use of those premises; and, in each case, the order is necessary to prevent the behaviour, nuisance or disorder from continuing, recurring or occurring (ABCPA 2014 s80(5)).

6.33 The effect of a closure order is that anyone is prohibited from entering the premises either at all, or only at specified times or in specified circumstances, unless expressly given permission to do so in the order (ABCPA 2014 s80(7)). In contrast to a closure notice (see para 6.31), the order can exclude someone from his or her home. The order lasts for three months but may be extended on application by the police or the local authority up to a maximum of six months (ss80(6), 82).

6.34 **Criminal offence.** A person commits an offence if he or she remains on, or enters, premises in contravention of the order without reasonable excuse (ABCPA 2014 s86). In the magistrates' court, the offence is punishable by a maximum of three months' imprisonment and/or an unlimited fine.

6.35 **Appeal.** A person served with the closure notice or any other person with an interest in the premises may – within 21 days – appeal against the order to the Crown Court (ABCPA 2014 s86).

6.36 **Compensation.** Provision is made for a person to claim compensation out of central funds on application to the magistrates' court (or to the Crown Court if there is an appeal) at any time up to three months after the closure order ceased to have effect (ABCPA 2014 s90). Compensation can only be awarded where the court is satisfied: that the applicant is not associated with the use of the premises, or the behaviour on the basis of which the closure order was made; that if the applicant is the owner or occupier of the premises, that he or she took reasonable steps to prevent that use or behaviour; that the applicant has incurred financial loss in consequence of the order; and, that having regard to all the circumstances it is appropriate to order compensation.

6.37 **Ground for possession.** Where a closure order has been made (and not overturned on appeal), the landlord has a mandatory ground for possession (see paras 2.108–2.212 – secure tenancies; para 2.270(8) – assured tenants).

Noise nuisance

6.38 One of the most common complaints people have about their neighbours is excessive noise, usually loud music but often loud arguments or noise from DIY. A person suffering from noise nuisance has a number of remedies. He or she may bring an action him- or herself against the neighbour for nuisance (see para 5.50(3)) and obtain an injunction prohibiting the noise. If the perpetrator is a tenant, he or she can complain to the landlord: most responsible landlords will warn their tenants about such behaviour and, if the nuisance persists, apply for an injunction to restrain the nuisance or bring possession proceedings on the ground of nuisance and annoyance (secure tenancies – see para 2.98(2); assured tenancies – see para 2.169(5); Rent Act tenancies – see para 2.218(2)). If the landlord is a local authority, PRP or RSL or charitable housing trust, an anti-social behaviour injunction could be sought (see paras 6.3–6.27). In addition, however, local authorities have specific powers to deal with noise nuisance: complaining to the local authority's environmental health department is often the best way to achieve a fast result.

Noise abatement notices

6.39 Local authorities have powers (and duties) to deal with 'statutory nuisances' under the Environmental Protection Act (EPA) 1990. Noise emitted from premises so as to be 'prejudicial to health' or a nuisance is a statutory nuisance (EPA 1990 s79(1)(g)). Nuisance in this context means a nuisance at common law, ie unreasonable interference with a person's enjoyment of his land (see para 5.50(3)). Prejudicial to health means 'injurious or likely to cause injury to health' (EPA 1990 s79(7)).

6.40 The law relating to statutory nuisances in a housing context is considered in more detail at paras 13.9–13.32. Given the relationship between anti-social behaviour and noise, the specific provisions which allow local authorities to deal with noise quickly and effectively are considered here.

6.41 **Noise abatement notice.** If an authority is satisfied that the noise is a statutory nuisance, or that there has been noise nuisance in the past which is likely to recur, it is obliged to take action (EPA 1990 s80(1)). The authority may serve a noise abatement notice on the person responsible for the noise (s80(1)). This is the person to 'whose act, default of sufferance, the noise is attributable (s79(7)). The abatement notice merely has to require that the noise ceases immediately and/or does not recur. Instead of serving an abatement notice, the authority may take appropriate steps to persuade the person responsible to abate the nuisance or prohibit its recurrence (s80(2A)). If it chooses to take this course, it must serve an abatement notice if the nuisance recurs at any time within seven days of the date when the authority was first satisfied that the nuisance existed (s80(2A)–(2E)). Failure, without reasonable excuse, to abate the comply with a noise abatement notice is a criminal offence (see further para 13.18).

6.42 *Seizure.* If the notice is not complied with, the authority may abate the nuisance themselves (EPA 1990 s81(3)). This power includes the right to seize and remove any equipment which appears to be being used in the emission of the noise (Noise Act (NA) 1996). It is an offence to obstruct an officer of the authority in the exercise of these powers (NA 1996 s10(7)). The equipment can be retained for 28 days and, if the authority chooses to prosecute, the authority keeps it until conclusion of the proceedings, if allowed to do so by an order of the magistrates' court (NA 1996 Sch paras 2(1), 5). On conviction, the court may order forfeiture of the equipment (NA 1996 Sch paras 3, 4).

Noise at night

6.43 NA 1996 also contains powers for authorities to deal with excessive noise from residential properties during the night. These powers only apply if the authority decides to adopt them (NA 1996 s1) but, once adopted, the authority is under a duty to investigate any complaint from someone in a dwelling in their area about excessive noise from another dwelling during night hours (s2). The 'night hours' are between 11 pm and the following 7 am (s2(6)). 'Dwelling' is defined to include any garden, yard, etc belonging to the dwelling (s11(2)), so the powers may be used to stop noise from parties outside the house itself.

6.44 **Warning notice.** The authority must measure the noise to see if it exceeds the permitted level, which is set by the secretary of state (NA 1996 s5). If so, the authority may serve a notice (s2(4)) on the 'person responsible' for the noise (defined as in EPA 1990; para 6.41). This warns the person responsible that he or she must reduce the noise to below the permitted level within a specified time (not less than ten minutes) and that the noise must be kept below that level until the following 7 am (s3).

6.45 **Enforcement.** Failure to comply with a warning notice is an offence (NA 1996 s4), punishable by a fine up to level 3 on the standard scale (currently £1,000). Instead of prosecuting, the authority has the option of issuing the offender with a fixed penalty notice of £100 (s8). If that is paid within 14 days, the authority cannot prosecute for the offence, unless the noise exceeded the permitted level again later that same night (s9). Authorities have the same powers to enter premises and remove and retain equipment as are available in statutory nuisance cases (s10(1); para 6.42).

Human rights

6.46 Some of the powers discussed in this chapter can lead to a person being evicted, eg an anti-social behaviour injunction or a closure order may exclude a tenant from his or her own home (see paras 6.20; 6.33). The exercise of such powers, however, is likely to be justified by the need to protect the community from severe forms of anti-social conduct. Likewise, although local authorities' powers to seize equipment under NA 1996 (see paras 6.42 and 6.45) are an interference with the owner's right to peaceful enjoyment of his possessions under Article 1 of the First Protocol to the European Convention on Human Rights (ECHR), such interference is plainly justified in light of the impact of excessive noise on neighbours.

6.47 One issue is whether a victim of anti-social behaviour could argue that his right to respect for the home under Article 8 ECHR has been breached by a public authority (see paras 1.321–1.322) which fails to use its powers to control such behaviour. The courts have been extremely reluctant to find that a public authority owed a common law duty of care in negligence (see para 11.110) to a victim of anti-social behaviour (*Mitchell v Glasgow City Council*, 2009; *X v Hounslow LBC*, 2009; *Hussain v Lancaster City Council*, 1998), recognising the difficult decisions which landlords face when considering what action to take against perpetrators and to protect victims. There is no reason in principle, however, why a claim for breach of Article 8 is not possible and the European Court of Human Rights has upheld such claims in a number of cases: *Moreno Gomez v Spain*, 2005 and *Dees v Hungary*, 2013 – failure to protect from noise nuisance; *Lopez Ostra v Spain*, 1994 – failure to protect from fumes and smells; *Smirnova v Ukraine*, 2016 – failure to prevent campaign of harassment.

CHAPTER 7

Domestic breakdown

Introduction

7.1 In this chapter, we consider in outline some of the law as it relates to housing in the event of a domestic breakdown. Normally, this refers to the break-up of a relationship between partners, but in some circumstances, it goes somewhat wider (see paras 7.15–7.27). This is in one sense an artificial study, because decisions cannot and will not be taken on the basis of housing law, or law itself, alone. There will be many other considerations to bring to bear, including that of the desirability of exercising particular rights and (always) the best interests of any children involved. The law affecting domestic breakdown is substantial, and a study in its own right; the purpose of this chapter is merely to indicate some of its possibilities.

7.2 The provisions considered are not mutually exclusive: it will be common for provisions contained in more than one Act to apply in the same case; in addition, the courts with jurisdiction over these issues have a fairly broad discretion to make such orders as are considered appropriate at any stage in proceedings; interim orders are commonplace. It is also necessary to consider the common law position, and the rights of any spouse or cohabitee under trust law (see paras 1.106–1.113). It may be noted that there are recent proposals to simplify and speed up operation of the law on domestic violence, which – if enacted – are likely to change some of the provisions considered in this chapter.

Relevant provisions

Matrimonial Causes Act 1973

7.3 The Matrimonial Causes Act (MCA) 1973 contains the broad powers pursuant to which a court can divide up matrimonial property when a marriage is in the course of breaking up or has broken up. These powers are only exercisable between married partners. They can be exercised in the course of divorce, separation or nullity proceedings. The court has power to apportion property between the parties and, if necessary, to order that property, including a home, be transferred from the name of one party to that of another or be sold: MCA 1973 ss24 and 24A. (Note that the Family Law Act (FLA) 1996 contains amendments to these provisions, which amendments are still not, however, yet in force).

7.4 These rights are mainly of interest to owner-occupiers, as rights under FLA 1996 considered below are usually considered more appropriate, although a court can order the transfer of a tenancy under them (*Hale v Hale*, 1975; *Newlon Housing Trust v Alsulaimen*, 1998) regardless of whether the tenancy is within a class of protection or not, but only if there is no provision in the tenancy agreement prohibiting assignment (see para 1.80). The powers cannot be used in connection with a licence, however, as a licence does not constitute 'property' which a court can transfer (see para 1.114). The provisions may be used to divide up matrimonial property, including the matrimonial home, in proportions which do not necessarily reflect the limited financial or quasi-financial considerations to which the common law will be limited (see para 1.106–1.113).

7.5 When deciding whether or not to make an order, for adjustment or sale, MCA 1973 s25 sets out a number of matters to which the court must have regard. These include the income, earning capacity and other financial resources each party has or is likely to have in the forseeable future, the financial needs, obligations and responsibilities each party is taking on, the age of the parties and duration of the marriage, any physical or mental disability, and the conduct of the parties (whatever its nature), but only if it is such that in the opinion of the court it would be inequitable to disregard it.

7.6 By way of anti-avoidance, MCA 1973 s37(2) prevents one spouse trying to dispose of or otherwise deal with the assets once the other spouse has commenced proceedings. Section 37(2)(b) allows a court to set aside a 'disposition' of property but it has been held that this does not include setting aside a tenant's notice to quit: *Newlon Housing Trust v Alsulaimen*, 1998. It has been suggested, however, without being decided, that section 37(2)(a), which provides a broader power to prevent 'dealing' with the property, and/or the inherent powers of the court, may be used to prevent its service in the first place (*Bater v Greenwich LBC*, 1999).

Civil Partnership Act 2004

7.7 The court has similar powers to divide up property when a civil partnership is in the course of breaking up or has broken up under the Civil Partnership Act (CPA) 2004 Sch 5. These powers may be exercised during the course of dissolution, separation or nullity proceedings.

7.8 As under MCA 1973 (see paras 7.3–7.6), the court has power to apportion property between the parties and, if necessary, to order that a home be transferred from the name of one civil partner to the other (CPA 2004 Sch 5 Pt 2) or be sold (CPA 2004 Sch 5 Pt 3). When deciding whether or not to make an order for adjustment or sale, the court must have regard to the same factors as are relevant under the MCA 1973 (CPA 2004 Sch 5 Pt 5; see para 7.5). Likewise, there are provisions preventing a civil partner disposing or otherwise dealing with assets once the other civil partner has commenced proceedings (CPA 2004 Sch 5 Pt 14 para 13).

Home rights under the Family Law Act 1996

7.9 **Home rights.** FLA 1996 introduced the concept of 'matrimonial homes rights'. These rights are now called 'home rights', as they are now also enjoyed by civil partners. The rights arise where one spouse or civil partner has the right to occupy a dwelling-house by ownership, tenancy or contractual licence, and the other does not. 'Dwelling-house' is defined to include not only houses and flats but also mobile homes and houseboats (FLA 1996 s63(1)). In these circumstances, the spouse or civil partner who does not have legal rights over the property has the right not to be excluded by the other from occupation of the home without an order of the court (FLA 1996 s30(1), (2)). The restriction also applies to anyone who shares the legal right over the property with the spouse or partner (*Abdullah v Westminster City Council*, 2011).

7.10 Such an order will normally be made in the course of matrimonial or dissolution proceedings dealing with a number of considerations, but it could be made on application under FLA 1996 alone. The court also has power to make an order permitting a spouse or civil partner who has been wrongfully evicted or excluded from the home to re-enter. The court can make the order in respect of part only of the premises, eg excluding one spouse from the residential part of the premises but allowing him or her to carry on his or her business in another part.

7.11 **Security of tenure.** As we saw in chapter 2, security of tenure is only afforded to tenants if they occupy premises as their home; whether as their 'only or principal home' under Housing Act (HA) 1985 (see para 1.175) or HA 1988 (see para 1.230) or as their 'residence' under the Rent Act (RA) 1977 (see para 1.290). If the tenancy is in the sole name of the departing spouse or civil partner, the remaining spouse or partner's occupation of the premises is therefore deemed to satisfy any of these residency requirements (FLA 1996 s30(4)).

7.12 These rights do not prevent a tenant from otherwise validly terminating his or her tenancy. Thus, if the spouse who is the tenant surrenders the tenancy (*Sanctuary Housing Association v Campbell*, 1999) or serves a notice to quit (*Harrow LBC v Johnstone*, 1997), there are no rights which can be protected under this provision (*Derwent Housing Association Ltd v Taylor*, 2016). Departing tenants often serve notices to quit which are invalid: an invalid notice to quit served by a sole tenant may still be treated as valid by the landlord, although a notice served by one of a number of joint tenants (see para 2.50) cannot (*Hounslow LBC v Pilling*, 1993). A non-tenant could prevent this by starting proceedings and seeking an immediate order from the court preventing the tenant surrendering or giving notice to quit until the application can be heard.

7.13 **Payments**. Where the person with home rights (see para 7.9) takes over mortgage or rent payments under these provisions, the landlord or mortgage company is obliged to accept them as though they were made by the owner-occupier, tenant or licensee (FLA 1996 s30(3), (5)).

7.14 **Registrable right of occupation**. A person who has home rights (see para 7.9) over an owner-occupied home is entitled to register these rights as a charge on the dwelling (FLA 1996 s31). The effect of this is that, if the house is sold, the purchaser buys it subject to the right of occupation and is deemed to have known that the person was and can remain in occupation. This is to prevent, for example, one spouse selling the home over the head of the other before a court has an opportunity to make any order for transfer.

Occupation rights under the Family Law Act 1996

7.15 **Spouses, cohabitees and associated persons**. FLA 1996 also makes provision for occupation rights to be enforced where the parties are already divorced or where they are merely cohabiting; these rights are available in other circumstances, where parties are only 'associated persons' (see para 7.16).

7.16 **Associated person**. A person is associated with another if:

1) they are or have been married to each other;
2) they are or have been civil partners of each other;
3) they are cohabitants or former cohabitants, ie a couple who, although neither married to each other nor civil partners, are living together as husband and wife or as if they were civil partners (FLA 1996 s62(1));

4) they live or have lived in the same household, otherwise than merely by reason of one of them being the other's employee, tenant, lodger or boarder;
5) they are relatives;
6) they have agreed to marry one another;
7) they have entered into a civil partnership agreement;
8) they are both parents of, or have or had parental responsibility for, the same child; or
9) they are both parties to other family proceedings (FLA 1996 s62).

7.17 **Applicants with legal rights.** Where an applicant has a legal right to occupy the home (as an owner, tenant or contractual licensee), or is entitled to occupy under home rights (see para 7.9), he or she may apply for an occupation order in relation to a dwelling-house which was or is his or her home or was intended to be his or her home, eg where a home has been bought for renovation but not moved into, against an ex-spouse, former civil partner, current or former cohabitee or another associated person (see para 7.16).

7.18 The court has power to make one of the following orders (FLA 1996 s33):

1) enforcing the applicant's entitlement to remain in occupation;
2) requiring the associated person to permit the applicant to enter and remain in the home;
3) regulating occupation by either or both parties;
4) limiting the legal right to occupy of the associated person;
5) requiring the associated person to leave the home; and/or
6) excluding the associated person from a defined area around the home.

7.19 In deciding whether to make an order under section 33, the court must have regard to all the circumstances, including: the housing needs and housing resources of each of the parties (including any prospects of re-housing by the local housing authority – *Guerroudj v Rymarczyk*, 2015) and of any relevant child; the financial resources of the parties; the likely effect of any decision on the health, safety or well-being of the parties or any relevant child; and, the conduct of the parties towards each other. An order may be made for a specified period or until further order (FLA 1996 s33(10)).

7.20 The same point made above (see para 7.12) in relation to matrimonial homes rights – that a tenant may nonetheless validly terminate the tenancy despite a court order (which it may be possible to prevent by seeking an immediate order of the court pending the full application) – also applies to occupation rights.

7.21 **Former spouses and civil partners without legal rights.** Where a former spouse or civil partner does not have legal rights but is in occupation of the home, he or she may apply for an order for a specified period excluding the other former spouse or civil partner from the home, and/or giving him or her the right not to be evicted or excluded (FLA 1996 s35). If not in occupation, the applicant may be given the right to enter and occupy. In either case, any of the orders at para 7.18(3)–(6) may also be granted.

7.22 The criteria to be applied in making an order where the applicant is a former spouse or civil partner are as set out in para 7.19, with the addition of: the length of time since the parties ceased to live together; the length of time since the marriage or civil partnership was dissolved or annulled; and, the existence of any pending proceedings which will adjust the legal rights in the home, eg under MCA 1973 or CPA 2004 (FLA 1996 s35(6)). The order must to expressed to last for a maximum of six months, although may be extended (on one occasion or more) for an additional period not exceeding a six months (s35(10)).

7.23 In the unlikely event that neither party has any legal rights to occupy the home, eg where a mortgage company has obtained a possession order but is allowing a period of grace, an order excluding one former spouse or civil partner and allowing the other into possession may be made under FLA 1996 s37. Again, an order lasts for a maximum of six months, although may be extended (on one or more occasion) for an additional period not exceeding a six months (s37(5)). This could also apply to squatters whose occupation appears to be long-term, including a case where it is sought to establish a right to property by way of adverse possession (see paras 1.146–1.154).

7.24 **Cohabitant without legal rights.** Where one cohabitant has legal rights to occupy the home, and the other does not, the party with no rights may apply to the court for any of the orders set out at para 7.18(3)–(6) (FLA 1996 s36). Former cohabitants may also apply.

7.25 The criteria to be used in deciding whether to make an order are the same as those set out at para 7.19, above, together with the following: the nature of the parties' relationship (including the level of commitment involved in it); the length of time during which they have cohabited; whether there are or have been any children who are children of both parties or for whom both parties have or have had parental responsibility; the length of time which has elapsed since the parties ceased to live together; any pending legal proceedings in relation to the home, eg under the Children Act (CA) 1989 (see para 7.37).

7.26 As with former spouses or civil partners, if neither has any legal occupation rights (see para 7.23), an order may still be made (FLA 1996 s38). Orders under either section 36 or section 38 last for a maximum of six months, although may be extended (on one occasion or more) for an additional period not exceeding six months (section 36(1) and section 38(6)).

7.27 **Additional orders**. When making an occupation order (other than in cases where neither party has any legal occupation rights), the court may also require one party to repair and maintain the home and pay the rent or mortgage, or other outgoings (FLA 1996 s40). The court may also order the party who is given occupation to make payments to the other party, where that person would otherwise be legally entitled to occupy the home. Orders may also be made in relation to furniture (FLA 1996 s40). As in the case of a person with home rights (see para 7.9), security of tenure is preserved despite the tenant or licensee's departure (see para 7.11) and the landlord or mortgage company is obliged to accept payments from a person with an occupation order as though they were made by the owner-occupier, tenant or licensee (see para 7.13) (FLA 1996 ss35(13), 36(13), and 37(4)).

Non-molestation orders under the Family Law Act 1996

7.28 A non-molestation order is one which prohibits a respondent from molesting another person with whom he or she is associated (see para 7.16) and/or from molesting a relevant child (FLA 1996 s42(1)).

7.29 Molestation is not defined by the Act, nor was it in earlier legislation. It is a wider term than violence, and can include pestering and harassment (*Vaughan v Vaughan*, 1973). In *Horner v Horner*, 1982, it was held that handing the claimant menacing letters and intercepting her on her way to work amounted to molestation. In *Johnson v Walton*, 1989, sending partially nude photographs of the claimant to a national newspaper, to cause her harm, was also molestation.

7.30 An application for a non-molestation order may be made by a person associated with the respondent or in the course of other family proceedings (FLA 1996 s42(2)). An order can be made without notice where the court considers it just and convenient to do so (FLA 1996 s45).

7.31 **Power of arrest**. The court has power to 'back' an order for arrest. This means that a police officer can arrest, without warrant, any person whom he or she suspects is in breach of an order under the Act. The person must be brought back before the judge within 24 hours. This power can, however, only be used where there has been actual violence or the threat of violence (FLA 1996 s47). In the context of domestic breakdown, 'violence' includes not only physical violence but also threatening and intimidating behaviour and any other form of abuse which, directly or indirectly, may give rise to the risk of harm (*Practice Direction (Fam Div: Residence and Contact Orders: Domestic Violence and Harm) (No 2)*, 2009).

Transfer of tenancy under the Family Law Act 1996

7.32 **Transfer of tenancy.** The court has power to order the transfer of tenancies under FLA 1996 s53 and Sch 7, between spouses, former spouses, civil partners, former civil partners, cohabitants and former cohabitants. The tenancy must have been the home of the parties concerned. The tenancies which may be transferred are secure tenancies (including flexible tenancies – see paras 1.181–1.189) under HA 1985 (see paras 1.160–1.189), introductory tenancies within HA 1996 (see para 1.203), assured (see para 1.220), assured shorthold (see para 1.246) and assured agricultural occupancies (see para 1.304) within HA 1988, protected or statutory tenancies under the Rent Act 1977 (see para 1.269) protected shorthold tenancies under HA 1980 (see para 1.299) and statutory tenancies under the Rent (Agriculture) Act 1976 (see para 1.304). There is no power to transfer demoted tenancies (see para 1.252) or family intervention tenancies (see para 1.262).

7.33 In deciding whether to order a transfer, the court must consider the circumstances in which the tenancy was granted, and the criteria set out at para 7.19 above. Where cohabitants are involved the courts must also consider those at para 7.25.

7.34 **Residence requirements.** Although transfer may take place after divorce, or dissolution or the end of the cohabitation, the law is unclear as to whether a transfer order can effectively be made after decree absolute or dissolution, when the occupation of the former spouse or civil partner will no longer be treated as that of the tenant (see para 7.11), if a former Rent Act protected tenancy has become statutory (see para 1.269) and the tenant-spouse or civil partner is himself or herself no longer in occupation. From the one case which has touched on this (*Lewis v Lewis*, 1985), it would seem that it cannot. For this reason, it is essential to seek the transfer order before the divorce or dissolution becomes final. The same point applies to secure (see para 1.160) and assured (see para 1.220) tenancies, as the tenancy may cease to be secure or assured if the tenant is not occupying it as his or her only or principal home – paras 1.175 and

1.230) and the marriage or partnership has ended, so that the occupation of the former spouse or civil partner is no longer treated as that of the tenant (see paras 1.179, 1.223).

Matrimonial and Family Proceedings Act 1984

7.35 The Matrimonial and Family Proceedings Act (MFPA) 1984 is intended to deal with divorce or legal separation in another country but which is entitled to be recognised as valid in this, where one of the parties is domiciled or has been habitually resident in this, or either or both of the parties had at the date of application under the Act an interest in a dwelling-house in this country which has at some time during the marriage been a matrimonial home (MFPA 1984 ss12 and 15).

7.36 The Act permits applications for financial relief, of various kinds, including (MFPA 1984 s17) a property adjustment order or sale under MCA 1973 ss24 and 24A (see paras 7.3–7.6) (MFPA 1984 s22) or transfer of tenancy under FLA 1996 (see paras 7.32–7.34).

Children Act 1989

7.37 Under CA 1989 there is a number of specific orders –'contact order', 'prohibited steps order', 'residence order' and 'specific issue order' – which may be sought in proceedings under any of the above Acts, or under the inherent jurisdiction of the High Court in relation to children, some of which orders eg 'an order settling the arrangements to be made as to the person with whom a child is to live', ie a residence order, will concern housing.

7.38 If such an order is sought during proceedings under these Acts, the general principles of CA 1989 s11 will be applied, under which the court sets a timetable regulating the actions of the parties, and ancillary powers will be available, eg a family assistance order under section 16.

Further considerations

The Family Court

7.39 Formerly, a number of complex rules governed which court could hear the applications considered in this chapter. In 2014, the Family Court was established to simplify court procedure. The country is divided into a number of regions each with its own designated family centre. All applications can be made to the family centre which then allocates the case to the appropriate level of judge (in the High Court, county court or magistrates' court) under the Family Court (Composition and Distribution of Business) Rules 2014 SI No 840.

Rehousing

7.40 **Homelessness.** A person who leaves the domestic home because of violence or the fear of violence is considered to be homeless for the purposes of HA 1996 Part 7 (see paras 10.35–10.36). As in other domestic breakdown cases (see para 7.31), violence is not limited to physical violence and includes threatening and intimidating behaviour and any other form of abuse which, directly or indirectly, may give rise to the risk of harm (*Yemshaw v Hounslow LBC*, 2011). In deciding whether it was reasonable for the applicant to continue to occupy the home for the purposes of deciding homelessness or intentional homelessness, authorities may not take into account the fact that the applicant could have taken proceedings under the provisions considered in this chapter, unless they are in fact proceedings which have commenced or which are going to commence (*Bond v Leicester City Council*, 2001; see para 10.35).

Discrimination

7.41 The Equality Act (EqA) 2010 ss33 and 34, make it unlawful for landlords and managing agents to treat a woman any less favourably than they would treat a man, eg by adding a term such as a demand for a guarantor for rent or mortgage payments.

7.42 These provisions do not apply to those engaged in 'positive action' (EqA 2010 s158), eg a housing association set up to provide accommodation for the needs of one sex only, eg female victims of domestic violence or male ex-prisoners or mental patients.

7.43 Unlawful discrimination can be the subject of a normal county court action (EqA 2010 s114).

Human rights

7.44 The provisions considered in this chapter often interfere with a person's existing property rights, eg where one spouse's tenancy is transferred to the other. In such cases, the interference with the owner or tenant's right to quiet enjoyment of his possessions under Article 1of the First Protocol to the European Convention on Human Rights (ECHR) will usually be justified, eg where the transfer is necessary to provide the couple's children with a home.

7.45 One issue which arises in domestic breakdown cases is where the departing tenant terminates the tenancy by notice to quit and the remaining partner therefore becomes a trespasser in the premises. Public authority landlords often ask tenants who flee from their homes to end their tenancies in this way, so as to be able to evict the remaining partner, particularly if the authority has to rehouse (see chapter 10).

7.46 In *McCann v UK*, 2008, the European Court of Human Rights (ECtHR) held that the remaining partner was entitled to challenge the proportionality of the decision to evict him or her by way of a court hearing. That decision was influential in the acceptance by the Supreme Court in *Manchester City Council v Pinnock*, 2010 and *Hounslow LBC v Powell*, 2011 of the right to a proportionality hearing (see paras 1.319 and 2.250). In *McCann*, the owner of the property was a local authority and the ECtHR was critical of the authority for advising the departing tenant to serve notice to quit rather than seeking possession using the ground for possession based on domestic violence (see para 2.98(3)). The Supreme Court later held, however, that the procedure for terminating tenancies by tenant's notice to quit is compatible with the remaining tenant's right to respect for his or her home under Article 8 ECHR and his or her rights under Article 1 of the First Protocol ECHR (*Sims v Dacorum LBC*, 2014).

CHAPTER 8

Regulation of social landlords

Introduction

8.1 In this chapter, we consider ways in which the decisions and actions of landlords of social housing – local authority and otherwise – are regulated. As discussed in chapter 1 (see paras 1.161–1.162), in addition to local authorities, there has long been a number of bodies which provide social housing; these are now registered with a special committee of the Homes and Communities Agency (HCA) (in England) or the Welsh Ministers (in Wales). Landlords registered with the HCA are known as PRPs (private registered providers of social housing) and those registered with the Welsh Ministers are RSLs (registered social landlords). By registering, a landlord qualifies for grant assistance ear-marked for social housing: in England, from the HCA or the Greater London Authority; in Wales, from the National Assembly for Wales; the price of this is regulation by the HCA or Welsh Ministers. The policy of successive governments has been for local authority housing stock to be transferred to PRPs and RSLs, including by a process called a large scale voluntary transfer (LSVT).

8.2 In this chapter, we identify certain key terms relating to landlords before considering how they may become registered. We then briefly consider the LSVT process, by which social landlords often acquire housing stock, before turning to how social landlords are regulated. We then consider how decisions of landlords, including PRPs and RSLs (see paras 1.321–1.327), may be challenged by an individual under either the principles of public law or through complaint to an ombudsman.

Key terms and bodies

8.3 **Non-profit-making.** Traditionally, social landlords have been non-profit-making bodies and, indeed, in Wales a landlord must be in order to register with the Welsh Ministers. In England, it is no longer necessary for the landlord to be non-profit-making to register with the HCA but where the landlord is a 'commercial' landlord, the HCA's regulatory powers are limited to its non-profit-making activities. A landlord is non-profit-making if it does not trade for profit or its constitution or rules prohibit the issue of capital with interest or dividend exceeding an amount prescribed by the treasury (Housing and Regeneration Act (H&RA) 2008 s115; Housing Act (HA) 1996 s2(1); Housing Associations Act (HAA) 1985 s1(1)).

8.4 **Housing association.** For many years, PRPs and RSLs were known as registered housing associations, then registered with the Housing Corporation. Most PRPS and RSLs are still housing associations. A housing association is a company, or a society, or a trust, which is non-profit-making (see para 8.3), the objects of which include the provision, management, construction or improvement of housing: HAA 1985 s1.

8.5 **Housing trust.** A 'housing trust' is a body of persons (eg a partnership) or a corporation (a company or registered society), which is required by its constitution either to use the whole of its funds for the purpose of providing housing, or to use its funds for charitable purposes and in fact uses them for provision of housing (HAA 1985 s2). If the trust is also a charity registered with the Charity Commissioners, it is referred to as a 'charitable housing trust'.

8.6 **Charitable housing association.** A charitable housing association is a housing association which is also a charity registered with the Charity Commissioners (HA 1996 s58), which means that it needs to have a permissible charitable purpose. The permissible charitable purposes are listed in Charities Act 2011 s3. In the context of housing, the most relevant is 'the relief of those in need because of youth, age, ill-health, disability, financial hardship or other disadvantage' (Charities Act 2011 s3(1)(j)). It has been held that the provision of social housing is not itself a charitable activity; it is only charitable if it is provided for a recognised charitable purpose (*Helena Partnerships Ltd v Commissioners for Her Majesty's Revenue and Customs*, 2012).

8.7 **Registered society.** A registered society is a form of corporate body which is registered with the Financial Conduct Authority (FCA) under the Co-operative and Community Benefit Societies Act 2014. (These societies used to be known as Industrial Provident Societies and were registered under the Industrial and Provident Societies Act 1965, which was replaced by the 2014 Act). Many housing associations are incorporated in this way rather than as companies under the Companies Act 2006.

8.8 **Fully mutual housing association.** A full mutual housing association is a housing association (see para 8.3), the rules of which restrict membership to persons who are tenants or prospective tenants of the association and which preclude the grant or assignment of tenancies to persons other than members (HAA 1985 s1(2)). A fully mutual housing association which is also a registered society (which it will usually be) is a 'co-operative housing association' (HAA 1985 s1(2)).

8.9 **ALMOs.** Not all bodies registered with the HCA are PRPs. In England, local housing authorities (see para 1.164) must also be registered, as must Arms Length Management Organisations (ALMOs), which are companies established by local authorities to manage their housing stock under HA 1985 s27 (Housing and Regeneration Act 2008 (Registration of Local Authorities) Order 2010 SI No 844). An ALMO is usually a company limited by guarantee which is wholly owned by the local authority. In Wales, however, local authorities and ALMOs are not required to register with the Welsh Ministers.

Registration of PRPs and RSLs

England

8.10 **PRPs.** A wide range of bodies can register with the HCA, including registered charities, registered societies and companies (H&RA 2008 s79). In contrast to the position in Wales, it is not necessary for the body to be non-profit-making (see para 8.3 and compare para 8.12). The landlord must satisfy two conditions: (i) it must be (or will be) a provider of social housing; and, (ii) it must satisfy any criteria set by the HCA regarding its constitution, financial situation and management arrangements (H&RA 2008 s112).

8.11 **Social housing.** There are two types of social housing: 'low cost rental accommodation' and 'low cost home ownership accommodation' (H&RA 2008 s68). In both cases, the landlord's rules for allocating housing must ensure that it is available to people whose needs are not adequately served by the commercial market (H&RA 2008 s69). Low cost rental accommodation must be available for rent at below the market rate (H&RA 2008 s69(a)) and low cost home ownership accommodation must be available for occupation under one of a number of shared ownership schemes (H&RA 2008 s70). Under such shared ownership schemes, the tenant initially pays part of the full purchase price for the property but his or her agreement will allow him or her to buy a greater share in the property in stages – a process commonly called 'stair-casing' – until he eventually owns the property outright. In the mean time, the tenant pays rent (and service charges), the amount of which reflects the amount he or she has contributed to the full purchase price, ie the larger his or her share, the lower the rent.

Wales

8.12 **RSLs.** Only bodies with registered addresses in Wales can register with the Welsh Ministers (HA 1996 ss1A, 2(1)). A registered society or company principally concerned with Welsh housing can register provided it is non-profit-making and meets certain conditions. First, the landlord's constitution must include among its powers the provision, construction, improvement or management of either: dwellings available for letting; dwellings available for occupation by members of the landlord body; or, hostels. Secondly, any additional purposes of the landlord's constitution must be limited to certain specified activities (s2(4)), which in general terms concern the provision of shared ownership accommodation (see para 8.11) and various housing services. A body is not to be ineligible for registration as a social landlord simply because it has power to acquire (or repair or improve) commercial premises or businesses which are incidental to its principal activities (s2(5)). Charitable housing associations (see para 8.6) are automatically eligible for registration as they are by their nature non-profit-making.

LSVT

8.13 The policy of large scale voluntary transfer (LSVT) is primarily responsible for the significant increase in the amount of social housing owned by PRPs and RSLs. Many PRPs and RSLs have been created specifically for the purpose of an LSVT. To qualify as 'large scale', over 499 dwellings must be included in the transfer (HA 1985 s34(4AB)). For this purpose, properties let under long leases – which will be properties disposed of to tenants, whether under the right to buy or a voluntary sales programme – are disregarded (s34(4C)). The disposal of housing by a local authority requires the consent of the secretary of state (in England) or the Welsh Ministers (in Wales) (HA 1985 s32): before any disposal takes place, the authority must consult its tenants (HA 1985 s105, Sch 3A); the consultation process includes a ballot of the tenants and if a majority of the tenants who vote in the ballot vote against the transfer, consent cannot be given (Sch 3A para 5. As to the requirements of consultation more generally, see para 4.91).

Regulation

England

8.14 **Accounts and finance.** The HCA has a number of powers to regulate the financial affairs of a PRP. It may give directions about the preparation of accounts, which must be sent to the HCA (H&RA 2008 s127). Companies, registered societies and charities are usually obliged to have their accounts audited under other regulatory frameworks. Those PRPs which do not have to do so may be required to have their accounts audited by the HCA (H&RA 2008 ss129–140).

8.15 **Economic matters.** The HCA has power to set standards for PRPs (but not local authorities) relating to the management of their financial and other affairs (H&RA 2008 s194, as amended by the Localism Act (LA) 2011), including levels of rent. The standards are *Governance and Viability Standard* (April 2015), *Value for Money Standard* (April 2012) and the *Rent Standard* (April 2015). The HCA has power to arrange for an inspection of a PRP's affairs (H&RA 2008 s201). If mismanagement is suspected, an inquiry may be held (H&RA 2008 s206). There are numerous forms of enforcement action which the HCA may take where it decides that a PRP's finances have been mismanaged. These are considered below (see paras 8.19–8.20) in relation to the HCA's broader powers to regulate a PRP's performance of its functions.

8.16 **Rents.** The restrictions on rents charged by PRPs are considered in chapter 3 (see paras 3.11–3.19).

8.17 **Consumer matters.** The HCA may set managements standards requiring local authorities and PRPs to comply with rules about: allocating accommodation, tenancy terms, maintenance, complaints procedures for tenants, consultation with tenants, involvement of tenants in management issues, assisting tenants to exchange tenancies, anti-social behaviour policy, contributing to the social and economic well-being of their areas, and estate management (H&RA 2008 s193, as amended by LA 2011). The standards are contained in *Tenancy Involvement and Empowerment Standard, Home Standard, Tenancy Standard, Neighbourhood Standard* and *Community Standard* (all published in April 2012).

8.18 **Enforcement.** Where financial or management standards have not been met, the HCA may serve an enforcement notice on the PRP or local authority requiring it to take remedial action (H&RA 2008 s220). There is a right of appeal to the High Court (s223). If the notice is not complied with, the HCA must consider using one of its other enforcement powers (s225) but service of an enforcement notice is not a precondition for doing so. The HCA can also fine a PRP (but not a local authority) up to £5,000 or, if the PRP has committed a criminal offence, impose any fine that a criminal court could impose (ss226, 229). Local authorities and PRPs can be required by the HCA to pay compensation to a tenant who has suffered as a result of the landlord's failure (s237). Before imposing such a requirement, it must inform the landlord of its decision and allow the landlord to make representations (ss242–243). There is a right of appeal to the High Court (s45).

8.19 **Management transfer.** In cases of severe mismanagement, the HCA has power to require a PRP or a local authority to put its management functions out to tender with a view to them being transferred to another landlord, usually a PRP (H&RA 2008 ss247–250A). Before doing so, the HCA must consider representations from the landlord, and consider the views of the landlord's tenants and, in the case of a PRP, the views of local authorities in whose area the PRP provides housing. Again, there is a right of appeal to the High Court (s248). An order requiring a transfer can only be made with the Secretary of State's consent (s249(3)). Ultimately, again with the Secretary of State's consent, the HCA can even require a PRP (but not a local authority) to transfer its stock to another PRP (s253).

Wales

8.20 **Accounts and finance.** The Welsh Ministers have power to set accounting standards for RSLs and detailed provision is made for auditing their accounts, depending on the nature of the landlord (HA 1996 Sch 1 para 16). They may also issue guidance on the governance of RSLs, effective management and establishing and maintaining financial viability. (HA 1996 s33B).

8.21 **Housing management standards.** Since December 2011, as a result of the Housing (Wales) Measure 2011, the Welsh Ministers now have much greater regulatory powers. After consultation with the RSLs, the Welsh Ministers may publish performance standards relating to any RSL housing function (HA 1996 s33A) and may publish guidance on those standards (HA 1996 s33B). The standards are contained in *Regulatory Framework for Housing Associations in Wales* (December 2011).

8.22 **Enforcement and management transfer.** Following the Housing (Wales) Measure 2011, the enforcement powers available to the HCA (see para 8.18) are now available to the Welsh Ministers where

RSLs have failed to comply with financial or management standards (HA 1996 ss50A–50V). Likewise, in cases of severe mismanagement, there are similar powers to require an RSL to transfer its management functions or even to transfer its land to another landlord (see para 8.19; HA 1996 Sch 1 paras 15B–15G, 20–24, 27). As in England, in each case, there is a right of appeal to the High Court.

Principles of public law

8.23 The decisions and actions of public bodies can be challenged on the principles of public administrative law, by way of judicial review, on an appeal where this is available by statute or by way of a defence to a claim, eg possession proceedings. As discussed in chapter 1 (see paras 1.321–1.327), local authorities are plainly subject to the requirements of public law; and, although not generally so subject, PRPs and RSLs are, in certain circumstances, also considered to be acting as public authorities, whose decisions and actions can therefore also be challenged on public law principles. It must be emphasised that the principles of public law are constantly evolving, particularly in light of the Human Rights Act (HRA) 1998, which tends to affect approaches to public law issues even where it does not directly apply: although in the context of housing law a traditional approach to public law challenges remains applicable, fundamental changes to the way in which courts consider all decisions of public authorities therefore remain possible. This is considered below (see paras 8.33–8.36).

8.24 **General principles.** A challenge to a decision under public law principles is not concerned with resolving factual disputes. Where a decision has been entrusted to a public authority, questions of fact are for the authority to decide and a court cannot substitute its own view of the facts for that of the authority (*R v Hillingdon LBC ex p Puhlhofer*, 1986). Exceptions to this general rule include cases where a breach of natural justice is alleged (see para 8.28(10) – *O'Reilly v Mackman*, 1982) or resolving a discrete issue such as a person's age (see para 10.29). Where a person's fundamental rights are engaged, a court may subject an authority's decision to a greater degree of scrutiny or even decide the facts for itself (see paras 8.33–8.36). Otherwise, a straightforward difference of opinion or judgment between an authority and an applicant as to what decision should have been reached will not suffice to justify the intervention of the courts. If Parliament has entrusted a decision to a local authority, it is that authority's view of what is reasonable which must prevail, rather than that of a court (*Associated Provincial Picture Houses Ltd v Wednesbury Corp*, 1947).

8.25 **Ultra vires.** What the principles invariably involve is that authorities should always approach their decisions in a lawful manner. If it can be shown that a public authority has approached a decision unlawfully, the decision will be void and the courts will not give effect to it. A decision improperly reached is *ultra vires*, ie outside the authority's powers, and without effect in law, whether it is because on the face of the statute there was no power to reach a decision or engage in an act at all, or because the statute has been misconstrued, or because the authority has misapplied the statute in another sense, eg by failing to use the powers to implement the purpose of the statute, or by reaching a decision under the statute by reference to something which is irrelevant – or in ignorance of something which is relevant – to the way the power under the statute is intended to be operated, or by reaching a decision so absurd that no reasonable authority could have reached it. Although the weight to be given to a relevant consideration is generally a matter for the decision-maker (*Tesco Stores Ltd v Secretary of State for the Environment*, 1995), it may be unlawful to accord too much weight to a particular factor (*R v Winchester City Council ex p Ashton*, 1991).

8.26 **Proper decision-making.** At the heart of the case-law is the proposition that Parliament intends that public bodies should always act properly, in the sense of reasonably and lawfully. That is not to say that they will always arrive at 'the' reasonable decision: one person's view of what is reasonable will often quite properly differ from that of another.

8.27 **Classification.** The principles of administrative law may be expressed, and classified, in a number of different ways. In *Council of Civil Service Unions v Minister for the Civil Service*, 1984, Lord Diplock re-classified them under three headings: 'illegality', 'irrationality' and 'procedural impropriety':

> By 'illegality' as a ground of judicial review I mean that the decision-maker must understand correctly the law that regulates his decision-making power and must give effect to it. Whether he has or not is par excellence a justiciable question to be decided, in the event of dispute, by those persons, the judges, by whom the judicial power of the state is exercisable.
>
> By 'irrationality' I mean what can by now be succinctly referred to as '*Wednesbury* unreasonableness' ... It applies to a decision which is so outrageous in its defiance of logic or of accepted moral standards that no sensible person who had applied his mind to the question to be

> decided could have arrived at it. Whether a decision falls within this category is a question that judges by their training and experience should be well equipped to answer, or else there would be something badly wrong with our judicial system ... 'Irrationality' by now can stand upon its own feet as an accepted ground on which a decision may be attacked by judicial review. I have described the third head as 'procedural impropriety' rather than failure to observe basic rules of natural justice or failure to act with procedural fairness towards the person who will be affected by the decision. This is because susceptibility to judicial review under this head covers also failure by an administrative tribunal to observe procedural rules that are expressly laid down in the legislative instrument by which its jurisdiction is conferred, even where such failure does not involve any denial of natural justice.

8.28 **Practical classification.** In practice, the principles tend to overlap with one another. They may be considered under one or more of the following.

1) A public body must take into account all relevant factors before making their decision, and must disregard the irrelevant: *Wednesbury*. See also *Bristol DC v Clark*, 1975.
2) The decision must be based on the facts; a decision totally at variance with the facts or for which there is no factual basis cannot be sustained:

   > If a judgment requires, before it can be made, the existence of some facts, then although the evaluation of those facts is for the Secretary of State alone, the courts must enquire whether those facts exist, and have been taken into account, whether the judgment has been made on a proper self-direction as to those facts, whether the judgment has not been made on other facts which ought not to have been taken into account. (*Secretary of State for Education and Science v Tameside*, 1976).

3) The authority must not act in bad faith or dishonestly: *Wednesbury*.
4) The authority must direct itself properly in law, so that a decision based on a misunderstanding or misapplication of the law will not have been reached properly: *Wednesbury*. This is the point in *Wednesbury* that is restated as 'illegality' in *Council of Civil Service Unions* (see para 8.27).
5) The authority must act so as to promote, and not to defeat, the objects or policy of the Act in question. Powers conferred for public purposes must be used in a way that Parliament can be presumed to have intended (*Padfield v Minister of Agriculture, Fisheries & Food*, 1968).

6) The decision must not be one to which no reasonable authority could have come: this is conclusive evidence that the decision is improper (or irrational): *Wednesbury*.
7) The authority must reach its own decision on each individual case; it must not fetter its discretion by approaching a decision with a predetermined policy as to how it will deal with any case falling within a particular class.

   The leading case on this is probably still *British Oxygen Co Ltd v Minister of Technology*, 1970. While a public authority can adopt a policy or limiting rule in order to guide the future exercise of its discretion if it thinks good administration requires it, the authority must nonetheless consider its application individually in every case where it is sought to make an exception (*Stringer v Minister for Housing and Local Government*, 1970).
8) It is the authority who is entrusted with the decision-making power and must make the decision. The authority cannot avoid its duties by adopting the decision of another person or body (*H Lavender & Sons v Minister for Housing and Local Government*, 1969).

   In the context of local authority decisions, a distinction must be drawn, however, between adoption of the decision of another person or body and use of the authority's resources when reaching a decision. The authority may employ staff (Local Government Act (LGA) 1972 s112), and have implied power to employ contractors or agents, and to enter into contracts with them (*Credit Suisse v Allerdale BC*, 1996). There is now an express power to contract (Local Government (Contracts) Act 1997 s1). These resources can all be used when reaching a decision. What cannot be abdicated is responsibility for the essential elements of a decision which are to determine what is to be done or what is to happen.
9) The authority's decision must be reached properly. Specific considerations arise here in relation to local authorities. Under LGA 2000, local authorities now function in what may be described as two parts: an executive (of one of three kinds: mayor and cabinet, leader and cabinet or – in Wales only – mayor and council executive: see LGA 2000 s11), and the full authority.

   Decisions not conferred on the full authority by statute, statutory instrument or (where the power is left to the authority to decide) conferred by the authority on itself under 'local choice' (LGA 2000 s13(3)(b)), must be taken by the executive (s13(2), (10)).

   Decisions to be taken by the executive may be dealt with in any way that LGA 2000 permits, which includes delegation to an individual member of the executive, or to a committee or sub-committee of the executive, or to an officer (or, in some circumstances, an area committee not of the executive but of the authority itself) (LGA 2000 ss14–16, 18). In some circumstances, therefore, individual decisions can properly be taken by an individual councillor.

Decisions which the authority is to take itself cannot, however, be delegated to an individual member, only to a committee, sub-committee or officer of the authority (LGA 1972 s101).

10) In all cases, an authority must act fairly, or in accordance with natural justice (*Ridge v Baldwin*, 1963). The extent of this duty will depend upon circumstances, and the nature of the decision.

The obligations of natural justice include a right to be heard where a person is the subject of action which adversely affects him or her. This has two elements: first, informing him or her about what is being said against him or her; secondly, affording an opportunity to answer it. This does not mean that he or she is always entitled to an oral hearing, unless required by statute, but where a decision is reached without a hearing, he or she must be given an opportunity to respond to adverse findings.

In many cases, statute imposes a duty on a public body to give reasons for its decision, see, eg applications by homeless persons (see para 10.146) and eviction of introductory tenants (see para 2.151). In the absence of a specific statutory requirement, whether reasons for a decision are required depends on what is fair in the circumstances of the case (*R v Secretary of State for the Home Department ex p Doody*, 1993). Where reasons are required, they must be proper, intelligible and deal with points raised by the person affected (*Re Poyser and Mills Arbitration*, 1963).

While there is no universal obligation to give reasons in all circumstances, the common law is moving to the position that, in general they should be given unless there is a proper justification for not doing so; reasons will be required where fairness requires it, or a particular decision is aberrant, where the failure to give reasons may frustrate a right of appeal, because without reasons a party will not know whether there is an appealable ground or not, and where a party has a legitimate expectation that reasons will be given: *Oakley v South Cambridgeshire DC*, 2017 at [30]–[31].

Even if a statute or other instrument contains its own procedural requirements to ensure fairness, including to give reasons for decisions, the courts may – if they consider that the circumstances of an individual case (or, presumably, class of case) call for it – impose yet further requirements to ensure that a matter has been decided fairly and/or give reasons (*Wiseman v Borneman*, 1969). This requirement means that, if relevant to the decision, an applicant must know what is being said against him or her (*Board of Education v Rice*, 1911).

The requirement of fairness will also mean that an authority must respect any legitimate expectations which an applicant may enjoy. Conventionally, the expression refers to a legitimate procedural expectation, ie as to how a matter is to be handled, such as an assurance that no decision will be taken at all on an aspect of a matter until there has been a further opportunity to comment, or until the authority has managed to contact someone, or that it will only be taken by an officer of a particular level of seniority, or by a panel (member or officer) (*Schmidt v Secretary of State for Home Affairs*, 1968; *R v Devon CC ex p Baker*, 1992), provided always that to do so would not interfere or conflict with the authority's statutory duty (*Attorney-General of Hong Kong ex p Ng Yuen Shiu*, 1983).

Less frequently it has been held to encompass a legitimate substantive expectation, ie of a particular outcome of a decision-making process, as opposed to its procedure, where there has been a clear and unambiguous statement, devoid of qualification, on which it was reasonable to rely (*R v IRC ex p MFK Underwriting*, 1989).

The court has to determine the nature of the legitimate expectation which has been engendered, and whether it would be an abuse of power for the court to frustrate it or whether there is a sufficient overriding interest to justify a departure from what had been promised (*R v North and East Devon Health Authority ex p Coughlan*, 1999).

Ombudsman

8.29 Tenants of social housing who are dissatisfied with their landlords may consider complaining to an ombudsman. In England, a complaint against a local authority or a PRP is to the Housing Ombudsman Service (HA 1996 s51 and Sch 2, as amended by LA 2011). In Wales, complaints about local authority landlords and RSLs are to the Public Services Ombudsman for Wales under the Public Services Ombudsman (Wales) Act (PSO(W)A) 2005.

8.30 In England, there are restrictions on the right to complain directly to the Housing Ombudsman Service (HA 1996 Sch 2 paras 7A–7C, inserted by LA 2011). A direct complaint is permitted eight weeks after the tenant has exhausted the landlord's internal complaints procedure. Otherwise, a complaint must be made through to an MP, a councillor, or a designated tenant panel – a group of tenants recognised by the landlord for referring complaints – unless the Ombudsman agrees otherwise or is satisfied that the person to whom the complaint was properly made has refused to refer it.

8.31 An Ombudsman is concerned with maladministration, ie faulty administration or inefficient or improper management of affairs (*R v Commissioner for Administration ex p Bradford City Council*, 1978). The Ombudsman will usually require the complainant to have tried to resolve his or her grievance with the landlord using its own internal complaints procedure (HA 1996 Sch 2 para 7B; PSO(W)A 2005 s9). If the dispute remains unresolved, the Ombudsman investigates the complaint and, if maladministration is made out, may make recommendations as to what the authority should do. An ombudsman has power to recommend that the landlord pay compensation to a successful complainant (PSO(W)A 2005 s15: HA 1996 Sch 2 para 7). In England, once amendments by LA 2011 are in force, the Secretary of State will be able to make regulations providing that an ombudsman's decision can be enforced by a court or tribunal (HA 1996 Sch 2 para 7D).

8.32 There is an overlap between the Ombudsman's powers to investigate and resolve complaints against a PRP and the HCA's regulatory powers (see paras 8.14–8.19). A Memorandum of Understanding, dated 21 April 2017, governs how the two will seek to work together to ensure that a complaint is handled by the more appropriate body.

Human rights

8.33 As discussed in chapter 1 (see paras 1.321–1.327), local authorities are subject to the provisions of HRA 1998, as are PRPs and RSLs when carrying out certain functions. The implications of the European Convention on Human Rights (ECHR) on a landlord's activities is considered at the conclusion of each chapter. Here, however, we are concerned with the development of domestic public law in light of HRA 1998.

8.34 In *Council of Civil Service Unions* (see para 8.27), Lord Diplock raised the possibility that domestic public law might one day import the European principle of 'proportionality' which is applied throughout Convention law, which is the doctrine that there must be a reasonable relationship between a public authority's action and its purpose in a given context. Even prior to HRA 1998, the courts had begun to cast doubt on whether the wide discretion given to decision-makers under the *Wednesbury* test considered above (see paras 8.24 and 8.27–8.28) was suitable in cases which involved fundamental rights, eg a person's liberty, and it was suggested that the test needed to be adapted so that such cases were subjected to what has been termed 'anxious scrutiny' (*R v Ministry of Defence ex p Smith*, 1995), requiring a somewhat closer degree of factual scrutiny.

8.35 Three possible standards of review have been suggested, within which there is a sliding scale of judicial scrutiny depending on the gravity of the decision's impact on the applicant (*R (Mahmood) v Secretary of State for the Home Department*, 2001):

a) the conventional *Wednesbury* approach;
b) an approach based on fundamental rights requiring the court to 'insist that that fact be respected by the decision-maker, who is accordingly required to demonstrate either that his proposed action does not in truth interfere with the right, or, if it does, that there exist considerations which may reasonably be accepted as amounting to a substantial objective justification for the interference'; and,
c) an approach based on claims which directly engage rights guaranteed by the ECHR, which requires the court to decide for itself whether there has been a violation of a convention right.

8.36 In cases involving fundamental rights, the courts continue to endorse an approach based on proportionality: see eg *Pham v Secretary of State for the Home Department*, 2015, which involved a decision to remove British citizenship. In contrast, in the context of decisions on applications for homeless persons (see para 10.160), the traditional public law approach remains applicable (*Runa Begum v Tower Hamlets LBC*, 2003; *Hines v Lambeth LBC*, 2014). Indeed, the European Court of Human Rights has held that this approach comprises sufficient protection of an applicant's right to a fair determination of his civil rights under Article 6 ECHR (*Fazia Ali v UK*, 2015). Although it has been suggested that it is now time to dispense with the *Wednesbury* approach (*Association of British Civilian Internees (Far East Region) v Secretary of State for Defence*, 2003), it has been suggested in the Supreme Court that a decision to replace *Wednesbury* rationality with a structured proportionality assessment would require a panel of nine Supreme Court justices (who usually sit in a panel or five or seven) because of the far-reaching implications such a change would have in constitutional terms (*R (Keyu) v Secretary of State for Foreign and Commonwealth Affairs*, 2015).

CHAPTER 9

Mobile homes and houseboats

continued

Introduction

9.1 In England, three statutes govern the rights of occupiers of mobile homes. The Caravan Sites and Control of Development Act (CSCDA) 1960 creates a licensing scheme for mobile home sites, which is the principal means of regulating physical conditions on sites. The Caravan Sites Act (CSA) 1968 Pt 1 protects occupiers of mobile homes both from eviction without court order and from acts of harassment. It applies to owners of mobile homes who rent a pitch, and to those who rent both mobile home and pitch, from the site owner. The Mobile Homes Act (MHA) 1983 contains a statutory code regulating the relationship between owners of mobile homes and site owners. All three Acts used to apply in Wales but the Mobile Homes (Wales) Act (MH(W)A) 2013 brought the law together into one Act. The statutory schemes in both countries are therefore similar but are contained in different sources. This chapter also considers the limited rights which are available to occupiers of houseboats.

Mobile homes

9.2 Both CSCDA 1960 and CSA 1968 use the term 'caravans' whereas MHA 1983 and MH(W)A 2013 refer to 'mobile homes'. Both terms are defined identically (CSCDA 1960 s29(1); CSA 1968 s16(1); MHA 1983 s5(1); MH(W)A 2013 s60(1)). For simplicity, this chapter uses the term 'mobile home', which is:

> ... any structure designed or adapted for human habitation which is capable of being moved from one place to another (whether by being towed, or by being transported on a motor vehicle or trailer) and any motor vehicle so designed or adapted but does not include (a) any railway rolling stock which is for the time being on rails forming part of a railway system, or (b) any tent.

9.3 A structure that satisfies the first part of this definition is a mobile home even if it does not accord with the ordinary usage of the phrase; accordingly, a chalet that can be moved from one place to another is a mobile home (*Wyre Forest DC v Secretary of State for the Environment*, 1990). *Note:* in one case, a county court decided that a houseboat was a mobile home: although the Court of Appeal strongly doubted whether this was correct (*Roy Crimble Ltd v Edgecombe*, 1981), on the wording of the definition, it is clearly arguable that a houseboat does fall within the definition. At present, it is nonetheless generally believed that the provisions considered in this chapter governing mobile homes do not apply to houseboats. The position of occupiers of houseboats is therefore considered separately, below (see paras 9.77–9.79).

Site licensing

9.4 The principal means of controlling conditions on mobile home sites is the licensing scheme in CSCDA 1960 and MH(W)A 2013 Pt 2. Licensing is administered by local authorities. For the purposes of these provisions, local authorities are:

1) unitary authorities;
2) other district councils;
3) London borough councils;
4) the Common Council of the City of London;
5) the council of the Isles of Scilly;
6) Welsh county or county boroughs (CSCDA 1960 s29; MH(W)A 2013 s62).

9.5 The following do not require a licence:

a) a mobile home used in conjunction with a dwelling-house and situated in the grounds of the house;
b) a mobile home used by someone travelling which is on the site for no more than two nights;
c) a site of less than five acres on which no more than three mobile homes are pitched for no more than 28 days in a year;
d) sites with an exemption certificate from the secretary of state or the National Assembly for Wales;
e) sites used by agricultural or forestry workers;
f) mobile homes used on building or engineering sites; and
g) sites owned by local authorities (CSCDA 1960 s2 and Sch 1; MH(W)A 2013 s2 and Sch 1).

9.6 In any other case, a licence must be obtained before land is used as a mobile home site and anyone who causes or permits land to be used as such without a licence commits an offence, punishable by an unlimited fine (CSCDA 1960 s1; MH(W)A 2013 s5; Legal Aid, Sentencing and Punishment of Offenders Act (LASPO) 2012 s85(1)). A licence can only be granted if the land has planning permission for use as a mobile home site (CSCDA 1960 s3(1); M(W)HA 2013 s7(1)). The application must include specified information about the site and its owner (MHA 1983 s3(5A) and Mobile Homes (Site Licensing) (England) Regulations 2014 SI No 442; MH(W)A 2013 s6(2)–(4)).

9.7 A licence can include any condition which the authority considers necessary or desirable in the interests of those living on the site or the public (CSCDA 1960 s5(1); MH(W)A 2013 s9(1)). Standard conditions have been published by both the Secretary of State and the National Assembly for Wales: *Model Standards 2008 for Caravan Sites in England: CSCDA 1960 – Section 5* (2008) and *Model Standards 2008 for Caravan Sites in Wales: CSCDA 1960 – Section 5* (2008). Authorities have power to vary licence conditions (CSCDA 1960 s8; MH(W)A 2013 s13).

9.8 Authorities can enforce a breach of a licence condition by serving a 'compliance notice', specifying the action required to remedy the breach (CSCDA 1960 s9A; MH(W)A 2013 s17). Failure, without reasonable excuse, to comply with such a notice is a criminal offence punishable by an unlimited fine (CSCDA 1960 s9B; MH(W)A 2013 s18; LASPO 2012 s85(1)). Following conviction, the authority can itself take action to remedy the breach. Usually, the authority will serve a further notice warning of its intention to do so but if there is an imminent risk to the health and safety of occupiers, immediate action can be taken (CSCDA 1960 ss9D–9E; MH(W)A 2013 ss20–21). The authority's expenses of serving notices and of any remedial action are recoverable from the site owner (CSCDA 1960 ss9C and 9F; MH(W)A 2013 ss19 and 22). On a third conviction for breaching a compliance notice, the court can revoke the licence (CSCDA 1960 s9B(4); MH(W)A 2013 s18(4)).

9.9 There is a right of appeal against: the refusal to grant a licence, the imposition or variation of a licence condition, the service of a compliance notice, a decision to take action in default and a decision to recover expenses from the site owner. In England, an appeal is to the First-tier Tribunal; in Wales, it is to the residential property tribunal.

Protection from eviction

Possession proceedings

9.10 CSA 1968 Pt 1 and MH(W)A 2013 Pt 3 make provision for the protection from eviction for occupiers of mobile homes. The provisions apply to an occupier of a mobile home who has a 'residential contract', which is any licence or contract under which a person is entitled either to station a mobile home on a protected site (see para 9.11) and occupy it as his or her residence (see paras 5.5–5.9), or to occupy as his or her residence a mobile home stationed on the site (CSA 1968 s1(1); MH(W)A 2013 s40). The protection is accordingly given both to a mobile home owner who only rents his or her pitch and to an occupier who rents both pitch and mobile home.

9.11 A protected site is either a site in respect of which a site licence is required (see paras 9.4–9.5) or any site owned by a local authority (CSA 1968 s1(2); MH(W)A 2013 s2(2)). The inclusion of local authority sites is particularly intended to protect Gypsies and Travellers (see para 9.80).

9.12 Where a residential contract (see para 9.10) permits termination by notice to quit by either party, the notice must be given at least four weeks before the date on which it is to take effect (CSA 1968 s2; MH(W)A 2013 s41). The notice need not be in writing nor contain prescribed information; compare Protection from Eviction Act (PEA) 1977 s5 (see para 2.49).

9.13 An occupier under a residential contract (see para 9.10) can only be evicted by order of the county court (CSA 1968 ss3(1)(b) and 5; MH(W)A 2013 s42(3)). The court can suspend a possession order for up to a maximum of 12 months on such conditions, including payment of rent or other payments and/or arrears, as it thinks fit (CSA 1968 s4; MH(W)A 2013 s44). Either party can apply for a variation of the conditions, or for a reduction, extension or removal of the suspension, although no further extension can be granted that would take the order beyond the 12 months' maximum. In exercising its discretion, the court must have regard to all the circumstances, including any breaches of the residential contract, any unreasonable refusal by the occupier to enter into a new contract and any efforts by the occupier to find another mobile home to live in. If a suspended order is granted, costs should not be awarded against either party unless there are 'special reasons' for doing so in light of a party's conduct.

9.14 Spouses and civil partners of occupiers of mobile homes may have 'home rights' (see paras 7.9–7.14) under the Family Law Act (FLA) 1996 and a mobile home may be subject to an occupation order (see para 7.15–7.27) under FLA 1996 in favour of a spouse, civil partner or other associated person (see para 7.16). A person with home rights or the benefit of an occupation order can apply for a variation of the conditions or an extension of the suspension of an order as if he or she was the occupier under the residential contract; *cf* the position under suspended possession orders made against secure tenants (see para 2.119); assured tenants (see para 2.175) and Rent Act tenants (see para 2.221).

Unlawful eviction, harassment and false information

Unlawful eviction

9.15 Anyone who evicts an occupier who has a residential contract (see para 9.10) without a court order commits a criminal offence (CSA 1968 s3(1)(a), (b); MH(W)A 2013 s42(2), (3)). It is a defence to show that the defendant believed, and had reasonable cause to believe, that the occupier had ceased to reside on the site (CSA 1968 s3(4); MH(W)A 2013 s43(1)).

Harassment

9.16 There are also two offences of harassment of occupiers, modelled on similar offences under PEA 1977 (see paras 5.5–5.16). One offence can only be committed by the site owner or his or her agent; the other can be committed by anyone. Each offence has two elements: (i) the prohibited harassment; and, (ii) the perpetrator's state of mind.

9.17 Under both offences, the prohibited harassment comprises:

a) acts likely to interfere with the peace and comfort of a residential occupier or members of his or her household; or
b) persistent withdrawal or withholding of services or facilities reasonably required for occupation of the mobile home (CSA 1968 s3(1)(c), (1A); MH(W)A 2013 s42(4), (5)).

9.18 A person who commits any such act of harassment is guilty of an offence if he or she intended to cause the occupier of the mobile home:

i) to abandon occupation of the mobile home; or
ii) to remove it from the site; or
iii) to refrain from exercising his or her rights or pursuing any remedy in respect of the mobile home (CSA 1968 s3(1); MH(W)A 2013 s42(4)).

9.19 If the perpetrator of the harassment is a site owner or his or her agent, an offence is committed if he or she knew, or had reasonable cause to believe, that the actions would have any of those consequences (CSA 1968 s3(1A); MH(W)A 2013 s42(5)). It is a defence for the site owner or agent to show that reasonable grounds exist for interfering with the peace or comfort of the residential occupier or for withdrawing or withholding the services or facilities (CSA 1968 s3(4A); MH(W)A 2013 s43(2).

False information

9.20 A site owner, or his or her agent, commits an offence if he or she:

(a) knowingly or recklessly provides information or makes a representation which is false or misleading in a material respect to any person; and,

(b) knows, or has reasonable cause to believe, that doing so is likely to cause–

(i) the occupier to abandon the mobile home or remove it from the site; or

(ii) the occupier to refrain from exercising his or her rights in relation to the mobile home; or

(iii) a person considering whether to purchase or occupy the mobile home to decide not to do so (CSA 1968 s3(1AA); MH(W)A 2013 s42(6)).

Death of occupier

9.21 If the residential occupier has died, his or her surviving spouse/civil partner or, if none, any other member of his or her family who was residing with him or her at the time of death, enjoys the same protection against eviction without court order, harassment and the provision of false information (CSA 1968 s3(2); MH(W)A 2013 s42(8)). Family member is not statutorily defined and cases on succession under the Rent Act (RA) 1977 may be relevant to who may qualify as a member of someone's family (see para 1.279).

Penalty

9.22 In relation to any of the offences, the defendant is liable on conviction in the magistrates' court to an unlimited fine and/or to imprisonment for a maximum of one year; on conviction in the Crown Court, liability is to an unlimited fine and/or imprisonment for a maximum of two years (CSA 1968 s3(3); MH(W)A 2013 s43(3)).

Agreements for mobile home owners: privately owned sites

9.23 MHA 1983 and MH(W)A 2013 Pt 4 govern agreements under which a person ('the occupier') is entitled to station a mobile home on a protected site (see para 9.10) and to occupy it as his or her 'only or main residence'. The test is similar to the 'only or principal home' residence condition for security of tenure under both the Housing

Act (HA) 1988 and HA 1985 (see paras 1.176–1.179). For the provisions to apply, the occupier must only rent the pitch from the site owner, ie the mobile home itself must be owned by the occupier: the provisions therefore do not apply to agreements under which the occupier rents both pitch and mobile home from the site owner. Gypsies and Travellers occupying local authority sites have similar rights, considered below (see paras 9.59–9.76).

Tribunal

9.24 The majority of disputes arising under mobile home agreements are resolved by a tribunal. In England, this is the First-tier Tribunal; in Wales, it is the residential property tribunal.

Statement of terms

9.25 Before entering into an agreement, the site owner must give the occupier a written statement setting out the terms implied by statute into the proposed agreement (see paras 9.28–9.57), any express terms and certain specified information (MHA 1983 s1(2), (3) and Mobile Homes (Written Statement) (England) Regulations 2011 SI No 1006; MH(W)A 2013 s49(1) and Mobile Homes (Written Statement) (Wales) Regulations 2014 SI No 1762). The statement must be given at least 28 days before the agreement is entered into, unless the proposed occupier agrees in writing to a shorter time. If the site owner fails to give notice, the occupier can apply to the tribunal (see para 9.24) for an order requiring a statement to be given. Failure to serve the statement in time also prevents the site owner from enforcing any express term of the agreement other than a 'site rule' made under the statutory procedure (see para 9.27), unless the tribunal gives permission to do so.

9.26 Either party can apply to the tribunal (see para 9.24) within six months of the date of the agreement or the written statement (whichever is later) for a term to be implied, varied or removed (MHA 1983 s2; MH(W)A 2013 s50). The tribunal can only order the inclusion of terms relating to: (i) charges payable by the occupier, including when they are to be paid; (ii) an annual review of the charges; (iii) provision or improvement of services, including the occupier's rights to use such services; and, (iv) preservation of the amenity of the site (MHA 1983 Sch 1 Pt 2; MH(W)A 2013 Sch 2 Pt 2). On an application for variation or removal of a term, the tribunal can order what it considers 'just and equitable in the circumstances'.

Site rules

9.27 'Site rules' are rules made by the site owner relating to the management and conduct of the site (MHA 1983 s2C; MH(W)A 2013 s52). Detailed provision is made for consultation of occupiers before site rules are introduced (Mobile Homes (Site Rules) (England) Regulations 2014 SI No 5; Mobile Homes (Site Rules) (Wales) Regulations 2014 SI No 1764). The consultation process is concluded by the site owner providing the occupiers with the final version of the rules. Occupiers have a right of appeal to the tribunal (see para 9.24) against this final version within 21 days of receiving it. Site rules made under the statutory procedure are deemed to be included in any agreement for a pitch on the site, provided that the site owner has lodged with the local authority (MHA 1983 s2C(1), (4); MH(W)A 2013 s53(4)).

Implied terms

9.28 Both MHA 1983 and MH(W)A 2013 Pt 4 imply terms into agreements between site owners and occupiers which override any express terms that conflict with them (MHA 1983 s2(1): MH(W)A 2013 s50(1)).

Pitch fees

9.29 A 'pitch fee' is the amount that the occupier has to pay for the right to station his or her mobile home and for the use and maintenance of the site's common areas (MHA 1983 Sch 1 Pt 1 Ch 2 para 29; MH(W)A 2013 s62). It does not include payments in respect of utilities unless expressly included by agreement. A pitch fee can only be varied by agreement between the parties or by order of the tribunal (see para 9.24) (MHA 1983 Sch 1 para 16: MH(W)A 2013 Sch 2 para 17(1)).

Annual review

9.30 Detailed provision is made for an annual review of the pitch fee (MHA 1983 Sch 1 Pt 1 Ch 2 para 17; MH(W)A 2013 Sch 2 para 17). The site owner must give at least 28 days' notice of the proposed new fee before the review date, which is either a date specified in the agreement or, if no such date is specified, the anniversary of the commencement of the agreement. The notice must be accompanied by prescribed information (Mobile Homes (Pitch Fees) (Prescribed Form) (England) Regulations 2013 SI No 1505; Mobile Homes (Pitch Fees) (Prescribed Form) (Wales) Regulations 2014 SI No 1760). If the occupier agrees the new fee, it becomes payable from the review date. If it is not agreed, either party can apply to the tribunal (see para 9.24) for a new fee to be determined. The application must be made no earlier than 28 days after – but within three months of – the review date. Pending the application, the occupier must continue to pay the current fee. Once determined by the tribunal or agreed between the parties, the new fee becomes payable from the review date but the occupier is not treated as being in arrears until the 28th day after the date on which the new fee is decided or agreed.

Alternative procedure

9.31 If the owner misses the review date, a notice proposing a new pitch fee can still be served. The procedure after service of the notice is similar to that for an annual review (see para 9.30), save that any application to the tribunal (see para 9.24) can be made no earlier than 56 days and no later than four months after service of the notice; the tribunal has power to extend this time limit.

Amount

9.32 Any increase or decrease ordered by the tribunal (see para 9.24) must be in line with changes in the retail price index (in England) or the consumer price index (in Wales), unless that would be unreasonable in the light of:

(a) the site owner's expenditure since the last review date on improvements which-
  (i) are for the benefit of the occupiers;
  (ii) were the subject of consultation (see paras 9.43–9.44); and,
  (iii) to which a majority of the occupiers did not object in writing or which, in the case of such objection, are improvements that the tribunal orders should nevertheless be taken into account;

(b) any deterioration in the condition, and any decrease in the amenity, of the site or adjoining land occupied or controlled by the owner;

(c) any reduction or deterioration in the services provided by the site owner; and,

(d) any decrease in the amenity of the protected site since the last review date (MHA 1983 Sch 1 Pt 1 Ch 2 para 20(A1), (1); MH(W)A 2013 Sch 1 Pt 1 Ch 2 paras 18 and 20).

9.33 If the occupier pays an increased pitch fee but the notice of increase was invalid, the occupier can apply to the tribunal (see para 9.24) for an order that the site owner refunds the overpayment.

Quiet enjoyment and rights of entry

9.34 The occupier is entitled to quiet enjoyment (see para 5.49(1)) of both the mobile home and the pitch (MHA 1983 Sch 1 Pt 1 Ch 2 para 11; MH(W)A 2013 Sch 2 para 15). This is subject to the site owner's rights of entry for: (i) delivery of post and notices (between 9 am and 6 pm); (ii) reading utility meters (between 9 am and 6 pm); (iii) carrying out essential repairs or emergency works (on reasonable notice); and, (iv) any other reason for which the agreement allows the site owner to enter, provided that the occupier is given at least 14 days' written notice of the visit (MHA 1983 Sch 1 Pt 1 Ch 2 paras 12–15; MH(W)A 2013 Sch 2 para 16).

Repair and maintenance

Site owner's obligations

9.35 The site owner is responsible for: (a) repairing the base on which the mobile home is stationed; (b) maintenance of utility supplies and other services; and, (c) maintenance of parts of the site which are not the responsibility of any of the occupiers, eg access ways, boundary fences and trees (MHA 1983 Sch 1 Pt 1 Ch 2 para 21; MH(W)A 2013 Sch 2 para 21). The site owner must not do anything to impede the occupier's ability to keep the mobile home in repair or to keep the pitch clean and tidy (MHA 1983 Sch 1 Pt 1 Ch 2 para 23; MH(W)A 2013 Sch 2 para 21).

Occupier's obligations

9.36 The occupier must keep the mobile home in a sound state of repair and keep both the exterior of the mobile home and the pitch in a clean and tidy condition (MHA 1983 Sch 1 Pt 1 Ch 2 para 21; MH(W)A 2013 Sch 2 para 21).

Re-siting of mobile home

9.37 A site owner can require a mobile home to be moved to another pitch on the same site (MHA 1983 Sch 1 Pt 1 Ch 2 para 10(1)(a); MH(W)A 2013 Sch 2 para 14(1)(a)). Before requiring the occupier to move, the site owner must first obtain an order from the tribunal (see para 9.24) which determines both that it is reasonable for the home to be moved and that the alternative pitch is broadly comparable to the current one.

9.38 The occupier can also be required to move to a comparable pitch in order to allow the site owner to carry out essential repairs or emergency works. Under this ground for re-siting, in England, the site owner does not need to obtain an order from the tribunal before requiring the occupier to move. If the occupier refuses to move, the site owner can apply to the county court for an order forcing him or her to do so. In Wales, the site owner first needs an order from the tribunal determining both that the mobile home needs to be moved and that the alternative pitch is comparable to the current one unless the works are so urgent that it is impracticable to make an application. If the mobile home has to be moved for the site owner to carry out repairs to the base on which it stationed, the occupier or the tribunal, as the case may be, can require the home to be returned to its original pitch on completion of the works. The site owner must pay the occupier's costs of moving the mobile home to and from the other pitch.

Provision of information

Site owner's obligations

9.39 The site owner must, if requested, provide the occupier with details of the size of the pitch and the base on which the mobile home is stationed and provide documentary evidence to support and explain any charges under the agreement, including pitch fees and utility charges (MHA 1983 Sch 1 Pt 1 Ch 2 para 22(a); MH(W)A 2013 Sch 2 para 22(1).

Occupier's obligations

9.40 The occupier must, if requested, provide the site owner with documentary evidence of any costs or expenses in respect of which the occupier seeks reimbursement, eg the cost of re-siting the mobile home (see para 9.38) (MHA 1983 Sch 1 Pt 1 Ch 2 para 21; MH(W)A 2013 Sch 2 para 21).

Site owner's address

9.41 The site owner must by notice provide the occupier and any qualifying residents' association (see para 9.44) with an address in England or Wales at which notices may be served (MHA 1983 Sch 1 Pt 1 Ch 2 para 26(1); MH(W)A 2013 Sch 2 para 24). Pitch fees are not due until such a notice is given. (This provision is modelled on Landlord and Tenant Act (LTA) 1987 s48: see para 1.86).

9.42 Any demand for payment of pitch fees or service charges must contain the name and address of the owner and, if that address if not in England or Wales, an address in England or Wales at which notices can be served; if the site owner does not include this information, the fees or charges demanded are not due (MHA 1983 Sch 1 Pt 1 Ch 2 para 27; MH(W)A 2013 Sch 2 para 25. (This provision is modelled on LTA 1987 s47: see paras 2.33).

Improvements

9.43 Before carrying out any improvements to the site, the site owner must consult the occupiers (MHA 1983 Sch 1 Pt 1 Ch 2 para 22(e); MH(W)A 2013 Sch 2 para 22(1)(e)). The owner must give the occupiers a notice describing the improvements and explaining their benefit to the occupiers and how they may affect the pitch fees on the next review (see para 9.32). The notice must invite responses by a specified date at least 28 days after the date of the notice. If there is a qualifying residents' association (see para 9.44), it must also be consulted.

9.44 An association can only be a qualifying residents' association if all the occupiers of the site are allowed to be members of it and at least half of the occupiers have actually joined it as members (MHA 1983 Sch 1 Pt 1 Ch 2 para 28; MH(W)A 2013 s61). There is detailed provision governing the constitution of such associations.

Termination by the occupier

9.45 An occupier can terminate an agreement by giving four weeks' written notice (MHA 1983 Sch 1 Pt 1 para 3; MH(W)A 2013 Sch 2 para 2).

Termination by the site owner

9.46 There are three grounds available to the site owner for terminating an agreement. In each case, the site owner may terminate the agreement immediately if the ground is made out and the tribunal (see para 9.24) or the county court is satisfied that is reasonable for the agreement to be terminated. Guidance on reasonableness can be obtained from cases under the Housing Acts and the Rent Acts (see paras 2.99–2.107) about when it is reasonable to make a possession order.

Breach of term of the agreement

9.47 The site owner can terminate the agreement if the tribunal (see para 9.24) or county court is satisfied that the occupier has breached one of its terms and, after service of a notice to remedy the breach, the occupier has not complied with it within a reasonable time (MHA 1983 Sch 1 Pt 1 Ch 2 para 4; MH(W)A 2013 Sch 2 para 5). If the breach is so serious that it cannot be remedied, eg where the occupier is guilty of serious anti-social behaviour, the site owner does not need to serve notice and can apply straightaway to the tribunal or county court (*Telchadder v Wickland (Holdings) Ltd*, 2014).

Absence of occupier

9.48 The site owner can terminate the agreement if the tribunal (see para 9.24) or county court is satisfied that the occupier is not occupying the mobile home as his or her only or main residence (see para 9.23) and that it is reasonable to terminate the agreement (MHA 1983 Sch 1 Pt 1 Ch 2 para 5; MH(W)A 2013 Sch 2 para 6).

Detrimental effect on the site

9.49 The third ground for termination is that the tribunal (see para 9.24) or county court has decided that the mobile home is having a detrimental effect on the amenity of the site (MHA 1983 Sch 1 Pt 1 Ch 2 para 5A; MH(W)A 2013 Sch 2 para 7). If the effect can be remedied by the occupier carrying out repairs to the mobile home, the application can be adjourned on condition that he or she do so.

Automatic termination

9.50 In two circumstances an agreement comes to an end automatically:

1) where the site owner has a lease of a site and his or her lease expires; or
2) where planning permission for the site was time-limited and the permission has expired (MHA 1983 Sch 1 Pt 1 Ch 2 para 2; MH(W)A 2013 Sch 2 para 3).

Recovery of pitch fees

9.51 Where pitch fees are paid in advance, if the agreement is automatically terminated (see para 9.50) or terminated by the owner (see para 9.46–9.49), the occupier can recover any fees paid for the period after the termination date (MHA 1983 Sch 1 Pt 1 Ch 2 para 7; MH(W)A 2013 Sch 2 para 8).

Transfer by sale or gift

Sale

9.52 If the agreement was entered into before 26 May 2013 (in England) or 1 October 2014 (in Wales), special rules govern the first sale after that date (MHA 1983 Sch 1 Pt 1 Ch 2 paras 7A and 7B; MH(W)A 2013 Sch 2 paras 9 and 10). The occupier must give the site owner a notice of his or her intention to sell the mobile home, which has to be in a prescribed form (Mobile Homes (Selling and Gifting) (England) Regulations 2013 SI No 981; Mobile Homes (Selling and Gifting) (Wales) Regulations 2014 SI No 1763). The site owner then has 21 days to notify the occupier that an application has been made to the tribunal (see para 9.24) for an order preventing the sale. If the site owner does not give notice, the occupier can sell the mobile home. The tribunal can only stop the sale on certain specified grounds, eg if it decides that the purchaser would breach site rules (see para 9.27) about keeping animals or limiting the permitted number of vehicles permitted.

9.53 In relation to all other sales, the site owner's consent is not required (MHA 1983 Sch 1 Pt 1 Ch 2 para 7A(1); MH(W)A 2013 Sch 2 para 9(1)).

9.54 In relation to any sale, the purchaser must pay the site owner commission at a rate limited by the secretary of state or the Welsh Ministers (currently 10 per cent). The site owner cannot require any other payment from the seller or purchaser (MHA 1983 Sch 1 Pt 1 Ch 2 paras 7A(6) and 7B(9); MH(W)A 2013 Sch 2 paras 9(5) and 10(9)).

Gift to family members

9.55 An occupier can transfer his or her mobile home to a family member as a gift (MHA 1983 Sch 1 Pt 1 Ch 2 paras 8A–8C; MH(W)A 2013 Sch 2 paras 12–13). Family membership is defined in the same way as under the HA 1985 (see paras 1.200–1.202).

9.56 As with transfers by way of sale (see para 9.50), special rules apply to the first transfer of an agreement entered into before 26 May 2013 (in England) or 1 October 2014 (in Wales). The occupier must serve the site owner with notice of his or her intention to give the mobile home to a family member, which must in a prescribed form (Mobile Homes (Selling and Gifting) (England) Regulations 2013 SI No 981; Mobile Homes (Selling and Gifting) (Wales) Regulations 2014 SI No 1763). The notice must be accompanied by evidence of the family relationship. As with sales, the site owner has the right to apply to the tribunal to prevent the transfer and the tribunal can only prevent on the same, limited grounds.

9.57 In relation to other transfers by way of gift, the occupier does not need the site owner's consent but evidence of family relationship must be provided before the transfer. The site owner cannot require any payment for the transfer.

Succession

9.58 On an occupier's death, the deceased's surviving spouse/civil partner or, if there is no surviving spouse/civil partner, a member of the deceased's family can succeed to the agreement (MHA 1983 s3; MH(W)A 2013 s53). Family membership is defined in the same way as under HA 1985 (see paras 1.200–1.202). There can only be a succession if the deceased was occupying the mobile home as his or her only or main residence (see para 9.23) at the time of his or her death and the person claiming succession was residing with (see paras 1.196–1.197) him or her at that time. There is no limit on the number of successions that can take place.

Gypsies and Travellers

Introduction

9.59 Special considerations apply to Gypsies and Travellers, who are defined as:

> ... persons of nomadic habit of life, whatever their race or origin, but does not include members of an organised group of travelling showpeople, or persons engaged in travelling circuses, travelling together as such. (MHA 1983 Sch 1 Pt 1 Ch 1 para 1(4); MH(W)A 2013 s62)

9.60 To fall within the definition, there must be a connection between the person's travelling and the means by which he or she makes a living (*R v South Hams DC ex p Gibb*, 1994). Accordingly, 'New Age' Travellers do not qualify (*R v Dorset CC ex p Rolls*, 1994). Gypsies no longer able to travel because of ill health or age are also outside the definition (*Wrexham CBC v National Assembly for Wales*, 2003).

9.61 Local authorities can provide sites for Gypsies and Travellers (CSCDA 1960 s24; MH(W)A 2013 s55). They do not have the same rights as occupiers of privately owned sites. The extent of their rights depends on whether they have a 'permanent pitch' or a 'transit pitch'. A transit pitch is a pitch on which the occupier is entitled to station a mobile home for a fixed period of up to three months (MHA 1983 s2 and Sch 1 Pt 1 Ch 1 para 1(4); MH(W)A 2013 s55(1)). All other pitches are permanent pitches.

Permanent pitches

9.62 Occupiers of permanent pitches have broadly similar rights to those enjoyed by occupiers of privately owned sites.

Statement of terms

9.63 Occupiers have the same right to be provided with a statement of terms before an agreement is entered into; likewise the tribunal (see para 9.24) can vary the terms of the agreement on application (see paras 9.23–9.24).

Site rules

9.64 The provisions relating to site rules (see para 9.25) do not, however, apply so that occupiers have no right to be consulted before such rules are made (MHA 1983 s2C(1) and Sch 1 Pt 1 Ch 1 para 1(4); MH(W)A 2013 s55).

Implied terms

9.65 Numerous terms are implied into agreements for permanent pitches on local authority sites for Gypsies and Travellers (MHA 1983 Sch 1 Pt 1 Ch 4 paras 14–19 and 24–25; MH(W)A 2013 Sch 2 paras 47–50 and 53–54). In relation to the following, rights and obligations are implied which are directly comparable to those implied into agreements for pitches on privately owned sites.

a) Pitch fees (see paras 9.29–9.33)
b) Quiet enjoyment and rights of entry (see para 9.34)
c) Repair and maintenance (see paras 9.35–9.36)
d) Provision of information (see paras 9.39–9.40)
e) Notice of site owner's address (see paras 9.41–9.42)
f) Improvements (see para 9.43)
g) Qualifying residents' association (see para 9.44)
h) Termination by the occupier (see para 9.45)
i) Termination by the owner (see paras 9.46–9.49)
j) Automatic termination (see para 9.50)
k) Recovery of pitch fees (see para 9.51)

Re-siting of mobile home

9.66 The local authority can require a mobile home to be re-sited MHA 1983 Sch 1 Pt 1 Ch 4 para 8; MH(W)A 2013 Sch 2 para 44). The grounds and procedure for doing so are similar to those available to the owner of a private site (see paras 9.37–9.38), save that the alternative pitch does not have to be on the same mobile home site.

Transfer – England

9.67 In England, no rights to transfer a mobile home are implied by MHA 1983; any transfer rights are governed by the express terms of the agreement.

Transfer – Wales

9.68 In Wales, an occupier has an absolute right to assign his or her agreement to a family member (MH(W)A 2013 Sch 2 para 41(1)(a)). Family membership is defined in the same way as under the HA 1985 (see paras 1.200–1.202).

9.69 With the authority's prior written consent, an occupier can transfer his or her home to another occupier of a permanent pitch on the same site or another site owned by the authority (MH(W)A 2013 Sch 2 para 41(1)(b)). If the authority wishes to withhold consent, it must do so by notice, giving reasons for the refusal, within 28 days of the occupier's request. Consent can be granted on a conditional basis if the occupier is in arrears with pitch fees or has breached another term of the agreement. If the authority fails to serve a notice or consent is refused, the occupier can apply to the tribunal (see para 9.24) for an order approving the transfer. The burden is on the authority to show that refusal is reasonable.

Succession

9.70 Spouses, civil partners and family members of occupiers of permanent pitches have the same rights of succession as relatives of occupiers of privately owned sites (see para 9.58).

Transit pitches

9.71 Occupiers of transit pitches have relatively few rights, reflecting the short-term nature of their agreements.

Statement of terms

9.72 Although an occupier of a transit pitch must be provided in advance with particulars of the agreement, the particulars can be provided at any time before it is entered into (MHA 1983 s1(8A), (8B); MH(W)A 2013 s49(8)).

Site rules

9.73 The provisions relating to site rules (see para 9.27) do not apply so that the occupiers have no right to be consulted before such rules are made (MHA 1983 s2C(1) and Sch 1 Pt 1 Ch 1 para 1(4); MH(W)A 2013 s55).

Implied terms

Termination

9.74 The agreement continues until either the fixed term (see para 9.61) expires or it is determined by one of the parties (MHA 1983 Sch 1 Pt 1 Ch 3 para 1; MH(W)A 2013 Sch 2 para 26). The occupier can terminate the agreement by giving such notice as is required by the agreement (MHA 1983 Sch 1 Pt 1 Ch 3 para 2; MH(W)A 2013 Sch 2 para 27). The authority can end the agreement by giving four weeks' written notice (MHA 1983 Sch 1 Pt 1 Ch 3 para 4(a); MH(W)A 2013 Sch 2 para 29(a)). If the occupier breaches a term of the agreement, the authority can serve a notice requiring remedy of the breach within a reasonable time; if it is not remedied, the authority can terminate the agreement immediately if it considers it reasonable to do so (MHA 1983 Sch 1 Pt 1 Ch 3 para 4(b); MH(W)A Sch 2 para 29(b)).

Other terms

9.75 Certain other terms are implied into any agreement for a transit pitch (MHA 1983 s2 and Sch 1 Pt 1 para 1(2) and Sch 1 Pt 2 Ch 3; MH(W)A 2013 s50(1) and Sch 2 para 1(2) and Ch 3). In relation to the following, rights and obligations are implied which are directly comparable to those implied into agreements for pitches on privately owned sites.

i) Quiet enjoyment and rights of entry (see para 9.34).
ii) Automatic termination (see para 9.50).
iii) Recovery of pitch fees (see para 9.51).
iv) Notice of site owner's address (see paras 9.41–9.42).

Succession

9.76 Spouses, civil partners and family members of occupiers of transit pitches have the same rights of succession as are available to relatives of occupiers of privately owned sites (see para 9.58).

Houseboats

9.77 Unless it is accepted that a houseboat may fall within the statutory definition of mobile home (see para 9.2), which is considered arguable (see para 9.3), occupiers of houseboats do not have security of tenure and their rights are therefore governed by the terms of their agreement with the owner of the mooring site. Where the mooring to which the houseboat is attached is owned by a public authority, if the owner requires the occupier to remove the houseboat, the occupier may be able to rely on the Human Rights Act (HRA) 1998 (see para 9.82).

9.78 If a houseboat is immobile and cannot be removed from the land to which it is attached without demolishing it, the houseboat can become a dwelling-house, to which HA 1985 (see paras 1.160–1.209), or HA 1988 (see paras 1.220–1.295) or RA 1977 (see paras 1.268–1.293) would apply (*Chelsea Yacht & Boat Co Ltd v Pope*, 2000), depending on the identity of the owner of the mooring. Whether the houseboat has become a dwelling-house is determined by looking at the position at the beginning of the mooring agreement, *ie* if the only reason why the houseboat cannot be moved is that it has fallen into disrepair it will not be a dwelling-house (*Tristmire Ltd v Mew*, 2011).

9.79 Spouses and civil partners of occupiers of houseboats may have 'home rights' (see paras 7.9–7.14) under FLA 1996 and a houseboat may be subject to an occupation order (see paras 7.15–7.27) under FLA 1996 in favour of a spouse, civil partner or other associated person (see para 7.16).

Human rights

9.80 HRA 1998 has had a significant impact on the rights of Gypsies and Travellers living on local authority sites (see paras 9.59–9.76). Originally, the county court's power under CSA 1968 to suspend a possession order against an occupier (see para 9.11) did not apply to orders made against Gypsies and Travellers. In *Connors v UK*, 2004, a family was evicted from a local authority site following a court order. The European Court of Human Rights held that there had been a breach of the family's right to respect for the home under Article 8 of the European Convention on Human Rights (ECHR), because the family had no opportunity to challenge the proportionality of the eviction. As a consequence, HA 2004 amended CSA 1968 to extend the county court's power to suspend possession orders in proceedings brought by local authorities against Gypsies and Travellers.

9.81 At that time, however, Gypsies and Travellers did not have any of the rights given to occupiers of mobile homes under MHA 1983 (see paras 9.23–9.58). The concern remained that this might breach their rights under Article 8 or be unlawful discrimination under Article 14. Amendments were therefore made to MHA 1983 by the Housing and Regeneration Act 2008 so that occupiers of permanent pitches now have similar rights to occupiers of privately owned sites (see paras 9.59–9.74). Indeed, had those amendments not already been prepared, the House of Lords would have held that the exclusion of Gypsies and Travellers from MHA 1983 was incompatible with Article 8 (*Doherty v Birmingham City Council*, 2008).

9.82 As noted above (see para 9.77), an occupier of a houseboat has no security of tenure. An occupier of houseboat who is required by a public authority (see paras 1.321–1.322) to remove his or her houseboat can argue that the removal would be breach his or her right to respect for the home under Article 8 (*Jones v Canal & River Trust*, 2017).

CHAPTER 10

Homelessness and allocations

continued

Introduction

10.1 Since 1977, local authorities have been under a duty to secure that accommodation is made available for many of those who are homeless. The provisions, first contained in the Housing (Homeless Persons) Act 1977, were later consolidated into Part 3 of the Housing Act (HA) 1985. Major changes were made by HA 1996 Pt 7 and further amendments by the Homelessness Act 2002 and the Housing and Regeneration Act (H&RA) 2008. HA 1996 Pt 7 used to apply in Wales but, from 27 April 2015, homelessness duties of authorities in Wales have been governed by Part 2 of the Housing (Wales) Act (H(W)A) 2014. Many features of the two Acts are similar. In Wales, H(W)A 2014 contains provisions imposing duties on authorities to prevent homelessness; once the Homelessness Reduction Act 2017 is in force, HA 1996 will be amended to contain similar duties in England: references in this chapter to 'new HA' sections are to provisions of HA 1996 as they are to be amended by the Homelessness Reduction Act 2017.

10.2 This chapter starts by considering the broader duties on local authorities to establish strategies for dealing with homelessness, including co-operation between authorities and other organisations, before turning to the specific duties to homeless persons currently contained in HA 1996 Pt 7 and H(W)A 2014. To understand the specific duties, it is first necessary to explain certain key concepts, which determine what duty applies in a given case. It is then necessary to consider how local authorities' decisions on homelessness applications may be challenged.

10.3 Although HA 1996 and the H(W)A 2014 are the primary sources of duties towards the homeless, other provisions are also relevant for children and vulnerable adults, such as the Children Act (CA) 1989, the Care Act 2014, the Social Services and Well-being (Wales) Act (SSWB(W)A) 2014, the Local Government Act (LGA) 2000 and the Localism Act (LA) 2011 which are also considered in this chapter. Finally, this chapter considers HA 1996 Pt 6 which governs the allocation of local authority housing in both England and Wales.

Homelessness: general provisions

Local authorities

10.4 Both Acts refer (HA 1996 s217; H(W)A 2014 s99) to three classes of authority: local housing authorities, relevant authorities and social services authorities. In a two-tier area of local government, 'local housing authority' means the district council while 'social service authority' means the county council; a unitary authority (including, in Wales, the county or county borough council), a London Borough Council and the Common Council of the City of London, will all be both the local housing and the social service authority (HA 1985 s1). 'Relevant authority' means both types of authority (HA 1996 s217; H(W)A 2014 s80).

10.5 Most of the functions of a local housing authority may, however, be contracted out to an external body: see Local Authorities (Contracting Out of Allocation of Housing and Homelessness Functions) Order 1996 SI No 3205. These are any functions under Parts 6 and 7 except those specified, the effect of which is to prevent the authority contracting out key functions such as deciding who qualifies for an allocation, adopting or altering an allocation scheme, providing homelessness advisory services and co-operation between authorities and other bodies.

Strategic duties and powers

10.6 Both the Homelessness Act 2002 and H(W)A 2014 impose a duty on local housing authorities to carry out a homelessness review (see para 10.7) in their areas and formulate and publish a homelessness strategy (see para 10.10) based on the results of that review (Homelessness Act 2002 s1(1)). The first strategy had to be published within 12 months of section 1 coming into force (31 July 2003 in England; 30 September 2003 in Wales), and thereafter a new one must be published at least every five years (Homelessness Act 2002 s1(3), (4); H(W)A 2014 s50(2)).

10.7 **Review.** For these purposes a homelessness review means a review of the following (Homelessness Act 2002 s2(1), (2); H(W)A 2014 s51(1)).

1) The level (and likely future levels) of homelessness in the authority's area.
2) The activities which are carried out in the area to: prevent homelessness; secure that accommodation is or will be available for

people in the area who may become homeless; and, provide support for people in the area who are or may become homeless or who have been homeless and support to prevent it from happening again.

3) The resources available to the authority, the social services authority, other public authorities, voluntary organisations and other persons for such activities.

10.8 In England, where different from the housing authority, the social services authority (see para 10.4) must assist in the review and in formulation of the strategy (Homelessness Act 2002 s1(2)). The strategy must be taken into account by both authorities in the exercise of their functions (Homelessness Act 2002 s1(5), (6)).

10.9 On completion of the review, the authority must arrange for the results to be available for inspection at its principal office, at all reasonable hours, without charge, and provide (on payment of a reasonable charge, if required) a copy of the results (Homelessness Act 2002 s2(3); H(W)A 2014 s51(2)). In Wales, the copy of the results must be published on the authority's website.

10.10 **Strategy.** A homelessness strategy means one formulated for: preventing homelessness in the authority's area; securing that sufficient accommodation is and will be available for people in the area who are or may become homeless; and, securing that there is satisfactory provision of support for people in the area who are or who may become homeless or who have become homeless and need support to prevent them becoming homeless again (Homelessness Act 2002 s3(1); H(W)A 2014 s52(1)).

10.11 The strategy may include specific objectives to be pursued as well as specific action planned to be taken in the course of the exercise of the authority's housing functions and also of the functions of the social services authority for the district (Homelessness Act 2002 s3(2); H(W)A 2014 s52(2)). The strategy may also include specific action which the authority expects to be taken by any other public authority or by any voluntary organisation or other person who can contribute to the objectives of the strategy, although such action can only be included with the approval of the body or person concerned (Homelessness Act 2002 s3(3), (4); H(W)A 2014 s52(3), (4)). The authority must consider how far the objectives of the strategy can be met by joint action between its housing and social services departments, the social service authority or any other body or persons (Homelessness Act 2002 s3(5); H(W)A 2014 s52(5)).

10.12 In Wales, the strategy must include general and specific actions planned by the authority, including actions expected to be taken by other public authorities and voluntary organisations, in relation to those who may be in particular need of support if they are or may become homeless, including prison-leavers, young people leaving care or youth detention centres, people leaving the armed forces, people leaving hospital after receiving treatment for mental disorder and people receiving community mental health services (H(W)A 2014 s52(6)).

10.13 The strategy must be kept under review and may be modified (Homelessness Act 2002 s3(6); H(W)A 2014 s52(6), (7)). Before adopting or modifying the strategy, the authority must consult such public or local authorities, voluntary organisations or other persons as they consider appropriate (Homelessness Act 2002 s3(8); H(W)A 2014 s52(8)). Any modification must be published. A copy of the strategy must be available at the authority's principal office for inspection at all reasonable hours, free of charge, and provided to members of the public on request, on payment (if required) of a reasonable charge (Homelessness Act 2002 s3(9); H(W)A 2014 s52(9)).

Co-operation between authorities

10.14 In England, a local housing authority (see para 10.4) may, in the discharge of its functions under HA 1996 Pt 7 or H(W)A 2014 Pt 2, request assistance from another local housing authority, a new town corporation, a PRP (private registered provider of social housing) or RSL (registered social landlord (HA 1996 s213(1)(a), (2); H(W)A 2014 s95(2), (5)). An English authority may also request assistance in relation to Scotland from a Scottish local authority, development corporation, registered housing association or Scottish Homes (HA 1996 s213(1)(a), (2)). It may also ask a social services authority (in England, Wales or Scotland) (see para 10.4) to exercise any of its functions on its behalf (HA 1996 s213(1)(b)). The other authority or body must co-operate with the housing authority, by rendering such assistance as is reasonable in the circumstances (HA 1996 s213(1)).

10.15 In Wales, where all authorities are unitary and therefore have both housing and social services functions, the corresponding provisions require each authority to make arrangements to promote co-operation between those of its officers who exercise its social services functions and those who exercise its functions as the local housing authority, with a view to achieving the following: prevention of homelessness, suitable accommodation available for people who are or may become homeless, satisfactory support for people who are or may become homeless, and effective discharge of its functions under H(W)A 2014 Pt 2 (H(W)A 2014 s95(3)).

10.16 In addition, a local authority in Wales may request the co-operation of the following bodies (whether in Wales or England): a local housing authority, a social services authority, an RSL or a PRP (H(W)A 2014 s95(5)). The body is bound to comply with the request unless it considers that doing so would be incompatible with its own duties, or would have an adverse effect on its functions. If the authority seeks information from the body, it must likewise comply unless it considers that doing so would be incompatible with its own duties or would otherwise have an adverse effect on the exercise of the person's functions. In either case, a body which decides not to comply with the request must give the local housing authority which made the request written reasons for its decision.

10.17 Although an authority may request assistance under HA 1996 s213, or H(W)A 2014 s95, it may not delegate its substantive duty to inquire under HA 1996 s184, or to carry out an assessment under H(W)A 2014 s62, (see paras 10.78–10.85) except as expressly permitted (under the regulations permitting contracting out: see para 10.5): *R v West Dorset DC ex p Gerrard*, 1994. So long as the key decision-making function is preserved by the authority, however, inquiries may be carried out by another body on its behalf without needing to contract the function out: *R v Hertsmere BC ex p Woolgar*, 1995.

Advice, information and voluntary organisations

10.18 In England, provision is made for grants, loans, premises or goods in kind to voluntary organisations concerned with the homeless (HA 1996 s180). The assistance may be given on terms and subject to conditions and undertakings as to the use of the assistance (HA 1996 s181). In addition, English authorities have an obligation to ensure that advice and assistance about homelessness and its prevention are available to any person in their areas, free of charge (HA 1996 s179(1)). This duty can be discharged by providing assistance (grant or loan, use of premises, furniture or other goods, or making staff available) through another person (not necessarily a voluntary organisation, although on the same terms and conditions as would apply to a voluntary organisation): (HA 1996 ss179(2), (3) and 181(1)).

10.19 In England and Wales, an authority must ensure that there is a service available providing free information and advice about homelessness and its prevention (HA 1996 s179(1); H(W)A 2014 s60). In

Wales, and in England once amendments to HA 1996 s179 by the Homelessness Reduction Act 2017 are in force, the authority must work with other public authorities and voluntary organisations to ensure that the service is designed to meet the needs of groups at particular risk of homelessness, including people leaving prison, young people leaving care or youth detention centres, people leaving the armed forces and people receiving treatment for mental health and, in England, victims of domestic violence (see paras 10.34–10.36).

Code of guidance

10.20 In the exercise of their homelessness functions, authorities are bound to have regard to such guidance as may from time to time be given by the secretary of state or the Welsh Ministers (HA 1996 s182; H(W)A 2014 s98). In England, the current code is the *Homelessness Code of Guidance for Local Authorities*, July 2006, as supplemented by *Supplementary Guidance on Intentional Homelessness* (August 2010); *Supplementary guidance on the homelessness changes in the Localism Act 2011 and on the Homelessness (Suitability of Accommodation) (England) Order 2012* (November 2012); and *Supplementary guidance on domestic abuse and homelessness* (November 2014). In Wales, see *Code of Guidance for Local Authorities on Allocation on Accommodation and Homelessness*, (March 2016). Authorities are not bound to comply with its contents in the way that they are bound to comply with legislation (*De Falco v Crawley BC*, 1979); guidance is, rather, something they are bound to take into account (see para 8.28(1)). Failure to comply with the guidance is not unlawful; the issue is whether the authority acted reasonably having had regard to it (*R v Brent LBC ex p Macwan*, 1994).

Code of practice

10.21 In England, once amendments to HA 1996 by the Homelessness Reduction Act 2017 are in force, the Secretary of State will also have power to issue Codes of Practice relating to homelessness or homelessness prevention to local housing authorities, in particular concerning the exercise by a local housing authority of functions under Part 7, staff training relating to the exercise of those functions and monitoring by the authority of the exercise of those functions (HA 1996 s214A(1)). A local housing authority must have regard to a Code of Practice when carrying out these functions: again, this will not bind an authority but it must take it into account (see para 8.28(1)).

Discrimination

10.22 **Equality Act (EqA) 2010.** In exercising their functions, including their functions under HA 1996 Pt 7 and H(W)A 2014 Pt 2 (*Hotak v Southwark LBC*, 2015), local authorities are under a duty to eliminate discrimination against persons on the grounds of race, gender, disability and other specified characteristics (EqA 2010 s149(1); paras 4.108–4.109). They must advance equality of opportunity for persons who may be discriminated against on one of those grounds (s149(2)). Authorities have to be aware of these duties in formulating their homelessness strategy and exercising their functions under Part 7, eg by ensuring that suitable interpretation facilities are available for members of minority ethnic groups. There is also a specific duty to take steps to take account of the needs of disabled persons (s149(4)).

Homelessness: duties under Housing Act 1996 Part 7

Definitions

10.23 The key concepts in HA 1996 and H(W)A 2014 which determine what duty may be owed to a homeless person are:

i) eligibility for assistance;
ii) homelessness;
iii) priority need;
iv) intentional homelessness; and,
v) local connection.

Eligibility for assistance

Persons from abroad

10.24 'Persons from abroad' are ineligible for assistance if they are subject to immigration control under the Asylum and Immigration Act 1996, unless requalified by regulations (HA 1996 s185(1), (2); H(W)A 2014 s61, Sch 2 para 1). In general terms, a person is subject to immigration control if he or she requires a visa to come to the UK. A visa is required by anyone who is not a national of the European Economic Area ('EEA') which comprises all the member states of the European Union, plus Iceland, Norway, Liechtenstein and Switzerland. The regulations govern requalification based on issues of immigration status. Examples of those who are subject to immigration control but who are nevertheless eligible for assistance include refugees and those who have been granted humanitarian protection: Allocation of Housing and Homelessness (Eligibility) (England) Regulations 2006 SI No 1294 reg 5 or Allocation of Housing and Homelessness (Eligibility) (Wales) Regulations 2014 SI No 2603 reg 5.

10.25 In addition, the regulations provide that certain persons from abroad who are not subject to immigration control are ineligible for assistance: SI 2006 No 1294 reg 6 or SI 2014 No 2603 reg 6. The primary effect of the provisions is to exclude from assistance EEA nationals unless they are exercising their rights under the Immigration (European Economic Area) Regulations 2006 SI No 1003, eg to work in the UK.

Ineligible household members

10.26 It is also necessary for the authority to consider the immigration status of the members of the applicant's household, as this may affect whether an applicant is homeless (see para 10.27), whether he or she has a priority need (see para 10.36) and how the authority may discharge its duty to the applicant (see para 10.121(9)). If the applicant is subject to immigration control but is eligible because he or she has been given leave to remain in the United Kingdom, eg a refugee, household members are not to be taken into account (HA 1996 s184(4), (5); H(W)A 2014 Sch 2 para 2).

10.27 If, however, the applicant is either not subject to immigration control or is an EEA national, ineligible household members are to be taken into account (HA 1996 s185(4), (5); H(W)A 2014 Sch 2 para 2). If they are themselves 'restricted persons,' ie a person who is ineligible in his or her own right and subject to immigration control who either does not have leave to enter or remain in the United Kingdom or who has such leave but subject to a condition of no recourse to public funds (HA 1996 s184(7); H(W)A 2014 Sch 2 para 2), and the authority would not otherwise be satisfied that the applicant was homeless (see para 10.27) or had a priority need (see para 10.36), the application is a 'restricted case' (HA 1996 s193(3B); H(W)A 2014 Sch 2 para 2). There are discrete provisions governing how an authority may discharge its duty in a restricted case (see para 10.121(9)).

Information

10.28 In order to reach a decision on eligibility, a local housing authority may seek such information as is required from the secretary of state, who is bound to provide it (and – whether or not the original request for information was in writing – to provide it in writing if the authority in writing asks for it so to be provided) (HA 1996 s187(1) and (2); H(W)A 2014 Sch 2 para 3). The secretary of state is also under a duty to notify the authority in writing if it subsequently appears that any application, decision or other change of circumstance has affected the status of a person about whom information had previously been provided (HA 1996 s187(3); H(W)A 2014 Sch 2 para 3).

Asylum-seekers

10.29 Since 3 April 2000, all new asylum-seekers have been ineligible for assistance under the homelessness provisions. Instead, they may obtain assistance from Migrant Help, an agency run by the Home Office, under the Immigration and Asylum Act (IAA) 1999 Pt 6. No support can be provided if the claim for asylum was not made as soon as reasonably practicable after the asylum-seeker arrived in the UK, unless it is necessary to provide assistance in order to prevent a breach of a person's rights under the European Convention on Human Rights (ECHR), eg the prohibition on degrading treatment in Article 3 (Nationality, Immigration and Asylum Act (NIAA) 2002 s55; *R (Limbuela) v Secretary of State for the Home Department*, 2004). Assistance under IAA 1999 Pt 6, can only be provided to adult asylum-seekers. If an asylum-seeker is under 18, however, he or she will usually be entitled to assistance from a local authority as a child in need (see para 10.176). The age of an asylum-seeker is a difficult decision, and the authority must take care to ensure that it adopts a fair procedure when interviewing an applicant (*R (SO) v Barking and Dagenham LBC*, 2010). As an exception to the general rule that a court cannot substitute its own view of the facts for that of the authority (see para 8.24), a person's age is for the court to decide (*R (A) v Croydon LBC*, 2009).

Homelessness

10.30 A person is homeless for the purposes of Part 7 if he or she has no accommodation in the UK or elsewhere. A person is deemed to lack accommodation if there is no accommodation which he or she:

1) is entitled to occupy by virtue of an interest in it, eg ownership (see paras 1.7–1.16) or tenancy (see paras 1.17–1.55); or
2) is entitled to occupy under a court order, eg in the course of domestic proceedings (see chapter 7); or
3) has an express or implied licence to occupy (see paras 1.114–1.130), eg family members (*Hemans v Windsor and Maidenhead RBC*, 2011) or service occupants; or

4) is occupying as a residence by virtue of any enactment or rule of law giving him or her the right to remain in occupation or restricting the right of any other person to recover possession of it, eg Protection from Eviction Act (PEA) 1977 (see para 5.5) (HA 1996 s175(1); H(W)A 2014 s55(1)).

Accommodation

10.31 Under the equivalent provisions of HA 1985, it was held that the only gloss which can be put on the word 'accommodation' is that which the statute imports, ie availability (see para 10.32) and reasonableness to continue to occupy (see paras 10.33–10.36). Other than that, it simply means 'a place which can fairly be described as accommodation', per Lord Hoffman in *R v Brent LBC ex p Awua*, 1995. *Note.* Although a person may not be homeless because of this low-level test, he or she may still be threatened with homelessness: see para 10.38. In *R v Waveney DC ex p Bowers*, 1982 (approved in *Awua*), a man who usually slept in a night shelter on a day-to-day basis but who could be turned away if the shelter was full at the time of his arrival was homeless.

Available accommodation

10.32 Accommodation is only available for an applicant's occupation if it is available for him or her, together with any other person who normally resides with the applicant as a member of his or her family, and any other person who might reasonably be expected to reside with the applicant (HA 1996 s176; H(W)A 2014 s56). This does not necessarily mean a single unit of accommodation for the whole household: two units of accommodation can suffice if they are located near enough that the household can live together in practical terms (*Sharif v Camden LBC*, 2013). Household members who are ineligible for assistance are not to be taken into account if the applicant is only eligible for assistance because he or she has been granted leave to remain in the United Kingdom, eg a refugee (see para 10.24). Accessibility to accommodation, eg whether the applicant can travel to it, is a relevant factor in determining whether it is available (*Nipa Begum v Tower Hamlets LBC*, 1999).

Accommodation reasonable to continue to occupy

10.33 Accommodation is disregarded if it is not accommodation which it would be reasonable to continue to occupy (HA 1996 s175(3): H(W)A 2014 s55(3)), eg if it is in such bad condition that no one could be expected to stay in it. When deciding whether or not it would be reasonable for a person to remain in occupation, an authority to which an application has been made can take into account the general housing circumstances prevailing in its area (HA 1996 s177(2); H(W)A 2014 s57(3)), ie whether others are living in accommodation just as bad. Before accepting an application, an authority can ask an applicant questions to clarify whether his or her current home is in such a condition that it may not be reasonable to continue to occupy it, ie not every complaint about the condition of a property will lead an authority to conclude that an applicant may be homeless (*R (Edwards) v Birmingham City Council*, 2016). The meaning of the term 'reasonable to continue to occupy' is also considered below, in relation to intentional homelessness (see paras 10.66–10.68).

10.34 The fact that it may be reasonable for a person to remain in accommodation for a little while longer does not prevent him or her from being homeless; the question is whether it is reasonable for the applicant to continue to occupy it for so long as he or she would have to do so until the authority takes action in respect of the homelessness (*Ali v Birmingham City Council; Moran v Manchester City Council*, 2009). Accordingly, in most cases, a woman who has left her home because of domestic violence remains homeless even if she has found temporary accommodation in a woman's refuge (*Moran*). See also *R v Ealing LBC ex p Sidhu*, 1982. *Note*. The House of Lords in *Ali* and *Moran* declined to comment on whether a prison cell or a hospital ward could amount to accommodation.

10.35 It is also not reasonable to continue to occupy accommodation if it is probable that to do so will lead to 'violence' (in England) or 'abuse' (in Wales), whether domestic or otherwise, against the applicant, or against someone who normally resides with the applicant as a member of his or her family, or against anyone else who might reasonably be expected to reside with him or her (HA 1996 s177(1); H(W)A 2014 s57(1)). For these purposes the terms violence and abuse are interchangeable as the courts have held that violence includes not only physical violence but any threatening or intimidating behaviour or other form of abuse which, directly or indirectly, may give rise to the risk of harm and the definition of abuse reflects this case law (see *Yemshaw v Hounslow LBC*, 2011; *Hussain v Waltham Forest LBC*, 2015; H(W)A 2014 s58(1)). Threats of such behaviour which are likely to be carried out fall within the provision (HA 1996 s177(1A); H(W)A 2014 s58(1)). In deciding whether it is reasonable for an applicant to continue to occupy under section 177(1), the only question the authority may ask is whether it is probable that continued occupation of the accommodation will lead to violence against that person; that is purely a question of fact devoid of value judgments about what an applicant should or should not do, eg whether he or she should take out an injunction against the perpetrator: *Bond v Leicester City Council*, 2001.

10.36 Violence or abuse is only domestic if it is from a person who is associated with the victim (HA 1996 s177(1A); H(W)A 2014 s58(1)). Persons are associated if they are or were: married to each other; engaged to be married to each other; in a civil partnership; in an agreement to enter into a civil partnership; cohabitants; persons with joint parental responsibility for child; or relatives. Relatives are parents, grandparents, children, grandchildren, siblings, uncles, aunts, nephews and nieces (including step-relations and half-relations) (HA 1996 s178; H(W)A 2014 s58). In Wales, the definition of associated persons also includes two people who 'have or have had an intimate personal relationship with each other which is or was of significant duration' (H(W)A 2014 s58(2)(h)).

Additional categories of homelessness

10.37 In addition, a person will be homeless even if he or she has accommodation which he or she is entitled to occupy, which is available for occupation and which it is reasonable to continue to occupy, but he or she cannot secure entry to it, eg a victim of illegal eviction (HA 1996 s175(2)(a); H(W)A 2014 s55(2)). Likewise, a person is homeless if he or she is entitled to occupy accommodation which consists of a moveable structure, vehicle or vessel, designed or adapted for living in, ie a houseboat or caravan (see chapter 9), and there is no place where he or she is entitled or permitted both to place it and reside in it (HA 1996 s175(2)(b); H(W)A 2014 s55(2)).

Threatened with homelessness

10.38 A person is threatened with homelessness if it is likely that he or she will become homeless within 28 days (England) or within 56 days (Wales) (HA 1996 s175(4); H(W)A 2014 s55(4)). The the Homelessness Reduction Act 2017 will extend the period in England to 56 days in line with Wales. In addition, in England, a person will be threatened with homelessness if he or she is an assured shorthold tenant (see paras 1.246–1.251) who has been given a valid notice under HA 1988 s21 (see paras 2.195–2.205) which will expire within the next 56 days (new HA 1996 s175(5)).

Priority need

10.39 A person has a priority need for accommodation if he or she falls into one of the following categories (HA 1996 s189; H(W)A 2014 s70).

1) **Dependent children.** The applicant has dependent children who are residing with him or her, or who might reasonably be expected to reside with him or her.
2) **Vulnerability.** The applicant, or anyone who resides or might reasonably be expected to reside with him or her, is vulnerable as a result of old age, mental illness or handicap or physical disability or other special reason.
3) **Pregnant women.** She is a pregnant woman, or the applicant resides or might reasonably be expected to reside with a pregnant woman.
4) **Emergency.** The applicant is homeless or threatened with homelessness as a result of an emergency such as flood, fire or other disaster.

Dependent children

10.40 Dependent children are usually treated as those still in full-time education or training, or otherwise up to the age of 16: *R v Kensington and Chelsea RLBC ex p Amarfio*, 1995. Even where a 16- or 17-year-old is financially independent, however, it is possible for him or her to be dependent in other ways (*Amarfio*). The concept of a dependent child connotes a parent/child or analogous relationship so that an applicant with a 17-year-old wife could not claim to be in priority need on the basis of her dependency on him (*Hackney LBC v Ekinci*, 2001). Likewise, an 18-year-old applicant, whose 17-year-old sibling was dependent on him, was held not to be in priority need (*R (Lusamba) v Islington LBC*, 2008). A dependent child is not entitled to apply under the Act in his or her own right, and will not qualify as vulnerable (see paras 10.42–10.46) simply because of youth or any disability. Dependent children are expected to be provided for by those on whom they are dependent (*R v Oldham LBC ex p G*, 1993).

10.41 The issue of residence is one of fact: are dependent children residing, or are there dependent children who ought reasonably to be expected to reside, with the applicant? In *Holmes-Moorhouse v Richmond upon Thames LBC*, 2009, the separated parents of four children agreed to a shared residence order under which the three youngest children would spend alternate weeks and part of each school holiday with their father. The father applied to the authority relying on the shared residence order to show that he had a priority need. The House of Lords held that whether children can be reasonably expected to reside with an applicant is a matter for the authority and is not determined by the terms of a residence order, although the authority must take such an order into account when making its decision. An authority must decide whether it is reasonably to be expected that children who already have a home with their mother should be able also to reside with their father. That question is to be addressed in the context of a scheme for housing the homeless, ie in the context of allocation of a scarce resource. Only in exceptional circumstances, therefore, will it be reasonable to expect a child who has a home with one parent to be provided with another under Part 7 or Part 2 so that the child can live with both of them.

Vulnerability: England

10.42 There is no definition of vulnerability in HA 1996 Pt 7. In *Hotak v Southwark LBC*, 2015, the Supreme Court held that a person is vulnerable if he or she is significantly more at risk of harm without accommodation that an ordinary person would be. For these purposes, an ordinary person is 'an ordinary person who is homeless', not 'an ordinary homeless person'. The significance of this distinction is that, prior to *Hotak*, some authorities had been comparing applicants' circumstances only with those of other homeless people: thus, in *Ajilore v Hackney LBC*, 2014, the authority decided that the applicant's depression and suicidal ideation did not make him vulnerable because statistics showed that significant numbers of homeless people had similar conditions; this approach is no longer correct.

10.43 An applicant who would otherwise be vulnerable might not be so if, when homeless, he or she would be provided with support and care by a third party, eg a family member, although even if substantial support is provided it does not necessarily follow that an applicant is not vulnerable (*Hotak*).

10.44 The Supreme Court also held in *Hotak* that, in deciding whether a person is vulnerable, an authority must have its duty to disabled persons under EqA 2010 s149, in mind (see para 10.22). The authority should focus on: whether the applicant is under a disability; the extent of such disability; the likely effect of the disability when taken together with any other features on the applicant, if and when homeless; and, whether the applicant is vulnerable as a result.

Vulnerability: Wales

10.45 In Wales, a person is vulnerable if:

> ... having regard to all the circumstances of the person's case-
> (a) the person would be less able to fend for himself or herself (as a result of that reason) if the person were to become street homeless than would an ordinary homeless person who becomes street homeless, and
> (b) this would lead to the person suffering more harm than would be suffered by the ordinary homeless person ... (H(W)A 2014 s71(1)).

10.46 An applicant is 'street homeless' if he or she has no accommodation available for occupation which he or she is entitled to occupy by virtue of an interest in it or a licence to occupy it or under any statutory right or rule of law (H(W)A 2014 s71(2) (see para 10.30).

Medical advice

10.47 An authority is entitled to obtain its own medical advice as to an applicant's medical condition (*Hall v Wandsworth LBC*, 2004). If the medical adviser does not him- or herself examine the applicant, his or her advice cannot ordinarily constitute expert evidence of the applicant's condition and the advice needs to take the lack of examination into account (*Shala v Birmingham City Council*, 2007). If the medical adviser is less qualified than the applicant's expert, eg where the applicant has obtained a report from a consultant psychiatrist, the authority must not fall into the mistake of thinking that it is comparing like with like (*Shala*). If the authority's advice raises new issues or calls the applicant's medical evidence into question, the applicant should be allowed an opportunity to comment on it. If it is merely intended to assist the authority in assessing the applicant's medical evidence, however, the authority does not have to disclose its advice before making a decision on the application (*Hall*). Representations from the applicant's medical adviser in response to the authority's advice need not be considered by the authority's medical adviser if they do not significantly add to the earlier advice (*Simms v Islington LBC*, 2008). An authority must reach its own decision and must not merely 'rubber-stamp' a medical opinion on the applicant's medical condition, unless that condition is decisive of the question (vulnerability) that it is considering, eg where the existence of a medical condition is the only relevant issue (*R v Lambeth LBC ex p Carroll*, 1987 and *R v Wandsworth LBC ex p Banbury*, 1986).

Other special reason

10.48 In *R v Kensington and Chelsea RLBC ex p Kihara*, 1996, the Court of Appeal rejected an argument that 'other special reason' was limited to the applicant's mental or physical characteristics. The category is free-standing, unrestricted by any notion of physical or mental weakness other than that which is inherent in the word 'vulnerable'. The word 'special' imports a requirement that the housing difficulties faced by an applicant are of an unusual degree of gravity, enough to differentiate the applicant from other homeless persons; it does not include financial impecuniosity by itself: an absence of means does not mark out one case from the generality of cases to a sufficient degree to render it 'special'.

Emergency

10.49 A person who has been unlawfully evicted from his or her home is not in priority need due to an emergency. If not flood or fire, the emergency must be of a similar nature which – while not needing to be a natural disaster – must encompass some physical damage to the home: *R v Bristol City Council ex p Bradic*, 1995 (see also *Noble v South Herefordshire DC*, 1983).

Further classes

10.50 The Secretary of State may specify further classes of person as having a priority need for accommodation, or may amend or repeal any of the present classes (HA 1996 s189(2)). In England, additional classes have been specified in the Homelessness (Priority Need for Accommodation) (England) Order 2002 SI No 2051. In Wales, a number of similar classes are included in the definition of priority need in H(W)A 2014 s70.

1) In England, all 16- and 17-year-olds, provided they are not a relevant child (as defined by CA 1989 s23A) or owed a duty under CA 1989 s20 or SSWB(W)A 2014 s76 (see para 10.157). In Wales, any 16- or 17-year-old child, or someone who is reasonably expected to reside with him or her.
2) In England, any person who is aged 18 to 20 who at any time while 16 or 17 was, but is no longer, looked after, accommodated or fostered but not a relevant student (as defined by CA 1989 s24B(3)). In Wales, any person who is aged 18 to 20 who was looked after, accommodated or fostered at any time while under the age of 18, or someone who is reasonably expected to reside with him or her.

3) In England, those aged 21 or over who are vulnerable because they have previously been looked after, accommodated or fostered. There is no equivalent in Wales.
4) In England, those who are vulnerable as a result of service in Her Majesty's regular armed forces. In Wales, any member of the regular armed forces have a priority need, ie there is no need for him or her to be vulnerable, or someone who is reasonably expected to reside with him or her.
5) In both England and Wales, those who are vulnerable as a result of having served a custodial sentence, having been committed for contempt of court or having been remanded in custody.
6) In England, those who are vulnerable because they have had to cease to occupy accommodation because of violence or threats of violence which are likely to be carried out. In Wales, a person who is homeless as a result of being subject to domestic abuse or someone who is reasonably expected to reside with him or her.
7) In Wales, any person aged between 18 and 21 who requires help in obtaining or retaining accommodation and who is at particular risk of sexual or financial exploitation, or someone who is reasonably expected to reside with him or her.

Ineligible household members

10.51 Household members who are ineligible for assistance (see paras 10.26–10.27) are not to be taken into account in determining priority need if the applicant him- or herself is only eligible for assistance because he or she has been granted leave to remain in the United Kingdom, eg because he or she is a refugee (see para 10.24) (HA 1996 s185(4), (5); H(W)A 2014 Sch 2 para 1(6)). Such members are taken into account if the applicant is neither subject to immigration control nor an EEA national (see para 10.24) but this will affect how the authority may discharge its duty to the applicant (see para 10.127(9)).

Intentional homelessness

10.52 A person becomes homeless intentionally if he or she deliberately does anything or fails to do anything in consequence of which he or she ceases to occupy accommodation which is available for his or her occupation and which it would have been reasonable for him or her to continue to occupy (HA 1996 s191(1); H(W)A 2014 s77(1)). In England, becoming threatened with homelessness intentionally is similarly defined (HA 1996 s196(1)). (There is no equivalent in

Wales). There is no distinction in principle between the two concepts (*Dyson v Kerrier DC*, 1980). (All future references to intentional homelessness may accordingly, and save where an express distinction is drawn, be taken to refer also to becoming threatened with homelessness intentionally.) If there is any doubt about whether or not someone has done a sufficiently direct act to qualify as intentionally homelessness, it should be resolved in the applicant's favour (*R v Thurrock BC ex p Williams*, 1982). In every case, it is for the authority to satisfy itself that a person became homeless intentionally, not for an applicant to satisfy the authority that he or she did not do so (*Lewis*; *Williams*).

10.53 The definition incorporates a number of elements.

1) Something must be done deliberately, or there must be a deliberate failure to act.
2) The act or omission must have a consequence.
3) The consequence must be that accommodation ceases or will cease to be occupied.
4) That accommodation must be, or have been, 'accommodation available for [the] occupation' of the homeless person (see para 10.65); and
5) It must have been reasonable to continue in occupation of that accommodation (see paras 10.66–10.68).

Act or omission

10.54 The definition does not require that the applicant deliberately became homeless so much as that he or she deliberately did (or failed to do) something as a result of which he or she became homeless. The word 'deliberate' only governs the act or omission (*Devenport v Salford CC*, 1983). The link between the act and the homelessness must be judged objectively (*Robinson v Torbay BC*, 1981).

Deliberate

10.55 An act or omission in good faith, on the part of a person who was unaware of any relevant fact, eg the availability of financial assistance towards rent, the right to remain in occupation after notice to quit or expiry of tenancy, is not to be treated as deliberate for these purposes (HA 1996 ss191(2), 196(2)). Good faith in these circumstances can encompass honest blundering and carelessness, eg in a business deal, and should be contrasted with dishonesty (*R v Hammersmith and Fulham LBC ex p Lusi*, 1991; *Ugiagbe v Southwark LBC*, 2009) and willfully disregarding the obvious (*Ugbiagbe*; *F v Birmingham*

City Council, 2006). Whether an act is in good faith, and whether it is done in ignorance of relevant facts, are two questions which the authority must therefore consider separately (*O'Connor v Kensington and Chelsea RLBC*, 2004; *Gibbons v Bury MBC*, 2010).

10.56 One preliminary question may be whose conduct is to be taken into account, when an application is by or on behalf of more than one person. In *R v North Devon DC ex p Lewis*, 1980, a woman lived with a man by whom she had a child. He quit his job and in consequence lost his tied accommodation. When he applied as homeless, he was held to have become homeless intentionally. The woman then applied in her own right. The authority argued that: (a) it did not have to consider her application, because she was governed by the decision on his application; and (b) she had in any event acquiesced in his decision to quit his job, so that she, by association, had committed an act of intentionality in her own right. The court rejected the authority's first argument but upheld the second on the facts of the case. It would not, however, have been appropriate for her to be deemed to have acquiesced if she had done all she could to prevent his conduct, but he had gone ahead notwithstanding, eg a woman who has done all she can to prevent her husband spending the rent money on drink or otherwise.

10.57 Thus, in *R v West Dorset DC ex p Phillips*, 1984, *Lewis* was applied so as to compel an authority to house a woman who turned on her husband during their homelessness interview and attacked him for spending money on drink. In *R v Mole Valley DC ex p Burton*, 1988, the authority failed to consider that a wife had acted in good faith when she had believed her husband's assurances that they would be re-housed if he quit his job and accordingly lost his tied accommodation, for which reason the authority's decision was not upheld. In *R v East Northamptonshire DC ex p Spruce*, 1988, it was said that a spouse's mere knowledge of, for example, rent or mortgages arrears would not be enough to amount to acquiescence: he or she might have learned so late that the arrears were too big to do anything about.

10.58 In other cases, however, attempts to apply the *Lewis* principle have failed. In *R v Nottingham City Council ex p Caine*, 1995, in particular, the Court of Appeal held that an authority was entitled to infer that the applicant had known of her partner's conduct in withholding the rent, even though there was no direct evidence that she had done so. (The intentionality of parents cannot be circumvented by a child's application, as a dependent child is not in priority need in his or her own right: *R v Oldham LBC ex p G*; para 10.40). The acquiescence principle is not confined to cohabitants. An applicant may be found to be intentionally homeless where failure to control the conduct of his or her children or lodgers leads to his or her eviction (*Smith v Bristol City Council*, 1981; *Devenport v Salford City Council*, 1983; and, *R v East Hertfordshire CC ex p Bannon*, 1986).

In consequence

10.59 The homelessness must be 'in consequence of' the deliberate act or omission. This is a question of 'cause and effect' (*Dyson v Kerrier DC*, 1980; *Din v Wandsworth LBC (No 3)*, 1983). The principal issue which has arisen in practice is the attribution of present homelessness to past act or omission. That is to say there is commonly a past act which has or could have been the subject of a finding of intentionality, and the argument then becomes whether or not that act or omission is the cause of the present homelessness. There may be several potential causes, in which case the authority has to make a careful judgment as to the true cause of the homelessness, bearing in mind that it is the applicant's responsibility for the homelessness that is in question (*Watchman v Ipswich BC*, 2007; *Noel v Hillingdon LBC*, 2013). In *Watchman*, the authority was entitled to find that the applicant lost her home because she took on a mortgage that she was never going to be able to afford. The fact that her husband subsequently lost his job, on which the applicant sought to rely instead, did not cause the loss of their home; it merely accelerated the inevitable eviction.

10.60 Commission of a criminal offence may be considered deliberate conduct, and lead to a finding of intentionality where it can properly be regarded as having caused the homelessness, eg where subsequent imprisonment leads to repossession of the home, ie for want of ability to pay rent. The test is whether the loss of accommodation could reasonably have been regarded at the time as a likely consequence of the commission of the offence (*R v Hounslow LBC ex p R*, 1997; *Stewart v Lambeth LBC*, 2002). A young person may be intentionally homeless where his or her parents have asked him or her to leave the family home because of his or her behaviour: in deciding intentionality, the authority must consider the nature of the behaviour and the reasonableness of the parents' house rules which they imposed on the child (*Denton v Southwark LBC*, 2007).

10.61 It will not always be appropriate to treat someone who has quit or been dismissed from his or her job and thus lost tied accommodation as intentionally homeless. There must be a sufficient link, or proximity, between the act which caused the loss of job, and the loss of accommodation (*R v Thanet DC ex p Reeve*, 1981). A direct act, eg theft from an employer, which could reasonably be foreseen to lead to loss of job and accommodation, may well amount to intentional homelessness; loss of job through, for example, a period of incompetence, should, however, not do so. The fact that someone appears voluntarily to have quit employment does not necessarily mean that he or she has become homeless intentionally: he or she may have been forced into it, so that the resignation was constructive dismissal (*R v Thurrock BC ex p Williams*, 1982).

10.62 Rent arrears, non-payment of mortgage instalments, and nuisance and annoyance causing eviction (see para 2.98(1) and (2)) can qualify as acts of intentional homelessness, although in each case there must be sufficient proximity, or foreseeability, between act and loss of home. In each case, too, ignorance of ways of avoiding loss of the home will be a defence. In *R v Hillingdon LBC ex p Tinn*, 1988, it was said that it could not be reasonable to continue to occupy accommodation if an applicant could not pay the rent or mortgage without depriving himself of the ordinary necessities of life, such as food, clothing, heat and transport. Authorities must therefore consider whether the applicant has adequate resources when deciding whether failure to pay the rent amounts to a deliberate act: *R v Wandsworth LBC ex p Hawthorne*, 1994. In *R v Leeds City Council ex p Adamiec*, 1991, however, a sale before the commencement of possession proceedings by a building society was upheld as intentional, even though it was likely that, in the long run, the applicant would not have been able to afford to continue living in the house. See now the regulations relating to affordability which authorities in England must consider (the Homelessness (Suitability of Accommodation) Order 1996 SI No 3204) and the statutory duty in Wales: H(W)A 2014 s59(2) – see para 10.119.

10.63 A causal link may continue to subsist following the act of intentionality even though the applicant ceases to be homeless in the interim, eg because he or she finds some temporary accommodation from which he or she is subsequently evicted: *R v Brent LBC ex p Awua*, 1995. The authority has to look back to the original cause of the homelessness and determine whether it was intentional (*Din*) unless a later event (which is not itself an act of voluntary homelessness) supersedes the earlier conduct, so that it cannot reasonably be said that 'but for' that earlier conduct, the applicant would not have become homeless. In such a case, the causal link between current homelessness and earlier conduct will have been interrupted. In the absence of such an event, the question is whether the proximate cause of the homelessness is an event which is unconnected to the earlier conduct (*Haile v Waltham Forest LBC*, 2015.

10.64 One way of breaking the chain of causation between the earlier conduct and present homelessness is a period of 'settled accommodation' (*Din*; *Awua*). There is no judicial or other definition of settled accommodation but accommodation which is indefinite at its outset should qualify, although an intention that it should be indefinite will not always be sufficient where the accommodation is of a precarious nature, eg where the applicant was living with relatives or a resident landlord (*Gilby v Westminster City Council*, 2007; *R v Merton LBC ex p Ruffle*, 1988). An assured shorthold may be settled depending on the circumstances of the case, eg whether the applicant knew that the tenancy was only for a fixed term of six months and would not be renewed (*Knight v Vale Royal BC*, 2003). Even if not settled, the link may nonetheless be broken by other events, eg separation from husband or reduction in housing benefit payments, provided that the event is unconnected with the temporary nature of the accommodation (*R v Harrow LBC ex p Fahia*, 1997, in the Court of Appeal).

Available accommodation

10.65 Accommodation is only available for a person's accommodation if it is available for him- or herself and for anyone with whom he or she might reasonably be expected to reside (HA 1996 s176; H(W)A 2014 s56) (see para 10.29).

Reasonable to continue to occupy

10.66 This is the same phrase as applies when considering homelessness itself (see paras 10.33–10.36). Much of the case law on it arose, however, in relation to intentionality. Because the authority is entitled to have regard to the general circumstances prevailing in relation to housing in its own area (HA 1996 s177(2); H(W)A 2014 s57(3)), authorities can claim that applicants should have remained in what objectively may be considered appalling conditions; it means in practice that people can rarely safely quit their current accommodation on account of its physical condition without a real likelihood of a finding of intentionality.

10.67 In *R v Hammersmith and Fulham LBC ex p Duro Rama*, 1983, it was said that 'reasonable to continue to occupy' involves a range of questions, not confined to the condition of the housing formerly occupied, and in *R v Tower Hamlets LBC ex p Monaf*, 1988, that it calls for a 'balancing exercise' between the reasons for leaving accommodation and coming to the area where the application has been made, and housing conditions in that area. In *R v Hillingdon LBC ex p H*, 1988, political and racial harassment was considered relevant to the question of reasonable to continue to occupy. When applicable, the provisions relating to violence will make it not reasonable to continue to occupy accommodation (see paras 10.35–10.36).

10.68 Where an applicant obtained a tenancy by deceiving the landlord and, on discovering the deception, the landlord seeks to evict the applicant, it is not reasonable for the applicant to remain in occupation (*R v Exeter City Council ex p Gliddon*, 1984; *Chishimba v Kensington and Chelsea RLBC*, 2013).

Collusive arrangements

10.69 There is one 'added' definition of intentional homelessness. A person becomes homeless intentionally, or threatened with homelessness intentionally, if he or she enters into an arrangement under which he or she is required to cease to occupy accommodation which it would have been reasonable to continue to occupy, the purpose of which arrangement is to enable him or her to qualify for assistance under Part 7, and there is no other, or independent, good reason for the actual or threatened homelessness (HA 1996 ss191(3), 196(3); H(W)A 2014 s77(4)).

Wales

10.70 Local housing authorities must choose whether to apply the intentionality test in their areas (H(W)A 2014 s78). If an authority chooses to do so it must publish a notice to that effect and must then apply the test. The Welsh Ministers can limit the application of the test to certain categories of applicant. Currently, the test cannot be applied to an applicant who has a priority need (Homelessness (Intentionality) (Specified Categories) (Wales) Regulations 2015 SI No 1265).

Local connection

10.71 A person has a local connection with an area:

1) because he or she is, or in the past was, normally resident in it and that residence was of choice; or
2) because he or she was employed in it; or
3) because of family associations; or
4) for any special circumstance (HA 1996 s199(1); H(W)A 2014 s81(2)).

Note. In England, amendments made by the Homelessness Reduction Act 2017, when in force, will mean that a child taken into local authority care obtains a local connection with that authority's area provided that he or she lived there for at least two years, part of which must fall before his or her sixteenth birthday. A local connection with an area depending solely on this ground ceases when the care leaver becomes 21.

10.72 The overriding term is 'local connection', which must be attributable to one of the specified 'grounds'; merely demonstrating that there is, for example, employment or family connection, without a finding sufficient to amount to a 'local connection' will not be enough (*Re Betts*, 1983). Residence is not 'of choice' if it is in consequence of detention under an Act of Parliament, eg imprisonment or compulsory in-patient (HA 1996 s199(3), (4); H(W)A 2014 s81(3)). An applicant housed in temporary accommodation by an authority (under, for example, HA 1996 s188, or H(W)A 2014 s68(1)); see para 10.83) will nonetheless be normally resident – 'of choice' – in that accommodation, which may assist the applicant as local connection (as eligibility, homelessness and priority need – *Bull v Oxford City Council*, 2011) is determined as at the date of the authority's decision (or, if a review – para 10.148, as at the date of the review) rather than the date of the application itself (*Mohamed v Hammersmith & Fulham LBC*, 2001), ie a local connection may be acquired because of a delay between application and (final) decision. A former asylum-seeker has a local connection with an area in England or Wales in which he or she was provided with accommodation under IAA 1999 (see para 10.29) unless he or she was subsequently provided with accommodation under that Act in another authority's district or the accommodation was in an accommodation centre provided by Migrant Help (HA 1996 s199(6), (7); H(W)A 2014 s89(6)).

10.73 Operation of the local connection provisions is considered below (see paras 10.128–10.141). It may usefully be noted here, however, that they only come into play if an applicant has no local connection with the area of the authority to which the application has been made, and does have a local connection with the area of another authority, does not run the risk of domestic violence/abuse (see para 10.35) in that area, and has not suffered non-domestic violence/abuse in that area (if it is also probable that his or her return to it will lead to further violence against him or her of a similar kind) (see para 10.129). Accordingly, there is no test of whether there is a greater local connection with one area or another.

Duties under HA 1996 Pt 7 and H(W)A 2014 Pt 2

Preliminary duties

Applications

10.74 Preliminary duties arise where a person applies to a housing authority for accommodation, or for assistance in obtaining it, or (in Wales) for help in retaining accommodation, and the authority has reason to believe that he or she may be homeless or threatened with homelessness (HA 1996 s184(1); H(W)A 2014 s62(1)). There is no provision for any particular form of application, or even that the application should be in writing (*R v Chiltern DC ex p Roberts,* 1990). For example, where a person makes a housing application under Part 6 (see para 10.187), facts may be included in the application form which give the authority reason to believe that he or she may be homeless, in which case duties arise under HA 1996 Pt 7 or H(W)A 2014 Pt 2 (*Gibbons v Bury MBC,* 2010).

10.75 As noted above (see para 10.40), the applicant must have sufficient capacity to understand and respond to the offer of accommodation, and to undertake its responsibilities: *R v Bexley LBC ex p B; R v Oldham MBC ex p G,* 1993.

Repeat applications: England

10.76 An applicant who has made an unsuccessful application for assistance may seek to make a new application soon afterwards. Authorities do not have to process a repeat application based on exactly the same facts as an earlier application (*R v Harrow LBC ex p Fahia,* 1998). It is for the applicant to identify in the new application why he or she contends that there has been a change in the facts (*Rikha Begum v Tower Hamlets LBC,* 2005). If the new facts relied on are, to the authority's knowledge, not new – or are fanciful or trivial – it may reject the application. Otherwise, it must accept the new application; it is not open to the authority to investigate the accuracy of the alleged new facts before deciding whether or not to accept it, even if it suspects that the facts are inaccurate.

Repeat applications: Wales

10.77 In Wales, the authority does not have to accept a new application from a person who has previously been assessed under H(W)A 2014 Pt 2, as to whom there has been no material change in his or her circumstances and no new material information since the earlier assessment (H(W)A 2014 s62(2)).

Enquiries/assessment

Enquiries: England

10.78 Where the authority has reason to believe there is actual or threatened homelessness (see paras 10.30–10.38), it must make such enquiries as are necessary to satisfy itself whether the applicant is eligible for assistance (see paras 10.24–10.27) and, if so, what – if any – duty is owed to him or her under Part 7 (HA 1996 s184(1)), which automatically imports whether or not the applicant is homeless, whether he or she is in priority need (see paras 10.39–10.51) and whether he or she became homeless intentionally (see paras 10.52–10.70). The authority may also make further enquiries as to whether there is a local connection (see paras 10.71–10.73) with the district of another authority (HA 1996 s184(2)).

10.79 Enquiry duties arise when there is 'reason to believe' that there is actual or threatened homelessness but the decision is whether the authority is 'satisfied' that the applicant is homeless and in priority need, and 'not satisfied' that he or she became homeless intentionally (HA 1996 s193(1); H(W)A 2014 ss62(1), 75(2)); satisfaction is a higher standard than having reason to believe, although the reversal of the burden of the decision in relation to intentionality should be noted (*R v Gravesham BC ex p Winchester*, 1986). (It may also be noted that the authority needs only 'consider' or be of 'the opinion' that the local connection provisions apply – HA 1996 ss198(1), 200(1); H(W)A 2014 ss80(1); 82(1) – which may be thought to fall somewhere between the two).

10.80 The duty is immediate; the authority cannot avoid it by keeping its offices shut for prolonged periods – in the major cities, authorities may be expected to maintain a 24-hour service, ie an emergency, out-of-hours service as well as a normal office service (*R v Camden LBC ex p Gillan*, 1988). Nor can an authority postpone a decision in the hope of a change of circumstances that will reduce its duty (*R v Ealing LBC ex p Sidhu*, 1982). Where an applicant is a young person who has been required to leave the family home, many authorities operate a mediation service intended to achieve reconciliation between the family members: authorities cannot, however, delay making a decision pending mediation (eg in the expectation that the applicant will pass a relevant age – see para 10.50), as mediation forms no part of their enquiries – they are different exercises (*Robinson v Hammersmith & Fulham LBC*, 2006).

10.81 What enquiries are necessary is a matter for the authority (*R v Kensington and Chelsea RLBC ex p Bayani*, 1990). An authority which has made enquiries can only be attacked for failing to make more if it failed to make an enquiry which no reasonable authority (see para 8.28(6)) could have failed to regard as necessary (*R v Nottingham City Council ex p Costello*, 1989). In general terms, an authority cannot be criticised for failing to enquire into a matter either which did not obviously have to be considered or which it was not asked to consider (*Cramp v Hastings BC, Phillips v Camden LBC*, 2005; *Williams v Birmingham City Council*, 2007). This principle requires some qualification where the applicant is a disabled person because – even if not invited to consider an applicant's disability – 'obvious' sets too high a standard, although authorities are not required in every case to make enquiries as to whether an applicant is disabled, ie if there is nothing to put it on notice that he or she may be (*Pieretti v Enfield LBC*, 2010).

Assessment: Wales

10.82 In Wales, if it appears to the authority that an applicant may be homeless or threatened with homelessness, it must carry out an assessment of the his or her case (H(W)A 2014 s62). The assessment must consider whether the applicant is eligible. If he or she is eligible, the assessment must then address: how the applicant has become homeless or threatened with homelessness; his or her housing needs and those of anyone with whom he or she lives or might reasonably be expected to live; the support required to meet those needs; and, whether or not the authority has any duty under Part 2 to the applicant. The assessment must seek to identify what the applicant wishes to achieve with the authority's help and the authority must consider whether the exercise of any of its powers under Part 2 can contribute to that outcome. The assessment must be kept under review.

Pre-decision accommodation

10.83 Enquiries and/or assessment may take some time. If the authority has reason to believe that the applicant may be eligible for assistance (see paras 10.24–10.27), homeless (see paras 10.30–10.38) and in priority need (see paras 10.39–10.51), then – pending its decision – it is obliged to secure that accommodation is made available (HA 1996 s188(1); H(W)A 2014 s68(1), (2)). This is so whether or not the applicant may have a local connection with another authority (HA 1996 s188(2); H(W)A 2014 s68(4)). The accommodation must be made available for the applicant and for any other family member who normally resides with the applicant, or anyone else who might reasonably be expected to reside with him or her (HA 1996 ss176, 188(1);

H(W)A 2014 ss56, 68(1)). The duty ceases on notification of decision, even if the applicant requests a review (see paras 10.148–10.161), but the authority has a discretion to continue to house pending the review (HA 1996 s188(2), (3); H(W)A 2014 s69).

Initial assessment and plan

10.84 In England, once the Homelessness Reduction Act 2017 comes into force, there will be a new duty to assess an applicant's case if the authority is satisfied that the applicant is homeless (see paras 10.30–10.37) or threatened with homelessness (see para 10.38) and eligible for assistance (10.24–10.29) (new HA 1996 s189A). It therefore arises at a later stage than the corresponding Welsh duty (see para 10.82). The assessment must include an assessment of the circumstances which resulted in the applicant's homelessness or being threatened with homelessness, his or her housing needs, and his or her needs for support in order to be able to have and retain suitable accommodation (the mandatory considerations). The assessment may include other matters. The authority has to notify the applicant in writing of the assessment it makes.

10.85 The authority must try to agree with the applicant what steps he or she is to be required to take in order to secure that he or she has and is able to retain suitable accommodation, and what steps the authority is to take under Part 7 (new HA 1996 s189A). If the authority and the applicant reach an agreement, it must be recorded in writing. If they cannot do so, the authority have to record in writing why they could not agree, what steps it considers it would be reasonable to require the applicant to take, and what steps the authority is to take under Part 7, for those purposes. Until the authority decides that it owes the applicant no duty under any of the remaining provisions of Part 7, the authority has to keep the assessment under review, as also must the appropriateness of any agreement reached or steps recorded be kept under review. If the assessment of the mandatory considerations (see para 10.84) changes, the authority must notify the applicant, in writing, of how its assessment has changed (whether by providing a revised written assessment or otherwise); the same is true if the authority's assessment otherwise changes in a way that it considers it appropriate to notify the applicant. If the authority considers that any agreement reached or any step recorded under it is no longer appropriate, it must notify the applicant in writing to this effect and that any subsequent failure to take a step that was agreed or recorded is to be disregarded.

Threatened with homelessness: England – Homelessness Reduction Act 2017

10.86 In England, once amendments made by the Homelessness Reduction Act 2017 are in force, if an authority is satisfied that an applicant is threatened with homelessness (see para 10.38) and eligible (see paras 10.24–10.29), it must 'take reasonable steps to help to secure' that accommodation does not cease to be available to the applicant (new HA 1996 s195(1), (2)). This duty cannot be used to prevent the authority itself obtaining vacant possession of any accommodation; accordingly, it cannot be raised as a defence by a tenant in possession proceedings by the authority (new HA 1996 s195(4)). In deciding what steps to take, the authority must have regard to its assessment of the applicant's case (see paras 10.84–10.85).

10.87 The authority can notify the applicant that the duty has come to an end in the following circumstances.

1) The authority is satisfied that the applicant has become homeless (in which case further duties will arise – paras 10.99–10.125).
2) The authority is satisfied that the applicant is no longer threatened with homelessness and suitable accommodation (see paras 10.113–10.122) is likely to remain available (see para 10.32) for the applicant's occupation for at least another six months.
3) The applicant refuses an offer of accommodation, having been notified in writing of the possible consequences of its refusal or acceptance, provided that the authority is satisfied that the accommodation was suitable (see paras 10.113–10.122) for the applicant and was likely to be available (see para 10.32) for at least the next six months.
4) The applicant has become homeless intentionally from any accommodation that has been made available to him or her under Part 7.
5) The authority is no longer satisfied that the applicant is eligible (see paras 10.24–10.29).
6) The authority is satisfied that the applicant has withdrawn the application.
7) The authority is satisfied that the applicant is unreasonably failing to co-operate with it. (H(W)A 2014 ss67 and 79; new HA 1996 s195(8), (9)).

Failure to co-operate

10.88 A detailed procedure will govern notification by an authority that its duty has to an end because of the applicant's failure to co-operate (see para 10.87(7)) (new HA 1996 ss193B). The applicant must have deliberately and unreasonably refused to take one more of the steps which were either agreed or recorded by the authority as reasonable for the applicant to take as part of the assessment (see para 10.85). The notice ending the duty must explain why it is being given and its effect and inform the applicant of the right to request a review of the decision and the time within which the request for a review must be made (see para 10.151).The notice cannot be given unless the authority has given the applicant a prior 'warning notice', advising that, if the applicant refuses to take steps specified in the warning notice, it will notify him that the duty has come to an end.

10.89 Notification that the duty has come to an end must be in writing and, if not received by the applicant, is treated as having been given if made available at the authority's office for a reasonable period for collection by the applicant or someone acting on his or her behalf (new HA 1996 s195(9)): if unreceived, therefore, the burden is on the applicant to go to the authority's offices and ask for it.

Initial help duty

Wales

10.90 In Wales, if an authority is satisfied that an applicant is homeless (see paras 10.30–10.37) and eligible for assistance (see paras 10.24–10.29), whether or not he or she has a priority need or may be homeless intentionally, it must help to secure that accommodation is available for the applicant (H(W)A 2014 s73). The duty does not arise if there is a local connection referral (see paras 10.128–10.137) to another authority in England or Wales (s73(2)).

10.91 An authority can help to secure that suitable accommodation is available either by providing something itself or arranging for someone else to provide it (H(W)A 2014 s64(1)). Examples in the Act of what may be provided or arranged are: grants or loans; guarantees; support in management of debt, mortgage or rent arrears; security measures for applicants at risk of abuse; advocacy or other representation; accommodation; information and advice; and, other services, goods or facilities (H(W)A 2014 s64(2)).

10.92 This duty lasts for 56 days (H(W)A 2014 s74(2)), although the authority can decide on a shorter period if reasonable steps to secure accommodation for the applicant have been taken to no avail (H(W)A 2014 s74(2)). After the 56 days (or that shorter period) have expired, further duties (see paras 10.111–10.122) may still be owed to the applicant depending on whether he or she has a priority need (see paras 10.39–10.51) and/or became homeless intentionally (see paras 10.52–10.70).

10.93 Notice that the duty has come to an end must provide reasons for the authority's decision and inform the applicant of the right to request a review of the decision to bring the duty to an end and of the time within which such a request must be made (H(W)A 2014 s84). The duty comes to an end if one of the following occurs (H(W)A 2014 ss74(3)–(8), 79).

1) The authority is satisfied that the applicant has suitable accommodation available for occupation, and the accommodation is likely to be available for occupation by the applicant for a period of at least six months.
2) The applicant refuses an offer of accommodation from any person, having been notified in writing of the possible consequences of its refusal or acceptance, provided that the authority is satisfied that the accommodation was suitable (see paras 10.113–10.122) for the applicant and was likely to be available for at least the next six months.
3) The authority is satisfied that the applicant has ceased to be eligible.
4) The authority is satisfied that the applicant has withdrawn the application.
5) The authority is satisfied that the applicant is unreasonably failing to co-operate with it.
6) The authority is satisfied that a mistake of fact led to the authority's notifying the applicant that it owed him or her a duty to help to secure accommodation for the applicant.

England

10.94 In England, Once the Homelessness Reduction Act 2017 comes into force, a similar duty will apply where the authority is satisfied that an applicant is homeless (see paras 10.30–10.37) and eligible for assistance (see paras 10.24–10.29) (new HA 1996 s189B). The duty will not arise where the authority refers the application to another local housing authority under the local connection provisions (see paras 10.128–10.141). The duty is to take reasonable steps to help the applicant to secure that suitable accommodation (see paras 10.113–10.122) becomes available for his or her occupation for at least six months or such longer period as may be prescribed. In deciding what steps to take, the authority must have regard to its assessment of the applicant's case (see paras 10.84–10.85).

10.95 Where the authority is satisfied that the applicant has a priority need (see paras 10.39–10.51) and is not satisfied that the applicant became homeless intentionally (see paras 10.52–10.70), the duty comes to an end 56 days following the day the authority was first satisfied that the applicant was homeless and eligible (new HA 1996 s189B). The authority may also give notice bringing the duty to an end when it is satisfied that one of the following apply (new HA 1996 s189(B))(5), (7)).

1) The applicant has suitable accommodation which is available for his or her occupation and there is a reasonable prospect of him or her having suitable accommodation available for at least six months from the date of the notice.
2) The authority has complied with the duty to take reasonable steps and the period of 56 days beginning with the day that the authority is first satisfied that the applicant was homeless and eligible has ended (whether or not he or she has secured accommodation).
3) The applicant has refused an offer of suitable accommodation and, on the date of refusal, there was a reasonable prospect that suitable accommodation would be available for occupation by the applicant for at least six months or such longer period as may be prescribed.
4) The applicant has become homeless intentionally from any accommodation that has been made available to him or her as a result of the authority's exercise of its functions under this duty.
5) The applicant is no longer eligible for assistance.
6) The applicant has withdrawn the application for accommodation or assistance in obtaining it.

10.96 The notice must specify which of the circumstances applies and inform the applicant that he or she has a right to request a review of the decision to bring the duty to an end and of the time within which such a request must be made (new HA 1996 s189B(6)).

10.97 The duty will end if the applicant, having been informed of the possible consequences of refusal and of the right to request a review of the suitability of accommodation (see para 10.148), refuses either a written final offer of a Part 6 allocation (see paras 10.187–10.188), or a 'final accommodation offer' which the authority was satisfied was suitable for the applicant (see paras 10.113–10.122) (new HA 1996 s193A(1)(b)(i), (5), (6)). A final accommodation offer is an offer of a fixed-term, assured shorthold tenancy (see paras 1.246–1.251) from a private landlord, which is made with the authority's approval (new HA 1996 s193A(4)). The term must be for at least six months. If a final accommodation offer or a final Part 6 offer is refused, then the full housing duty under section 193 (see paras 10.111–10.121) does not arise (s193A(3)).

10.98 The duty can also be brought to an end where the applicant is unreasonably refusing to co-operate with the authority (new HA 1996 s193B – paras 10.88–10.89) but this will not end a right to accommodation for an applicant who is homeless, eligible, in priority need and not homeless intentionally (new HA 1996 s193C).

No full housing duty

Priority need but homeless intentionally

10.99 In England, if the authority is satisfied that an applicant is homeless (see paras 10.30–10.37) and in priority need of accommodation (see paras 10.39–10.51), but it is also satisfied that he or she became homeless intentionally, it has two duties:

1) to secure that temporary accommodation is made available – for the applicant and for any other family member who normally resides with the applicant or anyone else who might reasonably be expected to reside with him or her (HA 1996 s176) – for such period as it considers will give the applicant a reasonable opportunity to secure his or her own accommodation (HA 1996 s190(2)(a)); and
2) to assess the applicant's housing needs and provide the applicant (or secure that he or she is provided) with advice and appropriate assistance (s190(2)(b), (4)).
   Note. Once amendments made by the Homelessness Reduction Act 2017 are in force, there will be no need for an assessment of housing need at this stage because one will already have taken place (see paras 10.84–10.85). In giving advice and assistance, however, the authority will have to have regard to that earlier assessment (new HA 1996 s190(4)).

10.100 What constitutes a reasonable opportunity for securing accommodation depends on the applicant's circumstances; when determining this issue, authorities cannot take into account the extent of their resources and other demands on them (*R (Conville) v Richmond upon Thames LBC*, 2006). If the authority provides its own accommodation, it will not be secure unless and until the authority notifies the applicant otherwise (HA 1985 Sch 1 para 4; para 1.180(6)), which it may not do otherwise than in accordance with the allocation provisions considered below (see paras 10.187–10.220). If the authority secures accommodation through a landlord whose tenants are not secure, then this temporary accommodation will likewise not be within statutory protection for a year from when the authority first gave notification of its decision (see para 10.144), or – if there is a review (see paras 10.148–10.161) or an appeal to the county court (see paras 10.162–10.168) – from its final determination, again unless the tenant is previously notified by the landlord that it is to be regarded either as an assured shorthold or a fully assured tenancy (HA 1996 s209(2)). The advice and appropriate assistance must include information about the likely availability in the authority's area of types of accommodation appropriate to the applicant's housing needs, including as to the location and sources of such types of accommodation (HA 1996 s190(5)).

Priority need but threatened with homelessness intentionally

10.101 In England, if the authority is satisfied that the applicant is threatened with homelessness intentionally (see para 10.52), eligible for assistance (see paras 10.24–10.29) and in priority need (see paras 10.39–10.51), then the advice and appropriate assistance duty (see para 10.99(2)) arises (HA 1996 s195(5)(b), (6), (7)), on the basis that, once the homelessness itself occurs, an application will entitle the applicant to a period of temporary accommodation. *Note.* Once amendments made by the Homelessness Reduction Act 2017 are in force, this duty will be replaced by the new section 195 duty considered in paras 10.86–10.87.

No priority need

10.102 In England, If the authority is satisfied that the applicant is homeless (see paras 10.30–10.37) – whether intentionally (HA 1996 s190(3)) or not (s192) – or threatened with homelessness (see para 10.38) – intentionally or not (s195(5)(a)) – and eligible for assistance (see paras 10.24–10.29), but it is also satisfied that he or she is not in priority need, it owes the advice and appropriate assistance obligation (see para 10.92(2)) to the applicant, but no accommodation duty. *Note.* Once the amendments made by the Homelessness Reduction Act 2017 are in force, the advice and assistance obligation under section 190(3) (no priority need and intentionally homeless) will only arise once the authority's duty under section 189B (see paras 10.94–10.98) has come to an end. The duty under section 195(5)(a) will be replaced by the new duty to an applicant threatened with homeless (see paras 10.106–10.107). The duty under section 192 (no priority need, not intentionally homeless) will be repealed reflecting the new duty under HA 1996 s189B (see paras 10.94–10.98).

10.103 In addition, if the authority is satisfied that the applicant is not in priority need (see paras 10.39–10.51) and also that he or she is unintentionally homeless, it has a power to secure that accommodation is made available for occupation by the applicant (HA 1996 s192(3)), even if no duty. Likewise, an applicant not in priority need who is unintentionally threatened with homelessness may benefit from the authority's power to take reasonable steps to secure that accommodation does not cease to be available for his or her occupation (s195(9)). Even if unlikely to be used, eg because of financial constraints, and/or even if there is a guidelines policy not to use them, the authority must consider using these powers in each case to which they are potentially relevant (see para 8.28(7)). *Note.* These powers will no longer exist once amendments made by the Homelessness Reduction Act 2017 are in force because of the new duty under HA 1996 s189B (see paras 10.94–10.98).

Priority need and unintentionally threatened with homelessness: England

10.104 In England, if the authority decides that the applicant is threatened with homelessness and eligible for assistance, and has a priority need, but did not become threatened with homelessness intentionally, its duty is to take reasonable steps to secure that accommodation does not cease to be available for his or her occupation (HA 1996 s195(1) and (2)), ie either to help the applicant remain in his or her current accommodation (s195(2)), or else to secure other accommodation for him or her once homelessness occurs.

10.105 This duty cannot be used to prevent the authority itself obtaining vacant possession of any accommodation (HA 1996 s195(3)), so that it cannot be raised as a defence by a tenant in possession proceedings by the authority. If the authority provides its own accommodation when the homelessness itself occurs, then section 193 applies in the same way as it applies to those who apply when already homeless (see paras 10.30–10.37) (s195(4)). *Note.* The provisions considered in this paragraph and the last will be replaced by a new section 195 once amendments made by the Homelessness Reduction Act 2017 are in force (see paras 10.86–10.87).

Threatened with homelessness: Wales

10.106 In Wales, if an authority is satisfied that an applicant is eligible (see paras 10.24–10.27) and threatened with homelessness (see para 10.38), it is under a duty to help to secure that accommodation does not cease to be available to the applicant (H(W)A 2014 s66(1)). This duty cannot be used to prevent the authority itself obtaining vacant possession of any accommodation; accordingly, it cannot be raised as a defence by a tenant in possession proceedings by the authority. The duty requires the authority to take reasonable steps to help, having regard to (among other matters) the need to make the best use of its resources; it does not require the authority to offer accommodation (s65).

10.107 An authority can help to secure that suitable accommodation does not cease to be available either by providing some assistance itself or arranging for someone else to provide it (H(W)A 2014 s66). Examples of assistance given in the Act are: mediation; grants or loans; guarantees; support in management of debt, mortgage or rent arrears; security measures for applicants at risk of abuse; advocacy or other representation; accommodation; information and advice; and, other services, goods or facilities.

10.108 The authority can notify the applicant that this duty has come to an end in the following circumstances (H(W)A 2014 ss67, 79, 84).

1) The applicant has become homeless.
2) The applicant is no longer threatened with homelessness and suitable accommodation is likely to remain available for his or her occupation for at least another six months.
3) The applicant refuses an offer of accommodation from any person, which accommodation the authority is satisfied was suitable and was likely to be available for at least the next six months, having been notified in writing of the possible consequences of refusal or acceptance of the offer.
4) The applicant ceases to be eligible.
5) A mistake of fact led to authority to notify the applicant that it owed him or her a duty to help to secure accommodation for the applicant.
6) The applicant has withdrawn the application.
7) The applicant is unreasonably failing to co-operate with the authority.

Other Acts

10.109 Other statutory provisions may be available to provide housing when there is no duty, or no full duty, under HA 1996 or H(W)A 2014 (see paras 10.170–10.186).

Charges

10.110 Authorities have a general power to make reasonable charges for the provision of their own accommodation under HA 1985 Pt 2 (HA 1985 s24 – see para 3.3). HA 1996 and H(W)A 2014 likewise entitles them to make reasonable charges to a homeless person for accommodation which they provide, or for or towards accommodation which they arrange for some other person to provide, under HA 1996 Pt 7, or H(W)A 2014 Pt 2 (HA 1996 s206(2); H(W)A 2014 s90).

Full housing duty

Full duties

10.111 In England, if the authority is satisfied that the applicant is homeless, eligible for assistance, in priority need and not intentionally homeless, then its duty is (subject to the possibility of referral to another authority, paras 10.128–10.141) to secure that accommodation is made available for his or her occupation (and, therefore, for any other family member who normally resides with, or anyone else who might reasonably be expected to reside with, the applicant: HA 1996 s176) (HA 1996 s193(2)). In addition, the authority must give the applicant a copy of the statement included in their allocation policy (see para 10.200) on offering choice (see para 10.201) to people allocated housing accommodation under Part 6 (HA 1996 s193(3A)). In Wales, the full duty is owed to an applicant who is homeless, eligible for assistance and in priority need (H(W)A 2014 s75(2)): the fact that the applicant is intentionally homeless is irrelevant (see para 10.70). There is, however, no similar requirement to provide information about the authority's allocation scheme.

10.112 In Wales, and in England once amendments made by the Homelessness Reduction Act 2017 are in force, the duty does not, however, arise until the authority's initial duty to help secure accommodation (see paras 10.94–10.98) has come to an end, ie the 56-day period must have elapsed (H(W)A 2014 s75(1); new HA 1996 s193(1)).

Suitability

10.113 The duty to secure that accommodation is made available for the applicant's occupation can be discharged by making available suitable accommodation held by the authority under HA 1985 Pt 2; or by securing that the applicant obtains suitable accommodation from some other person; or by giving the applicant such advice and assistance as will secure that he or she obtains suitable accommodation from some other person (HA 1996 s206(1); H(W)A 2014 s64(1)). When determining whether accommodation is suitable, the authority must have regard to HA 1985 Pts 9 (see paras 12.46–12.52) and 10 (see paras 14.2–14.9) (slum clearance and overcrowding) and HA 2004 Pts 1–4 (see paras 12.44 and 14.9–14.71) (hazardous housing, houses in multiple occupation and selective licensing of accommodation); and, in Wales, H(W)A 2014 Pt 1 (see paras 14.74–14.96) (regulation of private rented housing) (HA 1996 s210; H(W)A 2014 s59(1)). The obligation is, however, only to 'have regard' to the statutory provisions: provided they take them into account, the authority may still decide that a property is suitable even if it offends one of them, eg because it is statutorily overcrowded (*Harouki v Kensington and Chelsea RLBC*, 2007). The accommodation does not have to be suitable at the time it is offered provided that it will be before the applicant moves in, eg where adaptations are to be carried out to the property to facilitate access for a disabled person (*Boreh v Ealing LBC*, 2008).

10.114 In determining suitability, the authority must take into account the particular circumstances of the applicant and his or her family, eg medical evidence (*R v Brent LBC ex p Omar*, 1991). If the applicant is disabled, the authority's duty under EqA 2010 s149 (see para 10.22), requires it: to recognise that the applicant has a disability; to focus the applicant's impairments to the extent that they are relevant to the suitability of the accommodation; to focus on the disadvantages the applicant might suffer when compared to a person without those impairments; to focus on the applicant's accommodation needs arising from those impairments and the extent to which the accommodation met those needs; and, to recognise that the applicant's particular needs might require him or her to be treated more favourably than a person without a disability (*Hackney LBC v Haque*, 2017).

10.115 The accommodation must be adequate as regards size for the family's needs as well as having regard to such other factors as nature of area and employment prospects (*R v Wyre BC ex p Parr*, 1982). Accommodation will not be suitable if it is located in an area where the applicant would be at risk of violence (*R v Haringey LBC ex p Karaman*, 1996; *R v Lambeth LBC ex p Woodburne*, 1997) but an authority is entitled to take into account the size of the area concerned and the fact that the risk is only associated with a part of the area which is some distance from the accommodation (*Watson v Wandsworth LBC*, 2010).

10.116 In *Ali v Birmingham City Council*, 2009, the authority had a policy under which an applicant who had accommodation but who was homeless because it was not reasonable to continue to occupy it (see paras 10.33–10.36) was required to remain in that accommodation until it discharged its duty to the applicant by an offer under HA 1996 Pt 6 (see paras 10.125(4)). Although the Supreme Court held that the authority was not entitled to leave the applicants in their current homes indefinitely pending a Part 6 offer, it was accepted that there are degrees of suitability. What may not be suitable for occupation in the medium or long term may nonetheless be suitable in the short term, even though there is bound to come a time when the accommodation could no longer be described as suitable.

10.117 In England, the Homelessness (Suitability of Accommodation) Order 1996 SI No 3204 also requires the authority to take into account: the financial resources available to the applicant, including all state benefits (*Samuels v Birmingham City Council*, 2015); accommodation costs; any payments being made under a court order to a spouse or former spouse; payments made to support children under a court order or the Child Support Act 1991; and, the applicant's other reasonable living expenses. This requires the authority to undertake a careful analysis of the applicant's individual circumstances (*Balog v Birmingham City Council*, 2013; *Farah v Hillingdon LBC*, 2014). In Wales, the authority must likewise have regard to whether accommodation is affordable (H(W)A 2014 s59(2)).

10.118 In both England and Wales, there are additional regulations governing suitability: Homelessness (Suitability of Accommodation) Order 2012 SI No 2601; and Homelessness (Suitability of Accommodation) (Wales) Order 2015 SI No 1268. Both sets of regulations require authorities to take into account the following when considering suitability of accommodation for an applicant in priority need or a member of the applicant's household: the specific health needs of the person; the proximity and accessibility of the support of the person's family or other support services; any disability; the proximity and accessibility of medical facilities and other support services which are currently used by or provided to the person and which are essential to the person's well-being; where the accommodation is situated outside the authority's area, the distance of the accommodation from that area; the significance of any disruption which would be caused by the location of the accommodation to the employment, caring responsibilities or education of the person; and, the proximity of alleged perpetrators and victims of domestic abuse.

10.119 Both sets of regulations also require that accommodation offered to an applicant under a private rented sector offer (see para 10.125(8)) must be in a reasonable physical condition and comply with certain specific requirements, eg in relation to the safety of gas and electrical appliances. Once amendments made by the Homelessness Reduction Act 2017 are in force, these requirements will also apply to final offers of accommodation (see para 10.99).

Bed and breakfast

10.120 In England, the use of bed and breakfast accommodation is restricted by the Homelessness (Suitability of Accommodation) (England) Order 2003 SI No 3326. It is not suitable for families or pregnant women unless there is no other accommodation available and then only for a period not exceeding six weeks (or for periods not exceeding six weeks in total). Accommodation owned or managed by an authority, a PRP or voluntary organisation is exempt from this prohibition, ie does not class as a B&B. In Wales, bed and breakfast or shared accommodation is unsuitable for a person who is, or who may be, in priority need unless: offered in response to an emergency (eg fire, flood) when no other accommodation is reasonably available; or the applicant has been offered other suitable accommodation but has chosen bed and breakfast; or it is used for less than a fixed period (two weeks, or six weeks if the accommodation meets a higher standard defined in the Order which takes into account, inter alia, room size, heating facilities, storage facilities, toilet and washing facilities) (Homelessness (Suitability of Accommodation) (Wales) Order 2015 SI No 1268).

Accommodation in area

10.121 So far as reasonably practicable, authorities are bound to secure accommodation within their own areas (HA 1996 s208(1); H(W)A 2014 s91(1)). In *Nzolameso v Westminster City Council*, 2015, the authority offered the applicant and her five children, accommodation in Milton Keynes. The Supreme Court held that, when considering offering accommodation outside its district, an authority must have particular to the needs of an applicant's children. Where it is not reasonably practicable to secure accommodation in its area, the authority must try to place the applicant as near as possible to his or her previous home. Authorities with insufficient housing in their areas should have policies explaining what will be taken into account in deciding whether to secure accommodation outside their areas. (See also the regulations considered in para 10.118).

10.122 If the authority nonetheless places an applicant in another area, it must give notice to the local housing authority with responsibility for that area, stating: the name of the applicant; the number and description of any other persons who might reasonably be expected to reside with the applicant; the address; the date on which the accommodation was made available to him or her; and, what function the authority was discharging when securing the accommodation for him or her (HA 1996, 208(2), (3); H(W)A 2014 s91(2), (3)). The notice must be given in writing within two weeks from when the accommodation was made available (HA 1996 s208(4); H(W)A 2014 s91(4)).

Security

10.123 Where an authority provides its own accommodation in discharge of the full duty, it cannot be a secure tenancy (HA 1985 Sch 1 para 4; see para 1.180(6)), but continues to be provided under HA 1996 Pt 7, or H(W)A 2014 Pt 2 (hence the expression 'Pt 7' or 'Pt 2' accommodation, in contrast to accommodation allocated under Part 6 – para 10.160).

Charges

10.124 The charging powers discussed in relation to temporary accommodation apply to accommodation under the full duty (see para 10.110).

Cessation of duty

10.125 The duty continues to be owed to an applicant until it is brought to an end by any of the circumstances set out in HA 1996 s193 (HA 1996 s193(3)) or H(W)A 2014 ss76, 79 and 84 (H(W)A 2014 ss76(1), 79(1)).

1) **Refusal of Part 7 offer.** The duty will end if the applicant refuses an offer under HA 1996 Pt 7, or H(W)A 2014 Pt 2 (ie under the homeless provisions themselves (see paras 10.111–10.121)), which the authority is satisfied is suitable for him or her (see paras 10.109–10.118), and the authority has informed the applicant that if or she does not accept the offer it will regard itself as having discharged the duty (HA 1996 s193(5); H(W)A 2014 s76(3)(a)). The warning of the consequences of refusal does not have to be given when specific accommodation is offered; it may be given some time prior to the offer but if too long a period has elapsed between warning and offer section 193(5) may not be satisfied (*Vilvarasa v Harrow LBC*, 2010).

   These provisions are directed towards the Part 7 or Part 2 offer, which is to say the accommodation that the application will occupy until allocated a permanent home; it is in this sense 'temporary', although that is misleading, because it can be a matter of years (even a decade or more) before such a 'final' offer is made, and there can be more than one such 'temporary' home.

An authority may discharge this duty by securing an assured shorthold tenancy (see paras 1.246–1.251) from a private sector landlord (*Griffiths v St Helens MBC*, 2006). In offering the tenancy, the authority should explain to the applicant that if the landlord lawfully exercises his or her right to recover possession (and there has been no intervening event bringing the duty to an end under one of the following sub-paragraphs), it will still be obliged to secure that accommodation is available. (This may be compared with a final offer or a private rented sector assured shorthold tenancy, at (7) and (8), below.)

Where an authority notifies an applicant that its duty has ended because an offer of suitable accommodation has been refused, it is not obliged to keep the accommodation available during the period when the applicant has the right to request a review (see para 10.148) or until the authority has reached its review decision (*Osseily v Westminster City Council*, 2007).

2) **No longer eligible.** The duty will end if the applicant ceases to be eligible for assistance (see paras 10.24–10.27) (HA 1996 s193(6)(a); H(W)A 2014 s79(2)).
3) **Intentionally homeless from Part 7 accommodation.** The duty will end if the applicant becomes homeless intentionally (see paras 10.52–10.70) from the Part 7 (see paras 10.111–10.121) accommodation (HA 1996 s193(6)(b); H(W)A 2014 s76(6)).
4) **Allocation.** The duty will end if the applicant accepts an allocation (see paras 10.187–10.189) under HA 1996 Pt 6 (HA 1996 s193(6)(c); H(W)A 2014 s76(2)(b)).
5) **Assured tenancy.** The duty will end if the applicant accepts an offer of an assured tenancy (see paras 1.220–1.245) from a private landlord, ie one whose tenants are not secure (see paras 1.160–1.161) (HA 1996 s193(6)(cc); H(W)A 2014 s76(2)(b)). In England, the tenancy must not be an assured shorthold tenancy (see paras 1.246–1.257), which is governed by its own provisions (see (9), below), but in Wales acceptance of any assured shorthold tenancy brings the duty to an end.
6) **Cessation of occupation of Part 7 accommodation.** The duty will end if the applicant ceases to occupy the Part 7 accommodation as his or her only or principal home (see paras 1.176–1.179) (HA 1996 s193(6)(d); H(W)A 2014 s76(7)).
7) **Refusal of Part 6 offer.** The duty will end if the applicant, having been informed of the possible consequences of refusal and of

the right to request a review of the suitability of accommodation refused (see para 10.148), refuses a written final offer of a Part 6 allocation, which the authority was satisfied was suitable (10.113–10.122) (HA 1996 s193(7), (7A), (7F); H(W)A 1996 s76(3)(c)).

In England, a Part 6 offer may bring the duty to an end even though the applicant is currently under a contractual or other obligation in respect of existing accommodation, if (but only if) he or she can bring that other obligation to an end before being obliged to take up the offer (HA 1996 s193(8)); accordingly, the offer must run from no earlier than the first date when the obligation can be brought to an end. There is no similar provision in the H(W)A 2014.

8) **Assured shorthold tenancy – private rented sector offer.** The duty will end if the applicant accepts or refuses a 'private rented sector offer' of accommodation (HA 1996 s193(7AA); H(W)A 2014 s76(3)(b). A private rented sector offer is an offer of a fixed-term, assured shorthold tenancy from a private landlord, which is made with the authority's approval (HA 1996 s193(7AC); H(W)A 2014 s76(4)). In England, the term must be for at least 12 months, or for such longer minimum period as may be prescribed (HA 1996 s193(7AC), (10)); in Wales, the minimum term is six months (H(W)A 2014 s76(4)(c)). An authority may not make a private rented sector offer unless it is satisfied that the accommodation is suitable for the applicant (HA 1996 s193(7F); H(W)A 2014 s76(3)).

   In England, save in a restricted case – see (9), below – if an applicant who accepted a private rented sector offer re-applies as homeless within two years, the authority will still owe the applicant the full housing duty even if he or she no longer has a priority need (see para 10.39; HA 1996 s195A(1), (3)). Pending inquiries into the application, he or she will be entitled to interim accommodation (see para 10.83; HA 1996 s188(1A)). If the applicant then accepts a second private rented sector offer and later re-applies as homeless from that accommodation, however, the applicant will only be owed the full housing duty if he or she has a priority need (HA 1996 s195A(6)).

   When making a private rented sector offer, the authority must inform the applicant of the consequences of refusal or acceptance and of the right to request a review of the suitability of the accommodation (HA 1996 s193(7AB); H(W)A 2014 s76(3)).

9) **Restricted cases.** If the authority only owes the full housing duty to the applicant because of a restricted person (see para 10.27),

it *must*, so far as is reasonably practicable, bring the duty to an end by making a 'private sector offer' (see (8), above) (HA 1996 s193(7AD); H(W)A 2014 s76(5)).

Local connection

10.126 The local connection (see para 10.71–10.73) provisions allow one housing authority ('the referring authority') to shift the burden of duties under HA 1996 Pt 7, or H(W)A 2014 Pt 2, to make accommodation available onto another housing authority.

10.127 For an authority to refer an applicant to another authority, one of the following conditions must apply.

1) In England, the applicant was – within the previous five years – placed in accommodation in the referring authority's area by the authority which it intends to notify in pursuance of that other authority's Part 7 functions (HA 1996 s198(4)); Allocation of Housing and Homelessness (Miscellaneous Provisions) (England) Regulations 2006 SI No 2527 reg 3; see para 10.122 for the notification requirements imposed on the other authority at the time of the placement).
2) In England and Wales, the referring authority considers that *all* of the following conditions apply:
   (i) neither the applicant nor anyone who might reasonably be expected to reside with him or her has a local connection with its area; and
   (ii) the applicant or a person who might reasonably be expected to reside with him or her does have a local connection with the area of another housing authority; and
   (iii) neither the applicant nor any person who might reasonably be expected to reside with him or her will run the risk of domestic violence/abuse in the area of that other authority (HA 1996 s198(1), (2); H(W)A 2014 s80(3));
   (iv) but the conditions are not met if the applicant or any person who might reasonably be expected to reside with him or her has suffered non-domestic violence/abuse in the area of the other authority, and it is probable that the return of the victim to that area will lead to further violence/abuse of a similar kind against him or her (HA 1996 s198(2A); H(W)A 2014 s80(4)).
3) (i) In England, the application is made within two years of the applicant accepting a private rented sector offer (see para 10.125(8)) from the authority which the referring authority intends to notify. In contrast with condition 1, the private

rented sector offer need not have been in the referring authority's area (HA 1996 s198(2ZA)(a)). Thus, if the earlier application was made to authority A and it discharged its duty by a private rented sector offer of accommodation in authority B and the applicant now applies to authority C, authority C can refer the applicant to authority A.

(ii) The condition is not, however, met if the applicant or any person who might reasonably be expected to reside with him or her has suffered non-domestic violence in the area of the other authority, and it is probable that the return of the victim to that area will lead to further violence of a similar kind against the applicant (HA 1996 s198(2ZA)(b)). Violence and domestic violence/abuse are defined in the same terms as when determining whether or not it is reasonable to remain in occupation (HA 1996 s198(3); H(W)A 2014 s58; paras 10.35–10.36).

England: pre-Homelessness Reduction Act 2017

10.128 In England currently, where the authority would be under the full housing duty under section 193, ie duty to an applicant who is eligible, in priority need and not intentionally homeless, it may refer the applicant to another authority if it considers that the conditions for referral are met (HA 1996 s198(1)). If an applicant has no local connection with anywhere in England, Scotland or Wales, however, the local connection provisions simply do not apply, and the burden of housing will remain with the authority to which application is made (*R v Hillingdon LBC ex p Streeting*, 1980).

10.129 The housing duty passes to the other authority if the conditions are satisfied (HA 1996 s200(4)). That authority's obligation is to house under HA 1996 s193 (see para 10.111).

10.130 If the conditions are not satisfied, the housing duty under section 193 remains with the authority to which the application was made (HA 1996 s200(3)). Pending resolution of the question of which authority will have final responsibility, it is that authority which must provide temporary accommodation (HA 1996 s200(1)). Once the question has been decided, it is also that authority which must notify the applicant of the decision and of the reasons for it, as well as of the right to request a review and the time within which it must be requested (see para 10.148–10.161) (HA 1996 s200(2)). The temporary housing duty ceases when the notification is given, even if a review is requested, although the authority still has a discretion to continue to provide it pending review (HA 1996 s200(5)).

10.131 The decisions of the authority to which the application has been made on the issues of homelessness, priority need and intentionality are binding on an authority to which it is able to refers the application. This is so even if the applicant had formerly applied to one authority, been found homeless intentionally and moved on to apply to another authority; the second authority can still reach a decision, different from that of the first authority, that the applicant did not become homeless intentionally, and invoke the local connection provisions to refer the applicant back to the first authority (*R v Slough BC ex p Ealing LBC*, 1980). The proposition illustrates how views may differ as to whether or not someone has become homeless intentionally. There is nothing to stop an applicant applying to authority after authority in the hope of a favourable decision.

10.132 In the absence of any intervening change of circumstances, however, the authority to which a later application has been made must treat the application carefully and must give the authority which had made the earlier decision, and to which the applicant is liable to be returned, an opportunity of discussing the case and, above all, of discussing any discrepancies in the explanations offered for the homelessness by the applicant (*R v Tower Hamlets LBC ex p Camden LBC*, 1988). Before deciding to refer, the second authority must take into account the general housing circumstances in the area to which it is proposing to pass the application (*R v Newham LBC ex p Tower Hamlets LBC*, 1990). An authority which finds that an applicant is unintentionally homeless and which then refers the applicant to another authority cannot change its mind on intentionality simply because the referral is unsuccessful and the applicant comes back to it (*R v Beverley DC ex p McPhee*, 1979).

Wales

10.133 The position in Wales is slightly different in that the duty which passes to the other authority is the initial help duty under H(W)A 2014 s73 (see para 10.90), ie the duty which arises if the authority is satisfied that the applicant is eligible and homeless. For an application to be referred to another authority, however, the referring authority not only has to consider that the referral condition (see para 129(2)) is met but also that, if the case is not referred, it would be under a section 73 duty to an applicant who is in priority need and not intentionally homeless (s80(1)). Accordingly, the only applicants who can be referred are those considered by the referring authority to have a priority need and to be unintentionally homeless. Consequently, although the duty which passes is the initial help duty, if the authority to which the application is referred does not manage to help the applicant to secure accommodation, it will subsequently owe the applicant the full housing duty under section 75 (see para 10.111).

10.134 As in England, the duty will remain with the notifying authority if the conditions are not satisfied (H(W)A 2014 s82(3)). Pending a decision on final responsibility, the authority to which the application is made must provide temporary accommodation (H(W)A 2014 s82(1)). Once the issue has been decided, it is that authority which must notify the applicant of the decision and of the reasons for it, as well as of the right to request a review and the time within which it must be requested (see paras 10.148–10.161) (s82(2)). The temporary housing duty ceases when the notification is given, even if a review is requested, although the authority still has a discretion to continue to provide it pending review (H(W)A 2014 ss82(5), (6)).

England: post- Homelessness Reduction Act 2017

10.135 After the provisions of the Homelessness Reduction Act 2017 come into force, an English authority will still be able to avoid the full housing duty be making a local connection referral (see paras 10.128–10.141) but it will be able to consider local connection at an earlier stage. If the authority to which the application is made would be subject to the initial help duty (see paras 10.94–10.98), and considers that the conditions for referral are met, it will not be subject to that duty, but may instead notify the other authority of its opinion (new HA 1996 s198(A1)).

10.136 As under the other provisions considered above, the duty will remain with the notifying authority if the conditions are not satisfied (new HA 1996 s199A(4)). It it is the referring authority that must notify the applicant of the final decision and of the reasons for it, as well as of the right to request a review and the time within which it must be requested (new s199A(3)). The referring authority ceases to be under any duty to provide interim accommodation (see para 10.83) but is instead subject to the same duty to secure that accommodation is available although only until the applicant is notified of the decision as to whether the conditions for referral are met (new s199A(2)); the authority does, however, have a discretion to continue accommodation pending the decision on review (new HA 1996 s199A(6)).

Disputes between authorities

10.137 These provisions are a breeding ground for differences of opinion between authorities. Part 7 provides a process for the determination of disputes between them either by agreement or, if necessary, by reference to an arbitrator (HA 1996 s198(5)). An arbitration decision can nonetheless be the subject of internal review, and thence appeal on a point of law to the county court (see paras 10.162–10.168) (HA 1996 ss198(5) and 202(1)(d), (e)). The Act specifically provides that if the conditions for referral are met, the notified authority is bound by any decisions of the reefing authority not only as to eligibility and homelessness but also intentionality, unless satisfied that the circumstances have changed or that further information has come to light since the notifying authority made the decision (new HA 1996 s199A(5)).

10.138 Part 7 and Part 2 provide a process for the determination of disputes between authorities either by agreement or, if necessary, by reference to an arbitrator (HA 1996 s198(5); H(W)A 2014 s80(5)). An arbitration decision can nonetheless be the subject of internal review, and thence appeal on a point of law to the county court, on the part of an applicant dissatisfied with the outcome (see paras 10.162–10.168) (HA 1996 s202(1)(d), (e); H(W)A 2014 s85(1)(c)).

10.139 As a first stage, authorities will try to reach agreement as to which of them should house the applicant (HA 1996 s198(5); H(W)A 2014 s80(5)(a)). In default of agreement, disputes are to be resolved in accordance with arrangements made by the secretary of state or Welsh Ministers by order. The current arrangements are to be found in the Homelessness (Decisions on Referrals) Order 1998 SI No 1578 and the agreement reached between the relevant association of local authorities (the Local Authority Agreement). The terms of the latter do not bind anyone, not even an authority which is party to it: it is a voluntary guideline, for administrative purposes only, and if an authority chooses to depart from it in a particular case, it is free to do so; indeed, it will be irrelevant to any court or arbitration proceedings which may arise under the 1998 Order (*R v Mr Referee McCall ex p Eastbourne BC*, 1981).

Protection of property

10.140 If an authority is or has been under a (temporary or permanent) duty under HA 1996 ss188 (see para 10.83), 190, 193, 195 (see paras 10.101–10.107) or 200 (see para 10.130), or H(W)A 2014 ss66 (see para 10.83), 68 (see para 10.83), 73 (see para 10.90), 82 (see para 10.134), it may also be under a duty to take reasonable steps to prevent the loss of an applicant's property, or to prevent or mitigate damage to it (HA 1996 s211(2); H(W)A 2014 s93(2)). If the authority has not been under one of the identified duties but has reason to believe there is such a danger, it nonetheless has power to protect property (HA 1996 s211(3); H(W)A 2014 s93(5)).

10.141 The applicant's personal property, for these purposes, includes that of any person reasonably to be expected to reside with him or her (HA 1996 s211(5); H(W)A 2014 s93(6)). The duty arises if the authority has reason to believe that there is a danger of loss of, or damage to, property because of the applicant's inability to protect or deal with it and that no other suitable arrangements have been or are being made (HA 1996 s211(1); H(W)A 2014 s93(1)). Danger of loss or damage means a likelihood rather than a mere possibility of harm (*Deadman v Southwark LBC*, 2000).

10.142 The authority may refuse to take action under these provisions other than on such conditions as it considers appropriate, including for reasonable charges and the disposal of property (HA 1996 s211(4); H(W)A 2014 s93(4)). If the applicant asks the authority to move the property to a nominated location, the authority may (if it considers that the request is reasonable) discharge its responsibilities under these provisions by doing so, and treat its responsibilities as being at an end (HA 1996 s212(2); H(W)A 2014 s94(4)). In connection with these provisions, the authority has power, at all reasonable times, to enter any premises which are or were the usual or last usual place of residence of the applicant, and to deal with his or her property in any way that is reasonably necessary, including by way of storage (HA 1996 s212(1); H(W)A 2014 s94(1)), eg when someone is homeless or as a result of illegal eviction (see para 10.37).

10.143 Duties and powers end when the authority considers that there is no longer any danger of loss or damage, by reason of the applicant's inability to protect or deal with his or her personal property, although if the authority has provided storage, it has a discretion to continue to do so (HA 1996 s212(3); H(W)A 2014 s94(6), (7)). Where the authority's responsibilities end, it must notify the applicant, and of the reasons why (HA 1996 s212(4); H(W)A 2014 s94(8)). Notification may be given by delivery, or by leaving it or sending it to the applicant's last known address (HA 1996 s212(5); H(W)A 2014 s93(9)).

Decisions

10.144 If the authority makes enquiries or an assessment, it must, on their completion, notify the applicant of its decision, and 'so far as any issue is decided against [the applicant's] interests', ie not eligible, not homeless, not in priority need, intentionally homeless, to refer to another authority – it must inform the applicant of the reasons for the decision (HA 1996 s184; H(W)A 2014 s63(1)). The same notification requirements arise where an authority decide that the following duties have come to an end: helping to prevent an applicant from becoming homeless (in Wales – see para 10.106); initial help duty (see paras 10.90–10.98); and, duty to those threatened with homeless (Wales – see para 10.82). Notification must also inform the applicant of the right to request a review (within 21 days) (HA 1996 s184(5); H(W)A 2014 s63(4)(a); see para 10.148). There is no obligation to give reasons for a decision which is favourable to the applicant (*Akhtar v Birmingham City Council*, 2011).

10.145 Notification must be in writing. If the applicant does not receive the notification, he or she will, however, be treated as having done so if the notice is made available at the authority's office for a reasonable period, for collection by the applicant or by someone acting on his or her behalf (HA 1996 s184(6); H(W)A 2014 s63(4)(b)). The burden is therefore on the applicant who does not receive the decision to go to the authority's office and ask for it. If the applicant is represented by solicitors, it is sufficient to notify them rather than the applicant (*Dharmaraj v Hounslow LBC*, 2011).

10.146 The purpose of the obligation to give reasons for the decision is to enable the applicant to see whether they might by challengeable in law (*Thornton v Kirklees MBC*, 1979; *R v Croydon LBC ex p Graham*, 1993; *R v Brent LBC ex p Baruwa*, 1997). The reasons given must be 'proper, adequate and intelligible' (*Baruwa*). It is not appropriate, however, for the court to subject the decision to the sort of technical analysis that may be applied to a contract or a statute (*Osmani v Camden LBC*, 2004; *Holmes-Moorhouse v Richmond upon Thames LBC*, 2009; *Poshteh v Kensington and Chelsea RLBC*, 2017). Nonetheless, where a decision-maker fails to address an issue 'so startling that one would not expect it to pass without individual comment', the court may infer that it has not received any proper consideration (*R v Brent LBC ex p Bariise*, 1998).

10.147 Decisions as to eligibility, homelessness, priority need and local connection are reached as at the date of the decision – or, if a review (see paras 10.148–10.161), as at its date – rather than as at the date of the application (*Mohamed v Hammersmith & Fulham LBC*, 2001; *Bull v Oxford City Council*, 2011), although a decision as to intentionality relates to the date of the act which caused (see paras 10.59–10.64) the homelessness (*Din v Wandsworth LBC (No 3)*, 1983).

Challenging decisions

Review

10.148 Applicants have a statutory right to request an internal review of a decision on any of the following (HA 1996 s202(1); H(W)A 2014 s85(1)).

1) Eligibility for assistance (see paras 10.24–10.27).
2) In England, what duty (if any) is owed (see paras 10.74–10.125). In Wales, a decision as to whether an applicant is owed a duty under H(W)A 2014 ss66 (see paras 10.106), 73 (see para 10.90) or 75 (see para 10.111) or a decision that such a duty has come to an end.
3) Notification to another authority (see paras 10.126–10.127).
4) Whether the conditions for referral are met (see paras 10.127).
5) What duty is owed following a local connection referral (see paras 10.128–10.136).
6) Any decision as to suitability of accommodation offered in discharge of duty, including a Part 6 offer (see paras 10.113–10.122).
7) In England, once the Homelessness Reduction Act 2017 is brought into force, decisions as to the steps the applicant is to take under s189B(2) (see para 10.85) or that the duty under that section has come to an end (see para 10.87), that an applicant is refusing to co-operate with the authority (see para 10.88), and as to the steps the applicant is to take under section 195 (see para 10.88) or that the duty under that section has come to an end (see para 10.89).

10.149 An applicant may request a review of the suitability of accommodation even if he or she accepts the offer of accommodation (HA 1996 s202(1A); H(W)A 2014 s85(3)). The date at which suitability of accommodation should be considered depends on whether the offer is accepted or refused. If accepted, the authority should consider the facts at the date of the review because the accommodation is still available; if refused, the suitability of the offer is to be judged at the date of the original decision (*Omar v Westminster City Council*, 2008).

10.150 The right of review does not entitle the applicant to a review of an earlier review (HA 1996 s202(2); H(W)A 2014 s85(4)). This does not prevent an authority from further reconsidering a decision if it is minded to do so (*R v Westminster City Council ex p Ellioua*, 1998), although if an applicant wishes still to challenge the decision after such a further review, it must be by way of appeal to the county court against the original review decision (*Demetri v Westminster City Council*, 1999) as the reconsideration does not comprise a review in itself.

10.151 A request for a review must be made within 21 days of notification of the decision (see para 10.144), or such longer period as the authority may in writing allow (HA 1996 s202(3); H(W)A 2014 s85(5)). In exercising the discretion to extend time, the authority should consider the length of delay in making the request and the reasons for it. The merits of the applicant's case on review are relevant but, even if those merits are strong, the authority does not have to extend time if it thinks that the delay has been too long or is unjustifiable (*R (C) v Lewisham LBC*, 2003).

10.152 The request for a review sets the agenda for what the authority needs to reconsider. Often, the applicant will not have legal representation at this stage and a request must be looked at in a common sense way and a broad view taken of what aspects of an authority's decision are being challenged (*Nzamy v Brent LBC*, 2011).

10.153 The secretary of state and the Welsh Ministers have power to regulate the review procedure, including requiring the review to be conducted by a person of 'appropriate seniority ... not involved in the original decision', and the 'circumstances in which the applicant is entitled to an oral hearing, and whether and by whom [the applicant] may be represented at such a hearing' (HA 1996 s203(2); H(W)A 2014 s86(2)). In England, procedure is governed by the Allocation of Housing and Homelessness (Review Procedures) Regulations 1999 SI No 71; in Wales, the equivalent regulations are the Homelessness (Review Procedure) (Wales) Regulations 2015 SI No 1266.

10.154 Both sets of regulations require that an officer of the authority conducting a review should not have been involved in the original decision; in England, the reviewer must be senior to the original decision-maker. The applicant has the right to a face-to-face oral hearing, with his or her representative present, and the authority cannot require oral representations to be made in another way, eg over the telephone (*Makisi v Birmingham City Council*, 2011). The hearing is not intended to be a trial: it is a relatively brief opportunity for the applicant to make oral representations to the reviewing officer, who is entitled to determine where and when the hearing takes place and the procedure to be followed. The applicant is not entitled to insist on third parties being called to give evidence or to cross-examine any third parties.

10.155 The regulations (see para 10.153) provide that the review must generally be carried out within eight weeks, although a longer period is permitted in the case of local connection reviews. The parties may agree a longer period between themselves. Authorities may contract out their review duties (see para 10.5; *De-Winter Heald v Brent LBC*, 2009).

10.156 In carrying out the review, the reviewer must usually have regard not only to the information available at the time of the original decision but also to that obtained thereafter and to matters occurring after the initial decision: *Mohamed v Hammersmith and Fulham LBC*, 2001. This is not the case, however, if the original decision by the authority was unlawful. In *Robinson v Hammersmith and Fulham LBC*, 2006, the authority wrongly decided that the applicant was not in priority need, notwithstanding that she was only 17 years old at the time. By the time of the review, she was 18 and no longer in priority need (see para 10.50). The authority therefore sought to uphold its original decision. It was held that the reviewing officer should have decided that the original decision was unlawful and that it had denied the applicant the rights to which she was entitled; to be given those rights on review, she should therefore have been found to be in priority need.

'Minded to' letters

10.157 If the reviewer considers that there is a 'deficiency or irregularity' in the original decision, or in the manner in which it was made, but is minded nonetheless to make a decision against the applicant's interests, the reviewer must notify the applicant of the decision he or she is minded to make, giving reasons. The applicant must be informed that he or she, or a representative, may make representations to the reviewer orally and/or in writing (1999 SI No 71 reg 8(2) (England); 2015 SI No 1266 reg 5(2) (Wales)). 'Deficiency' means 'something lacking' that is sufficiently important to justify this extra procedural safeguard (*Hall v Wandsworth LBC*, 2004), such as a significant factual error in the original decision (*Bury MBC v Gibbons*, 2010). A change in circumstances or new information after the original decision may require the authority to make further enquiries with the result that a 'minded to' letter may have to be given (*Banks v Kingston upon Thames RLBC*, 2008; *NJ v Wandsworth LBC*, 2013; *Mohamoud v Birmingham City Council*, 2014).

Decision

10.158 The authority has to notify the applicant of the outcome of the review and, if it is adverse to his or her interests, or confirms a local connection referral, of the reasons for it (HA 1996 s203(4); H(W)A 2014 s86(3)). In any event, it must notify the applicant of the right to appeal to the county court on a point of law (HA 1996 s203(5); H(WA) 2014 s86(5)). If either of these requirements is not fulfilled, the notification is treated as not having been given (HA 1996 s203(6); H(W)A 2014 s86(5)). Otherwise, notification is given in the same way as under HA 1996 s184 or H(W)A 2014 s63 (HA 1996 s203(8); H(W)A 2014 s86(7); para 10.83).

Accommodation pending review

10.159 Pending the outcome of the review, the authority may – but does not have to – provide accommodation for the applicant (HA 1996 s188(3); H(W)A 2014 s69(11)). In contrast to a review decision itself (see para 10.121), the decision whether to provide accommodation pending review may be made by the officer who made the original decision (*R (Abdi) v Lambeth LBC*, 2007). As there is no provision for appeal against a decision not to house pending review, a challenge can only be made by judicial review (*R v Camden LBC ex p Mohammed*, 1997).

Appeal to the county court

10.160 If the applicant is dissatisfied with the outcome of the review, or if he or she has not been notified of the outcome within any time that may be prescribed (see para 10.155), there is a right of appeal to the county court (HA 1996 s204(1)). Exercise of the right to a review is therefore an essential precondition of appeal. Appeal lies only on a point of law (see paras 10.163–10.164), whether it arises from the original decision or the decision on review (HA 1996 s204(1); H(W)A 2014 s88(1)).

10.161 The appeal must be brought within 21 days of notification or of when the applicant ought to have been notified (see para 10.155) of the outcome of the review (HA 1996 s204(2); H(W)A 2014 s88(2)). The court may give permission for appeal out of time where there is good reason for failure to bring the appeal in time (HA 1996 s204(2A); H(W)A 2014 s88(3)). If there is no good reason for extending time, the merits of the appeal itself are irrelevant; the merits are only relevant to the court's exercise of its discretion once a good reason has been established (*Short v Birmingham City Council*, 2004).

Accommodation pending appeal

10.162 Pending an appeal (and any further appeal), the authority may continue to provide accommodation (HA 1996 s204(4); H(W)A 2014 s88(5)). If the authority refuses to do so, the applicant may appeal that decision to the county court (HA 1996 s204A; H(W)A 2014 s89). The court may order accommodation to be made available pending the outcome of the appeal (or such earlier time as it may specify) (HA 1996 s204A(4)(a), (b); H(W)A 2014 s89(4)). In considering whether or not to do so, the court must apply the same principles (see paras 8.23–8.28) that would be applied by the High Court on an application for judicial review (s204A(4); *Francis v Kensington and Chelsea RLBC*, 2003). As applied to interim accommodation pending appeal, this requires the authority to carry out a balancing exercise, to which the following will always be relevant (although other factors may also be): the merits of the claim that the authority's decision is wrong (including grounds of appeal – *Lewis v Havering LBC*, 2006); the extent to which the original decision appears to be contrary to the merits or to involve a fine degree of judgment; whether new material needs to be considered; whether there is a new argument which would change the original decision; and, the applicant's personal circumstances (*R v Camden LBC ex p Mohammed*, 1997). An order to accommodate pending appeal may, however, only be made if the court is satisfied that failure to do so would substantially prejudice the applicant's ability to pursue his or her substantive appeal (s204A(6)(a)).

Powers of court on appeal

10.163 The court may make such an order as it thinks fit, confirming, quashing or varying the decision (HA 1996 s204(3); H(W)A 2014 s88(4)). The right of appeal is, however, on a point of law rather than an appeal on the facts, a distinction which is not always straightforward, in so far as a conclusion of fact for which there is no, or insufficient, evidence may in itself comprise an error of law (see para 8.28(2)). Point of law includes issues of jurisdiction or powers. For practical purposes, the grounds on appeal are the same as those which are available (in homelessness or otherwise) on a claim for judicial review (see paras 8.23–8.28) (*Runa Begum v Tower Hamlets LBC*, 2003).

10.164 It follows that it is not sufficient merely to know what rights and duties are set out in Part 7 or Part 2 , or of knowing what the Code of Guidance under either HA 1996 s169 (see para 10.212) or HA 1996 s182 or H(W)A 2014 s98 (see para 10.20) suggests is appropriate in a particular case. The principal duties only arise when the authority has 'reason to believe', 'consider' or is 'satisfied' that a certain state of affairs exists. An applicant's rights therefore only arise and can only be enforced once the authority's satisfaction, belief or view has been established (*Cocks v Thanet DC*, 1982) and it is, accordingly, essential to distinguish between the actual – undisputed, or indisputable – facts of a particular case, and whether the authority is 'satisfied', has 'reason to believe' or is 'of the opinion' that those facts exist. It is here that the principles that have evolved – and that have been discussed (see paras 8.23–8.28) – known as the principles of domestic public law come into play. There is a very substantial body of case-law in relation to homelessness challenges, all of which are in one way or another an illustration of what is meant by 'point of law', but which cannot effectively be summarised because they turn so extensively on their own facts and/or on the way the court approached them: see Arden, Bates and Vanhegan, *Homelessness and Allocations* (10th edn, LAG, 2017).

Human Rights Act 1998

10.165 As public authorities within the meaning of the Human Rights Act (HRA) 1998 s6, local housing authorities must act in a way which is compatible with the ECHR. Two Articles of the Convention are potentially relevant in homelessness cases. First, Article 6 provides that in the determination of his or her civil rights, everyone is entitled to a fair and public hearing within a reasonable time by an independent and impartial tribunal. Although the Supreme Court held that homelessness rights are not civil rights within Article 6 (*Ali v Birmingham City Council*, 2010), the European Court of Human Rights held (on an application by the same homeless person) that they are civil rights but that the right to challenge an authority's decision by review and appeal to the county court complied with Article 6 (*Ali v United Kingdom*, 2015). Despite this, the Supreme Court subsequently declined to overrule its decision in *Ali v Birmingham City Council* that homelessness rights are not civil rights, deciding instead to await full consideration by a Grand Chamber of the European Court of Human Rights before considering whether (and if so how) to modify its position (*Poshteh v Kensington and Chelsea RLBC*, 2017).

10.166 Secondly, while Article 8 (see para 1.319) confers a right to respect for the home, this does not amount to a right to housing to be provided by the state (*Chapman v UK*, 2001; *Lambeth LBC v Kay*, 2006).

Judicial review

10.167 Decisions which are not subject to review (see para 10.148) may nonetheless be challenged by judicial review, which is a claim in the High Court (Administrative Court) which can only be brought with the permission of the court itself, sought without delay and in any event within three months. It is not practicable to describe here how such proceedings may be commenced beyond what has already been noted, but the principles will be the same as those already referred to (see paras 8.23–8.28; paras 10.163–10.164).

Criminal offences

10.168 **False statements.** It is a criminal offence knowingly or recklessly to make a statement which is false in a material particular, or knowingly to withhold information which an authority has reasonably required in connection with the exercise of its functions under Part 7, with intent to induce an authority to believe that the person making the statement, or any other person, is entitled to accommodation or assistance (or accommodation or assistance of a particular kind) (HA 1996 s214(1); H(W)A 2014 s97(1)). In England, the offence is punishable in the magistrates' court by a fine of up to an unlimited amount (HA 1996 s214(4); Legal Aid, Sentencing and Punishment of Offenders Act (LASPO) 2012 s85(1)); in Wales, it is punishable by a fine of up to level 4 on the standard scale, ie £2,500 (H(W)A 2014 s97(6)).

10.169 **Change of circumstances.** An applicant has a duty to notify an authority as soon as possible of any material change of facts material to his or her case which occurs before receipt of notification of the authority's decision on the application (HA 1996 s214(2); H(W)A 2014 s97(2)). The authority is under a corresponding obligation to explain to an applicant, in ordinary language, the nature of this duty, and the effect of the statutory defence to a charge of non-compliance (HA 1996 s214(2); H(W)A 2014 s97(3)). It is a defence to a charge of non-compliance that no such explanation was given, or that although such an explanation was given there is some other reasonable excuse for non-compliance (HA 1996 s214(3); H(W)A 2014 s97(5)). In the absence of such a defence, it is a criminal offence to fail to comply with the duty to notify of material changes, punishable in England on summary conviction by a fine of up to an unlimited amount (HA 1996 s214(4); LASPO 2012 s85(1)) or, in Wales, by a fine of up to level 4 on the standard scale, ie £2,500 (H(W)A 2014 s97(6)).

Duties under other Acts

Social services legislation

10.170 As well as discharging their duty under HA 1996 Pt 7 or H(W)A 2014 Pt 2, authorities may also provide assistance to the homeless under other statutory provisions, such as housing in a care home under the Care Act 2014 Pt 1 (England) or SSWB(W)A 2014 Pt 4 (Wales), or else, in the case of a minor, by using powers under the CA 1989 Pt 3 (England) or the SSWB(W)A 2014 (Wales). A duty may arise under either of these provisions, even though no duty – or, in practice, no full housing duty – exists under HA 1996 Pt 7 or H(W)A 2014 Pt 2. Duties under these Acts are imposed on social service authorities (see para 10.4). Decisions may be challengeable by judicial review (see paras 8.23–8.28).

Children

10.171 In England, CA 1989 s17 provides:

> (1) It shall be the general duty of every local authority...
> > (a) to safeguard and promote the welfare of children within their area who are in need; and
> > (b) so far as is consistent with that duty, to promote the upbringing of such children by their families by providing a range and level of services appropriate to those children's needs.

10.172 Although this section does not positively require authorities to provide accommodation, it does comprise a 'safety net' power permitting authorities to assist a family, including with the provision of accommodation (*R (W) v Lambeth LBC*, 2002, following *AG ex rel Tilley v Wandsworth LBC*, 1981 and *R v Tower Hamlets LBC ex p Monaf*, 1988).

10.173 In Wales, local authorities have a duty to meet the care and support needs of a child (SSWB(W)A 2014 s37). The duty arises where a child needs meet 'eligibility criteria' and the authority considers that those needs have to be met to protect the child from actual, or the risk of, abuse or neglect or other harm. The child's needs meet the eligibility criteria if: (i) the need arises from the child's physical or mental ill-health, age, disability, dependence on alcohol or drugs, or other similar circumstances, or is a need that if unmet is likely to have an adverse effect on the child's development; (ii) the need relates to one or more of a list of specified matters; (iii) the need is one that neither the child, the child's parents nor anyone else in a parental role is able to meet; and, (iv) the child is unlikely to meet one or more of his or her personal outcomes (defined in section 21(4)(b)) unless care and support is provided (Care and Support (Eligibility) (Wales) Regulations 2015 SI No 1578). In order to meet needs, authorities may provide accommodation (s34(2)).

10.174 Both CA 1989 s20, and SSWB(W)A 2014 s76 provide that:

> (1) Every local authority shall provide accommodation for any child in need within their area who appears to them to require accommodation as a result of–
>
> ...
>
> (c) ... the person who has been caring for him being prevented (whether or not permanently, and for whatever reason) from providing him with suitable accommodation or care...
>
> ...
>
> (3) Every local authority shall provide accommodation for any child in need within their area who has reached the age of sixteen and whose welfare the authority consider is likely to be seriously prejudiced if they do not provide him with accommodation.

10.175 The effect of the section is to impose a duty on social services authorities to house children in the circumstances set out in subs(1) and to house young people in the circumstances set out in subs(3). The duty is exclusive to the child and does not confer a duty (or even a power) on the authority to accommodate a child's family: *R (G) v Barnet LBC*, 2001.

10.176 Where not itself also the housing authority, as it will be in unitary authorities and London borough councils (see para 10.4), social service authorities may request assistance in discharging their duties under the CA 1989 (CA 1989 s27(1)). An authority whose help is requested 'shall comply with the request if it is compatible with their own statutory or other duties and obligations and does not unduly prejudice the discharge of any of their functions' (CA 1989 s27(2)).

10.177 In Wales, a local authority may request the co-operation of various bodies in discharging its duties, including other local authorities, an NHS trust and the Youth Offending Team (SSWB(W)A 2014 ss162, 164). The body is bound to comply with the request unless it considers that doing so would be incompatible with its own duties, or would have an adverse effect on its functions (s164). If the authority seeks information from the body, it must likewise comply unless it considers that doing so would be incompatible with its own duties or would otherwise have an adverse effect on the exercise of its functions. In either case, a body which decides not to comply with the request must provide the local housing authority which made the request with written reasons for its decision.

10.178 In *Smith v Northavon DC*, 1994, the housing authority found the applicant to be intentionally homeless and sought to evict him from his temporary accommodation. The applicant applied to the social services authority for assistance. The social services authority considered that the applicant's children would be in need when the eviction took place and therefore requested the housing authority to provide accommodation. The housing authority declined. The House of Lords refused to quash ITS decision. The request of the social services authority did not give the applicant any priority over other homeless persons or waiting-list applicants for housing. In the event of the housing authority being unable to provide assistance, the social services authority remained under a responsibility to protect the applicant's children.

10.179 Specific provision is made for applicants with children who are not owed a full duty under HA 1996 Pt 7 or H(W)A 2014 Pt 2 to be referred to social services. Where a local authority has reason to believe that an applicant with whom children reside or normally reside may be ineligible for assistance (see paras 10.24–10.27), may be homeless intentionally (see para 10.52), or may be threatened with homelessness intentionally (see para 10.52), it must make arrangements for ensuring that the applicant is invited to consent to the referral of his or her case to the social services authority (or department in the case of a unitary authority) and, if consent is given, must make the social services authority/department aware of the facts of the case and the subsequent decision in relation to it (HA 1996 s213A(1), (2); H(W)A 2014 s96(1), (2)).

10.180 Following a referral, the social services authority/department may request the housing authority to provide it with advice and assistance in the exercise of its functions under CA 1989 Part 3, and the housing authority/department must provide it with such advice and assistance as is reasonable in all the circumstances (England) (HA 1996 s213A(5), (6)) or such advice and assistance as the housing department may reasonably request (Wales) (H(W)A 2014 s96(4)).

Adults

10.181 Adults with needs for care and support may be provided with residential care by local authorities under the Care Act 2014 (England) or SSWB(W)A 2014 (Wales) which replaced the long-standing and well-known National Assistance Act 1948. Under both Acts, local authorities have duties and powers to provide care and support to meet a person's needs, including accommodation in a care home or accommodation of some other kind (Care Act 2014 s8(1)(a); SSWB(W)A 2014 s34(2)(a).

10.182 Where it appears to a local authority that an adult may have needs for care and support, the authority must assess whether he or she does in fact have such needs and, if so, what they are (Care Act 2014 s9(1); SSWB(W)A 2014 s19(1) (Wales)). If the authority is satisfied, on the basis of the assessment, that a person has needs for care and support, it must determine whether those needs meet the certain eligibility criteria and, if so, it must consider what can be done to meet those needs (Care Act 2014 s13; SSWB(W)A 2014 s32).

10.183 A local authority may not meet the needs for care and support of an adult who is subject to immigration control (unless re-included by regulations para 10.24) if his or her needs for care and support have arisen solely because of destitution (Care Act 2014 s21(1); SSWB(W)A 2014 s46(1)). Their needs are, instead, intended to be met under IAA 1999 by Migrant Help (see para 10.29).

10.184 In the case of asylum seekers whose need for care and attention does not arise solely because of destitution but because, for example, of disability, responsibility for meeting their care needs remains with the local authority (*R (Westminster City Council) v Secretary of State for the Environment, Transport and the Regions*, 2001). If the applicant's need for care and attention is to any extent made more acute by some circumstance (eg age, illness or disability) other than lack of accommodation or funds, he or she qualifies for assistance (*O v Wandsworth LBC*, 2001; *R (Mani) v Lambeth LBC*, 2003).

Local Government Act 2000 and Localism Act 2011

10.185 A further safety net may be available under general powers given to all local authorities, whether housing or social services (see para 10.4). LGA 2000 s2 introduced the 'well-being power' for authorities, which power remains applicable in Wales, but in England, on 1 April 2012, it was replaced by a 'power of general competence' by LA 2011 s1. A decision not to use either power to assist is challengeable by judicial review (see paras 8.23–8.28). The power of general competence is intended to be even wider than the well-being power and – subject to qualification – *prima facie* allows authorities to do 'anything that individuals generally may do' (LA 2011 s1(1)). LGA 2000 s2 provides (likewise subject to qualification) that:

> Every local authority are to have power to do anything which they consider is likely to achieve any one or more of the following objects–

(a) the promotion or improvement of the economic well-being of their area,
(b) the promotion or improvement of the social well-being of their area, and
(c) the promotion or improvement of the environmental well-being of their area.

10.186 In *R (J) v Enfield LBC*, 2002, it was held that – in order to ensure that there was no breach of an applicant's right to respect for family under Article 8 ECHR (see para 10.149) – section 2 could be used to provide financial assistance and, if no other power was available, that the authority would have to use it in order to assist; the same would be true of LA 2011 s1. In *R (Morris) v Westminster City Council*, 2005, however, it was concluded that although the authority had power to provide accommodation under section 2, they were not under a duty to do so even when there would otherwise be a breach of Article 8.

Allocation duties

Definition of allocation

10.187 When allocating housing, local housing authorities are obliged to comply with the provisions of Part 6 (HA 1996 s159(1)). As a result of amendments made to Part 6 by LA 2011, there are some differences between the rules that apply in England and in Wales.

10.188 For these purposes, allocation means the following.

1. **Selecting a secure (see paras 1.160–1.209) or introductory (see paras 1.210–1.219) tenant for their own accommodation.** Any form of secure tenancy qualifies so that selecting a person for the grant of a his or her first flexible tenancy (see paras 1.181–1.189) or, once the provisions of the Housing and Planning Act (HPA) 2016 are in force, selecting a person for his or her first new-style fixed-term secure tenancy (see paras 1.190–1.191) is an allocation. Notifying an existing tenant or licensee (see para 1.168) that his or her tenancy is to be secure (HA 1996 s159(3)), eg under HA 1985 Sch 1 paras 2 (employment-related accommodation), 5 (temporary accommodation for people taking up employment), or 10 (student accommodation) is also an allocation.
2. **Nominating a person to be a secure or introductory tenant of another landlord.** Nomination includes both formal and informal arrangements (HA 1996 s159(4)).

3. **Nominating a person to be an assured tenant (see paras 1.220–1.251) of a PRP or RSL (HA 1996 s159(2)).** Nominating has the same meaning as under the last heading.

10.189 Allocations to existing secure or introductory tenants are excluded so that a decision to grant a replacement flexible tenancy (see paras 1.181–1.189) or replacement new-style fixed-term tenancy (see paras 1.190–1.191) to follow on from the original tenancy is not an allocation. The exception is where the allocation involves a transfer of housing accommodation for that tenant made on his or her own application (HA 1996 s159(4A), (5)), ie management transfers initiated by the authority, to which the tenant accedes (or which are ordered by the court: see paras 2.113–2.117), are not allocations within Part 6. In England, management transfers for assured tenants of PRPs and RSLs are also excluded (HA 1996 s159(4A), (4B)) reflecting the fact that many local authorities do not have housing stock of their own as a result of the policy of LSVT (see para 8.13) so that all the social housing in their areas is owned by PRPs or RSLs. There may be circumstances where the authority or PRP may wish to initiate a transfer to make better use of housing stock, eg where the authority needs a large property to accommodate a homeless family and a PRP tenant in a suitable property is willing to move to smaller accommodation.

10.190 In addition, there is a number of other cases which are not treated as an allocation: succession and devolution on death (see paras 1.192–1.203), or assignment to a potential successor (see para 1.207); assignment by way of exchange (see paras 4.135–4.139); grant of a new tenancy by way of exchange (see paras 4.140–4.143); vesting under a number of family or domestic provisions (chapter 7); and, any other cases that may be prescribed by regulations (HA 1996 s160). This power has been exercised to exclude allocations to persons:

1) entitled to rehousing under Land Compensation Act 1973 s39 (see para 12.72);
2) whose homes are repurchased from former council tenants who bought defective dwellings from the authority under HA 1985 ss554–555;
3) who are family intervention tenants (see para 1.262)

(Allocation of Housing (England) Regulations 2002 SI No 3264 reg 3; the Allocation of Housing (Wales) Regulations 2003 SI No 239 reg 3).

Eligibility and qualification

10.191 **Persons from abroad.** Any person may be allocated housing, provided that he or she is not ineligible under section 160A (HA 1996 s160A(1), (2)). An allocation may not be made to two or more persons jointly if even one of them is ineligible (s160A(1)(c)). Eligibility has the same meaning (see paras 10.24–10.27) as in relation to homelessness (HA 1996 s160A; Allocation and Homelessness (Eligibility) (England) Regulations 2006 SI No 1294) and Allocation of Housing and Homelessness (Eligibility) (Wales) Regulations 2014 SI No 2603).

10.192 **Qualifying persons.** In England, the Secretary of State may prescribe categories of person who are or who are not qualified for accommodation under Part 6 (HA 1996 s160ZA(8)). Subject to these provisions, authorities can decide categories of qualifying and disqualified persons for themselves (s160ZA(7)). It has been held, however, that an authority cannot disqualify a person entitled to a reasonable preference (see para 10.202) (*R (Jakimaviciute) v Hammersmith and Fulham LBC*, 2014). Subject to this, disqualified persons could, for example, include applicants whose behaviour has been such that they would be unsuitable tenants, as suggested in *Allocation of accommodation: guidance for local housing authorities in England* (June 2012), para 3.22 (see para 10.194). In deciding whether to disqualify an applicant on this ground, an authority cannot rely on convictions which have become spent under the under the Rehabilitation of Offenders Act 1974 (*R (YA) v Hammersmith and Fulham LBC*, 2016).

10.193 An authority cannot disqualify the following applicants solely the basis that they have no local connection (see paras 10.71–10.73) with its area.

1) Someone serving in the regular forces, or who has served in the regular forces within five years of the date of application.
2) Someone who has recently ceased, or will cease, to be entitled to reside in accommodation provided by the Ministry of Defence following the death of that person's spouse or civil partner, which spouse or civil partner had served in the regular forces and whose death was attributable (wholly or partly) to that service.
3) Someone who is serving or has served in the reserve forces and who is suffering from a serious injury, illness or disability which is attributable (wholly or partly) to that service; or,
4) A secure or introductory tenant or an assured tenant of a social landlord

- who is to be given reasonable preference (see para 10.202) because he or she needs to move to a particular locality in the authority's district,
- where failure to meet that need would cause hardship; and
- who needs to move because he or she works in the authority's district or has been offered work in its district and has a genuine intention of taking up the offer.

(Allocation of Housing (Qualification Criteria for Armed Forces) (England) Regulations 2012 SI No 1869 and Allocation of Housing (Qualification Criteria for Right to Move) (England) Regulations 2015 SI No 967).

10.194 **Conduct.** In Wales, a local authority may decide that an applicant is to be treated as ineligible if it is satisfied that the applicant (or a member of his or her household) has been guilty of behaviour serious enough to make the applicant unsuitable to be a tenant of the authority and that, by reason of the circumstances at the time the application is considered, he or she is unsuitable to be a tenant of the authority because of that behaviour (HA 1996 s160A(7)). This is so even if that person has a right to a reasonable preference (see para 10.202), ie the decision in *Jakimaviciute* (see para 10.192) does not apply.

10.195 Unacceptable behaviour is that which would (if the applicant was a secure tenant of the authority) entitle the authority to a possession order under HA 1985 s84, on any of Grounds 1–7 of Schedule 2 to that Act (see para 2.98), or the absolute ground for possession in HA 1985 s84A (see paras 2.108–2.112) or behaviour by a member of the applicant's household which would (if he or she were a person residing with a secure tenant of the authority) entitle the authority to such a possession order (HA 1996 s160A(8)).

10.196 An applicant who is treated as ineligible because of unacceptable behaviour may (if the applicant considers that he or she should no longer be so treated) make a fresh application (HA 1996 s160A(11)).

10.197 **Decisions.** If the authority decides that an applicant is ineligible for an allocation, or disqualified from an allocation, it must notify the applicant of that decision and of the grounds for it (HA 1996 s160A(9); new s160ZA(9)). Notification must be given in writing, and, if not received by the applicant, shall be treated as having been given if made available at the authority's office for a reasonable period for collection by the applicant or someone acting on his or her behalf (s160A(10)), ie if unreceived, the burden is on the applicant to go to the authority's offices and ask for it.

Applications

10.198 Authorities must ensure that there is free advice and information available in their area about the right to make an application for an allocation of housing (HA 1996 s166(1)(a)). Authorities must also ensure that any necessary assistance in making an application is available free of charge to those who are likely to have difficulty in doing so without assistance (s166(1)(b)). Authorities must ensure that applicants are aware of their right to request information about the likely availability of accommodation (s166(2)).

10.199 Every application for an allocation of housing made in accordance with the procedural requirements of the authority's allocation scheme must be considered by the authority (HA 1996 s166(3)). The fact that a person is an applicant for an allocation may not, without the applicant's consent, be divulged by the authority to any member of the public (s166(4)).

Allocation schemes

10.200 **Allocation scheme.** The authority must maintain an allocation 'scheme' governing priorities and procedures (including all aspects of the allocation procedure, including by whom decisions may be made) (HA 1996 s166A(1) (England); s167(1) (Wales)). Any allocation of a property by an authority must be in accordance with the scheme (HA 1996 s166A(14) (England); s167(8) (Wales)). If not, the allocation may be quashed by the court as being *ultra vires* (*Camden LBC v Shardid*, 2004). It has been held that a tenancy granted pursuant to an *ultra vires* allocation is, however, not invalid (*Birmingham City Council v Qasim*, 2009).

10.201 **Choice.** The allocation scheme must include a statement of the authority's policy on offering people who are to be allocated housing a choice of housing accommodation or the opportunity to express their preferences about the housing accommodation to be allocated to them (HA 1996 s166A(2) (England); s167(1A) (Wales)).

10.202 **Priorities.** The scheme must be framed to ensure that a reasonable preference is given to the following categories of person.

1) The homeless (see para 10.30–10.37).
2) Persons who are owed a duty by a local housing authority under HA 1996 s190(2) (see para 10.99), 193(2) (see para 10.111), or 195(2) (see para 10.104) or under H(W)A 2014 s66, 73 or 75 (or under the analogous duties in the predecessor legislation, HA

1985) or who are occupying accommodation secured by any such authority under s192(3) (see para 10.103).

3) Persons occupying insanitary or overcrowded housing or otherwise living in unsatisfactory housing conditions.
4) Persons who need to move on medical or welfare grounds; and
5) Persons who need to move to a particular locality in the authority's area, where failure to meet that need would cause hardship to themselves or to others (s166A(3) (England); s167(2) (Wales)).

10.203 Reasonable preference must not, however, be given to an applicant who only falls within any of the reasonable preference categories because his or her household includes a restricted person (see para 10.27).

10.204 To afford a reasonable preference means that the criteria must be an 'important factor in making a decision about the allocation of housing' (*R v Lambeth LBC ex p Ashley*, 1996), and that 'positive favour should be shown to applications which satisfy any of the relevant criteria' (*R v Wolverhampton MBC ex p Watters*, 1997). More recently, to afford reasonable preference has been described as providing those who fall within the relevant categories with a 'reasonable head start' over other applicants (*R (A) v Lambeth LBC*, 2001). 'Reasonable preference does, however, imply a power to choose between different applicants on 'reasonable grounds' ... it is not unreasonable to prefer good tenants to bad tenants' (*R v Newham LBC ex p Miah*, 1995).

10.205 Preference does not imply prospects of success, which depend on many factors, of which the most significant is the fact that demand for housing greatly exceeds supply: it is quite possible for a scheme to give reasonable preference to a person and for that person never to be allocated housing; indeed, as it is the scheme which must afford the reasonable preference, assessed in itself rather than according to its outcome, it is even possible for someone with no preference to be allocated accommodation ahead of someone with a preference (*Lin v Barnet LBC*, 2007). Although persons within the categories of need are to be given a reasonable preference, it is not necessary for them to be given an absolute priority over everyone else. Authorities are entitled to allocate properties to persons who do not fall within a category of reasonable preference (*R (Ahmad) v Newham LBC*, 2009).

10.206 **Additional preference.** The scheme may be framed so as to give additional preference to those within these categories who have an urgent housing need (HA 1996 s166A(3) (England); s167(2) (Wales)). Additional preference means giving those applicants 'additional weight' or 'an extra head start', but it does not require an allocation to be made to applicants entitled to it ahead of all others (*R (A) v Lambeth LBC*, 2001). In *R (Ahmad) v Newham LBC*, 2009, the House of Lords held (contrary to earlier decisions of the lower courts) that allocation schemes did not have to include any mechanism for giving added preference to those who fell within more than one of the categories in para 10.202.

10.207 The scheme may include provision for determining priorities between those within the reasonable preference categories, taking into account: the financial resources available to a person to meet housing costs; any behaviour of a person (or a member of his or her household) which affects his or her suitability to be a tenant; and, any local connection which exists between a person the authority's area (HA 1996 s166A(5) (England); s167(2A) (Wales)).

10.208 **Unacceptable behaviour.** In Wales, the scheme does not have to provide for any preference to an applicant where the authority is satisfied that the applicant (or a household member) has been guilty of unacceptable behaviour (see para 10.194) serious enough to make him or her unsuitable to be a tenant of the authority and that, in the circumstances at the time the application is considered, he or she deserves by reason of that behaviour not to be treated as a member of one of the groups to whom a reasonable preference is to be given (HA 1996 s167(2C), (2D)).

10.209 **Regulations.** The secretary of state and the Welsh Ministers have power to add to, amend or repeal any part of the list of those to whom a reasonable preference is to be accorded (HA 1996 s166A(7) (England); s167(3) (Wales)) and also have power to specify factors which are not to be taken into account when allocating housing (s166A(8) (England); s167(4) (Wales)). In England, additional preference (see para 10.206) must be given to a person who falls within one of the reasonable preference categories (see para 10.202) and who:

a) is serving in the regular armed forces and is suffering from a serious injury, illness or disability attributable (wholly or partly) to the person's service;
b) formerly served in the regular forces;
c) has recently ceased, or will cease to be entitled, to reside in accommodation provided by the Ministry of Defence following the death of that person's spouse or civil partner who has served in the regular forces and whose death was attributable (wholly or partly) to that service; or

d) is serving or has served in the reserve forces and is suffering from a serious injury, illness or disability which is attributable (wholly or partly) to the person's service.

(Housing Act 1996 (Additional Preference for Armed Forces) (England) Regulations 2012 SI No 2989).

10.210 **Other allocations.** Subject to the reasonable preference categories, the scheme may contain provision about the allocation of particular accommodation to a person who makes a specific application for it – the authority's choice policy (see para 10.201) – and to persons of a particular description, whether or not they are within the reasonable preference categories (HA 1996 s166A(6) (England); s167(2E) (Wales)).

10.211 **Changing the scheme.** Priorities are otherwise in the discretion of the authority (HA 1996 s166A(11) (England); s167(6) (Wales)). Before adopting or making any major policy change to a scheme, the authority must send a copy of it in draft to every PRP or RSL with which it has nomination arrangements, and afford them a reasonable opportunity to comment (s166A(13) (England); s167(7) (Wales)). English authorities also have to consider their homelessness strategies (see para 10.10) and their tenancy strategies (see para 1.184); London borough councils also have to consider the London housing strategy published by the Greater London Authority. If the authority does make a major policy alteration to its scheme, it has to take such steps as it considers reasonable to bring the effect of the alteration to the attention of those likely to be affected by it (s168(3)).

10.212 **Code of Guidance.** As under Part 7 (see para 10.20), there is provision for the secretary of state and the Welsh Ministers to issue guidance to which authorities must have regard (HA 1996 s169). In England, see *Allocation of accommodation: guidance for local housing authorities in England* (June 2012), *Providing Social Housing for Local People: Statutory Guidance* (December 2013); *Right to Move: Statutory guidance on social housing allocations for local housing authorities in England* (March 2015). In Wales, see the *Code of Guidance to Local Authorities on the Allocation of Accommodation and Homelessness 2016* (March 2016).

10.213 **Information.** An authority must publish a summary of its scheme, and provide a copy of it free of charge to any member of the public who asks for it (HA 1996 s168(1)). The full scheme must be made available for inspection at the authority's principal office, and a copy must be made available to any member of the public who asks for it, on payment of a reasonable fee (s168(2)).

Procedure

10.214 The scheme must be framed so as to give an applicant the right to request general information that will enable him or her to assess the following:

1) how his or her application is likely to be treated under the scheme (including whether the applicant is likely to be regarded as in one of the reasonable preference categories); and
2) whether accommodation appropriate to his or her needs is likely to be made available to him or her and, if so, how long it is likely to be before such accommodation becomes available for allocation (HA 1996 s166A(9) (England); s167(4A)(a) (Wales)).

10.215 The secretary of state and the Welsh Ministers may require that the procedures are framed in accordance with such principles as may be prescribed (HA 1996 s166A(10) (England); s167(5) (Wales)). In both England and Wales, a councillor cannot be involved in a decision to allocate accommodation to a person living in his or her ward or a decision to allocate accommodation in his or her ward; in Wales, housing officers must be included in the persons making allocation decisions unless the authority has decided not to delegate such decisions to them (Allocation of Housing (Procedure) Regulations 1997 SI No 483 and Local Housing Authorities (Prescribed Principles for Allocation Schemes) (Wales) Regulations 1997 SI No 45). Procedures are otherwise in the discretion of the authority (s166A(11) (England); s167(6) (Wales)).

10.216 **Decisions.** In Wales, the scheme must be framed so that an applicant is notified in writing of any decision that he or she is a person who is to be given no preference because of a decision as to his or her behaviour (see para 10.208) (HA 1996 s167(4A)(b)).

10.217 **Review and challenge.** The scheme must include the right for applicants to request a review of a decision as to whether they are to be given no preference under section 167(2C) (see para 10.208), about the facts of their case or that they are considered ineligible under section 160A (see para 10.191) or disqualified under section 160ZA (see para 10.192) (HA 1996 s166A(9)(c) (England); s167(4A)(d) (Wales)). There are, however, no regulations governing the conduct of reviews, nor is there any appeal to the county court. It follows that any challenge to the review, or challenge to any other decision or aspect of the scheme, can only be by way of judicial review, according to the principles of domestic public law (see paras 8.23–8.28).

10.218 **Co-operation.** When an authority asks a PRP or RSL to offer accommodation to people with priority under the authority's allocation scheme, such landlords are bound to co-operate to such extent as is reasonable in the circumstances (HA 1996 s170).

Criminal offences

10.219 It is a criminal offence knowingly or recklessly to make a statement – in connection with the exercise by an authority of its functions under Part 6 – which is false in a material particular, or knowingly to withhold information which an authority has reasonably required in connection with the exercise of its functions under Part 6 (HA 1996 s171(1)).

10.220 The offence is punishable on summary conviction by a fine of up to an unlimited amount (HA 1996 s171(2); LASPO 2012 s85(1)).

CHAPTER 11

Disrepair: contract and tort

Introduction

11.1 **Civil proceedings.** In this chapter, we consider civil proceedings for disrepair, primarily from the viewpoint of the occupier who suffers its effects. Proceedings are also available to the local authority to counter bad housing, including disrepair, under the Housing Acts 1985 and 2004, and under the Environmental Protection Act (EPA) 1990, which are considered, respectively, in chapters 12 and 13. Within each of those sets of powers, an occupier may be able to take steps either to initiate action (by way of complaint to a justice of the peace under Housing Act (HA) 2004 s4 that a house is hazardous – see para 12.87) or to take action him- or herself, which is particularly relevant when the landlord is the local authority (by way of summons for statutory nuisance, under EPA 1990 s82 – see paras 13.20–13.27).

11.2 **Repair and improvement.** In practice, there can be an overlap between what is or is perceived to be an issue of disrepair and what is considered to be improvement. Although the overlap between each of these is considered in this chapter (see paras 11.20–11.27), improvement powers – and financial assistance for their exercise – have already been considered in chapter 4, within the framework of rights generally available to occupiers.

11.3 **Cumulative remedies.** It should, however, be remembered that all these other possibilities remain available, and that they, as well as other remedies considered in the final three chapters of this book, are additional to those considered in this.

11.4 **Contract and tort.** In this chapter, we are concerned with remedies in contract and tort. Contract will assist when there is a specific agreement governing repairs, whether express or implied; tort is the body of law governing relations between individuals where harm is alleged to have been suffered, where there is no contractual relationship, or where the contractual relationship does not itself cover the harm in question.

Contract

Contractual and statutory provisions

11.5 The starting point will always be what – if anything – is set out in any written agreement that may exist. In the main, it is landlords who draw up letting agreements and consequently the object of the agreement will be to impose upon the tenant the most extensive obligations that the law permits, while limiting the landlord's own obligations.

11.6 In a number of cases, however, the law will intervene. These circumstances are considered in context but it should be noted that in short leases and periodic tenancies any such attempts by a landlord – referable to repair – are likely to contravene the provisions of Landlord and Tenant Act (LTA) 1985 s11 (see paras 11.52–11.63), that other leases at low rents may have to comply with the provisions of LTA 1985 s8 (see paras 11.48–11.51), and that relief may be obtainable under the provisions of the Unfair Contract Terms Act 1977 or the Consumer Rights Act 2015 (see paras 4.93–4.100). Further, remedies in tort may be available where there are none in contract (see paras 11.109–11.140).

Notice of disrepair

11.7 There is one principle that is common to almost all of the provisions to be considered under this heading: a landlord's obligation to repair does not arise until he or she has had actual notice of conditions such as to put him or, if not on actual notice of what is in disrepair, then at least on sufficient notice to cause him or her to inspect and find out. The only exception to this is the case of an express repairing covenant which does not state that the tenant has to give notice (*Minchburn v Peck*, 1987).

11.8 The leading cases on the need for notice usefully illustrate its operation. In *O'Brien v Robinson*, 1973, works had been executed to a ceiling several years before it fell down. There had been no further complaint or warning, by tenant or otherwise, to the landlord between times and the landlord was, accordingly, held not to be in breach of the obligation to repair.

11.9 On the other hand, in *Sheldon v West Bromwich Corp*, 1973, a plumber employed by the defendant corporation inspected a water tank. The tank was corroded although it was not yet weeping. Subsequently, it burst. It was held that the condition of the water tank at the time of the inspection, even without the weeping (which would be a sure and final sign of corrosion calling for repair), was sufficient to put the corporation on notice that something needed to be done.

11.10 In *McGreal v Wake*, 1984, a notice was served on the landlord by the local authority requiring works to the property. When the landlord did not carry out the works, the local authority carried them out in default (see chapter 12). For the period from after the landlord had a reasonable opportunity to comply with the notice until the authority completed the works, the landlord was held to be in breach of his or her obligation to repair.

11.11 From these and other cases (see also *Dinefwr BC v Jones*, 1987; *Hall v Howard*, 1988) the following propositions emerge.

1) **Actual notice.** Notice need not come from the tenant. It is sufficient that the landlord has actually had notice, eg by way of a notice under one of the many provisions considered in the next three chapters.
2) **On notice.** Notice must be sufficient to warn the landlord that there may be a problem. It is not necessary for the tenant actually to identify causes, or to specify defects in such detail to serve as a schedule of (necessary) works.
3) **Unequivocal notice.** Notice must, however, be unequivocal. Where a tenant gave notice of disrepair, saying that he would subsequently provide the landlord with the details, the landlord was entitled to await the further information (*Al-Hassani v Merrigan*, 1987).

11.12 **Common parts.** The rule that notice has to be given does not apply in relation to any part of the premises still in the landlord's control (*British Telecommunications Plc v Sun Life Assurance Society Plc*, 1995; *Edwards v Kumarasamy*, 2016). In *Passley v Wandsworth LBC*, 1996, the landlord authority was held responsible for burst pipes, even though it had no notice of any defect, because the pipes were located in a roof space above a top floor flat which was a part of the property which was not within the flat but within a part of the property under its control.

Terminology

11.13 There is a number of different expressions which will be used in relation to disrepair, the meaning of which needs to be considered.

Structure and exterior

11.14 Some repairing obligations apply specifically or only to the structure and/or exterior of a property (see, in particular, LTA 1985 s11 – paras 11.52–11.63).

Structure

11.15 A house is a complex whole, and anything which touches upon that complex unit may properly be deemed to be part of the structure

(*Pearlman v Keepers and Governors of Harrow School*, 1978), including internal plasterwork on walls and ceilings (*Grand v Gill*, 2011). The roof of a block of flats or a house converted into flats may be part of the structure of the top floor flat, but then again it may not, depending on, for example, whether there is a roof space or an attic not part of the top floor letting (*Douglas-Scott v Scorgie*, 1984).

Exterior

11.16 A dividing wall between two terraced houses will be part of the exterior of each (*Green v Eales*, 1841), and the walls of a flat – whether to the outside or the inside of the building – and the ceiling and floor, will all be part of the exterior for the purpose of the covenant (*Campden Hill Towers Ltd v Gardner*, 1976).

Windows

11.17 Windows are part of the exterior (*Quick v Taff Ely BC*, 1985; *Ball v Plummer*, 1979; *Boswell v Crucible Steel Co*, 1924; *Irvine v Moran*, 1990). That is not to say that a landlord will be liable for a breakage by the tenant, which would be the tenant's responsibility as part of his or her duty to use the premises in a tenant-like manner (see para 4.111(3)), but it does mean that breakage by someone else, or because, for example, the frame broke or warped or a sash snapped causing the window to fall and the glass to break, would be the liability of the landlord.

Disrepair to structure or exterior

11.18 A repairing obligation affecting the structure or exterior means disrepair *to* the structure or exterior, not resulting from it. Thus, dampness caused by a leak or defective brickwork will mean that the structure or exterior is in disrepair, but where the construction of the structure and exterior results in dampness from ordinary use of the premises, ie 'condensation dampness', without actual disrepair, this will not class as disrepair within a covenant (*Quick v Taff Ely BC*, 1985; *Lee v Leeds City Council*, 2002).

11.19 Thus, in *Stent v Monmouth DC*, 1987, it was held that if a door 'merely' fails to keep out water, there will be no disrepair to the structure, although if the water ingress damages the door itself, there will be. In *Staves v Leeds City Council*, 1990, condensation dampness meant that the physical condition of the plaster required renewal. It was conceded that the plaster was part of the structure and it therefore followed that there was disrepair. In *Irvine v Moran*, 1990, however, it was held that internal wall plaster was not part of the structure of a dwelling-house since it was more in the nature of a decorative finish than an essential material element of the house.

Repair

11.20 Most covenants will govern 'repair' (see, in particular, LTA 1985 s11 – see paras 11.52–11.63). A covenant to keep something in repair means that it must also be put into repair, for that which is not in repair at the commencement of the tenancy can hardly be kept in repair (*Saner v Bilton (No 1)*, 1878).

11.21 For many years, it was believed that the proper way to define the word repair in a repairing covenant was by distinguishing it from such other terms as 'improvement', 'renewal' or 'replacement', ie if the works needed to cure the problem amounted to improvement, renewal or replacement, they would not comprise a repair. For this reason, it was commonly believed that an inherent defect could not be cured within a repairing obligation, because that would comprise an improvement.

11.22 The key test was – and to an extent remains – whether the works executed would result in the delivery up of something different in quality to that which was originally let. Thus, for example, it was thought that a repairing obligation could not be used to require a landlord to introduce a damp-proof course (*Pembery v Lamdin*, 1940), or to provide underpinning (*Sotheby v Grundy*, 1947).

Extent of works

11.23 More recently it was held, however, that these older cases turned on their own facts rather than setting precedents as to what works are or are not within a covenant to repair: *Ravenseft Properties Ltd v Davstone (Holdings) Ltd*, 1978, a case involving the same block of flats as the subject of the action in *Campden Hill Towers v Gardner*, 1976.

11.24 In that case, the block had been constructed without expansion joints to retain a stone cladding once natural movement ('settling') commenced. Accordingly, the stone cladding threatened to fall away. The only proper way to rectify this, however, was by the introduction of the missing expansion joints. It was argued that such works to the structure, involving the introduction of a new method of construction and the curing of a construction defect, could not be within the covenant to repair. Having regard to the sort of works involved (which were not, in comparison to the whole block, that extensive), to the necessity for the joints, and to the cost of the works compared to the value of the block as a whole, it was held that the works could be compelled within the repairing obligation.

Contemplation of parties

11.25 In another case (*Smedley v Chumley and Hawkes*, 1981), a riverside restaurant was built on a pier, or raft. It was a recent construction, and there was inadequate underpinning. The restaurant threatened to sink into the river. The court asked itself what had been in the contemplation of the parties, and was influenced by the fact that these were modern premises, not an old and deteriorating property: it was therefore held that underpinning could be compelled within a covenant to repair.

Principles in practice

11.26 How do these principles work in housing? In *Wainwright v Leeds City Council*, 1984, the older authorities prevailed. In *Elmcroft Developments Ltd v Tankersley-Sawyer*, 1984, and in *Quick v Taff Ely BC*, 1985, however, the Court of Appeal upheld the *Ravenseft* approach. Accordingly, where a modern property is in issue, works can be required within LTA 1985 s11, even though they comprise works to cure an inherent or constructional defect and which involve the introduction of a new construction method; and, where an older house is in issue, the courts – having regard both to contemporary values and to the comparatively small cost of such works as damp-proof coursing (*Uddin v Islington LBC*, 2015), perhaps also influenced by the modern emphasis on retention in use of older housing stock – are also now prepared to order whatever works are necessary to keep a house in a reasonable condition, provided they are not so extensive or expensive as to comprise virtual reconstruction or such overall improvement as will turn the old house into a new dwelling. Thus, in *Murray v Birmingham City Council*, 1987, it was held that the covenant could (in principle) extend to the provision of a new roof, although in that case such extensive works were in fact not considered necessary.

Three tests

11.27 In *McDougall v Easington DC*, 1989, the Court of Appeal considered whether a major rehabilitation programme requiring over £10,000 worth of works to each property, but only increasing their value from £10,000 to £18,000, amounted to their repair, and concluded that the works amounted to an improvement not within the repairing obligation. The court identified three tests which could be applied separately or concurrently to decide whether works amounted to a repair within LTA 1985:

1) **Whole or subsidiary structure** – whether the alterations went to the whole or substantially the whole of the structure or only to a subsidiary part;
2) **Character** – whether the effect of the alterations was to produce a building of a wholly different character than that which had been let; and
3) **Cost** – the cost of the works in relation to the previous value of the building and their effect on the value and life span of the building.

Proper working order

11.28 Some covenants require a landlord to keep installations, eg for gas, electricity or the use of water, in proper working order (see, in particular, LTA 1985 s11 – see paras 11.52–11.63). It is not a defence to an allegation that installations are not in proper working order to show that they suffer from a design defect (*Liverpool City Council v Irwin*, 1976) and a change in the nature of the supply may require the landlord to modify the installations to ensure that they continue to function (*O'Connor v Old Etonian Housing Association Ltd*, 2002).

Repairing obligations

11.29 Repairing obligations may be found in the contractual terms, ie those express terms which may be found in tenancy agreements; or, they may be found in terms implied by law, which may be additional to those expressed in an agreement or may provide a basic and minimum statement of liabilities when there is neither written nor verbal agreement between the parties; or, they may be found in terms implied by statute, which may override what has expressly been agreed or may operate where nothing express has been agreed.

Express terms

11.30 Although most landlords seek to limit their repairing obligations to a minimum, this is not always the case. Some local authorities have expressly agreed to higher standards than those imposed by LTA 1985 s11 (see para 11.55). In *Welsh v Greenwich LBC*, 2000, the authority covenanted to keep the premises in 'good condition', which was held to include liability for severe condensation dampness that would not have fallen within a mere covenant to repair (see paras 11.20–11.27).

11.31 Another term concerned a covenant to 'take all reasonable steps to keep the estate clean and tidy'. It was held that this was not discharged by the mere appointment of outside contractors, however competent, without also putting in place an adequate system for the landlord to monitor the contractor's performance and effectiveness (*Long v Southwark LBC*, 2002).

Terms implied by law

Fitness for habitation

11.32 There is no general term implied into contracts for the letting of residential accommodation either that a dwelling is fit for human habitation at the start of the tenancy or that it will be so kept by the landlord during the tenancy (*Hart v Windsor*, 1843). It is, however, implied that a furnished lettings will at the start of the tenancy be fit for human habitation (*Smith v Marrable*, 1843). It would seem likely that a similar covenant will be implied into a licence of furnished accommodation (*Smith v Nottinghamshire CC*, 1981), although there could be cases where it would not be consistent with the nature of the licence to do so, eg temporary accommodation as a caretaker or 'guardian' of property in disrepair, until works can be undertaken.

11.33 Fitness for these purposes means fitness at common law, not fitness for human habitation as defined in LTA 1985 (see para 11.48). What is meant by fitness, therefore, must be considered as a matter of common law, although statute may on occasion afford a helpful guide to contemporary standards: it is clear that what one generation means by fitness is not the same as another.

Weekly tenancies

11.34 Nor, in the absence of any express agreement as to repair, will the courts necessarily assume that under a weekly or monthly periodic tenancy, the landlord will take responsibility for 'major' repairs, even though the courts readily accept that it is unlikely to have been intended that the tenant will do so instead, for want of any sufficient interest in the property to merit substantial expenditure (*Mint v Good*, 1950; *Sleafer v Lambeth LBC*, 1959).

11.35 Under a weekly, or probably other short periodic tenancy, the landlord will, however, have a right to do repairs, and correspondingly to enter to view the state of the property, but whether or not it is implied at law that he or she is obliged so to do will depend on whether anything was written or said, or otherwise on the court's view as to what was intended.

11.36 In *Barrett v Lounova (1982) Ltd*, 1988, where the tenant was liable for internal repairs but nothing had been agreed or said about structural or external repairs, the court concluded that it must have been intended that the landlord would have liability, in order to make the agreement work effectively, ie to give it business efficacy, because the tenant could not otherwise comply with his or her own (internal) obligations.

11.37 In practice, this issue rarely arises today, because lacunae in responsibility are cured by the provisions of LTA 1985 s11, although there remain in existence a number of tenancies which predate its predecessor (HA 1961 s32), and to which, accordingly, its provisions do not apply, as in *Barrett*.

Licences

11.38 In the case of a licence, it will not only be the case that the landlord will usually be assumed to undertake liability to keep the property in repair (*Smith v Nottinghamshire CC*, 1981), but it may be considered inconsistent with the nature of licence for the licensee to be under any significant repairing obligation (*Addiscombe Garden Estates v Crabbe*, 1957). There could, however, be exceptions if some particular aspect of the licence so suggested, eg a licence to a builder allowing him or her to occupy premises while 'doing them up'.

Common parts

11.39 A clear distinction must be drawn between the premises which are the subject of the tenancy and other parts of a house or building which are not included in the letting. These parts, eg stairs, roof, halls, corridors, foundations and – in some houses – bathrooms and toilets, are kept in the landlord's possession and control and are consequently his or her responsibility. He or she is wholly responsible for their upkeep (*Cockburn v Smith*, 1924) and must keep them reasonably safe (*Dunster v Hollis*, 1918). Where they form the means of access to a house, flat or room, and in the absence of any express agreement to the contrary, he or she is to keep them in a reasonable condition (*Liverpool City Council v Irwin*, 1976; *King v South Northamptonshire DC*, 1991), probably in a condition reasonably approximating that in which they were at the commencement of the letting. (It is thought that this obligation is related to, or derived from, the landlord's obligation not to derogate from grant, which has already been discussed (see para 4.111(1)).

Non-derogation from grant

11.40 Where the tenant occupies property which adjoins property retained by landlord (eg common parts), the landlord must not act in such a way as to interfere with the tenant's use of the property for the purpose for which it was let. This obligation on the landlord not to 'derogate from the grant' has already been discussed (see para 4.111(1)).

Quiet enjoyment

11.41 This has already been discussed (see para 4.111(2)). This covenant may be a useful catch-all where, for example, repairs take an undue time to complete or are executed with such disregard for the tenant's convenience that it may be said unreasonably and unnecessarily to interfere with his or her use of the premises. There is no reason why disrepair should not also be considered breach of the covenant for quiet enjoyment (*Gordon v Selico Co*, 1986).

11.42 The covenant can only be used, however, in relation to a complaint about conditions arising after the grant of the tenancy. The tenant takes the premises in the physical conditions in which he or she finds them and subject to the uses contemplated for those premises. Thus, everyday noise from neighbouring flats arising because of a lack of soundproofing does not amount to a breach of the covenant (*Southwark LBC v Mills*, 1999).

Estoppel and rent registration

11.43 In some circumstances, even where one party has no direct or express legal rights against another, the law will stop the other party denying an obligation. This is known as 'estoppel' (see also paras 1.129–1.130).

11.44 One such circumstances relates to repairs and was at one time quite common, although is of decreasing contemporary relevance. It is noted below (see para 11.53) that the provisions of LTA 1985 s11, apply only to tenancies granted after 24 October 1961. Where a tenancy commenced before that date, therefore, there might have been no repairing obligations implied into the tenancy at all (as in *Barrett v Lounova (1982) Ltd*, 1988; see paras 11.36–11.37). Over time, however, if (as it is likely to have been) the tenancy came within the protection of the Rent Acts and therefore (on their introduction) qualified for registration of a fair rent (see paras 3.53–3.61), it is possible – perhaps even likely – that the rent officer (see para 3.53) will have assumed, or even been informed, either that section 11 applies or that the landlord is in any event responsible for major and structural repairs, and will have assessed the rent on this basis.

11.45 As the tenant will therefore be paying – and the landlord receiving – a higher rent than if the tenant were responsible for the major repairs, or than if no-one had any such responsibility, the landlord will be 'estopped' from denying the liability (*Brikom Investments v Seaford*, 1981), although he or she can subsequently apply for a variation in the registration in which case the estoppel will not guarantee future responsibility.

11.46 In an appropriate case, estoppel may override even the express terms of an agreement, ie where the tenant has paid on the basis of a repairing obligation imposed on the landlord, or has acted to his or her detriment because of an assumption that the landlord is not liable to repair (*Brikom Investments Ltd v Carr*, 1979).

Use in a tenant-like manner

11.47 This has already been discussed (see para 4.111(3)).

Terms implied by statute

LTA 1985 s8 – fit for human habitation

11.48 Contrary to the normal rule (see para 11.32) that there is no covenant that premises are fit for human habitation at the commencement of a tenancy or that they will so be kept throughout the tenancy, statute implies just such a term into tenancies at a very low rent (LTA 1985 s8). For these purposes, a property is unfit if it is not reasonably suitable for occupation because it is defective in respect of one or more of the following: repair, stability, freedom from damp, internal arrangement, natural lighting, ventilation, water supply, drainage and sanitary conveniences, facilities for preparation of food and for the disposal of waste water (LTA 1985 s10).

11.49 The covenant is implied into both short lettings and, unless excluded, into longer leases. It is not implied into a lease for three years or more if it contains a term requiring the tenant to put the premises into a condition reasonably fit for human habitation, unless the lease can be determined at the option of either party before the end of the first three years, ie under a break clause (see para 1.27) (LTA 1985 s8(5)).

11.50 As discussed above (see para 11.57), there will be no obligation until the landlord has had notice of the disrepair (*Morgan v Liverpool Corp*, 1927), and the term has no application where the premises is incapable of being rendered fit for human habitation at a reasonable expense (*Buswell v Goodwin*, 1970). In the case of a Rent Act protected tenancy (see paras 1.268–1.293), the term will, however, carry over into a statutory tenancy. (In the case of an assured tenancy (see paras 1.220–1.251), the low rent level will preclude application of section 8 – para 11.51). The term carries with it a right on the part of the landlord, on not less than 24 hours' notice in writing, to enter to view the state and condition of the premises (LTA 1985 s8(2)).

11.51 The covenant is, however, implied only into tenancies at such low rents that it is today rarely encountered in practice. The rent levels are as follows.

1) Where the contract was made before 31 July 1923, the rent at the beginning of the tenancy must not have been more than £40 pa in the administrative county of London, nor more than £26 pa in a borough of an urban district outside London, nor elsewhere more than £16 pa.
2) In relation to contracts made on or after that date, but before 6 July 1957, the rent at the commencement of the tenancy must not have been more than £40 pa in the administrative county of London, nor more than £26 elsewhere.
3) In relation to contracts made on or after that date, the rent at the commencement must not have been more than £80 pa in what was until 1 April 1965 the administrative county of London and thereafter Greater London, or £52 pa elsewhere.

LTA 1985 s11 – principal repairing covenant

11.52 This is the principal repairing covenant now implied into most lettings of residential accommodation. It does not usually apply if the letting is for a term of seven years or more (LTA 1985 s13), which means seven years from the commencement of occupation, either under the tenancy or under a binding agreement for a tenancy (*Brikom Investments v Seaford*, 1981). The Localism Act (LA) 2011, however, has recently amended section 13 to apply to secure tenancies and assured tenancies granted by PRPs in England even if they are for a term of seven years or more. This amendment does not apply to shared ownership leases (see para 8.11) granted by PRPs. Similarly, once in force, the Housing and Planning Act (HPA) 2016 will amend section 13 to apply to introductory tenancies for a term of seven years or more. The intention is to ensure that tenants with longer secure tenancies (see paras 1.190–1.191), longer flexible tenancies (see paras 1.181–1.189), or similar fixed-term assured tenancies granted by PRPs (see para 1.183), have the same rights as other secure and assured tenants.

11.53 The section applies only to tenancies granted after commencement of the HA 1961, when what is now section 11 was first introduced (24 October 1961). A periodic tenancy is not for seven years or more, even though it may last or have lasted that long or longer, so that the covenant accordingly does apply to it. If the tenancy is a Rent Act protected tenancy, it will carry over into any statutory tenancy (see para 1.269); if a fixed-term (see para 1.18) assured (see para 1.220), into a statutory periodic tenancy (see para 2.161).

11.54 LTA 1985 allows the parties to apply to the county court for an order excluding or modifying the operation of section 11 (s12(2)), but in the absence of any such order the Act overrides the express terms of any agreement, and any contract purporting to exclude the provisions of section 11 – or to penalise the tenant because the landlord has to comply with them – is void and of no effect (s12(1)). In relation to periodic tenancies such orders are rare.

11.55 The term is that:

> In any lease of a dwelling-house, being a lease to which this section applies, there shall be implied a covenant by the lessor–
> (a) to keep in repair (see paras 11.20–11.27) the structure and exterior (see paras 11.14–11.19) of the dwelling-house (including drains, gutters and external pipes); and
> (b) to keep in repair and proper working order (see paras 11.28) the installations in the dwelling-house–
> (i) for the supply of water, gas and electricity, and for sanitation (including basins, sinks, baths and sanitary conveniences but not, except as aforesaid, fixtures, fittings and appliances for making use of the supply of water, gas or electricity), and
> (ii) for space heating or heating water.

11.56 The provision applies as much to part of a house or building – even as little as a single room – as to a house (LTA 1985 s16). In *Brown v Liverpool Corp*, 1969, it was held that the obligation extended to essential means of access to the premises. The decision in *Brown* has been overruled (*Edwards v Kumarasamy*, 2016) but the unusual facts of *Brown* must be borne in mind: the disrepair was a broken step more than seven feet away from the front door of the tenant's house. Although the Supreme Court in *Edwards* decided that the step could not be part of the house's exterior, the repairing obligation may still apply to means of access connected to the fabric of the building, eg steps down from a front door.

11.57 Where only a part of a house or building is involved, the covenant extends to an obligation to keep the structure and exterior of the house or building of which it is a part in repair, and to keep in repair and proper working order an installation (for the same purposes – see para 11.55) which serves the part of the house which is the subject of the tenancy, provided it forms part of a building in which the landlord has an interest or the installation itself is owned by the landlord or is under his or her control (LTA 1985 s11(1A), added by HA 1988 s116; *Niazi Services Ltd v Van der Loo*, 2004). (For a landlord's specific duties in relation to gas appliances, see paras 11.106–11.108).

11.58 This extended obligation only arises, however, where the disrepair actually affects the tenant's enjoyment of his or her property or of the common parts (LTA 1985 s11(1B)). It only applies to a tenancy granted on or after 15 November 1988 (unless pursuant to an earlier contract).

11.59 The provisions do not, however, go so far as to require the landlord to do works for which the tenant is liable under the duty to use premises in a tenant-like manner (see para 4.111(3)), nor do they require him or her to rebuild or reinstate the premises in the case of destruction or damage by fire, tempest, flood or other inevitable accident, nor to keep in repair or maintain such of the tenant's own belongings as he or she is entitled to remove from the property (LTA 1985 s11(2)).

11.60 It is a defence to an action based on failure to repair a building in which the premises are situated, or installations outside the premises but which service them, that the landlord was unable to obtain sufficient rights to do the works (LTA 1985 s11(3A)), eg under the Access to Neighbouring Land Act 1992 (see para 11.140).

11.61 Unless the defect arises in a part of the premises which is not let to the tenant, there will only be a breach of the covenant if the landlord has had notice of disrepair (see paras 11.7–11.12; *Edwards v Kumarasamy*, 2016).

11.62 LTA 1985 provides that regard shall be had to the age, character and prospective life of the property, and the locality in which it is situated (LTA 1985 s11(3)). This may mean that patch repairs are adequate even where a higher standard of repair would be desirable (*Trustees of Hungerford Charity v Beazeley*, 1993).

11.63 The covenant carries with it a right on the part of the landlord, on giving not less than 24 hours' notice in writing, to enter to view the state of the premises (LTA 1985 s11(6)). (There are also covenants implied into Rent Act statutory and Housing Act assured tenancies allowing entry for repair – see para 11.64).

RA 1977; HA 1988

11.64 Though the Rent Act (RA) 1977 and HA 1988 are not directly concerned with repairs, they contain a number of provisions affecting the subject.

1) **Continuation of covenants.** Both a Rent Act statutory tenancy (see para 1.269) and a Housing Act assured statutory periodic tenancy (see paras 2.161) are on the same terms as the preceding contractual tenancy (RA 1977 s3(1); HA 1988 s5), from which it follows that any express or implied repairing obligations will be continued (*McCarrick v Liverpool Corp*, 1946).
2) **Access.** It is an implied term of all Rent Act protected tenancies (whether contractual or statutory: para 1.269), and of all Housing Act assured tenancies (see paras 1.220–1.251), that the tenant will afford the landlord all reasonable facilities for access and the execution of any repairs which the landlord is entitled to carry out (RA 1977 ss3(2), 148; HA 1988 s16). This is wider than the right to enter to view the state of the premises (see para 11.63).
3) **Grant-aided works and court order.** Where a landlord wishes to carry out works which qualify for a grant under the Regulatory Reform (Housing Assistance) (England and Wales) Order 2002 SI No 1860 (see para 4.168) or the Housing Grants, Construction and Regeneration Act 1996 (see para 4.177), and a Rent Act protected tenant (see para 1.269) will not consent to their execution, the landlord may apply to the court for an order compelling the tenant's consent, which may be subject to terms, eg housing during works, and which will be granted or refused bearing in mind such alternative accommodation, the age and health of the tenant, and any disadvantages that might be expected to result to the tenant from such works (RA 1977 s116). There is no equivalent provision under HA 1988, although suitable alternative accommodation to enable extensive works may constitute a ground for possession (see para 2.170).

LTA 1954

11.65 On termination of a long lease, a tenant at a low rent may become a statutory tenant under RA 1977 (see paras 2.74–2.77). Under the long lease, the tenant will usually have been responsible for repairs. It would be inconsistent with the nature of a statutory tenancy for the tenant to retain such an obligation, but on the other hand it might be considered unfair were the landlord suddenly to find him- or herself having to rectify breaches of the tenant's covenant, ie the tenant's failure to repair during the lease.

11.66 To this end, amongst the provisions governing 'conversion' of the long leaseholder to the status of statutory tenant, is to be found provision for the execution of 'initial repairs' (LTA 1954 s7). The notice proposing the statutory tenancy (see para 2.76) must itself propose what initial repairs are to be carried out and what the balance of repairing obligation is to be during the statutory tenancy. There are no equivalent provisions where the termination of the long tenancy falls to be dealt with under the Local Government and Housing Act 1989 Sch 10 (see paras 2.78–2.83).

11.67 The issue of initial repairs is to be agreed between landlord and tenant at least two months before the statutory tenancy comes into existence, or otherwise application must be made to the county court for a determination (LTA 1954 s7).

11.68 The purpose of the provision is to ensure that the property is in an acceptable state for the commencement of the statutory tenancy, for which purpose it is assumed that the state will be the same as if the tenant had fulfilled all his or her contractual obligations. The burden of initial repairs will commonly fall on the tenant. Unless the tenant is willing to have them carried out him- or herself, however, the court cannot order him or her to do so; instead, the landlord is ordered to execute the works, and the tenant to pay for them. The works are required to be to a maximum standard of 'good repair', or such higher standard of works as the landlord indicates he or she is willing to attain (LTA 1954 s9). The court may order payment for the initial repairs in instalments, or in a lump sum (LTA 1954 s8).

11.69 The court can also determine the balance of obligations to follow the initial repairs, but cannot order the landlord to maintain the premises at a higher standard than as at the completion of the initial repairs or, if there are no initial repairs, than the state of the premises at the date of the court's hearing (LTA 1954 s9). The court is under no obligation to make any order governing continuing repairing obligations (LTA 1954 s8). It is, however, common to order or agree that the balance will be as under LTA 1985 s11 (see paras 11.52–11.63).

Leasehold Reform Act 1967

11.70 On the extension of a lease under this Act (see paras 4.15–4.25), there is a general provision for variation of the repairing terms of the original lease by consent or by court order (Leasehold Reform Act (LRA) 1967 s15).

Contractual remedies

11.71 Either the landlord or the tenant may wish to obtain a remedy against the other for breach of a repairing obligation. If the tenant breaks his or her obligations, the landlord may seek possession of the premises by way of an action for forfeiture (see paras 2.29–2.44) and/or under RA 1977 (see para 2.194), HA 1985 (see para 2.98) or HA 1988 (see para 2.169). He or she may also seek damages. More commonly, it is the tenant who will be seeking redress against the landlord: here, possession will not be in issue, but the tenant will want an order for works to be executed and may also seek compensation for the period of disrepair.

Damages for breach by landlord

Unfitness

11.72 If furnished premises are not fit for human habitation, the tenant can quit and will not be liable for the rent. Unfortunately, that is rarely an option available for most tenants, especially as this could lead to a finding of intentional homelessness under HA 1996 Pt 7 or Housing (Wales) Act (H(W)A) 2014 Pt 2 (see paras 10.52–10.70).

11.73 It would seem at the least arguable that if premises are not fit at the commencement of the tenancy, the breach by the landlord should today be treated in the same way as breach of any other repairing obligation, ie that the tenant can remain in occupation, press for repairs to be executed and claim damages.

Disrepair

11.74 Where a landlord is in breach of a repairing covenant, the tenant is entitled to damages which, so far as money can, will put the tenant in the position in which he or she would have been but for the breach of covenant (*Pembery v Lamdin*, 1940; *Calabar Properties Ltd v Stitcher*, 1983).

Special damages

11.75 The tenant is entitled to special damages for any losses such as the cost of alternative accommodation while repairs are carried out, the value of damaged belongings, or the costs of redecoration (*Calabar*).

General damages

11.76 The tenant will also usually be entitled to an award of general damages to reflect any discomfort, inconvenience and ill health suffered.

Such an award may include damages for the tenant's mental distress (*Personal Representatives of Chiodi v De Marney*, 1988). Prior to the decision in *Wallace v Manchester City Council*, 1998, the Court of Appeal had approved a number of different approaches to the assessment of general damages.

1) **Diminution in value.** This was an award for the diminution in the value of the property to the tenant calculated by reference to a proportion of the rent payable (*McCoy & Co v Clark*, 1982).
2) **Discomfort and inconvenience.** This was a global assessment of the discomfort and inconvenience suffered made without reference to the rent payable (*Personal Representatives of Chiodi v De Marney*, 1988).
3) **Combination.** This was a combination of the above (*Sturolson & Co v Mauroux*, 1988).

11.77 In *Wallace*, the Court of Appeal restated the principles for awarding general damages to a periodic tenant, as follows.

1) **In occupation.** For periods when the tenant remains in occupation of the property, the loss requiring compensation is the loss of comfort and convenience which results from the disrepair.

   Expert evidence is of no assistance in assessing this figure; the question is the monetary value of the discomfort and inconvenience suffered by the tenant, which is a question for the judge. It may be ascertained in a number of different ways, including diminution in value assessed as a notional reduction in the rent. Some judges prefer to use that method alone; some prefer a global award for discomfort and inconvenience; others may prefer a combination of the two. The judge is not, however, bound to assess damages separately under heads of both diminution in value and discomfort and inconvenience; they are alternative ways of expressing the same concept.

   A judge who decides to assess the award on a global basis should cross-check the prospective award by reference to the rent payable for the period during which the landlord is in breach of covenant. A court may award a tenant general damages at a level which exceeds the amount of the rent which was payable by the tenant during the relevant period but the court must give clear reasons for doing so, and the facts of the case – in particular, the landlord's conduct – must warrant the award (*Shine v English Churches Housing Group*, 2004).

   The source of the money used to pay the rent is irrelevant to the amount of compensation; it is therefore irrelevant that the rent is paid by housing benefit. The quality of the accommodation is relevant to the amount of damages. A tenant who pays a high rent for high-class accommodation will be awarded damages reflecting the standards he or she is entitled to expect (*Niazi Services Ltd v Van der Loo*, 2004).

2) **Out of occupation.** If the tenant has to move out of the property because it is uninhabitable or to allow repairs to be carried out, damages will be awarded to reflect the inconvenience of having to move and live in temporary accommodation (*Lubren v Lambeth LBC*, 1987).

   If the tenant rented the property to sublet, provided the landlord was aware of the intention to sublet and the disrepair means that it can only be sublet at a reduced rent, the tenant is entitled damages measured by the loss of rental income (*Calabar*; *Wallace*).

Long-leaseholders

11.78 A long-leaseholder (see para 2.72) is in a different position to a periodic tenant, as his or her property is not only a home but is also a significant investment. If he or she sells or sublets the property, he or she is entitled to damages either reflecting the reduction in the purchase price or the reduction in the rent obtained for the sub-letting (*Calabar*; *Wallace*). Long-leaseholders usually only have to pay a small 'ground rent' (see para 2.33) so that if the leaseholder remains in the property, his or her general damages for distress and inconvenience have to be assessed by using a notional market rent for the property (*Earle v Charamboulos*, 2006). Even if the leaseholder does not suffer discomfort and inconvenience as a result of the disrepair, he or she is entitled to some general damages reflecting loss of enjoyment of his or her property rights (*Moorjani v Durban Estates Ltd*, 2015).

General damages uplift

11.79 Many claims for general damages are brought by claimants who have a conditional fee agreement with their lawyers (often called 'no win no fee'), ie the lawyer receives nothing if the claim fails but if it succeeds the lawyer receives a 'success fee' above his or her normal fee. On 1 April 2013, changes made by the Legal Aid, Sentencing and Punishment of Offenders Act (LASPO) 2012 mean that lawyers can no longer recover more than their normal fees from the unsuccessful party. To compensate claimants for not being able to recover success fees, after calculating general damages under the usual principles, the court must now increase the award by 10 per cent; this principle applies even in cases where there is no conditional fee agreement (*Simmons v Castle*, 2012).

Redecoration

11.80 Finally, the tenant is entitled to require the premises to be reinstated, including by way of any internal redecoration necessitated by the landlord's works (see para 11.75), and in the absence of such reinstatement or redecoration will be entitled to damages for having to do them him- or herself (*McGreal v Wake*, 1984; *Bradley v Chorley BC*, 1985).

Damages for breach by tenant

Reversionary interest

11.81 The principles governing a breach of an obligation to repair on the part of a tenant are different. The amount which the landlord can recover is the amount by which his reversionary interest in the premises, ie the interest which he or she enjoys on account of his or her future repossession of the premises, has depreciated (*Smith v Peat*, 1853; *Drummond v S & U Stores*, 1980; LTA 1927 s18(1)).

11.82 If the landlord has already repossessed the premises, the damages represent the depreciation in the value of that of which he or she has recovered possession compared to what he or she ought to have got back (*Hanson v Newman*, 1933). If the landlord intends to carry out the repairs which the tenant should have carried out, the damages will usually be the cost of those repairs together with loss of rent for the period during which the repairs are to be carried out (*Jones v Herxheimer*, 1950). The depreciation in value may, however, be substantially less if the landlord does not intend to do all, or intends to do only some of, the repairs (*Landeau v Marchbank*, 1949), eg if the future use to which the landlord intends to put the premises means that the repairs are not needed. If the landlord intends to demolish the premises, or redevelop the premises by carrying out works which are so extensive that works to remedy the disrepair would be valueless, he or she cannot obtain any damages (LTA 1927 s18(1)).

11.83 If the tenant is to remain in occupation, eg as a statutory tenant on account of LTA 1954 (see paras 2.74–2.77), then it would seem that unless 'initial repairs' (see paras 11.66–11.69) serve to eliminate any deterioration in the value of the landlord's reversion, the valuations of repaired and unrepaired property are to be based on the lower values representing a sitting tenant in occupation (*Jeffs v West London Property Corp*, 1954).

Set-off and counterclaim

11.84 One of the most common responses by tenants to repairs inactivity by the landlord is to withhold the rent. This is the principle of 'set-off,' reflecting the close connection between the obligations to pay rent and to carry out works. The essence of set-off is that rent is – for that reason – not due. Accordingly, if the landlord makes a claim for arrears against which the tenant can establish a set-off, the landlord's claim will fail (to the extent of the set-off). Where a landlord claims arrears (or any other sum), and the tenant seeks to deduct other monies he or she claims are due, not by way of damages for disrepair, the tenant's response is not by set-off but by counterclaim. (*Note.* The same is true if the tenant's claim for disrepair damages is greater than the landlord's claim for arrears, and the tenant wants to be paid the difference rather than setting it off against future rent).

11.85 At one time, set-off was thought to be confined to money actually expended by the tenant on carrying out works (that were the landlord's responsibility) in default (*Lee-Parker v Izzet*, 1971), and only after the landlord had been given a warning, an opportunity to review estimates, and the money was to be taken out of future rent. Subsequently, it was held that the same principle could apply in relation to past rent withheld, ie rent arrears (*Asco Developments Ltd v Lowes*, 1978). Finally, it was held the tenant could also set-off his or her general damages (see paras 11.76–11.79) (*British Anzani (Felixstowe) v International Marine Management (UK)*, 1978; *Televantos v McCulloch*, 1990).

11.86 Where there has been a change of landlord and the new landlord brings a claim for rent arrears, however, the tenant cannot set off damages relating to the time when the former landlord still owned the property (*Edlington Properties Ltd v Fenner & Co Ltd*, 2006), unless the former landlord has assigned the tenant's rent arrears to the new landlord as part of the sale (*Muscat v Smith*, 2003). (*Note.* Such an assignment is, in residential accommodation, common).

A note of caution

11.87 A tenant should, if possible, withstand the temptation to resort to set-off as a way of trying to force the landlord to carry out repairs. It is much better to pay the rent, and then to assert the right or counterclaim damages in the course of proceedings, calculated as described above (see paras 11.74–11.80), for there is otherwise the risk that the tenant will lose the monetary claim and find him- or herself in arrears. While it is true that, where there is a discretion, a court is unlikely to find it reasonable to make an order for possession if rent has been withheld because of a genuine dispute over repairs (*Lal v Nakum*, 1981, but compare *Haringey LBC v Stewart*, 1991), even where the tenant fails to prove his or her case, the risk remains and a court may take the view that the tenant should have put the money aside and have it available against the possibility of losing. Furthermore, while there is invariably such a discretion in relation to a secure tenant (see para 2.98) and a Rent Act protected or statutory tenant (see para 2.169), in the case of an assured tenant there are both discretionary grounds (see para 2.169) and the mandatory ground 8 (see para 2.170), in which case there will be no room for the exercise of discretion by the judge.

11.88 Set-off should accordingly, if possible, be confined to two cases: either where there is a clear breach, and the tenant, after giving his or her landlord warning of his or her intentions, causes the work to be carried out in default; or when the tenant puts the full rent aside. Even so, in the first circumstance there will continue to be a danger that the tenant will be incorrect as to his or her rights (and the landlord's obligations), for which reason if withholding can be avoided, it should be; and, in the second, there is the residual risk that a court could nonetheless make an order. Where the tenant is already in arrears, however, and lacks the money to pay them off, set-off may of course, and in an appropriate case should be, raised.

Specific performance and injunctions

11.89 An order for specific performance is an order of the court requiring someone to fulfil a contractual obligation; an injunction is an order to do something, which may or may not arise under contract, ie it may also be used in relation to tort (see para 11.109). There is no practical difference between the two remedies: either may be sought in the county court (LTA 1985 s17, governing specific performance; County Courts Act 1984 s38, governing injunctions).

11.90 A landlord's want of financial ability to comply with an order is no defence (*Francis v Cowcliffe*, 1976). Although it was formerly considered that neither class of order could be made against a tenant (*Hill v Barclay*, 1811; *Regional Properties v City of London Real Property*, 1981), a more recent case suggests that this is no longer the case (*Rainbow Estates Ltd v Tokenhold* Ltd, 1998) and it is hard to see a principled basis on which it would be refused today.

Court procedure

11.91 Where the tenant does not claim an injunction and the value of a claim is less than £5,000, a matter will normally be dealt with in the county court on the small claims track. Where, however, there is a claim for an order requiring the landlord to carry out work, it will not be allocated to the small claims track if the cost of the works is estimated to be more than £1,000 and the financial value of the remainder of the claim is more than £1,000 (CPR 26.6(1)(b)).

Appointment of manager or receiver

11.92 This has already been discussed (see paras 4.76–4.80). It is as available where the landlord's failure relates to repairs as to any other failure to discharge his or her obligations and is, indeed, one of the principal circumstances when it will be sought and considered a just and convenient order. It is not, however, available against a local authority (see para 4.78).

Tenant's right to repair

11.93 Certain local authority tenants have the 'right to repair' (HA 1985 s96). The right is available both to secure (see paras 1.160–1.201) and introductory tenants (see paras 1.210–1.219). The Secretary of State and the National Assembly for Wales have power to apply the right to demoted tenants (see paras 1.252–1.260) but neither has done so. The detailed provision of the scheme is contained in the Secure Tenants of Local Housing Authorities (Right to Repair) Regulations 1994 SI No 133. The intention is to ensure that authorities carry out repairs within a reasonable time. In outline, where the right applies and a tenant asks the authority for a repair to be carried out but the authority fails to do the work within prescribed time-limits, the tenant has the right to require the authority to use a different contractor. If that contractor also fails to do the work in time, the tenant is entitled to compensation.

11.94 The right to repair only applies if the authority has at least 100 properties let to secure or introductory tenants on the day they receive the request for a repair from the tenant (reg 3(2)). The tenant ceases to be entitled to his or her rights under the regulations if he or she informs the landlord that he or she no longer wants the repair carried out, or, although given a reasonable opportunity, he or she fails to provide details of the arrangements for the contractor to obtain access to the dwelling-house, or to provide access for an inspection or for the repair to be carried out (reg 3(3)).

11.95 The right only applies to specified defects (reg 4 and Sch): loss of electricity (total or partial); unsafe power to a light socket or electrical fitting; loss of water or gas supply (total or partial); blocked flue to fire or boiler; loss of space or water heating (total or partial); blocked or leaking drain or soil stack; blocked or leaking toilet pan or non-flushing toilet (but only if there is no other working toilet in the property); blocked sink, bath or basin; tap which cannot be turned; leaks from water or heating pipe, tank, cistern or roof; insecure external window, door or lock; loose or detached bannister or handrail; rotten timber flooring or stair tread; door entryphone, or mechanical extractor fan in internal kitchen or bathroom, not working.

11.96 If the tenant asks for a repair to be carried out, the authority has to decide whether it is a 'qualifying repair' and therefore has the right to inspect the property to find out whether it is (reg 5). Only a repair to a specified defect (see para 11.95) is a qualifying repair and any repair costing more than £250 does not qualify (reg 4). If the authority decides that the repair does not qualify, it must write to the tenant explaining why; if it decides that it does, it must write providing contact details for the authority's contractor (which can be an in-house repairs team) who will be doing the works and specifying the date by which the works must be completed (reg 5).

11.97 The time-limit for completing the works depends on the nature of the defect and varies between one working day and a week (reg 2 and Sch). In some cases, different time-limits apply during different times of the year, eg between 31 October and 1 May, the time-limit for restoring space or water heating is one day but between 30 April and 1 November, it is three days. If the works are not done in time, the tenant can write to the authority asking it to use a different contractor (reg 6) and the authority has a second period of the same length (reg 2 and Sch) to carry out the works. Time-limits can be suspended if the works cannot be done because of circumstances beyond the authority's or contractor's control (reg 8).

11.98 If the works are not completed before the end of the second time-limit, the tenant is entitled to compensation: £10 plus £2 per day from the final date for the repair up to when the repair is completed, subject to a maximum of £50 (reg 7). If the tenant is in rent arrears, the authority can credit this sum to his or her rent account.

11.99 Disputes may be determined by the county court (reg 10).

Forfeiture

11.100 Forfeiture is one of the means of bringing a tenancy to an end (see paras 2.29–2.44). There is no right to forfeit a tenancy unless such a right is expressly reserved in the agreement. The right is, however, commonly reserved in most written tenancy agreements, and is commonly drafted in terms that apply on breach of a tenant's repairing obligation.

Waiver

11.101 If the obligation in question is to put (but not also to keep) the premises in repair, a landlord who has known of a breach by the tenant but has so conducted him- or herself as to be considered to have waived (see para 2.41) the breach, will also have waived his or her right to forfeit the tenancy (*Doe d. Morecraft v Meux*, 1824). If, however, the obligation is also to keep the property in repair, both the obligation and the breach continue so long as the tenant fails to repair, and there is, accordingly, no waiver (*Doe d. Hemmings v Durnford*, 1832).

Remedying the breach

11.102 Before seeking to forfeit, the landlord must serve notice specifying his or her complaint and, assuming as it usually will be that the breach is capable of remedy, requiring remedy and demanding compensation (Law of Property Act (LPA) 1925 s146; para 2.46). The landlord must allow sufficient time.

Leasehold Property (Repairs) Act 1938

11.103 In relation to a long lease (see para 2.72) of which at least three years remain, the section 146 notice must also advise the tenant of his or her right to claim, by way of counter-notice, the protection of the Leasehold Property (Repairs) Act 1938, under the terms of which the landlord cannot proceed with an action for forfeiture based on disrepair other than with the leave of the court. The court will not grant leave unless an immediate remedy is needed in order to prevent a substantial reduction in the value of the landlord's interest, or where remedy now would be cheap compared to remedy later, or in order to comply with any statute governing condition (eg under HA 2004 or EPA 1990, see chapters 12 and 13), or where the tenant is not in occupation and repair is needed for the protection of other occupiers, or where in all the circumstances the court considers it just and equitable to grant leave.

Relief

11.104 Where a landlord seeks to forfeit a tenancy, the tenant can usually apply to the court for relief from forfeiture (see paras 2.37–2.46), which, however, will almost invariably be on conditions, here requiring the tenant to rectify the breach, although not if the court considers that the extent of the obligation is unreasonable (LPA 1925 s147).

Possession order

11.105 Even if a tenancy is determined by forfeiture, or where – without forfeiture – proceedings against either a secure (see para 1.160), or assured (see para 1.213) tenant, Rent Act protected or statutory (see para 1.220) tenant, are based on breach of the tenant's repairing obligation, it will still be necessary to prove that it is reasonable to make an order for possession (see paras 2.98; 2.169; 2.218).

Gas safety regulations

11.106 The Gas Safety (Installation and Use) Regulations 1998 SI No 2451 impose duties in relation to the maintenance of gas fittings, including appliances such as boilers and fires and pipework serving the appliances. The Regulations are made under the Health and Safety at Work, etc Act (HSWA) 1974. The duties apply to any landlord, defined as someone who has let premises for residential purposes either under a lease for a term of less then seven years (including all periodic tenancies (see para 1.18) and Rent Act statutory tenancies – para 1.269) or under a licence (reg 36(1)).

11.107 The landlord is under a duty to ensure that appliances and pipework are maintained in a safe condition so as to prevent risk of injury to any person (reg 36(2)). He or she must also ensure that each appliance is inspected once every 12 months by a Gas Safety registered engineer and that a record in kept of the inspection (reg 36(3), (4)), which must be retained for two years (reg 36(3)(c)) and a copy provided to any occupier on request (reg 36(5)). The landlord's duty extends to appliances and pipework which serve the premises even if they are not let to the tenant, eg communal boilers. Failure to comply with any duty imposed by the regulations is a criminal offence (HSWA 1974 s33(1)) punishable in the magistrates' court by imprisonment for a maximum of 12 months and/or an unlimited fine; in the Crown

Court, by a maximum of two years' imprisonment and or an unlimited fine (HSWA 1974 Sch 3A).

11.108 In England, if the tenancy is an assured shorthold tenancy (see para 1.246) which was granted on or after 1 October 2015, the landlord must provide the tenant with a copy of record of the inspection free of charge and – until he or she does so – cannot serve a section 21 notice (see para 2.197(3)). From 1 October 2018, this requirement will apply to all English assured shorthold tenancies whenever they were granted.

Tort

Causes of action

11.109 In this section, we briefly consider remedies for disrepair, or other unacceptable housing conditions, which arise independently of contract. Accordingly, these remedies may be available not only to the tenant, or, eg a licensee of the landlord, but others, such as visitors or those living with the tenant. These remedies arise in 'tort' (which means, literally, 'wrong'). There is a number of torts which may touch on housing conditions.

Negligence

Duty of care

11.110 Action in negligence only arises when there is a legal duty of care. This means:

> ... you must take reasonable care to avoid acts or omissions which you can reasonably foresee would be likely to injure your neighbour. Who, then, in law is my neighbour? The answer seems to be: persons who are so closely and directly affected by my act that I ought reasonably to have them in contemplation as being so affected when I am directing my mind to the acts or omissions which are called into question. (*Donoghue v Stevenson*, 1932, per Lord Atkin).

Duty to tenants and visitors

11.111 Thus, in addition to the landlord's contractual duty to make sure that common parts are kept reasonably safe (see para 11.39), he or she also owes a duty of care to tenants or others who may visit premises to ensure that they are safeguarded against damage from any danger in the common parts of which he or she knows, or ought to have known (*Cunard v Antifyre Ltd*, 1932).

Duty of builders

11.112 Anyone carrying out work on premises is under a general duty to use reasonable care for the safety of those whom he or she knows or ought to know might be affected by those works, or who are lawfully in the vicinity of those works (*AC Billings & Son v Riden*, 1957). A builder of a house, whether or not he or she is also the landlord, owes a duty of care in the construction of the building to potential occupiers of it, but the liability only extends to personal injury and not to economic loss, ie because, for example, it is worth less than was paid for it (*Murphy v Brentwood DC*, 1990) or cannot be used for the purpose for which it was acquired. A builder's liability to his or her client is primarily contractual and absent a specific assumption of responsibility by the builder, he or she does not owe a duty in tort in addition to his or her contractual obligations (*Robinson v Jones*, 2011).

Developers

11.113 Developers (whether or not also the owner) of, for example, housing for sale, owe a duty of care to ensure that purchasers are reasonably safe from personal injury (*Sutherland v Maton (CR) & Son*, 1976; *Batty v Metropolitan Property Realisations*, 1978; *Rimmer v Liverpool City Council*, 1983; *Targett v Torfaen BC*, 1991).

Building professionals

11.114 Architects, engineers, surveyors, and others involved in the construction of a dwelling owe a similar duty to future occupiers to take reasonable care in the execution of their functions (*Cedar Transport Group v First Wyvern Property Trustees Co*, 1980). In the light of *Murphy*, any such liability will be limited to damages for personal injury, and not extend to economic loss (*Preston v Torfaen BC*, 1993).

Works by the landlord

11.115 A landlord may also be responsible in negligence for other works, eg for the manner of carrying out his or her repairing obligations (*Sharpe v Manchester City Council*, 1977) or for the quality of works done prior to the commencement of a letting.

11.116 Whether the landlord has complied with his or her duty of care will normally turn on whether, in selecting a particular design or materials for the repair or maintenance, the landlord has acted 'in accordance with a practice accepted as proper by a reasonable body of ... men skilled in that particular art' (*Adams v Rhymney Valley DC*, 2000). There is no negligence, however, in failing to carry out works before a letting (*Arden v Pullen*, 1842).

Home purchase

11.117 A further, and important, illustration of negligence arises in the course of home purchase. Most people buying their own homes – whether freehold (see para 1.7) or under a long lease (see paras 1.11) – will take advice from a surveyor and a solicitor. The surveyor will report on the condition of the house: if he or she does so negligently, he or she will be liable for the effects of his or her default. A solicitor will have a number of legal functions to carry out, including finding out information about the purchaser's title, making inquiries of the environment agency (eg about risk of flooding or subsidence) and checking the local authority's register of local land charges (see para 12.28) which may show a wide range of restrictions on the property, including planning controls, improvement notices (see paras 12.18–12.26) or prohibition orders (see paras 12.33–12.43) made under HA 2004, and asking the authority whether it has any plans, eg for clearance (see paras 12.54–12.55), which may adversely affect the purchaser's intended occupation. He or she, too, may be liable in negligence

Report to building society

11.118 Where a purchaser failed to have his or her own survey carried out, but instead relied on the fact that a building society was willing to advance the mortgage, knowing that the building society had themselves sought a survey, the surveyor was held liable to the purchaser, even though the purchaser never saw his report to the building society (*Yianni v Evans (Edwin) & Sons*, 1981; see also *Smith v Bush*, 1987; *Harris v Wyre Forest DC*, 1987; *Davies v Idris Parry*, 1988). The surveyor is deemed to know that the consequences of his or her negligence would not only affect the building society's decision on mortgage but also the purchaser's decision as to whether or not to buy. In practice today, many building societies (and banks) release such reports to the borrower. This principle only applies to prospective owner-occupiers and not apply to buy-to-let purchasers, who are more likely to obtain their own valuations (*Scullion v Royal Bank of Scotland, trading as Colleys*, 2011).

Local authorities

11.119 Local authorities may be negligent in the execution of their functions. Alternatively, they may be liable for breach of statutory duty, which is technically a separate tort, for failing properly to carry out their obligations under an Act of Parliament if (but only if) on a proper construction of the statute, the court considers that Parliament intended that a person harmed by the way the authority has carried out its duty under the statute should be able to bring a claim against the authority (*X (minors) v Bedfordshire CC*, 1995).

11.120 Thus, where an authority was obliged to inspect property in the course of construction to see whether there had been compliance with Building Regulations (see also para 11.123), and were alleged to have done so negligently, action was available at the instigation of the first buyer or any subsequent owner (*Anns v Merton LBC*, 1977). Whether an authority can be liable in these circumstances has, however, subsequently been doubted, and it is clear that any liability is limited to damages for personal injury and does not extend to economic loss (*Murphy v Brentwood DC*, 1990).

Causation

11.121 The fact that there is a defect, however, is not enough to give rise to action: that defect must be caused by an act which a reasonable man would not have done, or an omission to do something which a reasonable man would have made sure was done (*Bolton v Stone*, 1951).

11.122 The act or omission must cause the harm (or the likelihood of harm). There must be a line of causation between act or omission and harm, so that the latter is not too remote a consequence of the former. Another way of putting the same proposition is that it must have been reasonably foreseeable (which is not to say reasonably foreseen) that harm of the order which has resulted would result.

Breach of building regulations

Building Act 1984 s38

11.123 In a large number of cases where housing is constructed, improved or altered, or its use changed, it will be obligatory to comply with the building regulations. Under the Building Act 1984 s38 (replacing HSWA 1974 s71) anyone who is obliged to comply with the regulations and who fails to do so will, save where the regulations themselves otherwise specify, be liable to an action in tort at the instance of a person harmed by his or her failure. This section, however, has yet to be brought into force and, after more than 30 years, it must be doubted whether it ever will be. That does not rule out negligence or another cause of action, but mere failure to comply will not be actionable unless and until it (or a replacement provision to like effect) is brought into force.

Defective premises

DPA 1972 s1

11.124 The Defective Premises Act (DPA) 1972 imposes a duty of care on anyone doing any work for or in connection with the provision of a dwelling by erection, conversion or enlargement (s1). The section only applies to works which provide a new dwelling: works of extension to, or refurbishment of, an existing dwelling only fall within section 1 if they result in a new dwelling, the identity of which is wholly different from the old one (*Jenson v Faux*, 2011). The duty of care is to see that work is done in a workmanlike manner and with proper materials or – if the person involved is a professional, eg architect, engineer – that it is done in a professional manner, so as to ensure that the dwelling will be fit for habitation when completed.

11.125 The duty is owed to, among others, purchasers and tenants. The duty is additional to the duty of care in negligence (see paras 11.110–11.122) but applies only to work following the commencement of the Act (1 January 1974).

DPA 1972 s3

11.126 Formerly, there was a common law rule that sellers of land or landlords could not be liable in negligence for building or other work on land which they carried out *before* the sale or letting (*Otto v Bolton*, 1936). Section 3 abolished that rule by providing that where work of construction, repair, maintenance or demolition, or any other work is done in relation to premises, any duty of care owed to anyone who might reasonably be expected to be affected by resulting defects in the state of the premises persists through any subsequent sale or letting.

11.127 The section does not apply to works carried out prior to a sale or letting which took place before the commencement of the Act (1 January 1974).

DPA 1972 s4

11.128 Further, whenever a landlord is under an obligation to repair (however arising, ie implied by law (see paras 11.32–11.47); implied by statute (see paras 11.48–11.70); or express), he or she owes:

> ... to all persons who might reasonably be expected to be affected by defects in the state of the premises a duty to take such care as is reasonable in all the circumstances to see that they are reasonably safe from personal injury or from damage to their property. (DPA 1972 s4).

11.129 The duty arises whenever the landlord knows of the defect, or ought to have known of it, so that it may be an appropriate cause of action if, for want of notice (see paras 11.7–11.12), action cannot be taken under a contractual obligation. Accordingly, a landlord was held to be in breach where his tenant suffered from carbon monoxide poisoning caused by a defective gas fire because, in breach of his obligations under the Gas Safety Regulations (see paras 11.106–11.108), the landlord had failed to have the fire inspected; the amount of damages was reduced, however, on the basis of contributory negligence by the tenant because he had failed to notify the landlord of the defect (*Sykes v Harry*, 2001). The duty is owed both to tenants, and to the tenant's visitors.

11.130 The duty only arises, however, in relation to 'relevant defects'. A relevant defect is one arising from or continuing because of an act or omission by the landlord which actually constitutes a breach of his or her repairing obligation, or which would have constituted a breach of his or her repairing obligation if he or she had had notice of it. In substance, this means any defect which is within the obligation to repair, of which the landlord knew, or ought to have known.

11.131 Even if the extent of the repairing obligation is unclear, however, if the landlord has at least a right to repair (as distinct from a duty), he or she is treated for these purposes as if under a repairing obligation (DPA 1972 s4(4); *McCauley v Bristol City Council*, 1991; *Lafferty v Newark & Sherwood DC*, 2016), so that in weekly tenancies, Rent Act protected and statutory tenancies, and Housing Act assured tenancies, and those to which LTA 1985 s8 (see para 11.48) and s11 (see para 11.52) apply, there will be an obligation for the purposes of this provision, in relation to any class of works which the right of entry is designed to permit the landlord to execute. The landlord's obligation, however, is only to put right something which is in disrepair and does not require him or her to carry out alterations to make the property safe (*McNerny v Lambeth LBC*, 1988; *Alker v Collingwood Housing Association*, 2007; *Dodd v Raeburn Estates Ltd*, 2016; *Sternbaum v Dhesi*, 2016).

Occupiers' liability

Occupiers' Liability Act 1957 s2

11.132 The occupier of premises is the person in possession and control of them (*Wheat v Lacon & Co Ltd*, 1966). Thus, a tenant is an occupier, but only of the premises which are the subject of the letting. In a block of flats, the landlord is the occupier of the block, just as in a house let out in bedsitting-rooms or flats the landlord retains possession and control of the house itself.

11.133 An occupier owes a common duty to take such care as is reasonable in all the circumstances of the case to see that 'visitors' to premises will be reasonably safe in using the premises for the purposes for which he or she was allowed in (Occupiers' Liability Act 1957 s2). The term 'visitors' includes those on the premises with the express or implied permission of the occupier, eg a tenant or licensee of some part, or the tenant's or licensee's own visitors. The extent of the duty may vary with circumstances, including factors affecting the class of visitor eg the elderly or children. In some circumstances, there may even be a duty of care to someone not lawfully on the premises, ie a trespasser: see the Occupiers' Liability Act 1984.

Nuisance

Act or state of affairs

11.134 Like breach of the covenant for quiet enjoyment (see paras 11.41–11.42), a landlord's control of neighbouring property may in appropriate circumstances be such that it interferes with the tenant's reasonable use of the premises let and, as such, in law a nuisance. To constitute a nuisance, there must be some act or state of affairs in one set of premises, which adversely affects use and enjoyment of another. One example is where an infestation of pests in the common parts of a building spreads into the tenant's premises (*Sharpe v Manchester City Council*, 1997 and *Siveter v Wandsworth LBC*, 2012). A claim in nuisance can only be brought by someone in possession of land, which certainly includes a tenant but may include a licensee if he or she has an exclusive right to occupy the premises. It is, however, only the person with the interest in the land who can sue, not other family members: *Hunter v Canary Wharf*, 1997. The effect of the nuisance on family members is nonetheless to be taken into account in assessing damages (*Dobson v Thames Water Utilities Ltd*, 2009). The fact that a person may have lawful authority to carry out an activity does not prevent it from being a nuisance, eg foul smells from a licensed waste disposal plant can still be the subject of a claim (*Barr v Biffa Waste Services Ltd*, 2012) or activities authorised by planning permission (*Lawrence v Coventry*, 2014).

Waste

Alteration of nature of premises

11.135 An act of waste is an act by the tenant which alters the nature of the premises let. It is a tort peculiar to the law of landlord and tenant. In some ways, it may be considered the equivalent in tort of the tenant's contractual duty to use premises in a tenant-like manner (see para 4.96).

11.136 Normally, waste will be an act of deterioration of the premises, eg cutting down a tree or knocking down an outhouse, or any other act of damage, including to the premises themselves. Technically, it can also be something which might otherwise be regarded as an improvement, eg an alteration. There will be no waste, however, if the landlord's consent to the act in question has been secured, and an act of waste will only give rise to a claim for possession if it is also an act of deterioration (see paras 2.98, 2.169, 2.218).

Remedies

11.137 If one person commits a tort which causes harm to another, that other is to be put in the position he or she would have been in had the tort not occurred. Thus, damages will be available for such harm as has ensued. There are broadly two categories of damages. 'Special damages' are those which are identifiable, such as loss of earnings, loss of property, including clothing, medical expenses, alternative accommodation, travelling expenses. In addition, there are 'general damages', for pain and suffering, personal injury, and nervous shock, although not, as a general rule, for inconvenience or discomfort (compare paras 11.76–11.79). In a number of cases involving defects in houses, however, damages for inconvenience and discomfort have been awarded (*Perry v Sidney Phillips*, 1982; *Watts v Morrow*, 1991).

11.138 Two points on damages are of importance to occupiers of housing. First, there is no reduction in a claim for damages because the claim is against a public body, engaged in a socially useful task, such as the discharge of their housing functions (*Taylor v Liverpool Corp*, 1939). Secondly, where the claim is in relation to damage to a house, eg by an owner-occupier suing someone who has negligently advised on the purchase (see para 11.117), damages will be the cost of repairs, assessed as at the date when, having regard to all the circumstances, the repairs could reasonably have been undertaken, rather than when the harm occurred: in this connection, the financial ability or inability of the person suing may be a factor in requiring the deferral (and so the increased cost) of repairs (*Perry v Sidney Phillips & Son*, 1982). In some cases, however, eg where a claim is brought against a local authority for failing to carry out building inspections correctly, any claim will be limited to damages for personal injury and will not cover any loss of value in the house or cost of repairs (see para 11.120; *Murphy v Brentwood DC*, 1990).

11.139 **Injunction.** In principle, there is no reason why an injunction should not be sought, either to prevent harm arising from a tort, or to rectify it. Although the prospect of harm should not be too remote, it is not necessary to wait until a building is about to collapse, and assistance may be secured by way of injunction as soon as it is clear that if something is not done, the harm feared will indeed occur (*Anns v Merton LBC*, 1977; *Crump v Torfaen BC*, 1982).

11.140 **Access to Neighbouring Land Act 1992.** Where, in order to preserve the condition of land, works are required to neighbouring land, it is possible to obtain an order for access to that neighbouring land in order to carry out the required works (Access to Neighbouring Land Act 1992).

Limitation

11.141 As a general rule, actions both in tort or contract must be brought within six years of the date on which the cause of action accrued, ie when the right to sue arose (Limitation Act (LA) 1980 ss2, 5). If, however, the claim includes personal injuries, it must be brought within three years (LA 1980 s11), from when the person injured knew of the injury, knew that it was serious enough to merit action, knew that it was attributable to the landlord's default, and knew who the landlord was (LA 1980 s14), although the court can extend this time limit (LA 1980 s33). Time does not, however, start to run against a minor until he or she achieves his or her majority (18) (LA 1980 s28).

11.142 An obligation to keep property in repair is a continuing breach, not only at its outset, so that time can run from any point until the landlord rectifies the defect.

11.143 **Latent damage.** More problematic is from when time runs if a defect is not obvious, perhaps for many years. In such a case, the limitation period will be the longer of the usual six-year period, accruing from the date when the damage came into existence, or three years from the date when the complainant discovers (or could have discovered) the damage (LA 1980 s24A). An overriding time limit (or 'long-stop') of 15 years is, however, applicable (LA 1980 s24B). A successor in title, who buys in ignorance of the damage, may also benefit from the extended time limits (Latent Damage Act 1986 s3).

Human rights

11.144 The right to respect for the home (see paras 1.319–1.328) required by Article 8 of the European Convention on Human Rights may be breached if a person's home is in very severe disrepair (*Lee v Leeds City Council*, 2002); accordingly, a failure to repair by a landlord which is a public authority (see para 1.321) is potentially actionable under the Human Rights Act 1998. It is likely, however, that conditions will have to be extremely bad before a court will require action to be taken under that Act where it would not otherwise have done so. The steps which the authority may be required to take to comply with Article 8 must be determined in each case, having regard not only to the needs of the occupiers but also to the limits on the resources available (*Lee*).

CHAPTER 12

Housing conditions: standards

Introduction

12.1 **Housing Health and Safety Rating System.** Local authorities have long had powers to ensure that buildings used for housing are of an acceptable standard. Formerly, the principal standard relating to housing conditions was that of fitness for human habitation, as most recently defined in the Housing Act (HA) 1985. HA 2004 Pt 1 introduced the Housing Health and Safety Rating System ('HHSRS') which set new standards for housing conditions. Whereas action could only be taken under the fitness provisions in relation to a limited number of housing defects, eg structural instability, serious disrepair and lack of sanitation, HHSRS allows authorities to address a range of housing problems in respect of which they could not previously take action.

12.2 **Private sector.** This chapter is primarily concerned with enforcement of standards in the private sector. The mechanism for enforcing HHSRS is by service of notices on those required to take action to remedy conditions. Local authorities cannot serve notices on themselves (*R v Cardiff City Council ex p Cross*, 1982). The provisions of HHSRS, therefore, only assist tenants of local authorities to a limited extent (see para 12.87 – complaint to magistrate), although they may have other remedies for disrepair (considered in chapter 11) or under the Environmental Protection Act (EPA) 1990 (see para 13.20).

12.3 **Grants.** Financial assistance for owners of land to carry out works – which may include those needed to respond to a notice under HHSRS provisions – may be available from authorities by way of grants under the Regulatory Reform (Housing Assistance) (England and Wales) Order 2002 SI No 1860, 'the Regulatory Reform Order'. This has been considered in chapter 4.

Local authorities

12.4 For the purposes of these provisions, local authorities are:

i) unitary authorities;
ii) other district councils;
iii) London borough councils;
iv) the Common Council of the City of London;
v) Welsh county or county boroughs;
vi) the sub-treasurer of the Inner Temple or the under-treasurer of the Middle Temple; and
vii) the council of the Isles of Scilly (HA 2004 s261(1)).

12.5 Under HA 2004 s3(1) these authorities are obliged at least once a year to consider the housing conditions in their areas with a view to deciding what action they ought to take under the provisions to be considered in this chapter (and in chapter 13). The secretary of state may give the authority directions as to exercise of this duty, with which directions the authority is obliged to comply.

12.6 To assist them in discharging their functions under the Act, authorities have a number of powers: the power to enter properties (HA 2004 s239); prosecution of offences of obstruction of authorities in exercising any of their powers under the Act (HA 2004 s241); and, the power to use housing benefit and council tax records (HA 2004 s237).

12.7 Action under the provisions considered in this chapter and those considered in the next is not mutually exclusive: for example, statutory nuisance procedure (see paras 13.15–13.19) is no substitute for procedure under HA 2004 (*R v Kerrier DC ex p Guppy's (Bridport)*, 1985) and even though an area may be declared a clearance area (see paras 12.54–12.60) under HA 1985 Pt 9, the authority will still be bound to take action under the EPA 1990 if such action is otherwise called for (*Salford CC v McNally*, 1975).

Health and Housing Safety Rating Standard

Definitions

12.8 **Residential premises.** Duties under HA 2004 Pt 1 arise in relation to 'residential premises', which are (HA 2004 s1(4)): dwellings; houses in multiple occupation (HMOs); unoccupied HMO accommodation; and, common parts of a building containing one or more flats.

1) **Dwellings** A dwelling is a building or part of a building intended to be occupied as a separate dwelling (HA 2004 s1(5); see para 1.171).
2) **HMO.** HMO is defined in the same way as for the provisions which govern their use (see paras 14.10–14.18) which are additional to the general provisions governing housing conditions considered in this chapter, which also apply to them.
3) **Unoccupied HMO accommodation.** This is a building or part of a building constructed or adapted for use as an HMO (see para 14.10) but which is currently not an HMO because it is either unoccupied or only occupied by a single household (see para 14.11(2)).

4) **Common parts.** These include the structure and exterior of a building containing flats and any common facilities provided to the flats (HA 2004 s1(5)).
5) **Flat.** A flat is a separate set of premises which is constructed or adopted for use as a dwelling and which forms part of a building (HA 2004 s1(5)).

12.9 **Person to be served.** Notices under these provisions has to be served on different persons, depending on the provision in question. Those persons may be the person having control, person managing or owner.

1) **Person having control.** The person having control is defined in relation to a dwelling or HMO as the person in receipt of the 'rack rent', defined as not less than two-thirds of the full net annual value of the premises, whether on his or her own account or as agent or trustee for another, or who would be in receipt of the rack-rent were the premises let at a rack rent (HA 2004 s263).
2) **Person managing.** The person managing is the owner or lessee of the house who receives – directly or through an agent or trustee – rents or other payments from persons who are tenants of parts of the premises or who are lodgers. The manager remains so even if the rents or other payments are being paid to another person, who is not the owner or lessee, whether voluntarily or in pursuance of a court order. 'Other payments' includes the collection of meter monies from gas and electricity meters used by tenants (*Jacques v Liverpool City Council*, 1996).
3) **Owner.** Owner means the freeholder or someone holding a lease of three years or more (HA 2004 s262(7)).

Hazards

12.10 **Hazard.** A hazard is any risk of harm to the health or safety of an actual (or potential) occupier of a dwelling or HMO which arises from a deficiency in the dwelling or HMO or in any building or land in the vicinity (HA 2004 s2(1)). 'Health' includes mental health (HA 2004 s2(5)). Hazards fall into two categories, depending on their severity: Category 1 and Category 2.

12.11 **Prescribed hazards.** The Housing Health and Safety Rating System (England) Regulations 2005 SI No 3208 or the Housing Health and Safety Rating System (Wales) Regulations 2006 SI No 1702 ('HHSRS Regulations') prescribe 29 hazards and circumstances giving rise to them. They are as follows.

1) Damp and mould growth – exposure to house dust mites, damp, mould or fungal growths.
2) Excess cold – exposure to low temperatures.
3) Excess heat – exposure to high temperatures.
4) Asbestos and MMF – exposure to asbestos fibres or manufactured mineral fibres.
5) Biocides – exposure to chemicals used to treat timber and mould growth.
6) Carbon monoxide and fuel combustion products – exposure to carbon monoxide, nitrogen dioxide or sulphur dioxide and smoke.
7) Lead – the ingestion of lead.
8) Radiation – exposure to radiation.
9) Uncombusted fuel gas – exposure to uncombusted fuel gas.
10) Volatile organic compounds – exposure to volatile organic compounds.
11) Crowding and space – a lack of adequate space for living and sleeping.
12) Entry by intruders – difficulties in keeping the dwelling or HMO secure against unauthorised entry.
13) Lighting – a lack of adequate lighting.
14) Noise – exposure to noise.
15) Domestic hygiene, pests and refuse – poor design layout or construction such that the dwelling or HMO cannot readily be kept clean; exposure to pests; inadequate provision for the hygienic storage and disposal of household waste.
16) Food safety – inadequate provision of facilities for the storage, preparation and cooking of food.
17) Personal hygiene, sanitation and drainage – inadequate provision of facilities for maintaining good person hygiene and for sanitation and drainage.
18) Water supply – inadequate supply of water free from contamination, for drinking and other domestic purposes.
19) Falls associated with toilets, baths, showers and other washing facilities.
20) Falling on any level surface or falling between surfaces where the change in level is less than 300 millimetres.
21) Falling on stairs, steps or ramps where the change in level is 300 millimetres or more.
22) Electrical hazards – exposure to electricity.
23) Falling between levels – where the difference in levels is 300 millimetres or more.

24) Fire – exposure to uncontrolled fire and associated smoke.
25) Flames, hot surfaces, *etc.* contact with controlled fire or flames, hot objects, liquid or vapours.
26) Collision and entrapment – collision with, or entrapment of body parts in, doors, windows or other architectural features.
27) Explosions at the dwelling or HMO.
28) Position, location and operability of amenities, fittings and equipment.
29) Structural collapse and falling elements – the collapse of the whole or part of the dwelling or HMO.

12.12 **Assessing severity.** The HHSRS Regulations set out the method by which the seriousness of the hazard is to be calculated and, accordingly, into which category it falls. This involves three stages.

1) **Likelihood of harm.** First, the authority must assess of the likelihood, during a period of 12 months beginning with the date of the assessment, of an occupier suffering any harm as a result of the hazard. The assessment must place the likelihood within the range of ratios set out in the regulations.
2) **Class of harm.** The second stage is to assess from which of the four classes of harm a relevant occupier is most likely to suffer during the 12-month period. The classes of harm range from extreme harm, such as death in Class I, to moderate harm, such as slight concussion or a broken finger in Class IV. The likelihood of any of the harm classes occurring as a result of the hazard must be assessed in accordance with a formula set out in the regulations.
3) **Hazard-rating score.** The third stage is to combine the figures obtained under the first two stages in accordance with a formula, so as to produce a hazard-rating score. The score is then assigned to one of 10 bands (A–J), with A being the highest scores (5,000 or more) and J the lowest (9 or less). A hazard falling within bands A, B, or C (1,000 and above) is a Category 1 hazard; a hazard within any other band is a Category 2 hazard.

Enforcement action

12.13 **Duty or power.** If a Category 1 hazard exists in a property, the authority is under a duty to take enforcement action (HA 2004 s5(1)); where there is a Category 2 hazard, it has power to do so (HA 2004 s6(1)).

12.14 There are six forms of enforcement action available.

1) Hazard awareness notice.
2) Improvement notice.

3) Emergency remedial action (Category 1 only).
4) Prohibition order.
5) Emergency prohibition order (Category 1 only).
6) Demolition order.

Note. Instead of a prohibition or demolition order, an authority may make serve a purchase notice (see para 12.49). Both types of order may be appealed (see para 12.52).

12.15 **Choice of action.** If there is only one course of action available in relation to a Category 1 hazard, the authority must take it (HA 2004 s5(3)). Where more than one course of action is available, the authority must take that which is the most appropriate (HA 2004 s5(4)). Authorities must make the choice taking into account guidance given by the secretary of state in *Housing Health and Safety Rating System: Enforcement Guidance* or by the National Assembly for Wales in *Housing – Enforcement Guidance: (Housing Act 2004, Part 1 – Housing Health and Safety Rating System)* (HA 2004 s9). Both sets of guidance are updated on a regular basis.

12.16 **Hazard Awareness Notice.** A hazard awareness notice may be served in relation to either a Category 1 or Category 2 hazard (see para 12.12). It advises the person served of the existence of the hazard which arises as a result of a deficiency on the premises (HA 2004 ss28(2) and 29(2)). It does not require any action but warns the person served of the risk and advises what action may be appropriate. The person on whom a hazard awareness notice is to be served depends on the nature of the property (HA 2004 Sch 1).

1) **Licensed dwellings and HMOs.** Where a dwelling or HMO is licensed under HA 2004 Pts 2 or 3 (chapter 14), the notice must be served on the licence-holder.
2) **Unlicensed dwellings and HMOs which are not flats.** In the case of all other HMOs and dwellings which are not flats, the notice must be served on the person having control (see para 12.9) of the dwelling or HMO, or in the case of an HMO the person managing it (see para 12.9).
3) **Flats.** Where the premises are a flat, the notice must be served on the person who is an owner (see para 12.9) of the flat who in the opinion of the authority ought to take the specified action. If the flat is also an HMO, the notice may be served on the person managing it (see para 12.9).
4) **Common parts.** Where a notice applies to the common parts serving flats, it must be served on the person who is an owner (see

para 12.9) of the premises who in the opinion of the authority ought to take the specified action.

12.17 In addition, the authority must serve a copy of the notice on every other person who, to its knowledge, is a freeholder, mortgagee, lessee or occupier of the premises concerned (HA 2004 Sch 1 para 5). Service must be effected within seven days of the service of the hazard awareness notice.

12.18 **Improvement notice.** An improvement notice may be served where a Category 1 or Category 2 hazard (see para 12.12) exists (HA 2004 ss11, 12). The person on whom notice is to be served is the same as for a hazard awareness notice (see para 12.16).

12.19 An improvement notice requires the person on whom it is served to carry out remedial action as specified in the notice to remove or reduce the hazard. In relation to Category 1 hazards, the remedial action must at least ensure that the hazard in the premises ceases to be a Category 1 hazard but it can require more (HA 2004 s11(5)), ie it may ensure that the hazard ceases to exist. An improvement notice may relate to more than one category of hazard on the same premises or in the same property; a notice relating to a Category 2 hazard may be combined with one relating to a Category 1 hazard, where they both require remedial action.

12.20 Remedial action is action which will remove or reduce the hazard (HA 2004 s11(8)). This will usually take the form of works but could include the removal of hazardous waste from the premises. In the case of premises containing flats, remedial action may be required in relation to the common parts or any part of the building containing the flats (which may include another flat), but only if the authority is satisfied that the deficiency from which the hazard arises is situated in the common parts of the building, and the action is necessary to protect the health or safety of any actual or potential occupiers of one or more of the flats in it (HA 2004 ss11(3), (4), 12(3)).

12.21 Although HA 2004 allows for forms to be prescribed (HA 2004 s244), neither the secretary of state in England or the National Assembly in Wales has yet exercised this power. HA 2004 sets out certain requirements in section 13. An improvement notice must specify:

1) whether it is served in relation to a Category 1 and/or Category 2 hazard;
2) the nature of the hazard and the residential premises on which the hazard exists, eg dwelling, HMO;
3) the deficiency giving rise to the hazard;

4) the premises in relation to which the remedial action is to be taken and the nature of the remedial action;
5) the date when the remedial action is to be started, which is to be no earlier than 28 days after service of the notice (*Odeniran v Southend-on-Sea BC*, 2013);
6) the period within which the remedial action is to be completed, or – if more than one action is required – the period within which each is to be completed; and
7) that there is a right of appeal to the First-tier Tribunal (England) or the residential property tribunal (Wales) and that there is a 21-day time limit for appealing.

12.22 An improvement notice may be suspended by the authority (HA 2004 s14) for a particular period of time, or until the occurrence of a particular event. Provision is made for termination of suspension where the nature of the occupancy of premises changes, eg where an occupier considered less vulnerable to the hazard is replaced by one who is more vulnerable. There may also be a suspension where the authority accepts an undertaking from the person on whom the notice is served, eg where the landlord promises to carry out works to the premises as a part of a programme of repairs. The suspension may be terminated if that undertaking is breached and the authority notifies the person accordingly. The authority may review a suspended notice at any time and must do so at intervals no greater than every 12 months (HA 2004 s17).

12.23 Revocation or variation of an improvement notice may occur either following an application made by the person on whom it was served or on the authority's own initiative (HA 2004 s16(8)). Decisions may be appealed to the First-tier Tribunal (England) or the residential property tribunal (Wales). A notice must be revoked once the authority is satisfied it has been complied with (HA 2004 s16(1)). In addition, the authority may revoke a notice where it considers it appropriate to do so and (in the case of a Category 1 hazard) where it considers that there are special circumstances which justify revocation. Detailed provision is made for the procedure to be adopted by the authority either where it decides to vary or revoke a notice or where it refuses to vary or revoke a notice at the request of the person on whom it was served (HA 2004 Sch 1).

12.24 A person served with an improvement notice may appeal to the First-tier Tribunal (England) or the residential property tribunal (Wales) (HA 2004 s15 and Sch 1 Pt 3). An appeal may be brought on any grounds, which may include that someone else should take the remedial action or that another form of enforcement action would be the best course of action to take. There is also a right of appeal against an authority's decision to revoke (or refuse to revoke) or to vary (or refuse to vary) a notice. An appeal against a notice must be lodged within 21 days of service. The time limit for any other appeal is 28 days. In each case, the tribunal has power to extend the time limit for 'good reason'.

12.25 Unless there is an appeal, the notice becomes operative 21 days from service. Failure to comply with the notice without reasonable excuse is a criminal offence punishable in the magistrates' court by a fine up to an unlimited amount (HA 2004 s30(1); Legal Aid, Sentencing and Punishment of Offenders Act (LASPO) 2012 s85(1)). Non-compliance means not commencing and completing within the time allowed (subject to the right to appeal: para 12.24). If the person served agrees to them doing so, or neither appeals nor complies with the notice in the permitted time, the local authority may take the remedial action itself and can recover the expenses of doing so (HA 2004 Sch 3).

12.26 In England, the First-tier Tribunal can make a rent repayment order against a landlord who is convicted of failure to comply with an improvement notice, provided the offence was committed on or after 6 April 2017, (Housing and Planning Act (HPA) 2016 s40). The procedure governing a rent repayment order for failure to comply with an improvement notice is the same as that which applies to rent repayment orders made in unlawful eviction and harassment cases (see paras 5.29–5.35).

12.27 Once the provisions of HPA 2016 Pt 2, are in force it is expected that local housing authorities will be able to apply to the First-tier Tribunal for a banning order against anyone convicted of failing to comply with an improvement notice, which will prevent that person from being involved in letting or managing residential property (see paras 5.82–5.102). A person against whom a banning order is made will be entered on a database of 'rogue landlords' (see paras 5.103–5.111).

12.28 Once the notice becomes operative (see para 12.25), it is a local land charge (HA 2004 s37), ie it is a restriction on the property which should be recorded on a register kept by the local authority. A local land charge is enforceable against a purchaser even if it has not been registered but if it was not registered and the purchaser actually checked the register before he or she bought the property, he or she may be entitled to compensation (Local Land Charges Act 1975 s10).

12.29 In England, where the improvement notice relates to a dwelling let under an assured shorthold tenancy, or to common parts of the building in which it is situated, the landlord is prevented from using the mandatory ground for possession under HA 1988 s21, for six months after the improvement notice was served (see para 2.199). In addition, if a landlord serves a section 21 notice following a complaint from the tenant about the condition of his or her home (or the common parts in which it is situated) and, after the section 21 notice is served, the authority serves an improvement notice on the landlord which relates to the subject matter of the tenant's earlier complaint, the section 21 notice becomes invalid (see para 2.200).

12.30 **Emergency remedial action.** An authority may only take emergency remedial action in relation to a Category 1 hazard (see para 12.12). Remedial action is any action that may be required under an improvement notice, eg the carrying out of works (see para 12.19). The authority must be satisfied that the hazard involves an imminent risk of serious harm to the health and safety of any of the occupiers of the premises concerned or any other residential premises (HA 2004 s40(1)).

12.31 Where an authority decides to take emergency remedial action, it may commence that action immediately and may recover its costs (HA 2004 s42(2)). Not later than seven days after the start of the action, it must serve a notice on the same person on whom an improvement notice must be served (see para 12.18). That notice must specify (HA 2004 s41(2)):

1) the nature of the hazard and the residential premises on which the hazard exists, eg dwelling, HMO;
2) the deficiency giving rise to the hazard;
3) the premises in relation to which the remedial action has been (or is to be) taken and the nature of the remedial action;
4) the power under which the remedial action has been (or is to be) taken;
5) the date of the start or intended start of the remedial action; and
6) that there is a right of appeal to the First-tier Tribunal (England) or the residential property tribunal (Wales) and that there is a 28-day time limit for appealing.

12.32 In England, where the notice of emergency remedial action relates to a dwelling let under an assured shorthold tenancy, or to common parts of the building in which it is situated, the landlord is prevented from using the mandatory ground for possession under HA 1988 s21, for six months after the notice was served (see para 2.199). In addition, if a landlord serves a section 21 notice following a complaint from the tenant about the condition of his or her home (or the common parts in which it is situated) and, after the section 21 notice is served, the authority serves a notice of emergency remedial action on the landlord which relates to the subject matter of the tenant's earlier complaint, the section 21 notice becomes invalid (see para 2.200).

12.33 **Prohibition order.** An authority may make a prohibition order where a Category 1 or Category 2 hazard (see para 12.12) exists (HA 2004 ss21, 22). An order may relate to more than one category of hazard in the same building; a notice relating to a Category 2 hazard may be combined with that relating to a Category 1 hazard where they both impose prohibitions relating to the same premises (HA 2004 s21(5)). The person on whom a prohibition order is to be served depends on the nature of the premises (HA 2004 Sch 2).

1) **Houses.** Where the property is a house which is not divided into flats, or an HMO which is not a flat, the order must be served on every person who is an owner (see para 12.9), and on an occupier of the whole or part of the premises, and on anyone who is authorised to permit persons to occupy the property, eg a letting agent, or a mortgagee.
2) **Flats and common parts.** Where the premises consist of one or more flats, or common parts, the order must be served on every person who is an owner (see para 12.9) or occupier of the whole or part of the building, and on anyone who is authorised to permit persons to occupy the whole or part of the premises, eg a letting agent, or a mortgagee.

12.34 The order must be served within seven days of being made. In the case of occupiers, service can be effected by fixing the order to some conspicuous part of the premises. If the hazard exists in a house which is not divided into flats, or an HMO which is not a flat, the order may prohibit the use of the property. In the case of a hazard in a flat or flats, the order may prohibit use of the building containing the flat(s), or a part of the building, or any external common parts. If the hazard is in the common parts of a building containing one or more flats, the order may prohibit use of the building, of any part of it or of any external common parts (HA 2004 ss20(3), 21(3)). The authority may serve a purchase notice instead of a demolition order (see para 12.49).

12.35 A prohibition order must specify the following (HA 2004 s22):

1) whether it is served in relation to a Category 1 and/or Category 2 hazard;

2) the nature of the hazard and the residential premises on which the hazard exists, eg dwelling, HMO;
3) the deficiency giving rise to the hazard;
4) the prohibitions imposed;
5) the premises in relation to which the prohibitions are imposed;
6) any remedial action which the authority considers would, if taken, result in its revoking the order; and
7) that there is a right of appeal to the First-tier Tribunal (England) or the residential property tribunal (Wales) and that there is a 28-day time limit for appealing.

12.36 The order may prohibit use for all purposes or permit limited approved purposes (HA 2004 s22(4)). Accordingly, the order may limit the number of occupiers or prohibit occupation by particular descriptions of persons, eg children or the elderly. The authority must not unreasonably withhold approval to a particular use (HA 2004 s22(7)); if it refuses approval, it must notify the person who has applied for it (HA 2004 s22(8)). A notice refusing approval must include reasons for the decision, and inform the recipient of his or her right to appeal to the First-tier Tribunal (England) or the residential property tribunal (Wales) and of the 28-day time limit for appealing.

12.37 Where a prohibition order prohibits the use of the whole of any premises for all purposes other than one approved by the authority, compensation is payable to every owner (see para 12.9) of the premises (HA 2004 s24(7) and HA 1985 s584A). If possession is required to comply with the order, tenants in premises which are the subject of a prohibition order lose any HA 1988 (see paras 2.158–2.173) and Rent Act (RA) 1977 (see paras 2.214–2.222) protection they may enjoy (HA 2004 s33), but, as other occupiers, they will gain rights to re-housing (see para 12.71) and to compensation (see para 12.81). The fact that statutory protection has been lifted does not, however, mean that the landlord can recover possession without terminating the contractual tenancy (*Aslan v Murphy*, 1989).

12.38 An authority may suspend a prohibition order, either for a particular period of time, or until the occurrence of a particular event (HA 2004 s23). Provision is made for termination of suspension where the nature of the occupancy of premises changes, eg where an occupier considered less vulnerable to the hazard is replaced by another who is more vulnerable. Suspension may also occur where the authority accepts an undertaking from the person on whom the notice is served, eg a promise that a bedroom in which a hazard exists will in future only be used as storage space. The suspension may be terminated if that undertaking is breached and the authority give notice. The authority may review a suspended order at any time and must do so at intervals no greater than 12 months (HA 2004 s26). Following a review, the authority's decision must be served on the same persons who are required to be served with the order itself (see para 12.33).

12.39 Revocation or variation of a prohibition order may occur either on application by the person on whom it was served or on the authority's own initiative (HA 2004 s25(8)). An order must be revoked if the authority is satisfied that the hazard no longer exists on the premises (HA 2004 s25(1)). In addition, the authority may revoke an order where it considers it appropriate to do so and (in the case of a Category 1 hazard) where it considers that there are special circumstances which justify revocation (HA 2004 s25). Where a notice deals with more than one hazard, the order can be revoked in relation to certain hazards, and varied in relation to the rest (HA 2004 s25(3)). An order may be varied with the agreement of the person on whom it was served (HA 2004 s25(6)), and a person may request variation of an order, eg for an approved use of the property (see para 12.37). The authority may unilaterally vary a suspended prohibition order so as to alter the time or events which bring the suspension to an end (HA 2004 s25(4)) and, thus, activate the order. Detailed provision is made for the procedure to be adopted where an authority decides to vary or revoke a prohibition order (HA 2004 Sch 2). Decisions may be appealed to the First-tier Tribunal (England) or the residential property tribunal (Wales).

12.40 An owner (see para 12.9), occupier, managing agent or mortgagee may appeal against the making of a prohibition order or any decision by the authority to revoke (or refuse to revoke) or vary (or refuse to vary) an order (HA 2004 s24 and Sch 2 Pt 3) (see para 12.39). Unless there is an appeal, the order becomes operative 28 days from service (HA 2004 s24). A person commits an offence if he or she uses the premises in contravention of the order or permits the premises so to be used (HA 2004 s32(1)). The offence is punishable by an unlimited fine, and £20 for each day after conviction on which the order continues to be breached (HA 2004 s32(2); LASPO 2012 s85(1)).

12.41 In England, the First-tier Tribunal can make a rent repayment order against a landlord who is convicted of failure to comply with a prohibition order, provided that the offence was committed on or after 6 April 2017, (HPA 2016 s40). The procedure governing a rent repayment order for failure to comply with an improvement notice is the same as that which applies to rent repayment orders made in unlawful eviction and harassment cases (see paras 5.29–5.35).

12.42 Once it becomes operative (see para 12.40), a prohibition order is a local land charge (see para 12.28) so it is enforceable against a purchaser of the property (HA 2004 s37). A local land charge is enforceable against a purchaser even if it has not been registered but if it was not registered and the purchaser actually checked the register before he or she bought the property, he or she may be entitled to compensation (Local Land Charges Act 1975 s10).

12.43 Once the provisions of HPA 2016 Pt 2, are in force it is expected that local housing authorities will be able to apply to the First-tier Tribunal for a banning order against anyone convicted of failing to comply with a prohibition order, which will prevent that person from being involved in letting or managing residential property (see paras 5.82–5.102). A person against whom a banning order made will be entered on a database of 'rogue landlords' (see paras 5.103–5.111).

12.44 **Emergency prohibition order.** An authority may only make an emergency prohibition order in relation to a Category 1 hazard (see para 12.12). The authority must be satisfied that the hazard involves an imminent risk of serious harm to the health and safety of any of the occupiers of the premises concerned, or other residential premises (HA 2004 s43(1)). An emergency order takes immediate effect (HA 2004 s43(2)). The prohibitions on use of the premises are the same as for other prohibition orders (see para 12.36). The order must be served on the same persons as a normal prohibition order (see para 12.33). It must be served on the day that it is made or, if that is not possible, as soon as possible thereafter (HA 2004 s43(4)). The order must specify (HA 2004 s44):

1) the nature of the hazard and the residential premises on which the hazard exists, eg dwelling, HMO, etc;
2) the deficiency giving rise to the hazard;
3) the prohibitions imposed;
4) the premises in relation to which the prohibitions are imposed;
5) any remedial action which the authority considers would, if taken, result in its revoking the order; and
6) that there is a right of appeal to the First-tier Tribunal (England) or the residential property tribunal (Wales) and that there is a 28-day time limit for appealing.

12.45 The provisions relating to compensation (see para 12.81), revocation and variation (see para 12.39), and enforcement (see para 12.40) governing normal orders also apply to emergency orders (HA 2004 s43(5)).

12.46 **Demolition order.** A demolition order can only be made in relation to a Category 1 (see para 12.12) hazard (HA 1985 s265(1)). The order must specify a time, not less than 28 days after the order becomes operative, within which the building is to be vacated and a time within which it is to be demolished, which is to be within six weeks of the premises being vacated or such longer period as the authority may specify (HA 1985 s267). Within seven days of the order being made, it must be served on any owner of the premises (see para 12.9), any occupier, any person authorised to let the premises and every mortgagee (HA 1985 s268(1)). If, after a demolition order has become operative but before the house is demolished, the house becomes a listed building under the Planning (Listed Buildings and Conservation Areas) Act 1990 s1, the authority must substitute a prohibition order (HA 1985 s304). The authority may serve a purchase notice instead of a demolition order (see para 12.49).

12.47 Demolition may be deferred to allow an opportunity for the Category 1 hazard to be dealt with by an owner (see para 12.9), or anyone else who appears to the authority to be in a position to put such a proposal into practice (HA 1985 s274). If the works are completed to the authority's satisfaction, the demolition order is then determined. Once a tenant is obliged to quit, he or she loses any HA 1988 (see paras 2.158–2.173) and RA 1977 protection (see paras 2.214–2.222) he or she enjoys (HA 1985 s270(3)), although, as other occupiers, will be entitled to re-housing (see para 12.71) and to compensation (see para 12.81). Compensation is payable to every owner of the premises (HA 1985 s265(9)).

12.48 Unless there is an appeal (see para 12.52) against a demolition order, it becomes operative 28 days after service (HA 1985 s268). person who knows of the demolition order and who enters into occupation of the property after it is made, or who permits someone else to enter, commits an offence, punishable by an unlimited fine and an additional £5 for every day on which occupation continues after conviction (HA 1985 s270(5)). Not only can the landlord seek possession of the premises from an occupier but so also can the local authority (HA 1985 s270(2)). The authority has power to cleanse the building of vermin before demolition, should it appear to be necessary (HA 1985 s273). If the owner does not proceed to demolish the building, the authority may itself do so in default (HA 1985 s271), and recover its costs.

12.49 **Purchase notice.** In place of either demolition or prohibition order, the authority may serve a purchase notice if it appears to it that the premises are, or can be, rendered capable of providing accommodation which is adequate for the time being (HA 1985 s300). It cannot purchase premises which are a listed building (HA 1985 s300(7)).

12.50 The purchase notice becomes operative 28 days after service, unless there is an appeal (see para 12.52), in which case it will become operative on the final determination of the appeal (HA 1985 s300(4)). If the owner will not agree to sell the house to the authority, the authority may, with central government consent, purchase it compulsorily (HA 1985 s300(6)). Compensation will be available to owner-occupiers, tenants and/or other occupiers when they are actually moved (see para 12.81), at which point they will also acquire rights to re-housing (see para 12.71). During the intervening period, any HA 1988 protection (see paras 2.158–2.173) is lost (HA 1988 s1, Sch 1 para 12) as is any Rent Act protection (see paras 2.214–2.222) (RA 1977 ss14, 19), but occupiers do not become secure tenants (see paras 1.160–1.204) of the authority (HA 1985 s79 and Sch 1).

12.51 The standard to which a property that has been purchased is to be maintained for the time being is lower than that required by the HHSRS, and the provisions of LTA 1985 s8 (see paras 11.48–11.51) are expressly disapplied (HA 1985 s302). The purpose of the power is to do no more than provide temporary accommodation: the power cannot be used to add to the authority's permanent housing stock (*Victoria Square Property Co Ltd v Southwark LBC*, 1977). The provisions of EPA 1990 (chapter 13) will, however, continue to apply, and the authority must prevent the property from becoming a statutory nuisance as long as it remains in use (*Salford CC v McNally*, 1975).

12.52 **Appeals.** A demolition order or purchase notice can be appealed to the First-tier Tribunal (England) or the residential property tribunal (Wales) (HA 1985 ss269(3), 300(4)). The appeal must be lodged within 28 days of service of the appropriate notice; pending the appeal, the authority is to carry out no action in relation to the notice (HA 1985 s269). A tenant may not appeal if in occupation under a lease with less than three years to run, eg a periodic tenant (HA 1985 s269(2)), although in the rare circumstances when a challenge can be made on principles of administrative law (see paras 8.23–8.28), such a tenant may seek judicial review of the authority's decision (*R v Maldon DC ex p Fisher*, 1986; *R v Woking BC ex p Adam*, 1995).

12.53 It is a specific ground of appeal that an alternative course of action, eg improvement notice or prohibition order, would have been the best course of action (HA 1985 s269A). If the tribunal decides to allow the appeal on this basis, the authority may ask it to include in its decision a specific finding as to the best course of action, and the tribunal must do so.

Slum clearance

12.54 Clearance areas were once the principal means of dealing with large areas of poor housing. Today, renewal (see paras 12.61–12.69) is more probable, although clearance has recently enjoyed a resurgence to deal with areas of uneconomic housing where the private market has collapsed and properties have been left vacant. Clearance areas are made under HA 1985.

Conditions for declaration

12.55 A declaration of a clearance area may be made in the following circumstances.

1) **Health and safety.** The authority must be satisfied that:
   (i) each of the 'residential buildings' in the area contains a Category 1 hazard and any other buildings in the area are dangerous or harmful to the health or safety of the inhabitants of the area; or
   (ii) the residential buildings in the area are dangerous to the health of the inhabitants because the buildings themselves or streets are badly arranged and any other buildings are also dangerous to the health of the inhabitants; or
   (iii) each of the residential buildings in the area contains a Category 2 hazard and any other buildings in the area are dangerous to the health or safety of the occupiers.
2) **Representations.** Before making a declaration, the authority must consult those with an interest in the buildings, and the occupiers of any residential buildings, and consider any representations in response.
3) **Alternative accommodation.** The authority must be satisfied that it can provide or secure alternative accommodation for those displaced prior to demolition.
4) **Resources.** The authority must be satisfied that it has sufficient resources to carry out the clearance programme (HA 1985 s289).

Compulsory purchase

12.56 The principal stage in the clearance procedure is compulsory purchase (HA 1985 s290). The authority is entitled not only to seek to purchase the houses and other buildings in the area but also any land (including houses and other buildings) surrounded by the area, or adjoining the area, which is necessary in order to acquire a cleared area of convenient shape, or in order satisfactorily to develop the area (HA 1985 s290(2)). The authority may include in the proposals any land which it already owns, which qualifies either under the principal criteria (see para 12.55) or would qualify as added land under section 290(2) (HA 1985 s293).

12.57 Compulsory purchase will require central government approval, which will normally mean an inquiry into the proposals. At any time before the compulsory purchase order is confirmed, application can be made for the exclusion of land from the order on the ground that the owner will him- or herself execute the demolition and that the authority does not, in those circumstances, actually need the land for the purpose of redevelopment of the area (HA 1985 s292).

Displacement

12.58 Once the land has been purchased, the authority's main obligation is to cause all the buildings to be vacated 'as soon as may be'. Thereafter, the authority must either demolish all the buildings within six weeks (or such period as it considers reasonable) and either sell or let the land for redevelopment or itself redevelop, the land (HA 1985 s291).

12.59 Historically, clearance area land was often left untreated for many years, which may sometimes still remain the case. If satisfied that the houses are, or can be rendered, capable of providing accommodation 'at a standard which is adequate for the time being', the authority may postpone demolition and retain the housing in use (HA 1985 s301).

12.60 Tenants and other occupiers displaced by the programme will be entitled to re-housing (see para 12.71) and to compensation (see para 12.81). Tenants will lose any status as assured (see paras 2.158–2.173) under HA 1988 (HA 1988 s1 and Sch 1 para 12) once the authority becomes their landlord, as well as any Rent Act (see paras 2.214–2.222) protection (RA 1977 ss14, 19), but do not become secure tenants (see paras 1.156–1.192) of the authority (HA 1985 s79 and Sch 1 para 3).

Renewal areas

12.61 The provisions governing the declaration of and powers and duties in renewal areas are to be found in the Local Government and Housing Act (LGHA) 1989 Pt 7, as amended by the Regulatory Reform Order 2002 (see para 4.167).

Report

12.62 The starting point for the declaration of a renewal area is a 'report' requested by the local housing authority, which should contain a reasoned recommendation that the renewal area should be declared (LGHA 1989 s89). The report may include any matters which the authority considers relevant, and in particular must include particulars of the following matters.

1) **Living conditions:** the living conditions in the area concerned.
2) **Improvement:** the ways in which conditions may be improved (whether by the declaration of a renewal area or otherwise).
3) **Powers:** the powers available to the authority if the area is declared.
4) **Proposals:** the authority's detailed proposals for the exercise of those powers during the period that the area will be a renewal area.
5) **Costs:** the costs of the proposals.
6) **Resources:** the financial resources available, or likely to be available, to the authority for implementing the proposal.
7) **Representations:** any representations (see para 12.66) made to the authority in relation to the proposals.

Conditions for declaration

12.63 A renewal area may be declared if the authority is satisfied, on the basis of the report (see para 12.62), that the living conditions in an area within its district which consists primarily of housing accommodation are unsatisfactory and can most effectively be dealt with by declaring a renewal area (LGHA 1989 s89(1)). In reaching this decision (or a decision to extend the life of the area), the authority must have regard to central government guidance issued (LGHA 1989 s89(5)), although there is currently no guidance in force.

12.64 Prior to declaration, the authority must take steps to secure that the proposals are brought to the attention of persons residing or owning property in the proposed area, and that those persons are informed of the name and address of the person to whom inquiries and representations concerning the proposals should be addressed (LGHA 1989 s89(6), (7)).

Duration

12.65 It is for the authority to determine for how long the renewal area is to last (LGHA 1989 s89(4)(a)). It may decide to extend the period (LGHA 1989 s89(4)(b)) or may decide to bring the area to an end at an earlier date, or to exclude land from it (LGHA 1989 s95). Both prior and subsequent to such a resolution, the authority must fulfil requirements as to publicity and consideration of representations.

Duties and powers

12.66 As soon as possible after the declaration or any subsequent extension, the authority must take steps designed to secure that its decision is brought to the attention of persons residing or owning property in the proposed area, and that those persons are informed of the name and address of the person to whom inquiries and representations concerning action to be taken should be addressed (LGHA 1989 s91). As well as the duty to publicise the declaration, the authority is under a continuing duty to bring to the attention of residents and property owners information about the proposed and existing action in the area, and any assistance available for the carrying out of works (LGHA 1989 s92), eg grant-aid (see paras 4.167–4.199).

12.67 Local housing authorities may by agreement or, with the consent of the secretary of state, compulsorily acquire land in a renewal area which comprises premises consisting of or including housing accommodation. The purchase must be (LGHA 1989 s93) for the improvement or repair of premises, either by the authority or by someone, eg a PRP or RSL to whom it proposes to dispose of them, or for the proper and effective management and use of housing accommodation, again either by the authority itself or by another, or for the well-being of residents in the area. The authority may also compulsorily acquire any land in the area in order to improve the amenities in the area, whether to carry out improvements itself or to dispose of the land to someone else to do so (LGHA 1989 s93(4)).

12.68 Tenants of premises acquired will lose any status as assured (see paras 1.220–1.251) under the 1988 Act (HA 1988 s1 and Sch 1 para 12) once the authority becomes their landlord, as well as any

Rent Act (see paras 1.269–1.293) protection (RA 1977 ss14, 19), but will become secure tenants (see paras 1.160–1.209) of the authority. Where the authority requires vacant possession to carry out the improvements, it may rely on HA 1985 Sch 2 Grounds 10 or 10A (see para 2.113).

12.69 The authority has power to carry out works on any land it owns in the area (whether acquired under its powers of acquisition outlined above, or not) (LGHA 1989 s93(5)). This power may be delegated to a PRP, RSL or other person. There are also powers allowing it to extinguish rights of ways over highways (LGHA 1989 s94) and powers of entry, backed up by offences of obstruction, in order to survey and inspect (LGHA 1989 s97).

Re-housing and compensation

12.70 Works to address housing conditions can, and frequently do, displace existing occupiers. They will usually be entitled to re-housing, and sometimes to compensation, from the authority taking the relevant action.

Re-housing

12.71 The rights to be considered under this heading are separate from and additional to those provided under HA 1996 Pt 7 considered in chapter 9. Thus, for example, it is not necessary for a displaced occupant qualifying under these provisions to show that he or she has a priority need for accommodation (see paras 10.39–10.51). Nor is re-housing under these provisions an allocation under HA 1996 Pt 6 (see paras 10.187–10.220) (Allocation of Housing (England) Regulations 2002 SI No 3264 reg 3; or Allocation of Housing (Wales) Regulations 2003 SI No 239 reg 3.

12.72 Unless suitable alternative residential accommodation is otherwise available, on reasonable terms, a person displaced from land in consequence of a series of public actions will be entitled to re-housing from or arranged by the local authority (Land Compensation Act (LCA) 1973 s39) in the following circumstances:

1) displacement in consequence of compulsory purchase (see paras 12.56–12.57);
2) displacement in consequence of a housing order, ie a prohibition order under HA 2004 Pt 1 (see paras 12.33–12.43), or a demolition order under HA 1985 Pt 9 (see paras 12.46–12.53);

3) displacement by an authority which has previously acquired the land, and which now decides to redevelop or improve it (see para 12.58).

12.73 The entitlement is not to immediate permanent re-housing: the authority has to do no more than their best, and if this means that the displaced occupant is provided with a series of short-life dwellings pending permanent re-housing, the authority will properly have discharged its duty (*R v Bristol Corp ex p Hendy*, 1973).

12.74 For an occupier to qualify on the ground that he or she has been displaced to allow the authority to improve the land, the displacement must be permanent (LCA 1973 s39(6A)). An occupier is only entitled to re-housing as a result of a housing order (see para 12.72) if he or she was in occupation at the time the order was made (LCA 1973 s39(6)), or as a result of compulsory purchase (whether or not the land has continued to be used in the meantime) (see para 12.59) unless in occupation when proceedings to purchase the land were commenced (LCA 1973 s39(6)). Only a person in lawful occupation will qualify, not a trespasser, nor will there be qualification by someone to whom permission has been given to use the property pending demolition or improvement, ie short-life user (LCA 1973 s39(3)). The Act contains powers for the local authority to advance money to a displaced owner-occupier (LCA 1973 s41); an owner-occupier who avails him- or herself of this power cannot also claim the right to re-housing (LCA 1973 s39(4)).

12.75 Analogous re-housing provision is made for caravan dwellers displaced by the same public activities (LCA 1973 s40).

Home loss payment

12.76 A home loss payment will be available in the same circumstances as those in which rehousing is available (see para 12.71–12.75). In addition, it is available:

1) in the event of permanent displacement of a PRP or RSL tenant (see para 1.162) on the carrying out of improvement to the dwelling or redevelopment of the land by the landlord; and,
2) to those evicted following an order under Ground 10 or 10A of HA 1985 Sch 2 (see para 2.113) (LCA 1973 s29(1)).

12.77 While the payment is normally made by the local authority, it must be made by the PRP or RSL if under either of these additional grounds (LCA 1973 s29(1)(e)).

12.78 Home loss payments are limited to those with a legal interest in the dwelling, ie freeholders (see para 1.7), leaseholders (see paras 1.18) and tenants (see paras 1.20–1.55), as well as statutory tenants (see paras 1.269–1.277), those with a restricted contract (see paras 1.298–1.303), and those with a right to occupy the dwelling under a contract of employment (see paras 1.131–1.140) (LCA 1973 s29(4)). A spouse or civil partner with home rights under the FLA 1996 (see paras 7.9–7.14) may also claim (LCA 1973 s29A). The claimant must have been in occupation of the dwelling for a minimum of one year, ending with the date of displacement (not of purchase proceedings or other action; compare para 12.74).

12.79 Occupation must have been as or with a tenant or other person entitled to payment, as an only or main (see paras 1.176–1.179) residence and of the whole dwelling or a substantial part of it (LCA 1973 ss29(2), 32(3)). Where the claimant has been in occupation of different rooms in the same building, eg a series of bedsitting-rooms, he or she is entitled to be treated as if he or she had remained in one room (LCA 1973 s32(5)). Where the displacement is by compulsory purchase (see para 12.56), the claimant does not have to remain in occupation until required to leave by the authority: provided his or her qualifying period is fulfilled, he or she may leave at any time after the date when the authority was given consent to make the compulsory purchase (LCA 1973 s29(3)).

12.80 The home loss payment must be claimed within six years of displacement (LCA 1973 s32(7A)). The amount is, in the case of an owner, 10 per cent of the market value of the interest, to a maximum of£53,000; in all other cases, the amount is £5,300 (LCA 1973 s30). These figures may be amended by regulations (LCA 1973 s30(5)). Where there are two or more persons equally entitled to the payment, eg joint tenants (see paras 1.48–1.56), they each get an equal share (LCA 1973 s32(6)).

Compensation for prohibition and demolition orders

12.81 Where a prohibition (see para 12.33) or demolition order (see para 12.46) is made, every owner of the premises is entitled to compensation (LGHA 1989 s584A). The amount of compensation is determined as at the day the order is made and is the diminution in the compulsory purchase value of the owner's interest as a result of the order. If a demolition order is subsequently substituted for the closing order, then the compensation already paid is to be deducted from that paid for the demolition order. Where the demolition or prohibition order is revoked, the recipient must, on demand, repay the compensation to the authority (LGHA 1989 s584B). Where the closing order is determined in relation to part only of the premises, provision is made for the amount repayable to be determined by apportionment.

Disturbance payment

12.82 A disturbance payment is an additional amount representing 'the reasonable expenses of the person entitled to the payment in removing from the land from which he or she is displaced' (LCA 1973 s38(1)). These words mean more than mere removal costs and include the costs of setting up in the new home. Many local authorities purport to fix amounts for disturbance payments, by scale, by maxima, or by limiting the matters for which payment will be made. There is no legal power to do this: the amount may be small or it may be large, and each case is to be judged on its facts. A dispute may be referred to the Upper Tribunal (LCA 1973 s38(4)).

12.83 A disturbance payment is available in the same circumstances as a home loss payment (see para 12.76) and is payable by the same body (see paras 12.76–12.77) (LCA 1973 s37(1)). If displaced by compulsory purchase without intervening use (see para 12.53), the claimant must have been in lawful possession of the land at the date when notice was first published of the intention compulsorily to purchase; if with intervening use (see para 12.59), when proceedings towards the purchase were begun; or, if by an order (see para 12.56), at the date when the order was made, notice was served, or undertaking accepted (LCA 1973 s37(3)). No payment is available if the claimant is entitled to compensation for the making of a prohibition or demolition order (see para 12.81).

12.84 If there is no entitlement under these provisions, and no compensation available under any other enactment (including home loss payments – paras 12.76–12.80), the local authority still has a discretion to make a disturbance payment in any event (LCA 1973 s37(5)).

Occupier action

12.85 **Judicial review.** If an authority refuses to take action under the provisions in this chapter despite receiving complaints from an occupier which showed that action should be taken, an occupier could seek to compel the authority to take action by judicial review. It is not possible in this book to specify the circumstances in which an authority can be so compelled by the courts, but it should be noted that public bodies must act within the ambit of legislation, and that the courts will intervene (using their powers of judicial review) if authorities misunderstand or misapply the law, act in bad faith or otherwise fail to take relevant matters into account or disregard the irrelevant, or fail to take decisions in individual cases where they were obliged to do so (see paras 8.23–8.28). In such cases, the authority acts *ultra vires* (outside its powers).

12.86 It is imperative to bear in mind that a court (other than a court given express powers on appeal) reviewing the conduct of a public body does not intervene merely because it disagrees with the authority's decision, nor because its (or the claimant's) view of what is reasonable is different from that of the authority, but only because the authority has acted wrongly in one of the ways illustrated in the last paragraph, or so unreasonably that no reasonable authority, properly approaching the matter, could have so acted (see para 8.28).

12.87 **Complaint to a JP.** HA 2004, however, does provide the occupier with one express and additional recourse: he or she may complain to a magistrate that a category 1 or category 2 hazard exists in any residential premises in an authority's area (HA 2004 s4). If the magistrate is satisfied that the complaint is correct, perhaps following a visit to the premises or area, he or she will in turn complain to the proper officer of the authority. It is this officer's duty then to inspect the house or area, and report to his or her authority (or appropriate committee). That is as far as the obligation goes. There is no sanction. The officer or committee is free to disagree with the magistrate. The procedure is, however, a useful way of making the authority inspect, and, if the inspection reveals a Category 1 hazard, it will be bound to take action (see para 12.13).

Human rights

12.88 As noted in chapter 11 (see para 11.144), the right to 'respect for the home' required by Article 8 of the European Convention on Human Rights, by which public authorities (see paras 1.321–1.322) are bound, may be breached by a home (see para 1.320) being in severe disrepair (*Lee v Leeds City Council*, 2002). The steps which an authority is required to take to comply with Article 8, however, must be determined in each case, having regard not only to the needs of the occupiers but also to the limits on the resources available to the authority (*Lee*). In cases of serious interference with an occupier's right to respect for the home, eg through environmental pollution, the ECtHR has imposed a positive duty on member states to take action (*Powell and Rayner v UK*, 1990; *Lopez Ostra v Spain*, 1994; *Hatton v UK*, 2003; *Taskin v Turkey*, 2004). Accordingly, in cases involving extremely bad housing conditions, it is possible that a failure to act by a local authority under one the duties or powers discussed in this chapter could be considered a breach of Article 8, which could be actionable against the authority under the Human Rights Act 1998 s6.

CHAPTER 13

Housing conditions: environmental health

Introduction

13.1 This chapter is concerned with a series of powers now to be found principally in the Environmental Protection Act (EPA) 1990, which consolidated much of the law formerly contained in the Public Health Act (PHA) 1936 and the Public Health (Recurring Nuisances) Act 1969. It also briefly considers some related powers to be found in the Building Act (BA) 1984 and in various public health Acts. The provisions are not aimed exclusively at housing. The approach of this chapter is, accordingly, necessarily selective.

13.2 It may also be noted that before the introduction of the Housing Health and Safety Rating System (HHSRS) (chapter 12), local authorities' powers to regulate private sector housing conditions were much more limited. Many of the problems which previously could only be addressed using the powers considered below, if at all, can now more effectively be resolved using those under the Housing Act (HA) 2004, eg the removal of vermin (see paras 13.73–13.75).

Local authorities

13.3 As in the last chapter, and in the next, we are here concerned primarily with duties imposed on local authorities, rather than rights as between individuals. Local authorities for these purposes are the same authorities who have duties under the Housing Acts (see para 12.4).

13.4 Where duties arise under EPA 1990, the Secretary of State for the Environment has power to declare that an authority is in default of its duties, and may direct it to carry out actions to remedy its default, or even take over its obligations (EPA 1990 Sch 3).

13.5 Authorities are obliged to inspect their districts with an eye to the performance of their duties in relation to statutory nuisances (see paras 13.9–13.31), the main class of action with which we are concerned in the present chapter (EPA 1990 s79).

13.6 Action under the provisions considered in this chapter and in the last is not mutually exclusive (see para 12.7).

13.7 Whether the purpose is in order to inspect premises, or in order to carry out works which they are entitled to do, local authorities have a general power of entry into premises, which may be exercised at any reasonable hour (EPA 1990 Sch 3 para 2). Authorities also have power to enter unoccupied premises in order to prevent them being or becoming a danger to public health (Local Government

(Miscellaneous Provisions) Act 1982 s29), although they are obliged to give an owner of the premises 48 hours' notice of intention of so doing.

13.8 Obstruction of an officer of the authority executing duties under the Acts is a criminal offence (EPA 1990 Sch 3 para 3).

Statutory nuisance

Definition

13.9 Relative to housing, a statutory nuisance means 'any premises in such a state as to be prejudicial to health or a nuisance' (EPA 1990 s79(1)). The limbs are alternative, so that statutory nuisance may be established by way of either prejudice to health or nuisance. There can be a statutory nuisance even although the landlord is not in breach (see chapter 11) of any repairing obligation (*Birmingham DC v Kelly*, 1985). Noise emanating from premises can also qualify as a statutory nuisance (see paras 6.38–6.44).

13.10 **Prejudicial to health.** Prejudicial to health is defined as meaning 'injurious or likely to cause injury to health' (EPA 1990 s79(7)). The courts have attributed a narrow meaning this phrase so that there must be some feature in the premises which is, in itself, prejudicial to health, in that it is a source of possible infection or disease or illness. Examples include dampness, mould or dirt (*Oakley v Birmingham City Council*, 2000). Accordingly, the arrangement of the rooms in a house cannot mean that the house is prejudicial to health, notwithstanding that the arrangement could lead to the risk of cross-infection (*Oakley*). Likewise, a steep internal staircase which presents a serious risk of falling cannot be prejudicial to health (*R v Bristol City Council ex p Everett*, 1999) nor can a flat with inadequate sound insulation (*R (Vella) v Lambeth LBC*, 2005).

13.11 **Dampness.** Dampness including condensation dampness, is capable of causing injury to health (*GLC v Tower Hamlets LBC*, 1983; *Dover DC v Farrar*, 1980; *Birmingham DC v Kelly*, 1985; *Birmingham DC v McMahon*, 1987; *Southwark LBC v Simpson*, 1998). The persons best equipped to determine prejudiciality to health are doctors and environmental health officers (*O'Toole v Knowsley MBC*, 1999). Whether or not premises are injurious to health, although a question of fact, may to an extent be a technical question, so that magistrates cannot (without controverting evidence) simply substitute their own opinions for those of a qualified person, unless, of course, they disbelieve the evidence (*Patel v Mehtab*, 1980).

13.12 **Nuisance.** To qualify as a nuisance within the definition, it must be shown that there is what is identifiable as a nuisance at common law (*National Coal Board v Thorne*, 1976). It follows (see para 11.134) that the nuisance must emanate from one set of premises and create an effect in another. Thus, a leaking roof will of course be (at least) a nuisance to the occupier of the house but unless it is injurious to his or her health it will not be a statutory nuisance. If, however, the effect of the leak spreads to the next-door property, there will be a nuisance, and as such a statutory nuisance, in the leaking premises, actionable in relation to the next-door house.

13.13 In this connection, it should be noted that where what is occupied is a flat or a room, or anything less than a whole building, the common parts of the building will remain in the landlord's possession and for this purpose will constitute another set of premises, eg roof, halls, stairs, corridors. It is therefore important to define the premises which suffer the nuisance: where there was condensation throughout a block of flats, it was nonetheless each flat which suffered the nuisance, not the block as a whole (*Birmingham DC v McMahon*, 1987).

13.14 Not every activity which affects neighbouring land is a nuisance; only activity which unreasonably interferes with use of the neighbouring land is actionable. Whether interference is unreasonable is a question of fact and degree in each case, and a court is not bound by the expert opinion of environmental health officers on that aspect or issue (*R (Hackney LBC) v Rottenburg*, 2007).

Abatement proceedings

By authority

13.15 If an authority is satisfied that there is a statutory nuisance, or that there has been and that the nuisance is likely to recur, it is obliged to take action (EPA 1990 s80). It must serve an abatement notice on the 'person responsible' for the nuisance. This is the person to 'whose act, default or sufferance' the nuisance is attributable (EPA 1990 s79(7)). If that person cannot be found, then the authority may serve the notice on either the owner (see para 13.16) or the occupier although, if the abatement notice requires structural works, it can only be served on the owner (EPA 1990 s80(2)(b), (c)). If there is no fault on the part of either owner or occupier, and the authority cannot find the person responsible in order to serve an abatement notice on him or her, it may instead execute works itself to abate the nuisance (see para 13.19) and to prevent its recurrence (EPA 1990 s80(2A)). If the abatement can be effected without works, eg simply by the removal of some object causing the nuisance, the authority needs do no more than require abatement; if works are needed, however, then the authority must specify what works it requires (EPA 1990 s80; *Kirklees MBC v Field*, 1997). The authority should allow a reasonable time for abatement, which it should state in the notice.

13.16 'Owner' is not defined in the EPA 1990; under PHA 1936, it was defined in similar terms to a person having control under the Housing Acts (see para 12.9) and that definition should still be applied (*Camden LBC v Gunby*, 1999). In many cases this will be the authority itself. In such a case, the authority cannot serve a notice on itself (*R v Cardiff City Council ex p Cross*, 1982: para 12.2), although the occupier will still be able to take his or her own proceedings against it (see paras 13.20–13.27).

13.17 A person served with an abatement notice may within 21 days appeal it to a magistrates' court (EPA 1990 s80(3)). Appeal is by way of complaint and there is a further right of appeal to the Crown Court (EPA 1990 Sch 3). The grounds of appeal are set out in the Statutory Nuisance (Appeals) Regulations 1995 SI No 2644 and include that the notice was not justified, that it should have been served on another person and that the time given to comply was not long enough. On hearing the complaint, the magistrates' court may quash the notice, vary it in favour of the appellant or dismiss the appeal (SI 1995 No 2644 reg 3(5)).

13.18 If without reasonable excuse the abatement notice is not complied with, and any appeal is unsuccessful, the recipient may be prosecuted. The offence is punishable by a fine of up to an unlimited amount and up to £500 for each day the offence continues after conviction (EPA 1990 s80(4), (5)). A nuisance is not abated just because the premises have been vacated (*Lambeth LBC v Stubbs*, 1980). Prosecution is a criminal proceeding, and does not lie within the residual civil jurisdiction of the magistrates' court: it should, accordingly, be commenced by information and summons, rather than by complaint (*R v Newham East Justices ex p Hunt*, 1976).

13.19 Where an abatement notice has not been complied with, the authority may, either additionally or instead of prosecution, abate the nuisance itself and carry out any necessary works (EPA 1990 s81(3)). Any expenses incurred may be recovered from the person by whose act or default the nuisance was caused (EPA 1990 s81(4)). Where the expenses are recoverable from the owner, they become a charge on the premises (see para 1.91), and may be repaid by instalments (EPA 1990 ss81A and 81B).

By occupier

13.20 There is a special procedure which can be used by an individual instead of the authority (EPA 1990 s82). The individual must be a 'person aggrieved' by the nuisance, ie someone suffering its effects, not – as it were – a mere busybody. A person cannot be aggrieved in relation to a whole block of flats, only in relation to the flat he or she occupies (*Birmingham DC v McMahon*, 1987). Public funding is not, however, available for the prosecution of criminal offences. Initial assistance may be available under the 'legal help' scheme, and solicitors are permitted to enter into conditional fee arrangements to take action under section 82 on the basis of recovering their costs under section 82(12) (see para 13.27) (Courts and Legal Services Act 1990 s58).

13.21 There are two circumstances in which an occupier is likely to want to use section 82: when the authority will not take action against a private landlord; and, more commonly, when the landlord is the authority itself. It is well-established that section 82 permits proceedings against a local authority, including the authority which would otherwise be responsible for taking action (*R v Epping (Waltham Abbey) Justices ex p Burlinson*, 1947).

13.22 Action is to be taken against the person responsible or the owner in the same way as with an abatement notice (see para 13.15; EPA 1990 s82(4)). Prior to taking any proceedings under this section, the occupier must give 21 days' notice in writing to the proposed defendant (EPA 1990 s82(6), (7)). Proceedings are commenced by 'laying an information' before the magistrates. Having heard the case, the magistrates' court may do one or more of the following: make a nuisance order requiring the defendant to abate the nuisance and/or execute works to prevent its recurrence (EPA 1990 s82(2)); impose a fine of up to an unlimited amount (EPA 1990 s82(2); Legal Aid, Sentencing and Punishment of Offenders Act (LASPO) 2012 s85(1)); if the nuisance renders the premises unfit for human habitation, prohibit the use of the premises for that purpose (EPA 1990 s82(3)); or, where neither the person responsible for the nuisance nor the owner or occupier can be found, direct the local authority to do anything which the court would have ordered that person to do (EPA 1990 s82(13)). If without reasonable excuse the nuisance order is not complied with, further proceedings may be taken against the person in default and the court may impose a fine of up to an unlimited amount, and up to an additional £500 for each day the offence continues after conviction (EPA 1990 s82(8); LASPO 2012 s85(1)).

13.23 The works to be included in a nuisance order can include structural works (see para 13.15). An order should be as detailed and as specific as possible (*Salford City Council v McNally*, 1975). The court has a relatively generous discretion as regards time. Thus, although the fact that Housing Act action is to be taken (eg by way of clearance – see paras 12.54–12.60) does not exclude the court's duty to make a nuisance order (see para 13.22), it may still influence the amount of time allowed for compliance (*Nottingham Corporation v Newton*, 1974). There is also a discretion as to extent of works: if the premises are shortly to be demolished, fewer works than otherwise may be ordered, provided what is ordered is sufficient to abate the nuisance for the period for which the property is likely to remain in use (*Lambeth LBC v Stubbs*, 1980; *Coventry City Council v Doyle*, 1981). The fact that the premises are to be vacated does not, however, mean that the nuisance will be abated for, in the absence of an order prohibiting use (see para 13.22), the premises might otherwise be used again in their current state of statutory nuisance (*Lambeth LBC v Stubbs*, 1980).

13.24 There is no express limitation on what works can be ordered. In one case (*Dover DC v Farrar*, 1980), a magistrates' court ordered the installation of gas heating in place of electric heating in premises suffering severely from condensation dampness. The Divisional Court quashed this order but only because the reason the electric heating was not being used was not that it did not work but that the tenants could not afford to use it. It is clear, however, that the order could have been within the power of the magistrates if the electric heating had not worked, or if it had been wholly unsuitable to eliminate the dampness even if fully and properly used by the tenants.

13.25 In the *Dover* case, the landlord was held not to be responsible for the nuisance, as it was the fault of the tenants that the heating that had been provided was not used (see para 13.24). In another case (*GLC v Tower Hamlets LBC*, 1983), however, the GLC owned a corner flat situated on the ground floor of a block, but at a raised level, with three sides and the whole of its underneath open to the air, so that an exceptionally large part of the flat was exposed to the elements. Originally, the flat had an open solid fuel fire but this was subsequently blocked up and replaced with an electric heater, itself later removed. The flat suffered from severe condensation dampness. It was held that the flat was prejudicial to the health of the occupants because of dampness caused by the failure of the landlord to take necessary precautions, either by way of ventilation or insulation, or by providing any special form of heating, for a property wholly exceptionally vulnerable to condensation.

13.26 A landlord has to apply his or her mind to the need for ventilation, and, if need be, to insulation and heating, and must provide a combination of these factors to make a house habitable for the tenant. Once the landlord has done so, it is the tenant's responsibility to use the facilities and if the cause of continuing condensation is the tenant's unwillingness to do so, the landlord cannot be held responsible. A landlord will not be held responsible where the reason works have not been done to abate the nuisance is refusal by the tenant to allow access (*Carr v Hackney LBC*, 1995).

Expenses

13.27 The court has a discretion (EPA 1990 s82(12)) to order a defendant to pay the person bringing the proceedings an amount it considers reasonably sufficient to compensate him or her for any expenses (including legal expenses) properly incurred in the proceedings, but only if the alleged nuisance existed at the date of making the complaint. If the case was funded by a conditional fee agreement (see para 13.20), the complainant can only recover the costs which he or she agreed to pay his or her solicitor even if the case is lost; he or she cannot recover the solicitor's success fee (see para 11.79). When considering whether to make an order for costs, magistrates are entitled to take into account any failure on the part of the person bringing the proceedings to allow the landlord access to the flat prior to the complaint being made (*Jones v Walsall MBC*, 2002).

Compensation

13.28 The court must also consider (LASPO 2012 s63) awarding compensation under the Powers of Criminal Courts (Sentencing) Act 2000 s130 (*Botross v Hammersmith & Fulham LBC*, 1994). There is no limit on the amount that may be awarded. Where proceedings are instituted by a person aggrieved, compensation can only be awarded from the date of the existence of the nuisance indicated in the summons, provided it was not before whichever is the later of (a) the date when the statutory notice expired (see para 13.22) and (b) a date not more than six months before the information was laid (see para 13.22) (*R v Liverpool Crown Court ex p Cooke*, 1996).

Urgent statutory nuisances

13.29 In view of the length of time which normal court proceedings can take, the local authority also has power to use a special, speedy procedure when it appears to it that premises are in such a defective state as to be a statutory nuisance, and that there would be unreasonable delay were the abatement procedure to be used (BA 1984 s76). In one case (*Celcrest Properties Ltd v Hastings BC*, 1979), the difference between four weeks under one of the Public Health Acts and 11–12 weeks under normal abatement procedure was an unreasonable delay, sufficient to justify use of this procedure.

13.30 The procedure commences with a notice of intent served by the authority on the same person as an abatement notice would be served on (see para 13.15). The notice has to state what works the authority intends to execute. The notice must be served at least nine days before their commencement. During the seven days following service, the person served is entitled to serve a counter-notice on the authority, stating that he or she intends him- or herself to remedy the defects which have been specified by the authority. The authority is then debarred from using this speedy procedure unless the person who has served the counter-notice does not commence or progress with the works within what appears to it to be a reasonable time.

13.31 The owner's remedy against use of this procedure is to do nothing: after the works have been completed, the authority will issue civil proceedings (generally in the county court) to recover its expenses; it is a defence to such a claim to show that no unreasonable delay would have flowed from use of the abatement procedure, and, if upheld, the authority will recover none of its expenditure, even though the owner will have benefited to the extent of the works executed (BA 1984 s76(4)). The owner may also defend a claim for the authority's expenses if he or she served a counter-notice (see para 13.30) but the authority entered to do works on the ground of unreasonable time, by proving to the court that the time taken to start or complete the works would not have been unreasonable (BA 1984 s76(4)).

13.32 BA 1984 procedure is not available if the works would contravene a building preservation order under the Planning (Listed Buildings and Conservation Areas) Act 1990, designed for the protection of buildings of special historic or architectural interest (BA 1984 s76(6)). BA 1984 procedure can be used, however, even though the works to be carried out could have been ordered by way of an improvement notice under HA 2004 s11 or s12 (see paras 12.18–12.25).

Other controls

Dangerous buildings

13.33 A dangerous building is any building in such a condition, or used to carry such a load, that it is dangerous (BA 1984 s77).

13.34 The normal way for an authority to deal with a dangerous building is by application to the magistrates' court for an order requiring the owner (see para 13.16), at his or her own election, either to carry out works to obviate the danger or to demolish the building or its dangerous part (BA 1984 s77). Works to obviate the danger means something in the nature of a permanent or semi-permanent remedy, rather than shoring it up (*London CC v Jones*, 1912) or securing the doors against entry and excluding the tenants (*Holme v Crosby Corp*, 1949). Though the court does not have to specify the exact works needed, it needs to specify a time for compliance, as no offence of non-compliance can arise until the time allowed has elapsed, nor will the authority acquire its rights to carry out the works in default (BA 1984 s77). No provision is made for the removal, re-housing or compensating of tenants.

13.35 In an urgent case, there is a procedure similar to that available in relation to urgent statutory nuisances (see paras 13.29–13.32). There is, however, no provision for a counter-notice (see para 13.30), and the authority needs only serve notice of intention if it is reasonably practicable to do so (BA 1984 s78). It is a defence to the authority's proceedings to recover its costs to show that the normal procedure (see para 13.34) could reasonably have been used and, if successful, the authority recovers no part of its costs (BA 1984 s78(5)). There is again no provision for removal, re-housing or compensation of tenants.

Dilapidated buildings

13.36 A dilapidated building is one which is seriously detrimental to the amenities of the neighbourhood, eg unsightly or a health hazard, by reason of its ruinous or dilapidated condition (BA 1984 s79).

13.37 Procedure is by way of notice requiring the owner (see para 13.16) either to carry out works of repair or restoration or, at his or her own election, to demolish the building or a part of it. This procedure is subject to the special appeals and enforcement provisions contained in BA 1984 Pt 4, which permit the owner to challenge the notice by way of appeal on specified grounds, which allow the authority to do works in default of compliance with the notice, and which create offences of non-compliance. No provision is made for removing, re-housing or compensating tenants.

Fire precautions

13.38 Fire is a prescribed hazard under the HHSRS (see para 12.11): where residential premises are a fire risk, local authorities are likely to use their powers under HA 2004. The Regulatory Reform (Fire Safety Order) 2005 SI No 1541 imposes duties on persons responsible for premises to take fire safety measures, which duties are enforceable by the fire service. The provisions of the order, however, do not apply to 'domestic premises', ie private dwellings (article 6(1)(a)). Accordingly, the provisions do not apply to living accommodation although they do apply to the common parts of buildings containing flats or bed-sitting rooms (*Westminster City Council v Select Managements*, 1985). The fire service may serve a prohibition notice restricting the use of such common parts (article 31) and has powers of inspection to enable it to do so (article 27).

13.39 **Smoke and carbon monoxide alarms.** In England, the Smoke and Carbon Monoxide Alarm (England) Regulations 2015 SI No 1693 reg 4, requires landlords to ensure that smoke and carbon monoxide alarms are fitted in properties let by them. The duty applies where a landlord grants one or more persons the right to occupy premises as their only or main residence at a rent (reg 2). Whether a dwelling is someone's only or main residence is similar to the 'only or principal home' residence condition for security of tenure under both HA 1988 and HA 1985 (see paras 1.176–1.179).

13.40 The duty does not apply to local authority landlords or PRPs (reg 3). Certain types of properties are also exempt, including accommodation shared by the occupier with his or her landlord or a member of the landlord's family, long leases (see para 2.72), student halls of residence, hostels and refuges (reg 2 and Sch 1). The duty also does not apply to HMOs licensed under HA 2004 Pt 2 (see paras 14.19–14.47), or houses licensed under HA 2004 Pt 3 (see paras 14.61–14.73) as the mandatory conditions for such licences require the licence-holder to ensure that smoke and carbon monoxide alarms are installed in the licensed properties (see paras 14.42 and 14.72).

13.41 The landlord must ensure that there is a smoke alarm on each storey of the premises on which there is a room used wholly or partly as living accommodation (reg 4). Living accommodation includes a bathroom or lavatory. The landlord must also ensure that there is a carbon monoxide alarm in any room used as living accommodation which contains a solid fuel burning combustion appliance. This term is not defined but is likely to include a coal fire or a wood-burning stove. The landlord must see that checks are made to ensure that such alarms are in proper working order on the day that a new tenancy begins.

13.42 Local housing authorities are responsible for enforcing the regulations. Where an authority has reasonable grounds to believe that a landlord is in breach of one of the duties, it must serve a remedial notice specifying the action that the landlord is required to take within 28 days (reg 5). If the landlord fails to comply with the notice, the authority must itself carry out the remedial action (provided that the occupier allows it to do so).

13.43 The authority may also require the landlord to pay a penalty charge of up to £5,000 (reg 8). The authority must serve a penalty charge notice on the landlord within six weeks of the day on which it became satisfied that the landlord was in breach of the duty to take remedial action. The notice must give reasons for imposing the charge, specify the amount of the charge and notify the landlord of his or her right to a review of the penalty charge notice, which must be requested within 28 days.

13.44 If the landlord requests a review within the 28 days, the authority must consider any representations made by the landlord and decide whether to confirm, vary or withdraw the penalty charge notice (reg 10). The authority's review decision must be notified to the landlord, who must also be informed of his or her right to appeal to the First-tier Tribunal against a decision confirming or varying the notice. An appeal to the First-tier Tribunal may only be brought on the following grounds: the decision was based on an error of fact; the decision was wrong in law; the amount of the penalty charge is unreasonable; or, the decision was otherwise unreasonable (reg 11). The appeal must be made within 28 days of the date of the authority's review decision. The tribunal can quash, confirm or reduce the penalty charge notice but cannot increase the amount.

13.45 In Wales, licences granted by Rent Smart Wales to landlord or managing agents must include conditions (see para 14.92) requiring them to ensure that smoke alarms are installed their properties and that they keep such alarms in proper working order and supply to the local housing authority, on demand, a declaration as to the condition and position of any such alarm.

Electrical safety

13.46 Exposure to electricity is a prescribed hazard under the HHSRS (see para 12.11): where residential premises contain unsafe wiring, local authorities are likely to use their powers under HA 2004.

13.47 Once Housing and Planning Act (HPA) 2016 s122, is in force, the secretary of state will be able to make regulations imposing duties on residential landlords to comply with electrical safety standards. Local housing authorities will primarily be responsible for enforcing these duties but the regulations may also provide for terms to be implied into a tenancy agreement to enable enforcement by a tenant him- or herself.

13.48 In the case of HMOs licensed under HA 2004 Pt 2 (see paras 14.19–14.47), or houses licensed under HA 2004 Pt 3 (see paras 14.61–14.73), the mandatory conditions for such licences require the licence-holder to keep electrical appliances provided by him or her in a safe condition and to supply the local housing authority, on demand, with a declaration by him or her as to their safety (see paras 14.42 and 14.72).

Energy efficiency

13.49 Exposure to excess cold is a prescribed hazard under the HHSRS (see para 12.11) and, where residential premises are poorly insulated, local authorities can use their powers under HA 2004.

13.50 **2012 Regulations.** The Energy Performance of Buildings (England and Wales) Regulations 2012 SI No 3118 require landlords to have an energy performance certificate (EPC) for their properties. An EPC specifies a band for the property from A to G, with A representing the most efficient properties in terms of energy usage and G the least efficient.

13.51 Where a house or flat is to be rented out, the landlord must provide a prospective tenant with an EPC at no charge (reg 6). There is no such requirement where only a room in house or flat is to be let out so this duty does not apply to a prospective tenant of a room in an HMO.

13.52 The landlord must also ensure that an EPC is given, without charge, to anyone who actually becomes a tenant of a house or flat (reg 6(5)).

13.53 Local authorities are responsible for enforcing the 2012 Regulations. An authority can require a person who appears to be, or to have been, under a duty to provide an EPC to a prospective tenant or to someone who becomes a tenant to produce for a copy of a valid EPC (reg 35). Unless he or she has a reasonable excuse for not doing so, that person must comply within seven days.

13.54 If an authority believes that a person has breached any of these duties (see paras 13.50–13.52), it may serve a penalty charge notice (reg 36). This may be given during the period of six months beginning with the day on which the breach was committed and must state that the authority believes that the breach has occurred, give particulars of it, state the amount of the charge (£200 for each beach of duty) and notify the landlord of his or her right to a review of the penalty charge notice, which must be requested within 28 days.

13.55 If the landlord requests a review within the 28 days, the authority must consider any representations made by the landlord and decide whether to confirm, vary or withdraw the penalty charge notice (reg 39). The authority's review decision must be notified to the landlord, who must also be informed of his or her right to appeal to the First-tier Tribunal against a decision confirming or varying the notice (reg 40). An appeal to the First-tier Tribunal may only be brought on the following grounds: the appellant did not commit the breach of duty; the notice was not given within the six-month period after the breach of duty was committed or does not comply with some other requirement imposed by the Regulations; in the circumstances of the case, it was inappropriate for the notice to have been given.

13.56 In England, a landlord cannot give notice requiring possession under HA 1988 s21, to an assured shorthold tenant (see paras 1.246–1.251) granted on or after 1 October 2015, until he or she has provided him or her with an EPC (see para 2.197(3)). From 1 October 2018, this restriction will apply to all assured shorthold tenancies in England whenever granted.

13.57 **2015 Regulations.** The 2012 Regulations do not impose any minimum energy efficiency requirements for a property. Once in force, the Energy Efficiency (Private Rented Property) (England and Wales) Regulations 2015 SI No 962 will, however, require residential properties let in the private sector to have an energy efficiency rating of A to E. Subject to exceptions, eg where the rating cannot be improved, a private sector landlord will not be able to let a residential property if the rating is F or G.

13.58 From 1 April 2018, a landlord of a 'domestic PR property' in England or Wales must not grant a new tenancy, or renew an existing tenancy, if the property is 'sub-standard', ie it has an energy performance indicator of below E (reg 22). From 1 April 2020, the landlord must not continue to let a property if it is substandard (reg 23).

13.59 A 'domestic PR property' is a property let under an assured tenancy (see para 1.220–1.261), including an assured shorthold tenancy (see para 1.246–1.251), a Rent Act tenancy (see paras 1.268–1.293), or any other form of tenancy specified by the secretary of state or the Welsh Ministers (reg 19). Properties let by local authorities, PRPs and RSLs are exempt. Detailed provision is made for properties which cannot be improved.

13.60 Local authorities will be responsible for enforcing the 2015 Regulations through compliance notices and/or penalty notices (regs 37–38).

13.61 From 1 April 2018, a compliance notice may be served where the landlord appears to the authority to be, or to have been within the preceding 12 months, in breach of the prohibition on letting sub-standard domestic PR property. The notice may request such information as the authority considers necessary to monitor compliance with the regulations (reg 37).

13.62 A penalty notice may be served where the authority is satisfied that the landlord is, or in the preceding 18 months has been, in breach of the prohibition on letting sub-standard domestic PR property or has failed to comply with a compliance notice (reg 38). The penalty notice must specify the regulation that has been breach, giving particulars of the breach, specify the amount of the penalty and notify the landlord of his or her right to a review of the penalty notice, which must be requested within 28 days.

13.63 The amount of the maximum penalty for letting sub-standard domestic PR depends on whether the breach lasted for less than three months (maximum £2,000) or more than three months (maximum £4,000) (reg 40). The maximum penalty for failing to comply with a compliance notice is £2,000.

13.64 The provisions governing the conduct of any review (reg 42) are similar to those governing a review of a decision to issue a penalty charge notice under the 2012 Regulations (see para 13.55). Likewise, the landlord will have similar rights to appeal a penalty notice (regs 43–44) to the First-tier Tribunal (see para 13.55).

Sanitary accommodation

13.65 Inadequate provision for sanitation is a prescribed hazard under HHSRS (see para 12.11) so that authorities can use their powers under HA 2004 to require the installation of adequate sanitary facilities. In addition, however, local authorities have a duty to serve notice on an owner (see para 13.16) of premises, requiring the provision of closets, either when the building has insufficient sanitary accommodation or when any part of the building occupied as a separate dwelling (see para 1.171) has insufficient sanitary accommodation (BA 1984 s64 as amended). They also have a duty to serve a similar notice if they are satisfied that such sanitary accommodation as exists is in such a state as to be prejudicial to health or a nuisance (see paras 13.9–13.14) and cannot be rendered satisfactory without reconstruction (BA 1984 s64).

13.66 For the purposes of the latter provision, local authorities not only enjoy their usual powers of entry (see para 13.7), but are also entitled to apply tests or otherwise examine the closet's condition (PHA 1936 s48). If, on examination, the authority comes to the conclusion that the closet can be rendered satisfactory without reconstruction, it serves notice requiring the execution of such works as may be necessary (PHA 1936 s45). Such a notice may be served on either the owner or occupier.

13.67 These provisions are subject to the appeals procedure contained in the BA 1984 Pt 4 (see para 13.37), which will entitle the person served to challenge a notice by way of appeal, but which also entitle the authority to carry out works in default, and which create offences of non-compliance. In addition, there are three specific offences related to sanitary accommodation.

1) **Flushing or deodorizing:** failure to keep the convenience supplied with water for flushing, or in the case of an earth closet with dry earth or other suitable deodorising material (PHA 1936 s51).
2) **Injury, fouling and obstruction:** when a convenience is used by more than one family, anyone who injures or improperly fouls the convenience, or anything used in connection with the convenience, or who wilfully or negligently obstructs the drain leading from the convenience, commits an offence (PHA 1936 s52).
3) **Insanitary state:** when a convenience is used by more than one family, leaving the convenience or the approach to the convenience in an insanitary state, for want of cleaning or attention, is an offence (PHA 1936 s52.).

Drains and sewers

13.68 Local authorities enjoy wide powers to require owners (see para 13.16) to make satisfactory provision for drainage and sewage, eg if a drain or sewer admits subsoil water, or is prejudicial to health or is a nuisance (BA 1984 s59). In addition, inadequate drainage is a prescribed hazard under HHSRS (see para 12.11) in respect of which authorities may take enforcement action under HA 2004.

13.69 In some circumstances, the authority may require remedial action by an occupier as well as, or instead of, by an owner, eg in the case of a blockage (Public Health Act 1961 s17). In this last case, the authority can require removal of a blockage within 48 hours, in default of compliance with which it may enter and carry out the works in default, recovering its expenses of so doing.

13.70 An authority may also secure repair of a drain or sewer, if it concludes that it is not sufficiently maintained and kept in good repair and that it could be repaired at a cost of less than £250 (Public Health Act 1961 s17). This power proceeds by way of notice of intention to carry out the works itself, and recover the costs of so doing.

13.71 There is no appeal against either of the last two classes of notice but in each case the authority's decision can be challenged by way of defence to the claim for recovery of expenses. Local authorities have additional discretionary powers to cleanse drains at the request and cost of an owner or occupier (PHA 1961 s22).

Food storage

13.72 Inadequate provision for the storage of food is a prescribed hazard under HHSRS (12.11) and authorities may therefore take enforcement action under HA 2004. In addition, local authorities have power to require the provision of sufficient and suitable accommodation for the storage of food in houses, or in parts of a building occupied as separate dwellings (BA 1984 s70). The power proceeds by way of notice on the owner (see para 13.16), who may challenge it under BA 1984 Pt 4 (see para 13.37), which also gives the authority power to execute works in default and to recover the costs of so doing.

Vermin

13.73 Vermin are harboured by filth. It follows that, not uncommonly, the property most in need of repair will be verminous, for it can be difficult if not impossible as a matter of practice to keep the premises clean. Exposure to pests is a prescribed hazard under HHSRS (see para 12.11) and authorities may take enforcement action under HA 2004. In addition, if the local authority is satisfied that premises are so filthy, or in such an unwholesome condition, as to be prejudicial to health (see paras 13.10–13.11) or verminous, it is bound to take action (PHA 1936 s83, as amended).

13.74 Action is by way of notice served on either the owner (see para 13.16) or the occupier. The notice may require such steps as may be necessary to prevent the prejudice to health, or to remove and destroy the vermin, which steps can include, if necessary, the removal of wallpaper and other wall-coverings, papering or repapering, painting and distempering, at the option of the person served (PHA 1936 s83, as amended). In the event of non-compliance, the authority may execute works in default, and seek to recover its costs from the person served, though it will be a defence to such an action to show either that the notice was not necessary or that as between owner and occupier, it is the other who should have been served (PHA 1936 s83(2)).

13.75 In some cases, the premises may be in such a condition that a gas attack is called for. A gas attack is carried out by, and at the cost of, the authority, which must give notice to both owner and occupier of its intention to proceed. It may require the premises (and neighbouring premises) to be vacated during the attack, in which event it must provide alternative temporary accommodation, free of charge (PHA 1936 s83; PHA 1961 s36). A notice requiring the premises to be vacated may be appealed, but subject to the right of appeal it is an offence not to comply with it (PHA 1936 s83).

Disease

13.76 Formerly, the Public Health (Control of Disease) Act 1984 Pt 2, contained specific provisions for dealing with 'notifiable diseases', such as cholera and typhus, some of which were relevant to housing. With effect from July 2010, Part 2 was repealed by the Health and Social Care Act 2008, and replaced by a new Part 2A, which contains wide-ranging powers for local authorities and other public bodies to prevent the spread of disease. These powers extend to any infection or contamination which could present a significant harm to human health.

13.77 A justice of the peace has power to order 'health measures' in respect of premises, if satisfied that the premises may be infected or contaminated, that the infection or contamination presents a significant risk of harm to human health, that there is a risk that the premises might infect people and that it is necessary to make the order to remove or reduce the risk (Public Health (Control of Disease) Act 1984 s45I(1)). 'Premises' is widely defined so as to include any buildings, houseboats and even caravans (s74). The justice of the peace may order closure or destruction of the premises concerned, or require their disinfection or decontamination (s45I(1)). The order may also require the owner (see para 13.16) or occupier to provide information about the premises and issues relating to the infection or contamination (s45I(1)).

13.78 An application for an order may be made by a local authority. Before doing so, the authority must make reasonable inquiries to ascertain the identity of the owner (see para 13.16) and the occupier of the premises and, where those inquiries are successful, it must give them notice of the application (Health Protection (Part 2A Orders) Regulations 2010 SI No 658 reg 3 or Health Protection (Part 2A Orders) (Wales) Regulations 2010 SI No 1544 reg 3.

13.79 Local authorities also have power to disinfect or decontaminate premises (see para 13.77) at the request of either the owner (see para 13.16) or the tenant of those premises (Health Protection (Local Authority Powers) Regulations 2010 SI No 657 regs 6 and 7 or Health Protection (Local Authority Powers) (Wales) Regulations 2010 SI No 1545. Provided he or she is forewarned before the works are carried out, the person who makes the request may be charged for the costs involved.

Human rights

13.80 The observations made at para 12.88 apply in the same way to the powers under consideration in this chapter.

CHAPTER 14

Housing conditions: overcrowding, multiple occupation and licensing

continued

Introduction

14.1 This chapter brings together a number of additional local authority powers to maintain proper management standards and maintenance of housing accommodation in their areas: overcrowding, under the Housing Act (HA) 1985; houses in multiple occupation (HMOs) under HA 2004; licensing under HA 2004; empty dwellings under HA 2004; and, private sector licensing in Wales under the Housing (Wales) Act (H(W)A) 2014.

Overcrowding

14.2 Levels of permitted overcrowding under the provisions of HA 1985 were set nationally in 1935 and are now considerably out of date. HA 2004 s216, allows the secretary of state and the National Assembly for Wales to change the standards through regulations but they have yet to exercise that power. As overcrowding is also a hazard which may be dealt with under the Housing Health and Safety Rating System (HHSRS) (see para 12.8), which allows authorities to impose stricter requirements using the provisions of that Act, they are now used in preference to those of HA 1985. As, however, HA 1985 remains in force, and creates its own offences, it continues to be necessary to consider it.

Definition

14.3 The HA 1985 overcrowding provisions apply to premises used or suitable for use as a separate dwelling (see para 1.171) (HA 1985 s343). As much as a house could be overcrowded, or as little as a single room. There are alternative tests. If either is offended, the premises are overcrowded in law.

1) **Room standard.** There is overcrowding whenever there are so many people in a house that any two or more of them, being 10 or more years old, and of opposite sexes, not being persons living together as husband and wife, have to sleep in the same room (HA 1985 s325). For this purpose, children under 10 may be disregarded.

   A room means any room normally used in the locality as either a bedroom or a living room (HA 1985 s325). Kitchens used to be considered a living room, and might still so be held in this connection, at least if big enough to accommodate a bed (*Zaitzeff v Olmi*, 1952) as well as all necessary kitchen utilities, but it must be said that there is a tendency for courts to adopt modern criteria when addressing issues such as how housing is used (consider *Uratemp Ventures Ltd v Collins*, 2001: see paras 1.171 and 1.172), and a person positively seeking to establish that his or her household is overcrowded may now be able to persuade an authority (or a court on a challenge) to ignore a kitchen as a room for this purpose.

Note. There is overcrowding not when two or more people actually sleep in the same room, as proscribed, but when the number of rooms means that they have to do so. Thus, a couple, with two children of opposite sexes and 10 years old or more, with two living rooms, are not overcrowded, because the couple could occupy separate rooms, each with one of the children (of the appropriate sex).

2) **Space standard.** This alternative standard operates by calculating the permitted number for the dwelling in one of two ways: the lower number so calculated is the permitted number for the dwelling (HA 1985 s326).
   - One test is based on the number of living rooms in the dwelling (disregarding a room of less than 50 square feet):
     - one room, two persons;
     - two rooms, three persons;
     - three rooms, five persons;
     - four rooms, seven and a half persons;
     - five rooms or more, ten persons plus two for each room in excess of five rooms.
   - The other test is based on floor areas of each room size:
     - less than 50 square feet, no one;
     - 50 to less than 70 square feet, half a person;
     - 70 to less than 90 square feet, one person;
     - 90 to less than 110 square feet, one and a half persons;
     - 110 square feet or larger, two persons.

   Note. The reference to a 'half person' is because, for these purposes, a child below the age of one counts not at all, and a child from one year old but who has not yet reached 10 counts as a half.

Permissible overcrowding

14.4 There are four circumstances in which overcrowding, although offending the above criteria, is still permissible.

1) **Licensed overcrowding.** On the application of an occupier, or an intending occupier, of a dwelling (but not on the application of the landlord or of the local authority itself), a licence may be issued (in prescribed form), which lasts for no more than one year at a time (HA 1985 s330).

   The licence is issued by the local authority, having regard to exceptional circumstances, expedience and, where appropriate, seasonal increases in population. The licence must state how many people are to be permitted. A copy must be served on the landlord. It may be revoked at any time by one month's notice.
2) **Temporary overcrowding.** There is no overcrowding if additional members of the occupier's family are staying with him or her temporarily (HA 1985 s329).
3) **Natural growth.** Natural growth occurs when a child achieves a relevant age (see para 14.3). If the occupier applies to the local authority for alternative accommodation, either before the child reaches the relevant age or before any prosecution is instigated (or possession proceedings; compare para 14.7), there will be no illegal overcrowding until either there is an offer of suitable alternative accommodation by the authority, which the occupier fails to accept, or the opportunity arises (after the child reaches the relevant age) of asking someone else living in the house, who is not him- or herself a member of the occupier's family, to leave, which opportunity the occupier fails to take (HA 1985 s328).

   Although the phrase 'suitable alternative accommodation' is used in HA 1985 (see paras 2.114–2.116) and HA 1988 (see para 2.169) and the Rent Act (RA) 1977 (see para 2.218(10)), the term has its own meaning in the context of overcrowding. Alternative accommodation is only suitable for these purposes if: the occupier and family can live in the house without overcrowding; the authority certifies it as suitable to his or her needs and the needs of his or her family as regards security of tenure, proximity to work, means, and otherwise; and, if the house belongs to the authority, it can certify it as being suitable to his or her needs as regards extent of accommodation (HA 1985 s342). The authority can only certify extent if it provides a house with two bedrooms for four people, three bedrooms for five, and four bedrooms for seven. It is, accordingly, a higher standard than that set by the overcrowding limits themselves.

   An occupier need only ask someone else to leave if it is reasonably practicable for that person to do so, which is to be considered in all the circumstances, including whether or not there is suitable alternative accommodation available to him or her. The exemption only continues to apply provided all the people sleeping in the house are those who were sleeping there at the date on which the child reached the relevant age which meant that the accommodation became overcrowded, or their children.

4) **Original overcrowding.** This refers to premises which were overcrowded when the provisions themselves first applied to the house (Housing (Consequential Provisions) Act 1985 Sch 4). As the provisions have applied throughout the country since 1935, this exemption is highly unlikely to be relevant today.

Offences

14.5 There are three sets of offences created by the overcrowding provisions.

1) **Rent book offences.** Every rent book or similar document (see para 1.85) must contain:
   (a) a summary of the overcrowding offences;
   (b) a statement of the power of the authority to licence overcrowding (see para 14.4(1)); and
   (c) a statement of the permitted number of occupants (see para 14.3) (HA 1985 s332).

   Either the occupier or the landlord can ask the authority for a written statement of permitted number at any time. The authority can require the occupier to produce his or her rent book for inspection and – provided the occupier has it – it is an offence to fail to do so (HA 1985 s336). It is also an offence to fail to provide the summary and statements, although it is a defence to a charge based on the insertion of an incorrect permitted number that it was the number provided by the authority (HA 1985 s332).
2) **Landlord's offences.** A landlord who causes or permits a dwelling to be overcrowded commits an offence (HA 1985 s331). This may occur when the landlord has reasonable cause to believe there might be illegal overcrowding, or by failing to make enquiries as to the number intending to occupy a dwelling, or, if the authority serves notice on the landlord that there is illegal overcrowding, by failing to take possession proceedings (see para 14.7; HA 1985 s331). Finally, unless the authority already knows of the overcrowding, the landlord is obliged to notify the authority once he or she learns of it (HA 1985 s333).

3) **Occupier's offences.** The occupier commits an offence when he or she causes or permits premises to be illegally overcrowded (HA 1985 s327).

   The authority has power to seek information from the occupier as to numbers in a dwelling, failure to comply with which demand, or providing an answer which the occupier knows to be false in a material particular, is also an offence (HA 1985 s335).

14.6 The local authority may itself commit an offence under these provisions. No one but a local authority may prosecute an overcrowding offence committed by a private individual, but a private individual may prosecute an authority, albeit only with the consent of the Attorney-General (HA 1985 s339); this will not easily be forthcoming.

Possession proceedings

14.7 Rent Act protection (see paras 1.268–1.293) is lost to occupiers whose premises are illegally overcrowded (see para 1.287; RA 1977 s101). It is, however, only illegal overcrowding that removes Rent Act protection, so that permissible overcrowding will allow the occupier to remain in the premises. The landlord must still determine the tenancy at common law (*Aslan v Murphy*, 1989). There is no equivalent removal of security (see paras 1.160–1.209) for secure tenants (including flexible tenants – paras 1.181–1.189) under HA 1985 (see paras 1.204–1.208) or introductory tenants under HA 1996 or for assured tenants under HA 1988 (see paras 1.220–1.251). There is a specific ground for possession against a secure tenant whose dwelling is illegally overcrowded (HA 1985 Sch 2 Ground 9) (see para 2.113). No grounds for possession are required to seek possession against an introductory tenant, so the landlord can evict for illegal overcrowding under the usual procedure applicable to introductory tenancies (see paras 2.148–2.157). Landlords of assured tenants commonly include a term in their tenancy agreements prohibiting illegal overcrowding so that if this term is breached, there is a ground for possession available (HA 1988 Sch 2 Ground 12) (see para 2.169(3)).

14.8 The authority may itself bring proceedings for possession of premises illegally overcrowded, and recover its costs of doing so from the landlord (HA 1985 s338). The authority must serve prior notice on the occupier, giving him or her 14 days within which to abate the overcrowding.

Houses in multiple occupation

14.9 HA 2004 introduced licensing of HMOs (Part 2), which fixes a permitted level of occupation for the HMO, and under which standards of management and maintenance can be imposed as conditions of the licence. Authorities must have a licensing scheme for certain 'high-risk' HMOs, and may extend their scheme to other HMOs. Management standards in HMOs are also controlled by management regulations, and levels of occupation in unlicensed HMOs may be controlled by service of overcrowding notices. (*Note.* Because these provisions are to be found in HA 2004, which is the same Act as that governing the HHSRS, some definitions are the same and are imported by reference). There is also provision for a management order to be made in relation to an HMO in some circumstances (see paras 14.122–14.134).

Definition

14.10 A building (or part of a building) is an HMO if it satisfies one of a number of tests: the standard test; the self-contained flat test; the converted building test; there is an HMO declaration in force in respect of it; or, it is a converted block of flats, which satisfies certain requirements (HA 2004 s254). There is, however, a number of exemptions applicable to properties which would otherwise qualify as an HMO.

Standard test

14.11 This includes the majority of HMOs encountered in practice, eg bedsitting-room accommodation and shared houses. Each one of six conditions must be satisfied (HA 2004 s254(2)).

1) **Not self-contained flats.** The premises must consist of one or more units of living accommodation which are not in themselves a self-contained flat. A self-contained flat is a separate set of premises which forms part of a building in which all the basic amenities are available for the exclusive use of its occupants. The basic amenities are: (a) toilet; (b) personal washing facilities, eg bathroom or shower-room; and (c) cooking facilities.
2) **Not single household.** The accommodation must be occupied by persons who do not form a single household. Persons do not form a single household unless they are either all members of the same family, or they fall within prescribed circumstances.

Family members include: spouses; cohabitees who live together as husband and wife; same-sex couples who are in an equivalent relationship; parents; grandparents; children; grandchildren; brothers; sisters; uncles; aunts; nephews; nieces; and, cousins. Half-blood relationships are treated as full-blood relationships; step-children are treated as children (HA 2004 s258).

Regulations prescribe certain categories of persons as being part of a single household even though they are not family members, eg carers, foster children and live-in employees, such as au pairs and nannies (Licensing and Management of Houses in Multiple Occupation and Other Houses (Miscellaneous Provisions) (England) Regulations 2006 SI No 373 regs 3 and 4; or Licensing and Management of Houses in Multiple Occupation and Other Houses (Miscellaneous Provisions) (Wales) Regulations 2006 SI No 1715 regs 3 and 4).

3) **Only or main residence.** The occupiers must occupy the living accommodation as their only or main residence. The test is similar to the 'only or principal home' residence condition for security of tenure under both HA 1988 and HA 1985 (see paras 1.176–1.179).

   Certain occupiers are deemed to be occupying property as their only or main residence (HA 2004 s259): (a) students occupying the property for the purpose of undertaking a full-time course of further or higher education; (b) people living in refuges; and, (c) certain migrant or seasonal workers and asylum seekers (Licensing and Management of Houses in Multiple Occupation and Other Houses (Miscellaneous Provisions) (England) Regulations 2006 SI No 373 reg 5 or Licensing and Management of Houses in Multiple Occupation and Other Houses (Miscellaneous Provisions) (Wales) Regulations 2006 SI No 1715 reg 5.

4) **Sole use.** Occupation of the living accommodation must constitute the only use of that accommodation by the occupiers, with the consequence that all the occupiers must occupy the HMO as their only or main residence. In some circumstances, the population of a property may fluctuate, or the nature of the population's occupation may be uncertain or variable, so that it cannot be said – at any rate with confidence – that that the property is the only or main residence of each and every occupier, eg in an hotel which provides both holiday and longer-term hostel accommodation. There is a presumption that the requirement is satisfied, but this may be rebutted by evidence from the landlord. To avoid the

problem altogether, authorities may declare a property to be an HMO, provided certain criteria are met (see para 14.15).

5) **Consideration.** At least one of the occupiers must be liable either to pay rent or to provide other consideration for occupying the property, eg services or something else of value.
6) **Sharing or lack of facilities.** Two or more of the households which occupy the living accommodation must share one or more basic facilities, ie toilet, personal washing facilities or cooking facilities, or else the living accommodation must be lacking in one or more of those facilities.

Self-contained flat test

14.12 The self-contained flat test is concerned with flats in multiple occupation. The only difference between the self-contained flat test and the standard test (see para 14.11) is that the relevant premises must be a self-contained flat and therefore a separate part of a building. It is satisfied where a self-contained flat meets conditions (2) to (6), in para 14.11 (HA 2004 s254(3)).

Converted building test

14.13 This test is concerned with buildings (or parts of buildings) which have been partly converted into self-contained flats but which also include living accommodation that is not a self-contained flat (HA 2004 s253(4)). Thus, the test is applicable to properties comprising both self-contained flats (which may not fulfil the self-contained flat test, ie which may not be HMOs in their own right) and bedsitting-room accommodation which would satisfy the standard test and would be an HMO in itself; the effect of this test is that the whole building, including the self-contained flats, is subject to the controls of the HMO legislation.

14.14 A converted building is a building (or part of a building) consisting of residential accommodation in which one or more units have been created since the building (or relevant part) was constructed. For a building to satisfy the converted building test:

1) it must be a converted building;
2) it must contain one or more units of living accommodation which are not self-contained flats (whether or not it also contains a self-contained flat or flats);
3) the living accommodation must be occupied by persons who do not form a single household (see para 14.11(2));

4) the living accommodation must be occupied by those persons as their only or main residence (see para 14.11(3));
5) their occupation must constitute the only use of that living accommodation (see para 14.11(4)); and
6) at least one of the occupiers must be liable either to pay rent or to provide other consideration for occupying the property (see para 14.11(5)).

HMO declaration

14.15 To satisfy any of the three tests set out above, it is necessary for the sole use of the living accommodation to be occupation by people as their own or main residence (see para 4.11(3)). Where the property's population fluctuates, or the nature of that population's occupation is uncertain or variable, an authority may – to remove doubts about the property's status – make an HMO declaration (HA 2004 s255). Before making a declaration, the authority must be satisfied: that the standard test (see para 14.11), the self-contained flat test (see para 14.12), or the converted building test (see para 14.13) would be satisfied but for the fact that the sole use condition (see para 14.11(4)) is not satisfied; and, that occupation as an only or main residence (see para 14.11(3)) by persons who do not form a single household (see para 14.11(2)) is at least a significant use of the property.

14.16 The authority must serve notice of its decision on: (a) any person who has an estate or interest in the premises (save a tenant under a lease with less than three years to run); (b) a person managing the premises (see para 12.9); and (c) any person having control of the premises (see para 12.9). That notice must inform the recipient of his or her right to appeal to the First-tier Tribunal (England) or the residential property tribunal (Wales) within 28 days of the date of the authority's decision. There is no power to extend this time limit. If no appeal is brought in time, the declaration comes into force on the date specified in the notice.

Converted block of flats

14.17 A converted block of flats is a building (or part of a building) which has been converted into and consists of self-contained flats (HA 2004 s257(1)). The effect is to bring within the HMO regime properties which have inadequate fire separation between flats. To qualify as an HMO, a converted block of flats must satisfy two conditions.

1) **Conversion works.** The conversion works must fail to comply with the 'appropriate building standards' (if the conversion was completed before 1 June 1992, the standards contained in the original form of the Building Regulations 1991 SI No 2768 or, if completed later, the standards which applied at the date of completion).
2) **Low level of owner-occupation.** Less than two-thirds of the flats must be owner-occupied. A flat is owner-occupied if it is occupied by a freeholder or a long leaseholder (see para 2.72) or members of their families.

Exemptions

14.18 Certain properties which otherwise qualify as HMOs on the basis of one or other of the above definitions (see paras 14.11–14.17) are nonetheless exempt for the purposes of the application of the licensing regime and the application of certain other powers (HA 2004 Sch 14). Such properties are only HMOs for the purposes of the application of HHSRS (chapter 12).

1) **Exempt landlords.** Buildings managed by local authorities, PRPs and RSLs or certain other specified public bodies and certain co-operative societies are exempt.
2) **Other controls.** Buildings which are subject to the control of other, specified regulatory schemes, eg care homes.
3) **Education.** Buildings occupied by full-time students at specified educational institutions, where the person managing (see para 12.9) or having control of (see para 12.9) the building is the educational institution or another specified person.
4) **Religion.** Buildings occupied by religious communities.
5) **Owner-occupiers.** Buildings predominantly occupied by owner-occupiers, ie freeholders (see para 1.7) and long leaseholders (see para 2.72): the building may be occupied by no more than two persons who are not owner-occupiers or members of their families.
6) **Two households**. Buildings occupied by only two persons who form two households.

Licensing

14.19 Local authorities must have a licensing scheme for those HMOs which present the greatest risk of death by fire because of their size; they also have power to impose licensing for other HMOs. The following provisions apply whether the licence is pursuant to the mandatory scheme for risk of death by fire or otherwise.

14.20 Failure to obtain a licence for an HMO which has to be licensed may have serious consequences for the landlord: failure to obtain a licence for an HMO without a reasonable excuse is a criminal offence (see para 14.97); while the HMO remains unlicensed, there are restrictions on the landlord's right to obtain possession (see para 14.103); and, the First-tier Tribunal (England) or the residential property tribunal (Wales) may make a rent repayment order, which requires the landlord to repay rent, housing benefit or universal credit which was paid during a period when the HMO should have been licensed (see paras 14.104–14.115). These consequences are considered below, under their own heading.

14.21 In England, once the provisions of Housing and Planning Act (HPA) 2016 Pt 2, are in force, it is expected that local housing authorities will be able to apply to the First-tier Tribunal for a banning order against anyone convicted of failing obtain a licence for an HMO which has to be licensed (see para 14.97), which will prevent that person from being involved in letting or managing residential property (see paras 5.82–5.102). A person against whom a banning order made will be entered on a database of 'rogue landlords' (see paras 5.103–5.111).

14.22 Although there was no licensing of HMOs before HA 2004, authorities were – under HA 1985 – able to make 'registration schemes', which required registration of HMOs (as then defined) in their area. Such schemes could include control provisions limiting the number of households or occupiers in an HMO and/or special control provisions regulating management standards. Accordingly, many authorities were operating a *de facto* form of licensing before HA 2004. Detailed transitional provisions were made to convert such registration schemes into licensing schemes.

14.23 Authorities are under general duties to make arrangements to secure effective implementation of the licensing regime and to ensure that all applications for licences are determined within a reasonable time (HA 2004 s55). As soon as reasonably practicable after a licence application is made, and within five years of that application, they must satisfy themselves as to whether they ought also to take action under the HHSRS (chapter 10).

Mandatory licensing

14.24 All authorities must operate a licensing scheme in respect of HMOs which:

1) comprise three storeys or more;
2) are occupied by at least five persons; and

3) are occupied by persons living in two or more single households (see para 14.11(2)) (Licensing of Houses in Multiple Occupation (Prescribed Descriptions) (England) Order 2006 SI No 371 or Licensing of Houses in Multiple Occupation (Prescribed Descriptions) (Wales) Order 2006 SI No 1712).

14.25 Both sets of 2006 regulations contain detailed provisions for the calculation of the number of storeys. Where the HMO is situated above or below business premises, the storeys comprised in the business premises are taken into account. Business premises are defined as any premises not used as an integral part of living accommodation so that not only commercial premises but also premises which are out of use are included. Where the HMO is such because it fulfils the self-contained flat test, however, other residential storeys above or below the flat are not included in the calculation (*Islington LBC v The Unite Group plc*, 2013). A basement or attic is included where it is used wholly or partly as living accommodation, or it has been constructed, converted or adapted for use wholly or partly as living accommodation. In addition, a basement is included if it is the only or principal means of entry into the HMO from the street; an attic is included if it is being used as an integral part of the HMO. Any other storey that is used as an integral part of the HMO is also taken into account but this does not include a staircase providing access to a flat which is not on the ground floor (*Bristol City Council v Digs (Bristol) Ltd*, 2014).

Additional licensing

14.26 Local authorities have power to require licensing of HMOs which are not within the mandatory regime by making a designation. The designation may apply by location or by particular categories of HMO and can be of all HMOs in an authority's area. Authorities must ensure that any exercise of their power to require additional licensing is consistent with their overall housing strategy and must adopt a co-ordinated approach in dealing with the overlapping issues of homelessness, empty properties and antisocial behaviour in the private sector (HA 2004 s57).

14.27 To make a designation, the authority must consider that a significant proportion of the HMOs which it intends to include are being managed so ineffectively as to give rise, or to be likely to give rise, to problems either for the occupiers of the HMOs or for members of the public (HA 2004 s56(2)). Accordingly, additional licensing is not only about regulating the housing conditions but also about controlling the behaviour of occupiers of HMOs and their visitors. Before making a designation, the authority must take reasonable steps to consult persons who are likely to be affected by it, and must consider any representations made in response (HA 2004, 56(3)). Failure to carry out proper consultation may result in a subsequent designation being invalid (*R (Peat) v Hyndburn BC*, 2011). If the designation is intended to cover the whole of an authority's area, persons in the areas of neighbouring authorities may have to be consulted (*R (Regas) v Enfield LBC*, 2014).

14.28 A designation must be confirmed by the secretary of state or the National Assembly for Wales (HA 2004 s58). Confirmation may either be specific or by way of a general approval. Following confirmation of the designation, the authority must take steps to publicise it, which are specified in regulations.

14.29 A designation must specify how long it is to last, to a maximum period of five years (HA 2004 s60). The authority must periodically review the operation of the scheme and may revoke it if considered appropriate. If a designation is revoked, the authority must comply with prescribed publicity requirements.

Temporary exemption notices

Temporary exemption notice

14.30 A person having control of (see para 12.9), or a person managing (see para 12.9), an HMO which needs to be licensed (whether under the mandatory or an additional scheme) may notify the authority of his or her intention to take steps to ensure that the house no longer requires to be licensed, eg by reducing the number of persons or households occupying the property (HA 2004 s62). If so, the authority may serve a 'temporary exemption notice', the consequence of which is that the HMO does not have to be licensed while the notice is in force. Such a notice remains in force for three months but it can be extended for a further three months.

14.31 If the authority refuses to issue a temporary exemption notice, it must give the applicant written reasons for its decision and inform him or her of the right to appeal to the First-tier Tribunal (England) or the residential property tribunal (Wales) within 28 days (HA 2004 s62(6)). There is no power to extend this time limit.

Applications

14.32 A licence is required for each HMO to which the licensing requirements – mandatory (see paras 14.24–14.25) or additional (see paras 14.26–14.29) – apply (HA 2004 s68). Licences are not transferable: on sale of the HMO, the new landlord has to apply for a new licence. An application for a licence must be made to the authority and must conform with any requirements which the authority may impose, including payment of a fee. Specified information must be contained in the application: Licensing and Management of Houses in Multiple Occupation and Other Houses (Miscellaneous Provisions) (England) Regulations 2006 SI No 373 reg 7 and Sch 2, or Licensing and Management of Houses in Multiple Occupation and Other Houses (Miscellaneous Provisions) (Wales) Regulations 2006 SI No 1715 reg 7 and Sch 2. In particular, the application must include:

1) details about the person managing (see para 12.9) the HMO and the person having control (see para 12.9) of the HMO;
2) details about the layout of the HMO and facilities provided; and
3) declarations that furniture and gas appliances in the HMO meet relevant safety requirements.

14.33 The form must also include questions designed to elicit information as to whether the proposed license holder and proposed manager are 'fit and proper persons' (see para 14.36). The applicant and the proposed licence holder (if different) must both sign the form, which application must be accompanied by signed declarations as to the truth of its contents. A person knowingly supplying any information in the form which is false or misleading, or supplying such information reckless as to whether it is false or misleading, commits an offence (HA 2004 s238(1)).

Decisions

14.34 Before granting a licence, the authority must be satisfied of five matters (HA 2004 s64(3)).

1) **Suitability of property.** The HMO must be reasonably suitable for occupation by not more than a specified maximum number of households or persons, or can be made so suitable by the imposition of conditions. (The maximum number is either that specified in the application or a number determined by the authority).
2) **Fit and proper licence-holder.** The proposed licence holder must be a fit and proper person to be the licence holder and must be the most appropriate person to hold the licence.

3) **Manager.** The proposed manager must either be the person having control (see para 12.9) of the HMO or his or her agent.
4) **Fit and proper manager.** The proposed manager of the HMO must also be a fit and proper person.
5) **Management arrangements.** The proposed management arrangements for the HMO must be otherwise satisfactory.

Suitability for multiple occupation

14.35 This is determined by reference to standards prescribed by regulations: Licensing and Management of Houses in Multiple Occupation and Other Houses (Miscellaneous Provisions) (England) Regulations 2006 SI No 373 Sch 3, or Licensing and Management of Houses in Multiple Occupation and Other Houses (Miscellaneous Provisions) (Wales) Regulations 2006 SI No 1715 Sch 3. The regulations are detailed and set the appropriate level of facilities, eg for cooking and washing, for a given number of occupiers, for fire safety requirements.

Fit and proper person

14.36 Both the proposed licence holder and the proposed manager must be 'fit and proper' persons. In deciding this issue, authorities must take into account (HA 2004 s66(2)) any evidence that the person in question:

1) has committed any offence involving fraud or other dishonesty, or violence or drugs, or any offence listed in Sexual Offences Act 2003 Sch 3 (offences attracting notification requirements);
2) has practised unlawful discrimination on grounds of sex, colour, race, ethnic or national origins or disability in connection with carrying out any business;
3) has contravened any provision of the law relating to housing or of landlord and tenant; or
4) has acted otherwise than in accordance with any applicable approved code of practice for the management of HMOs.

   Note. Evidence of any such conduct by a person associated with, or formerly associated with, the proposed licence holder or manager, whether on a personal, work or other basis, must also be taken into account if it appears to be relevant to whether the person under consideration is a fit and proper person (HA 2004 s66(3)).

Management arrangements

14.37 In deciding whether other proposed management arrangements for the house are satisfactory, the authority must take into account (HA 2004 s66(5), (6)):

1) whether any person proposed to be involved in the management of the HMO is sufficiently competent;
2) whether any person proposed to be involved in the management is a fit and proper person; and
3) whether any proposed management structures and funding arrangements are suitable.

Grant and refusal

14.38 Detailed provision governs the procedure for granting or refusing licences (HA 2004 Sch 5 Pt 1). Before making a decision, the authority is obliged to consult 'relevant persons', ie any other person who has an estate or interest in the HMO (other than a tenant under a lease of three years or less to run) or any other person managing (see para 12.9) or person having control (see para 12.9) of the HMO.

14.39 On the grant or refusal of a licence, the authority must inform the applicant and any relevant person (see para 14.38) of its decision. There is a right of appeal to the First-tier Tribunal (England) or the residential property tribunal (Wales) within 28 days, eg against a refusal or terms contained in the licence. The tribunal has power to extend this time limit where it is satisfied that there is 'good reason'.

Level of occupation and conditions

Maximum occupation

14.40 The licence must identify the maximum number of persons and households who may occupy the HMO (HA 2004 s64(3), (4)).

Licence conditions

14.41 Every licence must include some conditions; others may be included by the authority if it considers them appropriate for regulation of the management, use and occupation of the HMO and its condition and contents (HA 2004 s67). The authority cannot, however, impose conditions requiring a change to the terms of the occupiers' tenancy or licence agreements (HA 2004 s67(6)).

Mandatory conditions

14.42 Every licence must include conditions requiring the licence holder:

1) to produce to the authority a gas safety certificate of the annual inspection required under the Gas Safety (Installation and Use) Regulations 1998 SI No 2451 (see paras 11.106–11.108);
2) to keep electrical appliances and furniture provided by him or her in a safe condition and to supply the authority, on demand, with a declaration by him or her as to their safety;
3) to install smoke alarms and keep them in proper working order and to supply the authority, on demand, with a declaration as to their safety; and
4) to supply the occupiers with a written statement of the terms under which they occupy.

Discretionary conditions

14.43 Illustrations of other conditions that the authority may impose are to be found in HA 2004:

1) restrictions or prohibitions on the use or occupation of particular parts of the HMO (which can include restricting the use of a room to a particular description of person, eg a student – *Parr v Nottingham City Council*, 2017);
2) requirements for taking reasonable and practicable steps to prevent or reduce anti-social behaviour by occupiers or their visitors;
3) provisions for facilities and equipment in the HMO to meet prescribed standards;
4) obligations to keep such facilities and equipment in repair and proper working order;
5) time limits for carrying out such works of repair; and
6) a requirement for the licence holder or manager to undertake training courses in relation to the standards which may be set out in an approved code of practice.

Hazards

14.44 A defect in an HMO may constitute a Category 1 or Category 2 hazard under HHSRS against which the authority could take enforcement action (chapter 12) but which could also be dealt with by imposing license conditions. Authorities should generally deal with Category 1 or Category 2 hazards by enforcement action rather than by imposing licence conditions (HA 2004 s68).

Duration

14.45 The licence comes into force on the date specified in the licence and, unless the licence holder dies or the licence is revoked, remains in force for a maximum of five years (HA 2004 s68).

14.46 A licence may, however, be varied or revoked at any time. An authority may revoke a licence either by agreement with the licence holder or in the following circumstances (HA 2004 s70).

1) **Breach of conditions.** The licence may be revoked where the authority considers that the licence holder or any other person has committed a serious breach of a condition of the licence or repeated breaches of such a condition.
2) **Licence holder.** The licence may be revoked where the authority no longer considers that the licence holder is a fit and proper person.
3) **Manager.** The licence may be revoked where the authority considers that the management of the HMO is no longer being carried out by persons who are fit and proper persons.
4) **No licence needed.** The licence may be revoked where the HMO ceases to need a licence.
5) **New licence would be refused.** The licence may be revoked where the authority considers that, were the licence to expire, it would, for a reason relating to the management structure for the HMO, refuse to grant a new licence to the licence holder on similar terms to the existing licence.

14.47 As with licensing decisions, detailed provision governs the procedure to be adopted before a licence can be varied or revoked (HA 2004 Sch 5). Before making a decision, the authority must consult the licence holder and any relevant person (see para 14.38). The authority must give reasons for its decision; there is a right of appeal to the First-tier Tribunal (England) or the residential property tribunal (Wales) within 28 days (which may be extended for good reason).

Management regulations

14.48 Under HA 2004 s234, regulations ('management regulations') may be issued to ensure that the person managing (see para 12.9) an HMO observes proper standards of management. For all HMOs other than converted blocks of flats (HA 2004 s257; see para 14.17), the management regulations are contained in the Management of Houses in Multiple Occupation (England) Regulations 2006 SI No 372 and the

Management of Houses in Multiple Occupation (Wales) Regulations 2006 SI No 1713.

14.49 The regulations require the person managing (see para 12.9) the HMO to:

1) provide contact details to all occupiers and display these in the house;
2) take safety measures, including fire safety measures;
3) maintain the water supply and drainage;
4) supply and maintain gas and electricity, including ensuring that appliances are tested and that certificates are provided to the local housing authority upon request;
5) maintain common parts, fixtures, fittings and appliances;
6) maintain living accommodation; and
7) provide waste disposal facilities.

14.50 Similar duties are imposed on a person managing a property which is an HMO because it is a converted block of flats (HA 2004 s257; see para 14.17) by the Licensing and Management of Houses in Multiple Occupation (Additional Provisions) (England) Regulations 2007 SI No 1903 or the Licensing and Management of Houses in Multiple Occupation (Additional Provisions) (Wales) Regulations 2007 SI No 3229. The manager's duty only extends to parts of the HMO over which it would be reasonable to expect the licence holder to exercise control (reg 3).

14.51 Duties are imposed on those living in the house to ensure that the manager can effectively carry out these requirements.

14.52 Failure to comply with a regulation without reasonable excuse is an offence punishable by a fine of up to an unlimited amount (HA 2004 s234(3); Legal Aid, Sentencing and Punishment of Offenders Act (LASPO) 2012 s85(1)).

Overcrowding controls

14.53 A licence for an HMO specifies a permitted level of occupation (HA 2004 s64) (see para 14.40). In addition, local authorities have power to regulate the level of occupation in HMOs outside their licensing scheme through service of overcrowding notices.

14.54 An authority may serve notice in respect of an HMO which appears to accommodate, or to be likely to accommodate, an excessive number of persons (HA 2004 s139). The notice must specify the maximum number who are to sleep in reach room in the HMO. The notice may also state that some rooms are unsuitable for use as bedrooms. The maximum stated may be age-related. The notice may be served on one or more 'relevant persons' (see para 14.38).

14.55 The notice must contain one of two further classes of prohibition, immediate or natural reduction.

1) **Immediate reduction.** The person served must not:
   (a) permit a room to be occupied otherwise than in accordance with the notice; or
   (b) allow so many people to live in the house that it is impossible for them to occupy without offending the notice, or without sleeping in parts of the house which are not rooms, or without two persons of the opposite sex and over the age of 10, not living together as man and wife, being obliged to sleep in the same room.
2) **Natural reduction.** The person served must not:
   (a) permit a room to be occupied by a new resident, other than in accordance with the notice; or
   (b) permit a new resident to occupy any part of the premises if it is not possible to do so without offending the notice, or without sleeping in parts of the house which are not rooms, or without two persons of the opposite sex and over the age of 10, not living together as man and wife, being obliged to sleep in the same room.

14.56 At least seven days before serving an overcrowding notice, the authority must inform every relevant person (see para 14.38) of its intention to serve the notice. At the same time, the authority must try to ensure that every occupier is also told of its intention.

14.57 A person aggrieved by an overcrowding notice, eg landlord or occupier, may appeal to the First-tier Tribunal (England) or the residential property tribunal (Wales) within the 21 days of service (HA 2004 s143). The effect of an appeal is to suspend the operation of the notice pending the outcome.

14.58 The notice may be revoked or varied by the authority at any time on the application of any relevant person (see para 14.38) (HA 2004 s144). A refusal to revoke or vary may also – within 21 days – be appealed to the First-tier Tribunal (England) or the residential property tribunal (Wales).

14.59 Breach of a notice without a reasonable excuse is a criminal offence (HA 2004 s139(7)), punishable by a fine on standard scale 4 (currently £2,500).

Codes of practice

14.60 Codes of practice may be issued laying down standards of conduct and practice to be followed with regard to the management of HMOs, including exempt HMOs (HA 2004 s233). Failure to comply with a provision of a code does not of itself render a person liable to any civil or criminal proceedings, but a code may be relevant in a number of circumstances, eg failure to comply with a provision of a code is relevant to whether a proposed licence holder is a fit and proper person (see para 14.36). The only codes of practice which have been issued relate solely to accommodation for students in halls of residence and other university buildings (see para 14.18(3)).

Selective licensing

14.61 Selective licensing of residential accommodation (HA 2004 Pt 3) is intended to address problems in areas of low housing demand. In some areas, an absence of owner-occupiers has led to an influx of speculative landlords, who may have little interest either in maintaining proper standards of accommodation for their tenants or in exercising any control over their tenants' behaviour. Part 3 allows authorities to designate areas within their district as being subject to selective licensing. All houses and flats within the designation area and to which the designation applies must be licensed. In some circumstances, a management order may be made in relation to a property which qualifies for licensing (see para 14.122–14.134).

14.62 Failure to obtain a licence for a house which has to be licensed may have serious consequences for the landlord: failure to obtain a licence for a house without a reasonable excuse is a criminal offence (see para 14.97); while the house remains unlicensed, there are restrictions on the landlord's right to obtain possession (see para 14.103); and, the First-tier Tribunal (England) or the residential property tribunal (Wales) may make a rent repayment order, which requires the landlord to repay rent, housing benefit or universal credit which was paid during a period when the house should have been licensed (see paras 14.104–14.115). These consequences are considered below, under their own heading.

14.63 In England, once the provisions of HPA 2016 Pt 2, are in force, it is expected that local housing authorities will be able to apply to the First-tier Tribunal for a banning order against anyone convicted of failing obtain a licence for a house which has to be licensed (see para

14.97), which will prevent that person from being involved in letting or managing residential property (see paras 5.82–5.102). A person against whom a banning order made will be entered on a database of 'rogue landlords' (see paras 5.103–5.111).

Application of scheme

14.64 A selective licensing scheme applies to houses and flats (HA 2004 s99). The scheme only applies to premises which are let out, although not necessarily under a single tenancy or licence (HA 2004 s79). An HMO which has to be licensed under Part 2 (see paras 14.19–14.47) does not, however, also have to be licensed under Part 3 (HA 2004 s85).

14.65 No licence is necessary where any part of the house is let under an 'exempt tenancy' (HA 2004 s79), ie a tenancy or licence granted by a PRP or RSL or a tenancy or licence specified in regulations. Specified exempt tenancies include:

1) tenancies or licences of houses managed by local authorities and other specified public bodies (see para 14.18(1));
2) long leases (see para 2.72) where the occupier is either the tenant under the lease, or his or her successor in title, or a family member of the landlord;
3) service tenancies and service occupancies (see paras 1.131–1.140); and
4) tenancies or licences granted by a resident landlord (see para 1.226(10)).

14.66 An authority may designate either the whole or part of its area as subject to a selective licensing scheme. Before making a designation, the authority must be satisfied that one of a number of conditions is met (HA 2004 s80; Selective Licensing of Houses (Additional Conditions) (England) Order 2015 SI No 977; Selective Licensing of Houses (Additional Conditions) (Wales) Order 2006 SI No 2825). The conditions are as follows.

England and Wales

1) The area is, or is likely to become, an area of low housing demand and making a designation will contribute to improvement of the social or economic conditions in the area.
2) The area is experiencing a significant and persistent problem caused by anti-social behaviour, which at least some of the

landlords in the area are failing to address, which – in the authority's opinion – will be eliminated or reduced by the designation.

England only

3) A high proportion of properties in the area are let by private sector landlords under either assured tenancies (see paras 1.213–1.242) or licences and, having reviewed the housing conditions in its area under HA 2004 s3 (see para 12.5), the authority intends to take enforcement action and making a designation will improve housing conditions.
4) The area is experiencing an influx of migration, those migrants occupy a significant number of the properties let under either assured tenancies (see paras 1.220–1.251) or licences by private sector landlords and making a designation will preserve or improve social or economic conditions in the area and ensure proper management of those properties.
5) There is a high level of deprivation affecting a significant number of properties let by private sector landlords under either assured tenancies (see paras 1.220–1.251) or licences in the area and making a designation will reduce the level of deprivation.

Wales only

6) At least 25 per cent of the housing in the area is let by private sector landlords and the authority has declared that the area is a renewal area (see paras 12.61–12.69) or the authority has provided grant assistance, eg an improvement grant, to any person in the area under the Regulatory Reform Order 2002 (see paras 4.167–4.176).

Note. PRPs and RSLs are not private sector landlords for these purposes.

14.67 Before making a designation, the authority must take reasonable steps to consult persons who are likely to be affected by it and consider any representations made in response, and must ensure that any exercise of their power to require selective licensing is consistent with its overall housing strategy (HA 2004 ss80(9) and 81(2)). If the designation is intended to cover the whole of an authority's area, persons in the areas of neighbouring authorities may have to be consulted (*R (Regas) v Enfield LBC*, 2014). A designation must be confirmed by the Secretary of State or the National Assembly for Wales. Confirmation may either be specific or by way of a general approval. Following confirmation of the designation, the authority must take steps to publicise it, which steps are specified in regulations (HA 2004 s82). The designation may last up to a maximum of five years (HA 2004 s84). The authority must periodically review its operation and may revoke it if it considers it appropriate to do so. Any revocation must be publicised in accordance with prescribed requirements.

Temporary exemption notice

14.68 There are analogous provisions to those considered in relation to HMOs which need licensing, where the person having control (see para 12.9) of, or a person managing (see para 12.9), a property which needs a licence notifies the authority that he or she intends to take action to ensure that it no longer does so (see para 14.30; HA 2004 s86).

Applications

14.69 The provisions governing applications are analogous to those governing HMO licences (see paras 14.32–14.33; HA 2004 ss85–89).

Decisions

14.70 The provisions governing decisions are also analogous to those governing HMOs, save for those which are specific to HMOs, eg there is no requirement (see para 14.34(1)) to be satisfied as to the suitability of the property, or to establish whether the proposed license holder or manager has acted in accordance with an approved HMO code when deciding whether or not he or she is a fit and proper person (see para 14.36(4)).

14.71 **Procedure.** The procedure governing the grant or refusal of a licence is identical to that for HMO licences (see paras 14.38–14.39).

Conditions

14.72 The provisions governing conditions are analogous to those which govern HMO licences (see paras 14.41–14.43; HA 2004 s90). The conditions which must be included are the same as those which must be included in every HMO licence (see para 14.42); the additional conditions may include the same conditions as for HMO licences (see para 14.43) save for training (see para 14.43(6)); the same point is made (see para 14.44) as to dealing with hazards.

Duration

14.73 The duration of the licence is the same as for an HMO licence (see para 14.44; HA 2004 s91). Likewise, procedure for variation or revocation is identical to that for variation of an HMO licence (see para 14.47), and the grounds for revocation (see para 14.46) are the same (HA 2004 ss92–94).

Licensing in Wales

14.74 In Wales, H(W)A 2014 Pt 1, introduced a registration scheme for private landlords and a licensing scheme for private landlords and managing agents. Both schemes are administered for the country by Rent Smart Wales, a department of Cardiff Council, and are in addition to HMO and selective licensing run by individual local housing authorities. Both schemes apply to lettings of houses or flats let as separate dwellings (see para 1.171) under 'domestic tenancies', namely assured tenancies (see paras 1.220–1.251) – except for long leases (see para 2.72) – or Rent Act tenancies (see para 1.268–1.293) (H(W)A 2014 ss1 and 2). A dwelling let, or marketed or offered for letting, under a domestic tenancy is a 'rental property' (H(W)A 2014 s2).

14.75 Failure to obtain a licence may have serious consequences: letting or managing properties without a licence is a criminal offence (see para 14.98) as is using an unlicensed agent to manage a property (see para 14.98); there are restrictions on an unlicensed landlord's rights to obtain possession (see para 14.103); the residential property tribunal may make a rent stopping order, which suspends the tenant's obligation to pay rent (see paras 14.116–14.120), and a rent repayment order which requires the landlord to repay rent, housing benefit or universal credit, which was paid during a period when the landlord should have been licensed (see paras 14.104–14.115). These consequences are considered below under their own heading.

Registration

14.76 A landlord must be registered if he or she is letting out a rental property or marketing it or offering a dwelling for letting under a domestic tenancy (H(W)A 2014 s4). Failure to register, without a reasonable excuse, is an offence punishable by a fine on standard scale 3 (currently £1,000).

Exceptions

14.77 RSLs and fully mutual housing associations (see para 8.7) do not have to register (H(W)A 2014 s5(d),(e)).

14.78 When a property is sold, the new landlord has 28 days during which he or she does not have to be registered and if he or she takes steps to recover possession within that time need not be registered for as long as he or she continues to seek possession diligently (H(W)A 2014 s5(b),(c)).

Application

14.79 An application for registration must be made in the standard form used by Rent Smart Wales and must be accompanied by payment of a fee (H(W)A 2014 s15(1)). The information required is set out in Regulation of Private Rented Housing (Information, Periods and Fees for Registration and Licensing) (Wales) Regulations 2015 SI No 1368 reg 4. This consists of details of the landlord and his or her managing agent (if any) and the addresses of all the landlord's rental properties. Provided that the landlord properly completes the form and pays the fee, Rent Smart Wales must register the landlord within four weeks (H(W)A 2014 s15(1)). A renewal fee is payable every five years.

Changes

14.80 Once registered, the landlord must notify Rent Smart Wales of: any change in the landlord's name or contact details; the appointment of a new managing agent or termination of a management agreement; and, any transfer of the landlord's interest in a rental property (H(W)A 2014 s16; Regulation of Private Rented Housing (Information, Periods and Fees for Registration and Licensing) (Wales) Regulations 2015 SI No 1368 reg 5. Failure, without reasonable excuse, to comply with this duty is an offence punishable by a fine on standard scale 1 (currently £250).

Revocation

14.81 Registration may be revoked if the landlord provided false or misleading information in his or her application, fails to notify Rent Smart Wales of changes or provides false information when notifying changes (H(W)A 2014 s17). Before revoking registration, Rent Smart Wales must notify the landlord of its intention to revoke, explaining why. The landlord must be given at least 28 days to make representations. If registration is revoked, Rent Smart Wales must notify any managing agents recorded on the register under the landlord's entry and any tenants or occupiers of the landlord's rental properties. The landlord has a right of appeal to the residential property tribunal against a decision to revoke, to be exercised within 28 days. The tribunal has power to extend this time limit where it is satisfied that there is 'good reason'.

Access to information

14.82 Members of the public can request Rent Smart Wales to provide them with the information kept on the register, including the contact details of a landlord or a managing agent, whether a landlord or a managing agent has a licence (see paras 14.83–14.96), and whether there is any rent stopping order recorded against a property (see paras 14.116–14.120) (H(W)A 2014 s14 and Sch 1).

Licensing

14.83 Landlords need a licence to carry out 'lettings activities' and 'property management activities'. Managing agents need a licence to carry out 'lettings work' and 'property management work'.

Landlords

14.84 A landlord must have a licence to do any of the following lettings activities: arranging or conducting viewings with prospective tenants; obtaining information about the suitability of prospective tenants (eg references or credit checks); preparing tenancy agreements; and, preparing inventories or schedules of condition (H(W)A 2014 s6).

14.85 Landlords who do not have to register (see paras 14.77–14.78) do not need a licence (H(W)A 2014 s8).

14.86 A landlord does not need a licence if he or she uses a licensed managing agent to carry out all lettings activities for him or her or if the landlord's only role is instructing a solicitor to draft a tenancy agreement (H(W)A 2014 s6(1)(b), (6)(b)).

14.87 A landlord must have a licence to do any of the following property management activities: rent collection; being the tenant's principal point of contact; arranging repairs or maintenance; arranging access with the tenant; checking the condition of the property or its contents (even if the tenancy has ended); and, serving notices to end the tenancy (H(W)A 2014 s7).

Managing agents

14.88 A managing agent requires a licence to undertake 'lettings work', which is defined to mean responding to instructions from prospective landlords or prospective tenants (H(W)A 2014 s10).

14.89 A managing agent requires a licence to do 'property management work', which includes all the activities which qualify as property management activities when done by a landlord (see para 14.87) (H(W)A 2014 ss11 and 12).

Applications

14.90 Application for registration must be in the form required by Rent Smart Wales and must be accompanied by payment of a fee (H(W)A 2014 s15(1)). The information required is set out in Regulation of Private Rented Housing (Information, Periods and Fees for Registration and Licensing) (Wales) Regulations 2015 SI No 1368 reg 4. A renewal fee is payable every five years.

Decisions

14.91 To grant a licence, Rent Smart Wales must be satisfied that the applicant is a fit and proper person (H(W)A 2014 s20; see para 14.36) and that the applicant has completed or will complete an approved training course (H(W)A 2014 s19(2); Regulation of Private Rented Housing (Training Requirements) (Wales) Regulations 2015 SI No 1366). Rent Smart Wales must reach a decision within eight weeks of receiving a valid application (Regulation of Private Rented Housing (Information, Periods and Fees for Registration and Licensing) (Wales) Regulations 2015 SI No 1368 reg 6).

Conditions

14.92 A licence must include a condition that the licence holder complies with any code of practice published by the Welsh Ministers (H(W)A 2014 s22), currently the *Code of Practice for Landlords and Agents licensed under Part 1 of the Housing (Wales) Act 2014* (October 2015). Rent Smart Wales may also impose any other conditions it thinks fit.

Appeals

14.93 There is a right of appeal to the residential property tribunal against a refusal to grant a licence and against any conditions in the licence

(H(W)A 2014 s27). The tribunal has power to extend this time limit where it is satisfied that there is 'good reason'.

Changes

14.94 A licence holder must notify Rent Smart Wales of any change in his or her contact details and of anything that might affect whether he or she remains a fit and proper person (see para 14.36) (Regulation of Private Rented Housing (Information, Periods and Fees for Registration and Licensing) (Wales) Regulations 2015 SI No 1368 reg 8).

Amendment and revocation

14.95 Rent Smart Wales can amend the licence conditions (H(W)A 2014 s24) and can also revoke a licence (H(W)A 2014 s25). Unless the licence holder agrees to revocation, a licence can only be revoked if the licence holder has breached a licence condition, Rent Smart Wales is no longer satisfied that the licence holder is a fit and proper person (see para 14.36) or the licence holder has failed to update his or her information (see para 14.94).

14.96 Before amending or revoking a licence, Rent Smart Wales must notify the licence holder of its intention to do so, explaining why. The licence holder has 21 days to respond with representations. Rent Smart Wales must give reasons for its decision; there is a right of appeal to the residential property tribunal within 28 days (which may be extended for good reason).

Failure to licence: consequences

Criminal offences

14.97 **Failure to obtain licence.** If an HMO (see paras 14.10–14.18) or house subject to selective licensing (see paras 14.60–14.71) is not licensed when it should be, the person having control of (see para 12.9), or managing (see para 12.9), the property commits an offence (HA 2004 s72(1) – HMO; s95(1) – selective licensing). No offence is committed if the defendant has an outstanding application for a licence or there is a temporary exemption notice or an outstanding appeal at the relevant time. It is also a defence that the defendant had a reasonable excuse. The offence is punishable by a fine of up to an unlimited amount.

14.98 In Wales, carrying out lettings activities or work (see paras 14.84 and 14.88), or carrying out property management activities or work (see paras 14.87 and 14.89), without a licence is a criminal offence punishable by a fine of up to an unlimited amount (H(W)A 2014 ss6(4), (5), 7(5), (6), 9(2), (3) and 11(3), (4)). In each case, it is a defence for the landlord or the managing agent to show that he or she had a reasonable excuse for not having a licence.

14.99 **Using unlicensed agents.** A landlord in Wales commits an offence if he or she uses an unlicensed managing agent to carry out any lettings work (see para 14.88) or property management work (see para 14.89) in relation to a rental property and the landlord knew or should have known that the agent did not have a licence (H(W)A 2014 s13). The offence is punishable by a fine on standard scale 4 (currently £2,500).

14.100 **Over-occupation.** In relation to HMOs, a person having control of (see para 12.9) or managing (see para 12.9) an HMO commits an offence if he or she – without a reasonable excuse – knowingly permits someone to occupy the HMO so that the house is occupied by more households or persons than permitted under the licence (HA 2004 s72(2)). The offence is punishable by a fine of up to an unlimited amount.

14.101 **Breach of conditions.** Failure without a reasonable excuse to comply with a licence condition is an offence (HA 2004 s72(3) – HMO; s95(2) – selective licensing). The offence is committed by the person on whom the condition is imposed (usually the licence holder). The offence is summary only and punishable by a fine of up to an unlimited amount.

14.102 A director or a manager of a company convicted of any of these offences can also be convicted of the same offence if it was committed with his or her consent or connivance or it is attributable to his or her neglect (HA 2004 s251; H(W)A 2014 s35). *Note.* This is not yet in force in relation to the offences under H(W)A 2014 Pt 1.

Restriction on possession

14.103 Most tenants in the private sector are assured shorthold tenants (see paras 1.246–1.251); a landlord is therefore entitled to recover possession provided he or she has served a notice in accordance with HA 1988 s21 (see para 2.195). In England, as long as an HMO or house which needs a licence remains unlicensed, however, the landlord may not serve a section 21 notice (HA 2004 s75 – HMO; s98 – selective licensing). Likewise, in Wales, an unregistered landlord cannot serve a section 21 notice and an unlicensed landlord cannot do so unless all his or her property management work is carried out by a licensed managing agent (H(W)A 2014 s44). There is nothing to prevent the tenancy being brought to an end by other means. Accordingly, the landlord may recover possession by serving a notice under HA 1988 s8 and relying on grounds for possession contained in HA 1988 Sch 2, as he or she could do were the tenancy not shorthold (see paras 2.168–2.170); or, the tenant may end the tenancy by surrender or notice to quit (see paras 2.24–2.28; 2.47–2.56).

Rent repayment orders

14.104 Failure to obtain a license when one is necessary can also lead to the making of a 'rent repayment order'. Such an order is made on application to the First-tier Tribunal (England) or the residential property tribunal (Wales), and may require the landlord to repay rent (or other payments) to the occupier, or, if the occupier was in receipt of housing benefit or universal credit, to repay the local authority. In relation to HMO licensing and selective licensing, the application may be made by the local authority or by an occupier; in relation to licensing in Wales, an application can be made by Rent Smart Wales, the local housing authority (if Rent Smart Wales consents) or the tenant. The application may be made against the 'appropriate person', defined as the person who was entitled to receive payments 'on his own account', ie usually the landlord rather than a managing agent (HA 2004 s73(10) – HMO; s96(10) – selective licensing; H(W)A 2014 s32(9) – licensing in Wales).

14.105 In England, the procedure governing an application for a rent repayment order made on or after 6 April 2017, is governed by HPA 2016 ss40–47 and is the same as that which applies to rent repayment orders made in unlawful eviction and harassment cases (see paras 5.29–5.35). Applications commenced in England before that date and applications in Wales are governed by the following procedure.

Application by local authority

14.106 A notice of intended proceedings must be served, warning the landlord of the authority's intention to make the application and inviting representations within 28 days. The notice must give reasons for making the application and provide a calculation for the money sought.

14.107 On an authority's application, the tribunal must, before making an order, be satisfied of three matters.

1) At any time within the period of 12 months ending with the date of the notice of intended proceedings, the appropriate person had committed the offence of failing to obtain a licence (see para 14.97 or para 14.98). It is not, however, necessary that there has been a prosecution or conviction.
2) Housing benefit or universal credit had been paid whether to the appropriate person (see para 14.102) or to someone else. (Whether the housing benefit or universal credit has been passed on is relevant to the amount of the repayment.)
3) Notice of intended proceedings (see para 14.106) had been served by the authority and the authority has considered any representations made in response (HA 2004 s73(6) – HMO; s96(6) – selective licensing; H(W)A 2014 s32(5) – licensing in Wales).

14.108 Subject to three qualifications (see para 14.109), the tribunal must order repayment of the total amount of housing benefit or universal credit paid during the relevant period if satisfied that:

1) a person has been convicted for failure to obtain a licence (see para 14.97 or para 14.98); and
2) housing benefit or universal credit was paid during the period when the offence was being committed (HA 2004 s74(2) – HMO; s97(2) – selective licensing; H(W)A 2014 s33(1) – licensing in Wales).

14.109 The three qualifications are as follows.

1) If the total amount received by the appropriate person is less than the housing benefit or universal credit paid, eg because the tenant or managing agent did not pay the housing benefit or universal credit over to the landlord, the amount of the repayment is limited to what was received.
2) The repayment cannot exceed the amount which the tribunal is satisfied that, by reason of exceptional circumstances, it would be reasonable for the appropriate person to have to repay.
3) The order cannot require repayment of an amount payable more than twelve months before the date of the notice of intended proceedings.

14.110 In addition, no benefit which is recoverable from the landlord under the ordinary provisions for recovering overpaid housing benefit or universal credit may be the subject of an order (Rent Repayment Orders (Supplementary Provisions) (England) Regulations 2007

SI No 572 reg 2 or Rent Repayment Orders (Supplementary Provisions) (Wales) Regulations 2008 SI No 254 reg 2 or Regulation of Private Rented Housing (Rent Repayment Orders) (Supplementary Provisions) (Wales) Regulations 2016 SI No 1022 reg 2), ie it is to be recovered as provided for by those Regulations rather than by these repayment provisions.

14.111 On an authority's application, the amount of the repayment to the occupier is such amount as the tribunal considers to be reasonable in the circumstances. In determining this, the tribunal must consider:

1) the amount paid during the time when it appears that an offence of failure to licence was being committed;
2) the extent to which that amount consisted of housing benefit and was actually received by the appropriate person;
3) whether the appropriate person has been convicted of an offence of failing to licence; and,
4) the conduct and financial circumstances of the appropriate person.

Application by occupier

14.112 Where the application is made by an occupier, the tribunal must be satisfied of three matters.

1) The appropriate person (see para 14.104) must either
   (a) have been convicted of an offence of failing to obtain a licence (see para 14.97 or para 14.98); or
   (b) there must be an existing rent repayment order in respect of housing benefit, ie the authority has already successfully obtained a rent repayment order.
2) In the case of HMO or selective licensing, the occupier had made payments to a person having control of (see para 12.9) or person managing (see para 12.9) the property during the relevant time; in the case of licensing in Wales, the tenant made payments to the appropriate person, ie usually the landlord rather than a managing agent (see para 14.104).
3) The application is made within 12 months of the date of the conviction or earlier order. If there have been both a conviction and a rent repayment order, the time limit runs from the later date (HA 2004 s73(8) – HMO; s96(8) – selective licensing; H(W)A 2014 s32(7) – licensing in Wales).

14.113 The amount of the repayment is whatever the tribunal considers reasonable taking into account the four considerations in para 14.111

and, by way of additional consideration, the occupier's conduct (HA 2004 s74(6) – HMO; s96(6) – selective licensing; H(W)A 2014 s33(6) – licensing in Wales).

14.114 The order cannot require repayment of an amount payable more than 12 months before the date of application (HA 2004 s74(8) – HMO; s96(8) – selective licensing; H(W)A 2014 s33(8) – licensing in Wales).

14.115 The Upper Tribunal has given guidance on rent repayment orders on applications made by occupiers (*Parker v Waller*, 2012). There is no presumption that an order should be for the full amount received by the landlord during the relevant time; and, the fact that the landlord is liable to be fined for a criminal offence should be taken into account. Professional landlords are likely to be dealt with more harshly than non-professionals. Although the order is limited to repayment of rent paid during the twelve months before the application (see paras 14.112), the fact that the tenant has been in occupation for longer may justify an award at the higher end of the scale. Where rent is inclusive of utility bills, these should be deducted from the amount repayable save in the most serious cases.

Rent stopping orders (Wales)

14.116 If an unlicenced landlord is carrying out property management activities (see para 14.85), or using an unlicensed managing agent to carry out those activities, Rent Smart Wales can apply to the residential property tribunal for a rent stopping order (H(W)A 2014 s30). The local housing authority for the property concerned can also apply for an order if Rent Smart Wales agrees. Before making the application, the applicant authority must write to the landlord and the tenant stating its intention to apply for an order and explaining why. The landlord must be given at least 28 days to make representations.

14.117 Before making an order the tribunal must satisfied that a warning letter notice was sent to the landlord (see para 14.116) and that the landlord has either committed the offence of carrying out management activities without a licence (see para 14.98) or the offence of using an unlicensed managing agent to carry out those activities (see para 14.99) (H(W)A 2014 s30(4)–(6)).

14.118 The effect of an order is that from a specified date (which cannot pre-date the order itself), the tenant does not have to pay rent or make any other periodic payments, eg service charges (H(W)A 2014 s30(3)). If the tenant makes any payments while the order is in force, he or she can recover them from the landlord (H(W)A 2014 s30(8)).

14.119 A rent stopping order must be recorded against the landlord's name in the register kept by Rent Smart Wales (see para 14.80; (H(W)A 2014 s14 and Sch 1).

14.120 The landlord or Rent Smart Wales or the local housing authority for the property concerned (if Rent Smart Wales agrees) can apply to the residential property tribunal for a rent stopping order to be revoked (H(W)A 2014 s31). Revocation is only permitted if the tribunal is satisfied that the landlord is no longer committing the offence (see para 14.117). Once revoked, rent and other periodic payments become payable again from a date specified in the order, which can pre-date the order itself.

Fixed penalty notices (Wales)

14.121 Once the relevant legislation is in force (H(W)A 2014 s29), Rent Smart Wales will be able issue a fixed penalty notice to someone committing an offence under Part 1. The landlord or managing agent will have a choice to pay the fine specified in the notice or face criminal proceedings.

Management orders

14.122 A management order – which is similar to the 'control orders' local authorities previously had power to serve under HA 1985 Pt 11 – allows an authority to take over the management of an HMO (see paras 14.10–14.18) or a house which should be subject to selective licensing (see paras 14.60–14.66). A management order is usually made because the authority considers that there is no reasonable prospect of granting a licence, which may be because an appropriate licence holder cannot be found. The general effect of a management order is that the authority takes possession of the property, although it does not acquire any legal interest in it. Existing tenancies and licences are binding on the authority and, in some circumstances, the authority is able to grant tenancies or licences of the property. The provisions governing management orders are contained in HA 2004 Pt 4 Ch 4.

Application

14.123 There are two forms of management order: interim and final. An interim order lasts for a maximum of 12 months. Its purpose is to secure that any necessary immediate steps are taken to protect the health and safety or welfare of the occupiers and to secure proper management of the house pending the grant of a licence or the making of a final management order. A final management order lasts a maximum of five years. Its purpose is to secure the proper management of the property on a long-term basis in accordance with a management scheme contained in the order. In each case, the order has immediate effect – there are no procedural preconditions, such as the service of a warning notice, as this could defeat some or all of the purpose, eg occupiers might be evicted.

14.124 An interim order must be made if the property is an unlicensed HMO or house subject to selective licensing and the authority considers that:

1) there is no reasonable prospect of it becoming licensed in the near future; or
2) an order is necessary to protect the health, safety or welfare of the occupiers, or persons occupying, or having an estate or interest in, any premises in the vicinity (HA 2004 s102).

14.125 Where the authority considers that on expiry of the interim order it will still be unable to grant a licence, it must replace the interim order with a final order (HA 2004 s113). The authority has power to make a final order where it is necessary for the protection of the health, safety, or welfare of occupiers or persons in the vicinity of the premises. On expiry of a final order, a further final order must be made if the authority is still unable to grant a licence and, in any event, may be made if it is necessary to do so to protect the health, safety, or welfare of occupiers or persons in the vicinity of the premises.

14.126 In some cases, an authority can make an order in relation to premises which do not need to be licensed (HA 2004 ss102(4) and 103). Such an order must be authorised by the First-tier Tribunal (England) or the residential property tribunal (Wales). In the case of an HMO, authorisation can only be given if the order is necessary to protect the health, safety, or welfare either of the occupiers or of persons in the HMO's vicinity (HA 2004 s102(5)). In the case of other premises, the tribunal must also be satisfied that the antisocial behaviour of the occupiers is causing significant problems in the area and that the landlord is failing to take action against it (HA 2004 s103(6)).

Procedure

14.127 The authority must consult any relevant persons and provide them with copies of the proposed order including the management scheme (see para 14.131) (HA 2004 Sch 6). A 'relevant person' is any person who has an estate or interest in the property (other than a tenant under a lease of three years or less to run) or any other person who, but for the management order, would be a person managing (see para 12.9) or person having control (see para 12.9) of the property (HA 2004 Sch 6 para 8).

14.128 As soon as practicable after making a management order (interim or final), the authority must serve the occupiers with a copy of the order together with a notice (HA 2004 Sch 6 para 7). Within seven days, the authority must also serve a copy on each relevant person (see para 14.127) together with a notice which informs him or her of the right to appeal to the First-tier Tribunal (England) or the residential property tribunal (Wales) within 28 days. If the authority is assuming control from a person who is a leaseholder, there is also provision for service of a notice on the superior landlord so that the authority can take over liability under the lease.

14.129 An order may be varied or revoked at any time (HA 2004 Sch 6 Pt 2). A relevant person (see para 14.127) has a right to request variation or revocation. Any relevant persons must be consulted before a decision to vary or revoke the order is taken. A decision to vary or revoke, or to refuse to vary or revoke, must be served on any relevant person. Reasons for the decision must be given and the authority must inform the recipient of the 28-day time limit for appealing to the tribunal. If there is an appeal, the variation or revocation is suspended pending its outcome.

Powers

14.130 While a management order is in force, the authority has power to do anything which anyone else in possession of the premises could do (HA 2004 ss107, 116). It may discharge its functions through managing agents. If it has assumed control from a person who was a leaseholder, the authority steps into his or her shoes. It may take over responsibility for any furniture in the property. It can take over the landlord's responsibility under contracts relating to the property and can conduct legal proceedings brought by or against him or her (HA 2004 s125).

14.131 While the order is in force, the authority has the right to enter any part of the house for the purpose of carrying out works (HA 2004 s131). If an occupier prevents the authority from carrying out the works, it may obtain an order from the magistrates' court ordering him or her to permit them to be done. A person who fails to comply with the order commits an offence, punishable by an unlimited fine (HA 2004 s131(5), (6); LASPO 2012 s85(1)).

14.132 **Rights of occupation.** In relation to existing tenancies, security under HA 1988 or RA 1977 (see paras 1.220–1.251; 1.268–1.293) will continue notwithstanding the management order (HA 2004 s124(7)). Any new tenancies granted by the authority will not be secure (see paras 1.160–1.209) or introductory (see paras 1.210–1.219) but will be assured (see paras 1.220–1.251) (HA 2004 s124), reflecting the proposition that the authority, although managing the property, does not actually have an interest in it, ie it is not the landlord so much as the landlord's agent. As the landlord will be a private individual, his or her tenants are assured.

14.133 During an interim order (see para 14.123), the authority can only grant a new tenancy with the consent of the person whom it has replaced as landlord (HA 2004 s107). Once a final order is in force, consent is not required unless the tenancy is a fixed-term tenancy (see para 1.18), which would expire after the proposed expiry date for the final order, or it is a periodic tenancy (see para 1.18) determinable by more than four weeks' notice (HA 2004 s116).

14.134 A final management order must contain a 'management scheme', which must set out how the authority intends to ensure proper management of the property and include details of any proposed works (HA 2004 s119). Provision is also made for detailed accounts to be drawn up and maintained by the authority (HA 2004 s119(7)) and for payment of compensation to certain persons affected by the order (HA 2004 s128(1)).

Empty Dwelling Management Orders

14.135 The purpose of an Empty Dwelling Management Order (EDMO) is partly to bring vacant dwellings in the private sector back into occupation at a time when demand for accommodation is high, and partly to address the impact that empty dwellings can have on a neighbourhood, eg because they attract vandals. The scheme for EDMOs is similar to that for management orders (see paras 14.122–14.134). As with management orders, there are two forms of EDMO: interim and final.

14.136 An EDMO can only be made in respect of a 'dwelling', which is:

1) a building intended to be occupied as a separate dwelling (see para 1.171); or
2) a part of a building intended to be occupied as a separate dwelling which may be entered otherwise than through any non-residential accommodation in the building, eg a flat is a dwelling unless entry to it is through commercial accommodation (HA 2004 s132).

14.137 If an EDMO is made, the authority assumes the position of 'the relevant proprietor', ie the freeholder or, if let, the leaseholder who is the lowest in any chain of leases who has an unexpired term of seven years or more (HA 2004 s132). An EDMO cannot be made, however, where the relevant proprietor is a local housing authority, PRP or RSL, police authority, fire and rescue authority or a health service body (HA 2004 s133). In addition, regulations prescribe a number of circumstances in which an EDMO cannot be made, including where the relevant proprietor is absent because of ill health or serving in the armed forces or where the property is a holiday home or is usually used for tied accommodation (Housing (Empty Dwelling Management Orders) (Prescribed Exceptions and Requirements) (England) Order 2006 SI No 367 reg 3.

14.138 Before making an EDMO, the authority must obtain authorisation from the First-tier Tribunal (England) or the residential property tribunal (Wales). This can only be given if the tribunal considers that the property has been 'wholly unoccupied' for at least six months (disregarding occupation by trespassers). The tribunal must be satisfied that no exemptions apply (see para 14.137) and that there is no real prospect of the property being let unless an order is made.

14.139 The position under an EDMO is similar to that under any other management order and discussion in relation to variation and revocation (see para 14.129), the authority's powers (see paras 14.130–14.131), rights of occupation (see para 14.132), powers of letting (see para 14.132) and accounting obligations (see para 14.131) applies equally to EDMOs.

Human rights

14.140 The observations made at para 12.82 apply in the same way to the powers under consideration in this chapter. It may also be noted that the exercise of a local authority's powers considered in this chapter can have a significant impact on the way in which properties are used by their owners, which might be considered to breach an owner's right to peaceful enjoy of his or her possessions under Article 1 of the First Protocol to the European Convention on Human Rights. That right does not, however, prevent the state from enforcing such laws as it deems necessary to control the use of property and member states have a wide margin of discretion in relation to matters concerning public health and control.

14.141 The exercise of these powers is accordingly likely to be compatible with Article 1 of the First Protocol: local authorities' former powers to regulate HMOs under HA 1985 Pt 11, were held to be compatible (*Stanley v Ealing LBC (No 2)*, 2003). Similarly, an authority's power to take control of empty property using EDMOs is likely to be considered compatible with Article 1 of the First Protocol, given that the owner is not using the property and there is a clear benefit to society in bringing empty property into use at a time of housing shortage.

Index